PENGUIN REFERENCE

The Penguin Dictionary of Critical Theory

'Remarkable for its comprehensiveness, mapping "theory" across a wide range of disciplines and art forms. It is certainly a reference book I will want to have on my own shelves' David Lodge

'Excellent . . . an unusual instance of an academic reference book that I do believe doubles quite effectively as a textbook for students and I would recommend it unreservedly to anyone with an interest in theoretical matters, or just in the history of ideas' Dr Duncan Wu, St Catherine's College, Oxford

'An astonishing encyclopedia of people, ideas and concepts . . . ideal as introductory essays on a thinker or concept that you want to get a handle on before reading further . . . the book also rewards browsers with entries on unpredictable things like "dead white European males" and "false memory syndrome" . . . a great purchase for students of cultural studies, literature or sociology' www.theory.org.uk

'Enlightening and fun: this dictionary is a treasure of easy, elegant erudition. From *abjection* to *zeugma*, Plato to Tarantino, it offers sustenance for focused critical enquiry *and* entices readers on more whimsical tours around the ideas' Dr Andrea Ashworth

'Splendidly done. It brings clarity to the world of difficult concepts and radical ideas that constitute modern and post-modern critical theory, covering the significant schools and bringing clear definitions' Malcolm Bradbury

ABOUT THE AUTHOR

Born in Sunderland in 1949 and educated at University College London, David Macey is a freelance writer and translator. He is the author of *Lacan in Contexts* (1988), *The Lives of Michel Foucault* (1993) and *Frantz Fanon: A Life* (2000). His many translations from the French include Alain Touraine's *What is Democracy?* (1997) and the same author's *Can We Live Together? Equality and Difference* (2000). David Macey lives and works in Leeds.

The Penguin Dictionary of
CRITICAL THEORY

David Macey

PENGUIN BOOKS

Margaret: *parce que c'est toi; parce que c'est moi*

PENGUIN BOOKS

Published by the Penguin Group
Penguin Books Ltd, 80 Strand, London WC2R 0RL, England
Penguin Group (USA) Inc., 375 Hudson Street, New York, New York 10014, USA
Penguin Books Australia Ltd, 250 Camberwell Road, Camberwell, Victoria 3124, Australia
Penguin Books Canada Ltd, 10 Alcorn Avenue, Toronto, Ontario, Canada M4V 3B2
Penguin Books India (P) Ltd, 11 Community Centre, Panchsheel Park, New Delhi – 110 017, India
Penguin Group (NZ), cnr Airborne and Rosedale Roads, Albany, Auckland 1310, New Zealand
Penguin Books (South Africa) (Pty) Ltd, 24 Sturdee Avenue, Rosebank 2196, South Africa

Penguin Books Ltd, Registered Offices: 80 Strand, London WC2R 0RL, England

www.penguin.com

First published 2000
Published in paperback 2001
12

Printed in England by Clays Ltd, St Ives plc

To be advised that one should 'go and read some theory' or, worse still, 'do some theory' can be an intimidating experience. This is in part quite simply because there is so much theory. Academic bookshops are full of it; journals abound in it. Yet there is no real consensus as to just what constitutes theory. Louis Althusser repeatedly insisted that there could be no revolutionary practice without revolutionary theory. Paul de Man wrote dismissively of the resistance to theory. Homi K. Bhabha writes of his commitment to theory and urges us to emulate it. They are, of course, all speaking of very different things and theories.

The plethora of theoretical discourses on offer is largely a product of the rise of interdisciplinarity within the modern human sciences, and interdisciplinarity can itself be seen as a product of the collapse, or calling into question, of the old disciplines. Uncertain of its role, literary criticism looks to linguistics and to psychoanalysis. New disciplines from film theory to women's studies all invoke a wide variety of theoretical discourse, and the field of knowledge grows more and more complex. It is easy to get lost or to feel intimidated.

Whilst the opposition between theory and practice can be traced back to ancient philosophy, the modern emphasis on theory arises from a cluster of circumstances. In Britain at least, it stemmed from an impatience with what passed for common sense and empiricism, and from an irritation at the continued belief that all a literary critic had to do was read books and trust his (the term is used advisedly) intuitive judgement. The Leavises and the angry young men of the New Left had little in common, but they did share the view that literature, philosophy and politics were all too serious to be left to academic amateurs. Leavisite criticism was non-theoretical in that it did not share the concerns of Russian formalism or its structuralist progeny, but its deep seriousness helped to create the modern definition of English Literature, and shaped the English departments in which theory continues to flourish. If the demand for theory was, in Iris Murdoch's words, a cry for a house that could provide shelter from empiricism, it was also a political demand born of the realization that theories are never politically innocent. They express political prejudices and reproduce them, even when they deny it. To reveal those prejudices in order to neutralize them was the great ambition of the critical theory of the Frankfurt School, of the Barthes who unmasked 'mythologies' with such sardonic glee, and of the feminist critics and historians who refused to go on being hidden from history.

The goal of this dictionary is to provide information about a number of theorists and theories relating to the domains of literature, philosophy, psychoanalysis, film and the visual arts, historiography and sexual politics. In chronological terms, it refers primarily to the twentieth century but that unit proves surprisingly difficult to define. In political terms, it is difficult to disagree with Eric Hobsbawm's description of it as a 'short century' spanning the period from the outbreak of the First World War to the collapse of communism, though many would add that it was also a classically Hobbesian century – 'poor, nasty, brutish . . .'. In intellectual terms, Hobsbawm's periodization is less satisfactory. Freud, Marx and Nietzsche were all children of the nineteenth century, yet they have had much more influence on the twentieth. In intellectual terms, our experience is always that of what Ernst Bloch calls non-contemporaneity and we live in a number of different times. Few if any discussions of realism and representation in the literary and visual arts can avoid reference to Plato and Aristotle's category of mimesis, whilst semiologists can still read St Augustine with profit. This dictionary does not include articles on Plato or Augustine, but they have to be discussed in the relevant contexts. Just as Shakespeare and Racine are still part of modern theatre, they are still part of modern thought.

Whilst the dictionary seeks to provide information, it can do little more than provide introductions. Few of the entries run to more than one thousand words in length, and the idea of summarizing the complete works of Heidegger or Freud in the space of a thousand words can scarcely be contemplated. Every entry here could probably be expanded into a book and probably has been the subject of a book, but entries do not seek to replace those books and nor do they seek to replace the authors and works they discuss. No dictionary of critical theory can or should be a substitute for the silent encounter of the reader with the theories and theorists it seeks to introduce. Whilst this dictionary is a work of reference, it is above all an invitation to enter the library and to read.

Small capital letters indicate cross-references to other entries. The references given under 'Reading' are to works not cited in the body of individual entries. Full details of all references are given in the Bibliography. Dates cited are those of first publication, but where a work has been translated into English, the title given is that of the published translation.

In early printings of this book, Mark Polizzotti is credited with writing *Vision and Difference: Femininity, Feminism and the Histories of Art*; *Generations and Geographies in the Visual Arts: Feminist Readings* and *Mary Cassatt: Painter of Modern Women*. The author is in fact Griselda Pollock.

My thanks are due to my editor Stefan McGrath, whose patience has been truly remarkable, to my copy-editor Antony Wood, to Margaret Atack who shared so much of the excitement with me, and to our children Aaron, John and Chantelle, who can now at last stop asking me: 'What letter of the alphabet have you got up to?'

abjection In Kristeva's post-Freudian theory of PSYCHOANALYSIS, abjection describes both the founding and traumatic moment of separation from the child's archaic and undifferentiated relationship with its mother, and the process of the expulsion from the body of substances such as excrement or menstrual blood (Kristeva 1980). At the same time, the experience of abjection establishes bodily boundaries by facilitating the introduction of a distinction between the inner and the outer, and then between the EGO and the non-ego. It encapsulates the memory of the violence of separation from a level of existence prior to the establishment of OBJECT-RELATIONS, and that memory is reactivated by the expulsion from the body of abjected substances. The abject is also evoked by the ritual ceremonies of defilement and purification that repeat and reinscribe the universal tendency to regress to the archaic level. The process that establishes boundaries also implies the threat that boundaries can be breached, that meaning can collapse and that the SUBJECT can be absorbed back into a suffocating relationship with an archaic image of the mother, who is feared as a potential cannibal. For Kristeva, modern literature from Dostoyevsky to Céline is haunted by the threat of the extinction or collapse of meaning and is therefore characterized by its constant and horrified evocation of the abject. In describing abjection, Kristeva draws heavily on the British anthropologist Mary Douglas's work on ritual pollution and taboo (1966).

abstraction One of the defining characteristics of the visual arts in the period of MODERNISM has been the retreat from MIMESIS or the realistic representation of the visible world and the human figure. Indeed, the influential critic Clement GREENBERG regards abstraction as the essential feature of the AVANT-GARDE, which typically aspires to creating self-contained and self-referential art-objects that respect the qualities of their media and, in the case of painting, the flatness of the canvas. For LYOTARD, abstraction in the visual arts marks the emergence of a new form of the SUBLIME. Abstraction can take many different forms, ranging from EXPRESSIONISM to the geometricism of Malevich and Mondrian and the biomorphism of Joan Miró, who also uses the dream imagery of SURREALISM, and of Henry Moore. For Wassily Kandinsky (1866–1944), the non-figurative use of pure colour was a means of exerting 'a direct influence on the soul' (1912). Both he and Paul Klee draw analogies between abstract painting and music; atonal music is often cited by ADORNO (1949, 1968) and others as an equivalent to abstraction in the visual arts.

Whilst abstract or non-figurative elements have been part of the European tradition for centuries (both the Jewish and Islamic traditions forbid the portrayal of living creatures), the emergence of a specifically abstract art is really a feature of the twentieth century. There is no one theory of abstraction, but the German writer Wilhelm Worringer's distinction (1908) between 'abstraction' and 'empathy' (*Einfühlung*) introduces some important themes. 'Empathy' is said to be characteristic of an organic and humanist art, whilst 'abstraction' and geometric stylization are described as typifying Byzantine and African art (an important point of reference for Picasso and post-cubism), and as expressing an 'anxious relationship' with the world. Paul Cézanne (1839–1906) appeared to make the case for abstraction when he spoke of 'treating nature by means of the cylinder, the sphere and the cone', but was in fact thinking more of the classical tradition of Poussin and the seventeenth century (Verdi 1992). His words do, however, hint at the neo-Platonist theory that informs those versions of abstract art which seek to capture the pure forms that lie behind observable reality. Significantly, both the Russian Kandinsky and the Dutchman Piet Mondrian (see the texts collected in Holtzmann and James 1987) were strongly influenced by mysticism and theosophy, and saw abstraction as a means of attaining a higher reality. Cézanne's words also appear to anticipate the views of the Italian sculptor Umberto Boccioni (1882–1916), who described sculpture as being based on the abstract reconstruction of the planes and volumes that determine form rather than upon its figurative value.

Both the cubism of Pablo Picasso and Georges Braque (see Cooper and Tinterow 1983) and FUTURISM's depiction of movement inaugurate a process of abstraction by introducing multiple-perspective images of the same object and thus breaking with the single-point perspective that dominated the Western tradition from the Renaissance onwards. Post-cubist abstraction moves in different directions, with the Fauves using pure colour and the Dutch De Stijl and German Bauhaus movements using strictly defined pure geometric forms and anticipating INTERNATIONAL STYLE. In the early twentieth century, abstraction is often associated with utopianism. Mondrian dreamed of creating a new art for a new world, and the same social optimism is present in the many forms of abstract art that flourished in Russia immediately after the 1917 Revolution and before the rise of SOCIALIST REALISM and Zhdanovism (ZHDANOV; Grey 1962).

New York's Armory Show of 1912, which displayed contemporary European modernism alongside examples of an American art still dominated by realism, inspired a new abstractionism that was to culminate in the 'abstract impressionism' that Greenberg hailed as the true avant-garde in the 1950s. Its greatest exponent was Jackson Pollock (1912–56), whose enormous 'drip' paintings finally abolish the distinction between form and content: the skeins of paint are both subject and content of the painting.

The Royal Academy's exhibition *A New Spirit in Painting* (1980) was widely interpreted as marking a return to figurative art and the end of abstraction. Theorists of POSTMODERNISM are often highly critical of the puritanism of abstraction (Jencks

1996), but abstract art has been one of the defining features of the twentieth century.

READING: *Abstraction: Towards a New Art. Painting 1910–1920* (1980); Moszynska (1990)

absurdity The experience of absurdity is a common theme in the work of novelists such as Dostoyevsky and Kafka, as well as in the many varieties of EXISTENTIALISM. The early essays of Albert Camus (1942a) and his first novel *The Outsider* (1942b) are classic modern expressions of this experience. The realization that existence is absurd arises from the sense of futility and meaninglessness provoked by the perception that there is a divorce between the human aspiration towards infinity and the finite nature of actual human experience, or between the intellectual desire for rationality and the irrationality of the physical world. The world is experienced as something unintelligible, and as the product of random combinations of events and circumstances. Although the experience of the absurd can induce a suicidal despair, the realization that there is no God and that human beings are not immortal can also produce an exhilarating sense of freedom and inspire a revolt against the human condition. There is a somewhat tenuous connection between the literary-philosophical notion of the absurd and the themes of the THEATRE OF THE ABSURD.

READING: Sartre (1943b)

actant The basic unit in the structural-semantic analysis of narrative proposed by GREIMAS (1966a, 1966b), who draws on PROPP's morphological analysis of folk-tales (1928). An actant is not defined in psychological terms as a 'character', but as a functional unit with a predicate defined by what it does. Greimas identifies six such actants and orders them into the following binary oppositions: Subject/Object, Sender/Receiver, Helper/Opponent. Although Greimas's original analysis of the actant function refers to quest-narratives, the actant is assumed to be a universal feature of all narratives.

Adorno, Theodor Wiesengrund (1903–69) German philosopher, cultural critic and musicologist, and a leading figure in the FRANKFURT SCHOOL. Adorno is one of the most versatile and austere practitioners of CRITICAL THEORY and his writings, now collected in the twenty-three volumes of his *Collected Works* (1970–86), cover an extraordinary range of topics from the astrology column of the *Los Angeles Times* (1957) to the music of Alban Berg (1968), with whom he once studied composition. Although the late *Negative Dialectics* (1966) and the posthumously published *Aesthetic Theory* (1970) are the definitive accounts of Adorno's thought, both are forbiddingly dense texts; Adorno is best approached through the fragments and aphorisms of *Minima Moralia* (1951), the attractive essays in *Prisms* (1955) and the two volumes of *Notes to Literature* (1974). The classic *Dialectic of Enlightenment* (Horkheimer and Adorno 1947) also provides a concise introduction to his characteristic concerns and ambivalent relationship with the ENLIGHTENMENT tradition which both permits the domination of nature and induces an ALIENATION born of that very domination. Enlightenment sets human beings free, but it also tends to 'punish undisciplined gestures' (Adorno 1966).

Like that of the other members of the Frankfurt School, Adorno's MARXISM is highly cerebral and does not imply any allegiance to a party or a specific political programme. The themes of COMMODITY FETISHISM and alienation are Marxist-derived, but Adorno has relatively little interest in class and does not view the proletariat as the main agency of social change. He is highly critical of the way Communist parties have transformed Marxism into a dogmatic ideology, and the starting-point for *Negative Dialectics* is the dry observation that the invitation to 'change the world' contained in Marx's 'Theses on Feuerbach' (1845) has 'miscarried'. For Adorno there is no universal history that leads from savagery to humanitarianism; there is one that leads from the slingshot to the megaton bomb (1966). Adorno's version of critical theory is a 'melancholy science' born of the realization that philosophy can no longer perform its traditional task of teaching the good life, and can only offer 'reflections from damaged life' (1951). Freedom can be defined only in negative terms, as it always corresponds to specific forms of unfreedom. Adorno's thought is 'negative' in that it does not offer a blueprint for the future or for the good life, but responds to the 'darkening of the world' (1970) brought about by Fascism, Stalinism and the growth of an administered society in which false needs are met, not real ones. Whereas Marx held that alienation and commodity fetishism are characteristic of the capitalist MODE OF PRODUCTION, Adorno, with a pessimism rivalled only by that of MARCUSE, finds them everywhere. The entire world is becoming an 'open-air prison' (1966), and there is no escape from it.

Like BENJAMIN and KRACAUER, Adorno uses the essay form and the aphorism to great effect, and exploits apparently mundane phenomena such as an astrology column as a means of analysing the whole of the society that produced it. The use of the short philosophical essay, exemplified by *Prisms*, allows him to undertake an immanent CRITIQUE of cultural phenomena, examining their inconsistencies and contradictions from within. For Adorno there is no 'Archimedean' position that allows phenomena to be judged from outside; the cultural critic works within the culture he is criticizing, and is therefore always in danger of colluding with it even as he attacks it: no theory 'escapes the market place' (1966). The absence of any Archimedean position implies that there can be no portable methodology that can be applied from the outside, and that the critical understanding of society can never be complete. Hence the force of the aphorism 'The whole is the untrue', but hence too the insistence that 'intelligence is a moral category' (1951). There can be no total philosophy precisely because every general statement has to be dissolved by the critical examination of distinct entities.

Adorno's talent for aphorisms can also be used to stingingly critical effect. ANALYTICAL PHILOSOPHY is contemptuously dismissed as something that 'robots can learn and copy', whilst HEIDEGGER's philosophy is attacked as a 'jargon' of authenticity (1965) and memorably described as a 'highly developed credit system' in which concepts borrow from one another and in which 'Being' is exempt from criticism because it is neither a fact nor a concept (1966).

Adorno is probably best known for his scathing attacks on the CULTURE INDUSTRY (1991) and they go hand in hand with a qualified defence of MODERNISM. Whereas most forms of MARXIST CRITICISM cling to and defend, like LUKÁCS, a fairly traditional concept of artistic realism, the essays in *Notes to Literature* celebrate Proust, Joyce and Beckett, whilst *Aesthetic Theory* argues that even the most abstract art has a truth-content of its own. Adorno's essays on music (see Paddison 1993) adopt a similar stance, and contrast the 'progress' of Schoenberg with the 'restoration' brought about by Stravinsky (Adorno 1949). Stravinsky's neoclassicism combines ersatz modernism with the pseudo-archaism of *The Rite of Spring*, but perpetuates the traditional view that musical notes must sound as though they had existed since the beginning of time; Schoenberg's atonality both reveals the dissonances of modern society itself, and works on the raw material of music in an endless process of becoming rather than being. There is a parallel here with GREENBERG's influential theory of ABSTRACTION and the thesis that true art self-consciously works on its own materials in order to become an autonomous object. For Adorno the music of Schoenberg, like the art of cubism, disrupts the commodification of art and interrupts the eternal repetition of the culture industry in which the new is always the same, and which is typified by the repetitious rhythms of jazz (1955). Countering the common objection that Schoenberg's music is 'difficult', Adorno claims that it honours the audience by refusing to make any concessions to the listener. Yet even at its most abstract and difficult, the self-conscious work of art has a truth-content and hints at the concealed reality of the administered society. The art work thus functions as a critique of the IDEOLOGY that masks reality. Adorno remarks in *Notes to Literature* that Samuel Beckett's play *Endgame* (1957) typifies the dignity of modern art by examining, as though in a test-tube, the drama of an era which can no longer tolerate that which constitutes it: the dustbins in which the characters live are the emblems of the culture that was reconstructed after Auschwitz.

READING: Buck-Morss (1977); Held (1980); Jarvis (1998); Jay (1973)

affect Loan-word borrowed from the German *Affekt*. In nineteenth-century psychology the term is synonymous with emotion or excitement. Borrowing from that tradition, PSYCHOANALYSIS defines affect as a quantity of psychic energy or a sum of excitation accompanying events that take place in the life of the psyche. Affect is not a direct emotional representation of an event, but a trace or residue that is aroused or reactivated through the repetition of that event or by some equivalent to it. Like LIBIDO, affect is quantifiable and both DRIVES and images are therefore said to have a quota of affect.

In FREUD's earliest theory of HYSTERIA (the so-called SEDUCTION THEORY), the blocking of the affect corresponding to a traumatic event has a causal role; because it cannot be expressed or discharged in words, it takes the form of a somatic symptom. In his later writings Freud consistently makes a distinction between affect and representations, which may be either verbal or visual. The verbalization of the TALKING CURE thus becomes an intellectualized way of discharging affects relating to childhood experiences.

One of the criticisms levelled at LACAN by certain of his fellow psychoanalysts (for example Green 1977) is that he tends to pay little attention to affect.

affective fallacy An important notion in the NEW CRITICISM, derived from the title of an article by Wimsatt and Beardsley (1954b) which attempts to promote an objective form of criticism focused solely on the text, defined as a self-sufficient verbal icon (Wimsatt 1954), and which attacks semantic criticism for its psychological impressionism. To succumb to the affective fallacy is to mistake the poem for its emotional result, or to derive a standard of criticism from its psychological affects. As with the related INTENTIONAL FALLACY, the poem itself disappears as psychological speculation replaces criticism.

Afrocentricity (also known as **Afrocentrism**) A school of thought which builds upon the precedents of NEGRITUDE and the pan-Africanist writings of Marcus Garvey (1887–1940; see Garvey 1969), and which reacts against EUROCENTRISM by stressing the importance of classical African civilization and of the historical links between Ancient Egypt and modern African cultures. It is particularly strong in the United States. Afrocentrism can take many different forms, but most argue that Afro-Americans are a distinct nationality with a civilization of their own; some claim superiority over other ethnic groups. Following authors like DIOP and BERNAL, Afrocentrists such as Molefi Kete Asante (1988, 1990) insist that the Ancient Egyptians were black, and that Greek civilization, supposedly the source of European culture, was the product of interaction with African civilizations. Europe and Asia are therefore viewed as mere variants on the original African theme in philosophy and science. The theorists of Afrocentricity urge black people (described by Asante as 'overseas Africans'), and especially Afro-Americans, to reconnect with the African past and to develop a vigilantly Afrocentric consciousness. According to Asante, this implies a rejection of Islam on the grounds that its Arab origins imply the destructive adoption of non-African customs and values.

Asante's Afrocentricity has been criticized for its reliance on a simplistic notion of tradition and its appeal to a 'true self' which is transparently self-conscious. This quasi-Cartesian vision of black subjectivity has been unfavourably compared with the 'double consciousness' thesis elaborated by DU BOIS (Gilroy 1993a).

READING: Howe (1998)

aga saga Term applied, usually pejoratively, to a subgenre of popular novel (GENRE) set in a semi-rural area and centred on the domestic and emotional entanglements of affluent middle-class characters. It derives from the proprietary name of a type of stove which has come to symbolize a wealthy cosiness. According to the entertaining *Oxford Dictionary of New Words* (1997), 'aga saga' is a journalistic coinage current since the mid-1990s; it appears to have been applied originally to the popular fiction of British novelist Joanna Trollope; see her *The Rector's Wife* (1991).

agitprop A condensation of 'agitation and propaganda', often applied to radical forms of theatre (and particularly street theatre) developed in many countries in the 1960s and 1970s. The expression originates in the cultural practices of the early years of the Russian Revolution, when agit-trains and even agit-ships showing films and displaying poster art were used to spread propaganda amongst the rural population (Grey 1962; *Art in Revolution* 1971). The term is also applied to the political EPIC theatre developed in the 1920s by the German theatre director Erwin Piscator (1893–1966).

alienation The term is used widely and in a number of different senses, but always connotes a sense of loss or estrangement. In property law it refers to a transfer or loss of ownership. In psychology the word 'alienation' was used to mean insanity or the loss of mental faculties; in the mid-nineteenth century, 'alienist' replaced the earlier 'mad doctor' (Porter 1987). That usage is now archaic in English, but the equivalent terms still survive in the Romance languages (cf. the French *aliéné* and the Italian *alienato*).

The modern meaning of 'alienation' derives mainly from the early writings of Marx and especially from his 'Economic and Philosophical Manuscripts' (1844, first published in Moscow in 1932). Marx's theory of alienation owes much to the Hegelian and neo-Hegelian traditions in German philosophy. In *The Phenomenology of Mind* (1807), Hegel describes the 'unhappy consciousness' (*'unglückliches Bewusst-sein'*) typical of philosophical scepticism as an alienated soul which is conscious of itself as a divided being, or a doubled and contradictory being whose aspirations towards universality have been frustrated. In his *Essence of Christianity* (1841; the English translation of 1842 is by George Eliot), the neo-Hegelian Ludwig Feuerbach argues that the Christian God is a PROJECTION of a human essence that has been alienated or abstracted from human being, objectified and turned into an object of worship. Most subsequent descriptions of alienation combine the themes of estrangement and division with that of the inversion of a natural order.

For Marx, alienation is a characteristic feature of modern capitalism and of the COMMODITY FETISHISM whose devaluation of the human world is proportional to its overvaluation of things (Marx 1867). Because he does not own it, the product of the worker's labour appears to take on an alien and threatening life of its own. The labour process is therefore experienced not as a joyful act of creation, but as a loss of reality. The worker who creates the object of labour both loses it and becomes a slave to it, whilst the employer's appropriation of the product is experienced as estrangement and alienation. The alienation of labour estranges human beings from their own bodies, from the natural world and from their potentially universal essence. The abolition of the private ownership of the means of production and of the commodity system is, according to Marx, a prerequisite for the overcoming of alienation and for the emergence of a truly human society.

Ever since their publication the *Economic and Philosophical Manuscripts* have been of major importance to the tradition of WESTERN MARXISM and particularly to LUKÁCS and some of those associated with the FRANKFURT SCHOOL (who, like MARCUSE, tend to use the related term REIFICATION rather than 'alienation'). The great attraction of the manuscripts is that they appear to provide the theoretical basis for a socialist humanism and for a critique of the dogmatic DIALECTICAL MATERIALISM associated with Stalinism. Marx's theory of alienation is also a major influence on Guy DEBORD's caustic descriptions of the 'society of the spectacle'. In his attacks on humanism, ALTHUSSER, in contrast, argues (1960, 1961) that alienation is part of a pre-Marxist or Feuerbachian PROBLEMATIC, and that the scientific work of the mature Marx (and especially *Capital*) departs from that problematic thanks to a decisive EPISTEMOLOGICAL BREAK.

READING: Meszaros (1971)

alienation-effect A translation of the German *Verfremdungseffekt*, coined by the dramatist BRECHT (1949, 1962) to describe the effect produced by his EPIC theatre and the style of acting appropriate to it.

Brecht's dramaturgy breaks with the traditional values and conventions of naturalism and psychological realism, rejecting empathy, suspension of disbelief and unity of action on the grounds that they are expressions of a bourgeois IDEOLOGY that has no place in a scientific modern society. In order to create a revolutionary socialist theatre, a new style of writing and acting is essential. Brecht's objective is to encourage the audience to take a detached and critical attitude towards what they see on stage. The audience must be made aware that they are watching a *reproduction* of incidents drawn from real life, but must not be allowed to forget that they are in a theatre. The spectator's attention is drawn to the artificial theatricality of the play by the songs that interrupt the action, by the slogan-painted placards that are brought on stage, and by the actors who step out of character to address the audience directly. The audience are thus encouraged to think about what has caused the incidents they are watching.

The Brechtian actor must unlearn the lessons of STANISLAVSKY and the method-acting school. Rather than identifying with the character he is playing and disappearing into his part, the actor must make the audience aware that he is acting, and act in such a way that they are not emotionally carried away by the performance. The Brechtian actor is not playing a role, but showing or quoting a theatrical character.

To the extent that it involves an ALIENATION from theatrical conventions that are so familiar as to appear natural, Brecht's theory has something in common with RUSSIAN FORMALISM'S concept of *OSTRANENIE* or defamiliarization. Written at a time when he was actively promoting Brecht's theories as a model for popular theatre (1956), BARTHES' demystifying studies of the MYTHOLOGIES of everyday life (1957) are intended to produce a cultural alienation-effect.

allegory A form of narrative or a visual image whose literal or obvious meaning masks one or more other meanings, often with a didactic purpose. Allegory is often defined as an extended or sustained METAPHOR. The term is taken from the Greek *allegoria*, which derives from the verb *agoreuein* ('to speak publicly', as in the marketplace or *agora*) and the adverbial form of *allos* ('other').

Allegory is one of the most common and fertile of all the devices used in literature and the visual arts, and it can be argued that it is an integral part of the Western philosophical tradition that stems from Plato and the contention that appearances are the allegorical equivalents of a higher reality. Allegory cannot be defined as a specific GENRE, as it can be an element of many different genres and can appear in both comic and tragic modes and may take the form of either prose or verse. Satire may take an allegorical form (Orwell's *Animal Farm*, 1945), but so too can the celebration and inculcation of moral values in Renaissance painting. One of the classic examples of allegory in English literature is John Bunyan's *The Pilgrim's Progress* (1678), in which Christian's decision to leave home in search of the Celestial City indicates a formal kinship with the genre of the quest-narrative. Most of the public statuary to be observed in Western cities is allegorical in nature, and can represent either civic virtues or historical events (Warner 1985 provides a fascinating account of allegorical statues). A village pageant or even a school play may be allegorical; the elaborate masques favoured by European court society were also allegories. *Love's Triumph through Callipolis* written by Ben Jonson, designed and staged by Inigo Jones and performed in the Whitehall Banqueting Hall in January 1631, was a typical example in which Charles I took the part of Heroic Love and, attended by lords dressed as other forms of exemplary love, drove evil forms of sensuality out of the land in a celebration of both the Platonic virtues and royal power (see *The King's Arcadia*, 1973).

Allegory in painting and sculpture is one of the objects of study of ICONOGRAPHY. Renaissance and post-Renaissance painters often took their conventional devices from icon-books such as Cesare Ripa's *Iconologia* of 1593, which recommended that 'Good Counsel' should be represented as an old man holding a book on which there perches an owl (an ancient symbol of wisdom); he tramples on a bear representing anger, and a dolphin representing haste (see the essay 'Titian's *Allegory of Prudence*' in Panofsky 1939).

The literary critic Northrop FRYE notes (1957) that commentary and interpretation are forms of allegory to the extent that they attach ideas to the structure of poetic or verbal imagery and extract a general meaning from them. Allegorical interpretation was an important aspect of the process (studied by Warner 1985) that allowed the Christian world to appropriate the art of the pagan Ancient World. The figure of the Greek Athena, virgin goddess and dispenser of justice, is gradually transformed into the Roman Minerva or goddess of wisdom and is then allegorically interpreted as a representation of Christianity's Cardinal Virtue of Prudence. Allegorical interpretation of the type that transforms a pagan goddess into a Christian virtue, or the eroticism of the 'Song of Songs' into a spiritual text, is possible because almost all allegories can be read on more than one level without losing their narrative consistency. *The Pilgrim's Progress* can, that is, be read as the story of a man called Christian who meets a giant called Despair and crosses a swamp called the Slough of Despond; schoolchildren read *Gulliver's Travels* with pleasure and without suspecting that it has multiple layers of political meaning. Spenser's *The Faerie Queene* (1590–96) can be read and enjoyed both as a chivalric romance and as a eulogy of Elizabeth I. A modern allegory such as Camus's *The Plague* (1947) can be read as an account of an outbreak of plague that occurred in the Algerian city of Oran in 194*. It can also be read as an allegory both of the Nazi occupation of France and of the human condition itself. A successful allegory is consistent and coherent at all levels.

READING: Fletcher (1964); Fowler (1982)

Althusser, Louis (1918–90) French Marxist philosopher. Perhaps the most sophisticated of postwar Marxists, Althusser introduced a new degree of intellectual rigour into Marxist philosophy by reworking its basic concepts. His contributions to the theory of IDEOLOGY as INTERPELLATION, and his concept of the IDEOLOGICAL STATE APPARATUS (1970), have been particularly influential, as has his attempt to conceptualize a theoretical link between MARXISM and PSYCHOANALYSIS (1993).

Althusser owes his initial celebrity to the essays collected in his *For Marx* (1965) and to *Reading 'Capital'* (1965; written jointly with Balibar), which originated in a seminar held at the École Normale Supérieure in 1964–5. Their publication almost coincided with that of LACAN's *Écrits* (1966) and FOUCAULT's *Les Mots et les choses* (1966; Words and things, transl. as *The Order of Things*) and all three authors tended, to their chagrin, to be seen as major representatives of STRUCTURALISM. In retrospect, Althusser looks less like a structuralist Marxist than a Marxist heir to the epistemological tradition of BACHELARD and, in particular, CANGUILHEM.

The titles of the two publications of 1965 define the Althusserian project with remarkable accuracy. Just as Lacan proposes a 'return to Freud', Althusser insists on the need to go back to Marx himself, and that implies a rigorous critique of most aspects of the tradition of WESTERN MARXISM, and especially its humanist aspects. For Althusser, Marxism is not a humanism based upon the argument that a human essence can be freed from its ALIENATION; the ethical humanism/alienation themes of the early Marx (1844) belong to a pre-Marxist PROBLEMATIC that is still governed by Feuerbachian and Hegelian concerns. The work of the mature Marx, in contrast, contains a science of modes of production and opens up a new historical continent. Marx's concepts are not, however, simply given in the text and must be recovered through the work of SYMPTOMATIC READING. Althusser seeks to demonstrate that Marx's work is the site of an EPISTEMOLOGICAL BREAK or a COPERNICAN REVOLUTION that founds Marxism as a science. Marx's historical situation meant that he was obliged to think with 'borrowed concepts' that mask his true discovery; the work of theory is intended to uncover the philosophy of DIALECTICAL MATERIALISM implicit in his writings. A similar line of argument is apparent in the very influential essay on Freud and Lacan (1969b), where it is argued that Lacan's reading of Freud facilitates the extraction of a scientific core of concepts (see Macey 1994).

Althusser's primary objective is to recover and redefine the rational and scientific content of Marxism and to draw strict lines of demarcation between materialism and idealism (1967). The importance of theory is therefore paramount; the understanding of theory must precede the understanding of reality, and revolutionary practice cannot exist without revolutionary theory. What Althusser terms theoretical practice, or the elaboration of a rigorous dialectical materialism, is in itself a form of class struggle. Althusser strenuously denies that Marxism is a HISTORICISM or a philosophy of history in which there is an essential connection between events and human consciousness of those events. Individual SUBJECTS are the 'supports' and not the agents of historical processes, which are so impersonal as to have no subject. This thesis, together with Althusser's supposed allegiance to structuralism, has led to the accusation that he denies the importance – or even the existence – of history (Thompson 1978). More sympathetic readers might argue that Althusser's comments on the 'interlacing' of the different temporalities of the various levels of the social formation (the term is used in preference to the ideologically loaded 'society') are close to the historiography of the *ANNALES* historians in that they indicate that history is not a single process, but a complex combination of trends that develop in accordance with different rhythms. There is, that is, no simple correspondence between the history of economic modes of production and that of political events or ideological formations.

Active in Catholic youth organizations as a young man, Althusser was a member of the French Communist Party from the early 1950s onwards, but was never, as has sometimes been claimed, the Party's 'official' philosopher. He was in fact an isolated and often embattled figure, whose writings appealed to a younger generation of intellectuals sympathetic to recent developments in the human sciences, rather than to the Party leadership. The reasons for his relative isolation are both theoretical and political. In his view, most of the critiques of Stalin made after the Twentieth Congress of the Communist Party of the Soviet Union in 1956 (when Khrushchev denounced Stalin's crimes: Khrushchev 1956) were essentially critiques from the right which were designed to discredit the heritage of Lenin, who is philosophically rehabilitated in an essay written in 1968 (1969a). Althusser's enthusiasm for Mao Zedong also made for an uneasy relationship with a resolutely pro-Soviet Party which could easily be accused of REVISIONISM. The important essay on CONTRADICTION and OVER-DETERMINATION (1962a) is a major attempt to extract a philosophical lesson from the Chinese experience of communism, but it did little to endear its author to the French Party.

Althusser's influence in France was at its greatest in the period 1965–8 and it waned considerably after the student revolt of 1968. Always distrustful of spontaneity and spontaneism and a devout upholder of the Leninist thesis (1902) that the organized vanguard party, and not spontaneous class-consciousness, is the sole agent of revolution, Althusser was highly critical of the student movement, and the suspicion was mutual. The final controversies surrounding Althusser were personal rather than political. After murdering his wife in 1990, he spent most of the rest of the life in psychiatric institutions and was unable to write or publish. The posthumous publication of two autobiographical texts (1992a) was surrounded by scandal and unpleasant speculation, but did lead to a renewed interest in his work. Two volumes of political and philosophical essays have been published posthumously (1994, 1995), together with a collection of writings on psychoanalysis (1993) and a diary kept during the years he spent in a German prisoner-of-war camp (1992b). Althusser's letters to Franca Madonta (1998), with whom he had a lengthy affair, constitute a revealing personal and intellectual autobiography.

READING: Boutang (1992); Elliott (1987, 1994)

ambivalence A term widely (and often loosely) used in PSYCHOANALYSIS to describe the simultaneous existence of contradictory feelings towards a single OBJECT. In his discussion of the 'Rat Man' case (1909b), FREUD speaks of a battle between love and hate raging in the lover's breast; the same person is the object of both emotions. For Freud, ambivalence stems from the basic bisexuality of human beings and from the structures of the OEDIPUS COMPLEX, which means that a child can simultaneously love and hate both its parents.

Ambivalence takes on a much greater importance in Kleinian theory (KLEIN; and see in particular Klein 1937). According to Klein, ambivalence is present in the earliest OBJECT-RELATIONS established by the child. Love for the object is inseparable from the wish to destroy it, and this ambivalence induces an anguished form of guilt. The mechanism of PROJECTION allows love and hate to be split and identified with good and bad objects, such as the good breast which provides nourishment and the bad breast which withholds it. A child of four to six months is usually mature enough to integrate these fragmented perceptions as it enters the so-called depressive position, but there is also a danger that a damaged object will be produced if good and bad part-objects are brought together. The attempts that the child makes to emphasize the altruistic aspect of the ambivalent object-relation, and the fear that the object will be lost or damaged beyond repair, prefigure crucial aspects of mature relationships.

anaclisis Term used by FREUD (1905a) to describe the early relationship between the sexual and the self-preservative DRIVES. The sexual drives are not initially autonomous, and are 'supported' by the vital functions of nutrition and protection that supply them with an OBJECT and an aim. The relationship between the two is most apparent in the oral activity of a child at the breast; the pleasure associated with sucking is associated with the need for nourishment, but also establishes an erotic relationship with the breast. The need for repeating the sexual satisfaction gradually becomes detached from the physical need as the sexual drive takes on an independent existence. The expression 'anaclitic object-choice' (Freud 1914a) refers to a form of object-choice in which the love-object is selected because it in some way resembles the parental figure that once provided the child with food, care and protection. This is one of two major categories of object-choice, the other being the narcissistic choice in which the love-object represents some aspect of the desiring subject.

Like CATHEXIS, anaclisis is a pseudo-classical coinage; it is derived by Freud's English translator from a Greek verb meaning 'to lean on'. The German *Anlehnung* derives from the commonplace verb *anlehnen* ('to lean against') and has no classical overtones.

analytic philosophy One of the dominant strands within English-language philosophy in the twentieth century, sometimes described as 'linguistic philosophy' or even, and somewhat erroneously given that many major figures like WITTGEN-STEIN in fact worked at Cambridge, 'Oxford philosophy'. Although the expressions 'analysis' and 'logical analysis' or 'conceptual analysis' have been in common use since the 1930s, 'analytic philosophy' did not really become current until the 1950s; two of the classic anthologies do not use even the term in their titles (Feigl and Sellars 1948; Flew 1951). ORDINARY LANGUAGE philosophy and SPEECH ACT theory can both be seen as by-products of analytic philosophy. Despite its influence, it would be difficult to describe analytic philosophy as a school in the sense that one can speak of a 'Hegelian school'; it represents, rather, a shared attitude towards a number of problem areas relating mainly to language. No one figure has ever been dominant within analytic philosophy, but Russell, FREGE, WITTGENSTEIN and LOGICAL POSITIVISM were the main influences on its development. Michael Dummet (1925–; see Dummet 1973, 1978), Hilary Putnam (1926–; see Putnam 1988) and Willard Quine (1908–; see Quine 1953) are widely regarded as its most important contemporary spokesmen.

Analytic philosophy can be characterized in negative terms by its lack of interest in post-Kantian developments in European or CONTINENTAL PHILOSOPHY. Its scepticism about METAPHYSICS leads it to dismiss both Hegelian philosophy and PHENOMENOLOGY as so many exercises in speculation. As Wittgenstein argues in the *Tractatus Logico-Philosophicus* (1921), the task of philosophy is not to construct new theories, but to contribute to human understanding by clarifying the logic of language. There are two main tendencies within analytic philosophy. Influenced by Frege and the VIENNA CIRCLE, some practitioners are mainly concerned with artificially constructed languages or 'calculi'; others follow AUSTIN in concentrating on the intricacies of everyday language and claim that it holds the solution to many philosophical problems (see the essays collected in Chappell 1964). Although a concern with language is absolutely central to analytic philosophy, few if any of its advocates display any interest in linguistics as such.

Analytic philosophy can be seen in historical terms as an heir to the EMPIRICISM of Locke and Hume. 'Analysis', that is, is understood as meaning the reduction of complex ideas to their ultimate simple constituent ideas. Whereas the empiricists of the seventeenth and eighteenth centuries were attempting to establish a psychologistic EPISTEMOLOGY, the notion of 'analysis' is applied in the twentieth century to language and particularly propositions. The influence of G. E. Moore (1873–1958) and Bertrand Russell (1872–1970) is crucial here. In the *Principia Ethica* (1903) Moore argues that 'reality' consists of concepts that have been combined to form propositions, whilst Russell holds that the elementary propositions of logic are ultimate truths about the logical laws of reality (Russell and Whitehead 1910; Russell 1918). It follows that the task of philosophy is to clarify and verify those elementary or atomistic propositions and truths. Similar arguments are advanced by Frege, whose 'concept script' (*Begriffsschrift*) was designed as a logically perfect language which could, thanks to its high level of FORMALIZATION, reveal the structures of thought, which are obscured by natural languages. Both Wittgenstein and Russell argue on similar grounds that the true logical content of any proposition is concealed by ordinary language and that only reductive analysis can reveal it for what it is. The elementary propositions thus uncovered represent the world as it is. One of the major theses associated with varieties of analytic philosophy such as Wittgenstein's LANGUAGE GAMES, Austin's SPEECH-ACT theory and logical positivism is therefore the contention that philosophy has a curative or therapeutic function because what appear to be philosophical problems arise from the misuse or imprecise use of language. The primary task of philosophy is therefore not to supply truths about the universe (that task is left to the natural sciences) but to demonstrate to someone who is puzzled by a metaphysical question that the question is puzzling precisely because it is meaningless and therefore unanswerable.

The curative or therapeutic goals of analytic philosophy are well illustrated by Gilbert Ryle (1900–76), whose *Concept of Mind* (1949) demonstrates that the mind–body problem which has concerned philosophy since the seventeenth century is the product of a 'category mistake' (such as the attribution of the properties of colour to sound) or an error in the use of language. The model of body and mind dualism constructed by Descartes is described as the myth of the 'ghost in the machine', in which an immaterial soul interacts with a physical body. In order to describe their interaction, Descartes makes the category mistake of applying to mental phenomena the vocabulary that is employed to describe physical phenomena, and thus transforms the mind into a ghost of the material world rather than a distinct entity. Analytic philosophy is viewed by its supporters as a defence against such confusions. For its detractors, it represents an obsession with trivial linguistic puzzles and cannot provide a basis for a true philosophy, not least because many of the problems it addresses are specific to the English language.

READING: Feigl and Sellars (1948); Flew (1951); Hacker (1996a); Williams and Montefiore (1966)

anamorphis A device used in sixteenth- and seventeenth-century painting, involving a deliberate distortion of perspective. Anamorphic paintings depict an object in such a way as to make it unrecognizable when viewed in normal perspective; when viewed from a specific angle or in a curved mirror, it can be seen for what it is. One of the most famous examples is Holbein's *The Ambassadors* (1533, National Gallery, London). It portrays two richly dressed diplomats surrounded by symbols of wealth and worldly vanity. In the foreground is a strange elongated object resembling a cuttle-fish bone; when viewed from the correct angle, it can be seen to be a skull. Although the anamorphic effect is clearly intended to amuse, it also has a moral purpose. The concealed skull is a *memento mori* or a reminder of the inevitability of death.

anaphora In RHETORIC, a TROPE in which the same word is repeatedly used at the beginning of a sequence of clauses or sentences.

Anderson, Benedict (1936–) A distinguished specialist in South-East Asian studies (Anderson 1990), Anderson has received wide acclaim for his study of the origins and nature of modern nationalism (1983; revised edn 1991).

Anderson defines the nation as an imagined political community which is seen by its citizen-subjects as both inherently limited and sovereign. Its members do not know all their fellow nationals, but all share an image of their communion. A nation is limited in that finite, if elastic, borders divide it from other nations, and it is sovereign to the extent that is free and conceived as a deep horizontal comradeship. Its sense of identity is grounded in an imagined historical continuity which may be quite illusory; to claim that the English tradition is founded by Magna Carta is to ignore the fact that its signatories spoke Anglo-Norman and did not and could not regard themselves as Englishmen.

The origins of modern nationalism are traced back not to self-consciously held political ideologies, but to the decline of the religious communities and dynastic realms that preceded it. The decline of universal sacred languages such as Latin and their replacement by national vernaculars disseminated through print technology is a major feature of the emergence of nations. Modern nations become imaginable thanks to the interaction between the emergence of capitalism, technologies of communication and the fatality of linguistic diversity. The existence and promotion of national vernaculars play an important role in the emergence of an imagined national identity both in Europe and elsewhere. *Bahasa Indonesia* (literally 'Indonesian Language') was, for example, originally a lingua franca, but it has provided the means for the unification of a 'nation' comprising many ethnically distinct groups with no common identity prior to colonization.

Anderson's discussion of the imagined community has had a major influence on some forms of POSTCOLONIAL THEORY (Bhabha 1990a; Loomba 1998).

Anderson, Perry (1938–) British historian, long-time editor of *NEW LEFT REVIEW* and a key figure in the history of the British NEW LEFT.

The so-called Nairn–Anderson theses of 1963–4 (Anderson 1964; Nairn 1964) effectively set the New Left's agenda for the next decade by arguing that the incomplete nature of the English revolution of the seventeenth century had resulted in stultifying alliance between sections of the old nobility and the rising bourgeoisie which left social structures largely intact, and whose effects were still being felt. It had bequeathed a legacy of cultivated backwardness and empiricism, and had prevented the emergence in Britain of either an indigenous tradition of Marxism or a rigorous sociology. In the absence of a systematic history of British society, a fragmented anti-intellectualism had been allowed to flourish. The theses led to major polemic between the historian E. P. THOMPSON (1965) and Anderson (1966, 1968a), and to serious and lasting divisions between those who argued the case for an indigenous British tradition of radicalism and those who contended that the systematic analysis of British society required more sophisticated tools and turned to the broad tradition of WESTERN MARXISM in general and GRAMSCI in particular, the key texts here being Anderson's 'Introduction to Gramsci' (1968b) and 'The Antinomies of Antonio Gramsci' (1976b). A good account of all these developments is given by Anderson himself in his *Arguments within English Marxism* (1980); Thompson gives his rather different account in 'The Peculiarities of the English' (1965). In retrospect, the Nairn–Anderson theses can be seen as one of the sources of the call for THEORY that still echoes through so many areas of British cultural life.

Whilst Anderson and Nairn had called for a systematic examination of British history, Anderson himself actually embarked on the rather different and very ambitious project of examining the transition from Antiquity to feudalism and then absolutism in two wide-ranging studies of European history (1974a, 1974b). These were intended to be the prologue to a comparative history of the capitalist states of Europe. Whilst that project has not been completed, the two volumes of 1974 are classic examples of Anderson's erudition and critical engagement with the tradition of HISTORICAL MATERIALISM.

Anderson's later work consists mainly of essays surveying the development of Western Marxism (1976a) and its principal representatives, and more general studies in British politics (1992a) and intellectual history (1992b). As the radicalism of the 1960s and early 1970s subsided, his tone became more detached and even sceptical. By the mid-1980s, he was describing the Paris that had once been seen as a revolutionary storm-centre as the 'capital of European intellectual reaction', and speaking sardonically of the 'inflation of the signifier' brought about by STRUCTURALISM and its heirs (1983). A major contributor to the wide debate on the nature and politics of MODERNITY and POSTMODERNITY, Anderson is one of the most eloquent intellectual historians to have emerged from within the New Left. His essay on the origins of postmodernity (1998) provides a typically lucid survey of its subject-matter and introduces a historical dimension that is sometimes overlooked by participants in the debate.

READING: Elliott (1995); Lin Chun (1993)

angry young man The application of this term to someone who expresses dissatisfaction with traditional and establishment values has become a cliché. The phrase was first applied to the young British dramatists and novelists of the 1950s, and the original angry young man was Jimmy Porter in John Osborne's play *Look Back in Anger* (first performed at London's Royal Court Theatre in 1956). The source of his anger is the bitter realization that there are no good causes left to die for.

READING: Taylor, John Russell (1963)

Annales French history journal founded in 1929 by Lucien Febvre (1878–1956) and Marc Bloch (1886–1944). The original title *Annales d'histoire économique et sociale* was changed to *Annales: histoires, économies, civilisations* in 1946. Most of France's best known historians, including BRAUDEL and Le Roy Ladurie, have been associated with the journal. Although its title refers to 'civilizations' in the plural, the focus is almost exclusively French.

Annales was founded in reaction against the positivist tendency to reduce historiography to a trivial collection of facts pertaining mainly to a political history defined in the narrowest of senses, and it has always been characterized by a dismissal of 'factual' history, or *HISTOIRE ÉVÉNEMENTIELLE*, in favour of the *LONGUE DURÉE* or long-term structural trends. Initially, the journal concentrated on economic history but, partly because of the influence of the sociology of Emile Durkheim (see Lukes 1973), it also pioneered the HISTORY OF MENTALITIES. The journal's approach has always been resolutely interdisciplinary, and in keeping with Febvre's insistence that historians should also be geographers, sociologists and psychologists capable of writing the history of the entire range of human activities. Febvre also defined the new history as problem-oriented. Although its findings have been challenged, Febvre's own study of the problem of unbelief in the sixteenth century (1942) is a good example of problem-oriented historiography which attempts to demonstrate that modern atheism was quite literally unthinkable in the age of Rabelais.

Differences of opinion between individual authors make it difficult to speak of an *Annales* 'school', but there is a definite *Annales* spirit or style. It has, for example, become almost the norm for *Annales* historians to follow the example of Braudel's great study of the Mediterranean world (1949) by beginning their books with an essay in geohistory that sets the object of study in its physical and geographical environment. Although many of the studies published under the auspices of *Annales* are highly technical and rely heavily on the quantitative statistical analysis of, for example, the changing price of grain or salt, others, such as Philippe Ariès's histories of childhood (1960) and death (1985) or Le Roy Ladurie's best-selling *Montaillou* (1978), have enjoyed great popular success. The influence of *Annales* is not confined to professional academic historians; it is difficult to imagine FOUCAULT's histories of madness (1961) and prisons (1975) being written without the precedent it set.

READING: Burke (1990)

anophobia Neologism coined by GREER in her study of the menopause (1991), derived from the Latin *anus* ('old woman'), and defined as an irrational fear and loathing of old women. Anophobia finds its prime expression in the work of the male doctors and health professionals who use Hormone Replacement Therapy and other medical technologies in an attempt to eliminate the natural processes of aging and the menopause in order to keep all women perpetually appetizing and responsive to male sexual demands by perpetuating the MASQUERADE of eternal youth.

anti-psychiatry A radical tendency within clinical psychiatry that rose to prominence in the 1960s. It was highly critical of conventional methods of psychotherapy and questioned the very existence of mental illness. Although many of the themes of anti-psychiatry were outlined in articles published by the Hungarian-American Thomas S. Szasz from the 1950s (1961), its most prominent spokesmen were the British psychiatrists R. D. Laing (1927–89) and David Cooper (1931–86).

Anti-psychiatry originated in a rejection of classic therapies and especially drug therapies and electroconvulsive therapy. Claiming that doctors had a lot to learn from their patients, Laing and his colleagues dismissed conventional views about hospitalization and established small therapeutic communities, such as Kingsley Hall in East London, and lived there with their patients. Patients suffering from acute PSYCHOSIS were guided on a regressive journey back to infancy and then to a personal rebirth that produced a spontaneous cure (Berke and Barnes 1971). Mental illness was viewed not as a disease, but as a social label attached to certain individuals by an alienated society and the psychiatrists who were its agents; mental ALIENATION was explicitly equated with social alienation. Schizophrenia, in particular, was seen as the result of interactions within the family nexus, with the so-called schizophrenic being scapegoated for breakdowns in communication (Laing and Esterton 1964). The basic model of social interaction was clearly derived from SARTRE'S EXISTENTIALISM (Laing and Cooper 1964) and Gregory Bateson's descriptions of the 'double-bind' situation in which an individual is obliged by the family situation to respond to simultaneous but contradictory messages (Bateson et al. 1956; see also the essays collected in Bateson 1972).

Anti-psychiatry rapidly became part of the radical counter-culture of the late 1960s and early 1970s, especially when a parallel was drawn between the schizophrenic experience and the psychedelic ('mind-expanding') experience induced by hallucinogens such as L. S. D. Laing's *The Divided Self* (1960) and especially his *Politics of Experience* (1967) became central to a positive celebration of schizophrenia as a virtual liberation from the alienated society (hence such slogans as 'Do not adjust your mind; there is a fault in reality'). Ken Loach's film *Family Life* (1971), on which Laing worked as an adviser, accurately captures the climate of anti-psychiatry.

Outside Britain, the influence of anti-psychiatry was probably greatest in Italy, where Franco Basglia and the Psichiatria Democratica group established therapeutic communities based on the Laingian model (see Guattari 1970 and the introduction to Genosko 1996). In France, there was great enthusiasm for anti-psychiatric theories amongst the generation of 1968, but the movement had little practical impact, partly because even sympathizers like GUATTARI also remained true to the psychoanalytic tradition (Guattari 1976).

READING: Boyers and Orrill (1971)

anxiety of influence Term used by the American literary theorist Harold Bloom (1973, 1994) to describe the young author's experience of the UNCANNY when he recognizes the influence of his predecessors in his own work. The shock of recognition is so powerful that the author may despair of being able to write anything at all, or become convinced that he can only reproduce the work of his forebears. A strong poet such as Milton or Blake is able to overwhelm the literary tradition and to subsume it into his own original writing; weak poets are paralysed by the anxiety of influence. Strong literary originality and the ability to subsume tradition are the hallmarks of canonical texts (CANON). Bloom's theory is heavily influenced by Freudian PSYCHOANALYSIS (FREUD): the literary tradition is likened to the repressed material in the individual UNCONSCIOUS, and the quasi-Oedipal relations between the generations to a form of TRANSFERENCE.

Although certain feminist critics argue, like SHOWALTER (1977), that Bloom's theory is so reliant upon an Oedipal struggle between fathers and sons that it can scarcely be applied to women's writing, GILBERT AND GUBAR contend in their *Madwoman in the Attic* (1979a) that it can be modified to explore the way in which women writers from Jane Austen to Emily Dickinson have always struggled against the image of the 'woman writer' produced by male authors and male texts.

aphasia Loss or impairment of the faculty of speech and the ability to understand language. Drawing on the work of the British neurologist John Hughlings Jackson, the linguist Roman JAKOBSON argues (1941, 1956) that the phenomena associated with aphasia present an inverted image of the process of language-acquisition. The two main types of aphasia are similarity disorder and contiguity disorder, and they impair the ability to use metaphor and metonymy respectively. Aphasia thus provides a negative confirmation of the thesis that all language is structured around the twin poles or axes of METAPHOR/METONYMY.

aporia The literal meaning of the word is 'an unpassable path', and it is used in Greek philosophy to describe the perplexity induced by a group of statements which, whilst they are individually plausible, are inconsistent or contradictory when taken together (see Plato, *The Republic*, *Philebus* and *Protagoras*). In RHETORIC, the term is applied to the deliberate expression of doubt or uncertainty. The idea of aporia has been taken up by deconstructionists such as DERRIDA, who use it to describe the undecidability of terms that cannot be reduced to a play of binary oppositions. Derrida's exploration of the aporias present in Plato's use of the word *pharmakon*, which can mean both 'poison' and 'antidote', is the classic example of the deconstructionist use of the term (1968).

READING: Kofman (1983)

archaeology of knowledge A mode of historical and epistemological inquiry developed by FOUCAULT (1966, 1969a). Foucault explains (1971b) that he derives the term from the German *philosophische Archäologie*, the phrase used by Kant to designate 'the history of that which makes a certain form of thought necessary' (Bernauer 1990).

Foucault's archaeology of knowledge is concerned, not with the evolution of ideas, but with the emergence and transformation of DISCURSIVE FORMATIONS and with the underlying EPISTEME that governs relations between them. Archaeology deals with what Foucault terms the 'positive unconscious of knowledge', that is, with a level of knowledge that eludes the consciousness of individual scientists and thinkers but that provides their theories with underlying rules and structures. The archaeology undertaken by Foucault in *The Order of Things* demonstrates that Renaissance thinking was governed by an episteme for which the world was a vast syntactic system in which all beings communicated with their environment through a series of similarities and correspondences. In contrast, the thought of the classical age (the seventeenth and eighteenth centuries) is characterized or governed by a combination of *mathesis* (a general mathematical science of order), *taxonomia* (a more empirical form of classification) and genetic analysis. Foucault demonstrates that, although no single text produced in the period actually describes this episteme, its structures inform the work of the natural historians, political economists, grammarians and philosophers of the period.

In the early 1970s, Foucault begins to describe his methodology as a GENEALOGY of knowledge, but in general he appears to regard archaeology and genealogy as being complementary rather than mutually exclusive.

archetype A central term in JUNG's analytical psychology. It is conceptually related to the term IMAGO, introduced by Jung (1911) to describe an unconscious prototypical figure of a mother, father or sibling. In 1912 Jung begins to describe such figures as 'primordial images'; he introduces the noun 'archetype' in 1919. The adjective 'archetypal' is applied by Jungians to the overall pattern of a life-cycle that goes from childhood to early maturity, to the mid-life transition and finally to death.

Archetypes in the strict sense are primordial and universal images that make up the contents of the COLLECTIVE UNCONSCIOUS, and their existence is revealed by the regular patterns of imagery that reoccur in individual dreams, artistic productions and primitive religions and mythologies. Archetypes are by definition unconscious, but they can be activated by specific circumstances and can thus affect or even dominate the conscious life. They are held by Jung to be part of a collective memory and experience, and are described as spontaneous products of the psyche that are present within the individual psyche from birth onwards. One of the most powerful archetypes is the animus/anima figure (see Emma Jung 1957). The animus is a woman's archetypal image of man; the anima, man's archetypal image of woman. Both can take a wide variety of forms ranging from the wise old man to the virginal girl and the mother goddess. In more general terms, the anima can be described as the feminine side of the male psyche, and the animus as the masculine side of the female psyche.

Jung's theory of archetypes has influenced some literary theorists such as BACHEL-ARD and FRYE.

archive An important concept in the ARCHAEOLOGY OF KNOWLEDGE elaborated by FOUCAULT (1969a). The 'archive' is essentially the law governing what can and cannot be said in a given period or situation, or the general system that governs the formation and transformation of statements and sentences. In this model of DISCOURSE analysis, the archive is the second of three levels. The most general level is that of 'language' (*langue*; the term is adapted from SAUSSURE's *LANGUE/PAROLE* distinction), or the system that defines the sum total of all the sentences that it is possible to construct; the 'corpus' is a description of all the sentences that have actually been spoken. The intermediary level of the archive determines which sentences can be spoken, manipulated and analysed.

Arendt, Hannah (1906–75) German-American political philosopher. Arendt's career began with a thesis on the concept of love in St Augustine (1929), but her reputation rests on the studies in political philosophy produced after the Second World War. Forced into exile by German Fascism and anti-Semitism, she worked with Jewish refugee organizations in Paris and then the United States where she published numerous articles on Jewish politics and related essays (posthumously collected 1978b) in which she explores and analyses the twin stereotypes of 'the Jew as parvenu' and 'the Jew as pariah'.

Arendt's most significant work is the monumental *Origins of Totalitarianism* (1951). It represents an attempt to arrive at a pitiless but objective intellectual reconciliation with the absolute evil of the Holocaust. It also establishes a new typology of political states by identifying the common elements in communism and Fascism, seen as manifestations of the broader and historically unprecedented phenomenon of totalitarianism. Fascism and communism are analysed, that is, as variants on the same totalitarian model. Drawing on the crowd psychology of Gustave Le Bon and FREUD (1921) as well as Neumann's classic description of the Third Reich (1944), she describes totalitarianism as a force which abolishes both classes and CIVIL SOCIETY, and which transforms all social groups into a structureless mass of furious individuals. Once legality has been abolished, totalitarianism can establish the rule of History (communism) or Nature (Fascism) without translating it into a set of standards of right and wrong by which individuals can live their lives. Although Arendt's analysis of totalitarianism was very influential in the 1950s, it has often been pointed out that her analysis of Soviet communism is much weaker than that of German Nazism.

In a series of later studies (especially 1958, 1961), Arendt outlines a more general political theory centred on a triple distinction between 'labour' (meeting needs), 'work' (constructing a stable collective world) and 'action' (public activity in the public sphere). Her notion of public activity owes much to an idealized vision of the citizen-democracy of Ancient Greece, and defines political action as the noblest of activities. Politics is seen as a realm of freedom that transcends the world of labour and the mere satisfaction of needs. For Arendt, democracy is not defined by a political principle but by the action and will of its citizens, but it is the only defence against the threat of totalitarianism. The argument is expanded in the unfinished *Life of the Mind* (1978a), which tends to give greater importance to the contemplative life.

In 1961, Arendt covered the trial of Adolph Eichmann, who had been kidnapped and put on trial in Israel for his wartime crimes against humanity, for the *New Yorker*. Her report on the 'banality of evil' (1963) is a chilling account of the workings of Nazism, but continues to cause controversy because of her account of the role played by Jewish community leaders during the Holocaust. The phrase has often been misunderstood, and is not intended to suggest that the evil of Nazism was banal, but that those who committed it were banal human beings and bureaucrats like Eichmann, rather than the monsters portrayed in more lurid accounts.

READING: Young-Bruehl (1982)

Arielism A tendency within Latin American MODERNISM which takes its name from the essay *Ariel* published in 1900 by the Uruguayan José Henrique Rodó (1871–1917) and frequently reprinted throughout the continent. *Arielismo* takes its symbolism from Shakespeare's *The Tempest*, as reinterpreted by Ernest Renan (1823–92) in his philosophical drama *Caliban* (1878). For the French writer, Caliban represented the masses and the democracy that threatened to destroy the aristocratic culture embodied in Prospero and the life of the spirit (Ariel) that inspired it. Rodó uses the same symbolism but holds that democracy and equality of opportunity in education will lead to the emergence of a cultured elite, or a new Ariel who will lead Latin America to a higher civilization based on the best European values. The immense popularity of Arielism was due to a number of factors. It offered a cultural model which transcended national barriers, which appealed to the ideals of the white population and which seemed to be applicable to the whole continent, viewed as a supranational entity. Because it stressed the importance of intellectual and spiritual values, it also provided the basis for a critique of what was perceived as the gross materialism of the United States and for the comforting myth that, unlike Latin Americans, its citizens had no cultural standards. Arielism did not really survive the impact of the First World War, in which the supposedly higher civilizations of Western Europe devoted their energies to destroying one another.

READING: Franco (1970)

Artaud, Antonin (1896–1948) French poet, actor, theorist of the THEATRE OF CRUELTY (1938) and a major point of reference for KRISTEVA and the critics associated with *TEL QUEL*.

Artaud was associated with SURREALISM and produced a series of violent manifestos denouncing the rectors of European universities (coauthored with Michel Leiris, 1925a) and attacking Christianity (Artaud 1925b) but was expelled from the surrealist group by BRETON on the grounds that he was more interested in the transformation of the soul than in social and political revolution. Artaud was a heavy user of drugs, including the hallucinogens he discovered in Mexico, and spent long periods in psychiatric institutions. At its most intense, his poetry describes the painful disintegration of language, the mind and the body. His language does not 'describe' pain; it *is* itself the experience of physical and mental pain. It is this equation between the linguistic and the physical, or the exploration of language as physical-psychical reality, that makes him so appealing to Kristeva and others. As a film actor, Artaud played Marat in Abel Gance's *Napoleon* (1925) and Frère Massieu in Carl Dreyer's *The Passion of Joan of Arc* (1927), and the images of his face and staring eyes are amongst the most haunting in European silent film. The late self-portraits executed during his final years in a mental hospital (reproduced in *Paris Post-War*, 1993) have the same fearful intensity.

READING: Artaud (1976); Hayman (1977)

Auerbach, Erich (1892–1957) German-American critic. Auerbach is best known for his *Mimesis* (1946), which is one of the great classic studies in comparative literature.

Although its time-scale is immense and moves from Homer to Virginia WOOLF and Proust, *Mimesis* does not really elaborate a theory of literary realism. It examines, rather, the history of the representation of reality in literary texts and the structural concept of reality operating in the texts under consideration. Auerbach opens his study with close readings of the scene in Book XIX of the *Odyssey* where Odysseus is recognized by his housekeeper and sometime nurse, and of the biblical story of the sacrifice of Isaac. In the course of his readings he establishes that there is in Western literature a tension between the biblical and Hellenic traditions, or between sensory appearance and meaning. 'Meaning' refers not to the immediate semantics of the text, but to the deeper sense of experience governing the selection and articulation of its themes. Ultimately, it relates to a world-view: the differences between the narrow and repetitious parataxis of *La Chanson de Roland* and the looser structures of medieval German epics reflect the different structural concepts of reality characteristic of different societies.

Auerbach is not a particularly philosophical critic, but his methodological assumptions are grounded in a broadly Hegelian belief that a society and its culture form a totality and that their parts resemble the whole. He assumes, that is, that a series of randomly selected realistic texts from a given period will contain recurrent motifs that express a concept of reality common to writers and readers. Each of the twenty chapters of *Mimesis* therefore begins with a textual commentary in which philological, grammatical and semantic analyses are combined to reveal that concept of reality.

aura An important, but very ambiguous, term used by Walter BENJAMIN in his account of the work of art in the period of MODERNITY (1935, 1936). It refers primarily to that quality of a painting or sculpture seen in the immediacy of 'its here and now' (*sein Hier und Jetzt*), or its 'unique existence at the place where it happens to be' (Benjamin 1936). In his famous description of the work of art in the age of mechanical reproduction (meaning lithography and then photography), Benjamin remarks that not even the most perfect reproduction can capture this fleeting aura. In the earlier but related essay on photography (1931), the notion of aura is associated with the atmospheric character of early photographs; this too is destroyed as more perfect processes of reproduction strip the object bare. Aura is said to originate in the original ritual or cultic function of primitive works of art, and to be destroyed as mechanical reproduction transforms their ritual value into exhibition value. As Adorno remarks (1970), Benjamin appears to be both nostalgic for and critical of the phenomenon of aura. He both regrets the loss of the non-recuperable experience of perceiving the art work in its *Hier und Jetzt* and welcomes its liberation from parasitical dependence on ritual, arguing that it can now be based on the new practice of politics. The loss of aura is associated with the AVANT-GARDE practices of movements like DADA, which Benjamin describes as relentlessly destroying the aura of their own creations. It is clear from both essays that Benjamin also associated aura with the contemplation of nature and landscape. Elsewhere the term 'aura' is associated with the essence revealed by the 'profane illumination' (see Cohen 1993) induced by contemplating objects when under the influence of hashish.

READING: Buck-Morss (1977), (1989)

Austin, John Langshaw (1911–60) British philosopher, best known for his theory of the PERFORMATIVE and a major figure in the ORDINARY LANGUAGE debate. Austin's work, together with that of John SEARLE (1969), lays the foundations for the theory of SPEECH ACTS. He published only seven papers in his lifetime (collected with other materials 1970); both his books were reconstructed from lecture notes and published posthumously (1962a, 1962b). Austin is also the translator of FREGE's *Foundations of Arithmetic* (1884).

Austin has no general theory of philosophical method or of language and displays no interest in formal or technical linguistics. His major concern is to undertake a careful examination of how words are actually used in ordinary language, and his work is guided by the conviction that a sharpened awareness of words will lead to a sharpened perception of phenomena. Traditional philosophical problems tend to be dismissed by Austin on the grounds that they arise from verbal confusion and from a telescoping of meaning by philosophers. The careful analysis of shades of meaning is therefore a technique that can be used to dissolve philosophical doubts and worries. It is, according to Austin, philosophers, and not things, that are simple; a tendency to oversimplification is not the occupational disease of philosophers, but their actual occupation. Philosophy is, or should be, 'the fun of discovery, the pleasure of cooperation, and the satisfaction of reaching agreement'. Austin's wit and sense of fun are best displayed in his attack (1962b) on A. J. Ayer's claim (1940) that immediately perceived sense-data rather than physical objects provide the foundations of empirical knowledge.

The standard criticism of Austin (Gellner 1953; Graham 1977) is that the minimal differences of meaning – between, for instance, 'looks', 'seems' and 'appears' (Austin 1962b) – he discusses have no general philosophical significance and are merely variations in idiom that are irrelevant to anyone with a native COMPETENCE in English.

***auteur* theory** A theory of film associated mainly with the French critic André BAZIN and the younger critics who wrote for *CAHIERS DU CINÉMA* of the 1950s. *Auteur* ('author') theory holds that great film directors are artists on a par with the great novelists. Films made by a true *auteur* display a thematic consistency and an artistic development through time. The theory was developed mainly with reference to Hollywood cinema and is in part a reaction to the criticism that American films are almost anonymous products of the studio system and the CULTURE INDUSTRY. The original *auteurs* included Alfred Hitchcock, Vincent Minelli, Howard Hawks, Nicholas Ray and John Ford. The theory was gradually abandoned as the critics associated with *Cahiers* turned to STRUCTURALISM and SEMIOLOGY for their theoretical model.

Although the original pantheon of authors consisted of American directors, the debate about authorship was largely about the future of French cinema. The key text is Truffaut's 'A Certain Tendency in French Cinema' (1954), where he attacks the French tradition of 'quality cinema' in which the director was seen simply as the man who added the pictures to a preexistent literary scenario. The battle over authorship was decisively won by the young directors of the *NOUVELLE VAGUE*.

The original *Cahiers* critics spoke of a *politique des auteurs* ('author policy'), and the idea of a hierarchy of artistic merit was always present in their work. The more familiar '*auteur* theory' was popularized in English by the journal *Movie* and by Andrew Sarris's important study of American cinema (1968).

READING: *Cahiers du cinéma* vol. 1, 1985

authentic The standard translation of HEIDEGGER's *eigentlich*. For Heidegger (1927, 1975a), authenticity is the mode of being of those who seek to understand their existential situation and their freedom to realize their existential possibilities. Authenticity is contrasted with the inauthenticity of the mode of DASEIN in which individuals are tranquillized by the apparent familiarity of the world, are convinced that they understand everything, and thus drift into ALIENATION. The constant tendency to lapse back into inauthenticity is described as 'falling' (*verfallen, das Verfallen*). Authenticity draws back from falling to obtain a vision of the individual's situation, and implies a resoluteness in the face of BEING-TOWARDS-DEATH and the feeling of anxiety (*Angst*) or care (*Sorge*) it induces.

The term 'authenticity' (*authenticité*) is used by SARTRE (1943a) in a similar (and derivative) sense to describe a lucid and truthful awareness of a SITUATION, and the conscious assumption of the responsibilities and possibilities it affords. The individual subject moves towards authenticity by assuming or 'making his own' that situation as the basis of the freedom to which he is condemned. For both Heidegger and Sartre, authenticity is a future-oriented project rather than a state or condition. The statement 'I am authentic' signals a lapse into inauthenticity or BAD FAITH because it claims that the individual has, or has achieved, a timeless and changeless essence.

avant-garde The French term originally designated that section of an army which marched into battle ahead of the main body of troops (the 'van') but has come to be used in both French and English to describe pioneering or innovatory trends in the arts, and especially music and the visual arts. It originates in the work of the utopian socialist Henri de Saint-Simon (1760–1825), who applies it to the elite of artists, scientists and industrialists who will be the leaders of the new social order. The notion of an artistic avant-garde was reinforced by currents associated with the short-lived Revolution of 1848, and by Gustave Courbet's definition of the new realism as democracy in art (Nochlin 1968). The term acquired much greater currency in the early years of the twentieth century (Shattuck 1969).

The idea of avant-gardism implies that progress is always the result of a rebellion against an entrenched establishment. It is linked to the concept of innovation and MODERNITY encapsulated in the French poet Rimbaud's defiant cry (1873): '*Il faut être absolument moderne*' ('We must be absolutely modern'). Bürger's influential account of the theory of the avant-garde (1980) describes DADA and SURREALISM as typical avant-garde movements which attack the institutional status of art in bourgeois society. For many theorists of MODERNISM, the avant-garde and the self-consciously new are the only adequate defences against KITSCH (Greenberg 1941) or the commodified mass culture of the CULTURE INDUSTRY.

B

Bachelard, Gaston (1884–1962) French philosopher of science and literary theorist. It has rightly been said (Lecourt 1972) that there are two Gaston Bachelards: the austere philosopher of science who outlines the philosophy of concepts and EPISTEMOLOGICAL BREAKS that so influenced CANGUILHEM, ALTHUSSER and FOUCAULT, and the self-indulgent literary theorist who, in his studies of the IMAGINARY, reverts to the very PHENOMENOLOGY he criticizes in his work on the sciences. In a late essay on the POETICS of daydreaming (1960), Bachelard makes it clear that, in his view, this apparent duality reflects the duality of human knowledge itself. Human knowledge is organized around the contrasting poles of 'concepts' and 'images'. A scientific concept is purely intellectual, devoid of all images and afterimages, and has cast off its prehistory thanks to the epistemological break that wrests it out of an ideological past; a poetic image is a product of the imaginary that opens up an infinite future for both reader and writer.

Bachelard's scientific background was in mathematics and physics, and his historical studies tend to concentrate on those sciences. In a series of major works on the history of the sciences (1928, 1934, 1940, 1953), Bachelard traces a non-continuous history in which concepts emerge from earlier concepts through a process of correction and rectification. The history of science traces their emergence and reconstructs the breaks that made it possible. When we look at the sciences of the past, we do not find 'earlier versions' of modern concepts, but a different conceptual network defining different objects of knowledge that can be evaluated on the basis of later developments. Thus the word 'electricity' can be found in the physics of both the eighteenth and the nineteenth centuries, but the changing configuration of knowledge means that the concept of electricity changes dramatically. Bachelard takes a disparaging view of most forms of philosophy, arguing that philosophers tend to cling to outmoded scientific concepts and that modern science cannot be confined to any one doctrine such as idealism, realism or positivism. The truly scientific philosophy typified by the philosophy of physics is for Bachelard a 'philosophy of no' (1940) which refuses to be confined within any given doctrine and which therefore promotes an openness that is in keeping with the open and unfinished quality of scientific progress itself.

The opposite pole of Bachelard's epistemology produces an attractive series of studies (1942, 1943, 1948a and 1948b) of the archetypal dreams and daydreams associated with the themes of 'water' (repose), 'air' (movement) and 'earth' (will-power and work, but also rest). He has also produced fascinating studies of the typical reveries induced by watching a fire in the hearth (1938b) or the flickering flame of a candle which evokes reveries about the past (1961). The most coherent exposition of Bachelard's thematic and phenomenological poetics is found in *The Poetics of Reverie* (1960). Although Bachelard describes these studies as 'psychoanalytic', he is less concerned with Freudian dream analysis (FREUD) than with a study of reverie or daydreaming inspired largely by JUNG's theory of ARCHETYPES. Whereas a dream is beyond the dreamer's control, there is a flicker of consciousness in daydreaming, which generates poetic images as the daydreamer discovers an ideal world. The poetic image produces a sense of wonder and opens up an imaginary world of delights and of universal archetypes, and makes us read or listen to a poem as though we were hearing words for the first time. It is an expression of the basic human characteristic of 'imagining'. For Bachelard, daydreaming is a function of Jung's anima, or the female principle of repose that allows us to reach, when we are deep in reverie, the sleeping waters that lie within us.

READING: Tiles (1984)

bad faith   A major theme in the early phenomenological writings of SARTRE (e.g. 1943a), bad faith (*mauvaise foi*) is a form of self-deception and inauthenticity (INAUTHENTIC), and a denial of human freedom. Sartre makes an important distinction between lying and bad faith. The liar is in possession of the truth, denies it in the words he addresses to others, and then silently denies his own denial of the truth. The liar's consciousness can thus be said to be dual. An individual who is acting in bad faith masks the truth from himself or herself, and there is therefore no duality between the deceiver and the deceived; bad faith involves a unitary consciousness.

Sartre's illustrations of the mechanisms of bad faith are remarkably concrete. A waiter in a café plays the role of a waiter because he wishes to be a waiter in the same way that a table is a table, and thus denies the distinction between existence IN-ITSELF/FOR-ITSELF that is the foundation of human freedom. Although well aware of her suitor's intentions, a woman who is being seduced fears both his desire and her own sexuality. Constantly deferring the moment when she must decide how to respond, she finally abandons her hand to him as though it were a mere physical object. She thus denies and avoids her own freedom and responsibility. Living and acting in bad faith are an exploitation of the ambiguities of human existence, as the individual transforms freedom into contingency and FACTICITY. Good faith or authenticity is, obviously enough, the antithesis of bad faith, but it is a project rather than a state of existence. The statement 'I am authentic and acting in good faith' signals a lapse into bad faith precisely because it implies that I am an essence that exists in-itself.

According to Sartre, the existence of bad faith disproves FREUD's theory of the UNCONSCIOUS, which implies a dualistic structure of consciousness/unconsciousness. All the phenomena that Freud describes as unconscious can be adequately explained by the mechanisms of bad faith.

READING: Santoni (1995)

Bakhtin, Mikhail Mikhaylovich (1895–1975) Russian literary theorist. Despite his considerable influence on DISCOURSE analysis, Bakhtin remains an elusive and enigmatic figure. His writings are difficult to date with any certainty and some of his works have been lost; the fragment of the essay on the BILDUNGSROMAN (1936–8), for example, is all that remains of a much longer study that was never completed. There are also doubts as to just who was the major partner in the production of the coauthored texts on 'the formal method' (with Medvedev 1928) and Marxism and the philosophy of language (with Voloshinov 1929), and they are therefore sometimes attributed to 'the Bakhtin group'. Forced into internal exile in 1929, Bakhtin was always a fairly obscure figure in his native Russia. In the West, Bakhtin was discovered only at the end of the 1960s. An extract from his study of Rabelais (1965) published in *Yale French Studies* in 1968 generated a certain interest, but it was KRISTEVA's essay 'Word, Dialogue and Novel' (1969) and her preface to the 1970 French translation of his study of Dostoyevsky (1929) that both made Bakhtin a major point of reference and allowed Kristeva to elaborate her influential story of INTERTEXUALITY.

Bakhtin's earliest known works (1924; with Medvedev 1928; with Voloshinov 1929) both contain a critique of RUSSIAN FORMALISM and begin to outline the characteristic theme of 'dialogism'. Formalism is criticized for its abstraction, its failure to analyse the content of literary works and the difficulty it finds in analysing linguistic and ideological changes. The critique is then extended to linguistics as such and SAUSSURE in particular. According to Bakhtin, the purely linguistic approach to both language and literature is limited in that it isolates linguistic units or literary texts from their social context and offers no analysis of the relations that exist between both individual speakers and texts. He therefore proposes a historical POETICS or a 'translinguistics' (1934–5) which can demonstrate that all social intercourse is generated from verbal communication and interaction, and that linguistic signs are conditioned by the social organization of the participants. In Bakhtin's later work (1952–3), the notion of a historical poetics develops into a theory of 'speech genres' or 'typical forms of utterances', and it is claimed that the weakness of Saussure's linguistics is that it concentrates solely on individual utterances and cannot analyse how they are combined into relatively stable types of utterance. The theory of speech genres is incomplete, but was clearly extremely ambitious as it was intended to apply to everything from proverbs to multi-volume novels by analysing their common verbal nature.

Bakhtin's first major literary study was the long essay on Dostoyevsky, which established dialogism and polyphony as his main themes. Dostoyevsky's novels are said to be polyphonic in that there is no central 'voice' and in that their characters are characterized not by their temperament or their psychological make-up but by their ideas and the way they expound and discuss them. The reader remembers Ivan Karamazov, for example, as an embodiment of the proposition that 'if God does not exist, then everything is permissible' and not as a bundle of psychological traits. According to Bakhtin's analysis, Dostoyevsky describes a world in which the final word has never been spoken and in which the dialogue goes on perpetually. In this literary dialogue, there is no privileged point of view, and Bakhtin contrasts

Dostoyevsky's polyphony with the monological blocks of Tolstoy, which imprison the characters' words in the words of the author, notably in the long discourse on history at the end of *War and Peace*. Self-consciousness is a product of the dialogue in which Dostoyevsky's characters engage with themselves, their ideas and their inter-locutors; they do not exist in themselves or for themselves, but with and for others. The 'dialogic principle' explains the structural elements of Dostoyevsky's fiction, which is described as introducing a new GENRE and even as inaugurating a COPERNI-CAN REVOLUTION with respect to the monologism of Gogol and Tolstoy. Dostoyev-sky's novels are polyphonic in that the reader can sense in every utterance the nature of the social language that gives it its background, its overall meaning and its truth. At a much more general level, the dialogic principle provides the model for Kristeva's intertextuality by describing how texts and GENRES engage in a conversation that never ends. Cervantes is in constant dialogue with the novels of chivalry read by Don Quixote; Fielding, Smollet and Sterne converse with the genres and styles they parody. The polylinguistic structure of the novel uses, that is, the discourses of other novels and writers to refract its own discourse (Bakhtin 1934–5).

Bakhtin's late study of Rabelais again uses the dialogic model, but also expands upon the important theme of the carnivalesque. The tradition of carnival, whose history is traced back to the Roman saturnalia, is described by Bakhtin as abolishing the boundaries between the public and private spheres and between performers and spectators, and as establishing an inverted order in which fools and outsiders become kings for the day. It offers a mocking challenge to the 'serious' official culture of the Middle Ages and the Renaissance by destroying social hierarchies and making all social strata and all age-groups equal. For Bakhtin, carnival is a re-enactment of the ancient cults of fertility and rebirth; the mocking challenge to authority represents a popular force of renewal that opens the way to a new future. The characteristic features of Rabelais's fiction – the giants Pantagruel and Gargan-tua, with their enormous appetites and gluttony, the emphasis on excretion and the sheer verbal exuberance – are all explained as reflections of the spirit of carnival: Rabelais carnivalizes literature and in doing so challenges and demystifies the dogmatic serious culture of his times. Bakhtin's emphasis on the popular element in Rabelais has not found much favour with professional Renaissance specialists, not least because it tends to ignore the very serious theological themes in his work (on Rabelais's theology, see Screech 1958).

READING: Bernard-Donals (1994); Todorov (1981)

Barthes, Roland (1915–80) French literary critic and theorist. Barthes' prolific output (collected 1993–5) is so consistently innovative and inventive as to make him one of the most important and influential critics of the twentieth century. Although his work goes through a number of distinct phases, he often remarks that although the theoretical languages he uses change, his basic concerns remain relatively constant, as is evident from a reading of a selection (1981a) of the interviews given by Barthes between 1962 and 1980. His fundamental concern is with the relationship between language and the social world, and with the literary forms that mediate between the two. A taste for creating neologisms, a fascination with classificatory systems and a tendency to work with pairs of concepts, such as WRITERLY AND READERLY TEXTS (1970a) or pleasure and *JOUISSANCE* (1973a), are also constant features of his work. Whilst such pairs of concepts certainly reflect the importance of binary oppositions in STRUCTURALISM, they are also an index of the elegant sense of playfulness that is to be found in so much of Barthes' writing; for Barthes, concepts are in a sense intellectual playthings. As one of the best studies of Barthes notes (Knight 1997), there is an important utopian dimension to his work, and its presence is often revealed by the second of the paired concepts. A 'writerly' text, remarks Barthes (1970a), is unlikely to be found in a bookshop; it is both a utopia towards which he strives and a theoretical weapon that facilitates the critique of the banal 'readerly' text.

Barthes' concern with writing is apparent from his first major essay (1953), which demonstrates that no form or style of writing is a free expression of an author's subjectivity. Writing is always loaded with social and ideological values, and language is never innocent. A sense of the need for a CRITIQUE of forms of writing that mask the historical-political features of the social world by making it appear 'natural' or inevitable, together with a utopian longing for a different world and different forms of writing, provides the impulse behind the analyses of MYTHOLOGIES (1957) that first gave Barthes a non-academic readership.

The long analytic essay appended to *Mythologies* marks the beginning of what is usually seen as Barthes' structuralist or semiological phase. *Elements of Semiology* (1964a) played an enormously important role in making SEMIOLOGY an integral part of intellectual life, and soon came to have the status of a classic textbook, whilst Barthes' major contributions (e.g. 1966a) to the emerging science of NARRATOLOGY helped to make structuralism the dominant discourse of the period. The structuralist Barthes was also a controversial figure. His study of Racine (1963), which abandons the conventional author-and-works approach (and thus prefigures the announcement of the DEATH OF THE AUTHOR in 1968) in favour of an anthropological and psychoanalytic reading of canonical texts (CANON), drew down the wrath of the very traditionalist Raymond Picard (1965) and sparked a controversy that went to the heart of French intellectual life (see Doubrovsky 1966). The stakes were high, given that Racine is in some ways the French Shakespeare; Barthes' new criticism was denounced as an imposture. Barthes' predictable, and stinging, response (Barthes 1966b) was that criticism, like language itself, is never neutral and that the specificity of literature can be examined only within the context of a semiology or a general theory of signs. It was precisely the generality of semiology that attracted Barthes, who would speak (1971b) in retrospect of the euphoric dream of scientificity that it inspired; it inspired a sense of wonder at the potential of a system that seemed applicable to anything and everything. The most sophisticated product of the structuralist period is Barthes' study of the fashion system (1967). It does not examine fashion as such, but looks at the descriptions of garments contained in women's magazines and demonstrates that the implicit system operating there can be analysed as though it were a language. Individual garments are selected from a PARADIGM of types and styles, and combined in the SYNTAGM of an individual ensemble of clothes, just as Barthes had already selected items from a paradigmatic menu and combined them into a syntagmatic meal (1964a). With this analysis, Barthes' structuralism reaches its apotheosis in an exquisite exercise in classification and categorization that most readers find quite unreadable.

As the dream of scientificity fades, Barthes' fascination with classification takes the form of a close reading of the plethora of narrative codes he identifies in a short story by Balzac (1970a), and then of the strange systems of thought elaborated by Sade, the utopian socialist Fourier and the Jesuit Ignatius of Loyola (1971a). The text is no longer an object for cold scientific analysis, but rather a cause for a hedonistic celebration that has strong sexual overtones. The utopian strand reappears in an account of Barthes' travels to Japan (1970b), described as the 'empire of signs' and experienced (or rather constructed) as a utopia in which signs and signifiers finally escape the constraints of the Western system of meaning and become delicate objects to be played with. The theme of DESIRE comes to the fore in the delightful but deliberately misleading autobiographical study of *Roland Barthes by Roland Barthes* (1975), in which Barthes quietly hints for the first time at his homosexuality, and in the delicate fragments that analyse the longings, frustrations and pleasures of sexual love (1977). Like the old dream of scientificity before it, the utopian hedonism eventually fades into a melancholy of longing and loss which most commentators agree was provoked by the death of Barthes' mother in 1977. The great work of this late period is the elegiac study of photography (1980) published in the year of Barthes' death in a banal road accident.

READING: Calvet (1990); Culler (1983b); Lavers (1982); Wiseman (1989)

base/superstructure The classic Marxist theory of IDEOLOGY holds that there is a relationship of determination between an economic base (the forces and relations of production) and a superstructure made up of the state, and legal, political and ideological forms. Elements of a theory of base and superstructure are outlined in Marx and Engels's *The German Ideology* (1845–6), but the clearest exposition is to be found in the preface to Marx's *Contribution to the Critique of Political Economy* (1859). Here Marx argues that the MODE OF PRODUCTION of material life determines social, political and intellectual life: 'It is not the consciousness of men that determines their existence, but their social existence that determines their consciousness.' It follows that the ruling ideas or dominant ideology of any given historical period are the ideas or ideology of its ruling class. Changes at the level of the economic base of society will eventually transform the entire ideological superstructure. In his famous letter of 21/22 September 1890 to Joseph Bloch (in Marx and Engels 1965), Engels insists, however, that the base/superstructure model does not mean that the economic is the sole determinant of ideology, and that superstructural forms also have an influence on the course of historical struggles. Many of the debates that have taken place within WESTERN MARXISM focus on an attempt to avoid the crude economic determinism of the simpler forms of the base/superstructure model and the claim that ideology is no more than a distorted reflection of an underlying economic reality.

Bataille, Georges (1897–1962) French writer, critic, cofounder of the COLLÈGE DE SOCIOLOGIE and founding editor of the journal *CRITIQUE*. The publication of the

French edition of Bataille's collected works began in 1971, and now consists of twelve volumes covering topics as varied as cave painting (1955a), the art of Manet (1955b), eroticism (1957) and the theory of religion (1973). His writings range from erotic novellas (1928, 1941) to lengthy essays on what he calls the 'general economy' (1949). The influence of his work can be seen in that of FOUCAULT, DERRIDA and BARTHES, whilst his writings on eroticism have had a major impact on LACAN's work on sexuality and *JOUISSANCE*. As a result of his influence in these quarters, Bataille is often, and especially outside France, seen as a prototypical theorist of POSTMODERNITY, but his work is deeply rooted in the French thought of the interwar years. His concentration on the importance of the human recognition of the inevitability of death owes, for instance, much to KOJÈVE's reading of Hegel, even though he rejects the 'end of history' thesis as absurd. Bataille is also a member of the first generation of French writers to take Nietzsche seriously (1995).

In his early work published in the journal *Documents* (fifteen issues published in 1929–30), Bataille began to develop what was to become a characteristic concern with excess and with a 'base materialism' which celebrates everything that is foreign to aspirations towards human ideals (a good analysis is given in chapter 6 of Macherey 1990). In terms of sexuality, Barthes celebrates masochism and sadism as ways of feeling 'more human' and finds in degradation and humiliation a profoundly human experience. It is this concentration on the ignoble that offended BRETON and led to the difficult relationship between Bataille and the more orthodox adepts of SURREALISM. Bataille's own writings on surrealism, which are highly critical of the ideal aspiration signalled by the prefix *sur-* ('higher' or 'supra'), are collected in English as *The Absence of Myth* (1994).

The central theme that binds together Bataille's disparate and at times contradictory writings derives from the sociology of Durkheim (see Lukes 1973) and from Mauss's work on the gift relationship (Mauss 1923). The unifying element in society is the *sacred*, which both establishes cohesion and sets limits on individual behaviour. The sacred implies that the individual has a self-sacrificial relationship with the collectivity; human sacrifice, as exemplified by Aztec civilization, was one of the abiding interests of both Bataille and the other members of the Collège de Sociologie. The sacred is the forbidden element that lies on the margins of society, and no society can exist in its absence. According to Bataille, the presence of the sacred is manifested in extreme emotion, pointless activity such as play and non-reproductive sexuality, and body exhalations, or in other words in everything that a rational and homogeneous society would like to expel. The sacred also becomes apparent in festivals of waste and expenditure, such as the Native American cult of the potlach in which wealth is deliberately destroyed or wasted, and in those moments when taboos are transgressed. The notion of excess is the key to Bataille's concept of a general economy based upon the deliberate production of non-utilitarian goods such as luxuries, spectacular displays of wealth and weapons-systems.

For Bataille, human experience is the experience of limits and the recognition that death is an absolute limit. That recognition generates an anguish of being that can be assuaged through eroticism and reaffirmation of the life forces. Eroticism itself is also an experience of limits, as it leads to the dissolution of identity that occurs in the 'little death' of orgasm. This is the recurrent theme of Bataille's erotica, which have often been dismissed as pornography. The violent images of sexual degradation in *The Story of the Eye* (1928) are often greeted with derisive laughter and rejected as grotesque, but Bataille himself forestalls such objections in a prefatory note to *Madame Edwarda* (1941; in English translation, with other erotica, 1980) in which he warns his reader: 'If you laugh, it's because you're afraid.' In this novella Edwarda, an insane prostitute in a Parisian brothel, displays her genitals to the narrator, proclaims herself to be God, and then has an orgasm.

READING: Richardson (1994); *Yale French Studies* (1990)

Baudrillard, Jean (1929–) Originally a teacher of German, Baudrillard established himself as a sociologist in the late 1960s and is widely regarded as one of the most significant commentators on POSTMODERNITY. Baudrillard has moved from a Marxist-inflected critical commentary on the affluent consumer society to an ambiguous position which can be interpreted either as a bleakly lucid perception that there is no escape from what DEBORD calls the society of the spectacle, or as a horrified fascination with the shallowness of a postmodernist society in which the SIGN has become a SIMULACRUM that signifies nothing. Baudrillard's prolific output of books (most of them short), articles and interviews (see Gane 1993) has brought him enormous media attention. He is probably the only French sociologist to have become the subject of a feature-length article in a British colour supplement (Leith 1998).

Baudrillard's early studies of the consumer society (1968, 1970) are influenced by a variety of tendencies within sociology and philosophy, ranging from Marx's theory of COMMODITY FETISHISM to the BARTHES of *Mythologies* (1957) and *The Fashion System* (1967) and from Debord's denunciations of the 'society of the spectacle' to MCLUHAN's celebrated proclamation that 'the medium is the massage' (McLuhan 1967). Packard's classic study of the 'hidden persuaders' of the advertising industry (1957) is also an important point of reference. According to Baudrillard, the consumer society is dominated by a system of object-signs (consumer goods and gadgets) which circulate endlessly and constitute an order of signification which can be compared to the signs of SAUSSURE's linguistic system. Their use-value is less important than their ability to signify the status of their consumer; the possession of a washing machine allows one to wash clothes, but it also signifies membership of a social group. In a postindustrial society where the importance of economic production is in decline, it is consumption that binds society together. The society described by Baudrillard in these early studies is remarkably similar to that depicted by OULIPO-member Georges Perec in his novel *Things* (1965), in which an affluent couple live through the objects they purchase and consume.

With *Symbolic Exchange and Death* (1976), which provides the most sustained exposition of his later theory, Baudrillard departs completely from the quasi-Marxist framework of his early books. In the course of a far-ranging discussion of Saussure, Mauss's theory of the gift relationship (1923) and FREUD (which involves dubious descriptions of the impersonal code of DNA), Baudrillard now argues that, in the era of postmodernity, signs are replaced by simulacra, and the real by HYPERREALITY. Consumption itself gives way to the game of seductions in which nothing real is at stake, and to a simulation in which sexuality itself is absorbed into a vacuous hyperreal pornography which is more real than any actual sexual encounter could ever be. In this world, the MASQUERADE of sexuality described by Joan Rivière (1929) is the reality of sex (1979). Production and labour are now seen as quite irrelevant, and political hopes for political change are dismissed as a nostalgia for an era of signification typical of the lost industrial age.

Baudrillard is a deliberately provocative writer. His contention that the imaginary Disneyland is a construct designed to convince us of the reality of an America that now exists only as a hyperreal simulacrum of itself (1981, 1986) is seen by many as an entertaining paradox, but the claim that the Gulf War of 1990 would not take place (1991), followed by the assertion that it did not take place, seems to defy all logic. Such statements are anticipated by the earlier claim (1983) that the only future war would be a hyperreal and dissuasive war in which no events would take place because there was no more space for actual warfare. The underlying argument is that the Gulf War was a simulated war or a reproduction of a war. Whatever its human consequences, this was, for Baudrillard, a war which consisted largely of its self-representation in the real time of media coverage.

Baudrillard is a highly literate and literary stylist whose work contains some unexpected allusions. He revives the 'PATAPHYSICS, or science of imaginary solutions, of JARRY to describe (1983) the inexorable build-up of weapon-systems which are designed not to be used, and the notorious claims about the Gulf War appear to allude to the title of Jean Giraudoux's play *The Trojan War Will Not Take Place* (1935), which ends with the Greek army going off to war in a fulfilment of Cassandra's unheeded prophecy. Baudrillard's style – and style of thought – often resembles the cultivated and glacial dandyism of a Baudelaire, particularly in the fragmentary notations and observations of the three volumes of *Cool Memories* (1987, 1990, 1995). At other times, he appears to adopt the pose of a latter-day FLÂNEUR. Indeed, the Baudrillard who drives across a hyperreal America in a fast car seems to be the direct descendant of the figure celebrated by both Baudelaire and BENJAMIN. Like his ancestor, the postmodern flâneur is, by definition, male, and his fantasy of sacrificing a woman in the deserts of the West (1986) has done little to recommend him to feminist readers.

READING: Gane (1991a, 1991b, 1993); Kellner (1989); Leith (1998)

Bauman, Zygmunt (1925–) Polish-born British sociologist. Although Bauman's publishing career has been a long one and began with a study of British Welfare State socialism written in Polish while he was at the University of Warsaw (1956), he is best known for his series of works in POSTMODERNITY (1987, 1992, 1997). His most controversial book deals with the Holocaust (1989) and it was inspired by his response to his wife's devastating account of her life in wartime Poland (Janina Bauman 1986).

Like most writers on postmodernity, Bauman also provides a contrasting account of MODERNITY, though he stresses that the difference between the two is grounded in a change of attitudes and not simply a temporal shift. To that extent at least, modernity and postmodernity can coexist. Bauman's account of modernity is derived mainly from the work of Max Weber (1904–05) and stresses the role played by secularization and rationalization in the gradual disenchantment of the world. He also stresses, in terms reminiscent of FOUCAULT, that, despite its self-image, the ENLIGHTENMENT project of modernity was concerned not so much with the diffusion of education as with legislation; its intellectuals legislated on the basis of the laws of a supposedly universal reason. One of the outcomes of modernity was the PANOPTICISM of Foucault's disciplinary society (Foucault 1975); 'modernity was a long march to prison' (Bauman 1992). On a more domestic note, and borrowing a phrase from Ernest Gellner (Gellner 1983), Bauman also describes modernity as a 'garden culture' in which the weeding out of the undesirable is a constant activity. The notion that intellectuals have a 'legislative' vocation is, according to Bauman (1987), one of the characteristic traits of sociology, described as both the product and the theory of modernity. Sociology mediates between the political ambitions of the state and the agents of the management of social problems on the grand scale, viewing social engineering and problem-solving as an exercise in the total administration of society. That ideology finds its fullest expression in Talcott Parson's FUNCTIONALISM, but also in the communist vision of a society that is carefully designed, rationally managed and totally industrialized.

The effects of the transition to postmodernity are first visible in the arts, where the collapse of authority and the loss of a sense of tradition make pastiche, parody and borrowings the dominant style. At the same time, the globalization of the economy and the erosion of the power of nation-states result in a plurality of sites of authority. Since the early 1980s Bauman has argued (1982) that consumption and consumer culture have taken on the central role in the economy that once belonged to work. Increasingly, consumption becomes the social link between the LIFE-WORLD of individuals and the purposeful rationality of the system as a whole. The exacerbated individualism that results leads to still further social fragmentation. Bauman argues that postmodernity is in fact the new self-consciousness of an intellectual class that can no longer legislate and which now simply interprets and mediates between communities. It is a consciousness that modernity has failed in that the emancipation it promised has not been realized; the task of the intellectual is still to question consumerism and commodification in a search for new forms of emancipation.

Modernity and the Holocaust (1989) is largely an attempt to face up to the paradox whereby the emergence of the specialist academic discipline of Holocaust Studies has been accompanied by the virtual disappearance of the Holocaust from mainstream history, and to make it the central issue for both history and sociology. Arguing that the Holocaust is neither a 'Jewish problem' nor a 'German problem' nor, *contra* Adorno, the expression of an authoritarian personality (Adorno et al. 1950), Bauman insists that it was a project born of and implemented in a modern rational society, and that it is therefore a problem of modern rational society. Modern civilization was not the Holocaust's sufficient cause, but it was one of its necessary causes. Rational bureaucracy, scientific planning and scientific rationality in the service of absolute modern power created it; understanding the Holocaust is an essential task for any theory of modernity and the civilizing process that supposedly accompanies it.

Bazin, André (1918–58) French film critic and cofounder, in 1951, of *CAHIERS DU CINÉMA*. Bazin never published a systematic book on the theory of film; his influential *What Is Cinema?* (1958–62), which had a major impact on the young directors of the *NOUVELLE VAGUE*, consists of reviews and short articles published between 1945 and 1958. The four-volume French edition includes some sixty essays; almost half have been published in English in a two-volume selection (1967, 1971). Bazin is one of the first serious cinema critics and regards film as a language whose evolution can be traced through an examination of styles of editing and of the introduction of such new techniques as Gregg Toland's deep-focus photography, which is such a striking feature of Orson Welles's *Citizen Kane* (1941, but not shown in France until after the Second World War). Bazin's aesthetics of cinema is a realistic aesthetic. Like photography, cinema is described as creating an ideal world that is made in the image of the real. For Bazin, 'realism' does not refer to the subject-matter of the film, but the reality of the space without which moving pictures cannot become cinema. Cinema is the art of the real because it records the spatiality of objects and the physicality of the space in which they exist. Bazin's articles on Italian NEOREALISM, which he praised for its 'respect for reality', are particularly fine. Although incomplete and fragmentary, his study of the French director Jean Renoir (1894–1979) is an important contribution to the *AUTEUR* THEORY of cinema (1971).

READING: Andrew (1976); Andrew and Truffaut (1971)

Beauvoir, Simone de (1908–86) French philosopher, novelist and feminist. Her *The Second Sex* (1949) is generally regarded as one of the great manifestos of modern FEMINISM.

The underlying philosophical structure of *The Second Sex* is grounded in the Self–Other relationship described by SARTRE's classic essay on EXISTENTIALISM (1943a), but the emphasis placed upon GENDER introduces themes that are not present there. According to Beauvoir's schema, women have been turned into an objectified Other, whilst men have appropriated the Subject position and have thus made it impossible for women to live in the mode of the for-itself (see IN-ITSELF/FOR-ITSELF). The famous sentence 'One is not born, but rather becomes, a woman' is the starting-point for a detailed phenomenological description of 'becoming a woman' and for an attack on all the myths of the eternal feminine that reduce women to a timeless essence. Unlike Sartre, Beauvoir attaches great importance to the social and economic forces that determine women's existence, and demonstrates the oppressive effects of education, family structure, conventional marriage, housework and motherhood. *The Second Sex* is a powerful call for women to grasp freedom and independence, and insists that economic independence is an essential precondition for social and existential freedom. Paradoxically, Beauvoir did not regard herself as a feminist at the time of writing, and believed that some form of socialism would lead to women's emancipation. It was not until the 1970s that she openly identified with the feminist movement and became involved in campaigns for the right to contraception and abortion. Regrettably, the notoriously inaccurate English translation denies non-French speaking readers access to the full richness of Beauvoir's thought.

Beauvoir's status as one of the founding mothers of feminism has not gone unchallenged. Later writers such as KRISTEVA, CIXOUS and IRIGARAY are highly critical of her failure to place a positive emphasis on women's sexual difference and of her apparently negative descriptions of the female body. Her reliance on Sartrean theory, and the close relationship with Sartre himself, have also led to the accusation that she is a 'male-identified' woman. Many critics also deny that Beauvoir makes any original contribution to philosophy, but it has been argued (Vintger 1992) that her essays on ethics (1947a) offer an escape from Sartre's alleged SOLIPSISM by stressing that freedom can be achieved by a combination of willing-oneself free and an emotional fusion with the other. Despite the criticisms that have been addressed to Beauvoir, who is now more widely read in the English-speaking world than in France, it remains true to say that *The Second Sex* is a book of which many women can say: 'It changed my life' (Forster and Sutton 1989).

Like the best of her novels, *The Mandarins* (1954), Beauvoir's autobiographical works (1958, 1960, 1963, 1972) provide a remarkable chronicle of French intellectual life, and a self-portrait of 'the emblematic intellectual woman of the twentieth century' (Moi 1994). It is, however, clear from the posthumously published letters and diaries (1990a, 1990b) that there is an element of idealization and even self-censorship in the account of how an 'essential relationship' with Sartre could be freely combined with more transient and 'contingent' relationships with others.

READING: Bair (1990); Fallaize (1998); Forster and Sutton (1989)

Benjamin, Walter (1892–1940) Jewish-German critic, philosopher and man of letters. Benjamin is one of the most intriguing and elusive figures of the twentieth century, and his posthumous career has been both fascinating and a source of misunderstandings. The publication in 1955 of a two-volume edition of his works edited by ADORNO (since superseded by the seven volumes of the collected works, 1974–9) made him a significant figure for the German NEW LEFT and his reputation spread to the English-speaking world thanks to a collection edited by ARENDT (1969), who also selected the material included in the later *Reflections* (1978). His image of the FLÂNEUR (1939a, 1939b), his comments on the loss of aura of the work of art in the age of mechanical reproduction (1936), his discussion of photography (1931) and his characterization of Paris as the 'capital of the nineteenth century' (1935) have become familiar features of debates on the origins and nature of MODERNITY, whilst his essays on BRECHT (1973) have provided many readers with a good introduction to EPIC theatre. His occasional pieces on Naples (1924) and Marseille (1928b, 1928c), the autobiographical 'Berlin Chronicle' (1932) and the diary kept during a visit to Moscow in 1926–7 (1986) are major contributions to the literature of the modern city.

Whilst Benjamin is widely regarded as a key figure in WESTERN MARXISM, his relationship with the FRANKFURT SCHOOL (documented in Jay 1973 and Buck-Morss

1977) was always more difficult than this image may suggest, and he is best viewed as standing at the confluence of the very different traditions of Marxism, which he discovered when reading LUKÁCS's *History and Class Consciousness* in 1924, German Romanticism (Benjamin 1920; see in particular Bowie 1997) and the Jewish tradition of messianic mysticism; although he came from an 'assimilated' family, Benjamin was in contact with Zionist movements in his youth, and came into contact with the mystical current thanks to his friendship with Gershom Scholem (see the correspondence in Benjamin 1980). The 'Theses on the Philosophy of History' (1940) are typically ambiguous in that they juxtapose references to an orthodox HISTORICAL MATERIALISM and to the Jewish tradition that 'every second of time was the strait gate through which the Messiah might enter.' The coming of the Messiah will signal not the culmination of history, but rather a movement out of history into timelessness.

The ambiguity of Walter Benjamin is typified in the two major works published in his lifetime. One was a study of German baroque drama (1928a), which was intended to be the *Habilitation* dissertation which would guarantee him an academic career; in the face of academic hostility, he finally had to withdraw his application for a university position. *One-Way Street* (1928b), in contrast, looked very much like a classic example of Weimar AVANT-GARDE art: the cover design was a striking example of photomontage. Benjamin is a fascinating writer, but he is not an easy one, mainly because of his conviction that theory cannot be expounded in isolation – the exegetical texts on Brecht are very much the exception – and that factuality is already theory. *One-Way Street* does not expound any theory, but its constellations of images, aphorisms and juxtapositions are intended to be a form of thinking-in-pictures (*Bilddenken*) from which understanding emerges without having to be expounded. Benjamin claimed that he had nothing to say, 'only to show'. His book on German baroque drama, in contrast, is a dense and almost esoteric study of a group of 'royal martyr' plays in which Benjamin both outlines a theory of ALLEGORY, which is said to transcend profane reality by creating a realm in which everything can arbitrarily mean something else, and elaborates a quasi-theological theory of the nature of language. As in earlier essays (1916) Benjamin argues that there was once a paradisical state that knew only one language, and in which things coincided with their names. 'Naming' is the essential linguistical-philosophical act, and the Adam who gave names to the animals (Genesis ii.19–20) is the father of philosophy. The object of literary-philosophical criticism is, in Benjamin's view, to recover the theological immediacy in which things are redeemed by being regiven their true names.

Benjamin's texts on Baudelaire are the most familiar part of his oeuvre, but they are no more than part of the huge and unfinished project on which he worked from 1927 until his suicide in 1940. This was the '*Passagen-Werk*', usually known in English as the 'Paris Arcades Project', the notes and drafts for which are published in volume 7 of the collected works. There is no full English translation, though one has been announced by Yale University Press; the best accounts in English are *The Origins of Negative Dialectics* and *The Dialectics of Seeing* by Susan Buck-Morss (1977, 1991). The project was inspired by a reading of Aragon's *Paris Peasant* (1926) and Breton's *Nadja*

(1928a), two of the classic texts of SURREALISM which explore a mysterious and symbolic Paris; Benjamin greatly admired the surrealists for their 'radical concept of freedom' (Benjamin 1929; on Benjamin and surrealism, see Cohen 1993). Built from the 1820s onwards, the Paris arcades were both thoroughfares and centres for the luxury-goods trade, as well as for prostitution and gambling. They revealed the unconscious of nineteenth-century Paris, or in other words the COMMODITY FETISHISM, REIFICATION and ALIENATION that accompanied the development of a consumer society. For Benjamin, they were the 'ur-phenomena' of modernity. The term *Ur-phenomenon* ('originary phenomenon', as the term has become established in English) is borrowed from Goethe (Benjamin 1924–5), who uses it to describe the emergence of colours out of light and darkness. As in *One-Way Street*, Benjamin examines ephemera and fleeting images in which the 'total historical event' is to be discovered in an ur-history of the origins of the present historical moment. This use of the ephemeral and the fleeting should be compared with his friend KRACAUER'S thesis that the 'inconspicuous surface-level expressions' of a period say more about it than its judgements about itself; 'the true image of the past flits by' (Benjamin 1940). The time of the arcades is a deadening time in which the new, which the *flâneur* seeks so avidly, is 'always the same' (*Immergleiche*), but it is also pregnant with a partially-glimpsed future resembling BLOCH's not-yet (*Noch-Nicht*) consciousness: the time of the now is 'shot through' with 'chips of Messianic time' (Benjamin 1940). Only the fragmentary images produced by the true work of art can produce a glimpse of the redemptive world that will transcend the deadness of the present. The task of the critic is to rescue and preserve those fragments.

READING: Brodersen (1990); *New German Critique* (1979, 1986); Sontag (1978c); Wolin (1982)

Benveniste, Émile (1902–76) French linguist. Benveniste is an important figure in the transition from the historical approach to linguistics typified by PHILOLOGY to the emphasis on the systematic aspects of language that characterizes STRUCTUR-ALISM. He was also one of the first linguists to explore the linguistic implications of Freudian psychoanalysis in an important contribution to the first (1956) issue of *La Psychanalyse*, which was edited by LACAN and devoted to 'speech and language'; this was subsequently included in his major collection of papers (1966). His work on pronouns or SHIFTERS is of particular relevance to Lacan. Benveniste argues that it is only in and through language that the subject can be constituted, but also that the need to use shifters to signify subjectivity introduces a split into the heart of the subject. Thus, the pronoun 'I' is a signifier which designates but does not signify the subject because it is an empty sign. The 'I' constantly shifts between the level of the utterance (*énonciation*) and that of what is uttered (*énoncé*). Analysis of the *énoncé* is matter for abstract grammatical work; that of the *énonciation*, a matter for the analysis of the linguistic production of the 'I'. It is the gap between the subject of the enunciation and that of what is enunciated that allows Lacan to subvert the subject by noting (1957): 'I think where I am not, therefore I am where I do not think', and to establish the distinction between the EGO and the subject of the UNCONSCIOUS.

Bernal, Martin Originally a specialist in government studies at Cornell University, the British-born Bernal has written on Chinese politics (1976), but is now best known for his controversial investigations into the Afro-Asiatic origins of Classical Greek culture (1987, 1991). The stated political purpose of these studies is to lessen European cultural arrogance; they have had a major impact on Afro-American studies and theories of AFROCENTRICITY, especially in the United States.

Like DIOP, Bernal argues that the ancient Egyptians were black and that they transmitted their culture to Greece thanks to a combination of trade and colonization, whilst Greek thinkers absorbed the philosophy of Egypt during periods of study in that country. Bernal bases his argument on linguistic and archaeological evidence, and on the 'Ancient model' of Greek history supplied by Herodotus and others who describe the origins of their culture as Egyptian or Pharaonic. Widely accepted until the eighteenth century, the Ancient model was gradually replaced by the 'Aryan model', which attributes the origins of Greek culture to an invasion from the north and seeks to deny the existence of the Egyptian, Phoenician and Semitic heritage. The Aryan model is a product of the EUROCENTRISM and racism that accompanied the rise of colonialism. Having idealized Greece as the source of all European culture, the architects of the Aryan model were obliged by their own racism to falsify history by rejecting the Ancient model and its accounts of the sophisticated culture that once flourished in Egypt.

Bernal's many critics object that his use of fragmentary evidence – and particularly linguistic and archaeological evidence – is very tendentious and that it is a mistake to project the ethnic categories of the modern world onto ancient civilizations (Lefkowitz and Rogers 1996). It has also been objected that his reduction of cultures to a racial heritage is disturbingly reminiscent of nineteenth-century racism.

Bettelheim, Bruno (1903–90) Viennese-born American psychotherapist. Although his study of fairy-tales (1976) can be viewed as a significant contribution to the literature of PSYCHOANALYTIC CRITICISM, it is EGO PSYCHOLOGY rather than the classic PSYCHOANALYSIS of FREUD that provides the basis for Bettelheim's work as a therapist.

In 1938–9, Bettelheim was briefly incarcerated in Dachau and then Buchenwald and his descriptions of life in the concentration camps (1960, 1986) are widely regarded as an important, if controversial, part of the literature on the Holocaust. Bettelheim describes the camps as a world in which the death-DRIVE has taken over from the life-drive, and he makes the controversial claim that those Jews who walked into the gas chambers did so because they had been deprived of all hope and had been deserted by the whole world; they were no longer able to keep their death-drive in check, and turned it inwards against themselves. Conversely, he attributes the ability of some people to survive the camps to their success in safeguarding their EGO. After the war, Bettelheim worked at Chicago's Orthogenic School (from the Greek *orthos*, straight, and *genos*, origin); the therapeutic methods he developed for the treatment of severely disturbed and maladjusted children (1967) were based partly on his experience of the extreme situation of the concentration camp.

Bettelheim's study of fairy-tales is based on the thesis that they contain universal patterns that speak to the child's budding ego and that by portraying a world of struggle to overcome immense difficulties they provide a model for the child's development. 'Rapunzel', for instance, can be read as the story of conflict between a pubertal girl and a jealous mother who does not want her to gain the sexual independence she will eventually find with her prince. More importantly, fairy-tales are realistic in that they depict a world in which evil is a real force and in which good does not always triumph. Because they are so matter of fact in their presentation of evil, fairy-tales can help children to come to terms with their own unconscious feelings of aggression and hatred, and can help to defuse unconscious conflicts.

Bettelheim's *Freud and Man's Soul* (1983) provides an interesting critique of the Standard Edition translation of Freud and claims that it betrays Freud by replacing his homely German with a pseudo-scientific English; the banal *Ich* ('I') becomes the Latinate *ego* in the hands of a translator who is trying to confer the dignity of scientificity and classicism on the text.

After his death by his own hand, Bettelheim became the focus of a major scandal when it was claimed that he had lied about his experiences in the camps, and that he had inflicted physical violence on the children in his care. His biographer (Sutton 1995) reluctantly concludes that the charges are not unfounded, but that Bettelheim himself was as severely damaged as his patients.

Bhabha, Homi K. (1950–) The Indian-born Bhabha, together with SAID and SPIVAK, is widely recognized to be one of the most significant contributors to POSTCOLONIAL THEORY. His considerable reputation is surprisingly based upon only two books: an edited volume (1990a) and a collection of his own essays (1994), many of them previously published elsewhere and heavily revised. The essays are dense, richly eclectic and characterized by a style of writing that is so personal that it sometimes borders on the impenetrable.

The very influential *Nations and Narration* (1990a) takes its inspiration from Benedict ANDERSON's thesis (1983) that a nation is an 'imagined community' whose sense of identity is grounded in an imagined sense of historical community and continuity which may be quite illusory. It also takes inspiration from Ernest Renan's 'What is a Nation' (1882), in which the French historian (1823–92) argues that a nation is not based upon 'purity of race', but upon a collective will to live together and a combination of memory and amnesia. Every French citizen, writes Renan, 'has to have forgotten the massacre of Saint Bartholomew' in 1572, when thousands of Huguenots were murdered. The essays included in the collection explore the manner in which literary texts, and especially the CANON, contribute to the creation of the sense of imagined community, not least by establishing what can be remembered and what must be forgotten. Although Bhabha's preface speaks of 'an international perspective', the focus is in practice almost exclusively on the English-speaking world in the postcolonial period, the major exceptions being Doris Sommer's discussion of the 'founding fictions' of Latin America, and Martin Thom's valuable contextualization of Renan's essay.

Bhabha's own essays deal primarily with colonial discourse and the manner in which it produces and reproduces its OTHER, but the theme of cultural HYBRIDITY in the age of POSTMODERNITY becomes more dominant in his later work. His major points of theoretical reference are Said, FOUCAULT, DERRIDA, FANON (Bhabha prefaced the 1986 edition of his *Black Skin, White Masks*) and LACAN's psychoanalysis, but all are used critically. Bhabha is, for instance, sceptical of Foucault's EUROCENTRISM (curiously, the possibility that psychoanalysis itself might be eurocentric is not discussed), and critical of Said's account of ORIENTALISM on the grounds that it reproduces the very monolithic structure it is trying to explain and describes a unidirectional process in which the 'West' simply creates an 'Orient' which exists as a stable identity. One of Bhabha's most important insights is that the creation of stereotypes ('the inscrutable Oriental', 'the lascivious black') has to be repeated again and again, which implies that the stereotype is in fact unstable and requires constant reinforcement. He likens the perpetuation and recreation of the stereotype to FETISHISM and the reiterated denial of sexual difference. Colonial discourse, which is illustrated primarily by reference to nineteenth-century British writing on India, is thus revealed to be haunted by an uncertainty as to its own strength. Its deep uncertainties are revealed by the way in which it seeks to produce colonial subjects who are at once 'the same' as their colonizers (and thus amenable to being culturally assimilable) and 'different' from them (and thus amenable to colonization). Colonial discourse thus produces subjects that are almost the same, but not quite. Bhabha describes this as a kind of mimicry or a flawed MIMESIS in which to be anglicized is emphatically not to be English. At a more abstract level, the issue of a difference that is not quite the same arises in the claim that both English colonizers and their Indian subjects have common Aryan origins, and the simultaneous insistence that 'Indians are different'. Here Bhabha touches upon a major theme in British writing on India from Kipling to E. M. Forster's *Passage to India* and beyond; the difficulty is that the argument tends to be generalized and applied to the 'colonial experience' as a whole, rather than to specific colonial experiences. Just as Derrida contends that there is nothing outside the text Bhabha argues that there can be no knowledge outside representation, and his analysis of the postcolonial is textual in the extreme; the economics and politics of colonialism are rarely touched upon.

As hybridity emerges as the major theme of his more recent essays, Bhabha draws on a vision of postmodernity in which the compression of time and space produces complex patterns which undermine any sense of national or personal identity and in which class and gender cease to be primary categories. The West now has to cease perpetuating the narratives that are internal to its national identity, and listen to the postcolonial histories told by its migrants and refugees. The archetypal figure now becomes the migrant who lives in the transitional spaces where cultural differences clash. Bhabha suggests that the 'truest eye' may now be that of the migrant who lives, like the novelist Salman Rushdie, between cultures, but his sharper critics note that his migrant is 'remarkably free of gender, class and identifiable political location' (Ahmad 1995).

READING: Moore-Gilbert (1997); Young (1990)

Bildungsroman German noun formed from *Bildung* (education or cultivation) and *Roman* (novel) and used in all European languages to describe the sub-GENRE of novels about education. The classic *Bildungsroman* deals with the psychological and emotional development of a central character, and traces his or her evolution from youthful naïvety to maturity. The prototypical example is Goethe's *Wilhelm Meister's Apprenticeship* (1795–6). Familiar examples include Flaubert's *Sentimental Education*, Dickens's *David Copperfield* and Joyce's *Portrait of the Artist as a Young Man*.

In the German philosophical tradition, *Bildung* is associated with the idea of the cultivation or formation of the self, and with the Enlightenment notion of the 'cultivation of mankind' (*Bildung zum Menschen*).

READING: Bakhtin (1936–8)

biopolitics Biopolitics was the theme of the lectures given by Michel FOUCAULT at the Collège de France in 1978–9; only extracts have been published (1979). Biopolitics is Foucault's term for the attempts made by governments to rationalize the problems posed by the physical existence of a population, namely health, hygiene, birth-rates, longevity and race. Biopolitics is a matter of treating the social body, and it provides the rationale for the formulation of health policies from the eighteenth century onwards. Prevention becomes the primary goal as hospitals are transformed into the 'curing machines' that replaced the asylums and hospices of old, and as health comes to be defined in statistical terms. Life-styles and patterns of child-raising are increasingly viewed as areas for medical intervention, and medical practice is integrated into the economic and social management of society. Biopolitics places a new emphasis on childhood and medicalizes the family by generating an ethics of good health, whilst the new stress on hygiene makes medicine an agency of social control. Biopolitics affects the structures of urban space as hospitals are reformed, redesigned and rebuilt. It also has obvious effects on the population as a whole, the family unit and the bodies of individuals.

blaxploitation Coined from the words 'black exploitation' and used to describe a sub-GENRE of Hollywood films made in the 1970s. Deliberately designed to appeal to an urban black audience, films such as *Shaft* (1971) and *Superfly* (1972) use the conventions of the thriller and crime film and feature stereotypical pimps, drug-dealers and private investigators. Despite their popularity with their target audience, these films have been criticized for perpetuating a racist caricature of black America. It has also been argued that the dominant image of the black woman, with her 'Afro' hair, gun and revealing clothes, deliberately exploits and depoliticizes the image of the women militants of the Black Power movement of the 1960s (Robinson 1998). *Shaft* and *Superfly* are typical of the genre in that the soundtracks, by Isaac Hayes and Curtis Mayfield respectively, are more memorable than the films themselves. The expression 'blaxploitation' acquired a new currency in 1998 thanks to the release of Quentin Tarrantino's *Jackie Brown*, which is a virtual remake of *Foxy Brown* (1974).

Bloch, Ernst (1885–1977) German Marxist philosopher notable for his interest in utopian thought.

Whilst most Marxists follow Engels (1892) in denouncing utopianism and in defending Marxism as a scientific socialism, Bloch (1918) retains from his own earliest and pre-Marxist writings the thesis that it is 'the wish that builds up and creates the real' and constantly stresses the role played by the imagination and dreams, or 'the will to utopia' (1959), in the creation of the human future. Written over a long period of time and frequently revised, his most famous work is *The Principle of Hope* (1959). It is in part a vast historical survey of utopias from the Greeks onwards, and it is in this context that he outlines some of his most distinctive themes and concepts, and argues that all freedom movements are guided by utopian aspirations. We live, that is, surrounded by possibilities that have not yet been realized. Such possibilities are described as the Not-Yet-Become and they are apprehended by a Not-Yet-Consciousness associated with a rising class in a specific age and world. The Not-Yet-Consciousness is the vehicle for the utopian function whose contents are first glimpsed in imaginative ideas, as opposed to remembered ideas which simply reproduce past perceptions. This imaginative perception of the future in the present is described as a *Vor-Schein* or pre-appearance which both expresses discontent with the present and hope for the future. The future is, according to Bloch, visible at the *Front*, the most advanced point of an age or the point where the nature of the next age is decided; the related concept of the Novum describes the real possibility of the Not-Yet-Consciousness and the Not-Yet-Become. Bloch insists that his utopianism is a materialism, and defines matter in quasi-Aristotelian terms as that which exists and that which is possible. The 'will to utopia' is also described as a material force, and Bloch sees it as something akin to FREUD'S DRIVES.

It is the notion of *Vor-Schein* that explains Bloch's lasting interest in millenarianism, as expressed in his study of Thomas Münzer (c. 1489–1525), the visionary Anabaptist who was executed because of the role he played in the Peasants' Revolt of 1524–5 (1921). The stress on the historical importance of Christian millenarianism, with its apocalyptic image of a wrathful Christ driving the money-changers out of the Temple and announcing that he comes not to bring peace, but with a sword, means that Bloch's writings on religion have a great appeal for the theorists of Liberation Theology (see chapter 3 of Geoghegan 1996).

Bloch's concept of the Not-Yet (*Noch-Nicht*) is linked to his concept of Non-Contemporaneity and his contention that not all people live in the same Now, which he relates to the more classically Marxist-Leninist idea of unequal and uneven development. Non-contemporaneity is one of the major themes of *Heritage of Our Times* (1962), another text written and revised over a long period. In a series of vignettes and fragments, Bloch paints a grim picture of the rise of Nazism, and argues that its success owed a lot to its ability to exploit non-contemporaneity. Alongside the Not-Yet-Consciousness, there exist impulses and reserves from pre-capitalist times and old superstructures that are still at work. Nazism is thus able to resurrect and exploit folk-customs and traditional themes that Marxism has chosen to ignore at its peril. Fascism does not invent or create anything, but it can falsify and pervert older traditions and even virtues. Thus, the millenarian revolts of the Middle Ages were often accompanied by talk of a Third Reich or the Reich of the Third Gospel in which the rule of the Father and then that of the Son are transcended by the rule of the Holy Spirit; it is this vision and this product of the will to utopia that is perverted by the nightmare of Nazism.

Bloch's politics and cultural politics are deeply contradictory. A convinced Marxist, he was never a member of the German Communist Party. Although he defends EXPRESSIONISM (1938, 1959) – an instance of what he terms the Front – against the criticisms advanced by LUKÁCS, and takes a sympathetic interest in German popular culture (notably in the vignettes of Bloch 1962), he also attacks jazz, Hollywood cinema ('a poison factory') and other manifestations of 'American filth' in a style that would have pleased ZHDANOV, and contrasts them with the wholesomeness of Russian folk-dances. Bloch defended the Moscow Show Trials of 1937 in print (1937), but soon came into conflict with the communist authorities when he returned to the German Democratic Republic from his American exile in 1949. He scornfully described the compulsory courses in Marxism-Leninism at Leipzig University as 'the marxism of the narrow lane', criticized the GDR's Soviet orientation and was in turn accused of REVISIONISM and removed from his teaching post in 1957 (Bloch's years in the GDR are described in Ernst and Klinger 1997). By chance, Bloch was visiting the then West Germany when the building of the Berlin Wall began on 13 August 1961, and he did not return to the GDR.

BLOCK British journal of visual culture; fifteen issues on art history, design history and cultural theory were published between 1979 and 1989. *BLOCK*'s stated ambition was to address the problems of the social, economic and ideological dimensions of the visual arts in societies past and present. Produced by a group of young academics working mainly in art schools and what were then the polytechnics, *BLOCK* was an expression of a revolt against the anti-theoretical tradition of EMPIRICISM in art history. Whilst it did draw on the tradition of Marxist art history associated with Arnold Hauser and John Berger (Berger 1965, 1972), which had been revitalized by Clark's work on the nineteenth century (Clark 1973a, 1973b), the journal, like *SCREEN*, was also an important forum for discussions of PSYCHOANALYSIS and the cultural analysis of WILLIAMS and BOURDIEU. There was a significant overlap between its concerns and the developing discipline of CULTURAL STUDIES. *BLOCK* also provided one of the first platforms for interventions into art history by FEMINIST CRITICISM. The *BLOCK Reader in Visual Culture* (1996) reproduces a representative selection of articles from the journal.

Bloom, Allan (1930–) American philosopher and cultural critic. His controversial and bestselling *The Closing of the American Mind* (1987) and the essays collected in *Giants and Dwarves* (1990) make a polemical assault on the contemporary state of American universities, arguing that a relativist approach to cultural values, an insistence on minority rights, affirmative action to increase minority representation and a soft liberalism have destroyed their universalist vocation to instil in their students a taste for learning. The openness associated with the ENLIGHTENMENT once meant using reason to seek the good; to Bloom it means an uncritical acceptance of everything and anything, and he dismisses as folly John Rawls' attempt (1972) to make indiscriminateness or fairness a 'moral imperative'. The trivialization that is at work throughout modern culture means that words like 'creativity' and 'personality', which were once applied to Beethoven and Goethe, can now be applied to any schoolchild, because democracy insists that no one can be denied access to the good. Bloom's philippic against relativistic trivialization is grounded in his conviction that true education begins with an early acquaintance with the great books which reveal the permanent questions of the Western tradition that began with Socrates. Significantly, Bloom is the translator of both Rousseau's *Émile* and Plato's *Republic*.

Bloom's tirade against relativism derives in part from a universalist reading of the American Constitution which argues that it guarantees the rights of individual citizens of a universal republic, but not the differential rights of minorities defined by IDENTITY POLITICS, and his comments on the conformism of modern America owe a great deal to Alexis de Tocqueville's classic thesis that the main threat to a democracy is that it may become enslaved by the tyranny of public opinion (*Democracy in America*, 1835–40), but the main influence on him is Alexandre KOJÈVE. The two men were close, and Bloom prefaced the abridged American translation of Kojève's study of Hegel (Kojève 1947; Bloom 1969). The underlying argument of *The Closing of the American Mind* is that the crisis in the universities is an aspect of the post-historical experience in which men revert to an almost animal-like existence. The university which was once a road of learning that led to a meeting-place of the great is now the domain of the last man described by Nietzsche in section five of the prologue to *Thus Spoke Zarathustra* (1892). When he asks what is meant by love, creation or longing, the last man (or 'the ultimate man' in Hollingdale's translation) merely blinks: the earth has become small, and the last man makes everything small. As Nietzsche puts it: 'Everyone wants the same thing, everyone is the same.'

Bloom, Harold (1930–) American literary critic and theorist. Bloom's specialist field is English Romantic poetry (1959, 1961), but his enormous range is illustrated by his many contributions, from 1985 onwards, to Chelsea House's *Modern Critical Interpretations* and *Modern Critical Views* series. These make him one of the very few twentieth-century critics to cover the whole field of English literature. Bloom is also unusual in that he writes for both an academic and a popular audience; his panoramic survey and defence of the entire Western CANON (1994) is a rare example of successful popularization.

Bloom is probably best known for his Freudian-inflected theory (FREUD) of the ANXIETY OF INFLUENCE (1973) and its themes recur through his career, despite his many changes of direction. His early studies of Romanticism react against the NEW CRITICISM in two ways. On the one hand, Bloom deflects critical interest away from 'the line of wit' and metaphysical poetry (Brooks 1939), and towards Romanticism. On the other, he insists from the earliest stages of a long career that the poem is not an isolated verbal icon (Wimsatt 1954); for Bloom, there are no texts, but only relations between texts, and meaning itself is a product of their interaction. Whilst this vision of the relationship between texts obviously anticipates the INTERTEXTUALITY of KRISTEVA, it is also an early version of what Bloom will later call 'misreading' or 'misprision' (1975a) and 'REVISIONISM' (1982). The literary tradition is revisionist in that poets (and critics; Bloom sees no difference, in kind or degree, between the languages of poetry and criticism) inevitably reinterpret, re-envision, re-evaluate and revise the work of their precursors in a bid to overcome the anxiety of influence and their sense of belatedness, or the nightmare sense of coming after the event, and of trying to occupy the ground where powerful predecessors have stood. Strong poetry begins with a wilful act of misreading that allows the *ephebe* (the Greek term for a young citizen, used by Bloom to describe the new citizen of the poetic realm) to absorb and overcome the influence of his precursors. One of the most obvious and fertile examples of misprision is the Romantic reading, to which Bloom himself subscribes, that sees Satan as the true hero of *Paradise Lost*.

Bloom's idiosyncrasies and inconsistencies are many. Once closely associated with the so-called Yale school of DECONSTRUCTION (1979), he later dismisses deconstruction as the 'death-throes of German romantic philosophy' (1982). His borrowings from the traditions of RHETORIC, PSYCHOANALYSIS and Gnostic or Kabbalistic interpretation (1975b) are exemplary instances of misprision. He is wasp-ish towards his many rivals, dismissing 'source hunters' as 'the carrion-eaters of scholarship' (1975a) and generically describing Foucauldians, New Historicists and Feminists as the SCHOOL OF RESENTMENT, the object of their resentment being the authority and influence of the canon (1994). His pronouncements on FEMINISM are deliberately provocative; if the 'burgeoning religion of Liberated Woman' comes to dominate the West, the last links with the tradition of Homer will be broken and the canon will be destroyed (Bloom 1975a). Despite this anti-feminist stance, Bloom also argues in his bestselling *The Book of J* (1991) that the first books of the Bible were written by a woman at the court of Solomon, even though there is little or no evidence to support that claim. Exponents of FEMINIST CRITICISM such as SHOWALTER claim (1991) that Bloom's theory applies only to a male line of descent; others, like GILBERT AND GUBAR (1979a), have used it with profit, whilst PAGLIA is a self-confessed disciple. Bloom's choice of terminology can be so idiosyncratic as to appear eccentric or even quite arbitrary. One of the strategies of misreading is dubbed *clinamen*, described as the swerving away from a strong influence; this is the term used by Lucretius in Book II of *The Nature of the Universe* to describe how atoms swerve from their straight course and collide to form matter. Bloom's justification for such eccentricities is that every word in a critic's vocabulary should 'swerve from inherited words'.

Like *The Western Canon* (1994), Bloom's *Shakespeare* (1999) is a work of popular-ization and argues that Shakespeare is such a strong poet that his work already contains all the interpretations that can be made of it; that, indeed, Shakespeare, the key figure in the Bloomian canon, is such a strong poet that he created the modern sense of selfhood; that we cannot conceive of ourselves without making reference to Shakespeare's characters. To the extent that Bloom's reading of the plays concentrates on individual characters, it is strangely reminiscent of the much-derided character analysis of Bradley's *Shakespearean Tragedy* (Bradley 1904).

Although Bloom's theory of influence is based upon the notion of inter-generational conflict (*agon*), his survey of the canon (1994) gives the impression that the battle has been lost. Bloom does not view the ascendancy of the 'dismal social science' of cultural criticism with total dismay; if English and literature departments do shrink to the size of Classics departments, it may at last be possible to revert to the essential critical task of studying the inescapable canon.

READING: Allen (1994); Lentricchia (1980)

Bourdieu, Pierre (1930–) French sociologist. Bourdieu's earliest work, in which he introduces the important concept of HABITUS (1958, 1962, 1965), was on the conflict between modernization and tradition in Algeria and on peasant societies in France, but his reputation rests mainly on his work on the sociology of culture and cultural FIELDS (1966, 1982). He has written extensively on the sociology of taste (1979), on the culture of museums and their use (Bourdieu, Darbel and Schnapper 1969), and on higher education in France (Bourdieu 1984a, 1984b), but his major themes are already present in an earlier collaborative study of students and their relationship with culture (Bourdieu and Passeron 1964).

In *The Inheritors* (1964) Bourdieu and Passeron note that whilst French universities offer equal access to all, working-class children are seriously underrepresented. Their underrepresentation and failure to achieve good results are not the result of direct discrimination, but of their deficiency in 'cultural capital' or the extra-curricular culture that is recognized and valued, but not directly transmitted, by the educational institution. The universities' apparent function of transmitting information proves not to be their real function, which is to consecrate and reproduce values created elsewhere. The cultural capital required to ensure academic success and recognition is acquired by exposure to areas to which working-class students rarely have access: exhibitions, serious music such as contemporary compositions and jazz, and contemporary literature. Students from more privileged social strata are able to legitimize their cultural privileges thanks to the IDEOLOGY which represents socially determined cultural capital as an expression of individual talent and taste, and failure to acquire it as an individual failing. Much of Bourdieu's later work has been on the reproduction of the mechanisms that make culturally and socially determined positions of dominance appear to be the result of personal choices.

READING: Robbins (1991)

Braudel, Fernand (1902–85) French historian. One of the most important figures associated with the *ANNALES* school, Braudel is famous for his rejection of the purely chronological history of events (*HISTOIRE ÉVÉNEMENTIELLE*) and for his concentration on the long-term perspective (*LONGUE DURÉE*). In the preface to his great study of the Mediterranean world (1949), which began life as a study of Philip II of Spain's foreign policy and then developed into an immensely long study of 'the sea in all its complexity', he outlines a three-level model of history, which he likens to the three floors of a house. The first level is that of the *longue durée* or of a history whose passage is almost imperceptible. This is the history of man's relationship with the physical environment and of an almost timeless experience of constant repetition. The perceptible but still slow changes of social history in which social groups interact makes up the next level, and the lives of individuals the third. Historical time is thus broken down into geographical, social and individual time.

The structure of Braudel's books is consistent with the three-level model; they inevitably begin with physical geography, and gradually move on to examining the material history of everyday life and then into a study of the social dimension. Braudel's goal is to write a total history that moves from the basement of the environment to the attic where collective representations or MENTALITIES are studied, though he is in fact much less concerned with mentalities than some of his *Annales* colleagues.

The 'world' of the Mediterranean is the starting-point for the idea of a world-economy explored in the three volumes of *Civilization and Capitalism* (1975a, 1975b, 1979). The hyphenated 'world-economy' is not synonymous with 'world economy', which refers to a market spanning the universe, but designates an autonomous fragment of the world that can provide for most of its needs, and which relates to the rest of that world on that basis. Braudel thus outlines a history of multiple times and spaces. His concept of economic development is unconventional in that his reliance on very slow patterns of change precludes the notion of sudden ruptures or breaks. Capitalism is thus neither the product nor the harbinger of an industrial revolution, but results from slow cycles and patterns of accumulation observable in the fifteenth century or even earlier. Capitalism is an accumulation of power or a form of social parasitism, and Braudel contrasts it with the more informal exchanges that take place in the markets that continue to escape its control. The scope of Braudel's highly sophisticated work is immense, but his vision of history is impersonal in the extreme and accords little importance to human initiative. The large-scale study of the 'identity of France' (1986a) was left unfinished when Braudel died. His theoretical essays on historiography are collected as *On History* (1969).

READING: Burke (1990)

Brecht, Bertolt (1898–1956) German dramatist, director, poet and founder, in 1949, of the Berliner Ensemble. *The Life of Galileo* (1939), *Mother Courage and her Children* (1941) and the *Caucasian Chalk Circle* (1945) are classics of the twentieth-century theatre, whilst the bitter-sweet Weil-Brecht songs from *The Threepenny Opera* (1928) enjoy almost universal popularity. Brecht is unusual amongst twentieth-century dramatists in that, as well as producing a large body of work for the stage, he also produced a large body of theoretical texts in which he outlines his vision of a didactic EPIC theatre which uses the ALIENATION-EFFECT to help the audience take a detached and critical view of what they are watching, rather than empathizing and identifying with the characters on stage as they are invited to do by productions based upon STANISLAVSKY'S method acting. It is significant that Brecht began his career as a *Dramaturg*, which is the German term for a reader, adaptor and literary adviser employed by a theatre. Brecht's plays are grounded in his practical knowledge of stagecraft and of writing for the stage in the most direct and practical of senses.

Brecht's earliest plays, *Baal* (1918a) and *Drums in the Night* (1918b), are violent, almost melodramatic affairs, in which crime, alcohol and grim urban settings figure conspicuously. In this early period, Brecht sees the boxing match and the night-club performance as the models for a new theatre and the mood of his writing owes something to both DADA and EXPRESSIONISM. It is also characterized by a fascination with the 'exotic' and almost purely mythical image of an England seen through Kipling and the literature of Empire; it finds its final expression in *The Threepenny Opera* (1928), which adapts John Gay's *The Beggar's Opera* (1728) and transfers it to the criminal London of 1900, and the related *Threepenny Novel* (1934). A more didactic style emerges in the *Lehrstücke* or 'learning plays' of the late 1920s (in *Plays* 2). These were designed to make explicit political points; *St Joan of the Stockyards* (1929–31), for instance, uses an almost caricature image of the stockyards and commercial exchanges of Chicago to denounce the workings of the capitalist system in its entirety. The change of mood is influenced partly by Brecht's study of Marx, and partly by the general cultural shift to a more objective style signalled by the emergence of *NEUE SACHLICHKEIT*. The influence of Piscator's EPIC theatre now becomes all-important. In this version of political AGITPROP theatre, slogans on placards and documentary information projected on slides replace dramatic exposition, break up the flow of the play and make a serious assault on the conventions of psychological theatre. Brecht's own version of epic theatre, perfected in the best-known plays of his period of exile from Germany between 1933 and 1948, uses similar devices, but also develops a style of acting in which the players act 'in quotation marks' by adopting a 'gestural' style which literally points to the artificiality of what they are doing. The play itself becomes a sequence of loosely connected episodes interspersed with songs that comment on the action. The emphasis falls not on psychological characterization, as Brecht expressly rejects the classical or 'Aristotelian' thesis that drama should be based on an emotional CATHARSIS, but on a *Fabel*, a German term for 'story' that has unmistakably didactic overtones. The difficulties of creating a truly epic theatre in which the audience watches with a lucidly critical attitude are illustrated by *Mother Courage* (1941). Set in the Thirty Years' War of the seventeenth century, it is the story of a woman who follows the warring armies, selling them food from her wagon. She eventually loses all her children and is reduced to misery, but still continues her pursuit of profit. Although the audience is clearly meant to be critical of Mother Courage's search for economic gain, it invariably sympathizes with her in her plight.

Brecht's politics are surprisingly ambiguous. Although he thought of himself as a Marxist and had overt communist sympathies, he rarely followed any party line and was highly critical of the stance on realism taken by LUKÁCS during the BLOCH– Lukács debate over EXPRESSIONISM in 1936–9. The lucid irony of his dramatic style could not be further removed from orthodox SOCIALIST REALISM, with its 'positive heroes' who set examples for the reader. When a workers' uprising was put down with great brutality in June 1953, Brecht sent a notorious telegram expressing support for the government, but he also wrote a poem (unpublished in his lifetime) in which he opined that the solution to the crisis was for the government to dissolve the people and elect another one.

Brecht's influence on modern theatre is almost incalculable, as was the impact of the Berliner Ensemble's visits to Paris in 1954 and 1956 and to London in 1956. Although neither France nor Britain developed a truly Brechtian theatre, his influence is visible in John Osborne's *The Entertainer* (1957) and *Luther* (1960), in the work of Joan Littlewood's Theatre Workshop in the East End of London, and in French attempts to create a popular theatre in the 1960s (see O'Connor 1975). In Germany, Brecht's influence can be seen in the 'documentary' theatre of Rolf Hochhuth – *The Representative* (1963), *Soldiers* (1967). In the cinema, directors as diverse as Britain's Lindsay Anderson and France's Jean-Luc Godard have also been greatly influenced by Brecht (see SCREEN 1974, 1975/6).

READING: Benjamin (1966); Esslin (1980); Thomson and Sacks (1994); Willett (1977)

Bremond, Claude (1929–) French specialist in NARRATOLOGY. Bremond's work on the logic of narrative draws on and modifies PROPP's morphological analysis of folk-tales (1928), and has much in common with that of GREIMAS and the early TODOROV (particularly 1969).

Bremond adapts Propp's notion of function (the action of a character, defined in terms of its contribution to the unfolding of the plot) and redefines it as a 'role' played by a subject/character defined by a process/predicate. Roles can be subdivided into those played by 'patients' and 'agents'. Patients are affected by processes that modify or preserve their position and might be described as, for example, 'beneficiaries' or 'victims'. Agents such as informants, benefactors, dissimulators or seducers initiate the processes that affect patients. Both patients and agents are inserted into sequences which, at every point in the narrative, open up a set of alternative consequences. To take a hypothetical example: the king will or will not leave the castle, and if he does, will or will not set out on a perilous quest. A further set of possible consequences will then open up; some will be realized by the narrative whilst others will not. According to Bremond, all narratives can be analysed in terms of roles and sequences, which can be analysed in a quasi-grammatical manner. With disarming modesty (and honesty) he describes his major study in narratology (1973) as a tool or a 'catalogue of roles', adding that it is a text to be consulted rather than read.

Breton, André (1896–1966) French poet and principal theorist of SURREALISM. Breton's charismatic personality and his remarkable ability to coin manifesto-slogans such as 'Beauty will be convulsive or it will not be' (1928a) and 'The simplest surrealist act consists of going into the street, revolver in hand, and firing at random into the crowd for as long as one can' (1929), meant that he was always the dominant figure in the surrealist group. The authoritarian manner in which he excommunicated rivals or dissidents like ARTAUD and BATAILLE led to his being dubbed the 'Pope of surrealism'; he himself proclaimed: 'I *am* surrealism.'

The claim to being surrealism is not unfounded. The movement was always marked by Breton's personal tastes and interests. There are few surrealist novels because he scorned the novel as the basest form of literature (exceptions were made for Sade, Huysmans, Swift and the Gothic novel), and his total lack of interest in music did little to encourage experiments in that domain. In the hauntingly beautiful *Nadja* (1928a), an autobiographical account of obsessive love, photographs replace conventional descriptive passages, but it is not, as has sometimes been claimed, the first 'novel' to use photographs in this way; that distinction belongs to Georges Rodenbach's *Bruges-la-morte* (1892), which is one of the classics of symbolism. Breton had little formal education and his knowledge of philosophy (primarily Hegel and Marx) was limited. The interest in the unconscious and psychoanalysis that pervades surrealism stems largely from Breton's medical studies, which he never completed, and his work as an auxiliary doctor during the First World War, when he began to record and analyse the dreams of traumatized soldiers in the Val de Grâce military hospital, Paris.

Breton's poetry is characterized by its use of surprising imagery rather than any interest in the technicalities of versification, and is highly personal. The dominant themes of *amour fou* ('mad love') and the quest for the marvellous are autobiographical in origin (1928a, 1937). The sense for imagery also characterizes Breton's extensive writings on art (see in particular the sumptuous *Surrealism and Painting* of 1928, and its revised editions of 1946 and 1965), his talent as a collector and his production of 'poem-objects', which combine elements of collage, found objects and calligraphy (examples are reproduced in the exhibition catalogue *André Breton: La Beauté convulsive* of 1991). Breton's influence is not confined to poetry and the arts; SITUATIONISM'S practice of *DÉRIVE* owes much to Breton's quest for the marvellous and to his notion of 'objective chance', or the random encounter with the very thing one desires.

Breton's own account of the movement he founded is given in the radio conversations with Andrée Parinaud broadcast and published in 1952.

READING: Gershman (1969); Polizzotti (1995)

bricolage French for 'tinkering about' or 'do-it-yourself'; a *bricoleur* undertakes odd jobs and is a jack-of-all-trades, as distinct from a craftsman. Because of the difficulty of finding a strict equivalent, the French term has been retained by the translators of LÉVI-STRAUSS (1949, 1962b), who uses *bricolage* to describe a characteristic feature of mythical thought. Mythical thought, or the thinking that creates myths, expresses itself with a heterogeneous but limited repertoire of oddments left over from a variety of human endeavours. Its themes are a subset of a wider culture and already have their own meaning, but they can be rearranged in new combinations and contexts. Mythical thought uses them because it has nothing else to hand, and cobbles them together to create new myths and stories through a process of intellectual *bricolage*. *Bricolage* is not a primitive form of thought that is transcended through evolution, but a fundamental aspect of human intellectual activity; all societies use it to create their myths.

Butler, Judith P. (1956–) American feminist philosopher. Butler's first book was an important study of the Hegelian strand in contemporary French philosophy (1987), but she is best known for her subsequent work on GENDER (*Gender Trouble*, 1990) and her contributions to QUEER theory (*Bodies that Matter*, 1993).

In the course of a long and at times difficult dialogue with PSYCHOANALYSIS and theorists such as IRIGARAY, FOUCAULT and KRISTEVA, Butler argues that gender is a cultural meaning that is ascribed to human bodies and not an inherent attribute of personhood or subjectivity. The meaning of gender is inseparable from the cultural and political intersections within which it is produced and maintained, and it does not derive naturally from the biological sex of the individual. Applying the work of AUSTIN and SPEECH-ACT theory to the domain of sexual difference, Butler demonstrates that the production of gender is a matter of performativity. When applied to a neonate, the utterance 'It's a girl' inaugurates a process of 'girling' that is constantly reiterated through the rituals and INTERPELLATIONS that instil the norms of a female gender defined by a taboo on homosexuality. The performativity of gender does not refer to a single act, but to a long and repetitive process through which DISCOURSE produces the gender-effect it claims to name; there can be no gender outside or prior to the DISCOURSE that names it. 'Being a man' or 'being a woman' is an unstable affair, since the process of gendering is never complete. Having a gender is a matter of identification, but it also implies the loss of other potential genders or identifications. The instability of gender implies that it can always be subverted or 'queered' by practices such as drag and cross-dressing, and by the adoption of 'femme' and 'butch' roles in lesbian relationships. Butler is at pains to stress (1993) that, whilst drag can to some degree subvert gender norms, it can also be used to reinforce heterosexual stereotypes, as in films such as *Some Like it Hot* (dir. Billy Wilder, 1959).

Butler's *Excitable Speech* (1997) applies her theory of performativity to a discussion of pornography and HATE SPEECH, and argues that legal interventions based upon the MACKINNON-DWORKIN MODEL LAW would extend the definition of pornography by inaugurating a debate which would reproduce and reiterate in a pedagogical or juridical mode the very thing they are attempting to regulate. In Butler's view, the queering and reappropriation of terms of abuse and hate speech is preferable to legal regulation through the courts.

C

Cahiers du cinéma French film journal, founded by Jacques Doniol-Valcroze and André BAZIN and published monthly since April 1951. It is probably the most influential of all film journals.

Cahiers du cinéma (Cinema notebooks) was one of the first journals to begin to elaborate a serious theory of film, as opposed to publishing ephemeral reviews and essays in film appreciation. It is also unique in that many of the critics associated with the early *Cahiers*, such as Jean-Luc Godard, François Truffaut and Claude Chabrol, went on to become the major directors of the *NOUVELLE VAGUE*. In the 1950s, the *Cahiers du cinéma* critics were aggressive and often polemical defenders of *AUTEUR* THEORY and, although the journal subsequently turned to semiotic and Marxist-influenced theory in the late 1960s, its overall view of cinema has always been director-centred. It is very rare for a journal to be translated into another language, and the existence of a three-volume selection of articles in English (1985, 1986, 1990) is a tribute to *Cahiers du cinéma*'s lasting importance and influence.

Calvino, Italo (1923–85) Italian novelist, critic and member of OULIPO.

Outside Italy, Calvino is best known for his later stories and novels such as *Invisible Cities* (1972) and especially *If On A Winter's Night a Traveller* (1979) which, with their combination of realism and fantasy and their intricate but playful use of formal devices like *MISE-EN-ABYME*, are often regarded as classic examples of POSTMODERN-ISM, but his early fiction (1947) is very close to the aesthetic of NEOREALISM. In both his fiction and his criticism, Calvino gradually absorbs a host of influences ranging from PROPP to STRUCTURALISM, but all his work is characterized by a deep belief in the importance of story-telling, and he remarks that 'It all began with the first storyteller of the tribe' (1969). For Calvino, story-telling is the most basic way of bringing order and structure into the world, and all literary culture originates in the very old game that has always been played between story-teller and listener. His collection of Italian folk-tales (1956) is at once a monumental collection of folklore and a storehouse of delights. Sadly, only a small selection of the essays now collected in the two volumes of *Saggi* (Essays, 1995) is available in English translation (1982).

READING: Re (1990)

Canguilhem, Georges (1904–95) French philosopher and historian of science. Canguilhem succeeded BACHELARD at the Sorbonne, and became the most prominent representative of the French school of historical EPISTEMOLOGY. Whilst his reputation is based upon his detailed historical studies of the sciences, his influence extends far beyond his own academic sphere.

Canguilhem trained both as a philosopher and as a doctor of medicine, and most of his work deals with the history of biology and the life sciences. In 1943 he published his doctoral thesis on the concepts of the normal and the pathological (republished in a revised version 1950); this was followed by a major study of the concept of the reflex in the life sciences of the seventeenth and eighteenth centuries (1955). He has published major studies of Auguste Comte, Claude Bernard and Charles Darwin (1958b, 1959, 1960).

The central concept in Canguilhem's history of the sciences is that of the EPIS-TEMOLOGICAL BREAK which wrenches a science out of its prescientific past and allows it to reject that past as ideological. Canguilhem's history is a history of radical discontinuities and breaks that restructure whole fields of knowledge as concepts such as those of fever, normality or pathology emerge. This is not the history of a smooth progress towards knowledge, but one of errors that have been overcome. A science does not develop thanks to empirical discoveries alone, but through conceptual shifts and breaks. At any given moment in its history, a science or proto-science is not a picture of empirical reality, but a system of concepts organized by a PROBLEMATIC. It has sometimes been claimed that Canguilhem's notion of an epistemological break is related to KUHN's idea of a PARADIGM shift; Canguilhem strenuously rejects that suggestion, arguing (1976) that Kuhn works with a psych-ologistical notion of science, and that his 'NORMAL SCIENCE' is no more than a consensus that prevails within a given scientific community. It is also significant that Canguilhem habitually speaks of 'sciences' in the plural, and not of a single abstract Science. Although Canguilhem is both a militant anti-empiricist and a bitter opponent of subjective philosophies of existence such as EXISTENTIALISM, there is a profoundly humanitarian and even humanist strand in his work. He describes knowledge as the 'daughter of fear', and the role of the sciences as the improvement of human existence (1952).

Canguilhem's influence was at its height in the 1960s, when he became a figure of immense importance for certain tendencies within STRUCTURALISM. FOUCAULT quite accurately remarks (1978) that if we ignore Canguilhem, we shall understand little of developments in French philosophy at that time. His studies in scientific historiography had a major impact on ALTHUSSER and on the history of medicine elaborated in Foucault's *Birth of the Clinic* (1963a), whilst the famous essay in which psychology is dismissed as 'a philosophy without rigour', 'an ethics that makes no demands' and a 'medicine without controls' (1958a) provided valuable ammunition for those who were seeking to demonstrate the scientificity of the PSYCHOANALYSIS of LACAN.

READING: Canguilhem (1994); *Economy and Society* (1998); *Georges Canguilhem* (1993); Lecourt (1972)

cannibalism A tendency within Brazilian MODERNISM which takes its name from Oswald de Andrade's 'Cannibal Manifesto' of 1928 (see Johnson 1987). Andrade's notion of cultural cannibalism derives from the traditional customs of the Tupy Indians, who ate the bodies of their dead enemies so as to absorb their virtues and strength. His manifesto urges Brazilian writers and artists to devour European culture, to absorb its positive elements and to eliminate its negative aspects so as to create a synthetic but genuinely Brazilian culture. Cannibalism also implies a critique of Romantic myths which portrayed Brazilian Indians as noble savages.

Similar metaphors of cannibalism occur in other parts of Latin America and the Caribbean. Cannibalism is a theme in the early NEGRITUDE of Martinique's Aimé CÉSAIRE, whose wife Suzanne Césaire stated in 1942 that Martiniquan literature 'will be cannibalistic or will not exist'. She also spoke of the need to 'cannibalize' and digest SURREALISM rather than be passively influenced by it. In the 'author's note' to the 1988 edition of his novel *Palace of the Peacock* (1960), often seen as a classic example of MAGICAL REALISM, the Guyanese writer Wilson Harris exploits the myth of the spirit flute or bone flute (a musical instrument made by the Caribs from the bones of the conquistadores they had eaten) as a metaphor for the traditions that link pre-Columbian America to the contemporary Latin American states and their cultures. Here again, the dominant motif is that of the cycle of death and resurrection symbolized by the devouring, absorption and transformation of invasive European cultures.

canon The original theological meaning of the word is a law or decree promulgated by an ecclesiastical court and forming part of the body of canon law. By extension, the term applies to the set of books accepted by a church or faith as genuine or of true divine inspiration. The canon of the Old Testament was established in AD 90–100 by an assembly of rabbis; the current canon of the New Testament was first promulgated in 365. Those books that were not accepted as canonical were relegated to the Apocrypha.

In literary studies, the canon is made up of the great books by classic authors that go to make up the tradition of a national literature. In terms of English literature, the canon is usually accepted as including Chaucer, Shakespeare, Pope, Wordsworth, and so on. The opening sentence of F. R. LEAVIS's *The Great Tradition* (1948) is a classically canonical statement: 'The great English novelists are Jane Austen, George Eliot, Henry James and Joseph Conrad.' As Barthes remarks (1969), 'literature' is 'what is taught', and the canon is largely synonymous with the body of literature recommended for study in schools and universities. The formation of a canon is therefore the result of pedagogical decisions taken on the basis of received critical opinion as to what is legitimately part of a tradition, and a consensus as to the meaning of literary value. The successive editions of standard works such as the *Oxford Book of English Verse* and the Norton anthologies also play a major role in establishing and revising the canon.

The authority of the canon is regularly challenged on the grounds of its non-relevance to contemporary concerns and issues. As a canon is necessarily exclusive, demands for its revision often take the form of a demand that it should be expanded to include works by authors from minority or marginalized groups. Hence the POLITICALLY CORRECT criticisms of a canon that consists solely of the writings of

DEAD WHITE EUROPEAN MALES (Gates 1992; Morrison 1992). Harold BLOOM's *The Western Canon* (1994), with its strictures against the SCHOOL OF RESENTMENT, and the essays of Allan BLOOM (1990) are typical examples of the attempt to defend the canon against such criticisms.

captatio benevolentiae Latin phrase literally meaning 'the capture of good will'. It is used in treatises on rhetoric to describe the orator's initial attempt to win his audience's sympathy and attention by establishing a relationship of complicity, as in Mark Antony's 'Friends, Romans, countrymen, lend me your ears' in Shakespeare's *Julius Caesar* (III.ii).

catachresis In grammar, the improper use of a term or the application of a term to a thing to which it is inappropriate. Examples of the former sense given in the *New Fowler's Modern English Usage* include 'chronic' in place of 'habitual' or 'inveterate', and 'to infer' in place of 'to imply' or 'to suggest'. Book III of St Augustine's *De Doctrina Christiana* (On Christian teaching) provides a more entertaining definition of the TROPE: 'Don't we all refer to a swimming pool by the name *piscina*, which takes its name from fish (*pisces*) even though it does not contain fish and was not made for fish?' In RHETORIC, the term can apply to the improper use or inversion of a FIGURE or trope, but is also used to describe a violent or unexpected METAPHOR. The rhetorical function of catachresis is to inspire ironic doubts about either what is being characterized or the mode of its characterization. Catachresis is also a part of normal speech, and describes how a figurative or metaphorical term can be used when the available literal terms are inadequate. One speaks, for example, of 'the sails of a windmill', even though a windmill is not a sailing vessel. Catachresis is a device popular with the practitioners of DECONSTRUCTION, and SPIVAK describes it as a metaphor without a literal REFERENT which stands in for a concept that is a precondition for conceptuality. The opening words of Nietzsche's *Beyond Good and Evil* (1886) supply an example: 'Supposing truth to be a woman . . .'

catalogue raisonné French expression, literally meaning 'reasoned catalogue', current in English since the late eighteenth century (*OED*). A catalogue raisonné is a chronological listing of all the works of an individual artist, giving details of format, dimensions, medium and support, provenance, sales and exhibitions. The works themselves are often illustrated in small format. Commentary is usually minimal; the purpose of the catalogue raisonné, unlike that of an exhibition catalogue, is to establish the work's provenance and not to interpret it. Catalogues raisonnés are the standard works of reference in art history. Wildenstein's *Monet* (1996), which is the product of forty years' work, is a classic example, comprising a one-volume biographical study of the artist and a three-volume catalogue. Together with the monograph on a single artist (e.g. Scott 1992) or a single work (e.g. Isaacson 1972) and the exhibition catalogue, the catalogue raisonné is the fundamental GENRE of art history.

catharsis Derived from the Greek verb meaning 'to clean' or 'to purify', the term is used in Aristotle's *Poetics* to describe the purification or purgation of the emotions through a vicarious participation in the representation of events that inspire feelings of fear (*phobos*) and pity (*eleos*). Tragic drama is the typical form of cathartic MIMESIS. *Phobos* describes a cold shudder that makes the blood run cold; *eleos* the shiver of apprehension we feel as we watch Oedipus rushing to his destruction, and fear for him (Gadamer 1960).

In the history of PSYCHOANALYSIS, the adjective 'cathartic' is applied to the therapeutic method developed by FREUD in the period 1880–95, when he was still using techniques derived from older hypnotic treatments (Freud and Breuer 1903–05). The pressure of the hand to the forehead of the patient was used to convince the patient that a repressed traumatic memory could be recovered. The evocation of that memory allowed the patient to abreact the AFFECTS associated with it in a dramatic or cathartic discharge of emotion. The cathartic method was rapidly abandoned in favour of the FREE ASSOCIATION technique. Cathartic methods are still used in other forms of psychotherapy such as psychodrama, in which play-acting is used to effect a release from internal emotional conflicts (Moreno 1946).

cathexis James Strachey's rendering of FREUD's term *Besetzung*, and now a standard term in the psychoanalytic vocabulary of the English-speaking world. One of the meanings of *Besetzung* is the occupation of a town or territory. Like its French equivalent *investissement*, *Besetzung* is in common usage, and Freud's choice of terminology reflects his usual reluctance to use a highly technical vocabulary (Laplanche and Pontalis 1967; Bettelheim 1983). Like LIBIDO, 'cathexis', and the verb 'cathect', coined by Freud's English translator on the basis of a Greek verb meaning 'to occupy', have quasi-classical connotations that are not present in the original German.

Freud uses the term to describe the process whereby a quantity of psychical energy becomes attached to an OBJECT or idea. In his earliest writings (1895; Freud and Breuer 1903–05), Freud describes neurones as being cathected with a quantity of energy or a quota of AFFECT. There is some variation in usage in the later texts, but the basic notion of quantities of energy remains fairly constant. Thus, to say that an object is libidinally cathected means that it is charged with sexual energy deriving from sources internal to the psyche. In Freud's second TOPOGRAPHY, the ID, or the instinctual pole of the personality, is said to be the source of all cathexes.

Césaire, Aimé (1913–) French poet, dramatist and politician.

Together with SENGHOR and DAMAS, Césaire is one of the founding fathers of NEGRITUDE; his epic poem *Notebook of a Return to my Native Land* (1939) is generally regarded as that movement's poetic manifesto. The poem is at once a celebration of the positive values of Black African culture (this is largely an imaginary construct, as Césaire had not, at the time of writing, visited Africa) and a searing denunciation of the white colonialism that had blocked the development of a culture specific to Césaire's native Martinique. Césaire's poetic analysis of the ALIENATION induced by colonialism should be compared with the psychological and political analysis supplied by FANON. Both the *Notebook* and Césaire's later poetry (collected 1983) are strongly influenced by SURREALISM's critique of European rationality and its appeal to irrational values as a source of liberation. Although deeply rooted in the culture of Martinique and overtly political, Césaire's poetry is erudite, makes use of the rarest resources of the French language and makes no concessions to populism. The younger writers associated with the CREOLENESS school are highly critical of his reliance on the French poetic tradition and his refusal to use the Creole that is the first language of most of the population of Martinique (Bernabé, Chamoiseau and Confiant 1993; Confiant 1993).

Césaire represented Martinique in the French Assemblée Nationale from 1945 to 1993. Although he is an outspoken critic of colonialism (1955), he has never argued that Martinique should become independent. In 1946 he sponsored the legislation that transformed the former colony into a *département* like any in metropolitan France. He has, however, consistently demanded greater autonomy within the framework of the French nation.

READING: Toumson and Henry-Valmore (1993)

chiasmus In RHETORIC, a FIGURE of speech in which a second clause or phrase inverts the order of words used in the first, as in 'Man must eat in order to live and not live in order to eat.'

Chomsky, Noam (1928–) American linguist and political activist. It is extremely rare for a specialist in the highly technical field of linguistics to achieve the renown and even popularity enjoyed by Chomsky, but his combination of scholarly rigour and political radicalism has made him a public figure as well as an innovative linguist. One of the more popular aspects of Chomsky's work is that it provides a link between language and psychology that places great emphasis on human creativity. An initial link between his linguistics and his politics can be seen in the virulent polemical review (1959, reprinted in Fodor and Katz 1964) of B. F. Skinner's *Verbal Behaviour* (1957), which attempts to reduce language-use to patterns of stimulus and response, and conditioning and habit. Chomsky, in contrast, maintains that language is an expression of human creativity, and therefore of human freedom. Chomsky's COMPETENCE/performance model has proved very attractive to specialists working in other areas, and has, for instance, been incorporated into FISH's version of READER-RECEPTION THEORY. Chomsky's work on linguistics is very technical and relies heavily on the use of mathematically precise analyses and models; *Language and Mind* (1968) provides the clearest and least technical account of his theories.

Whereas the linguistics of SAUSSURE and his followers centres on the notion of a system of interacting individual SIGNS or units of meaning, Chomskyan linguistics is focused on the description of grammar. That term is not to be understood in the prescriptive sense, but in the sense of a description of an underlying structure governing language-use. To that extent, his work is, as Lyons demonstrates in his helpful introduction to Chomsky (1970), greatly influenced by specifically American traditions in linguistics. In the early part of the twentieth century, American linguistics was dominated by the attempt to record the numerous Native American languages. Those languages were recorded as objectively and exhaustively as possible, but in purely formal terms that made no reference to meaning. So-called Bloomfieldian linguistics (see Bloomfield 1923) took this tendency still further, arguing that it was possible to study the grammar of a language and to identify the structures and rules of its syntax and phonology without reference to semantics. Similar assumptions inform Harris's important work on DISCOURSE analysis (1951). Chomsky was to become very critical of this version of structural linguistics, but his early work is heavily influenced by it.

In his earliest work *Syntactic Structures* (1957) Chomsky makes a distinction between language and corpus, or between the potential to generate utterances and the actual utterances that have been made and are therefore available for analysis. The goal of linguistic analysis is to discover the grammar, or the 'device', that allows sentences to be produced or generated within the language under analysis. The influence of the Bloomfieldian thesis that a discovery device will reveal the unique grammar of every natural language is still apparent here. The great insight of this period is that, whilst a grammar is finite (and can therefore be codified), a language is not. A grammar can, that is, generate all, and only, the sentences that can be uttered by the native speaker of a language and that are acceptable ('correct') in the eyes of other native speakers. This insight is the source of the later competence-performance model that becomes the core of Chomskyan linguistics from 1965 onwards (1965, 1966a). Whereas the so-called language used by bees to indicate sources of pollen in their wagging dance is 'closed', human languages are characterized by their open-endedness and creativity. The creativity of language cannot be explained in terms of behavioural patterns. Whereas Bloomfield argued that speakers learn to make utterances on the basis of the utterances they have heard before, Chomsky contends that they have heard only a limited number of utterances, but can create an infinite number of new utterances for which there is no analogical precedent. It follows that grammatical competence is an innate aspect of the human mind and that linguistics merges imperceptibly into a psychology or philosophy of mind. Chomsky finds a historical precedent for his theory of generative grammar in the 'Cartesian linguistics' of seventeenth-century rationalist philosophy (1966b).

Chomsky's politics are based upon the conviction that intellectuals have a responsibility to speak the truth and to expose lies. He habitually does so on the basis of a meticulous study of official government documents. His *American Power and the New Mandarins* (1969) made a devastating attack on American policy in Vietnam and became a handbook for a generation of war-resisters. Chomsky continues to denounce the abuse of human rights and to criticize American foreign policy, and has played a major role in defending the cause of East Timor, the former Portuguese colony invaded and illegally occupied by Indonesia in 1975 (see, for example, the long essay on that topic in Chomsky 1996). Chomsky might be described as a libertarian socialist. He argues that there is a direct link between his linguistics and his politics (1973), contending that language is a basic criterion which demonstrates that human beings have a capacity for free thought and self-expression, but also a need for freedom from repressive authority. Chomsky is also a convinced rationalist who has strongly supported SOKAL's attack on what he regards as the abuse of science at the hands of certain French intellectuals.

READING: Barsky (1997); D'Agostino (1986)

chora The Greek term for a receptacle or an enclosed space, borrowed by KRISTEVA (1974a) from Plato, and effectively made synonymous with 'womb'.

In the *Timaeus*, Plato makes a distinction between three different forms of reality: the unchanging form that is the object of thought, the copy of that form which is apprehended by the senses, and the receptacle, which is described as the nurse of all becoming and all change. The latter is the *chora*. The *chora* is a space which is both eternal and indestructible, and it provides a position for everything that comes into being. The *chora* is apprehended not by the senses, but by what Plato terms a sort of 'spurious reasoning'.

In Kristeva's theory of the SEMIOTIC, the *chora* is a provisional and mobile articulation of movements and their ephemeral stases. It exists prior to spatiality, temporality and representation, and can be likened only to primitive vocal or kinetic rhythms. In psychoanalystic terms, the *chora* exists at the level where the child's archaic and primitive DRIVES are directed towards the mother. To the extent that it is a space that allows the child to separate itself from the mother, the *chora* is the SUBJECT's point of origin; to the extent that it is a receptacle that threatens the child with a suffocating enclosure, it is also the site of the subject's negation. Whilst all discourse is, ultimately, based upon the rhythmic articulations of the *chora*, discourse rejects it and struggles against it. The *chora* therefore reappears whenever discourse breaks down or when the literature of the poetic AVANT-GARDE reveals the tensions that exist within it.

cinéma vérité The French, which literally means 'truth-cinema', is now standard in English and describes a style of documentary film which deliberately allows the subjects to present themselves in their own words and avoids psychological analysis so as to allow viewers to form their own opinions. There is usually no intervention on the part of the film-maker, and no interviewer is present. The technique was made possible thanks to the development of light-weight 16 mm (and subsequently 8 mm) cameras with synchronous sound recording facilities. The expression was originally coined by the French sociologist Edgar Morin in an article entitled '*Pour un nouveau cinéma vérité*' (Towards a new truth cinema) in the weekly *France-Observateur* in January 1960. Morin then collaborated with the director Jean Rouch on the film *Chronique d'un été* (Chronicle of a summer, 1961). Their intention was to extract a truth, and they actually intervene in the film, which is a classic sociological investigation into Parisian life structured around a set of interviews. The film script, a press dossier and supplementary comments from the directors were subsequently published as Rouch and Morin (1962). The first classic example of what is usually understood by cinéma vérité is the Drew Associates *Primary* (1966), which chronicles the Wisconsin Primary. The most sustained example is perhaps D. A. Pennebaker's *Don't Look Back* (1966), a low-key black and white account of Bob Dylan's first (1965) UK tour.

It is also claimed that cinéma vérité is a literal translation of the Russian *Kino-pravda*, the term used by Dziga Vertov (1896–1954) to describe the twenty-three newsreels he produced between 1922 and 1925, and subsequent documentaries such as *One Sixth of the World* (1926) which documents the wealth and variety of the Soviet Union with film shot by ten teams of cameramen. The cameramen were known as *kinoki* or 'cinema-eyes', and one of Vertov's many manifestos (cited Armes 1974) begins: 'I am an eye. I am a mechanical eye. I, a machine, am showing you a world.'

READING: Leyda (1960); Musser (1996)

civil society The expression 'civil society' is commonly used to describe a sphere of human activity that is outside or apart from the structures of states and governments and in which free individuals form voluntary associations and establish pluralistic relations based upon affinities and common interests rather than coercion. The distinction between state and civil society is an old one but can take very different and even contradictory forms.

For seventeenth- and eighteenth-century theorists of the social contract from Hobbes (1651) to Rousseau (1762), the institution of civil society is in fact equivalent to the founding of the political state. It is the institution of civil society and the state that puts an end to the war of every man against every man which, in Hobbes's famous phrase, characterizes the condition of nature. Locke's second *Treatise on Government* (1690a) provides the classic description. Men are born free, equal and independent, but they forgo that natural freedom and put on 'the bonds of civil society' when they agree to enter a Commonwealth 'for their comfortable, safe and peaceable living one amongst the other'. When individuals agree to enter civil society, they adopt the principle of majority rule; they are at liberty to leave civil society but doing so means living in a state of nature that leaves them free but without any defence against others.

A rather different concept of civil society emerges from the Hegelian and Marxist traditions, which see it as something antithetical to the state. For Hegel (1821), civil society is a market society in which individuals enter into 'infinitely complex criss-cross movements of reciprocal production and exchange' and in which property rights are established by legally binding contracts. The danger is that the divergent interests at work in civil society will transform it into an indiscriminate multitude of individuals with conflicting and irreconcilable interests. The role of the state, defined as the embodiment of the principle of rationality, is to reconcile those divergent interests. It exists over and above civil society, and its agents or civil servants are defined as a universal class serving the interests of society as a whole. The ultimate destiny of civil society is its absorption into the rational state. In his early writings Marx (1843a, 1843b, 1843–4) both draws on and criticizes the Hegelian account of civil society; Lucio Colletti's introduction to the writings of the 'Early Marx' (Marx 1975) gives a good account of this stage in his thought. For Marx, who famously inverts the Hegelian schema, the constitution of the political state and the dissolution of civil society into independent individuals are one and the same thing, but the state 'overcomes' civil society, guarantees the property rights that promote and reproduce class divisions, and at the same time creates a class – the proletariat – that exists outside civil society and therefore has no claims to make on it. Its vocation is to abolish all classes and to become a universal class. Marx predicts the seizure of power by the proletariat and the withering away of the state that will result from the establishment of a society based upon free associations between individuals.

The most important Marxist contribution to the theory of civil society is that made by GRAMSCI, who argues (1971) that 'state' should be understood as meaning not only the apparatus of government, but also the 'private' sphere or the complex of structures in which the battle is waged for HEGEMONY or for cultural and ideological domination. The superstructures of civil society are, he writes, akin to the trench-systems of the First World War and are the site for a war of positions between the conflicting classes brought into being by capitalism. For Gramsci, the state's ultimate destiny is its destruction: political society will finally be absorbed back into civil society when the working class and its allies achieve hegemony and establish a free and self-governing society.

The term 'civil society' can also be used as a synonym for liberal democracy, seen as the best of all possible worlds. Gellner, for instance (1994), defines civil society as being based on a plurality of institutions which place checks and balances on the state, but which are also protected by the state. According to this view, which appears to be becoming increasingly common as the perceived threat of Islamic fundamentalism grows (Huntington 1996), the closed societies of the Islamic world are likely to replace communism as the main threat to the civil society enjoyed by the 'Atlantic world'.

Cixous, Hélène (1937–) French writer. Although she is best known outside France for her theory of *ÉCRITURE FÉMININE*, Cixous is also well known inside France as a playwright; her first major success as a dramatist was with a play based on Freud's 'Dora' case (Freud 1905c; Cixous 1976), and she has subsequently reached very wide audiences with plays about Cambodia (1985) and Indian independence (1987). She is also a prolific novelist: her first novel, *Inside*, was published in 1969 and her twenty-seventh in 1997. Closely associated with the *PSYCHANALYSE ET POLITIQUE* group, whose 'des femmes' publishing house has published all her work since 1975, Cixous was the founder, in 1974, of France's first and only postgraduate course in *Études féminines*, the closest thing to a women's studies course to exist in a country where neither women's studies nor gender studies have taken root. The weekly seminar run by Cixous on the poetics of sexual difference has for many years attracted a faithful international audience (selections from the papers read to it have been published in English as Sellers 1988). The best introduction to her work is *Rootprints* (Cixous and Calle-Gruber 1994), which includes lengthy interviews, a moving account of her childhood and an excellent bibliography.

Although she is often viewed, together with IRIGARAY and KRISTEVA, as an eminent representative of a distinctive French FEMINISM (Marks and Courtivron 1979), Cixous avoids the word 'feminist' and habitually uses 'feminine' on the grounds that feminism connotes a reformist demand for the equality of the sexes and places insufficient emphasis on sexual difference, and even speaks scornfully of 'feminist misogyny'. She also prefers not to speak of herself as French, claiming to have adopted an imaginary literary identity in 1955, the year in which she came to Paris after spending her childhood and adolescence in Algeria.

As used by Cixous, the word 'feminine' is not an adjective that can be applied solely to women; like Kristeva's SEMIOTIC it is, rather, a position that can be taken by individuals of both GENDERS and which reflects what PSYCHOANALYSIS sees as the basic bisexuality of human beings. Indeed, much of Cixous's writing can be read as an attempt to deconstruct, in terms reminiscent of the work of her friend DERRIDA, the binary opposition that constructs 'male' and 'female' as opposites. Her first critical work, based on her doctoral thesis, was on James Joyce (1969b); she regards his work as an instance of *écriture féminine*, and makes a distinction between the destructive 'war-man' and the creative 'mother-man'. The title of her novel *Neutre* (1972) plays in typical fashion on the Latin etymology (*ne* + *uter*: 'not' + 'either') in a further attempt to subvert a binary sexuality. Although the best known of her own explorations of *écriture féminine* is an exuberant demolition of the norms of 'male' syntax (1975), her novels are often deeply introspective and difficult explorations of subjectivity in which the narrating 'I' is never stable but constantly changes generation and gender. Although, like IRIGARAY, she is very suspicious of FREUD's theory of castration and contends that the psychoanalytic account of femininity is voyeuristic in that it makes women the object of a male GAZE, Cixous's work is heavily influenced by psychoanalysis. Many of her works explore the issues of loss and death, and writing is seen as a means of preserving life whilst at the same time recording the knowledge and experience of loss. In her early fiction, the loss involved tends to be that of the father (Cixous's own father died when she was eleven); her subsequent work concentrates, rather, on the separation from the mother that is both a loss and a precondition for becoming an individual SUBJECT.

READING: Sellers (1994, 1996); Shiach (1991); Wilcox et al. (1990)

code/message Central terms in the immensely influential model of linguistic communication elaborated by JAKOBSON (1956, 1960), partly on the basis of his studies of APHASIA. According to this model, six elements are involved in any act of linguistic communication: sender (or addressor), receiver (or addressee), message, code, contact and context. These elements correspond to the six linguistic functions involved and the nature of the message will vary as one or another function is stressed. The functions are described as expressive (stress on sender), vocative (stress on receiver), metalingual (stress on code), PHATIC (stress on the process of communication itself), referential (stress on context) and poetic (stress on the message itself). Any communication consists of a message passing from sender to receiver, and requires some form of contact between the two. The message must be formulated in terms of a code (encoded) and must refer to a context understood by both sender and receiver. The contact enables both to make sense of (or decode) the message. The phatic function ensures that communication is taking place. The message itself is made up of elements that have been combined from constituent parts (PHONEMES, words, sentences) of the code, or the repository of all the possible constituent parts available to both sender and receiver.

Selection corresponds to the paradigmatic pole of language (PARADIGM), and combination to the syntagmatic pole (SYNTAGM). A code is not a form of crypto-gram, but a system of constraints and possibilities that exists within any given language. In terms of this model, the 'message' is not synonymous with a 'content' defined solely by the quantity of information that is conveyed. In quantitative terms, the phatic function alone makes up a major part of any message, as in a telephone conversation which begins with 'Hello' and which is punctuated with 'Can you hear me?' or, when mobile phones are involved, 'Sorry, you're breaking up.' The two major descriptions of the model made by Jakobson differ slightly, as do the corresponding diagrams, but the underlying concepts remain the same. The final and most familiar diagrammatic representation of the communication model is

Referential

Poetic

Emotive   Conative

Phatic

Metalingual

collective unconscious One of the most significant differences between the PSYCHOANALYSIS of FREUD and the analytical psychology of JUNG is that the latter makes a distinction between the personal and the collective UNCONSCIOUS (1936). In Jungian terminology, the personal unconscious is a characteristic of the indi-vidual, and consists of repressed instinctual impulses, forgotten memories and subliminal perceptions. The personal unconscious is a shadowy realm existing on the fringes of consciousness, and its contents can be recovered by using techniques such as word association (1911). The collective unconscious exists at a much deeper level of the psyche, and its contents, which are derived from the whole of human history and recurrent life-situations, are common to the whole of humankind. They take the form of primordial images or ARCHETYPES. The existence of the collective unconscious is revealed by images or symbols – the theme of rebirth, the image of the wise old man – that appear in contexts as various as dreams, daydreams, works of the imagination and especially primitive religions and mythologies.

Collège de Sociologie Intellectual circle founded in Paris by Georges BATAILLE, Michel Leiris (1901–90) and Roger Caillois (1913–78), active in 1937–9. This was not a college in the educational sense but a *collegium* in the Latin sense of an association or partnership, and its founders were not professional sociologists. Bataille was a librarian, Leiris an anthropologist and poet, and Caillois a classicist with a sound knowledge of anthropology. The three founders were the main speakers at the fortnightly meetings; the most important contribution from an outsider was Pierre Klossowski's lecture on 'Sade and Revolution', later reworked as a chapter of his major study of Sade (1947, revised edn 1967). Characterized by simultaneously aesthetic and political ambitions, the Collège was an instance of the tradition of the AVANT-GARDE groups which are such a conspicuous feature of French intellectual life. SURREALISM is the prototypical example, but DEBORD and the Situationist Internationale and TEL QUEL are also part of the same tradition.

The Collège's main concern was with individual and collective manifestations of the sacred, as defined by Bataille's subversive readings of Mauss (1923) and Durkheim (1912) on the sociology of religion. It also played an important part in promoting a serious philosophical reading of Nietzsche (Schrift 1995). In his lecture on 'La Fête' (Festival), Caillois summed up the group's convictions by arguing that the revaluation of all values sought by Nietzsche would come about through a revival of the orgiastic and often murderous rites used by non-Western societies to bring about personal rebirth and social renewal. The publications of the Collège, the surviving texts of the lectures given and other related documents have been published by Denis Hollier (1979).

READING: Stoekl (1989)

collocation Term introduced into linguistics by J. R. Firth (1951) to describe the habitual co-occurrence of individual words such as 'spick and span' and 'neat and tidy'. One of the difficulties facing anyone learning a foreign language is the mastery of collocation and the avoidance of the false collocations ('chips and fish', 'butter and bread') that so often reduce native speakers to helpless laughter.

committed literature The normal translation of the French *littérature engagée*. The classic statement of the theory of committed literature is SARTRE's *What Is Literature?* (1947c). Sartre's essays on theatre (collected 1973) should also be consulted.

The Sartrean notion of commitment does not imply a commitment to some IDEOLOGY or to a predefined political line or policy, and committed literature is therefore not to be confused with SOCIALIST REALISM. It reflects, rather, the writer's necessary and inevitable involvement in the SITUATION that both defines and restricts his or her fundamental freedom. For Sartre, to write is to name and unveil the world, and to project an image of being in the world. The writer thus assumes a specific position within the context of a sociopolitical reality and is said to be committed to the extent of being lucidly conscious of involvement in the world. He or she is also under a moral imperative to disclose to the reader a reality in which the individual can be seen to be a historically situated being who is committed to a quest for authentic freedom. The idea of commitment establishes a full circuit of communication between reader and writer. Here, at least, the common criticism that Sartre lapses into SOLIPSISM does not really hold true.

In Sartre's 1947 essay it is made clear that the medium of committed literature is prose fiction and drama. For the poet, words are things; for the committed writer, they are instrumental signs which name the world with a view to changing it. In the preface to SENGHOR's important anthology of NEGRITUDE poetry (1948), in contrast, Sartre does concede that poetry can be a form of committed literature. Whereas European poets attempt to dehumanize and naturalize language, the poets of negritude play a political role and engage in a quest for freedom to the extent that they violently break down conventional associations and turn the French language against French colonialism.

In terms of Sartre's own works, the clearest example of committed literature is the *Roads to Freedom* trilogy (1945a, 1945b, 1949a) in which the characters, and the reader, are forced to come to terms with the necessity of choice and with the realization that the failure to choose is itself a choice made in BAD FAITH. Sartre's novels and plays also dramatize the situation of the intellectual who is sympathetic to the ideals of socialism but who cannot accept the dogma of a Communist party without betraying the ideal of freedom and authenticity. Stylistically, the trilogy of novels, with its fragmented narrative and shifting points of view, is heavily influenced by John Dos Passos's *USA* trilogy (1930–36); the philosophical corollary is that no one consciousness is in possession of the truth, and that all consciousnesses exist alongside and in conflict with others.

The Sartrean concept of a committed literature had considerable influence on the Italian novelists associated with the NEOREALISM of the decade following the Second World War.

READING: Goldthorpe (1984)

commodity fetishism An extreme form of ALIENATION induced by the structures of commodity-exchange in capitalist society. The classic description is to be found in the chapter on 'The Fetishism of the Commodity and its Secret' in the first volume of Karl Marx's *Capital* (1867). LUKÁCS subsequently extends Marx's theory into the more general theory of REIFICATION, which is an important theme for the whole of WESTERN MARXISM. Both DEBORD's theory of the 'society of the spectacle' and BAUDRILLARD's early writings on 'objects' are heavily influenced by the theory of commodity fetishism.

According to Marx's analysis, commodity fetishism arises from the twofold nature of the commodity itself. A commodity such as a coat has both a use-value and an exchange-value; it can be worn to provide protection against the elements, but it can also be exchanged for another commodity. The exchange itself takes no account of the specific qualities of the coat, or of the quantity of labour (value) that is embodied in its making. Similarly, the wage relationship between capitalist and worker takes no account of their respective social positions or of their social relations. The labour that is exchanged for a wage produces value in the form of a coat, but is treated as though it were an abstract commodity that is equivalent to any other commodity. The social characteristics of human labour thus take on the appearance of objects that appear to exist independently of social relations, whilst the products of labour appear to possess magical properties that bear no relationship to the labour that produces them. The characteristics of labour appear to be the natural properties of objects. A fetish is an object invested with supernatural powers by those who worship it; Marx holds that the commodities that are exchanged in a capitalist economy are invested with similar magical powers and an illusory autonomy. The psychoanalytic theory of FETISHISM also refers to the idea of a belief in the magical properties of an inanimate object and, like Marx's theory, derives from nineteenth-century European attitudes towards African religions.

Commonwealth literature Broadly defined as consisting of literary works written in English in the decolonized nations of the former British Empire.

The Nigerian writer Wole Soyinka describes (1976) how in 1973 he was appointed to a year-long Fellowship at Churchill College, Cambridge. His proposal for a series of lectures on literature and society was rejected, apparently because the Department of English did not believe in the existence of a 'mythical beast' known as African literature. The lectures were finally given in the Department of Social Anthropology. Soyinka was simultaneously Visiting Professor at Sheffield University, and here he found that African literature was taught at both undergraduate and postgraduate levels. His experience is illustrative of the ambiguous nature of Commonwealth literature.

The first conference on Commonwealth literature took place at the University of Leeds in 1964, and the subtitle of the published proceedings (Press 1965) sums up the assumptions that inspired its organizers: 'Unity and Diversity in a Common Culture'. It was assumed that all Commonwealth countries, from Nigeria to the white settler-dominions of Canada and Australia, shared a common history, a common culture and a common language, and that English literature provided a common standard of value. It was hoped that Commonwealth literature would contribute enrichment and new traditions to 'the great body of English literature'. The *Journal of Commonwealth Literature* began publication in September 1965 and its first editorial defined its field of study as 'imaginative writing in English in the various parts of the Commonwealth', adding in the next sentence that 'British authors' were excluded because 'in a literary sense at least, Britain is in a very different position.' It was, however, accepted that all writing that was 'recognizably' in English took its place within the great body of English literature and was to be judged by the criteria of excellence by which works in English were judged.

The new discipline of Commonwealth literature did promote awareness of the writing produced outside the metropolis. Its major institutional base was the very important *African Writers* series published by Heinemann from 1962 onwards; a *Caribbean Writers* series began publication in the 1970s, and there is now also an *Asian Writers* series. The notion of a Commonwealth literature soon began to be challenged in a number of ways. The Kenyan NGUGI WA THIONG'O has argued (1968) that the Heinemann series has indeed promoted the 'Afro-European novel' but has done nothing to revitalize the African tradition itself, and calls for African literature written in African languages to be made central to the CANON taught in Kenya. From the mid-1960s onwards, the rise of THIRD WORLD theories of revolution, the emergence of Black Nationalism in the United States and the appearance in English translation of FANON's incendiary attacks on colonialism all helped to undermine the notion of Commonwealth literature by insisting that, far from creating a common culture, colonization had actively destroyed cultures. In the English-speaking world, Walter Rodney's *How Europe Underdeveloped Africa* (1972) had a particularly powerful impact in that respect.

Although Commonwealth literature is still an object of study, it tends increasingly to give way to the notion of POSTCOLONIAL THEORY, but many of the problems raised in the earlier debates remain unresolved.

READING: Moore-Gilbert (1997)

communicative action The notion of communicative action is an essential feature of HABERMAS's theory of interpersonal communication and SPEECH ACTS (1981, 1987, 1988). Communicative action takes place with the LIFEWORLD, as opposed to the systems of power and money where strategic action holds sway, and allows subjects to arrive at a communality of mutual comprehension that facilitates shared action because they recognize the mutual compatibility of the validity claims they are putting forward. Because they are open to public scrutiny and recognized as being both comprehensible and sincere, these claims to be speaking the truth can be modified through argument and consensual persuasion. In theory, it is therefore possible to arrive at a full or ideal consensus.

Communist Party Historians' Group A small group of historians active in the Communist Party of Great Britain between 1948 and 1956 which began to publish the journal *Past and Present* in 1952. The most prominent members were Maurice Dobbs, Christopher HILL, E. J. HOBSBAWM, E. P. THOMPSON and a very young Raphael SAMUEL. Most left the Communist Party in 1956 in protest at the Soviet invasion of Hungary, and Samuel and Thompson went on to become prominent members of the British NEW LEFT.

Most of the group's collective work, published mainly as mimeographed pamphlets, was focused on the emergence of capitalism in England and on the factors which, from the Civil War onwards, made England the home of the first industrial revolution. The existence of an indigenous British radical tradition from the seventeenth-century Levellers onwards was also an important theme. Although the group was committed to Marxism, its members were anxious to move away from a mechanical interpretation of the BASE/SUPERSTRUCTURE model of historical causality and therefore stressed the historical importance of culture and IDEOLOGY. The group's work is an important stage in the transition from the early labour history of the Hammonds' studies of the village labourer (1911), the town labourer (1917) and the skilled labourer (1919) to the historiography of the HISTORY FROM BELOW movement and to HISTORY WORKSHOP.

READING: Kaye (1984); Samuel (1980)

competence Term introduced by CHOMSKY in *Aspects of the Theory of Syntax* (1965) to describe a native speaker's tacit or innate understanding of his or her own language. Whilst competence does hint at the existence of a universal faculty for language, it is also identified with the grammatical rules that can generate all and only those sentences that can be uttered by speakers of a given natural language. The term refers, that is, to all the possible grammatically correct sentences that the native speaker can utter simply by virtue of the fact of speaking his or her language. At this stage in his work, Chomsky defines the goal of linguistics as the development of theories of competence. Competence is contrasted with performance, or the utterance of specific sentences within a concrete situation. Errors at the level of performance, such as the utterance of ungrammatical sentences, no more invalidate the theory than an arithmetical error invalidates the theory of mathematics, as they can be explained simply as a wrong application of the laws of the language. In its most general sense, the competence/performance distinction is reminiscent of SAUSSURE'S *LANGUE/PAROLE* distinction.

According to Chomsky, competence is both the source of and the explanation for linguistic creativity or the ability, which is observable in very young children, to produce and understand grammatical utterances the speaker has never before encountered. The ability to produce such utterances cannot be explained in terms of a stimulus-and-response pattern of learning, but indicates the existence of an innate competence.

complex The term is used in both Freudian psychoanalysis and Jungian analytic psychology to describe organized sets of ideas and memories that are largely unconscious but have enormous affective power (FREUD, PSYCHOANALYSIS, JUNG, AFFECT). As Laplanche and Pontalis (1967) point out, the term is used by Freud and Breuer in their early work on hysteria (1893–5), but it is Jung's studies in word association (1911) that make it an integral part of the vocabulary of psychoanalysis by showing that specific stimulus-words can reveal the existence of stable and meaningful sets or complexes of associations. Within Freudian psychoanalysis, the term is used very sparingly and is normally restricted to the OEDIPUS COMPLEX and the related 'castration complex'. One of the reasons why it tends to be shunned by Freudians is that it was so widely popularized, or even vulgarized, by Jung and by such expressions as Adler's 'inferiority complex', which describes NEUROSIS as an attempt to escape a *feeling* of inferiority (Adler 1913) rather than as a symptom resulting from a failed *act* of REPRESSION. The noun 'complex' is used very widely in Jungian analytical psychology to describe the nuclei of associated ideas and affects that cluster around an IMAGO or ARCHETYPE. A 'father complex' will typically consist of both conscious and unconscious associations derived not only from an individual's actual experience of his or her real father, but also from the way in which the individual reacts to that experience, from fantasies and from associations with an unconscious father-ARCHETYPE.

compulsion to repeat Also referred to as 'repetition compulsion' and described by PSYCHOANALYSIS as a powerful process originating in the UNCONSCIOUS (Freud 1920a). Typically, an individual suffering from a compulsion to repeat repeatedly places himself or herself in a distressing or painful situation, but cannot recall the prototypical experience that is being compulsively repeated. Obsessional rituals, hysterical symptoms, traumatic dreams and recurrent nightmares are all examples of the ability of repressed materials to override the PLEASURE PRINCIPLE. The compulsion to repeat is often acted out in the TRANSFERENCE, and FREUD (1914d) establishes an important distinction between the compulsive repetition of material that has not been mastered or understood, and the recollection, verbalization and working-through characteristic of the TALKING CURE. For Freud, the compulsion to repeat is related to the DEATH-DRIVE and the desire to return to an inorganic state. It can also represent an attempt on the part of the EGO to control and overcome anxiety, as in the FORT-DA GAME.

LACAN's notion of the 'insistence of the letter' (1957), or of the compulsive repetition of certain signifiers or letters despite the SUBJECT's conscious attempts to repress them, is a development of Freud's 'compulsion to repeat', but it is also influenced by the idea of *automatisme de répétition* ('repetition automatism'), which, in the French psychiatric tradition of Pierre Janet (1859–1947; see Ellenberger 1970), refers to the compulsive repetition or reproduction of an internalized social structure. Lacan's tendency to use *automatisme de répétition* as a translation of Freud's *Wiederholungszwang* is a reminder of how much he owes to the school of psychiatry in which he was first trained.

condensation An essential aspect of the workings of the UNCONSCIOUS and especially of DREAM-WORK, as described by PSYCHOANALYSIS (Freud 1900). A single idea or image in a dream may represent the nodal point at which a number of chains of associations or ideas intersect, and can thus be a condensation of both their multiple unconscious meaning and their quota of AFFECT or emotional charge. The mechanism of condensation explains why the MANIFEST CONTENT of a dream is often so laconic or fragmentary: it is an abridged translation of the LATENT CONTENT. The second basic mechanism of the dream-work is DISPLACEMENT. Both mechanisms can be observed in other unconscious formations, and notably in symptoms of HYSTERIA and NEUROSIS; they are also important features of jokes (Freud 1905b). Following JAKOBSON (1956), LACAN (1957) likens condensation and displacement to the linguistic mechanisms of METAPHOR/METONYMY.

consciousness-raising The discussion of women's experiences in small and supportive women-only groups was one of the principal practices of the early WOMEN'S LIBERATION movement, and provided many women with a point of entry into FEMINISM. Originally developed in the United States in the late 1960s, the practice is sometimes said to have grown out of group psychotherapy, but other accounts (Eisenstein 1984) suggest that the real model was the Chinese practice of 'speaking bitterness' or denouncing in public the sufferings inflicted by the landlords of the prerevolutionary period, as described by Hinton (1966) in his popular description of revolutionary change in a Chinese village.

Consciousness-raising, often abbreviated to CR, is designed to allow women to realize that they are not alone and that their experiences (of, for instance, rape, abortion or male violence) are common to many women and are the product of PATRIARCHY rather than of the situation of individual women. It allows personal experience to be understood in broader terms, and has been described as 'what happened when women translated their personal feelings into political awareness' (Coote and Campbell 1982). A personal account of participation in a small CR group in London in the early 1970s can be found in Micheline Wandor's 'The Small Group' (in Wandor 1972).

constative Term used by AUSTIN (1962a) and in the theory of SPEECH ACTS to describe a form of statement imparting straightforward information about a body of facts or a set of circumstances. Unlike a PERFORMATIVE, a constative must be either true or false.

continental philosophy The expression is widely used in British and American philosophy to refer to such varied tendencies within European thought as EXISTEN-TIALISM, PHENOMENOLOGY, STRUCTURALISM, POSTSTRUCTURALISM, and the work of NIETZSCHE, the FRANKFURT SCHOOL and GRAMSCI. The phrase is not normally used in Europe, where, as Descombes has remarked (1983), the notion of 'continental philosophy' is viewed with as much wariness as the idea of a 'continental breakfast'. The notion of a divorce between Anglo-American and European developments in philosophy stems in part from the perceived isolation of ANALYTIC PHILOSOPHY, which has long been the dominant force within British universities but which was until recently largely ignored in Europe; it was only in the 1980s that French philosophers began to take a serious interest in the analytic tradition (Descombes 1983). The sense of a divorce is heightened by the fact that the vector for the importation into Britain of continental philosophy has not, with some exceptions, been philosophy departments, which tend to view Kant as the last good continental philosopher, but literary departments and centres for CULTURAL STUDIES.

Cambridge University's refusal to award DERRIDA an honorary degree in 1992 was widely viewed as a symptom of a wider problem. It was argued that this demon-strated analytical philosophers were scarcely in a position to evaluate the work of the followers of Derrida, and that this called the whole notion of 'peer review' into question. In 1993 a Society for European Philosophy was therefore established in Britain to counter the marginalization of European philosophical traditions and to affirm their expanding influence and vitality.

contradiction The motor of the DIALECTIC of HISTORICAL MATERIALISM, which holds that 'the history of all hitherto existing society is the history of class struggles' (Marx and Engels, 'The Communist Manifesto', 1847–8). Class struggle itself is an expression of the contradiction between the interests of classes whose positions are defined by the structure of a MODE OF PRODUCTION. In the capitalist mode, the primary contradiction is said to be that between the bourgeoisie which owns the means of production, and the proletariat (broadly defined as the industrial working class) which owns nothing but the labour-power it sells in order to live, but which is the source of all value. At a structural level, a contradiction exists between the forces of production (factories, mills) and the social relations of production. The large-scale industrialization that began to develop within feudal society requires both a labour force (the proletariat) and relations of production (the ability to sell labour-power and to buy commodities) that cannot develop within the framework of the small feudal estate. The contradiction 'bursts asunder' the old society and leads to the emergence of industrial society. ALTHUSSER remarks in his discussion of OVER-DETERMINATION that the contradiction between the bourgeoisie and the proletariat never exists in purely economic terms; it is further determined by historical conditions, as well as by political and ideological practices.

Copernican revolution Copernicus's *De revolutionibus orbium coelestium* (On the revolutions of the heavenly spheres, 1543) demonstrates that the sun is the centre of the solar system and thus destroys the earlier Ptolemaic system, which assumed that the heavenly bodies rotated around the earth. The so-called 'Copernican revolution' has therefore come to be seen as the archetypal example of a scientific revolution or EPISTEMOLOGICAL BREAK (see Kuhn 1957; Koyré 1961), and analogies with it play an important role in attempts to demonstrate or assert the scientific nature of emergent theories.

In the preface to the second edition of his *Critique of Pure Reason* (1787), Kant explains that he proposes to do for philosophy 'just what Copernicus did in attempting to explain the celestial movements'. Kant's Copernican revolution in METAPHYSICS reverses the traditional theory of cognition by demonstrating that knowledge does not conform to a realm of objects; objects conform, rather, to ways of knowing and it follows that we know them as they appear to us, and not as they exist in themselves.

FREUD describes PSYCHOANALYSIS (1916–17) as the last of three Copernican revolutions, or of three major blows to the self-love of man. Copernicus demonstrated that the earth was not the centre of the universe, and Darwin's theory of evolution dethrones man from his privileged place in creation. Psychoanalysis then delivers the most wounding blow of all, as the discovery of the UNCONSCIOUS reveals that the EGO is not master in its own house. According to LACAN (1955), Freud's Copernican revolution calls into question the entire humanist tradition, with its emphasis on the centrality of the conscious SUBJECT and the ego, by DECENTRING the subject and demonstrating that it is governed by forces outside its conscious control.

counterfactual The product of an excursion into imaginary or fictional history; a speculation about alternative outcomes or versions of events. A classic example is provided by Pascal's remarks that had Cleopatra's nose been shorter, 'the whole face of the earth would have been different' (1669). A modern anthology of counterfactuals (Ferguson 1997) includes speculative essays on 'What if there had been no American Revolution?' (J. C. D. Clark), 'What if Germany had invaded Britain in May 1940?' (Andrew Roberts and Niall Ferguson) and 'What if communism had not collapsed?' (Mark Almond). Although counterfactuals can be very entertaining, many professional historians take a dim view of them; E. P. THOMPSON, for instance, memorably describes counterfactual fictions as '*Geschichtenscheissenschlopff* – unhistorical shit' (1978). Others, like HOBSBAWM (1997), take a more charitable view, and accept that all history is full of implicit or explicit counterfactuals or speculations about alternative outcomes, and Ferguson notes that Hobsbawm's *Age of Extremes* (1994) is itself predicated on the unspoken question: 'What if there had been no Soviet Union to defeat Germany in the Second World War and to "rescue" capitalism?'

Outside the field of history, counterfactuals are an important feature of both imaginary literature (indeed, science fiction could scarcely be written without asking 'What if . . .') and the most banal daydreams ('What if I won the National Lottery?').

They are also an essential part of any form of planning or futurology that needs to include possible variables into its calculations. 'What if . . .' is an essential question for the planners and econometricians who construct models of the economy's future performance, and for the military planners who construct alternative scenarios in their war games.

creoleness Cultural-literary theory elaborated by a small group of French-speaking writers from the Caribbean islands of Martinique and Guadeloupe who state: 'Neither Europeans, nor Africans, nor Asians, we proclaim ourselves Creoles' (Bernabé, Chamoiseau and Confiant 1993). This use of the term 'creole' reflects the original sense of the Spanish *criollos*, which was applied to anyone born in the Americas or the Caribbean islands, regardless of colour or ethnicity.

Creoleness, which is strongly influenced by GLISSANT, is largely a reaction against the NEGRITUDE of Aimé CÉSAIRE, which is condemned for replacing the illusion that Caribbean culture is European with the illusion that it is African. Its supporters describe creoleness as an interactional or transactional aggregate of Caribbean, European, African, Asian and Levantine elements, united on the same soil by the yoke of a common history. More generally, creoleness is viewed as a model for a future multiculturalism which will transcend racial IDENTITY POLITICS.

The theory of creoleness has given rise to a lively literature which integrates elements of folklore and oral culture into novels that provide a rich picture of colonialism and postcolonialism in the French West Indies, and which blends creole rhythms and vocabulary with elements of standard French to produce a heady concoction reminiscent of the islands' Franco-Creole cuisine. Perhaps the best example is Patrick Chamoiseau's *Texaco* (1992), the saga of a shanty town (named after an oil-storage depot) that grows like some urban mangrove swamp on the outskirts of the capital of Martinique. *Texaco* won the prestigious Prix Goncourt for 1992.

READING: Walcott (1997)

Critical Inquiry American literary and theoretical journal, published quarterly by the University of Chicago's Department of English since 1974. Although the original subtitle – 'A voice for reasoned inquiry into significant creations of the human spirit' – has now been dropped, it still captures the spirit of a journal which was described by its founding editor Sheldon Sacks as not designed to appeal to literary critics who were not interested in GOMBRICH's *Art and Illusion*, or art historians who were bored by FRYE's *Anatomy of Criticism*. Resolutely pluralistic, interdisciplinary and international in its outlook, *Critical Inquiry* is notable for debates between well-known figures that can continue over several issues.

critical theory The term can be used quite loosely, as in the present dictionary, to refer to a whole range of theories which take a critical view of society and the human sciences or which seek to explain the emergence of their objects of knowledge. Much more specifically, it also refers to the major strand in the work of the FRANKFURT SCHOOL and particularly to the writings of ADORNO and HORKHEIMER. HABERMAS is critical theory's most important contemporary spokesman. Horkheimer's inaugural address (1931) to the Institut für Sozialforschung (Institute for Social Research) broadly defines critical theory as a human activity that takes society as its object, and that attempts to transcend the tensions between individual spontaneity and the work-process relationships on which society is based. In very general terms, the critical theory of the Frankfurt School can be described as a theory that seeks to give social agents a critical purchase on what is normally taken for granted and that promotes the development of a free and self-determining society by dispelling the illusions of IDEOLOGY. Critical theory takes as its starting-point the work of Marx and Freud, and an analogy is often drawn between the Marxist theory of ideology as illusion and the individual delusions analysed by Freud in *The Future of an Illusion* (1927b), where he speaks of the middle-class Viennese girl's delusion that a prince will come and marry her. Critical theory would seek to dispel her delusion by giving her a critical and self-critical awareness of why such a marriage is improbable in the extreme, but also showing her why she clings to that delusion (McCarthy 1993).

In a very useful survey of the work of Habermas and the Frankfurt School, Raymond Geuss (1981) describes critical theory as a theory that provides a guide for human action, is inherently emancipatory, has a cognitive content and, unlike a scientific theory, is self-conscious, self-critical and non-objectifying. Critical theory often takes the form of a CRITIQUE of ideology (*Ideologiekritik*) that seeks to explain why social agents accept or consent to systems of collective representations that do not serve their objective interests but legitimate the existing power structure, and exposes the falsity of non-cognitive beliefs (such as value-judgements) that are presented as cognitive structures. *Ideologiekritik* is not merely a moralistic denunciation of false perceptions but a cognitive undertaking that seeks to analyse how and why they arise in specific situations or contexts. The object of a critical theory such as Marxism is to supply the knowledge of the necessity of transforming the present social order into a classless society. It does not, however, predict the inevitability of that transformation and merely points to what *ought* to be done rather than to what *will* happen.

The distinction between scientific and critical theories is an important one here, and is basic to the whole notion of a DIALECTIC OF ENLIGHTENMENT. A scientific theory is objectifying and instrumental in that it constructs objects of knowledge with a view to manipulating the external world in accordance with what Horkheimer calls 'instrumental reason'. The object itself remains external to the theory; Newton's particle theory of physics is not itself a particle in motion, whereas critical theory is always bound up with, and critical of, the circumstances in which it is elaborated. The danger is that the objective or instrumental reason of scientific theory will be perverted into a subjective reason which defines rationality purely in terms of consumer-needs defined not by actual needs but by the 'false' needs determined by the workings of a consumer society (see Horkheimer 1947, 1967). The nightmare vision of the Frankfurt School, and especially of ADORNO and MARCUSE, is one of an 'administered' modern industrial society which has such ideological control over the deepest desires and feelings of its subjects that they are quite literally unaware of their exploitation, frustration and unhappiness.

The goal of critical theory is to preclude the emergence of such a society by demonstrating that a transition to a freer and more fulfilling society is objectively or theoretically possible, and then by demonstrating that the existing state of society is so unsatisfactory and frustrating that it *ought* to be transformed. Determinism is avoided by adding the important proviso that the transformation can come about only if social agents can accept the theses of critical theory as a form of self-consciousness that can act as a guide to emancipatory action.

READING: Held (1980); Jay (1973)

critique In the first (1781) preface to his *Critique of Pure Reason* (1787), Kant defines the goal of the critique of speculative reason as being to discover the source of that form of cognition and to expose the conditions of its possibility. In the Kantian sense, a critique is therefore an investigation into how a form of knowledge is possible. The word 'critique' is more usually used to mean a sustained criticism of an argument, film or book from a specific viewpoint, with the criticism also functioning as an explanation of what is being criticized. A critique of the racism of a film would not simply say 'This film is racist', but would seek to demonstrate why and in which sense it is racist. Marx uses the term in roughly this sense when he subtitles *Capital* 'A Critique of Political Economy'; his critique seeks both to explore the origins of political economy in order to expose its limitations and to supply a better explanation of the workings of capitalism.

ADORNO (1931) makes an important distinction between a 'transcendent critique' and an 'immanent critique'. Whereas a transcendent critique establishes its own principles and uses them to criticize a theory 'from the outside', an immanent critique uses a theory's internal contradictions to criticize it in its own terms.

Critique French literary journal founded by Georges BATAILLE and published monthly since June 1946. Subtitled 'General Review of French and Foreign Publications', *Critique* has long been an important feature of French cultural life and, although it has always kept alive the connection with Bataille and SURREALISM, has been a major conduit for the introduction of new currents of thought. Throughout the 1950s, its promotion of the 'new criticism' of BARTHES, RICHARD and Jean Starobinski helped to counterbalance *LES TEMPS MODERNES*' emphasis on EXISTENTIALISM and COMMITTED LITERATURE, and under the joint editorship of Jean Piel, Barthes and FOUCAULT it provided a platform for the structuralism of the 1960s. In more recent years, it has done much to promote a new French interest in ANALYTIC PHILOSOPHY.

cultural materialism Raymond WILLIAMS's term for the theory of culture he develops in the course of a long dialogue with MARXISM, and which ascribes a central importance to the role of STRUCTURES OF FEELING (see in particular Williams 1973b, 1977). Williams is critical of the BASE/STRUCTURE model so often used by Marxists to analyse cultural phenomena on the grounds that it makes, for example, literature dependent, secondary and superstructural, or subsumes it into the wider category of IDEOLOGY. Cultural materialism stresses that culture is a constitutive social process which actively creates different ways of life. Similarly, signification or the creation of meanings is viewed as a practical material activity which cannot be consigned to a secondary level or explained in terms of a primary level of economic activity. Consciousness itself is not a reflection of a basic or more material level of existence, but an active mode of social being. Williams is also critical of the technological determinism of theorists such as MCLUHAN who argue that communications media have independent properties that impose themselves automatically ('the medium is the message'). He does not deny that the functioning of the media is determined, but insists that its determination is social and always bound up with sociocultural practices.

cultural studies A flourishing interdisciplinary mode of studying aspects of culture, usually defined as 'popular' culture, and cultural production in the modern period. Originally pioneered mainly by Birmingham University's celebrated Centre for Contemporary Cultural Studies from 1964 onwards and subsequently by the Open University, cultural studies is now an internationally recognized discipline (see Kraniauskas 1998) supported by a host of journals ranging from *Cultural Studies*, *Social Text* and *New Formations* to the more recent *Parallax* (launched in 1995). Ironically, the original Birmingham Centre no longer has a truly independent existence and has been absorbed into Social Sciences. There is no one theory of cultural studies, and the discipline has always been characterized by a high level of eclecticism; whilst the 1970s were dominated by the theme of IDEOLOGY, the 1990s saw a marked shift towards POSTCOLONIAL THEORY. The contemporary state of cultural studies is best revealed by the six-volume series entitled *Culture, Media and Identities* (Gay et al. 1997a; Gay 1997b; Hall 1997a; MacKay 1997; Thompson 1997; Woodward 1997).

The Birmingham Centre was originally a postgraduate research unit founded within the University's English Department by Richard HOGGART in 1964 (Green 1982). Its work was greatly influenced by the 'left-Leavisite' tradition of studying popular culture (LEAVIS), but its members rapidly abandoned the mandarin approach of *Scrutiny* in favour of the more sympathetic stance adopted by Hoggart in his *Uses of Literacy* (1957). Raymond WILLIAMS was perhaps the most powerful single influence; if there is one idea that unites the many strands of cultural studies, it is his slogan 'Culture is ordinary' (see Green 1974). As Stuart HALL, who was the Centre's charismatic director from 1967 to 1979 (surely its most productive phase), put it in the introduction to the first issue of the important *Working Papers in Cultural Studies* (1971), cultural studies was essentially seen by its founders as an attempt to view the whole complex of social change from the point of culture, 'to make intelligible the real movement of culture as it registered in social life, in group and class relations, in politics and institutions, in values and ideas'.

In many senses, cultural studies was originally a product of the British NEW LEFT, and had a lot in common with the political-cultural networks that produced HISTORY WORKSHOP and the project of HISTORY FROM BELOW. Its development reflected the growing importance of a 'cultural politics' that goes beyond institutional politics and finds its base and expression in WOMEN'S LIBERATION and GAY politics. The new discipline flourished on a diet of the WESTERN MARXISM and CONTINENTAL PHILOSOPHY that began to be translated into English in the 1970s;

GRAMSCI's concept of HEGEMONY and ALTHUSSER, in particular, were crucial influences on how cultural studies approached the question of IDEOLOGY (the key text here is *Working Papers in Cultural Studies* 1977). The very broad definition of the discipline, the overlap with sociology, media studies and, latterly, women's studies and the plurality of the theorists invoked (BARTHES, FOUCAULT and so many others), made it possible to look at a whole range of subjects that had not traditionally been deemed worthy of academic attention. SUBCULTURE was an early object of interest, but also one of the first indications of the undoubted strand of populism in a discipline which sometimes takes the view that the popular nature of the subculture of motorcycle gangs (or, perhaps more accurately, their anti-bourgeois character) makes them inherently worthy of study, whilst more purist sociologists would argue that a high degree of romanticism is involved. The jokes that claim that some forms of cultural studies developed to give academics an intellectual justification for watching SOAP OPERAS or listening to their favourite rock music are perhaps not entirely without foundation.

Such half-humorous criticisms should not, however, distract from the real importance and major achievements of cultural studies. The focus on race or ethnicity, and the analysis of how media images of black people – and particularly black youth – were constructed into a menacing threat to the social order helped to set the terms of major political debates in the 1980s (Hall et al. 1979; Gilroy 1987), whilst studies of how working-class youths 'learn to labour' (Willis 1979) added a new dimension to sociology and at the same time returned to the concerns of ORWELL. The input from feminism has resulted in important examinations of how popular girls' weeklies influence the socialization of young women and govern representations of their sexuality (McRobbie 1991). Cultural studies starts out from the proposition that culture is ordinary in that it informs every aspect of day-to-day life; it demonstrates beyond doubt that culture is also very important indeed.

culture industry Term introduced into the CRITICAL THEORY of the FRANKFURT SCHOOL by ADORNO and HORKHEIMER in the 1940s. It refers primarily to the entertainment industry. In the draft notes for their *DIALECTIC OF ENLIGHTENMENT* (1947), Horkheimer and Adorno initially used the term 'mass culture', but that term was subsequently rejected on the grounds that it might seem synonymous with a contemporary form of popular art or a culture that is spontaneously created by the masses. Whilst *Dialectic of Enlightenment* is the *locus classicus* for the discussion of the culture industry, Adorno's later essays should also be consulted (1991). There is also a definite continuity with the essays of Siegfried KRACAUER's Weimar period (1963).

The traditional and ENLIGHTENMENT notion of culture implies a critical attitude towards the status quo, and Adorno and Horkheimer retain that notion by arguing that social freedom is inseparable from enlightened thought. The culture industry, in contrast, produces works of art whose every detail is tailored to the needs of mass consumption, devalues the experience of art and dulls the critical faculties of the consumer. In a mass culture, the individual consumer is said to be king, but his supposed cultural needs have been anticipated and shaped by the requirements of the industrialized constraints of an industry typified by Hollywood cinema, KITSCH, commercial radio, advertising and repetitious songs. Apparently differentiated products (such as A and B movies in the Hollywood system, or magazines sold at different prices) are characterized not by differences at the level of their actual subject-matter, but by the prior identification and classification of the differences between their probable consumers. Something is provided for everyone in order to ensure that no one escapes the dominance of the market. The culture industry thus inverts the schema of Enlightenment thought. For Kant, art was defined as purposefulness without purpose (1790); the principle of the culture industry is defined by Horkheimer and Adorno as 'purposelessness for the purposes declared by the market'.

The theory of the culture industry relies heavily upon a version of Marx's theory of COMMODITY FETISHISM. As in the capitalist economy as a whole, exchange-value is more important than use-value, and evaluation becomes the sole criterion of value. The fetishistic value placed upon conspicuously high production values and effects results in a situation where the consumer who buys a ticket for a Toscanini concert is worshipping the money he has paid for it.

The effect of the culture industry is to promote social and intellectual conformity. The inability to speak in the prescribed fashion, or to reproduce accepted formulae and conventional judgements, becomes a criterion for exclusion. Exclusion is also the fate that awaits serious artists like Schoenberg or Webern, who are prepared to express the anxiety or terror about MODERNITY that others evade by regressing to the norm. Their work will be either homogenized and adapted to the needs of the culture industry, or marginalized and denied an audience.

It is often claimed that Adorno in particular is a defender of an elitist MODERNISM who is scornful of a culture that is freely available to all. He himself consistently argues that both high and mass culture are marked by the stigmata of capitalism, and that they are the torn halves of an integral freedom that cannot be reconciled in modern society. The lost ideal is represented by works like Mozart's *The Magic Flute*, in which the utopia of the Enlightenment did coincide with the pleasures of light operatic song.

D

Dada One of the classic AVANT-GARDE movements of the early twentieth century, and a forebear of SURREALISM, Dada is also closely related to FUTURISM. Dada began its tumultuous existence at the Cabaret Voltaire in Zurich in 1916, when Hugo Ball, the Romanian poet Tristan Tzara (1896–1963) and others organized riotous performances designed to turn the ideals of art and culture into a programme for a variety show. The performances featured improvised music played on home-made 'noise-machines' and simultaneous poetry-readings in which a number of voices merged in a polyphonic cacophony. Abstract phonetic poems with no meaning were also read. Art objects were produced from ready-made or 'found' materials, and collages were made by assembling randomly sampled newspaper cuttings. The short-lived journal *Dada* (eight issues published between 1917 and 1921) rapidly abandoned conventional design in favour of a revolutionary and disconcerting use of typesetting, with words running diagonally across the page. Although it began in Zurich, Dada established outposts in Berlin, New York and Paris in the aftermath of the First World War. Participants included Arp, Marcel Duchamp, Picasso and André BRETON.

Dada was an attempt to destroy meaning itself, and a nihilistic reaction to the futility and destruction of the First World War. The word 'Dada', supposedly discovered after a dictionary was opened at random, was chosen as the group's name precisely because it was meaningless, or had so many meanings as to challenge the concept of 'meaning'. On 1 April 1916 Ball wrote (cited in *Dada and Surrealism Reviewed*, 1978): 'Dada is "yes, yes" in Romanian, "rocking horse" in French. For Germans, it is a sign of foolish naïveté, joy in procreation and preoccupation with the baby carriage.'

READING: Richter (1964); Tzara (1924)

Daly, Mary (1928–) American lesbian theologian, radical feminist and self-styled Positively Revolting Hag. In 1971, Daly was the first woman to be invited to preach at Harvard University's Memorial Church. At the end of her sermon on 'The Women's Movement: An Exodus Community', all the women in the congregation walked out together at the preacher's invitation (King 1989). Daly's refusal to accept questions from men, and then to allow male students to attend her classes, has brought her into regular conflict with the authorities at the Jesuit Boston College, where she began to teach in 1966, when it was a men-only institution. In May 1999, a judge ruled that the College had the right to dismiss her for defying its policy of keeping all courses open to both sexes.

Daly's earliest books (1968) are critical of the Church's failure to exorcize the devil of sexual prejudice and equate the women's revolution with a spiritual revolution (1973), but in *Gyn/Ecology* (1978) and its 'sister-volume' *Pure Lust* (1984), which are her most celebrated books, she moves far away from orthodox Christianity and into what is sometimes called post-Christianity. Christianity is now harshly criticized for having dismembered the older Goddess religion and for transforming the Tree of Life into the Cross, which is a fitting symbol for the necrophiliac world created by a Sado-Society or a phallocracy intent upon destroying both women and their sister Earth. The image of Mary, once an aspect of the Goddess, has been tamed and reduced to the abject figure of a woman who passively adores her own son.

Gyn/Ecology is divided into three sections or 'passages' representing a journey or a long process of CONSCIOUSNESS-RAISING. In the first, the woman traveller struggles to escape the myths of PATRIARCHY and then confronts the global dimension of Goddess-murder, or the extinction of the divine spark of female be-ing. The manifestations of Goddess-murder range from the Indian custom of suttee to European witch-hunts, the genital mutilation of women, and modern gynaecology and psychotherapy. In the third and final passage, the woman reader-traveller escapes into a realm of female creativity known as the Otherworld or Ecstasy.

Although no real political programme is drawn up by Daly, she is even more critical than most radical feminists of what she sees as reformism or tokenism. She is dismissive of most of the achievements of the WOMEN'S MOVEMENT on the grounds that equal rights amendments and equality of opportunity are tokens that integrate women into PATRIARCHY and sap true female energy, offering only a 'plasticized' feminism.

Daly is an extraordinary writer and her writings effectively create a new form of English – especially the *Intergalactic Wickedary* 'conjured in cahoots with Jane Capati' (1988). 'Negative' stereotypes such as 'hag', 'crone' and 'nag' are reclaimed and put to positive use in the creation of such neologisms as 'nagostics', whilst puns and multiple meanings are piled up to create double-edged words that can cut through 'the maze of man-made mystifications'. Daly exploits the multiple senses of 'race' to describe a nation or people of women rushing forward to meet in a strong current of water that restores them to an elemental communion. The manner in which she fragments and distorts the conventions of syntax, grammar and vocabulary to spin or weave her web of language makes her writing in this and other works the closest English equivalent to the French *ÉCRITURE FÉMININE*.

READING: Grimshaw (1988); Hodges (1996)

Damas, Léon-Gontran (1912–78) French poet and politician. Although less well known than either CÉSAIRE or SENGHOR, Damas is one of the classic poets of Francophone NEGRITUDE. He was born in French Guyana and *Pigments*, his first collection of verse (first published at the author's expense in 1937, reissued 1972), explores the cultural effects of French colonialism with wit and humour. One of the poems suggests that, rather than invading Germany, France's black colonial troops should 'invade' Senegal. The collection was banned on the grounds that it posed a threat to France's internal security.

Damas represented Guyana in the French Assemblée Nationale from 1946 to 1951, and subsequently worked as a cultural ambassador for both France and UNESCO.

READING: Racine (1983)

Dasein German compound noun formed from *da* ('there') and *sein* ('to be'), and literally meaning 'being there'. *Dasein* is a key term in the early philosophy of HEIDEGGER, and the decision of the translators of his *Being and Time* (1927) not to translate it has made it the standard term in English-language discussions of his work. The German convention of capitalizing the initial letter of a noun is followed in English, and the word is not usually italicized.

Heidegger's use of the term plays on the two senses of the German *Dasein*. In philosophy, the word is traditionally used to refer to any mode of being or existence; Kant, for instance, speaks readily of *Dasein Gottes* ('the existence of God'). In colloquial German, the term simply means 'to be present' or 'to be there', and is usually applied to people rather than inanimate objects. For Heidegger, *Dasein*, like *Existenz*, refers to the mode of being (*das Seiende*) of human beings, as opposed to the being (*Vorhandensein*, 'being at hand' or 'presence at hand') of things or entities. Albert Hofstadter's 'Translator's Appendix' to the translation of Heidegger's *Basic Problems of Phenomenology* (1975a) provides a helpful introduction to the complexities of Heidegger's use of *da* and *Dasein*.

dead white European males A derogatory way of referring to the figures traditionally associated with the literary, artistic and philosophical CANON. Often abbreviated to the acronym DWEM, the term derives from the criticisms of the canon made by those who, especially in American universities, seek to broaden the curriculum to include more feminist and non-European writers and thinkers and who challenge the relevance of studying only the accepted great figures of the past. Allan BLOOM and other critics of such proposals regard references to DWEMs as an extreme appeal to the idea of the POLITICALLY CORRECT that will lead to the cultural impoverishment of the universities. For his part, Harold BLOOM views the attempt to broaden the curriculum and canon in this way as an expression of the SCHOOL OF RESENTMENT.

Although references to DWEMs may seem to represent an excess of political correctness, the underlying issue is far from trivial. In a course of lectures on the history of American civilization given at Harvard in 1990, the novelist Toni Morrison, who was awarded the 1993 Nobel Prize for Literature, notes that the conventional 'knowledge' of literary critics and historians still holds that traditional or canonical American literature is still free of and unshaped by the four-hundred-year-old presence within the United States of Africans and then African-Americans (Morrison 1992).

death-drive (For the issues involved in the translation of Freud's *Instinkt* and *Trieb*, see the entry on DRIVE.) In his later writings FREUD (1920a) posits the existence of two broad categories of life instincts (*Lebenstriebe*, also known as 'Eros') and death instincts (*Todestriebe*, sometimes known as 'Thanatos', though Freud himself does not use that term). The former are concerned with the creation of cohesion and unity; the latter with the undoing of connections and the destruction of unity. The fusion of the two results in sadism. All drives are regressive in that they seek to return to an earlier state or to recover a lost OBJECT, and the death drive expresses the tendency, which is said to be found in all living beings, to annul all tension by reverting to an inorganic state. Initially inward-directed, the death drives first manifest their existence in the human tendency to self-destruction; as they subsequently turn to the outside world, they take the form of aggressive or destructive behaviour.

The theory of the death drive is, by Freud's own admission, speculative, and is grounded in descriptions of the COMPULSION TO REPEAT. The fact that Freud describes the death drive as 'silent' makes it difficult to supply concrete clinical evidence for its existence and the notion remains controversial, even though Freud continues to uphold it in his very last writings. Many post-Freudian analysts dismiss the notion of a death drive as mere speculation on Freud's part, but KLEIN (1933) adopts it whole-heartedly, regarding the tyranny of the early SUPEREGO as it crushes the young child's EGO as the first clinical manifestation of its power. LACAN tends to reject Freud's thesis of a duality of life and death drives, arguing (1978) that the death drive is an aspect or component of all drives. The death drive strives, in Lacan's view, to go beyond the PLEASURE PRINCIPLE and to attain the painful joys of *JOUISSANCE*.

death of man FOUCAULT's *Les Mots et les choses* (translated as *The Order of Things*, 1966) ends with the famous image of a face drawn in the sand that is about to be erased by the waves, and the comment that man is an invention of recent date and perhaps one that is nearing its end. The idea of the death of man makes an obvious allusion to the death of God, as proclaimed by Nietzsche in *Thus Spoke Zarathustra* (1892). According to Foucault, the classic image of 'man', or of a creature defined by the laws of philology, economics and biology, is a product of the EPISTEME of the modern age. It has always been dependent upon the notion of an anthropological human essence, and that notion is no longer tenable given the recent developments in the human sciences that deny the individual SUBJECT a constitutive or self-constitutive role and demonstrate that the subject is an effect of certain DISCURSIVE FORMATIONS rather than an anthropological point of origin.

death of the author The title of BARTHES' short article 'La Mort de l'auteur' (1968b) captures an important aspect of the aesthetic sensibility associated with STRUCTURALISM.

Barthes argues that the traditional notion of the author is a product of the rationalist and empiricist thought that ascribes a central importance to the individual human being. In literary studies, the author is traditionally invoked as the origin and explanation of the text, or as its final signified. The idea of the author is said by Barthes to be tyrannical in that it encloses the text within a single meaning and denies the importance of what KRISTEVA terms its INTERTEXTUALITY. Texts are not, that is, produced by authors, but by intertextuality and other texts. The death of the author signals the liberation of the reader, who no longer has to accept unquestioningly that a novel has a single meaning enshrined in the biography of its author.

The centrality of the author is challenged by the classic texts of MODERNISM. The poetry of Stéphane Mallarmé (1842–98) reaches the point at which language can be said to be 'speaking itself' through an impersonal WRITING, and it ceases to be either a psychological expression of the poet's subjectivity or a representation of something external to its own workings. Despite the supposed acuity of his psychological analyses, Proust has, according to Barthes, written the epic of modern writing. The narrator of *À la recherche du temps perdu* is, that is, a product of the text rather than its point of origin or its signified.

Similar issues are raised by FOUCAULT in his paper 'What is an Author?' (1969b), but he goes on to explore the notion of a historically variable author-function defined by a variety of DISCOURSES and institutions (and not least the law of copyright which determines the ownership of a text). The emergence of the author-function signals an individualization of writing that occurred quite recently; ancient EPICS do not have authors in the modern sense of the word. According to Foucault, the death of the author, which he links to the broader theme of the DEATH OF MAN, produces a feeling of indifference that is one of the ethical features of modern writing. This 'ethical indifference' emphasizes that writing is not something that can be completed and therefore appropriated, but an endless practice. Foucault illustrates his theme by citing Beckett: ' "What does it matter who is speaking," someone said, "What does it matter who is speaking?".'

Debord, Guy-Ernest (1931–94) French political activist, film-maker and, together with VANEIGEM, the principal theorist of SITUATIONISM.

Debord is best known for his *Society of the Spectacle* (1967) which, he remarked with some pride in 1993, remained in print almost continuously for twenty-five years, having been reprinted every eighteen months (it is still in print). The book, which anticipates many aspects of the work of BAUDRILLARD, describes in 221 numbered paragraphs the profound ALIENATION in which the circulation of images has become more important than the accumulation of material commodities. Life is no longer something to be lived, but a spectacle to be watched from a distance. The spectacle is not merely a set of images, but a social relationship between people that is mediated by images; it does not realize philosophy, but philosophizes reality. In the society of the spectacle, the concrete life of all is debased to being a speculative universe. Even violent revolt is liable to be incorporated into the constant and constantly changing spectacle. Debord's work is as deeply pessimistic as that of MARCUSE, but is relieved by the glacial elegance of his aphoristic style. He wrote relatively little, and in 1989 wryly – and quite accurately – described himself as one who had written much less than most people who write, but who had drunk much more than most people who drink.

READING: Plant (1992); Sadler (1998)

decentring Widely used to describe the COPERNICAN REVOLUTION that displaces the apparent source or focus of subjectivity and meaning away from the traditional SUBJECT. Different theories have combined to give decentring a complex sense in most forms of STRUCTURALISM and POSTSTRUCTURALISM, ranging from FOUCAULT'S DEATH OF MAN to LACAN's insistence that the seeming unity of the EGO is an illusion. It might be argued that they have a common source in section 17 of *Beyond Good and Evil* (1886), in which Nietzsche contends in arguing against Kant that it is false to say that the subject 'I' is the condition of the predicate 'think', and that 'it' (*das Es*; the ID) thinks unbidden by the 'I'.

In his *Introductory Lectures on Psychoanalysis*, Freud (1916–17) writes that 'the naïve self-love of men' has suffered major blows at the hands of the Copernican revolution and then the Darwinian revolution that demonstrated that man was descended from the animals and did not have a privileged place in creation. A third blow is struck by the psychoanalytic discovery of the UNCONSCIOUS, which reveals that the EGO is 'not even master in its own house' and that human beings are governed, not by their conscious thoughts, but by unconscious forces and DRIVES. The idea of a loss of the conscious self-control exercised by a rational SUBJECT is implicit in all theories of decentring. Structuralists note, for example, that meaning is an effect of differential SIGNS and not of a subjectivity that decides the meanings of words, whilst HEIDEGGER famously observes (1951) that whilst man acts as though he were 'the shaper and master of language', it is in fact language that is the master of man in that it determines his very existence.

Lacan follows Freud when he remarks (1978) that the core of our being does not coincide with the ego, and that the ego is an IMAGINARY structure in which the subject is alienated because it identifies with the illusory self-image of the MIRROR-STAGE. For Lacan (1949), psychoanalysis inaugurates a revolution against any philosophy based on the Cartesian *cogito* that states 'I think, therefore I am.' As he argues elsewhere (1957), the existence of the unconscious means that 'I think where I am not, therefore I am where I do not think.'

ALTHUSSER then incorporates this version of decentring into his Lacanian-influenced theory of IDEOLOGY by contending (1969b) that the ideological subject is decentred to that extent that it is created by a structure that has no centre except the imaginary recognition of the ego, or the ideological formation in which it 'recognizes' itself. More generally, Althusser also argues (1962a) that the social totality itself is decentred; the existence and effects of OVER-DETERMINATION at the economic, political and ideological levels mean that it has no essence and no single centre.

deconstruction A form of textual analysis associated mainly with the French philosopher Jacques DERRIDA, the American critic Paul DE MAN and his fellow 'Yale deconstructionists' Harold BLOOM, Geoffrey Hartman (1970, 1979) and J. Hillis Miller. One of the principal strands in POSTSTRUCTURALISM, deconstruction has had an immense influence on literary studies – though this is more marked in the English-speaking world than in France – philosophy and historiography. Thanks in part to Derrida's translator Gayatri Chakravorty SPIVAK, it has had a major impact upon

POSTCOLONIAL THEORY. It has also become an important element in QUEER theory.

Although the practitioners of deconstruction insist that it is not a 'theory' or 'philosophy' that can be applied, or even one that can be defined in a set of propositions, a number of general principles can be identified. All forms of deconstruction rely upon extremely close readings of the texts under analysis and tend to refrain from introducing external evaluative criteria; to that extent, deconstruction can be seen as an extreme form of immanent CRITIQUE. Indeed, De Man (1979) argues, in terms reminiscent of the NEW CRITICISM's veneration of the autonomy of the 'verbal icon', that deconstruction is not something that is added to the text; a literary text deconstructs itself because it simultaneously asserts and denies the authority of its own rhetoric. Little or no distinction is made between GENRES: philosophical texts are to be analysed in the same terms as literary texts, and one of the stated goals of deconstruction is to undermine philosophy's prestige by showing that it too is a rhetorical construct (in similar fashion, WHITE demonstrates that history is a rhetorical construct).

In strictly philosophical terms, deconstruction's ancestry can be traced to NIETZSCHE and his contention that there are no facts, only interpretations (1901), and to HEIDEGGER's critique of the priority that is traditionally given to the present tense in attempts to discuss the nature of being. One of Derrida's constant concerns is with the 'metaphysics of presence', which he regards as central to the history of Western philosophy, or the thesis that the SUBJECT can be self-understanding and can express itself fully in speech. In his earliest work (1967a, 1967b, 1967c), he makes a far-reaching critique of what he calls LOGOCENTRISM or phonocentrism, which assumes that speech exists prior to WRITING and which is typified by the biblical 'In the beginning was the Word.' By claiming that speech is the primal and full form of expression, logocentrism inevitably ignores or conceals the fact that, if writing is a SUPPLEMENT to speech (a theme that can be easily traced from Plato to SAUSSURE), something must be absent in the speech that has to be supplemented. Speech, that is, does not have a point of origin, but arises from an 'originary lack'. Derrida follows Saussure in describing language as a series of supplements and substitutions, but argues that the theory of the SIGN (a self-sufficient union of signifier and signified) is itself an instance of logocentrism. In his critique of the sign, Derrida introduces the crucial notion of *DIFFÉRANCE* (meaning both 'difference' and 'deferral') to demonstrate that language and meaning have no point of origin and no end: the 'meaning' is always the product of the difference between signs, and it is always 'deferred' by a temporal structural that never comes to an end. There is, moreover, no final or correct reading of a text; any reading generates a supplementary reading. The effect of this emphasis on a never-ending process of *différance* is to unsettle the binary oppositions that are so important to STRUCTURALISM (the most elementary being that between differential PHONEMES such as /f/ and /p/) by demonstrating both that one element (male as opposed to female; white as opposed to black) is always dominant and that they are inherently unstable because the implicit hierarchy can, in principle, be inverted. The universalist ambitions of structuralism are also challenged by deconstruction's emphasis on undecidable APORIAS which cannot be described in terms of sets of binary oppositions such as

Plato's *pharmakon* (meaning both 'poison' and 'antidote'). This is the subject of one of Derrida's most brilliant essays (1968).

Derrida's detailed reading of Saussure in *Of Grammatology* (1967a) exemplifies deconstruction's insistence on unravelling the logic and contradictions of the text itself. In one of his most lucid statements of principle, Derrida (1972c) explains that deconstructing a philosophical text means working through its concepts and logic in such a way as to discover and determine what it cannot describe, what its history has excluded in order to constitute it as what it is. De Man makes a similar point when he argues (1979) that, if they are to be coherent and self-consistent, literary texts must of necessity be blind to the METAPHORS and other figures of RHETORIC that constitute them as texts. Deconstruction's rigorous examination of those figures reveals the weakness of the links that hold them together.

Although deconstruction has become an extraordinarily, and somewhat bewilderingly, sophisticated exercise in reading, Derrida's early review (1963; see also the later discussion in Derrida 1991) of FOUCAULT's first major book, *Folie et déraison: Histoire de la folie à l'âge classique* (1961; translated into English as *Madness and Civilization: A History of Insanity in the Age of Reason*), illustrates many of its principles and some of the difficulties inherent in it. Foucault claims to be both writing the archaeology of the silence surrounding madness and the gesture that divorced reason from unreason by literally confining the mad in the asylums of seventeenth-century France. Derrida contends that Foucault has confused a singular event with the category of reason as such, and has misconstrued the meaning of the 'great confinement' of the insane; reason constitutes itself by expelling madness from the definition of subjectivity. The exclusion of madness is therefore not an event, but a precondition for the definition of reason. The categories of 'reason' and 'madness' are not mutually exclusive: a concept of madness is part of the constitutive definition of reason. Foucault's book inadvertently or blindly reproduces the structures that exclude madness. To attempt to write the archaeology of a silence is to breach that silence, to repeat the violence perpetrated against the insane; Foucault's book is itself a gesture of confinement, a Cartesian gesture for the twentieth century. It is 'Cartesian' in that classical reason's definition of madness derives from the certainty of not being mad. That certainty is founded upon the *cogito*, and the whole thrust of deconstruction is to undermine such certainties.

VATTIMO, who is by no means unsympathetic to deconstruction, remarks (1994) that it often resembles a form of virtuoso performance art, and a common criticism is that the authority of the virtuoso is the one thing that is unchallenged. Lentricchia, for instance, has commented (1980) unfavourably on the apparently unassailable authority and certainty displayed by De Man. In his belated reply to Derrida's criticisms of his *Histoire de la folie*, Foucault (1972) makes the more damning criticism that deconstruction gives the master a limitless sovereignty, and simply teaches students to repeat and reproduce his words.

READING: Culler (1983a); Hobson (1998); Norris (1982)

deictic Term commonly used in linguistics as a synonym for what JAKOBSON terms a SHIFTER. The term derives from the Greek *deiktos*, an adjective derived in turn from the verb *deiknunai* ('to show'), and is used in logic to describe a form of reasoning that provides direct or demonstrable proof of a thesis.

Deleuze, Gilles (1925–95) French philosopher. Deleuze's many works cover an extraordinary range of topics and take him well beyond the normal academic definitions of philosophy. Typically, his *Logic of Sense* (1969) explores the issues of meaning and non-meaning by establishing and reading a corpus of texts ranging from the Stoics and Plato to Lewis Carroll. He has also written on topics as diverse as Sacher-Masoch (1967), the cinema (1983, 1985) and the art of Francis Bacon (1981). The interviews collected as *Negotiations* (1990) and the dialogues with Claire Parnet (1977) provide points of entry into an extremely complex body of work, whilst a late collection of critical and clinical essays (1993) is a fine introduction to Deleuze's multiple concerns and interests.

Deleuze's early work comprises a series of monographs on authors from a conventional philosophical CANON, including studies of David Hume (with Cresson, 1952), Nietzsche (1962), Kant (1963) and Bergson (1966), as well as a fine study of Proust (1964) which illustrates his life-long interest in literature. The study of Nietzsche is widely regarded as playing a key role in making Nietzsche such an important point of reference in contemporary French philosophy (Schrift 1995). Deleuze's essay on Bergson foreshadows many of his own later themes, and it has often been argued (by, for instance, Watson 1998) that Deleuze's philosophy can be seen as a new Bergsonism. In his *Matter and Memory* (1896), Bergson departs from the Cartesian tradition by insisting that there is no separation of mind and body and that matter and movement of energy are all that exists. In his later work, Deleuze argues in distinctly similar terms that the body and brain form a material continuum which is in direct contact with the external world, and his concept of DESIRE has much in common with Bergson's *élan vital* or 'life force'.

In the late 1960s Deleuze entered into a remarkable long-term partnership with the radical psychoanalyst Félix GUATTARI which lasted until the latter died in 1992. The first product of their partnership, which coincided with a period of intense political activism and a close friendship with Michel FOUCAULT (celebrated in Deleuze 1976; for the context, see Macey 1993), was the monumental *Anti-Oedipus* (1972). Like its sequel, *A Thousand Plateaus* (1980), it is a sprawling and often exasperating book, but it is at times also a very funny one. It makes a full-scale assault on Freudian, and by implication Lacanian, psychoanalysis (FREUD, LACAN), and largely inaugurates the philosophy of desire that was so important in the 1970s. Psychoanalysis is criticized for its reduction of everything to a fundamental Oedipal triangle (father, mother and child), for promoting a conventional and repressive family structure, and for channelling a polymorphous desire into narrowly restrictive channels. Psychoanalysis's inability to recognize that desire takes multiple forms is, it is argued, typified by a famous passage in Freud's 'Wolf-Man' case history (1918). In his dream, the Wolf Man sees six or seven white wolves, but Freud interprets them all as representing his father: multiplicity is reduced to unity, and a potential proliferation of meanings is channelled back to the Oedipal triangle. Deleuze and Guattari replace both Freud's theatrical vision of the unconscious, or *'der andere*

Schauplatz' (1900), and Lacan's linguistic vision of an unconscious structured like a language, with that of a factory powered by impersonal DESIRING MACHINES. Elsewhere (1976), they liken the proliferating tangles of desire to the underground root system of a rhizome such as couch-grass. Unlike a plant with a single tap root, rhizomes spread in all directions, creating a chaotic network in which every point can be connected to every other point. The multiform workings of desire are, that is, as deep-rooted and as multidimensional as the roots of couch-grass, which, as all gardeners know, is almost impossible to eradicate.

Deleuze and Guattari's last collaborative work, *What Is Philosophy?* (1991), is very different in tone from their iconoclastic books of the 1970s. It is a quiet, almost mournful, attempt to answer the question 'What is philosophy?', and they answer it by stating that philosophy is a discipline that creates concepts, and not a form of contemplation, reflection or communication. The history of philosophy is that of the creation of 'signed concepts' such as Descartes' *cogito* or Leibniz's monad. Science, on the other hand, produces propositions and functions, and the arts, to which roughly one third of the text is devoted, are combinations of words, pigments or sounds that capture and encode sensory perceptions. Philosophers are 'friends of concepts' (and this definition must also be seen as a comment on the long friendship between a philosopher and a psychoanalyst). Whilst this late text appears to represent a rejection of the iconoclasm of *Anti-Oedipus* and its sequels, it can also be read (MacKenzie 1997) as proof that there is a profound continuity in Deleuze's work. There is a constant emphasis, that is, on creativity in all domains and a refusal to reduce philosophy to contemplation. The early monographs were attempts to preserve the Classical tradition, as well as to use it in new ways and to go beyond it. And as Smith points out in his valuable introduction to the English translation of *Critique et clinique* (1993), Deleuze's study of Sade and Sacher-Masoch (1967) was basically a study of how doctors use concepts and a conceptual symptomatology to 'isolate' the illnesses they identify and name. Deleuze was always a friend to concepts, and the consensus that emerged from the many affectionate tributes that appeared in the French press after he committed suicide in November 1995 was that philosophy had lost one of its best friends.

READING: Bogue (1989); Foucault (1977b); Patton (1996)

De Man, Paul (1919–83) Belgian-born American literary theorist and exponent of DECONSTRUCTION. Given his formidable reputation as a teacher (mainly at Yale University) and critic, it is surprising to recall that De Man published only two collections of essays in his lifetime (1971, 1979). Three posthumous collections (1986, 1989, 1996) now make it possible to trace the evolution of his thought from the early debts to SARTRE and the NEW CRITICISM to a most austere and demanding form of deconstruction. De Man's style is notoriously difficult, his use of terminology (and etymology) idiosyncratic, and his sense of authority and self-certainty awesome.

In the preface to *Allegories of Reading* (1979), which is his best known book, De Man remarks that he began to read Rousseau in preparation for a study of Romanticism but found himself 'unable to progress beyond local difficulties of interpretation'. The historical study therefore became an examination of the problematics of reading, or a rhetoric of reading. *Allegories* contains detailed textual studies of Rilke, Proust, Nietzsche and Rousseau; the study of Rousseau is also an encounter with DERRIDA's reading of the same author (1967a). Although De Man undertakes what he calls rhetorical readings of his chosen texts, he departs from the canonical definition (CANON) of RHETORIC in that he denies that it has a persuasive function; for De Man, rhetoric is the study of TROPES and FIGURES. A distinction is then made between literal (grammatical or referential) meaning (REFERENT) and figural meaning. Following Rousseau and the German Romantics, on whom he often wrote (1984), De Man takes the view that all language is inherently figural and that the figural is in conflict with the grammatical. It is the figural dimension of language, and the chains of SUPPLEMENTS it introduces, that makes it an autonomous structure that resists paraphrase and interpretation, and introduces the ever-present element of ambiguity or undecidability. The search for a literal meaning obscures the figural nature of the text, and makes both the reader and the text blind to it. Teasing out the relationship between the two dimensions is the primary task of deconstruction, which never seeks to establish a final meaning, but rather to demonstrate that there is and can be no final meaning. Meaning is no more than an allegory of reading.

De Man also insists that deconstruction is not a method that is applied *to* texts; it merely explores and unfolds ambiguities that are already present in the text. The final line of W. B. Yeats's poem 'Among School Children' is used to illustrate the argument. The line 'How can we know the dancer from the dance?' can be read literally as meaning that creator and creation, or SIGN and REFERENT, fuse imperceptibly into one. A more figural reading reads the question as a rhetorical plea to be told the difference between the dancer and the dance. It is not possible to make a decision that validates one reading as opposed to the other; they are dependent upon one another. In his *Resistance to Theory* (1986), similar deconstructive tactics are used to tease out all the ambiguities of the title of Keats's *Fall of Hyperion*: does it mean 'Hyperion's fall' or defeat by a newer power, or does it mean that 'Hyperion is falling', or is it an intertextual reference to the earlier *Hyperion* which implies that the failure of the first text is a condition for the success of the second?

Blindness and insight, and the inseparability of the two, are the themes of De Man's first major collection (1971) and form its title. Critics and readers are insightful in that they do identify meanings in texts, but in order to do so, they remain blind to their figural meanings and thus succumb to an 'aesthetic IDEOLOGY' (1996). In the programmatic essay 'Criticism and Crisis' (in De Man 1971), De Man remarks that fiction is not myth because it names itself as fiction. Nor is it a demystification, as it has already demystified itself as fiction. Critics who claim to be demystifying fiction, or the poetic text, are in fact being mystified by it as they are necessarily blinded both by their own activity and by the literal-referential dimensions that mask the figural. The blindness of critics and readers is reminiscent of the structures of SARTRE'S BAD FAITH, and a reminder that De Man's early work (collected 1989) is influenced by PHENOMENOLOGY.

The publication of De Man's wartime journalism (1988) provoked a scandal comparable with that surrounding the HEIDEGGER affair. Between 1940 and 1942, De Man contributed reviews and articles to German-controlled newspapers published in occupied Belgium. They reveal a strand of anti-Semitism and a sympathy for Nazism which, although relatively mild by the standards of the day, are still deeply disturbing. The suggestion that the deportation of the Jews to some isolated colony would have 'no deplorable consequences' for Europe has become particularly notorious. The question of the relevance of these youthful texts to his later work continues to be the subject of fierce controversy (see the 'responses' to his wartime journalism collected as Hamacher, Hertz and Keenan 1988; short accounts of the controversy are given in Donoghue 1989 and Kermode 1989). According to De Man's defenders, the wartime journalism has been exploited by the literary press as a means of discrediting deconstruction as a whole. It has also been suggested in other quarters that the complexities of deconstruction are in some way intended either to atone for or to conceal a compromising past. The irony is that so many of De Man's defenders, who would normally subscribe to DERRIDA's view that 'there is nothing outside the text', rely so strongly on biographical and even anecdotal evidence and so often stress, like Frederic Jameson (1991), that they (or colleagues) never heard him make anti-Semitic remarks.

READING: Gasché (1998); Lentricchia (1980)

denotation/connotation The terms describe two aspects of the meaning of a word. A word *denotes* a primary or dictionary meaning but also *connotes* a whole set of associated meanings. As Barthes puts it (1970a), connotations are all the meanings that are not in the dictionary.

The distinction between denotation and connotation plays an essential role in Barthes' analyses of what he calls MYTHOLOGIES. A picture on the cover of a magazine may denote a black soldier saluting the French flag, but it also connotes numerous associated meanings about 'France', 'Empire', 'race', 'army' and so on. At this stage in his evolution, Barthes associates connotation with mystification and even IDEOLOGY. In his important essay on SEMIOLOGY (1964a) he extends the analysis of connotation by borrowing from the work of the Danish linguist Louis Hjemslev (1899–1965), who describes language as a bi-planar system which combines a plane of expression consisting of signifiers, with a plane of content made up of signifieds (1943). Meaning is generated by the relationship between the two. Hjemslev argues that the two planes conform in formal systems such as mathematics, in which elements and relations between them always correspond to their semantic interpretations. Natural languages, in which neither plane constitutes a language itself, are described as 'denotative'. If, in contrast, the plane of content is a language, we are dealing with a METALANGUAGE. Where the plane of expression is a language, we are dealing with a 'connotative' language. These distinctions provide the starting-point for Barthes' contention that connotation is a second meaning: its signifiers consist of signs belonging to a first or denotative system. In *Elements of Semiology*, Barthes continues the analysis begun in *Mythologies* by putting the case for a 'linguistics of connotation'. Society constantly uses the 'first system' of human language to produce systems of secondary meanings, and the resultant accumulation of connotated signifiers solidifies into ideology. Barthes therefore calls for a historical anthropology of connotation. The task of the semiologist is to decipher the connotative signifiers that mask denotative signs by obscuring their historical origin and making them seem natural.

In his later work, in particular *S/Z* (1970a), Barthes takes a less harsh view of connotation, describing it as the starting-point for the codes that make up polysemic texts whose multiple meanings are to be celebrated rather than denounced. The change of tone marks the shift from the 'dream of scientificity' (1971b) that characterizes the early Barthes to the hedonism of the later work.

dérive French noun literally meaning 'drift', used by DEBORD and the other theorists of SITUATIONISM to mean 'locomotion without a goal'. The idea of *dérive* owes much to SURREALISM and its search for the encounter with the marvellous, and is related to BENJAMIN's image of the *FLÂNEUR*. It differs from both in that the object of exploring the city on foot is to investigate its 'psychogeography', and to discover those places that are conducive to specific emotions or which resonate with the DESIRE that can be harnessed to subvert what Debord calls the 'society of the spectacle'. The theory of psychogeography, which was never entirely serious, inspired the Situationists to make exquisite maps of cities like Paris by cutting up existing maps and reassembling the fragments to show a sequence of highly charged or symbolic psychogeographic sites (see the maps reproduced in Sadler 1998). Although these maps are extremely beautiful, it is impossible to use them to navigate one's way about Paris, as the important sites are separated from one another with white spaces, and there are no directions to indicate how they can be crossed. The very strange walks through London recorded in Iain Sinclair's *Lights out for the Territory* (1997) are motivated by a similar theory of *dérive* and psychogeography.

LYOTARD uses the term *dérive* to describe his own 'drift' away from Marx and Freud and towards a philosophy of DESIRE (1973a).

READING: Plant (1992)

Derrida, Jacques (1930–) French philosopher and principal theorist of DECON-STRUCTION. Derrida's first published work was a translation of and introduction to Husserl's *Origin of Geometry* (1962) and his thesis (written in 1953–4 and finally published in 1990) was devoted to the problem of genesis in that author's work. The simultaneous publication in 1967 of the three works that lay the foundations of deconstruction then pushed him to the forefront of the philosophical stage. The paper read to the famous Johns Hopkins conference of 1966 on 'The Languages of Criticism and the Sciences of Man' (1966a, in Macksey and Donato 1972) had already established him as a major figure in what has since come to be known as POSTSTRUC-TURALISM and marked the start of an American career that has been consolidated by numerous visiting professorships. With the possible exception of Paul RICOEUR, no other French philosopher has gained such prestige in both France and the United States. Derrida's French and Anglo-American reputations are, however, curiously different; the 'literary' Derrida associated with DE MAN and 'Yale deconstruction' is an almost totally American creation. In France, Derrida tends to be seen more as a philosopher working in the traditions of NIETZSCHE and HEIDEGGER.

Derrida's work is notoriously difficult, not least because he has written so much;

in early 1999, he had more than fifty titles in print. The secondary literature on him is also vast. Infuriating to some and playful to others, Derrida's style, with its complex network of puns, wordplay, neologisms (described by Derrida as 'neo-nymy') and allusions, is dense and demanding, whilst the philosophical erudition he deploys is formidable to the point of intimidation. None of Derrida's texts could be described as providing an easy introduction to his work, but the essays collected as *Margins of Philosophy* (1972b) provide some convenient starting-points, as do the selected interviews published as *Points* (1995). The collaborative *Jacques Derrida* (Bennington and Derrida 1991) surveys the whole of Derrida's work to date (with, it has to be said, a degree of self-satisfaction and self-indulgence), and also provides some rare biographical information.

With the three publications of 1967, which deal with topics as diverse as Rousseau's theory of the origins of language (1967a), Husserl (1967c), and the wide range of texts reviewed in the essays that make up *Writing and Difference* (1967b), Derrida launches his sustained attack on the LOGOCENTRISM and the neglect of WRITING that are characteristic of Western thought from the Greeks to STRUCTURALISM. Derrida habitually refers to this entire tradition as 'METAPHYSICS' or 'Western metaphysics'; the term remains ill-defined but is broadly synonymous with 'philosophy'. A critic has noted (Pavel 1989) that there is a surprising similarity between Derrida's use of 'metaphysics' and the VIENNA CIRCLE's dismissive use of the word as a synonym for 'pseudo-philosophical problems'. Derrida obviously does not subject pseudo-problems to empirical verification, but deconstructs metaphysics from within, dem-onstrating that theories of the SIGN, which assume that signifier and signified, or speaker and speech, are, or can be, transparent or 'self-present' in fact depend on the concealed or repressed logic of *DIFFÉRANCE* and SUPPLEMENTS which means that meaning has no one point of origin. The neologism *différance* conveys the sense of both difference and deferral: signs are meaningful because they are different, but the final meaning is always deferred by the endless chain of signifiers. Meaning is always in motion or in transit, and the workings of the postal system eventually (1980) become a METAPHOR for the endless series of relays that supports all language and meaning.

Derrida rarely makes methodological statements, partly because his terminology is in a permanent state of flux (see 1972a, where *différance* is supplanted by 'dissemin-ation'), but mainly because, like De Man, he does not regard deconstruction as a method to be applied to texts, but rather as a style of reading or criticism which works by teasing out the internal logics of the text. Derrida's characteristic mode of approaching texts is a combination of very close reading, quotation and interpret-ation. His books are not, that is, so many stages in the methodical application of a preexisting theory, but so many encounters with texts, and the mode of reading develops and changes in the course of those readings. As the internal logic, contra-dictions and unseen confusions of the text are unravelled, the stability of meaning is undermined as it is shown to depend upon such oppositions as 'inside' and 'outside', which can easily be demonstrated to be no more than a spatial metaphor. Given that 'inside/outside' is no more than a metaphor, deconstruction itself cannot be said to be 'outside' the logocentric tradition it is undermining; that work can be done only from within. The very notion of GENRE is subverted to such a degree as to blur all distinctions between philosophy, literature and criticism. Derrida has often been accused of reducing philosophy to nothing more than a sophisticated literary criticism; the whole thrust of his deconstruction is to argue that such criticisms rest upon the unthought assumption that philosophy is a higher form of DISCOURSE, whereas it in fact, like any literary text, consists of metaphors and figures and remains, as De Man would put it, blind to its own workings. The deconstruction of binary oppositions such as inside/outside, or male/female, has had an immense influence on the many forms of POSTMODERNISM and QUEER theory.

Derrida's deconstructions involve detailed readings of a wide variety of authors from Plato (1968) to FREUD (1966b), Nietzsche (1978b), Heidegger (1987), MARX (1994) and the fascinating French poet Francis Ponge (1978a; a selection of Ponge's work was published in translation in 1998). Whilst Derrida's brilliance as a reader cannot be questioned, doubts must arise as to the selection of the texts he reads. The choice of texts to be deconstructed seems almost arbitrary, especially in *Glas* (1974) where Hegel is discussed together with the French writer Jean Genet, and where both text and commentary are printed in parallel columns. Like De Man's authoritative interpretations, Derrida's choice of texts appears to be governed by little more than a personal authority that is, by the very nature of deconstruction, very difficult to challenge.

READING: Culler (1983a); Hobson (1998); Johnson (1993)

desire The concept of desire, thanks largely to LACAN, has become a vital category in contemporary thought, but in introducing it into PSYCHOANALYSIS Lacan draws on an old philosophical tradition as well as on the theories of FREUD. More specifically, the Lacanian concept of desire is inseparable from the reading of Hegel undertaken by KOJÈVE and from the postwar writings of French Hegelians such as Jean Hyppolite; in that sense, *désir* serves as a translation of Hegel's *Begierde* (longing, desire, appetite), and that term is very rarely used by Freud. In psychoanalytic terms, *désir* is, however, the normal French translation of Freud's *Wunsch*, which is rendered as 'wish' by James Strachey in the Standard Edition of Freud's works, whilst the *Wunscherfüllung* ('wish-fulfilment') that defines the function of dreaming (Freud 1900) becomes *réalisation du désir*. All Lacan's translators have opted to translate the word as 'desire', and whilst that choice is faithful to French usage, something of Freud's original sense begins to disappear, particularly as 'desire' tends to replace 'LIBIDO' in Lacan's texts from the 1950s onward. Paradoxically, the emphasis placed by Lacan on a very broad concept of desire tends to desexualize Freud's libido theory.

Desire begins to come to the fore in Lacan's seminar of 1954–5 on the ego (1978), and is discussed in very clear terms in section XVIII where the Freudian world is described as 'a world of desire as such', but it is in 1958 that the theory really crystallizes with the distinction between need, demand and desire (1958b). Lacan now speaks of demand as the verbalized expression of a fundamental need (such as the child's biological need for nutrition if it is to survive) and of desire as a longing that persists once needs have been satisfied. Ultimately, desire is not caused by the wish to possess an object: it is caused by 'a lack of being' that signals the split or division at the heart of the SUBJECT. Ultimately, the inherent dissatisfaction of desire is caused by the evanescent quality of what Lacan will call '*OBJET (PETIT) A*'. It is obviously possible to relate this triple structure to Freud's description of how the libido is gradually separated out from the biological DRIVES whose aims are self-preservation and nutrition, and acquires a sexual OBJECT of its own (Freud 1905a), but Lacan introduces a rather different note by adding that desire is an appeal to receive from the OTHER the complement to what it lacks. When he goes on to formulate the classic thesis that 'man's desire is the desire of the Other', it is clear that he is integrating into psychoanalysis Kojève's description of the dialectic of desire in which the slave seeks the recognition of the master and which generates the struggle for pure prestige. Lacan thus returns not so much to Freud as to the French Hegelianism of the 1940s, when Jean Hyppolite wrote (1947) that 'human desire is always a desire for the desire of an other'.

In making desire so central to psychoanalysis and defining it in terms of a founding lack or absence, Lacan effects a circuitous return to one of the oldest themes in Western philosophy. In Plato's *Symposium* Socrates forces Agathon to concede that love or desire exists only in relation to some object that it lacks. Spinoza defines desire (*cupiditas*) as 'nothing else than the very essence or nature of man' (1677), whilst Descartes describes it as 'an agitation of the soul' which disposes it to possess things it sees as agreeable but does not possess (1649).

Like Lacan, classical theories of desire define desire in negative terms, or in terms of something that is lacked by the desiring subject. That perspective is inverted by DELEUZE and GUATTARI and the other so-called 'philosophers of desire' such as LYOTARD. In this theory of desire, desire creates its objects and, rather than signifying a relationship determined by lack, opens up new possibilities. Guattari puts it very simply (1975a): an individual falls in love with someone or something in an apparently closed universe, and his or her desire opens up new and infinite possibilities. For Deleuze and Guattari, desire is not the product of an encounter with an object, however ephemeral, but a universal force or flow that exists prior to the establishment of the subject-object distinction and prior to representation (Guattari 1975a). Always resistant to representation and socialization, desire is a marginal and marginalizing force associated with outsiders; Guattari remarks (1975a) that in twenty-five years of psychiatric practice he never once encountered a heterosexual married couple who functioned in accordance with the perverse and polymorphous flows of desire. Yet even the proponents of such a radical theory of desire have to admit that they have their classical forebears; in the first chapter of their *Anti-Oedipus*, Deleuze and Guattari acknowledge (1972) that it was Kant who brought about the revolution in the philosophy of desire in the Introduction to the *Critique of Judgement* (1790) when he defined desire as 'a faculty which by means of its representations is the cause of the actuality of the objects of those representations'.

desiring machines Concept introduced by DELEUZE and GUATTARI in the course of their polemical assault on PSYCHOANALYSIS in *Anti-Oedipus* (1972). In *The*

Interpretation of Dreams (1900) and elsewhere, FREUD describes the UNCONSCIOUS as another scene or stage (*ein anderer Schauplatz*); Deleuze and Guattari replace the theatrical metaphor with that of impersonal machines at work in a factory. Guattari (1975b) explains that the introduction of the idea of the machine is intended to indicate that desire begins production at a stage at which there is as yet no question of a structure, of SUBJECT-positions or coordinates of reference. *Anti-Oedipus* opens with a description of one such machine. An organ-machine is connected to a source-machine which emits a flow; the breast is a machine that produces milk, and the mouth is a machine connected to it. A number of literary allusions are employed to describe the functioning of desiring machines; thus Deleuze and Guattari cite a line from ARTAUD's essay on Van Gogh (1947): 'Under the skin, the body is an overheated factory.' They also relate their desiring machines to the writing machine in Kafka's 'In the Penal Settlement' (1919), and to the machine constructed by the narrator of Beckett's *Molloy* (1950). The latter consists of sixteen 'sucking stones' kept in two coat-pockets and two trouser-pockets, and passed from one to the next via the mouth that sucks them in turn. The most surprising allusion is perhaps that to the love-making machine in JARRY's novel *The Supermale* (1902), which illustrates the proposition that the act of love is of no importance since it can be performed indefinitely.

dialectic   In Greek philosophy, a form of reasoning which uses the pattern of questions and answers exemplified by Plato's dialogues. Whereas RHETORIC is a way of establishing a plausibly convincing argument, dialectic is a method for arriving at the truth. In medieval philosophy, 'dialectic' was equated with the logic which, together with grammar and rhetoric, made up the trivium or lower part of a university course.

Although Kant uses the term 'dialectic' to describe pure reason's necessary but temporary reliance on self-contradictory ideas and the syllogisms in which there are no empirical premisses as it proceeds to greater certainty (1787), it is really with Hegel and MARXISM that the dialectic becomes an important notion in modern thought. For Hegel, both the development of subjectivity and self-knowledge (1807), and the development of world history (1837) are governed by a dialectic between conflicting and contradictory expressions of mind or spirit. Any stage of development is characterized by a tension between conflicting forces – most famously between the interest of master and slave – which will be resolved as a new synthesis is achieved. That synthesis will in its turn generate new internal contradictions, and then a further resolution. The process will cease only with the end of history (see KOJÈVE and FUKUYAMA) or, in the case of the mind, the emergence of the serene and complete self-knowledge of Absolute Spirit, which abolishes all CONTRADICTIONS (Hegel 1807).

Within the Marxist philosophy of DIALECTICAL MATERIALISM, the idea of the dialectic refers to the CONTRADICTION between classes, the forces and relations of production, and modes of production. As Marx and Engels put it in *The Communist Manifesto* (1847–8), the means of production and exchange on which the bourgeoisie built its power were actually created in a feudal society. The social relations of property-ownership became incompatible with the productive forces of industry and the factory-system: 'They became so many fetters. They had to be burst asunder; they were burst asunder.'

dialectic of Enlightenment For eighteenth-century philosophers such as Kant, the ENLIGHTENMENT was a linear process that would finally free human beings from the superstitions and tyranny of their self-incurred immaturity, and would reveal the existence of a rational humanity capable of infinite perfectibility (1784). One of the most significant critiques of this utopian rationalism is HORKHEIMER and ADORNO's contention that the Enlightenment is a DIALECTIC of contradictory tendencies (1947). Reason does free human beings from superstition, but it also establishes itself as a court against which there is no appeal, and the only objective that it recognizes as legitimate is the transformation of the world into an object that can be subjugated and manipulated. At this point, reason degenerates into an 'instrumental reason' governed solely by the logic of ends and means. The goal of humanist philosophy was to liberate human beings, but it also creates an unfettered market which does not obey rational principles, and the power of that market destroys reason. Increased power over nature leads to ALIENATION from a natural world which is reduced to being no more than a collection of resources to be exploited. Enlightenment can thus become a form of totalitarianism which establishes a tyranny of instrumental reason. The emblematic figure of the dialectic of enlightenment is, according to Horkheimer and Adorno, the eponymous heroine of the Marquis de Sade's novel *Juliette* (1798), who exploits the power of rational thought as an instrument of sadistic domination and pleasure. Juliette enjoys the exquisite pleasures of destroying the civilization of the Enlightenment with the very weapons it has created.

dialectical materialism The term is not actually used by either Marx or Engels, but came to mean 'Marxist philosophy' in the 1930s when texts such as Stalin's *Dialectical and Historical Materialism* (1938; whether or not this was in fact written by Stalin himself remains a matter for debate) and the *Textbook of Marxist Philosophy* prepared under the auspices of the Leningrad Institute of Philosophy (Shirikov 1937) began to codify the enormous body of work produced by the founders of MARXISM into a set of laws applying to both society and the natural world. The main sources are the later works of Engels, and especially *Anti-Dühring* (1878) and the posthumously published *Dialectics of Nature* (1875–82). Lenin's manuscript notes on Hegel's *Science of Logic*, written in 1914 and first published in 1929 (Lenin 1929), are also an important point of reference.

Dialectical materialism, often abbreviated to 'Diamat', asserts the primacy of matter over consciousness, and of the material conditions of existence over intellectual life. Change is asserted to be the outcome of a DIALECTIC between contradictory elements at every level from social revolution to alterations in the composition of matter itself. The dialectic is governed by three laws. The law of the unity and conflict of opposites states that all phenomena consist of mutually contradictory elements, and that change is the result of their internal contradictions. The law of the transition of quantity into quality describes how quantitative changes always lead to qualitative change. The movement that unites atoms into molecules is an example of the transition from quantitative to qualitative change in the physical sciences; the accumulation of capital that eventually destroys the social structures of feudalism illustrates the same process at the sociohistorical level. The third law is that of the negation of the negation, and it is derived mainly from the first volume of *Capital*. Every stage in the development of the private ownership of the means of production grows out of its predecessor and negates it. It is then negated in its turn by the development of its internal contradictions. Capitalism, that is, came into being by negating or destroying feudalism and will in turn be negated by the rise of socialism and communism.

In his influential essay on the materialist dialectic (1963), Althusser refers to dialectical materialism as 'theory', defined as a theory of scientific practices which transforms the ideological products of social practices into 'knowledges' or scientific truths.

Critics of orthodox Marxism point out that the attempt to transform dialectical materialism into a philosophy of nature, or even of the natural sciences, turns it into a form of POSITIVISM or SCIENTISM (Habermas 1973).

diaspora From the Greek verb *diaspirein*, meaning 'to disperse'. Since the late nineteenth century, the term has been widely applied to the dispersal of the Jews throughout the Gentile nations and to the Jewish community that lives outside the frontiers of the biblical Israel. It is now also used to refer to the experience of populations displaced by slavery, colonialism or forced migrations. The term 'black diaspora' is commonly used to describe the history and experience of black people living outside Africa (Segal 1995).

diegesis A term used by Plato to mean 'narration' and by Aristotle (in *Rhetoric*) to mean 'statement' (of a case). It is widely used in NARRATOLOGY, largely as a result of an important essay by GENETTE (1966). In Book III of *The Republic*, Plato makes a distinction between diegesis and MIMESIS or 'imitation'. In diegesis, the poet 'speaks in his own voice but does not try to make us think that the speaker is any one but himself'. In the diegetic passages of the *Iliad*, Homer speaks in his own voice and reports what others say in indirect speech; in the mimetic passages, he speaks in the voices of others by mimicking or imitating them. In *The Republic*, Plato shows a definite preference for diegesis; the mimetic poets who tell 'lies' are to be banished from the ideal city. Reading *The Republic* in tandem with the rather different theory of representation supplied by the *Cratylus*, Genette demonstrates that, even in the terms of Plato's own arguments, there can be no direct or pure narration or diegesis because any story is necessarily a verbal reproduction or imitation of events, real or imaginary. He can therefore equate mimesis with diegesis.

Genette uses the concept of diegesis to construct a typology of narration and narrators. A narrator who stands outside the story he is telling is said to be 'extradiegetic', and is part of an extradiegetic level of the text; the narrators of Fielding's *Tom Jones* or Balzac's *Père Goriot* are extradiegetic. A narrator who, like Conrad's Marlow, and Genette cites *Heart of Darkness*, is also a diegetic character in a story told by an extradiegetic narrator is described as 'intradiegetic'. The insertion of narratives into narratives produces a whole series of narrators whose function can be defined with reference to the basic diegetic level. Genette's classification of narrators and diegetic levels is a good example of the purely descriptive ambitions of narratology as it constructs its logic or grammar of narrative.

READING: Rimmon-Kenan (1983)

différance A key term in the theory of DECONSTRUCTION elaborated by Jacques DERRIDA from 1967 onwards and the central element in his CRITIQUE of LOGOCEN-TRISM. The word is Derrida's coinage and typifies the importance he attaches to undecidables or APORIA. Like the more usual *différence*, it is derived from the verb *différer*, which can mean both 'to differ' and 'to defer'. At the phonetic level, there is nothing to distinguish the standard *différence* from Derrida's *différance*, and the anomalous spelling is designed to signal the primacy of WRITING over speech. Derrida introduces the term in the course of a discussion of the logos and of Saussurean linguistics (SAUSSURE). The reference to difference takes up Saussure's argument that meaning is no more than the product of the differences between SIGNS, whilst the introduction of *différance* or deferral stresses that there is never any final meaning and that there is never any final or complete coincidence or correspondence between the signifier and the signified. The concept of *differance* is central to Derrida's critique of all theories of language which refer, implicitly or otherwise, to the metaphysical tradition of the logos, as in the invocation of the primal 'word' that opens the Gospel of St John, or which, like LACAN's theory of the PHALLUS and the NAME-OF-THE-FATHER, suggest that there can be a master signifier that halts the perpetual movement of signs.

READING: Derrida (1967b)

Diop, Cheikh Anta (?–1986) Senegalese nuclear physicist and historian.

As BERNAL's later 'Black Athena' hypothesis, Diop's extensive writings on African history and culture seek to demonstrate that the Ancient Egyptians were black and that all known civilizations have their origin in Africa (e.g. 1954, 1974). The Egyptology that developed in Europe after Napoleon's Egyptian expedition and after Champollion's decipherment of the Rosetta Stone is, in Diop's view, motivated by a desire to destroy the memory of black Egypt and to falsify African history by negating the black contribution to world history. Diop draws heavily on Ancient Greek historians, and especially Herodotus, and on comparative studies in lexicography and etymology that reveal similarities between Ancient Egyptian and modern African languages (especially Wolof). In political terms, Diop argues that the future of Africa lies in the creation of a continent-wide federal state.

Diop's work had a major influence on the Francophone poets of NEGRITUDE and the writers associated with *PRÉSENCE AFRICAINE*. It continues to influence the theory of AFROCENTRICITY (Asante 1988). Both Diop and Bernal have been criticized for their tendentious use of very fragmentary evidence (Lefkowitz and Rogers 1996).

dirty realism Term coined in Britain to describe a trend within American fiction, and especially the short story, that emerged in the early 1980s (*Granta* 8, 1983). Dirty realism is characterized by its pared-down style and its concentration on the mundanity of suburban life, petty crime and the bleak lives of characters who drift aimlessly through a depersonalized society. The most important authors associated with the trend are Raymond Carver (1939–88), Jayne Anne Phillips (1952–) and Richard Ford (1944–).

discourse Term traditionally used to designate a formal discussion of a topic, a treatise or homily, or an exposition of a thesis with a pedagogical or methodological purpose. The titles of Descartes' *Discourse on the Method* and Machiavelli's *Discourses on Livy* provide classic examples of that usage. In most forms of linguistics, 'discourse' is used to refer to an extended piece of text, or its verbal equivalent, that forms a unit of analysis. In the contemporary HUMAN SCIENCES, the term is widely, and often very loosely, used to describe any organized body or corpus of statements and utterances governed by rules and conventions of which the user is largely unconscious. The very wide use of the term reflects STRUCTURALISM's promotion of the linguistic model as a model for all communication; it thus becomes possible to speak of the discourse of advertising, or the discourse of Impressionist painting. Here, 'discourse' easily becomes a near-synonym for 'IDEOLOGY'. More generally, the new emphasis on discourse is influenced by the thesis that language, and symbolic systems in general, is not an expression of subjectivity, but rather the agency that produces subjectivity by positioning human beings as SUBJECTS. In all these senses, 'discourse' is heavily influenced by the French *discours*, which has extremely broad connotations and which, unlike its English equivalent, is part of everyday speech: *tenir un discours sur . . .* means little more than 'to talk about . . .'. Modern French thus retains the sense, now archaic or archly literary in English, of 'discourse' as 'conversation' or 'talk'. Something of that usage survives in LACAN's 'discourse of the unconscious'; this refers quite literally to 'what the unconscious is saying'.

  Within the human sciences, the most influential definition of the word 'discourse' is that given by the French linguist BENVENISTE. In the fifth section of *Problems of General Linguistics* (1966), which deals mainly with language and subjectivity, Benveniste defines the term 'discourse' in the broadest of senses as any utterance involving a speaker and a hearer, and an intention, on the part of the speaker, of influencing the hearer. Both a trivial conversation and a formal oration can thus be seen as instances of discourse. Benveniste also describes 'discourse' as a supra-linguistic phenomenon. The sentence is defined as the highest or most complex of the system of SIGNs that is language in that it is the product of the combination of more basic units such as PHONEMES and signs. With the analysis of the sentence, the domain of linguistics proper is abandoned and the analyst enters a universe in which language is an instrument of communication, with discourse as its form of expression.

  Although theories of discourse, from Foucault's DISCURSIVE FORMATIONS to PÊCHEUX's automatic (i.e. computerized) discourse analysis, vary considerably, most are informed by Benveniste's original formulations and stress that discourse is an intersubjective phenomenon, is not a direct product of subjectivity and has a constituent role in the production of the symbolic systems that govern human existence. Most would also agree that the analysis of discourse begins at the point where linguistics reaches the limits of its technical competence.

discursive formation A group of statements in which it is possible to find a pattern of regularity defined in terms of order, correlation, position and function. Discursive formations are the objects studied by FOUCAULT'S ARCHAEOLOGY OF KNOWLEDGE; the formations examined in his *Les Mots et les choses* (1966; translated as *The Order of Things*), where the term is used for the first time, include philology, biology and political economy. A more formalized description of discursive formations will be found in his *Archaeology of Knowledge* (1969a). Following Foucault, SAID analyses ORIENTALISM (1978) as a discursive formation that justified the West's dominance over the East in terms of its supposedly innate superiority.

Discursive formations are the products of DISCOURSES and of their formation of objects, SUBJECT-positions, concepts and strategies. Nineteenth-century psycho-pathology, for example, includes a wide variety of phenomena within the category of mental illness (which it constitutes as an object of knowledge), determines the role of subjects such as doctors and health administrators, produces concepts of the normal and the pathological, and then generates strategies for the treatment of the mentally ill. Relations of force and power are involved at every level of a discursive formation; for Foucault, knowledge is always a form of power.

Discursive formations do not refer to 'things' in the way that the linguistic REFERENT designates an extra-linguistic object; they both constitute their objects and generate knowledge about those objects. Although they constantly interact with non-discursive formations (institutions, political events and economic processes) and are therefore not completely independent of them, discursive formations are relatively autonomous and are not subject to the mechanical determination of the non-discursive. They do not have 'authors' in the traditional sense, and are constituted by ARCHIVES or anonymous collections of texts that have acquired a dominant role in their field.

Foucault's introduction of the concept of discursive formations extends the idea of the DEATH OF THE AUTHOR beyond the purely literary domain and provides a theory of IDEOLOGY that is not dependent upon a crudely mechanical model of BASE/SUPERSTRUCTURE.

displacement Like CONDENSATION, an essential feature of the workings of the unconscious and of DREAM-WORK, as described by PSYCHOANALYSIS (Freud 1900). The mechanism of displacement detaches the AFFECT or emotional charge of an unconscious idea and transfers it to a less intense idea which is linked to the first by a chain of associations. Both condensation and displacement can also be observed in other unconscious formations such as symptoms; they are also an important feature of jokes (Freud 1905b). Following JAKOBSON (1956), LACAN likens condensation and displacement to the linguistic mechanisms of METAPHOR/METONYMY.

dispositif An important term in FOUCAULT'S later work (1976a, 1977), where it tends to replace the earlier EPISTEME. It is difficult to translate and has often been sadly mistranslated, but approximates to 'apparatus' (and not 'deployment', as the translator of Foucault 1976 would have it, having mistaken the military sense – 'deployment of troops' – for the more general meaning). The term refers to a heterogeneous body of DISCOURSES, propositions, laws and scientific statements; the *dispositif* is the network that binds them together and governs the way they interact. A *dispositif* is a formation corresponding, at a given historical moment, to a major strategic function such as the regulation of sexuality. The grid of intelligibility constructed by the historian of sexuality can also be defined as a *dispositif*.

docudrama Abbreviated from 'documentary drama', a term used to describe a type of documentary developed by British television in the 1990s. The first significant example was a series on backstage life at the Royal Opera House, Covent Garden (*The House*, BBC, 1996). This was followed in 1997 by series dealing with Heathrow Airport (*Airport*) and a Liverpool hotel (*Hotel*). In all cases the producers were granted unprecedented access to private events and institutions and claimed to be pioneering a new style of fly-on-the-wall documentary or CINÉMA VÉRITÉ. Docudrama tends to focus on incidents rather than providing analysis, and the need for strong characters has led to the criticism that the individuals portrayed are very media-conscious and cannot resist the temptation to act up for the camera. It has also been claimed that some incidents are staged. Although docudrama continues to be immensely popular with audiences, critics have been quick to point out that the incident-driven narratives, the colourful characters, the characteristic half-hour format and the prime-time slot have a lot in common with the classic SOAP OPERA. By the end of 1997, the disparaging term 'docusoap' had almost become a journalistic cliché.

dream-work Term used in PSYCHOANALYSIS to describe the mechanisms that transform the raw materials of a dream into its MANIFEST CONTENT (Freud 1900). Typically, the raw materials will include physical stimuli, day's residues (elements from the day's waking state that appear either in the dream itself or in the dreamer's FREE ASSOCIATIONS) and dream-thoughts (LATENT CONTENT). The principal mechanisms of the dream-work are CONDENSATION and DISPLACEMENT. Considerations of representability select, transform and censor dream-thoughts so as to allow them to be represented – usually in the form of visual images – whilst secondary revision arranges them into a relatively coherent scenario or narrative. The dream-work does not create anything and merely transforms existing material. It is the dream-work and not the latent content that constitutes the essence of a dream.

drive The Standard Edition of the works of FREUD fails to register the important distinction he makes between *Instinkt* and *Trieb*. Increasingly, and largely as a result of the influence of LACAN, the latter term tends to be translated as 'drive', as this is the closest equivalent to the French *pulsion* (see Lacan 1973, chapters 10–13).

Freud normally uses the word *Instinkt* to refer to a relatively fixed set of behavioural patterns triggered by external stimuli; instincts are characteristic of animals, and are biologically defined (Freud 1905a, 1915a). Unlike an instinct, a drive or *Trieb* (from the verb *treiben*, 'to push') does not have a preordained goal and is characterized by the pressure it exerts within the psyche. The aims or goals of drives are extremely variable and are strongly influenced by the history of the individual. A drive is characterized by its source (a physical stimulus or erogenous zone), its aim (the elimination of the tension caused by stimulation) and its object (anything that enables it to fulfil its aim).

Freud's theory of drives is dualistic, and a distinction is made between ego-drives, which are directed towards self-preservation, and sexual drives. In his later work, Freud (1920a) introduces a further distinction between life-drives and the DEATH-DRIVE.

Du Bois, William Edward Burghardt (1868–1963) Black American writer, economist and cofounder, in 1909, of the National Association of Colored People.

Although he wrote extensively, Du Bois is best known for his *Souls of Black Folk* (1903), which is both an American classic and a founding text for black cultural studies. It is a complex work, combining a sociological account of black life in the rural South, personal reminiscences, polemic and a moving account of the 'sorrow songs' or spirituals, which Du Bois regards as the only truly American music and the most beautiful expression of human experience to have been created in America.

Du Bois' starting-point is the contention that the colour line is the greatest problem of the twentieth century. The colour line is described as a veil that both divides society and makes black people invisible. Du Bois thus anticipates by fifty years the central image of Ralph Ellison's great novel *Invisible Man* (1952). For Du Bois, black experience is characterized by the phenomenon of double consciousness: 'an American, a Negro; two souls, two thoughts, two unreconciled strivings; two warring ideals in one dark body, whose dogged strength alone keeps it from being torn asunder.' A form of double consciousness informs the very organization of the text. Each chapter is prefaced by two epigraphs: a quotation from the CANON of European literature (and in one case from the Bible), and a fragment from one of the sorrow songs discussed in the final chapter. Du Bois' theory of double consciousness has been described (Gilroy 1993a) as capturing both the core dynamic of racial oppression and the fundamental contradiction experienced by the people of the black DIASPORA. Du Bois' stress on education as a force for liberation is to be contrasted with Marcus Garvey's emphasis on economic self-improvement (1969), but is not without overtones of elitism as it suggests that the race will be saved by an 'educated tenth'.

Dworkin, Andrea (1946–) American radical feminist, anti-pornography campaigner (1974) and joint architect of the MACKINNON-DWORKIN MODEL LAW.

Dworkin is often derided as the archetypal man-hating feminist of the tabloid imagination but she has never, as it is sometimes claimed, said that all men are rapists or that all sex is rape. She does, however, paint a very bleak picture of heterosexuality at its most brutal and her denunciations of male violence against women are uncompromisingly harsh and couched in extreme terms. She views pornography both as the cause of male violence and as its true expression. Inherently violent, pornography – 'Dachau brought into the bedroom and celebrated' – reveals the inextricable link between male pleasure and the victimization and humiliation of women (1981). Lesbian pornography is seen as an expression of female self-hatred. Sexual intercourse is equated with violation and made synonymous with an almost literally military form of penetration, invasion and occupation (1987). Dworkin is also harshly critical of the liberal feminism of Naomi Wolf and others (Wolf 1990), arguing that their work serves the interests of middle-class women and ignores the violence inflicted on the less privileged and particularly on women coerced into working in the sex industry.

E

Eagleton, Terry (1943–) British literary critic, novelist and playwright. Although he has written very extensively (see the essays collected in 1986), it would be difficult to speak of an 'Eagletonian' school or of 'Eagletonism'. His studies of the Brontës (1975a) and of criticism and IDEOLOGY (1976) are interesting contributions to MARX-IST CRITICISM, but Eagleton's main role has been that of a popularizer who has increased awareness of BENJAMIN (1981) and others. His general introduction to literary theory (1983) is a very good survey of its field, and has found a wide audience, as has his introduction to the concept of IDEOLOGY (1991). Eagleton follows WIL-LIAMS in defining the role of the critic as the production of a deeper understanding of the symbolic processes through which political power is deployed, reinforced, resisted and, at times, subverted (1984), and his general concern to ground literature in its social conditions without reducing it to them is heavily influenced by CUL-TURAL MATERIALISM. In the 1990s Eagleton's interest turned increasingly to Ireland and he applied GRAMSCI's theory of HEGEMONY in a significant study of the Anglo-Irish 'Ascendancy' of the colonial period (1996).

Eagleton is a prolific reviewer, and at times a waspish one. Commenting on FISH's *Professional Correctness*, he characteristically described its author as 'deploying sophisticated theory for anti-theoretical ends' (1995).

École Freudienne de Paris (Psychoanalytic School of Paris) Psychoanalytic training institute established by Jacques LACAN in 1964 after years of dispute with the International Psychoanalytic Association over the methods he used in his training analyses. The EFP was unilaterally dissolved by Lacan in 1980.

READING: Roudinesco (1986, 1993)

écriture féminine An experimental form of writing developed in France in the 1970s and associated primarily with HÉLÈNE CIXOUS (1975). Discussions in English tend to retain the French term, but it can obviously be translated as 'feminine writing' and has also been rendered as 'writing the body'. There is a close association between *écriture féminine* and the *PSYCHANALYSE ET POLITIQUE* group and its 'édi-tions des femmes' publishing house. Some critics also relate it to the theoretical work of KRISTEVA and IRIGARAY and describe all three writers as representatives of 'new French feminisms' (Marks and Courtivron 1979). Cixous herself normally uses the term *féminine* in preference to *féministe* on the grounds that the latter term refers to a reformist demand for equality and not to the exploration of and insistence on sexual difference that is so characteristic of both her own work and that of *psychanalyse et politique*.

The major founding texts are Cixous' own 'The Laugh of the Medusa' (1975) and the two joint volumes *La Venue à l'écriture* (Coming to writing; written with Gagnon and Leclerc 1975) and *La Jeune née* (The newly-born woman; written with Clément Clément, 1975) published in a short-lived collection edited by Clément and Cixous. The cover of the second volume describes the project of the *Féminin futur* (Feminine future) collection as follows: 'Investigating and analysing the questions that arise in the emerging field of woman's History. Working in the sites where there is a conflictual articulation between femininity and the discourses, practices, or structures that seek to envelop it. Theories, practices, anticipation: opening up a space for the moves demanded by the feminine transformation.' *Écriture féminine* draws upon DECONSTRUCTION and elements of Lacanian theory (LACAN) to weave texts of extreme complexity which might best be described as 'theoretical fictions' in that traditional distinctions between theory and fiction are deliberately ignored or transgressed. Elements of autobiography merge into fantasies and polemic. Cixous celebrates 'the milk of love and the honey of my unconscious' and describes them as a language spoken amongst women themselves when there is no one there to correct them. Gagnon launches a polemical assault on the male science that has made women the object of phallic discourse, but never its subject, whilst Clément and Cixous celebrate the feminine revolt of witches and hysterics. The focus on the body, and especially the maternal body, has often provoked the criticism that *écriture féminine* can trap itself into an ESSENTIALISM that reduces femininity to biology. That criticism is countered by the claim that *écriture féminine* is, like Kristeva's SEMIOTIC, not a feature of an ascribed or fixed GENDER, but rather a SUBJECT-position that can be adopted by women and men alike.

Although *écriture féminine* is often seen as a quintessentially French, or even Parisian, phenomenon, Gagnon is in fact French-Canadian. *Écriture féminine* is an important strand within contemporary French-Canadian writing; the poetry and prose of Nicole Brossard (particularly 1989) are good examples.

READING: Moi (1985); Shiach (1991)

ego The central agency of the psyche, as described in FREUD's second TOPOGRAPHY. The ego is defined in general terms as the seat of perception, and as mediating between the contradictory demands of the ID and the SUPEREGO.

Although the ego is given a new importance in the 1920s, the term is used in some of Freud's earliest writings (1895). It is difficult to trace the evolution of the concept with any great precision as it sometimes refers to the individual personality as a whole, and sometimes to a specialized agency within the psyche (see the relevant article in Laplanche and Pontalis 1967). Freud deliberately plays on the different connotations of the word. Like its French and Spanish equivalents (*le moi; yo*), the German *Ich* is a commonplace pronoun transformed into a noun by the article *das* and has none of the Latinate overtones introduced by the English translation. The German word also has philosophical connotations; Kant applies *das Ich* to the subject of pure apperception and remarks that 'The *I think* must accompany all my representations.' It refers to a form of self-consciousness, and 'unaccompanied by it, no representation can exist *for me*' (1787). The term is also related to the *ego* of Descartes' *cogito* (1637): '*cogito, ergo sum*', or 'I am thinking, therefore I am.'

The ego described by Freud's second topography (1923a) is a product of a differentiation that occurs within the id as the psyche adapts to external reality, and of processes of identification and INTROJECTION. Part of the ego remains unconscious, and it is this that allows it to communicate with the id and to mediate between its instinctual demands and the stern imperatives of the superego. The ego is the seat of rational perception, and it fulfils a number of important functions. It instils a sense of time into mental processes, controls motility, is responsible for REALITY-TESTING, and imposes the norms of the external world on the DRIVES and unconscious impulses by giving the REALITY-PRINCIPLE precedence over the PLEASURE PRINCIPLE. The ego takes over the role of the 'censor' of the first topography, filtering unconscious ideas and impulses before allowing them access to the conscious mind. The ego is not, however, master in its own house, and is constantly threatened by the demands of the id and the superego, as well as by external reality and the threat of death. The phenomenon of NARCISSISM reveals (Freud 1914a) that the ego itself can become a love-OBJECT and a focus of sexual CATHEXIS.

According to LACAN, the discovery of the UNCONSCIOUS is a COPERNICAN REVOLUTION which means that the ego can no longer be regarded as the central agency of the psyche. To that extent, he follows Freud himself, but goes far beyond him when he then contends that the ego is an illusory product of the IMAGINARY identifications of the MIRROR-STAGE, a symptom and the site of resistances to analysis, that the SUBJECT, in contrast, is a product of the SYMBOLIC, and that psychoanalysis must therefore oppose any philosophy based upon the *cogito* (Lacan 1978).

For Kleinian psychoanalysts (KLEIN) the ego is present from birth and is not the product of a differentiation within the id. They therefore tend to use the term more loosely than Freud and to make it synonymous with the broader notion of the self.

ego-psychology An important strand within post-Freudian PSYCHOANALYSIS, derived mainly from child psychology, FREUD's second TOPOGRAPHY and ANNA FREUD's work on the ego and its defences (1937). The principal theorists of ego-psychology are Heinz Hartmann (1939), Rudolf Loewenstein and Ernst Kris (Kris 1951); its main journal is the American-based *Psychoanalytic Study of the Child*, published since 1945.

Ego-psychology holds that there exist within the EGO of the child the innate elements of a conflict-free sphere that can become autonomous vis-à-vis both the SUPEREGO and the ID (Hartmann, Kris and Loewenstein 1946). The conflict-free sphere neutralizes the DRIVES and harnesses them to the task of adaptation to the environment, adaptation being defined in terms of biological maturation and socialization. Treatment tends to be based on the establishment of a therapeutic alliance in which the patient identifies with the strong ego of the analyst. The developmental theory of ego-psychology provides the underpinning for BETTELHEIM's reading of fairy-tales.

Ego-psychology is Jacques LACAN's *bête noire* and he condemns it for reducing the distinguished practice of psychoanalysis to 'a theology of free enterprise' (1955a) and 'a label suitable to the "American way of life"' (1960).

READING: Blanche and Blanche (1974)

Eisenstein, Sergey Mikhaylovich (1898–1948) Russian film director and film theorist. Eisenstein's early films (*Strike*, 1924; *Battleship Potemkin*, 1925 and *October*, 1927) are amongst the greatest classics of the silent cinema. With *Alexander Nevsky* (1938) he made a successful transition to sound and in the second part of the unfinished *Ivan the Terrible* (Part 1, 1944; Part 2, 1946) he was equally successful in using colour stock for the first time.

Eisenstein was one of the most self-conscious and reflective directors of his generation and, although not always entirely coherent, his major collections of essays (*The Film Sense*, 1942; *Film Form*, 1949) are important contributions to film theory. Close to the Constructivists of the contemporary AVANT-GARDE, deeply committed to the Russian Revolution (though not always appreciated by its leaders) and influenced by the formal stylization of Japanese theatre and poetry, Eisenstein loathed the psychological realism of STANISLAVSKY's Moscow Art Theatre and sought to promote a formalist or 'machine' theory of film production. For Eisenstein, the basic unit or 'cell' of film is the single shot and he describes the assembling of shots into a sequence as 'collision montage'. The meaning of the sequence emerges, that is, not simply from its linear structure, but from the jarring juxtaposition of the individual shots that make it up. The collision of the images creates meaning or gives rise to a concept. In *Strike*, a shot of a crowd is juxtaposed with one of a bull being slaughtered; this both creates the idea of 'slaughter' by acting as a filmic metaphor and anticipates later events in the film. The composition of individual frames is calculated as a function of the relationship between the sequence of frames. Although the terminology of SEMIOLOGY was not available to him it is clear that Eisenstein had grasped the principle that a SYNTAGM is necessarily made up of a sequence of SIGNS which are meaningful because they are different.

Although Eisenstein's films look like documentaries and although their production involved the restaging of actual events from the revolutions of 1905 and 1917, they are really the products of long hours in the cutting room where multiple shots of the same objects, taken from different angles, were assembled to produce the greatest possible psychological effect on the viewer. Lighting, angles of shot, the gestures of the actors and even the subtitles (and after 1938 the sound and music) are orchestrated to produce the greatest possible psychological-political effect. Eisenstein's influence on the fast cutting between shots typical of the French NOU-VELLE VAGUE is almost incalculable.

READING: Andrew (1976); Leyda (1960)

empiricism A form of EPISTEMOLOGY which holds that all knowledge is derived from experience through the five senses. As its alternative name ('logical empiricism') indicates, LOGICAL POSITIVISM is a modern form of empiricism. The term derives from the Greek *empeirikos* ('experienced'), and the first 'empirics' were a sect of physicians who based the rules of their medical practice on their experience alone. So-called 'British empiricism' is associated mainly with John Locke (1632–1704), David Hume (1711–76; see Hume 1758), and John Stuart Mill (1806–73; see Mill 1843), and Locke's *Essay Concerning Human Understanding* (1690b) is generally regarded as its founding text. Locke strenuously denies the existence of innate ideas, is bitterly opposed to the rationalist claim that self-evident propositions can be derived from reason alone, and argues that at birth the human mind resembles a piece of 'white paper' on which impressions are literally imprinted. Ideas, defined as 'whatsoever is the object of the understanding when a man thinks', are derived from impressions or sense-data and may be either simple or complex. Simple ideas are unanalysable and cannot be broken down into smaller elements; they are combined into complex ideas such as substances representing things in the real world (a cat or a dog), modes (qualities or properties of substances) and relations between substances. Although all knowledge derives from experience, it is not simply *given* by the senses. Knowledge is a product of the human reason that establishes connections and associations between ideas.

For the original empiricists, knowledge is associated with a neutral and dispassionate observation of the world, and the term 'empiricism' is therefore commonly used to mean little more than a common-sense respect for 'the facts' and a distrust of speculation. In Britain at least, dissatisfaction and frustration with this weak empiricism was one of the impetuses behind the NEW LEFT's initial calls for 'THEORY'.

Empson, Sir William (1906–84) British literary critic and poet. Empson was a leading exponent of the practices of 'close reading' associated with both the PRACTICAL CRITICISM of RICHARDS and the NEW CRITICISM, but his work differs from both in a number of significant ways. Unlike the New Critics, and especially Cleanth Brooks (1947), Empson contends that paraphrase is an appropriate tool for analysing poetry and that a poem is not resistant to prose summary to the extent that the languages of poetry and prose are based upon the same underlying logic. Although he always acknowledges that Richards has a considerable influence on his own work, Empson rejects both the emotive stimulus/satisfied response model of I. A. Richards' *Principles of Literary Criticism* (1924) and the contention that poetry is emotive and has no logical structure. For Empson, poetry is a concentrated form of ordinary language and he has, perhaps, more in common with AUSTIN than with either Richards or New Criticism. Whereas Austin holds that a sharpened perception of language will lead to a sharper perception of reality, Empson argues (1930) that a moderate step forwards in the understanding of language would do a great deal to improve literary criticism.

Empson's understanding of language is based not upon a system of theoretical linguistics, but upon an intuitive realization that any word brings with it a body of meanings, and that no word can be reduced to a finite number of points of meaning. The method of analysis outlined in *Seven Types of Ambiguity* (1930) and further elaborated in *The Structure of Complex Words* (1951) consists in the careful analysis of very small units of text (a sentence, a line or a word) but Empson does not supply any explanation of his choice of texts. *Seven Types* examines the verbal nuances that provide the basis for alternative readings of the same piece of language, and implicitly argues that ambiguity is the hallmark of poetic and literary language. In *The Structure of Complex Words* the units of analysis are still smaller, with whole chapters being devoted to the multiple meanings of 'wit' in Pope's *Essay on Criticism*, 'honest' in *Othello* and 'all' in *Paradise Lost*. Although Empson seems at times to rely too heavily on dictionaries (and especially the *OED*), his interpretations are also based upon extensive reconstructions of the historical semantics of, for instance, 'blood' in Elizabethan literature. He is also very sensitive to the manner in which the canonical text (CANON) of Shakespeare's *Othello* has been shaped by generations of editors, and takes their shifting interpretations into account as he reconstructs the meaning of 'key words' such as 'honesty'.

The eclecticism apparent in Empson's selection of material for analysis becomes even more marked in the study of the GENRE of pastoral (1935), which encompasses readings of the proletarian literature of the 1930s, of Marvell's 'The Garden', 'The Beggar's Opera', and even Lewis Carroll's *Alice* books. It would be difficult to describe this study as providing a true theory of genre, but it does reveal an important theme in English literature, namely the idealization of relations between rich and poor. Pastoral, that is, transforms the feeling that life is inadequate to the demands of the human spirit into the insistence that anyone wishing to live the good life must avoid saying so. Pastoral describes the lives of 'low' people to an audience of wealthy people, and allows the latter to conclude: 'We are just like them.' It thus helps potentially antagonistic classes to see themselves as part of a larger unity.

Empson's general attitude to both literature and social questions has been described (Norris 1978) as a 'rationalistic humanism'. His humanism is most apparent in the late study of Milton (1961), in which Empson attempts to rescue Milton from the 'neo-Christians' he loathed so much by reading *Paradise Lost* in secular terms as a 'drama of rational dissent' (Norris 1978).

Empson's tendency to introduce personal comments about his age, and his sometimes flippant asides, can be disconcerting, as can the sometimes peremptory value-judgements (a footnote to *The Structure of Complex Words* dismisses Orwell's *1984* as a 'dreadful book'), but it is difficult to dislike a critic whose reading of Shelley's ode 'To a Skylark' suddenly turns into a knowledgeable and affectionate description of the flight pattern of the bird itself.

encyclopedia A work of reference, usually consisting of alphabetically arranged articles, dealing either with a specific subject or the entirety of human knowledge. Although examples can be found in Classical Antiquity (Pliny the Elder's *Natural History*), the modern encyclopedia is a product of the ENLIGHTENMENT era. John Harris published an alphabetically arranged *Lexicon Technicum* or *Technical Lexicon* in English in 1704, but Ephraim Chambers' *Cyclopaedia* of 1728 was the first to use cross-references to link the entries. The first edition of *Encyclopaedia Britannica* was published between 1768 and 1771. The French translation of Chambers (1743–5) provided the basis for the greatest of the Enlightenment encyclopedias. Produced under the general direction of Diderot and containing some 60,000 articles, the *Encyclopédie*, described by its subtitle as a 'reasoned dictionary of the arts, the sciences and the crafts', appeared between 1751 and 1772; contributors included Diderot, Rousseau and Voltaire. D'Alembert's 'Preliminary Discourse' or general introduction (1751) is a fine statement of the ideals of the Enlightenment. The great satire of encyclopedic knowledge is Flaubert's *Bouvard and Pécuchet* (1881), in which two hapless copy-clerks plunge into the never-ending labyrinth of accumulated knowledge, but constantly abandon their projects for self-enlightenment as they flit from archaeology to politics, philosophy or gardening. Appropriately enough, Flaubert did not live to complete the book.

The age of the printed encyclopedia is probably now over as the multi-volume work of reference is being replaced by CD-ROM, which is both cheaper to produce and easier to use.

Enlightenment A broad trend within European philosophy of the seventeenth and eighteenth centuries, associated mainly with Locke and the British deists, Voltaire, Diderot and the French Encyclopedists, and the critical philosophy of Kant. The period is often described as the Age of Reason. An important aspect of the Enlightenment period is the compilation of the first modern ENCYCLOPEDIAS, which claimed to provide a compendium of the whole of human knowledge.

Enlightenment philosophy is critical of all forms of traditional authority, and particularly of those associated with religion and feudalism. It seeks to replace fear and superstition with consent and truth and looks forward to the establishment of a social order based upon reason and natural law. Once the particularisms of local customs and beliefs are stripped away, a universal humanity will be revealed, and that humanity will be capable of infinite perfectibility. Kant famously defines the Enlightenment as man's emergence from a self-incurred immaturity and writes that the motto of Enlightenment is '*Sapere aude*: have courage to use your *own* understanding' (1784). The forty-eighth etching in Goya's *Los Caprichos* (Caprices) series of 1799 supplies an icon to match Kant's motto. A writer or philosopher has fallen asleep over his manuscript, and the air is filled with bats, owls and other nightmarish creatures. The caption reads: '*El sueño de la razón produce monstruos*' ('The sleep of reason produces monsters').

Philosophers such as Kant regarded the Enlightenment as a linear and irreversible process, but later writers such as ADORNO and HORKHEIMER argue that it was a DIALECTIC OF ENLIGHTENMENT with contradictory and sometimes dangerous effects. A wakeful reason, that is, can produce monsters of its own. The precise nature of the Enlightenment, the supposed universality of its values (rationality, tolerance, equality of rights) and the worth of its GRAND NARRATIVES of emancipation continue to be debated in discussions of the origins of modernity involving thinkers as diverse as HABERMAS and FOUCAULT. For LYOTARD, scepticism about the Enlightenment's GRAND NARRATIVES, which promise that humanity will be liberated by rational knowledge, is one of the hallmarks of the age of POSTMODERNITY.

READING: Cassirer (1932); Hampson (1968)

Entartete Kunst German expression meaning 'decadent art', and applied by the Nazi regime to most forms of MODERNISM from 1933 onwards. After 1937 the term tended to be replaced by *Kulturbolschewismus* ('Cultural Bolshevism').

On 19 July 1937 a large exhibition of 'decadent art' opened at the Munich Hofgarten. Designed as a propaganda exercise to demonstrate the superiority of Nazi 'Aryan' art (simultaneously exhibited in the 'House of German Art' constructed opposite the Hofgarten) by providing a negative example, it included 730 works by 112 artists such as Picasso, Gauguin, Kandinsky, Braque and Matisse. The works were deliberately badly hung and crowded together. Some were shown without frames. Derogatory captions and scrawled comments covered the walls, and pointed to the perceived association between modernism and idiocy, sexual depravity and Jewish influence. Attended by an estimated 20,000 people a day, *'Entartete Kunst'* is often said to have been the most widely-seen exhibition of modernist art ever held.

The implicit contrast was between the degeneracy of most non-German art and the Neoclassicism of the sculptor Arno Brecker and the architect Albert Speer, and focused on the image of the body. Whereas modern art from Impressionism and EXPRESSIONISM onwards was often characterized by the fragmentation or distortion of the body (a trend associated by Nazi IDEOLOGY with the 'sickness' of socialism), the art promoted by the Nazi regime was distinguished by its 'clarity' (*Klarheit*) and 'completeness' (*Geschlossenheit*). The clear, firm outlines of the sculpted nude, male and female, were both easily read and signified the organic wholeness of the totalitarian system, as well as the warrior values it sought to promote.

READING: Taylor and van der Wil (1990)

epic A long narrative poem or group of poems depicting great actions, often related to the founding of a nation or community. Although the Homeric epics of *The Iliad* and *The Odyssey* are often seen as the classic examples, they are predated by the Babylonian *Epic of Gilgamesh* (recorded on clay tablets in the seventh century BC, but probably older than *The Iliad* by at least one thousand years). The term is also applied to such poems or poem-cycles as the Sanskrit *Ramayana* and *Mahabharata* (third century BC) as well as the Anglo-Saxon *Beowolf*. Aristotle's *Poetics* provides the earliest formal description of the epic. Like a tragedy, an epic is a representation (MIMESIS), in dignified verse, of serious actions, but unlike tragedy, it does not use a single metre and there are no limits to the time-scale of the actions depicted. The Homeric epic supplies the model for one of the great GENRES of Western literature from Dante's *Divina Commedia* to Milton's *Paradise Lost*, whilst Joyce's *Ulysses* (1922) reworks it in the self-conscious mode typical of high MODERNISM (see Gilbert 1950). In film history, the term 'Hollywood epic' refers to films such as D. W. Griffiths' *Birth of a Nation* (1915) and Cecil B. DeMille's *The Ten Commandments* (1923, remade in 1956) and by extension to large-scale productions, usually of a historical nature.

The epic has often been described as the precursor of the novel. Lukác's early and influential study of the novel (1920) makes an important connection between the two, describing the epic as a product and reflection of a unified world in which there is no rift between the self and the world, and in which the actions of heroes have cosmic effects, and the novel as a genre in which a problematic individual seeks meaning in a contingent world.

In theatrical history 'epic theatre' refers to the innovations made by Erwin Piscator (1893–1966) in the Germany of the 1920s. Piscator's epic theatre was an elaborate form of communist-oriented AGITPROP drama, strongly influenced by early Soviet cinema, in which the new theatrical technology of lifts and revolves was combined with the projection of slogans and documentary material on slides to involve the audience in an event that resembled a public meeting rather than a classic performance (Piscator 1925; see Willett 1978). The term was subsequently employed by BRECHT to describe his own brand of political theatre, in which the ALIENATION-EFFECT was exploited to encourage the audience to take an objectively critical view of what was going on on stage rather than empathizing or identifying with the characters portrayed.

episteme The Greek word for 'knowledge', employed in Foucault's ARCHAEOLOGY OF KNOWLEDGE to describe the historical set of relations uniting the various discursive practices and DISCURSIVE FORMATIONS that generate the sciences and other forms of knowledge (Foucault 1966, 1969a). Foucault is at pains to stress that an *episteme* is not in itself a form or body of knowledge; it is a structure defining the conditions that both make knowledge possible and restrict its scope. Until the end of the Renaissance, for example, the knowledge that made up Western culture was governed by the *episteme* of 'resemblance'; the world was a microcosm reflecting a macrocosm, or a book of natural symbols that could be read and interpreted like any other book. In Foucault's later work, *episteme* tends to be replaced by the term *DISPOSITIF*.

epistemological break Defined in the history and philosophy of science elaborated by BACHELARD (1934, 1938a) and then CANGUILHEM (1962, 1970) as the moment of rupture that wrenches a science from its prescientific past and allows it to reject that past as ideological. A classical example is the discovery of oxygen, which demonstrates the non-scientific nature of the theory that substances burn because they contain a hypothetical inflammable substance, phlogiston, which is released at the moment of combustion. The history of a science is thus the history of the overcoming of epistemological obstacles or hindrances to knowledge; these might include opinions, popular images and perceptions or the accretion of unquestioned assumptions that have obscured the potential object of knowledge. An epistemological break is not simply a matter of new empirical discoveries or of an accumulation of scientific facts. It is a conceptual reorganization of a whole field of knowledge. Ohm's theory of electrical resistance reformulates in abstract mathematical terms (Ohm's law) the earlier theory that described the passage of electrical 'fluids' through substances in organicist and almost sensualist terms, and reinscribes them in a new network of concepts.

In the French thought of the 1960s, the concept of an epistemological break gains a new – and inflated – importance as it is invoked to demonstrate the scientific nature of both PSYCHOANALYSIS and MARXISM (Macey 1994). Whilst LACAN argues that the discovery of the UNCONSCIOUS is Freud's COPERNICAN REVOLUTION or epistemological break, ALTHUSSER contends that the scientificity of HISTORICAL MATERIALISM is established by the epistemological break between the work of the mature Marx and the young Marx, who was still under the sway of Hegel and Feuerbach. The core of scientific rationality common to Marxism and psychoanalysis allows them to be so articulated as to produce a unified theory of IDEOLOGY and the SUBJECT.

epistemology That branch of philosophy which deals with the theory, nature, scope and basis of knowledge (Greek *episteme*), or which investigates the possibility of knowledge itself. The French philosophical tradition makes a distinction between 'theory of knowledge' and 'epistemology', and defines the latter as the critical study of the principles, hypotheses and findings of the various sciences. Defined in that sense, epistemology seeks to determine the logical origins, value and objective import of the sciences. BACHELARD and CANGUILHEM are the great representatives of the French school of historical epistemology, which is a major influence on FOUCAULT.

Epistemology can take many different forms, ranging from Plato's doctrine of forms, which distinguishes between the unchanging form which is the object of thought, the copy of that form that is perceived by the senses, and the *CHORA* or receptacle that is the nurse of all change (*Timaeus*), to the Cartesian *cogito* which founds the certainty of knowledge by using a process of methodical doubt to conclude 'I am thinking, therefore I am' (Descartes 1637). The epistemology of EMPIRICISM, in contrast, derives all knowledge from the input of the senses and views the mind as a blank sheet or *tabula rasa* on which knowledge is imprinted.

Epistemology has traditionally been seen as sitting in judgement on other areas of philosophy or functioning as a court of appeal which rules on what can and cannot be known. Epistemology functions, that is, acts, as First Philosophy (Descartes 1641). It still plays that role with respect to the history of the sciences in the French tradition. Elsewhere, its traditional function has been redefined or challenged. The tradition of ANALYTIC PHILOSOPHY tends to displace the issue of epistemology towards the analysis of the nature, coherence and meaning of propositions. Critics of FOUNDATIONALISM like RORTY doubt the very possibility of a correspondence between knowledge and its objects and question the need for any theory of knowledge, whilst VATTIMO and WHITE propose the HERMENEUTICS of RHETORIC as an alternative to the cast-iron certainties of epistemology.

Feminist epistemology can take the form of the critiques of PHALLOCENTRISM and PHALLOGOCENTRISM put forward by CIXOUS, KRISTEVA or IRIGARAY, who attempt to map a specifically feminine IMAGINARY and a new sexual economy that can speak of and to women's needs and desires. It can also take the form of an attempt to GENDER knowledge by challenging the supposed objectivity and value-neutrality of knowledge, and especially science, and demonstrating that knowledge is always socially constructed, and therefore influenced by the social construction of gender (Harding 1976; Lennon and Whitford 1994). Such gender critiques have been particularly significant in the social, biological and medical sciences, and often take as one of their starting-points Foucault's thesis that any form of epistemology is also a regime of power.

epoche In Greek philosophy, the term refers to the withholding of assent or the suspension of judgement associated with scepticism. In twentieth-century philosophy, the term is synonymous with the 'bracketing' associated with the PHENOMENOLOGY of HUSSERL and with the method of phenomenological reduction (Husserl 1913). It refers both to the refusal to pass any judgement on the theoretical content of all previous philosophy, and to the 'putting out of action' of all theses as to the nature of spatio-temporal existence in order to arrive at a pure perception of phenomena that is devoid of all presuppositions or assumptions.

essentialism Term derived from 'essence', meaning the true or permanent nature of being of a phenomenon, as opposed to the accidents that may befall it. It might be argued that IDENTITY POLITICS is a contemporary variety of essentialism. One of the earliest and fullest accounts of essentialism is given by Aristotle in Book Gamma of *The Metaphysics*, where 'essence' is synonymous with the intrinsic properties of a phenomenon, and where it is stated that the task of philosophy is to get to know both the essence of things and their accidents. The ability to do so is assumed to be an intrinsic property of human reason or *nous*.

Although the term is still used in its traditional or technical sense, 'essentialism' can also be employed in a critical and pejorative sense, particularly within modern FEMINISM which has, from BEAUVOIR (1949) onwards, always challenged the view that there exists an unchanging or eternal 'female nature'. It is also argued that those forms of feminism that stress women's difference to the exclusion of everything else lapse into essentialism. IRIGARAY, for example, has been criticized for reducing women's sexuality to a biological essence (Sayers 1982) and for invoking a psychic essentialism by invoking an inherently female LIBIDO which perpetuates the myth of the eternal feminine (Segal 1987). Whilst SPIVAK is another critic of essentialism, she also insists that there is a need for a moment of 'strategic essentialism', when it becomes necessary to abandon universalism so as to speak 'as a woman' or 'as an Asian' in order to contest the HEGEMONY of colonial discourse.

ethnocentrism The tendency to judge the characteristics and cultures of other groups by the standards defined or recognized by the observer's own ethnic group. Cultural judgements made on an ethnocentric basis are inevitably negative and pejorative, and serve to justify the denigration of other cultures and to promote racism. Both EUROCENTRISM and AFROCENTRICITY are forms of ethnocentrism.

Eurocentrism A form of ethnocentrism which holds that Europe is the centre of the world and that its culture is by definition superior to all others. Eurocentrism is one of the issues at stake in debates as to what is POLITICALLY CORRECT, and fuels the controversy about DEAD WHITE EUROPEAN MALES. Hegel's notorious remark that Africa is 'no historical part of the world' (1822) is a classic instance of Eurocentric thinking, as is Marx's comment (1853) that India has no history and that one of the benefits of British colonialism is that it will bring the subcontinent into the narrative of Western history. The literary critic Harold BLOOM perpetuates the tradition when he opines (1975a) that America is the 'evening land' or 'the last phase of Mediterranean culture'.

existentialism The broadest definitions of existentialism would regard it as part of the broader tradition of the PHENOMENOLOGY of HUSSERL and HEIDEGGER, which is its main source, and would trace it back to Kierkegaard's insight that human beings have a special mode of existence (*existenz*; the word is used in both Danish and German) that distinguishes them from both animals and natural objects. There are, however, grounds for defining it in narrower terms as the dominant trend within the French philosophy of the 1940s and 1950s, when it began to be displaced by STRUCTURALISM. Its preeminent representative is Jean-Paul SARTRE, but the important contributions made by Simone de BEAUVOIR (1944, 1947a) should not be overlooked (see Vintges 1992). In the 'Letter on "Humanism"' (1946) addressed to his French translator Jean Beaufret, Heidegger is careful to distance himself from Sartre, objects to '*DASEIN*' being translated as 'human reality' ('*réalité humaine*') and places 'existentialism' in disdainful inverted commas (see Rockmore 1995). Ironically, Sartre himself had doubts about the advisability of using that term and preferred to speak of 'philosophy of existence' until popular pressure forced him to adopt the more popular term.

The classic text of French existentialism is Sartre's *Being and Nothingness* (1943a), but many of its themes are anticipated in his novel *Nausea* (1938). The 'nausea' refers to the feeling of disgust induced in the narrator by the sight of a chestnut tree in a park: the tree reveals the stark physicality of the meaninglessness of existence by simply being there. At the same time, it reveals the fundamental difference between the being of things and the being of human beings. Whilst the chestnut tree is always identical to itself, and exists solely IN-ITSELF, human beings exist both in themselves and for themselves. Because they exist for themselves and project themselves into a future existence by negating ('nihilating') what they are, human beings are free or, rather, condemned to freedom. The major ethical theses of Sartrean existentialism stem from the *in-itself/for-itself* distinction and from the insistence on human freedom. Freedom means that individuals have no destiny, and are obliged to choose freely what they become. To refuse to choose is in itself a choice, but it implies the self-deception of BAD FAITH, or a surrender to the temptation to exist in the in-itself mode of a natural object. At the same time, freedom is contingent upon or restricted by the SITUATION in which the individual exists and by the FACTICITY which defines him or her in terms of class, race and GENDER. Freedom or AUTHEN-TICITY does not mean freedom from a situation or facticity but the ability to assume it consciously. The ethic implicit in Sartre is a stark one: there are no excuses. Sartre's biographical exercises in EXISTENTIAL PSYCHOANALYSIS are lucid illustrations of the interplay between situation, facticity, authenticity and bad faith.

Sartrean existentialism is very much an individualist philosophy, and has often been criticized for its SOLIPSISM. Relations between SUBJECT and OTHER are antagonistic, and are typically structured by the GAZE which reduces the subject to the dimension of being-for-others, or to existing purely in terms defined by the Other.

FANON's description (1952a) of how his being-for-himself was reduced to objecthood or facticity when a white child looked at him, turned to its mother and said 'Look, a Negro' is a perfect illustration of the mechanism of the gaze. At the same time, Sartre does outline a theory of intersubjectivity via a critical comment of Heidegger's *Mittsein* ('being with') which claims that Heidegger understands 'being with' as meaning 'being alongside' in the sense that objects exist alongside one another. For Sartre, a distinctive 'we' appears when a group of individuals witness an event (or a theatrical performance) together and briefly fuse into a 'we' that watches it. Although Sartre does not expand on this in *Being and Nothingness*, the emergence of the 'we' anticipates the themes of SERIALITY and GROUP-IN-FUSION of his later work (1960).

Being and Nothingness is a technical and demanding study in philosophy. It was the popularized or even vulgarized summary given in the lecture on existentialism and humanism (1947b) that turned Sartre's version of existentialism into the fashionable philosophy that made him the most famous – and most vilified – thinker of the postwar decade. The popular perception was then that there was a close link between existentialism and the theory of the ABSURD associated with Camus (1942a, 1942b), even though that theory has none of Sartre's rigour. Nicely satirized by the novelist Boris Vian in his novel *The Froth on the Daydream* (1947), the vulgarized existentialism of Saint-Germain-des-Près, with singer Juliette Greco in 'existentialist' black, captured the intoxicating feeling of freedom after the Occupation, but had little to do with the austere and demanding vision of a world without pregiven moral values in which individuals are condemned to be free, but also to be responsible for how they use their freedom.

existential psychoanalysis A mode of analysis outlined by SARTRE in his classic essay on phenomenological ontology (Sartre 1943a). Its principles are derived from Sartre's EXISTENTIALISM and it supplies the basic methodology for his biographical studies of Baudelaire (1947a), Genet (1952) and Flaubert (1971–2) and for his essay in autobiography (1964).

Existential psychoanalysis differs from the PSYCHOANALYSIS elaborated by FREUD in a number of important respects. It has no therapeutic goal as such, even though elements of the theory do feed into the practices of ANTI-PSYCHIATRY, but is intended to provide a means of understanding individuals. Given the fundamental Sartrean contention that it is death alone that transforms a life into a destiny or something that can be fully understood, biography is its main field of application. Sartre explicitly rejects the postulate of the unconscious, arguing that all mental phenomena are coextensive with consciousness even though the mechanisms of BAD FAITH mean that the subject is not lucidly aware of them. Other aspects of Freud's metapsychology are criticized for their abstraction. DESIRE for an object is not, for example, a symbolization of some more fundamental sexual desire but a mode of consciousness expressing a desire *to be* or, ultimately, to achieve the impossible unity of being-in-oneself and being-for-oneself. The psychoanalytic reliance on symbolic equations, such as the unconscious equation between faeces and gold, is criticized for its failure to grasp the meaning of such equations for specific individuals in specific SITUATIONS by establishing a much more general and abstractedly universal symbolism. Similarly, Sartre holds that the concept of LIBIDO is meaningless unless it is referred to the experience of the individual; libido does not exist outside its concrete fixations.

In the opening pages of his monumental but unfinished study of Flaubert, Sartre defines the goals of his existential psychoanalysis by asking: 'What can we know of a man today?' Arriving at an understanding of what an individual is implies a reconstruction of a family and social situation, but also of the project that defines how the individual will live that situation. The basic thesis is that the individual is a totality or SINGULAR UNIVERSAL and not merely a collection of disparate phenomena and incidents. It follows that the most 'insignificant' details of behaviour express that totality and form part of the individual project in which the individual chooses his existence and life within the limits imposed by his or her situation. The genius of a Flaubert or a Genet is not a gift, but the way the writer chooses to escape from an impossible situation, the way in which he chooses his life and the meaning of his universe. Thus the ten-year-old Jean Genet is caught stealing and is told: 'You are a thief.' Defined by the OTHER and shamed by the other, he assumes that definition with the defiant 'I will be a thief', and the inversion of values implied in that assumption will define his aesthetics and ethics of betrayal and criminality because it signals the choice of a world and a mode of being in that world.

The term 'existential psychoanalysis' is also applied to the clinical theory of the Swiss psychiatrist, Ludwig Binswanger (1881–1966), though it is more properly described as *Daseinanalyse* (DASEIN-analysis; see Binswanger 1963). According to Binswanger, HEIDEGGER's concept of Dasein provides the therapist with a tool that frees him from the prejudices of scientific theory and allows him to describe the clinical phenomena he encounters in all their phenomenological depth. Mental illness is viewed not simply as a pathological disorder, but as a modified mode of being-in-the-world; what is lost in illness is Dasein's freedom to organize the world, and the goal of therapy is to restore that freedom. One of FOUCAULT's first publications (1954) was a lucid introduction to a French translation of Binswanger's *Traum und Existenz* (Dream and existence, 1930); the text and the introduction are now conveniently translated in one volume (Foucault and Binswanger 1993).

READING: Dobson (1993)

Expressionism A broad tendency within North European, and particularly German, painting, film and literature that developed before and after the First World War. The debate between Ernst BLOCH and Georg LUKÁCS over the nature of expressionism is one of the most significant discussions of realism and MODERNISM.

In art history, the term 'Expressionism' (in this context customarily capitalized) refers to the work of Kandinsky, Klee and others associated with the Blaue Reiter (Blue Rider; the name is derived from the title of Kandinsky's painting of 1903) group which held exhibitions in Munich in 1911 and 1912. Heavily influenced by the Swiss critic Worringer's comments on ABSTRACTION and rejecting both Impressionism and Naturalism, Expressionist painting uses distorted lines and perspective and forms and bold colours to express raw emotion and spirituality. Although the Blaue

Reiter group itself was short-lived, the Expressionist style became extremely popular after the First World War, and influenced the later NEUE SACHLICHKEIT school, as well as the cynical portrayal of the Weimar Republic in Georg Grosz's satirical drawings (1971), the photomontage of John Heartfield (Ades 1986) and the images of the modern city in the 'picture books' of uncaptioned woodcuts produced by the Belgian Frans Masereel (1925). The systematic distortion and introspection characteristic of the style resulted in its being derided and banned as ENTARTETE KUNST (degenerate art) by the Nazi regime.

Expressionist cinema is characterized by stark black and white contrasts, highly theatrical sets and screenplays that deal with the supernatural and the diabolic; the classic expressionist films are *The Golem* (1914, dir. Paul Wegener and Henrik Galeen) and *The Cabinet of Dr Caligari* (1919, dir. Robert Wiene), and the classic study is Lotte H. Eisner's *The Haunted Screen* (1965). Expressionist cinema supplies the iconography for many later horror films, such as the original *Frankenstein* (1931, dir. James Whale). Certain of BRECHT's plays, such as *Baal* (1918a) and *Drums in the Night* (1918b), are sometimes described as expressionist but the most significant literary manifestation of the tendency is Alfred Döblin's *Berlin Alexanderplatz* (1929), which uses techniques pioneered by James Joyce and John Dos Passos to paint a kaleidoscopic picture of Berlin.

The famous exchange between Bloch and Lukács took place in the pages of *Das Wort* (The word), an expatriate literary journal published in Moscow between 1936 and 1939. Ostensibly about expressionism, it is in fact a very broad debate about the politics of the AVANT-GARDE. Responding to an article in which Lukács reiterates his 'reflection theory' of realism, Bloch (1938) criticizes the Hungarian critic for having elaborated a doctrine of permanent neoclassicism that denies the very possibility of an avant-garde in capitalist society, and for dismissing any experimentation in the arts as being decadent because it abandons the classic realism of Balzac. Bloch himself argues that avant-garde movements ranging from expressionism to SURREALISM can be anticipatory and can provide a vision of a more human future. In his reply Lukács insists that all modern literary schools produce only a frozen and superficial image of reality because the social ALIENATION of modern writers means that they cannot discover the underlying truths about society. Expressionism is singled out for criticism on the grounds that it discourages revolutionary clarification. Its decadence is contrasted with the progressive realism of Thomas and Heinrich Mann and Maxim Gorky. In a coda to the debate which was not published in his lifetime, BRECHT for his part attacked Lukács's theory for its dogmatic formalism and its ahistorical reliance on a very limited range of novels (1967a). The original exchange between Bloch and Lukács, with Brecht's comments and later comments on the debate made by ADORNO, is translated with explanatory material in Bloch et al., *Aesthetics and Politics* (1977).

READING: Selz (1957); Washton Long (1993)

F

facticity Term derived from the German *Faktizität* and the French *facticité*, used in PHENOMENOLOGY to describe the fact that being always means being-in-the-world, or what HEIDEGGER terms the 'fact' or 'factuality' of DASEIN's being (1927). The word refers to the non-essential or contingent aspects of being. SARTRE defines it in terms of an individual's circumstances of birth, class, race, nationality, and in terms of the physiological and bodily structures that necessarily condition that individual's SITUATION or being-in-the-world (1943a). Whereas transcendence defines consciousness's movement away from any given state of being in order to achieve its freedom and realize its potential, facticity restricts and limits freedom by reintroducing the dimension of contingency or the fact of being in a situation that is not freely chosen or determined.

false memory syndrome Term used to describe the recovery, during psycho-therapy, of memories of childhood sexual abuse, usually at the hands of a male rela-tive, that did not actually occur. Typical cases involve adults accusing their parents of having abused them when they were children, or of having abused or even murdered other children. Critics of false memory syndrome claim that such accusations are often the result of persistent and leading questions by the therapist involved, of con-tamination by suggestion and of the assumption that the very absence of memories can be proof that abuse occurred. Resultant court cases have led to fathers being imprisoned despite their claims of innocence. A False Memory Foundation was estab-lished in Philadelphia in 1992 to defend parents who claim to be victims of the syn-drome, and a similar society was formed in Britain the following year.

The debate over false memory syndrome and RECOVERED MEMORY is a phenom-enon of the 1990s, and arose out of the realization in the previous decade of the wide extent of child sexual abuse in the wake of events like the Cleveland (UK) scandal in which almost two hundred children were taken into care after alleged abuse (for conflicting accounts of the case, see Bell 1988 and Campbell 1988). The serious criticism that PSYCHOANALYSIS is a sophisticated form of false memory syndrome has revived earlier controversies about the SEDUCTION THEORY (Crews et al. 1997). In 1998 the British Royal College of Psychiatrists published, after much debate, a report concluding that any memory recovered through hypnosis, dream interpretation or regression therapy is almost certainly false (Brandon, Boakes, Glaser and Green 1998).

falsifiability The principle of falsifiability, also known as the verification principle, has been popularized by POPPER (1935) and is the criterion used by the VIENNA CIRCLE to establish the scientific nature of a proposition or theory. The principle derives from the view that science makes no ultimate statements and does not recognize the existence of insoluble problems. Scientific theories cannot be verified in any absolute sense, but they can be refuted or falsified by new evidence. Scientists therefore test the validity of their theories by attempting to refute them, and do not look for evidence that confirms them. One of the standard criticisms of PSYCHO-ANALYSIS is that FREUD and his followers do not make use of the principle of falsifiability, but seek to confirm their theories.

family romance A form of fantasy in which a child imagines that it is not being brought up by its real parents and that its 'true' parents are of noble birth (Freud 1909a). In some variants, only one parent is involved in the fantasy. The child fantasizes that it is illegitimate and that one of its parents, usually that of the same sex, is unknown or has abandoned it. Family romance is often a means of warding off or controlling the incestuous fantasies and desires linked to the OEDIPUS COMPLEX. It can also be a way of dealing with sibling rivalry.

The French critic Marthe Robert (1914–96) uses Freud's short paper on family romance to construct a typological theory of the novel (1972). She identifies two archetypal heroes: the foundling, whose story illustrates the child's belief in the omnipotence of wishes, and the bastard whose story is an epic of self-reliance and self-creation. *Don Quixote* and *Robinson Crusoe* are Robert's prototypical novels.

Fanon, Frantz (1925–61) Psychiatrist and revolutionary activist. Born in the then French colony of Martinique, Fanon trained in France and subsequently worked as a psychiatrist in colonial Algeria, where he became actively involved in the Front de Libération Nationale's armed struggle for independence, which was finally victorious in 1962. Expelled from Algeria in 1957, Fanon worked in Tunis as a journalist and continued to practise as a psychiatrist. The unsigned articles written for the FLN's paper *El Moudjahid* were posthumously published in volume form (1964) and argue the case for a pan-African revolution in which Algeria would play a leading role.

Fanon's first book, *Black Skin, White Masks* (1952a; it should be noted that the published English translation is very unreliable), is an important study of the psychological and cultural ALIENATION induced by colonialism, and of the psychology of racism. An eclectic study which draws on a wide range of authorities from Adler to SARTRE and LACAN, it is deeply rooted in personal experience and dominated by the realization that, whilst he had always been taught – and had believed – that he was French, the average French citizen regarded Fanon as a racial inferior. It also reflects the experience of the North African and black soldiers who, like Fanon, fought with the French army in the Second World War. Having liberated their colonizers, they were then recolonized by them. Fanon's analysis of white racism draws on the model provided by Sartre's study of anti-Semitism (1946), and he also analyses the negrophobia of his fellow Martiniquans, who had internalized white stereotypes to such an extent as to deny their own blackness and to despise black Africans. Although there is no evidence to suggest that Fanon had ever read DU BOIS, there is a distinct similarity between his image of a black man wearing a white mask, and the latter's theory of double consciousness.

Like GLISSANT and others of his generation, Fanon was greatly influenced by CÉSAIRE and often cites his *Notebook of a Return to my Native Land* (1939). He is, however, highly critical of NEGRITUDE, which he regards as a mirage and an ESSEN-TIALISM. The basic thesis of *Black Skin, White Masks* is that whilst blacks must be liberated from their inferiority complex, whites must be liberated from an equally alienating superiority complex.

The Wretched of the Earth (1961) is widely regarded as one of the great classics of decolonization and of the THIRD WORLD's struggle for independence and liberation. Notorious for its apologia for the use of violence when all the alternatives have failed, it challenges MARXISM's traditional emphasis on the historical role of the industrial working class, and argues that the landless peasantry and the dispossessed of the shanty towns surrounding the cities of the THIRD WORLD are the only true agents of revolutionary change.

Fanon's clinical writings on psychiatry are often overlooked, or obscured by his fleeting references to PSYCHOANALYSIS, and have never been collected (the most important are reprinted in *L'Information psychiatrique* 1975; see also Fanon 1952b). Mainly concerned with the practicalities of constructing a truly transcultural psychiatry (Vergès 1996), they offer a virulent critique of the colonial psychiatry that regarded Algerians as primitives with an innate propensity for impulse and homicidal violence.

The Fanon of *The Wretched of the Earth* was a key figure in the Third Worldism of the 1960s (Macey 1998) and an inspiration to the American militants of the Black Power movement (Carmichael and Hamilton 1967); *Black Skin, White Masks* is now regarded (Bhabha, 1990b; Gordon, Sharpley-Whiting, Denean and White 1996; Read 1996) as a key text in POSTCOLONIAL THEORY.

READING: Gordon, Sharpley-Whiting, Denean and White (1996); Macey (2000)

feminism Although feminism, which became one of the most important forces in twentieth-century politics and thought, can take many different forms, its common core is the thesis that the relationship between the sexes is one of inequality or oppression. All forms of feminism seek to identify the causes of that inequality and to remedy it, but the issue of precisely which agency produces and reproduces inequality is the source of many of the differences between feminists. The long association between socialism and feminism leads the supporters of SOCIALIST FEMINISM to explain the inequality of the sexes in terms of the social relations and economic structures of capitalism, whilst RADICAL FEMINISM tends to argue that the nuclear family or PATRIARCHY – or even men in general – is/are to blame. The issue of equality itself is contentious, and the question of whether the emphasis should fall on the demand for equality or on the celebration of GENDER difference (as in ÉCRITURE FÉMININE and forms of LESBIAN FEMINISM) continues to arouse controversy.

The first recorded use of the French *féminisme* dates from the 1830s, and the term is usually agreed to have been coined by the utopian socialist Charles Fourier (1772–1837), for whom the degree of women's emancipation was the measure of the emancipation of society as a whole. 'Feminism' was in use in English by 1851, but became much more widely used in the 1890s when it became synonymous with 'advocacy of women's rights' and was associated with the suffragette movement led by the Women's Social and Political Union in the period 1906–14 (Liddington and Norris 1978). Limited suffrage was won in 1918, and full suffrage in 1928; in the United States, the nineteenth amendment to the Constitution gave women the vote in 1920.

Whilst the term 'feminism' dates from the 1830s, feminist or protofeminist thought is much older (see the materials anthologized in Schneier 1996). Whilst it can be argued that the attack on literary misogyny made by Christine de Pisan's *Book of the City of Ladies* (fourteenth century) is an early example of feminist thought, most historians would agree that modern feminism first emerges in the wake of the American and French Revolutions of the late eighteenth century. In 1791 Olympe de Gouges published a *Déclaration des droits de la femme et de la citoyenne* (Declaration of the rights of woman and of the female citizen); Wollstonecraft's *Vindication of the Rights of Woman* appeared a year later (see Tomalin 1974). Wollstonecraft argued that women were the slaves of men, but immediately added that slavery degrades both master and slave. Married women are memorably described as birds 'confined to their cages' with 'nothing to do but plume themselves'. Wollstonecraft was also the first to describe marriage as a form of legal prostitution; that theme runs through a whole socialist tradition – it is, for instance, present in the *Communist Manifesto* (Marx and Engels 1847–8) – and is perpetuated in the anti-marriage, anti-family line within socialist feminism (Barrett and McIntosh 1982). The association with slavery is not merely metaphorical; in both Britain and the United States there was a considerable overlap between abolitionism and feminism throughout the nineteenth century (Berg 1978; Ware 1992). The relationship was not always an easy one, and is seen by some as setting in motion the trend that equated 'women's liberation' with the liberation of white women, and 'black liberation' with the liberation of black men, but not necessarily black women (hooks 1981). Nor was the relationship with socialism easy. Although there was a connection in most countries between utopian socialism's desire to create a 'new moral world' and the aspiration of early feminists (Taylor 1983), and although the 'woman question' was supposedly high on the socialist agenda especially in Germany and Russia (Thönnersen 1969; Rowbotham 1972) the demand for 'equal pay for equal work' has not always been popular with male trade-unionists.

It has become conventional to describe the history of feminism as one of successive waves which peak and then recede. The various campaigns to obtain the vote have often been described as the first wave of modern feminism, and the WOMEN'S LIBERATION movement of the 1970s, which still dominates popular perceptions of feminism, as its second wave. The key figures for this period are GREER, MITCHELL, MILLETT and FIRESTONE, but BEAUVOIR and FRIEDAN are commonly seen as the first mothers of women's liberation (Beauvoir 1949; Friedan 1963). Mention should also be made of the somewhat neglected Hannah Gavron (1936–65), whose sociological study of 'captive wives' (1966) foreshadows later critiques of the domestic role imposed on so many women. The early women's liberation movement was predicated on the idea of sisterhood, or the theory that all women had interests in common (Morgan 1970). That utopian unity was undermined by the growing perception that the interests of black women were not necessarily identical with those of white women (Mirza 1997), as well as by differences over class and sexual orientation (Hirsch and Keller 1990).

The 1980s have been described as the decade of the backlash against feminism or of an undeclared war against women fought largely in the media, which claimed that feminism had 'gone too far' and was even to blame for women's discontents (Faludi 1991; for thoughtful discussion of the backlash thesis, see the essays in Oakley and Mitchell 1997). Yet the same period saw the emergence of women's studies or gender studies as a major academic discipline (Jackson et al. 1993; Robinson and Richardson 1997), the spectacular rise of feminist publishing houses and of FEMINIST CRITICISM, and a much more general awareness of the issues surrounding GENDER. The institutionalization of feminism does have its critics, who argue that it implies a rejection of the 'liberation' aspect of women's liberation (Curthoys 1997), but it can also be claimed that it makes feminism 'ordinary' in the sense that WILLIAMS describes culture as ordinary. This has sometimes led to the idea of a 'post-feminist' era in which young women enjoy the benefits won by earlier feminist struggles but either reject or know nothing of ideas such as sisterhood.

Whilst many of the debates inaugurated in the 1970s are still in a sense ongoing, a younger generation of women is also arguing for a new feminism. In the United States, Naomi Wolf (1962–) contends (1993) that women must abandon the old 'victim feminism' that portrayed them as helpless victims in favour of a 'power feminism' that views them as potent agents of change with many resources at their disposal. In Britain, Natasha Walter (1967–) also argues (1998) for a 'new feminism' (in which men too have a role to play) which will function as a spreading consensus or social movement promoting a long overdue economic equality with men, and not a female-centred culture. Her claim that Margaret Thatcher (Britain's first woman Prime Minister from 1979 to 1990) is the 'unsung heroine' of British feminism because she normalized female success has proved very controversial; survivors from that era point out that one of Margaret Thatcher's first acts was to restrict access to paid maternity leave.

feminist criticism The expression can be applied to an enormously wide and rich body of criticism covering literature, the visual arts and film. There is no one school of feminist criticism and it reflects the many tendencies that coexist within FEMINISM itself. Although there is always a commitment to some political definition of feminism, feminist criticism can take its methodological inspiration from theories as varied as MARXISM and SOCIALIST FEMINISM, STRUCTURALISM, PSYCHOANALYSIS and PSYCHOANALYTIC CRITICISM or DECONSTRUCTION. The gradual institutionalization of women's studies and gender studies in British and American universities from the mid-1970s onwards (Jackson et al. 1993; Robinson and Richardson 1997) has given feminist criticism such a high profile that it is easy to forget that it is a recent phenomenon.

Although Virginia Woolf (1929, 1979) can be seen as one of its most important predecessors and although Beauvoir's *The Second Sex* (1949) devotes much space to the discussion of literary texts, contemporary feminist criticism really emerges out of the WOMEN'S LIBERATION movement of the 1970s and coincides with the explosion of feminist art, literature and film. The first International Festival of Women's Films was held in June 1972, and London's National Film Theatre showed its first season of Women's Cinema a year later (Johnston 1973). Feminist literary criticism, helpfully surveyed in such studies as *Making a Difference: Feminist Literary Criticism* by Green and Khan (1985), *Feminist Literary Theory: A Reader* by Mary Eagleton (1986) and *Feminisms: An Anthology of Literary Theory and Criticism* by Warhol and Herndl (1992), has been neatly defined as combining the study of women writers with the analysis of women in literature (Kaplan 1986). That the Women's Movement discussed literature from its earliest beginnings is not surprising, given that major figures like GREER, MILLETT and MITCHELL all had an academic background in English literature. The third part of Millett's *Sexual Politics* (1969) is entitled 'The Literary Reflection' and examines the stereotypical representation of women in the writings of D. H. Lawrence, Henry Miller and Norman Mailer. Although Millett's account of male misogyny and PATRIARCHY is, by later standards, fairly crude, it does establish important precedents for the study of the representation of women. The issue of the stereotypical representation of women, and especially their sexuality, is a major component in critiques of advertising and in the campaign against pornography, and also informs texts like Molly Haskell's *From Reverence to Rape* (1974), which is an early survey of the depiction of women in film from the 1920s onwards. As a slogan coined in the 1970s put it, 'pornography is the theory; rape is the practice.'

Although individual women obviously made vital contributions to feminist theory, the collectivist ethos of 1970s feminism meant that much work was also done in small groups. One of the most significant was the Marxist Feminist Literature Collective (1975–7), which gradually worked through a reading list comprising MARXIST CRITICISM and 'French THEORY'. This group succeeded in turning theory into performance art when ten of its members gave a paper on nineteenth-century women's literature to the 1977 Conference on the Sociology of Literature at the University of Essex. The ten took the platform together, and then took turns to read out sections of the collective paper (Marxist Feminist Literature Collective 1978; see the account in Kaplan 1986).

One of the major themes of the Women's Liberation Movement is that women have been 'hidden from history' (Rowbotham 1973a), and it is reflected in the many attempts to rescue or rediscover a tradition of women's writing that has been marginalized or excluded from the CANON. This is also the major impetus behind the London-based Virago publishing house's extremely successful 'Virago Classics' series, which has made available numerous major but neglected texts. Moers (1976) celebrates the existence of a centuries-old tradition of 'great women writers'. The establishment of a female tradition is also the objective of SHOWALTER's *A Literature of their Own* (1977), whilst her theory of GYNOCRITICS proposes the existence of a specifically 'female' criticism of women's writing. Perhaps the most monumental contribution to the canon-making strand in feminist criticism is GILBERT and GUBAR's *Madwoman in the Attic* (1979a) and its successor volumes.

In the domain of art history, the problem of exclusion is a serious one: a standard work like GOMBRICH's best-selling *Story of Art* (1950) contains no references to women artists. As in the literary field, the initial feminist response was to insist that there have always been great women artists and to rediscover their hidden heritage (Tuft 1974; Nochlin and Harris 1976). Although subsequent critics are sceptical about this search for 'old mistresses', they acknowledge that it was a necessary preliminary to the feminist intervention within art history (Parker and Pollock 1981). Concentration on hidden traditions alone is seen by Pollock as problematic in that it leaves intact the very notions of authorship, creativity and genius that are undermined by structuralism, psychoanalysis and theories of IDEOLOGY. The feminist appropriation of psychoanalysis, and particularly of LACAN's concept of the GAZE, has had, since Mulvey's pioneering essay on visual pleasure (1975), a powerful impact on film studies and has allowed feminist critics to move beyond Haskell's early classificatory study of the representation of women to studies of how women are ideologically and sexually 'positioned' both within films and within the social institution of cinema (see Kuhn 1982).

In many areas feminist criticism overlaps with feminist art practice to such a degree that the two become virtually indistinguishable, as in the French concept of an *ÉCRITURE FÉMININE* that is at once a new form of writing celebrating femininity and a critical reflection on a society (and texts) dominated by the image of the PHALLUS. Here creative writing merges almost seamlessly with the theoretical work of women such as IRIGARAY and KRISTEVA (see Moi 1985). Feminist art criticism is inseparable from the creative work of inventing new networks of exhibition and distribution (Lippard 1976; see also the final chapter of Chadwick 1990 and the introductory chapter in Pollock 1996). The related art practices have often proved controversial; when the Swedish artist Monica Sjoo exhibited her painting *God Giving Birth* (1969, reproduced in Chadwick 1990) in England in 1971, she was threatened with prosecution on charges of blasphemy and obscenity. The ensuing protests led directly to the formation of the Women's Art History Workshop (see Parker and Pollock 1987). Other manifestations of the interplay between theory and creativity were more confrontational. The London Institute of Contemporary Arts' exhibition of women's images of men (*Women's Images of Men* 1980), partly inspired by Margaret Walters' major study of the 'forgotten' tradition of the male nude (1978), was a direct response to pop artist Allen Jones's exhibition in the same space of women transformed into furniture. Given the circumstances, many of the images of men on show at the ICA in 1980 were surprisingly tender.

fetishism In the psychoanalytic theory of sexual perversion, very broadly defined as any activity that deviates from heterosexual intercourse, a fetish is a non-sexual part of the body or an object such as a foot, a shoe, or a piece of fur or velvet which is highly cathected (CATHEXIS) with LIBIDO. A fetish is described by FREUD as a substitute for the mother's penis that the little boy once believed in (1927c). The realization that she does not in fact possess a penis gives rise to the child's 'sexual theory' (Freud 1908a) that she once possessed one and has been deprived of it, and to the child's fear that he too might be castrated. The fetish-object is thus both a means of denying the existence of sexual difference and a defence against the fear of castration. The typical fetishist simultaneously retains and has given up the belief in the maternal penis, and fetishism is usually accompanied by an aversion to the real female genitals. Fetishism is a typically male perversion and is very rare in women.

The term 'fetishism' was coined by the French psychologist Alfred Binet (1857–1911; see Sulloway 1979) and derives from European perceptions of the amulets used in traditional West African religions. Freud's remark to the effect (1905a) that fetish-objects can be 'likened to the fetishes in which savages believe that their gods are embodied' is, like the subtitle of his theoretical study *Totem and Taboo* (1913: 'Some Points of Agreement between the Mental Lives of Savages and Neurotics'), a reminder that psychoanalytic theory is reliant upon an evolutionary schema characterized by a high degree of EUROCENTRISM. Marx's theory of COMMODITY FETISHISM also invokes the notion of a magical belief in the power of inanimate objects.

Feyerabend, Paul (1924–94)   Austrian-American historian and philosopher of science. Feyerabend's early work (collected 1981a, 1981b) was on the philosophy of quantum physics and was heavily influenced by POPPER and LOGICAL POSITIVISM; in his later work (1975, 1992) he abandons his earlier positions and outlines what he terms an anarchistic methodology for an anarchistic science that functions in accordance with the principle of 'anything goes'.

For the later Feyerabend, the world, including the world of science, is a complex entity that cannot be explained by any one theory. The idea of a fixed scientific method or a fixed theory of rationality rests upon a naïve and restrictive view of the universe: all methodologies have their limits and nothing is ever settled. Scientists do not work with any one method. They break the rules of scientific method, speculate and work by rule of thumb, and their discoveries usually result from the convergence of disparate and often conflicting trends. Unanimity of opinion suits rigid churches and tyrannies; objective knowledge can only flourish when a variety of opinion exists. The power of science is social rather than epistemological, and Feyerabend contends that a free society is one in which science, like the church, is separated from the state. Although Feyerabend's claims may appear wild, they are underpinned by a thorough study of the history of science and of Galileo in particular.

Feyerabend's scepticism about the claims of science stems from two main sources. Working in an increasingly multicultural environment in California in the 1960s, he became uncomfortably aware that the 'universalist' history of science that he was teaching was in fact an extreme form of EUROCENTRISM. According to his own account (1995), AUSTIN'S work on ORDINARY LANGUAGE convinced him that, when examined with sufficient attention, scientific propositions were as meaningless as those of METAPHYSICS. Human activity can, he argues, survive without the cancers of general philosophy and the philosophy of science: anarchistic science and common sense will suffice.

field A central notion in the cultural sociology of Pierre BOURDIEU, first introduced in a discussion of the sociology of the creative project (1966) and gradually elaborated into a theory that can be applied to all literary, artistic, philosophical and scientific activities. In practice, Bourdieu has applied it primarily to literary production (1982, 1992).

The literary field is defined by Bourdieu as the social space that situates the agents who contribute to the production of cultural works. The field is autonomous and has its own rules, which must be obeyed by any aspiring literary figure, but it also overlaps with the semi-autonomous subfield made up of agents such as publishers, editors, distributors, critics and booksellers. Both the literary field and its subfield exist within a broader political field. All are 'fields of forces' in which a power struggle is waged. Within the political field, the struggle is for real power; within the literary field, it is one for the symbolic power conferred by the sites and agencies that confer legitimacy by legislating on what 'is' and 'is not' literature. Anyone who enters the literary field does so in a differential manner; the position of a successful playwright is not that of an AVANT-GARDE poet with a tiny readership. The struggle between such agents can take the form of a search for a heteronomy that coincides with the interests of the dominant powers within the political field, or the search for autonomy characteristic of the avant-garde. Here Bourdieu draws a parallel with literary activity and struggles over the allocation of funding to pure and applied research in the scientific field. Even though an avant-garde may meet with failure, its very defeat may be a source of symbolic capital, as commercial failure may be an index of a successful bid for autonomy.

Bourdieu likens his literary field to the old metaphor of the Republic of Letters, and the rise and fall of new movements to the revolutions that take place there. Typically, an avant-garde begins as an oppositional force that denounces a dominant DISCOURSE. STRUCTURALISM, for example, attacks the EXISTENTIALISM associated with Sartre by seeking alliances with its enemies in a form of positional warfare, denouncing it as old and repressive and gradually eroding its power by appealing to agents within the subfield that can promote its interests. It seeks to establish a monopoly by asserting the legitimacy of its own values and its own ability to determine the nature of the literary or cultural object. The literary field, like any other field, is a world in which 'to exist' means 'to be different'.

figure A device in RHETORIC involving the arrangement of the words of a sentence or clause into a structure that is natural but goes beyond the usual requirements of communication. Examples include variations in syntax, word play and ANAPHORA. The distinction between literal and figurative or figural language is basic to all theories of rhetoric. It is traditional to make a further distinction between figures and TROPES.

LYOTARD uses the term 'figure' (1971) to establish a distinction between discursive or textual signification ('meaning'), and a figural rhetoricity which can never be reduced to the BINARY OPPOSITIONS of discursive communication and which introduces an element of non-meaningful opacity into the signifier. The figural is at various times identified as the locus of DESIRE, of fantasy and of the UNCONSCIOUS itself. References to 'figure' also appear in Lyotard's discussions of the visual arts (especially 1984a), which owe a lot to MERLEAU-PONTY's phenomenology of perception. In this sense, 'figure' refers to the line of the painting, the plasticity of three-dimensional works, or to any element that is not reducible to simple communication. In introducing the idea of 'figure', Lyotard superimposes a third or visual-figural dimension onto the two-dimensional model of discursive textuality (1985).

READING: Readings (1991)

film noir French term, literally meaning 'black film' or 'dark film', widely applied to violent thrillers with a sinister atmosphere of personal and political corruption. The term was coined by two French film critics, apparently working independently of one another, in the autumn of 1946 (Nino Franck 1946; Chartier 1946), and was originally used to describe five Hollywood films that were first shown in Paris earlier that year: *The Maltese Falcon* (dir. John Huston, 1941), *Laura* (dir. Otto Preminger, 1944), *Double Indemnity* (dir. Billy Wilder, 1944), *Murder, My Sweet* (dir. Edward Dmytryk, 1944) and *The Woman in the Window* (dir. Fritz Lang, 1944). Howard Hawks's *The Big Sleep* (1946) and Robert Montgomery's *The Lady in the Lake* (1946) were also described as *films noirs* when they were released in France. The first study of the GENRE appeared in French in 1955 (Borde and Chaumeton 1955). Various explanations have been proposed for the choice of the term *noir*. It is sometimes seen as an allusion to the characteristically stark black and white photography, but has also been described as being modelled on *roman noir* – the standard French term for 'Gothic novel'. And it is surely no accident that the phrase was first used a year after the launch of Gallimard's *Série noire* ('black series') of detective novels and thrillers (there are now over 2,500 titles in the series).

The archetypal *film noir* hero is Philip Marlowe (Humphrey Bogart) in *The Big Sleep*, which is adapted from Raymond Chandler's novel of the same title (1939): cynical, hard-drinking, frequently assaulted by and unlucky with women, but still prepared to walk the mean streets of the corrupt city. Women tend to be portrayed in *film noir* as sexually predatory and dangerously attractive *femmes fatales* (the depiction of women is discussed in Kaplan 1980).

READING: Copjec (1993); Naremore (1998)

Firestone, Shulamith (1945–) Canadian-born American feminist writer. Her *Dialectic of Sex* (1971) is one of the founding texts of RADICAL FEMINISM.

Dismissing earlier feminists like FRIEDAN and their concern with legal inequalities such as employment discrimination as 'conservative', Firestone calls for a sexual revolution that will overthrow a male-run society that defines women as an inferior and parasitic class. The oppression and exploitation of women is biologically based;

Firestone contends that pregnancy and the dependency of small children have always worked to women's disadvantage and have allowed men to dominate them ever since the earliest human societies were formed. The existence of the sexual class system provides the model and prototype for every system of political and economic exploitation. The end-goal of feminist revolution is therefore not merely the elimination of male privilege, but the abolition of the sex distinction itself and the creation of a society in which genital differences will be of no cultural importance. It will begin with women's seizure of control over the means of reproduction. Firestone regards pregnancy as 'barbaric' and, with a very utopian faith in science and technology, looks forward to a future in which humans will reproduce by artificial means. Whilst many of Firestone's ideas, and especially that of a sex-class, were and are widely accepted by radical feminists, her vision of the technological future that will supposedly liberate women has always been very contentious.

Fish, Stanley (1938–) American literary critic. Originally a Milton specialist (1967), Fish is one of the leading representatives of a variety of READER-RESPONSE theory which he often describes as 'affective stylistics' (1980). He is highly critical of both conventional stylistic analysis, on the grounds that it merely strives to establish an inventory of fixed meanings, and of STRUCTURALISM, criticizing Lévi-Strauss and Jacobson's famous analysis of Baudelaire's poem '*Les Chats*' (1962) for its 'monumental aridity', and complains, not unreasonably, that the problem with PSYCHOANALYTIC CRITICISM is that it always reproduces the same text.

For Fish, the question 'What does this mean?' should be replaced by the question 'What does this poem or phrase *do*?' and literary analysis should focus on the logic of the reading experience. Meaning is not something that is extracted from the text, and does not exist in itself; it is an event that happens between the words and in the reader's mind, and the reader is an active mediating presence without whom there would be no text. Interpretation is the art of constructing, and not the art of construing. According to Fish, readers do not decode poems; they make them. Literature itself is the product of a community of agreement as to what counts as literature, and that agreement allows the members of the interpretive community to pay a certain attention and thus to create literature. Such communities are historically situated and historically variable. The communication that occurs between text and reader takes place within a situation, and the very existence of that situation implies that the members of an interpretive community are already in possession of the structures of understanding and practices deemed relevant to reading. Fish thus posits the existence of a literary competence analogous to the linguistic COMPETENCE described by CHOMSKY. Literary competence is not, however, innate. A competent or informed reader is one who is sufficiently experienced as to have internalized the properties of literary discourse, and who can therefore respond appropriately to texts that have never been encountered before.

In his 1993 Clarendon Lectures delivered in the University of Oxford (1995), Fish presents a witty defence of literary criticism as a professional discipline in its own right and attacks the idea of the POLITICALLY CORRECT in the name of 'professional correctness'. When specialists in cultural studies tell us to look elsewhere for the meaning of literary texts, Fish retorts that if we look elsewhere we shall see something else, in other words that we shall lose sight of literature. Whilst he does not deny the importance of the contribution made by gay, black or feminist critics, Fish argues that it is because gay, black and feminist politics are important outside the academy that they have established a role within it, and contends that no analysis of gender reversal in *Macbeth* will ever change anyone's views on the rights or wrongs of abortion. His advice to those academics who want to send a message that will be heard outside the academy is: 'Get out of it.' The study of literature has, according to Fish, no extra-literary purpose: 'Literary interpretation is, like virtue, its own reward.'

flâneur French noun best translated as 'stroller'. The figure of the *flâneur* has become one of the emblems of MODERNITY. In his essay 'The Painter of Modern Life' (1863), which is heavily influenced by Edgar Allan Poe's story 'The Man of the Crowd' (1840), the French poet and critic Charles Baudelaire describes the elegant *flâneur* as the ultimate consumer of the modern city who gathers fleeting but significant impressions as he strolls through the streets and arcades of the Paris that BENJAMIN describes as 'the capital of the nineteenth century' (1935, 1939a, 1939b). The figure of the *flâneur* is a common image in Impressionist painting and the literature of Naturalism (Herbert 1988). Although Baudelaire's painter of modern life was the GENRE artist Constantin Guys (1805–92), the most striking visual representation of the theme is Gustave Caillebotte's *Le Pont de l'Europe* (1876, Musée du Petit Palais, Geneva). It shows an elegantly dressed man in a top hat crossing the bridge by the Gare Saint-Lazare, and turning to glance at the woman he has just overtaken. The flicker of desire that seems to pass between them is a reminder that one of the attractions of the stroll was the possibility of an erotic encounter.

In the fragments of the *Passagen Werk* (Arcades project) that make up volume 7 of the collected works, Benjamin combines the figure of Baudelaire's stroller with motifs culled from the Parisian mythologies associated with the SURREALISM of Aragon and BRETON to produce one of the most haunting and influential images of early modernity (Cohen 1993). The mythological image of the *flâneur* is quite consciously appropriated by DEBORD and the theorists of SITUATIONISM as they elaborate their notion of *DÉRIVE* or 'locomotion without a goal'. It has often been observed by feminist critics that the *flâneur* is inevitably male and that certain of the pleasures of the urban culture he enjoys are not readily available to women (Wolff 1985; Pollock 1988; Wilson 1992). The woman in Caillebotte's painting is not *une flâneuse*, but she is clearly the object of the *flâneur*'s desire.

flow A term introduced by Raymond WILLIAMS in his innovatory study of television (1974), descriptive both of television programming and the experience of watching television. Whereas earlier cultural artefacts such as books were produced and consumed as discrete objects, television's typical mode of functioning is a planned temporal flow which includes both the advertised programmes and breaks such as adverts, announcements and trailers for future programmes. What is on offer is not so much the advertised programme-units as the overall continuous flow of sounds and images. Typically, rival channels or stations plan the flow by

broadcasting a popular programme such as an established soap opera at the beginning of the evening in the belief (for which there is some statistical evidence) that
viewers will go on to watch whatever follows. The ease with which one can speak
of the activity of 'watching television', as opposed to 'watching a programme', or
of 'an evening's viewing' indicates how deeply the notion of a flow is ingrained in
television culture. The introduction of MTV and of CNN's rolling news, in which
information is supplied on a continuous basis rather than in specific segments,
further highlights the importance of flow. British television's continuous or rolling
coverage of the funeral of Diana Princess of Wales on 6 September 1997 was a perfect
instance of television as flow.

Fordism/Postfordism The notion of Fordism, first identified as a distinctive
development within American capitalism by GRAMSCI in his notes on 'Americanism
and Fordism' in the *Prison Notebooks* (1971), was further elaborated by the French
'regulationist' theory of Marxist economics (Aglietta 1976; Lipietz 1987), which distinguishes between 'regimes of accumulation', or the modes in which capital is accumulated and profits maximized, and 'modes of regulation', or the institutional forms
that persuade economic agents to conform to the demands of those regimes. The
transition from Fordism to Postfordism is sometimes seen as the determining factor
in the move from MODERNITY to POSTMODERNITY (Harvey 1989).

Fordism develops out of the earlier stage of 'Taylorism', in which the application
of the principles of 'scientific management' breaks down the labour process into a
series of repetitive and unskilled tasks to be performed within limited periods of
time, destroys the traditional skills of craft workers and allows their knowledge to
be appropriated by a new class of managers and planners (Taylor 1914; Doray
1981). The principles of Taylorism were first applied in the slaughterhouses and
meat-packing plants of Chicago, but Fordism transposes them to the car plants of
Detroit. Henry Ford's great innovation was the moving assembly line which allowed
standard production models to be built as they moved through the factory.
Although Fordist production methods required a high level of capital investment,
they improved productivity levels to such an extent that it was possible to pay
relatively high wages, which allowed workers to purchase the very cars (the standard
Model-T Ford) they were building, and this promoted a new form of mass consumerism. High wages and the provision of social benefits had the further effect of
weakening trades unionism by producing the 'Fordman', who identified fully with
the factory, its products and its labour-intensive ethos. The classic description of
Fordism in action is Benyon's *Working for Ford* (1973).

Postfordism is the product of a number of factors ranging from the rise in oil prices
in the 1970s and inflation to the introduction of computerization and numerically
controlled machines. Advanced technology means that factories can be built
quickly, but also that production can be relocated in other countries if local political
conditions appear unfriendly. This decimates the Fordist work force, but also
requires more skilled workers organized into Japanese-style 'quality circles'. Whereas
the Fordist worker performed one strictly defined task, the Postfordist worker is
expected to be flexible, adaptable and mobile. Postfordism is further characterized

by a wide diversity of consumer choice, reflected in the postmodern image of a supermarket in which personal life-styles can be bought off the shelf and, for Harvey and others, in the characteristically fragmented experience of both space and time.

foreclosure The standard English translation of LACAN's *forclusion*, which is used to describe the psychical mechanism responsible for the triggering of PSYCHOSIS (Lacan 1957–8). The mechanism of foreclosure means that a primordial signifier such as the PHALLUS or the NAME-OF-THE-FATHER is expelled from the SYMBOLIC universe of the SUBJECT. Unlike a repressed signifier, a foreclosed signifier is not absorbed into the UNCONSCIOUS and therefore does not reappear in the psyche in the form of a neurotic symptom. It returns, rather, in the REAL, usually in the form of a persecutory hallucination.

foregrounding An important part of the conceptual terminology used in RUSSIAN FORMALISM and by the theorists associated with the PRAGUE SCHOOL. The concept of foregrounding derives from a phenomenological or Gestaltist description (GES-TALT) of visual perception: on perceiving an object, the viewer foregrounds certain elements and suppresses, or 'backgrounds', others. In terms of formalist POETICS (Mukarovsky 1932), foregrounding refers to the poem's drawing of the reader's attention to the artifices that give it *LITERATURNOST'* or 'literariness'. Repetition, parallelisms and foregrounded literary devices draw attention to the poetic function and defamiliarize the norms of language (see *OSTRANENIE*). In terms of Jakobson's diagrammatic representation of the CODE/MESSAGE model of communication (1956), foregrounding places the emphasis on the poetic function, whilst the referential or discursive function is undermined or backgrounded.

formalization The translation of a proposition or body of propositions into a more formal language, such as that of mathematics or symbolic logic, usually in order to clarify or explicate the information content, as in the MATHEME of LACAN. FREGE's concept script (*Begriffsschrift*), which was designed to 'break the power of the word over the human mind' (1879), is a classic example of formalization.

Fort-Da game The name of a game played by an eighteen-month-old boy, as observed by FREUD (1920a), has become an important theme in PSYCHOANALYSIS. Left alone in a bedroom by his mother, the boy repeatedly throws a wooden reel out of his cot and then retrieves it by means of the string attached to it. As he does so, he utters the sounds 'Oo' and 'Ah', which are interpreted by Freud as approximating to the words *fort* ('gone') and *da* ('there'). The game allows the child to control a physical object, and to achieve a symbolic mastery of the anxiety caused by his mother's absence. For Lacan (1953), the repeated 'Oo/Ah' represents differential PHONEMES and the game anticipates the use of a linguistic system based upon binary oppositions.

Foucault, Michel (1926–84) Although Foucault is often described as a French philosopher and historian, he himself provided a more accurate self-description when, on being elected to the Collège de France in 1970, he stated that he was a specialist in the history of systems of thought.

Foucault wrote on a wide variety of topics ranging from the history and philosophy of science to literature (1963b) – an aspect of his work that has rarely been studied in detail (see During 1992) – and the history of the prison system (1975). His work is resolutely interdisciplinary and therefore difficult to categorize in terms of the traditional divisions of knowledge, but certain constants do emerge despite the frequent changes of direction and the refusal to be defined that is encapsulated in the famous passage from the introduction to *The Archaeology of Knowledge* (1969a): 'Do not ask who I am and do not ask me to remain the same.' The question that is constantly being asked by Foucault himself is 'How have my objects of knowledge and the questions I address to them been produced?'

Insofar as he can be described as a historian, Foucault has much in common with both the historians of MENTALITIES associated with *ANNALES* and the historical epistemologists BACHELARD and CANGUILHEM. His first major work on the history of madness (*Folie et déraison*, 1961; the English translation of 1967 is brutally abridged; for a discussion of the effects of the abridgement see Gordon 1990) explores how madness is socially constructed by a wide variety of DISCOURSES that give rise to collective attitudes or mentalities defining insanity. Although the book has been criticized on the grounds that it is historically inaccurate (Stone 1982; Porter 1987), the basic thesis that, like the lepers of the Middle Ages, the mad are excluded in a gesture that helps to construct modern society and its image of reason did prove very attractive to the spokesmen for British ANTI-PSYCHIATRY and their counterparts in other countries. Canguilhem's influence on Foucault is most apparent in the latter's study of the origins of modern medicine (1963a), which demonstrates that the sciences of the past are not simply false constructs but coherent systems of concepts that define and determine which modes of thought are possible in a given historical period. Foucault's major works explore the question of why, in any given period, it is necessary to think in certain terms about madness, illness, sexuality or prisons. By implication, they therefore ask if it is possible to think about those topics in different ways.

In philosophical terms, Foucault works within the broad tradition established by NIETZSCHE, from whom he borrows the technique of GENEALOGY and the insight that the search for knowledge is also an expression of a will to power over other people. For Foucault, knowledge is always a form of power. Hence the ambiguity of new developments in psychiatry and mental-health care. They are presented as forms of liberation, but Foucault's critique of the REPRESSIVE HYPOTHESIS (1976a) demonstrates that they are also new technologies that categorize certain forms of social and sexual behaviour as deviant in order to control them. Like the confessor-priest, the psychoanalyst or psychiatrist who asks his patient to say what he desires is establishing a relationship of power and control. Similarly, the prison-reform movements of the post-Enlightenment period abolish legal torture and public executions, but they also establish a regime of PANOPTICISM in which Foucault sees power as not a matter of repression but of the constant surveillance of a population (1975). Foucault's thesis that power is not an 'object' that can be seized, held or lost, but a network of forces in which power always meets with resistance (1976a), can also be traced back to Nietzsche's *Will to Power* (1901).

Foucault's earliest writings reveal the influence of HEIDEGGER'S PHENOMENOLOGY

(Foucault and Binswanger 1954), but his rise to prominence is due to his perceived association with STRUCTURALISM. Published at the height of the structuralist boom, his *Les Mots et les choses* (1966; translated into English as *The Order of Things*) was commonly read as an exercise in structuralism, even though it makes little use of the Saussurean-derived linguistic model that underpins classical structuralism (SAUSSURE). The controversial themes of the DEATH OF THE AUTHOR (1969b) and the DEATH OF MAN (1966) are related to the anti-humanism of ALTHUSSER and others, but the crucial role played by the concepts of the EPISTEME and DISCURSIVE FORMATION (especially 1969a) indicates that Foucault's true concern is indeed with the formation and limitations of systems of thought.

Although Foucault's major works can seem abstract and even arcane and make few concessions to his readers, it is apparent from the materials collected in the four volumes of the posthumous *Dits et écrits* (Sayings and writings, 1994; a three-volume selection of 'essential works' has been made available in English, 1997–9) that they have surprisingly concrete and immediate implications. The author of the deeply pessimistic *Discipline and Punish* (1975), which suggests that the mechanisms of power are all-powerful, was also a political activist deeply involved in campaigns to publicize conditions in the French penal system. Foucault's greatest political virtue is that he never outlines programmes of reform, but constantly forces his reader to challenge everyday assumptions about the very nature of punishment, sexuality and mental health.

In his later works Foucault moves away from his earlier themes and, after a programmatic study of the history of sexuality (1976a), begins to write a history of the desiring subject and of the construction of personal and sexual identity by looking at the 'use of pleasure' (1984a) and the 'care of the self' (1984b) in both the Greek and Christian traditions. In these late studies the self is seen not as a personal essence, but rather as an aesthetic and ethical object to be created and cultivated, whilst pleasure is viewed as a disciplined form of self-government rather than an unbridled liberation of repressed desires. In his return to a version of the Stoic tradition, Foucault poses important and disturbing questions about sexuality: given that sexuality is not a matter of repressed essences, there can be no liberation of sexuality, and Foucault suggests that liberation *from* sexuality may be more import-ant than the unleashing of DESIRE. The theme of the care or government of the self merges with the broader theme of how human beings and their societies are gov-erned as Foucault returns to the ethical question of the relationship between self and society. The same concern for ethics appears in Foucault's defence of human rights and insistence that those who are governed must be freed from the will to power of those who govern them.

Whilst it would be a mistake to overestimate the influence of Foucault's homo-sexuality on his work (he laughed at the idea of being described as a 'gay philos-opher', as opposed to a philosopher who was gay), it is perhaps fitting that in the latest of his many incarnations, he has become an icon of QUEER theory (Halperin 1995).

READING: Bernauer (1990); During (1992); Macey (1993); Sheridan (1980)

foundationalism The philosophical thesis that knowledge is founded upon basic truths or insights that cannot be (or do not have to be) called into question and from which more general propositions can be inferred. Knowledge-claims can therefore be assessed by breaking them down so as to identify their ultimate foundations and assess their validity. Descartes provides a classic example of foundationalism when, in his *Discourse on the Method* (1637), he uses a process of methodical doubt to arrive at the indubitable *cogito* ('I am thinking; therefore I am') which provides the foundations for his philosophical system, and which is the basis for a 'first philosophy' (1641). In the post-Kantian tradition, it is often argued that philosophy itself is foundational in that, being grounded in reason, it can adjudicate and assess the validity of the claims to truth that go to make up a culture. All foundationalist arguments are vulnerable to the counterargument of infinite regress (Ryle 1949), which raises the question of what provides the foundations for the foundations. Critics of foundationalist EPISTEMOLOGY such as RORTY and VATTIMO query the need for a theory of knowledge and argue that HERMENEUTICS provides an alternative to the search for strong foundations or cast-iron epistemologies.

fragmented body The usual translation of LACAN's '*corps morcelé*', which can also be translated as 'body-in-pieces'. In his early paper on the MIRROR-PHASE (1949), Lacan refers to the IMAGO of the fragmented body, or images of castration and evisceration, which express the SUBJECT's feeling that the body lacks any substantial unity. The resultant anxiety stimulates the subject's identification with the complete image in the mirror, but the fragmented body always poses a threat to its unity. According to Lacan (1949), the imago of the fragmented body reappears when the analysis touches upon or provokes the aggressivity of the analysand, and its existence helps to explain hysterical symptoms such as paralysis of the limbs and the 'phantom limb' syndrome in which an amputee feels pain in a limb that has been removed. The image of the fragmented body does not derive from Freud. Lacan himself compares it to the hallucinatory imagery of Hieronymus Bosch; it has been suggested (Bowie 1991) that Lacan's imago is influenced by Hans Bellmer's photographs of a dismembered and rearranged doll (1936; reproduced in Chadwick 1985). They are inspired by the artist's sexual obsession with a young girl and appeared in a surrealist journal to which Lacan contributed. Bowie's suggestion is therefore highly plausible, and provides a reminder of Lacan's debt to SURREALISM.

francophonie Politically, the term is used to designate the loosely knit community of French-speaking nations around the world. Forty-nine countries were represented at the sixth Francophone Summit, held in Cotonou (Benin) in December 1995. This linguistically based community, which is in some ways analogous to the British Commonwealth, is an important vector for the dissemination of French culture or, as critics would put it, for the continued existence of French neocolonialism in Africa, the Caribbean and the Indian and Pacific Oceans. A 'Permanent Council of the Francophone Community' was established in 1992 in order to defend and promote the use of French. The journal *Notre Librairie* (Our Bookshop) covers the literature of *francophonie*, and is heavily subsidized by the Ministry for Cooperation and the Ministry of Foreign Affairs.

In cultural terms, francophone literature is generally understood as comprising the literature of the former colonies, France's overseas departments and territories, and French-speaking Canada; the literature of the francophone regions of Belgium and Switzerland is sometimes included in the same category. The distinction between French and francophone writing was not really made until after the Second World War, and the launch of *PRÉSENCE AFRICAINE* in 1947 and the publication of SENGHOR's anthology of Black and Malagasy poetry in 1948 are the first significant manifestations of literary *francophonie*. Francophone literature is rich and extremely varied, ranging from NEGRITUDE to the more recent CREOLENESS, but, although institutes for its study do exist in French universities, it does not have the same importance as the POSTCOLONIAL THEORY of the English-speaking world. Although French-speaking Canada has a highly developed publishing industry based in Québec and Montréal, most francophone literature is published in Paris. When, for instance, Algeria achieved independence in 1961 and established state publishing houses, most Algerian writers continued to publish in Paris as this gave them both greater freedom of expression and access to a wider audience. Whilst Rachid Boudjedra (1941–), widely regarded as one of Algeria's best novelists, began to write in popular Arabic rather than French in the 1980s, the dominance of French is perpetuated by events such as the annual Salon du Livre du Maghreb (Maghreb Book Fair), first held in Paris in 1994. A British-based *International Journal of Francophone Studies* began publication in 1997.

READING: Jack (1996); Judge (1996)

Frank, Manfred (1945–) German philosopher and literary theorist. Frank's work is grounded in the tradition of German Romanticism (1989) and of the HERMENEUTICS (Frank 1977) of Friedrich Schleiermacher (1768–1834). Frank has written extensively on Romantic philosophy, on the question of subjectivity in postmodern philosophy (1986) and on style in philosophy (1992a), and has produced important new editions of Schleiermacher's writings. Regrettably little of his work is available in English translation (1980, 1984, 1992b, 1997). Andrew Bowie's long introduction to the four essays translated as *The Subject and the Text* (1997) provides a good survey of Frank's main concerns; the same author's important *From Romanticism to Critical Theory* (1997) gives the best English-language account of the tradition in which Frank is working. Frank's criticisms of the DECONSTRUCTION of DERRIDA are all the more telling in that, unlike a number of critics, he is in many ways sympathetic to Derrida's project.

Frank's major concern is to reinstate the notion of the SUBJECT at the heart of philosophical and literary debates that have developed since the DEATH OF MAN and the DEATH OF THE AUTHOR was announced so loudly by FOUCAULT and BARTHES in the 1960s. This does not mean that he advocates a return to the 'Cartesian' subject of the *cogito* ('I am thinking, therefore I am'); on the contrary, Frank's concern with the status of the subject leads him to explore a philosophical tradition which has, he believes, been unjustly ignored – especially in France. He develops the Romantic conception which describes the subject as being never fully present to itself, but which also argues that it is not merely subject or subjected to the linguistic system into which it is inserted. Drawing on both this tradition and the structure of HERMENEUTICS, Frank argues that self-consciousness plays an active role in the understanding and use of language. Language does not simply impose 'its' meaning on subjects. At the level of spoken language, a system of signs functions only to the extent that a community of interpretation, or a hermeneutic community of individuals, has previously fixed the meaning of its use. Language-users are therefore by definition always involved in a hermeneutic exercise which is analogous to the creative acts of their interlocutors.

Frank further argues that a return to hermeneutics and a theory of active self-consciousness can be used to undermine the PARADIGM of the reflection theory of knowledge, which holds that knowledge mirrors nature (Rorty 1980) and which has dominated Western philosophy since Parmenides. Once the notion of truth-as-reflection is abandoned, all truth must be established in the actual processes of communication analysed by hermeneutics.

Drawing on the philosophy of Johann Gottlieb Fichte (1762–1814; see in particular Fichte 1794), Frank speaks of a 'self-positing subject' and refuses to describe the subject as a core of self-identical being that exists throughout a temporal continuum; the self-positing subject is born of the loss of the past and of the absence of the future. The present in which it exists is effectively a gap which it attempts to fill because it has a sense of the completion that would overcome it. This further undermines the reflective theory of knowledge and self-consciousness; the subject cannot recognize itself in a mirror without having a prior sense of what it is. The notion of a self-positing subject allows Frank to make a startling connection with the basic Sartrean thesis (SARTRE) that human beings are always what they are not, and that their mode of existence negates their being as they move towards a future project that can never be completed. Such sympathy for Sartre is highly unusual in contemporary philosophy, and when Frank describes *The Family Idiot* (Sartre 1971–2) as a masterpiece and favourably describes its thesis about the SINGULAR UNIVERSAL as a powerful and relevant contribution to Schleiermacher's notion yof 'the complete understanding of style', his comments help to point out just how badly Sartre has been neglected in recent French debates.

In the course of a long and densely detailed discussion of the debate between DERRIDA and SEARLE, Frank (1997) places Sartre within the Fichtean tradition, and effectively contends that Derrida simply overlooks it and concentrates instead on the more dominant tradition which defines individual subjectivity as a core of selfhood. Like Sartre, Frank argues that the contrary is true: the very nature of individual subjectivity is such that it has no essence precisely because it is born of a lack and because self-consciousness is constituted not by identity and self-presence, but by the absence or negation that complements it. Because Derrida's deconstructive work is fixated on the idea of the 'self-presence' of the subject and on the underlying principle of identity, it cannot take into account this alternative tradition.

Frankfurt School Collective term applied to the group of German philosophers, sociologists and economists associated with the Institut für Sozialforschung (Institute for Social Research) set up in Frankfurt am Main in 1923 and with the intellectual trend usually referred to as CRITICAL THEORY. The most important members of the Institut were ADORNO, HORKHEIMER and MARCUSE; BENJAMIN was always a more marginal figure. HABERMAS is the most important contemporary representative of the Frankfurt School.

The Institut was founded as an independently endowed research foundation within the University of Frankfurt. Its most productive period began in 1930, when Horkheimer was appointed Director. The Nazi Party's assumption of power in January 1933 forced the Institut, many of whose members were Jewish, into exile, first in Switzerland and then in the United States where, as the Institute for Social Research, it found a new home at Columbia University. In 1950 it was able to relocate in its native Germany; Adorno became Director in 1958. Good histories of the Frankfurt School are to be found in Jay (1973) and Held (1980).

The Frankfurt School was always Marxist in inspiration and had important links with the Moscow-based Marx-Engels Institute before the war, but its members were always critical of the institutionalized form of MARXISM known as DIALECTICAL MATERIALISM and of the suppression of the libertarian impulses within Marxism as it became a state IDEOLOGY in the Soviet Union. The institutionalization of Marxism, the rise of Fascism and the defeat of working-class movements in Germany led many of its members – particularly Marcuse and Adorno – to the conclusion that the proletariat could no longer be viewed as the agent of revolutionary change; that role now devolved upon the intellectuals or even upon Reason itself. The reliance on the rationalist tradition was tempered by the realization that Reason itself could be a source of oppression as well as liberation (typified by the idea of the DIALECTIC OF ENLIGHTENMENT), but has led to the accusation that the Frankfurt School simply perpetuates the German tradition of philosophical idealism (see, for example, Therborn 1970). Although critical theory was a major influence on the NEW LEFT, particularly in Germany, relations between the student radicals of the 1960s and the older generation were strained. In January 1969 the Institut's premises were occupied by student protesters; Adorno responded by calling the police and having them evicted (this incident is described in Leslie 1999; the article reproduces the relevant correspondence between Adorno and Marcuse). The Frankfurt School's attacks on the CULTURE INDUSTRY and distaste for popular culture have also resulted in the accusation that critical theory is a form of mandarin-elitism. The distaste for mass culture was no doubt heightened by the conviction, which is very marked in the work of Adorno, that the Frankfurt School's members were the defenders of an intellectual tradition grounded in both philosophical humanism and the literature and music of a high MODERNISM that was threatened both by Fascism and the mass culture encouraged by Hollywood and Tin Pan Alley. Of all the tendencies within WESTERN MARXISM, the critical theory of the Frankfurt School is the most austerely intellectual, and the most bleakly pessimistic.

In his inaugural address to the Institut, Horkheimer spoke (1931) of the need for an integration of disciplines such as philosophy, sociology, economics and history that could promote the development of a broad social philosophy (critical theory) capable of combining the study of individuals with that of society in such a way as to explore the contradictions and interconnections making possible the reproduction and transformation of society, culture, the economy and consciousness. Although a highly intellectualized Marxism provided the theoretical basis for the project, PSYCHOANALYSIS soon became an integral part of critical theory, thanks largely to the influence of FROMM and REICH's notion of character analysis. The work published in the journal *Zeitschrift für Sozialforschung* (Journal of Social Research; eight volumes published between 1922 and 1939, and superseded by *Studies in Philosophy and Social Science* from 1939 to 1941) combined theoretical approaches with empirical studies to great effect and foreshadowed the collective work undertaken in exile. The most sustained piece of collective work was *The Authoritarian Personality* (Adorno et al. 1950), which was originally intended to be part of a series of *Studies in Prejudice*. Rejecting the crude Marxist stress on the role of the economics of capitalism in the development of Fascism, the study used the statistical analysis of questionnaires to analyse the susceptibility of individuals to anti-democratic propaganda and to rigid, dogmatic and prejudiced thinking. Drawing on both a psychoanalytic theory of character and sociological analysis, the researchers elaborated the notion of a so-called 'F-scale' that could measure 'implicit prefascist tendencies' in individuals with an authoritarian personality characterized by adherence to conventional values, submission to peer-group moral authorities, aggression, a tendency to stereotypical thinking, and the projection of unconscious fantasies of destructiveness onto scapegoats. This personality, argued Adorno and his colleagues, was likely to be found in the middle classes of Europe. The effect of such studies was to make authoritarianism, and even Fascism, a psychological rather than a political phenomenon, but they also reflect the deep belief that the philosophical self-awareness and self-reflection promoted by critical theory was the best, if not the only, antidote to authoritarianism.

READING: Bronner and Kellner (1989)

free association An essential feature of the technique of PSYCHOANALYSIS, gradually developed by FREUD between 1892 and 1898. Curiously enough, no one paper by Freud is devoted in its entirety to describing the technique; its origins are described in 'On the History of the Psychoanalytic Movement' (1914d), and 'Two Encyclopedia Articles' (1922c) describe the technique itself.

The rule of free association states that a patient in analysis (or analysand) must verbally express whatever comes into his or her mind during the session, telling all and omitting nothing. A corresponding rule requires the analyst to listen to all the verbal associations made by the patient, giving no particular importance to anything but paying attention to everything. The analyst must listen with 'evenly suspended or poised attention' (Freud 1912b). The function of both rules is to prevent the conscious mind from censoring or blocking the process of interpretation.

Free Cinema The overall title of six programmes of film screenings at London's National Film Theatre between 1956 and 1959. The films shown included work by

French *NOUVELLE VAGUE* directors, Roman Polanski's *Two Men and a Wardrobe* and Lindsay Anderson's *Every Day Except Christmas* (a documentary about Covent Garden market), Karel Reisz's *We Are the Lambeth Boys*, and the collectively made *March to Aldermaston*, produced for the Campaign for Nuclear Disarmament in 1958. The programme notes, written mainly by Anderson, criticized British cinema for its failure to reflect anything but a metropolitan Southern English culture which excluded the rich diversity of the rest of Britain, and called for a cinema that could make ordinary people feel and celebrate their importance and dignity. Although Anderson subsequently argued that Free Cinema was a failure because it did not attract the support of the younger generation, it was the breeding ground for the most important directors of the period and ushered in a dynamic age in British cinema. The most distinguished films to emerge from Free Cinema were *Saturday Night and Sunday Morning* (1960, adapted from Alan Sillitoe's novel of 1958 by Karel Reisz), Tony Richardson's *Look Back in Anger* (1959, from John Osborne's play of 1956) and Anderson's own *This Sporting Life* (1963, adapted from David Storey's novel of 1960). Albert Finney's words at the end of the pre-credit sequence of *Saturday Night and Sunday Morning* sum up the revolt against a certain 'metropolitan Southern English culture' as effectively as John Osborne's ANGRY YOUNG MAN: 'What I'm out for is a good time. All the rest is propaganda.'

READING: Hewison (1988); Sussex (1969)

free indirect style A mode of narration in which subjective thoughts and feelings are expressed in the third person in such a way that it is impossible to tell if it is the character or the narrator who is speaking or thinking. The great master of free indirect style is commonly recognized to be the French novelist Gustave Flaubert (1821–80). When Flaubert went on trial for offences against public and religious morality in January 1857, the prosecutor himself complained that the use of the style in *Madame Bovary* was so effective that there was no vantage-point within the novel from which Emma Bovary could be considered (Lacapra 1989). A passage from part II, chapter 9 illustrates the transition from third-person narration to free indirect style: ' "I've a lover", she said . . . At last she would know the delights of love, the feverish joys of which she had despaired. She was entering a marvellous world where all was passion, ecstasy, delirium.'

Frege, Gottlob (1848–1925) German philosopher and mathematician. Although he was little read in his own lifetime, Frege is now regarded as one of the founders of modern logic and as a crucial influence on ANALYTIC PHILOSOPHY, thanks mainly to the way in which his ideas were refracted through Russell and Whitehead's *Principia Mathematica* of 1910. Frege's major studies in mathematics, which endeavour to prove that the principles of arithmetic can be derived from pure logical axioms (this thesis is known as 'logicism'), are *The Basic Laws of Arithmetic* (1884) and the two-volume *Foundations of Arithmetic* (1893, 1903), which has never been translated into English in its entirety. These are difficult works written for specialists in mathematics and logic; for most readers, Geach and Black's abridged *Translations from the Philosophical Writings of Gottlob Frege* (1952) will serve as an adequate introduction to Frege.

For linguistic or analytic philosophers, the most attractive feature of Frege's thought is the idea of the 'concept script' (*Begriffsschrift*), first introduced in a short pamphlet (1879) which some regard as the most important contribution to logic to have been made since Aristotle. The concept script is described as a formalized language of pure thought, and the object of this exercise in FORMALIZATION is to leave no scope for conjecture as to the nature or truth-value (true/false) of a proposition, and to 'break the power of the word over the human mind'. The concept script is designed to rid propositions of the confusions introduced by the relationship between subject and predicate, or active and passive verbs. The Battle of Hastings can be summarily described in one of two sentences: 'William defeated Harold' and 'Harold was defeated by William.' The differences between the two sentences may be pertinent in linguistic terms, but it does not affect what follows from them: the conceptual content is the same. In later papers (1892a and 1892b are the most important), Frege introduces the distinction between 'sense' (*Sinn*) and 'reference' (*Bedeutung*) in order to clarify the ambiguity inherent in the fact that the planet Venus can be described both as 'the evening star' and 'the morning star'; the *meaning* of 'evening star' is the same as that of 'morning star', but not the *reference*.

The original *Begriffsschrift* used a combination of Roman, Greek and Gothic letters, with the addition of a variety of strokes to symbolize judgement, predication, conditionals and so on. Because it was so difficult to print, it is no longer used in logic and has been replaced by other systems of notation, but its influence has been immense.

Although Frege's main influence has been on analytic philosophy, he has also affected the course of CONTINENTAL PHILOSOPHY. His critical review of HUSSERL's *Philosophy of Arithmetic* (1891), extracts from which appear in the *Translations*, was one of the factors that led Husserl to abandon his early 'psychologism', which held that arithmetic was grounded in 'mental acts', in favour of the Fregean view that numbers are conceptual and mind-independent objects.

READING: Baker and Hacker (1984); Kenny (1995)

Freud, Anna (1895–1982) Viennese-born British psychoanalyst, youngest daughter of Sigmund FREUD and founder, in 1947, of the Hampstead Child Therapy Clinic. Her *Selected Writings* (1998) provide a comprehensive introduction to her work.

Anna Freud is one of the pioneers of child psychoanalysis and of the psychoanalytic study of normal child development. Firmly grounded in Freud's second TOPOGRAPHY of ID, EGO and SUPEREGO, her work is one of the starting-points for the development of EGO-PSYCHOLOGY. Her main contribution to psychoanalytic theory is her description of the defence mechanisms used by the ego in its attempt to avoid anxiety, danger and unpleasure (1937). According to Anna Freud, the supergo originates in the mechanism of identification with the aggressor, as the child mimics and then identifies with the aggressive criticisms of its parents in such a way as to allow the ego to perceive its own faults. Anna Freud's description of the mechanism of altruistic surrender, in which an individual defends the ego by dedicating his or her life to others, and living through others rather than having independent experiences, is often assumed to be based on a rather rueful self-portrait.

Anna Freud's theory of child development (1966) is based upon the view that there is a normal sequence of libidinal phases (oral, anal and genital) and that a child who is going to be a harmonious personality should, at each stage of libidinal development, reach a corresponding stage of emotional maturity, physical independence, companionship and creative play. Unlike KLEIN's purely therapeutic play technique, Freudian child analysis always has an educational aim.

In 1943-4, the respective supporters of Anna Freud and Melanie Klein became embroiled in the so-called 'Controversial Discussions' which almost split the British Psychoanalytic Association and led to its recognition of three coexisting groups (Freudians, Kleinians and 'Independents'). The discussions focused on differences over play therapy, the chronology of the onset of the OEDIPUS COMPLEX and of superego formation, and the role of fantasy, with the Kleinians arguing that unconscious fantasies are dominant in the first years of life, and with Anna Freud insisting that environmental and mental factors are of equal importance. Although the points of disagreement may appear to be arcane, the central issue was in fact the question of just who was Freud's legitimate heir.

READING: Young-Bruehl (1988)

Freud, Sigmund (1856-1939) The founder of PSYCHOANALYSIS was born in Moravia but his family moved to Vienna in 1860, and that city was his home until 1938 when the *Anschluss*, the incorporation of Austria into the Nazi Reich, obliged him to make a reluctant departure for London. Although it is not strictly true to say that Freud 'discovered' the UNCONSCIOUS, as the idea that part of the mind is non-conscious or escapes the control of conscious thought has a long history in both philosophy and psychology (Ellenberger 1970), the influence of Freud's theory on twentieth-century thought has been enormous. Thanks in part to the 'return to Freud' advocated by LACAN, psychoanalytic theory has become an integral element in the modern HUMAN SCIENCES.

An ambitious student, Freud graduated as a doctor of medicine in 1881, and his early research and publications dealt with anatomy and physiology. In 1885-6, a modest bursary from his medical faculty allowed him to spend six months in Paris, where he studied at the Salpêtrière hospital under Jean-Martin Charcot (1825-93), widely regarded as the greatest neurologist of his day and sometimes described as the 'Napoleon of neuroses'. Charcot had established that HYSTERIA is a genuine disease and not merely a form of malingering; he had also demonstrated that, traditional views to the contrary notwithstanding, hysteria can affect men and women alike. Like many others, Freud was spellbound by Charcot's ability to use hypnosis to reproduce in his patients the physical symptoms of hysteria. On his return to Vienna, Freud set up in private practice as a specialist in nervous diseases. The rest of his career is synonymous with the history of psychoanalysis.

Freud's early career established what was to become a characteristic pattern of close collaboration with a male colleague or interlocutor, followed by a period of estrangement and then a hostile rejection of his former associate. The most famous instance of this is the story of the friendship and break with JUNG, as chronicled in their correspondence (Freud and Jung 1974). Splits and schisms originating in disagreements in which personal and theoretical differences are often inextricably linked are a recurrent feature of the history of psychoanalysis.

The origins of psychoanalysis lie in Freud's search for an aetiology or causal explanation for hysteria, and can be traced in his lengthy correspondence with Wilhelm Fliess (Freud 1985), an ear, nose and throat specialist with whom he was in frequent contact between 1887 and 1904. The initial explanation, further refined in collaboration with Joseph Breuer (Freud 1896; Freud and Breuer 1903–05), was that the origins of hysteria are sexual in nature and that hysterical symptoms are a somatic reproduction of the repressed memory of a traumatic sexual event. Repressed in childhood, the memory is reactivated, with traumatic effects, at puberty. Freud habitually describes the traumatic effect as 'seduction'; this is a euphemism for sexual abuse, rape or some other brutal encounter with an adult sexuality that the child does not understand. In this initial scenario, the child is the passive victim of an active adult, and the discovery of an active infantile sexuality is one of the factors that led Freud to abandon his early theory. Although he originally believed that all hysterics had suffered a traumatic seduction (1896), by 1897 Freud was forced to conclude in a letter to Fliess that his theory implied an improbably high incidence of incest and child abuse. His so-called abandonment of the SEDUCTION THEORY continues to cause controversy (Masson 1984), particularly in the light of revelations of the extent of the sexual abuse of children and in view of the controversies surrounding FALSE MEMORY SYNDROME and RECOVERED MEMORY treatment (Crews et al. 1997). It should, however, be recalled that Freud never denies that the sexual abuse of children does occur (1938).

Freud's mature theory of hysteria and NEUROSIS develops gradually and in tandem with the elaboration of the theory of stages of sexual development known as the LIBIDO theory, and culminates in the discovery of the OEDIPUS COMPLEX. A first TOPOGRAPHY of the psyche or mind is developed in the period 1900–15, as Freud explores the way in which the workings of the unconscious are revealed by dreams (1900), PARAPRAXES (1901) and jokes (1905b). His writings of this period are in part a product of the long and difficult process of his own self-analysis, which he never describes in any detail even though *The Interpretation of Dreams* (1900) abounds in autobiographical details (see Anzieu 1975). A second or 'structural' topography is developed from the 1920s onwards, and introduces the tripartite model of ID, EGO and SUPEREGO and the mature theory of DRIVES. After the introduction of the concept of a DEATH-DRIVE (1920a), the structure of Freud's theory of psychoanalysis remains largely unchanged.

Freud's last years were devoted mainly to the study of art and the origins of civilization and religion (1930, 1939). His writings on literature (e.g. 1927a) and culture provide the basis for the various schools of PSYCHOANALYTIC CRITICISM. Wide-ranging and, as he himself admits, highly speculative, Freud's writings on civilization and religion are deeply pessimistic and take the view that the achievements of culture are grounded in the repression or SUBLIMATION of instinctual and sexual drives that constantly threaten to undermine them. They are also marked by comments on 'primitive' religions and societies that reveal his evolutionary theory to be a classic expression of EUROCENTRISM.

Freud's work remains controversial. Although it is claimed by Lacan and others that psychoanalysis is a science of the unconscious, critics such as POPPER point out that Freud continually looks for confirmation of his theories and does not use the criterion of FALSIFIABILITY to test them. The Freudian theory of sexuality has been enormously influential but it too remains controversial for those feminists who, from MILLETT to IRIGARAY, argue that Freud, who viewed female sexuality as an unknown and unknowable 'dark continent' (1926a; see also 1931a and the chapter on femininity in 1933), always takes the boy as his developmental model and does not provide a comparable model for girls. The relationship between PSYCHOANALY-SIS AND FEMINISM is therefore a fraught one. In more general terms, it can be argued that Freud provides a liberating vision of sexuality in that he broadens its definition and refuses to restrict the word to meaning only genital or reproductive activity. Freud also demonstrates that, just as attenuated forms of neurotic behaviour are commonplace in 'normal' life, sexual perversions are not aberrations or indications of an inherent depravity, but part of the broad continuum of human sexual behaviour.

READING: Gay (1988); Laplanche and Pontalis (1967); Schur (1972)

Friedan, Betty (1921–) American feminist and cofounder, in 1966, of the National Organization of Women. She served as NOW's President until 1970.

Friedan's *The Feminine Mystique* (1963) is one of the founding texts of modern FEMINISM. The 'mystique' of the title is the creation of the sociologists, advertisers, neo-Freudian psychoanalysts and psychologists who convinced a postwar genera-tion of American women that the acceptance of their femininity would be a source of personal fulfilment, and that it implied an acceptance of sexual passivity and male domination, and a personal commitment to the provision of nurturing maternal love. It offered women a choice between being a woman or risking the pain of human growth. Friedan was one of the first to diagnose what she calls 'the problem with no name' or the 'housewife's syndrome': the vague and undefined wish for something more than a prosperous suburban domesticity. For Friedan, the solution lay in the education and professional training of women.

Although it is rightly seen as a classic of feminism, *The Feminine Mystique* has much in common with less GENDER-specific critiques of the American society of the 1950s and early 1960s, and especially with the 'lonely crowd' thesis that a salary was no longer an adequate source of identity, and that creative work that contributed to a wider human community was more likely to promote individual growth (Riesman et al. 1950).

Representatives of RADICAL FEMINISM such as FIRESTONE have always been critical of what they see as Friedan and NOW's conservatism, and Friedan has often been equally critical of their 'extremism'. Her *The Second Stage* (1981), which stresses the importance of the family circle and 'women's' sphere and recommends that women should abandon the campaign for equal rights in favour of personal involvement in the voluntary sector, has been described (Faludi 1991) as making a major contribution to the 1980s backlash against feminism.

READING: Horowitz (1998)

Fromm, Erich (1900–80) German-American theorist of a post-Freudian analytical social psychology.

As a member of the FRANKFURT SCHOOL in prewar Germany, Fromm was influential in making PSYCHOANALYSIS an important reference for the school's CRITICAL THEORY but rapidly distanced himself from Freud by challenging the central role ascribed to sexuality by the latter's LIBIDO theory and arguing, like JUNG, that it should be replaced by a more general and desexualized theory of psychic energy. In a series of popular works published after his departure for the United States (1941, 1956, 1963), Fromm outlines a theory of social psychology that combines elements of psychoanalysis with a quasi-Marxist theory of ALIENATION. His concept of the social unconscious allows various character traits (including the authoritarian personality and the marketing orientation) to be seen as resulting from the adaptation of the unconscious instinctual apparatus to specific socioeconomic situations. In his later works in particular, Fromm's description of the search for human happiness moves from a classic theory of alienation to a vaguely defined humanism that can accommodate theories as disparate as Zen Buddhism and the thesis that the hypothetical matriarchy that is sometimes held to have existed before the emergence of PATRIARCHY can provide the model for a caring society based upon human solidarity. *The Erich Fromm Reader* (1985) provides a clear and useful introduction to his work.

Frye, Herman Northrop (1912–91) Canadian literary theorist. A prolific and erudite scholar, Frye was originally a Blake specialist (1947) but also wrote significant studies of Shakespeare (1965a, 1967), Milton (1965b) and the Bible (1982). He is best known for the theory of literary archetypes elaborated in his monumental *Anatomy of Criticism* (1957), which makes a major contribution to the theory of GENRE. Frye has also written eloquently on the liberal humanist tradition in education (particularly in 1970 and 1971), arguing that the study of literature is the central component in the humanities. Frye's importance in the United States is difficult to overestimate. In 1965 the English Institute devoted a full session to his work (proceedings published as Krieger 1966), and Denham's *Enumerative Bibliography* (1974) catalogues the extraordinary number of articles and reviews that have been devoted to his work.

In the 'polemical introduction' to the *Anatomy*, Frye argues the case for examining literature in terms of a conceptual framework that can be derived from the inductive study of the entire literary field. By following what is later termed 'the critical path' (1971) the scholar should be able to arrive at a theory that can simultaneously account for the phenomena of literary experience and situate the role of literature within civilization as a whole. Unlike the literary critic, the scholar is not concerned with passing value-judgements on individual works, but with organizing our knowledge of past cultures. Nor does the scholar evaluate the past in terms of the present in terms of a temporal scale of values. Frye remarks (1971) that there are no dead ideas in literature; there are only tired readers. When released from the obligations of evaluative criticism, the serious critic is tolerant of the whole of literary culture and finds it impossible to express preferences for any one kind of poem.

For Frye, literature is an autonomous verbal structure in which words are used for their own sake, and in which their individual values and meanings are subordinate to a structure of interconnected motifs. Literary structures are not shaped by external forces. Frye often uses musical analogies to illustrate his argument, and contends that a literary form such as tragedy can no more exist outside literature than the sonata form can exist outside music. On the basis of perceived analogies of form across a vast range of literary material, Frye posits the existence of broad categories that are broader than or logically prior to genres, as understood in the conventional sense, and suggests that they should be studied by applying the methods pioneered by JUNG and Frazer (*The Golden Bough*, 1890–1915) in their studies of the folk-tales, ballads and rituals of oral cultures. Such broad categories are described as generic plots or *mythoi* (*mythos* is Aristotle's once-used term for 'plot' or 'narrative') and are said to be archetypal, though in later essays Frye uses the expression 'containing form' in preference to 'ARCHETYPE'. Four archetypal *mythoi* are identified: romantic, tragic, comic and ironic or realistic. The four correspond to the cycle of the seasons, comedy being equated with spring, ROMANCE with summer or the idealized world of wish-fulfilment, tragedy with autumn, and winter with IRONY and satire. Each has a typical plot, examples of which can be found in countless individual works. The archetypal plot of comedy-spring, for example, involves a young man whose desire for a young woman is frustrated, usually by her father, but who finally triumphs thanks to the resolution of the comic plot. Examples of the romance of summer, which involves a perilous journey, a struggle between hero and foe and the final triumph of the hero, and which takes place in an idealized world of beautiful heroines and wicked villains, range from the story of St George to the chivalric romances of the Middle Ages to the revolutionary romances of Soviet Russia.

Within this archetypal classification, Frye establishes five modes of fiction, each defined by the relationship between the hero and other men or the environment: a hero who is superior in kind to other men is the divine hero of a myth; the hero who is superior in degree is the hero of a romance who performs marvellous actions but remains human. In the high mimetic mode typified by epic and tragedy, the hero is a leader who is superior to other men, but not the environment, whilst the hero of the low mimetic mode (which includes most comedy and realist fiction) is superior to neither other men nor the environment. The hero who is inferior in power or intelligence belongs, finally, to the ironic mode. The main genres of literature are then categorized as drama, epic and lyric. In the final essay of the *Anatomy*, entitled 'Theory of Genres' (GENRE), the classifications and subclassifications proliferate to such an extent that one critic (Todorov 1970) is reminded of the lexicographers and dialectologists of the nineteenth century who scoured villages in search of rare or precious words.

Frye's vision of the central role of literary studies within the humanities is grounded in a classic liberal humanism, and it is significant that he was an ordained minister of the United Church. The role of learning, and particularly literary learning, is to fertilize life by promoting forms of scholarship that flow into a systematic development of taste and understanding. The humanities in general are viewed as expressing in the myths they recycle the very nature of human involvement with the human world.

READING: Denham 1978

Fukuyama, Francis (1950–) Originally a political analyst working for the RAND Corporation and specializing in the study of 'socialist-oriented states', Fukuyama first came to public notice when he published a short article tentatively entitled 'The End of History?' in *The National Interest* (1989). This was then expanded to form the bestselling *The End of History and the Last Man* (1992).

Fukuyama studied with Allan BLOOM and, like his teacher, is heavily influenced by Nietzsche and KOJÈVE's reading of Hegel: the title of his book alludes both to Kojève's thesis that history has come to an end, and to the description of the contemptible last man who 'makes everything small' in the prologue to Nietzsche's *Thus Spoke Zarathustra* (1892). In this context, 'history' is not synonymous with the sequence of mundane events that is still going on – these are mere skirmishes. Fukuyama reverts to the theory of Universal History associated with the Hegelian tradition: history is a single evolutionary process that takes into account the whole experience of all peoples in all times. The end of history is signalled by the emerging consensus that the American model of liberal democracy is the most desirable form of government, and that it has finally overcome the challenges of Fascism and communism. Liberal democracy can thus be regarded as the final form of human government, and we are living in 'the old age of mankind'. The end of history implies that the struggle for prestige characteristic of Kojève's master–slave dialectic is over, and is giving way to a desire to be recognized as equal. Liberal democracy's central dilemma focuses on the need to reconcile the wish for comfortable self-preservation characteristic of 'last men' who have reverted to an almost animal complacency, with the possibility that new battles for prestige will begin and that weapons of mass destruction will be used to wage them.

Fukuyama's later work is much more eclectic than *The End of History*, but combines economic and sociological arguments to make equally grandiose claims. His *Trust* (1996) pursues the end of history argument, but contends that the ideal society is one with a weak central state and a powerful CIVIL SOCIETY that can limit the effects of excessive individualism by establishing relations of trust and mutual dependence. *The End of Order* (1997) describes modern society as belonging to an age of Great Disruption brought about by the collapse of the nuclear family. The availability of contraception and the mass entry of women into the labour market has destroyed the prestige that once marked the status of men and removed the sense of obligation that bound them to the family. Fukuyama concludes that a reversal of this process and the restoration of male prestige and privilege would help to promote the nuclear family.

READING: Halliday (1992); McCarney (1993)

functionalism The term is used in slightly different but related senses in linguistics, sociology and architecture; the common semantic core is the stress on what words, societies and buildings do and how they function.

The linguistic STRUCTURALISM of the PRAGUE SCHOOL is described as 'functionalist' because it stresses that the nature of linguistic phenomena cannot be understood without regard to the functions they fulfil within the system to which they belong. Verbal communication has both a communicative function, which stresses the message that is being communicated, and a poetic function which stresses the form of the message at the expense of its REFERENT. The analysis of PHONEMES undertaken by JAKOBSON and by Trubetzkoy (1939) is functionalist in that it identifies these linguistic units on the basis of the functional differences that distinguish them from other units. The French linguist André Martinet describes this form of analysis as 'functional' or 'oppositional': phonemes function as linguistic units because they allow signs to be identified as different from all other signs (Martinet 1960).

In sociology, functionalism is associated mainly with the American Talcott Parsons (1902–79), who in a series of books (1937, 1951, 1971) outlines a very general theory designed to explain both individual behaviour and macrosocial processes. Any society is a system consisting of an integrated set of subsystems which strive to maintain themselves in a state of homeostasis or stability. All forms of behaviour and social action are said to be either functional or dysfunctional, depending on whether they serve or disrupt the needs of the system. The goal of the system itself is the functional integration of subsystems such as the family into a rationally ordered whole. Although immensely influential, Parsons' theory has often been criticized on the grounds that its stress on integration and stability is a conservative reaction to social change.

In architecture, functionalism is one of the basic characteristics of the MODERNISM of the INTERNATIONAL STYLE, which emphasizes the practical function of buildings rather than their aesthetic appeal. Form is thus subordinated to function. The classic expression of architectural functionalism is Le Courbusier's dictum that a house is a machine for living in, which implies that fitness for use is the sole criterion by which the value of a building can be judged.

fundamentalism Strict adherence to traditional or orthodox religious beliefs or, by extension, a dogmatic belief in an unchanging political or other credo. The term derives from the Protestant theological tradition, where it refers to an unalterable belief in the literal truth of Scripture and the Creeds. The equivalent French term *intégrisme* describes the doctrines of Archbishop Marcel Lefebvre and others who rejected, and still reject, the reforms instituted by the Second Vatican Council of 1962–5. Since the Iranian Revolution of 1979, which sought to establish a theocratic regime based upon Islamic law (*sharia*), it has become commonplace to speak of 'Islamic fundamentalism' or *intégrisme islamique*, rather as though Islamic theology and history were simply variants on the Western model. The closest Arabic equivalent is *saalfiyya* (which can be rendered as 'salafism'), which is a generic term implying a call for a return to the values of the Koran and for following the example of pious epigones (*salaf*).

READING: Al-Azmeh (1993)

futurism AVANT-GARDE poetic and artistic movement launched by the Italian poet F. T. MARINETTI in a series of violent manifestos (in Marinetti 1971), beginning with the 'Initial Manifesto' of 20 February 1909: 'We declare that the world's splendour has been enriched by a new beauty: the beauty of speed . . . A roaring motor car . . . is more beautiful than the Victory of Samothrace.' Futurism is in part a reaction against the weight of Italy's cultural past; Marinetti likened his country to an immense Pompei whitened with sculptures, and his followers wanted to fill in Venice's canals and to dredge and widen the Grand Canal in order to turn it into a vast commercial port. Futurist art and poetry are celebrations of speed, violence, war and the impersonal beauty of machines. Drawing on the techniques of cubism, the artists Umberto Boccioni (1882–1916), Carlo Carrà (1881–1966) and Giacomo Balla (1871–1958) all depicted movement by using simultaneous images of its successive phases, Boccioni's *Charge of the Lancers* (1915, reproduced in *Futurism 1909–1919*), with its strong diagonals, being a particularly good example. Although it has something in common with DADA, futurism was primarily an Italian phenomenon. The closest British equivalent is Vorticism, which is said to have taken its name from Boccioni's slogan to the effect that artistic creation results from a vortex of emotion (*Vorticism and its Allies*). Intensely nationalistic, the futurists were enthusiastic in their support for Italy's invasion of Libya in 1911 and are often seen as having helped to create the climate that gave birth to Fascism. The movement was short-lived, and futurism was a spent force by the end of the First World War.

Russian futurism was partly inspired by the Italian original but developed along rather different lines. The manifesto 'A Slap in the Face of Public Taste', written by Vladimir Mayakovsky and others in 1912, captures the provocative tone and a further manifesto of the following year, 'The Word as Such', speaks of the need to throw Pushkin, Dostoyevsky and Tolstoy overboard from the steamship of history. Rejecting with contempt the allusive tone of symbolist poetry, the Russian futurists sought to liberate the word from the weight of tradition, and to liberate the text from its old functions. Emphasizing both the phonic element in poetry and the visual power of experimental typography, Russian futurism stresses the value of the 'self-sufficient word'. The emphasis on the physical presence of the word is one of the sources of what RUSSIAN FORMALISM would call FOREGROUNDING. JAKOBSON'S early essays 'The Newest Russian Poetry' (1914) and 'Futurism' (1919) are important pointers to the links between futurism and formalism. Russian futurism is essentially a prerevolutionary phenomenon, but Mayakovsky and his fellows also devoted their considerable energies to defending the October Revolution through various forms of AGITPROP. The exhibition of his own work organized by Mayakovsky a year before he committed suicide in 1930 (and recreated as *Mayakovsky: Twenty Years of Work* in 1982) was an eloquent testimony to both the futurist heritage and the vibrancy of Soviet art before the rise of SOCIALIST REALISM.

READING: Erlich (1965); Hyde (1976); Markov (1969); Rawson (1976)

G

Gadamer, Hans-Georg (1900–) German philosopher, and the foremost contemporary exponent of HERMENEUTICS. Gadamer's reputation in Germany is long-established but he remained little known in the English-speaking world until his masterwork *Wahrheit und Methode* (1960) appeared in translation (*Truth and Method*, 1975; the revised translation of 1998 should be used in preference to the earlier version). Later collections of shorter essays (1976, 1981) provide a clear introduction to Gadamer's main themes. Gadamer is an extraordinarily lucid writer and, although this is obviously not its primary purpose, *Truth and Method* supplies a remarkable introduction to the history and technical vocabulary of modern German thought.

Written under the direction of HEIDEGGER, the *Habilitation* thesis on Plato's dialectical ethics (republished in a revised edition 1968), which qualified Gadamer to begin his academic career at the universities of Marburg and then Leipzig, introduces some characteristic themes by establishing dialogue as the primary mode of arriving at truth and agreement. The Socratic dialogue provides, that is, the model for the DIALECTIC that establishes truth through argument and conviction. More significantly, Gadamer argues here that theory 'precedes' facts in the sense that 'facts' cannot exist in the absence of the theoretical framework that allows them to be recognized as facts, and that theoretical frameworks are constructed through language. This argument can be seen as an early version of the thesis that understanding (*Verstehen*) is always a product of a preunderstanding or prejudice, defined in the sense of prejudgement about the nature of the object under investigation.

Like Heidegger, Gadamer regards language as the 'house of being' (Heidegger 1959) and the form in which understanding is achieved; language is both the fundamental mode of being-in-the-world and the all-embracing form that constitutes our world (1966a). Learning to speak does not mean learning to use a tool or to acquire the ability to designate objects that exist outside it; it means coming to terms with the medium through which we exist and perceive a world that has already been interpreted by a language and a tradition that establish a 'horizon' of knowledge. Growing up in the world means growing up in a world of language (1966b). Gadamer departs from the ENLIGHTENMENT tradition by arguing that prejudice is not something that can be dispelled by the progress of science. Prejudice, or a pregiven orientation towards the world, is the source of the questions that clarify our understanding of that world, defined as the LIFEWORLD of HUSSERL and the phenomenological tradition. Given that prejudice cannot be eradicated, because human existence or DASEIN is always/already historically situated, it follows that there can be no prior truth, 'first philosophy' or METAPHYSICS that establishes the certainty of knowledge; there is only the constant work of interpretation. Meaning is not something that can be 'extracted' from a text or other object, but rather an event that takes place through and in interpretation, and thus transforms the interpreter. Hermeneutics is Dasein's mode of being (1960). To exist as a human being is to exist as a member of a hermeneutic community.

The hermeneutical tradition, whose history is traced in *Truth and Method*, originated in PHILOLOGY and the textual study of scripture (largely as a means of avoiding false interpretations). Although Gadamer draws on this tradition, and extends it to the law (lawyers and judges interpret legal texts before applying them), he is also critical of its tendency to turn hermeneutics into an ancillary method or tool to be used in the human sciences (*Geisteswissenschaften*). As the general phenomenon commonly described as the LINGUISTIC TURN reveals that language pervades the entire human experience of the world, hermeneutics ceases to be a methodology; it becomes philosophy itself. Gadamer's criticisms of traditional hermeneutics overlap with the rejection of the claims of metaphysics and FOUNDATIONALISM. The rise of the empirical sciences, together with an increasingly specialized division of intellectual labour between different domains of knowledge, destroys the claims of philosophy and metaphysics to being the ultimate mode of knowledge or the 'queen of the sciences'; it is now hermeneutics, or even the interpretive understanding of works of art, that provides the model for human self-understanding. At the same time, the sciences themselves are freed from the model of 'comprehensive' knowledge elaborated by the metaphysical tradition that goes back to Aristotle. The empirical sciences offer not comprehensive knowledge, but a never-ending process of investigation based upon hypothesis and experimentation, and Gadamer remarks that testing a hypothesis is in fact a hermeneutical operation. Whilst there is a hermeneutical aspect to the sciences, they do not, however, provide 'understanding' (*Verstehen*) but merely 'explanation' (*Erklärung*). Their methods are inappropriate to the human sciences, which have no empirical object and in which the questions that are asked and the objects of research are constituted by the inquiry itself.

Gadamer's insistence on the centrality of language does not lead him to endorse the linguistics of SAUSSURE or CHOMSKY, which he criticizes on the grounds that they produce formal monologic grammars which take no account of the fact that the use of language always involves the speaker in a dialogue or conversation. To that extent, his thought is close to some aspects of SPEECH ACT theory, and insists that the individual is always part of a language community. It is language that allows the horizons of the past to influence our culture and present life, but it is also language that influences everything that can be hoped for, or feared, in the future. The encounter with language is therefore an encounter with an unfinished event; given the finitude of historical existence, it would be absurd to claim that there can be only one correct interpretation of that event. Hermeneutics can, on the other hand, ensure that individuals participate in a process of transmission which constantly mediates between past and present. Gadamer's hermeneutics leads him to rejoin the great tradition of humanism: the constant work of interpretation allows human action to be organized for the sake of a common tradition and order of things, and to ensure that all individuals know and acknowledge that tradition and that order as the common one.

READING: Sullivan (1989); Weinsheimer (1985)

Gates, Henry Louis Jr (1950–) African-American literary theorist. Gates's major project can be characterized as an attempt to synthesize elements of Western literary theory with a black vernacular tradition in order to produce a synthetic and self-sustaining African-American criticism. Although he is highly critical of the EUROCENTRISM of white critical theory, with its CANON of DEAD WHITE EUROPEAN MALES, Gates does not argue for its complete rejection, and nor does he argue for the celebration of an undifferentiated 'Black Experience'. The emblematic figure in Gates's influential studies (1987, 1988) is the 'signifying monkey'. This is the 'trickster' figure in the black oral tradition, who constantly outwits the more powerful lion by using the verbal strategy of a rhetorical double talk. According to Gates, the signifying monkey is a descendant of Essu-Elegbara, the Yoruba trickster figure to whom he was introduced by the Nigerian Wole Soyinka who, in Gates's view, provides the model for a new African literature. Signifyin(g) is the model for both musical and oral traditions; blues and jazz musicians constantly quote one another ('Signifying' is the title of a composition by Count Basie), and the black literary tradition can be described as one in which books talk to one another. Drawing on the fiction (1934) and anthropological work (1935, 1938) of Zora Neale Hurston, Gates also relates signifyin(g) to the old custom of the 'Dirty Dozens', in which a small group exchanges disparaging remarks (usually of a crudely sexual nature) about those they love; this is described in Oliver's classic study of the blues (1960). Signifying, quotation, mockery, imitation and double-talk are seen as the hallmarks of the African-American vernacular and literary tradition from the Harlem Renaissance of the 1920s (Huggins 1971; Baker 1987) to Ellison's *Invisible Man* (1952) and Alice Walker's *The Colour Purple* (1983).

The essays collected as *Loose Canons* (1992) cover the topics of canon formation and the role of the African-American intellectual in a very entertaining manner. Here Gates describes what he calls the 'taxi fallacy': the black intellectual's knowledge that 'race' is a construct is of little help when a taxi refuses to pick him up, and there is little point in shouting 'It's only a trope' at the taxi-driver.

As the general editor of the 'Schomburg Library of Nineteenth-Century Black Women Writers', Gates has played a major role in rediscovering, preserving and publicizing the many narratives in which black slaves 'wrote themselves into being'.

gay Synonym for homosexual, usually used in the masculine, as in 'lesbians and gay men'. In nineteenth-century slang the adjective 'gay' was applied to prostitutes and 'loose women', but had taken on its present sense in the United States by the mid-1950s. The term was occasionally used in Britain, but was usually thought to have upper-class connotations. 'QUEER' was used within the homosexual community, but was also widely used as a derogatory term of abuse. It was only at the end of the 1960s that 'gay' came into common use as a positive self-designation.

Although homosexual 'reform societies' existed throughout the twentieth century, it is widely accepted that the modern gay movement originates in the riots that erupted after police raided the Stonewall Inn in New York's Christopher Street in June 1969. Whilst police raids were not an unusual occurrence, this time the gay customers fought back. The New York Gay Liberation Front was formed in the aftermath of the riots (which are chronicled in Duberman 1993) and issued a manifesto stating: 'We reject society's attempt to impose sexual roles and definitions of our nature. We are stepping out of those roles and simplistic myths. WE ARE GOING TO BE WHO WE ARE' (cited Weeks 1977). The first Gay Pride march took place a year later. The example of the American Gay Liberation Movement, which was in part modelled on the WOMEN'S LIBERATION movement and the Black Power movement of the late 1960s, was soon imitated in most European countries and its vocabulary was widely adopted. The expression 'coming out', widely used to mean acceptance and open admission of one's homosexuality, derives from the American 'coming out of the closet', the closet being the symbol of concealment, oppression and self-oppression (Sedgwick 1985).

In Britain, the first meeting of the Gay Liberation Front was held in the autumn of 1970 and attracted only nine people; within a year up to five hundred were attending its weekly meetings (Weeks 1977). GLF itself was short-lived and did not survive the end of the counter-culture of the late 1960s and early 1970s. From the outset, there were internal political divisions between the advocates of lifestyle politics and the 'politicos', not to mention those between women, who were always in the minority, and men (Watney 1980). Its very existence did, however, indicate a change of mood. The adoption of the word 'gay', which tended to be replaced by 'queer' from the early 1990s onwards, signalled a rejection of the older reformist groups such as the Campaign for Homosexual Equality, which sought acceptance and equality, and the positive assertion of an uncompromising identity.

READING: Abelove, Barale and Halperin (1993); Cruikshank (1992)

gaze The expression *le regard* is used by both SARTRE and LACAN, but a certain confusion has arisen in English as the translator of Sartre's *Being and Nothingness* (1943a) has opted to translate it as 'the look', whilst Lacan's various translators render it as 'the gaze'.

Becoming the object of the look is, in Sartre's PHENOMENOLOGY, an important aspect of being-for-others (*être-pour-autrui*), which can be defined as the for-itself's (IN-ITSELF/FOR-ITSELF) mode of being when it apprehends itself as having become an object for another consciousness. Insofar as it is being looked at, the for-itself exists as an object like any other and is alienated from its potential freedom because it is no longer in control of the situation. Being the object of the other's look is often accompanied by a feeling of shame. Shame is a form of consciousness characterized by INTENTIONALITY, and implies the recognition or consciousness of being the object of the look: I am indeed the object that is being looked at and judged by the other. 'Being in the sight of God' is the ultimate instance of being-for-others as there is no escape from the all-seeing gaze of the divinity.

Visual perception is an important theme in Lacan's earliest paper; the infant-SUBJECT is, that is, entranced by its own image in the MIRROR-PHASE (Lacan 1936, 1949). In the first year of the seminar that began in 1954 (published 1975), Lacan describes the phenomenology of intersubjective relations in terms similar to those of Sartre's analysis of being-for-others, but he subsequently develops a different theory of the gaze and of the scopic DRIVE (1973). The gaze is now viewed as a property of the object rather than of the subject. As the subject gazes at the object of its perception, it senses that the object is gazing back at it from a point that lies outside the field of subjective perception. The subject is thus lured into the image of the object by the mechanism illustrated by the ANAMORPHIS of Holbein's *The Ambassadors* (1533, National Gallery, London). Lacan's analysis of the gaze has become an important element in feminist discussions of how women are constructed as the object of a male gaze in film and the visual arts (Mulvey 1975; Rose 1986).

Geertz, Clifford (1926–) American anthropologist. Whilst the monographs based on Geertz's fieldwork in Indonesia and Morocco (1960, 1968) are primarily addressed to a professional audience of fellow anthropologists, his essays (1973, 1983, 1988) have a much wider appeal which is in part due to his vivid style of writing. The description of Balinese cockfighting and its rituals (in Geertz 1973) is particularly memorable.

As a cultural anthropologist, Geertz adopts a broadly semiotic approach to his object of study and describes his work in Weberian terms as an interpretive science that is in search of meaning. The goal of the anthropologist is not to establish pseudo-scientific laws, but to gain access to a conceptual world that initially appears opaquely foreign, just as Weber (1904–05) enters the conceptual world in which Calvinists lived. Borrowing an expression from the British philosopher Gilbert Ryle (1966–7, 1967), Geertz refers to anthropology as an elaborate exercise in THICK DESCRIPTION that seeks to analyse the interwoven systems of signs that make up any culture. These are not mere superstructures, but organized systems without which human behaviour would be both ungovernable and incomprehensible because man is, ultimately, a symbolizing, conceptualizing and meaning-seeking animal.

Geertz is highly critical of the FUNCTIONALISM that reduces a work of art or a cultural artefact to the status of an elaborate mechanism for defining social relations, sustaining social roles or reinforcing social values, and insists, in terms that are influenced by the PHENOMENOLOGY of Alfred Schutz, that it materializes a way of experiencing the world (Schutz 1967).

Geertz also writes (1973) on the problems faced by the new states that emerged, like Indonesia, from postwar decolonization, as they struggle to integrate groups whose primordial loyalties are to tribes and clans or religious and even linguistic communities into a new and much more impersonal civil state. His sympathetic interest in the anthropology of social change leads him to criticize LÉVI-STRAUSS for his notorious lack of concern for history, his tendency to reduce sentiment to the shadow of intellect, and the minds of particular savages to a universal 'savage mind' whose structures are inherent in all human beings.

gender The term traditionally refers to both the classification of nouns and their corresponding modifiers as 'masculine', 'feminine' and 'neuter', and the sense of being male or female. A distinction between 'sex' and 'gender' began to be made in English in the 1970s, largely as a result of the impact of FEMINISM and WOMEN'S LIBERATION, and Gender Studies subsequently emerged as a specific academic discipline. The verb 'to gender' is sometimes used to describe the introduction of the issue of gender difference into a debate perceived as being dominated by the assumption that 'he' is a universal or neutral pronoun. In the mid-1980s references to gender difference began to be replaced by the broader and less dualistic term 'sexual difference', one of the key events that provoked the shift being the conference on sexual difference organized by the *Oxford Literary Review* at the University of Southampton in 1985 (the main papers were published in the *Oxford Literary Review* 1986).

Although she does not use the French equivalent of 'gender' (*genre* is still very rarely used in French to indicate sexual difference), Simone de BEAUVOIR anticipates many of the concerns of the gender-sex debate when she remarks that 'One is not born, but rather becomes, a woman' (1949) and argues that femininity is the product of contingent forces and not an eternal essence. The actual starting-point for the early feminist distinction between sex and gender was the research carried out by Robert Stoller (1924–91) at the California Gender Identity Center, where it was found that in cases where genital malformation resulted in erroneous gender assignment at birth, it was easier to undo the biological effects of the gender assignment than to unravel the psychological effects of having lived as the 'wrong' gender (Stoller 1968; Millett 1969). Sex could thus be defined in terms of biological differences at the level of the genitals, chromosomes and secondary sexual characteristics, whilst gender could be equated with socially constructed notions of femininity and masculinity. In England the distinction was widely popularized by feminists like Ann Oakley who argued (1972) that 'sex' was a biological term, and 'gender' a social and psychological term and (1974, 1996) that people are either male or female in biological terms, but in cultural terms are pressured to be or become masculine or feminine through processes of socialization.

Although the sex-gender distinction is widely accepted, theories as to how gender is produced and reproduced vary greatly. Studies such as Sharpe's account of how girls become women (1976) stress the differential socialization of girls and boys at home and in school, whilst authors like Lees (1993) stress that the construction of masculinity and femininity involves the reproduction of relations of power that define both domestic roles and forms of sexuality in terms detrimental to girls and women. Adopting a very different approach based upon SPEECH ACT theory rather than empirical sociology, BUTLER regards the ascription of gender as the result of a process of 'girling' or 'boying' that begins when it is said of a neonate that 'It's a boy/girl' and which is repeatedly reinforced by the use of PERFORMATIVES, though it should be added that ultrasound technology now means that girling/boying can begin before birth. The psychoanalytic contribution to the gender debate is a major issue in the often acrimonious dialogue between PSYCHOANALYSIS AND FEMINISM. Whilst Freudian psychoanalysis holds that human beings are innately bisexual and therefore come to adopt gendered 'attitudes' or 'positions', FREUD himself (and LACAN after him) tends to take a very normative view of masculinity and femininity, and to take the male child as the developmental norm. Freud's conviction that the girl who takes her father as her love-OBJECT is adopting a 'normal female attitude' indicates that he still relies on a normative thesis that equates gender with sex (see for example Freud 1931a).

The introduction of GAY sexuality and identity into discussions of gender tends to make the issue more complex as gay sexuality is not necessarily modelled on a binary masculine/feminine model, with one partner playing the 'male' role, whilst practices such as cross-dressing and deliberate role-playing (the theatrically 'butch' lesbian and her exquisitely hyper-feminine 'femme' partner) further unsettle gender differences. Talk of gender can, it is argued, actually perpetuate stereotyping by inadvertently promoting monolithic and unchanging models of masculinity and femininity (Watney 1986). Such criticisms, which lead to the emergence of QUEER theory, can be reinforced by appeals to DECONSTRUCTION and the theories of POSTMODERNITY that seek to undermine all binary oppositions and to free DESIRE from its constraints.

genealogy A mode of historical inquiry adopted by FOUCAULT from 1971 onwards and derived from the *wirkliche Historie* ('effective' or 'critical history') invoked in the second of Nietzsche's *Untimely Meditations* (Nietzsche 1874; Foucault 1971a); Foucault's choice of terminology also makes an obvious allusion to Nietzsche's *Genealogy of Morals* (1887), in which it is argued that the actual causes of a thing's origins and its eventual uses are worlds apart. Nietzsche speaks of the need to break up and dissolve the past, and Foucault's genealogies of power (1975) and sexuality (1976a) seek to demonstrate that bodies of knowledge do not have discrete points of origin and are not stable configurations. Genealogy uproots the traditional foundations of history and disrupts history's apparent continuity by concentrating on minor events and 'accidents' and insisting that knowledge is always rooted in power, but seeks to deny its own origins. There is no hidden or inner truth in a category such as GENDER, which is constructed by the bodies of knowledge (sexology, psychoanalysis) that claim to be able to explain it. A genealogical study of gender does not, therefore, look forward to the liberation of some repressed essence but, rather, to a liberation from the categories of gender. Ultimately, Foucault's genealogy enables him to ask (1980): 'Do we *truly* need a *true* sex?'

Although 'genealogy' tends to replace Foucault's earlier description of his methodology as an ARCHAEOLOGY OF KNOWLEDGE, he appears to regard the terms as being complementary rather than mutually exclusive.

Genette, Gérard (1930–) French literary theorist and, together with BARTHES and TODOROV, one of the major figures in French NARRATOLOGY and POETICS. Genette has written extensively and is best known for the elegant essays collected in the three volumes of *Figures* (1966b, 1969, 1972; selected essays in English translation 1982b).

Genette defines poetics as a theory of literary forms, or of the rhetorical codes, narrative techniques and poetic structures that combine to produce literary texts. Whilst such forms are constitutive of texts, they also transcend them and are not fully visible in individual works. The function of poetics is therefore to examine the forms and devices that make possible the existence of texts; Genette likens this process to taking an X-ray to reveal a skeleton. Individual texts are cited by Genette as instances of examples of overriding forms. In the classic narratological study of Proust included in *Figures III*, Genette uses *À la recherche du temps perdu* as a means of identifying and classifying forms and structures; unlike literary criticism, poetics is not concerned with using a judgement of taste to evaluate individual literary works.

Much of Genette's work has been devoted to the study of RHETORIC (1966), MIMESIS and DIEGESIS, and of the STORY/PLOT distinction. He distinguishes between *histoire* (story or diegesis), *récit* (text or plot) and *narration* (the act of narrating), and then identifies a number of levels of narration. An extradiegetic narrator stands outside or above the diegesis, like the narrator of the *Canterbury Tales* or *The Arabian Nights*; a narrator who is also an actor in the narrative is described as 'hypodiegetic'. Temporal levels of narration are identified as 'ulterior' (a story told after the event, as in *Tom Jones*), 'anterior' (a prophecy or prediction; this level is often an internal feature of a narrative and is exemplified, at its most banal, by such devices as 'As the hero was to learn . . .'), 'simultaneous' (as in a diary) and 'intercalated' (alternation between reported events and reactions to those events, as in an epistolary novel). Following SHKLOVSKY, Genette also stresses that narration itself is an event that takes place in time, but whose temporal nature is often overlooked. A favourite example is supplied by Sterne's *Tristram Shandy*, in which the narrator realizes that he has spent a year recording the first day of his life, and is therefore constantly in danger of falling behind his own narrative.

Genette's studies in poetics can at times look a rather aridly austere exercise in typology, and his terminological innovations and borrowings (PALIMPSEST, PARA-TEXT, HYPERTEXT, hypotext) can appear to border on the scholastic. His voluminous and endlessly erudite study of palimpsests in fact reveals him to be a man who greatly appreciates literary parodies, puns and jokes of all kinds (and not least those of OULIPO), and in possession of a nicely dry sense of humour. He was happy to accept that his summary of Proust's *À la recherche* ('Marcel became a writer') should be emended to read 'Marcel *finally* became a writer.'

genre French noun, current in English since 1816 (*OED*), used to describe a style or type of painting, book or film (such as *FILM NOIR*) characterized by a specific form, structure or thematic content. The discussion of genres is one of the oldest discourses on the arts, and can be either narrowly prescriptive or purely descriptive or classificatory. The term is cognate with 'genus', the basic taxonomic category used in biology to describe similar species of animals.

Aristotle is the earliest theorist of genre and his *Poetics* establishes a system of classification whose influence was still powerful in the early modern period. Aristotle's classification is based upon a distinction between poetic truth and historical truth, or between the kinds of things that might happen and things that have happened. Because it deals with universal truths about what might happen, poetry is superior to the history of particular facts. Within the domain of what would now be called 'literature', Aristotle then distinguishes between EPIC and tragic poetry, comedy and dithyrambic poetry, defining each genre in terms of the medium it uses, the objects it represents through MIMESIS and the manner in which it represents those objects. Tragedy represents an action that is complete in itself and worthy of serious attention. It takes the form of action rather than narration, and provokes fear and pity and then purges those emotions through CATHARSIS.

Writing on the art of poetry in the first century BC, Horace demonstrates how easily a descriptive classification can become a set of prescriptive rules for the aspiring poet, who is advised to use 'well-defined functions and styles of poetic forms'. He is also advised that a tragedy should have five acts, and that Medea must not butcher her children in the presence of the audience. Such rules are still observed in seventeenth-century classical French tragedies, in which no one dies or commits violence on stage. In the 'Discourse on Pastoral' that accompanies his four pastorals, Alexander Pope (1704) displays a similar sense of generic propriety when he remarks that his verses 'comprehend all the subjects which the critics . . . will allow to be fit for pastoral.'

The establishment of a classification of genres is rarely a purely taxonomic exercise and often introduces a hierarchy of values that grants greater literary or even moral worth to certain types of writing. For the Greeks, tragedy was 'more noble' than comedy; for a long time, the novel was viewed as a low or even immoral form of entertainment. In his wide-ranging examination of 'kinds of literature' Alastair Fowler (1982) demonstrates the historical variability of systems of generic classification. For Cicero (*De optimo genere oratorum*), the PARADIGM included 'tragic, comic, epic, melic and dithyrambic'; for Boileau (*L'Art poétique*, 1674) and Dryden (*Of Dramatic Poetry*, 1683), the CANON comprised 'epic, tragic, satiric, epigrammatic, lyric, elegaic and pastoral'.

The rise of the novel, which has been variously described as a true genre and as a subgenre of prose fiction, and its almost total dominance of the modern literary field, mean that such classifications are now largely redundant or of purely historical interest. Novels themselves can be classified on generic or subgeneric lines (science fiction, thrillers, horror, *BILDUNGSROMAN*, ROMANCE . . .), and the genres or subgenres are subject to both historical and local variations. The eighteenth-century Gothic novel is a recognizable historical genre. The English 'campus novel', inaugurated by Kingsley Amis's *Lucky Jim* (1954) and perpetuated by Malcolm Bradbury's *The History Man* (1975) and David Lodge's *Changing Places* (1975), demonstrates that genres do not always cross national boundaries: there are no equivalents to the campus novel in French or Italian.

Whilst there is still a classificatory strand in modern genre criticism, and especially in FRYE's archetypal theory of genre, the notion of an overt hierarchy of values is largely a thing of the past, though it survives in the critical commonplaces that dismiss a novel for being 'melodramatic', or a film for being 'stagy'. Such judgements are made so spontaneously that they must indicate that some notion of genre, however attenuated, is an integral part of the experience of reading. Fowler suggests that this is indeed the case when he remarks that genres are functional, and that our response to Christopher Marlowe's *The Jew of Malta* will vary depending on whether we see it as a tragedy or as a savage farce. TODOROV makes a similar point in his discussion of the fantastic (1970). The fantastic does have formal generic properties, such as a first-person narrator who knows only the laws of nature, witnesses something he or she cannot explain and hesitates, like the reader, between the natural and the supernatural explanation (does the governess in James's *The Turn of the Screw* see or imagine the ghosts?), but it also requires a reader who accepts the conventions of that structure and who does not read it as an ALLEGORY.

Art history understands genre in much the same sense as the literary tradition. Here too, genre was for centuries understood in a hierarchical sense; until the Impressionist revolution, history painting was deemed inherently superior to portraiture, landscape and the portrayal of contemporary life. The term 'genre' is also used more specifically to describe realist painting of everyday life, and especially the detailed interiors of seventeenth-century Dutch art (*Masters of Seventeenth-Century Dutch Genre Painting* 1984).

gestalt The German noun (plural: *Gestalten*) means shape, form or configuration, and is used in English because there is no precise equivalent. A 'gestalt' is usually understood as meaning a perceptual structure or unity which is functionally greater than the sum of its parts, and which cannot be understood by analysing its constituent elements. The gestalt psychology developed in Germany and then the United States, and associated primarily with Max Wertheimer (1880–1943), Kurt Koffka (1896–1941) and Wolfgang Köhler (1897–1967; see Köhler 1947), is essentially a theory of visual perception which challenges the stimulus-response model of behaviourism by stressing that perception involves the recognition and reorganization of whole structures rather than elements of structures. The basic model is that of the interplay between figure and ground: every act of perception involves the differentiation of a pattern or figure from the ground around. The 'good gestalt' is the pattern that finally supersedes all others. The perception of gestalts often involves a process of 'closure', meaning that incomplete perceptual patterns are transformed into wholes, even though that may distort elements of the whole. Later developments in gestalt psychology extend the theory to the whole of human behaviour. Thus psychoaffective disorders (AFFECT) can be described as incomplete gestalts which can be 'completed' or filled in by the therapeutic use of psychodrama.

Gestalt theory has often been applied to the study of the visual and literary arts, notably by GOMBRICH and ISER. Gombrich uses the figure/ground distinction in his psychology of the visual perception of organized patterns in the decorative arts (1960, 1979). For his part, Iser (1974, 1976) notes that meaning is not manifested in individual words and that reading is therefore not simply a matter of identifying individual linguistic signs. The reader's apprehension of a literary text is dependent upon the perception of configurative and gestalt-like groupings of words and other units of linguistic meaning. RUSSIAN FORMALISM'S notion of FOREGROUNDING is a literary variant on gestalt theory.

Gilbert, Sandra M. (1936–) and **Gubar, Susan** (1944–) American feminist literary critics and historians, best known for their collaborative studies of women's literature. Their *Madwoman in the Attic* (1979a), runner-up for a 1980 Pulitzer Prize and winner of the National Book Critics' Circle Award in Literature for 1979, is one of the great classics of FEMINIST CRITICISM. Their three-volume *No Man's Land* (1987, 1988a, 1988b) is a large-scale survey of women's writing from the mid-nineteenth century to the present. Gilbert and Gubar are also the editors of the influential *Norton Anthology of Literature by Women* (1985), and the editors of major collections of essays on women poets (1979b), and on women and modernism (1986). They habitually write on an epic scale, and combine great erudition and readability to remarkable effect.

Unlike SHOWALTER, Gilbert and Gubar argue that BLOOM's theory of the ANXIETY OF INFLUENCE can be usefully applied to the history of women's writing, and in *The Madwoman in the Attic* they modify it to explore how women from Jane Austen to Emily Dickinson have struggled against the image of the 'woman writer' produced by male authors and male texts. Although most of the discussion centres on canonical texts (CANON) and authors, the story of Snow White provides an important subtext symbolizing the woman writer's escape from the glass coffin, as well as the twin mythical figures of the beautiful evil Queen and the equally beautiful but innocent Snow White. At the end of the fairy-tale, the Queen dances her way to hell in burning iron shoes, and Snow White escapes the male mirror that defines her as the fairest of all. The title of *Madwoman* obviously alludes to *Jane Eyre*, and the book describes how women writers of the nineteenth century dance their way out of the mirror and the glass coffin of male texts that define them as either angels or monsters. Tracing subversive pictures behind respectable façades, Jane Austen demonstrates, for instance, that romantic fiction assumes that women's legitimate task is to love men, but subverts it by demonstrating that it is precisely that fiction which constructs women as deceitful, narcissistic and masochistic. Gilbert and Gubar agree with WOOLF when she argues (1931) that 'the angel in the house' must be killed if the woman writer is to emerge, but add that their role as historians and critics is to explore how the angel came into being in the first place.

The options facing the women novelists of the nineteenth century are described as submission to male myths, or strategies for survival and the eventual achievement of equality. One of the dominant myths and influences to be overcome is the romantic reading of *Paradise Lost*, with its powerful images of Eve (the cause of the Fall, or woman as terrifying source of evil) and the rebellious Satan. In *Wuthering Heights*, Emily Brontë creates Heathcliff as 'a woman's man', a male figure onto whom she can project a rebelliousness that springs from her own anxiety about the social role that is forced on her by the 'social disease of ladyhood'. Genres such as the *BILDUNGSROMAN* are exploited to tell a tale of female emancipation as the madwoman in the attic is revealed to be Jane Eyre's ferocious secret self (a reading contested by SPIVAK), whilst Charlotte Brontë's *Villette* fuses the *Bildungsroman* and the mystery to suggest that growing up female requires a careful demystification of an enigmatic and male-dominated world. George Eliot's novels suggest that male–female relations are dominated by a struggle between a transcendent male and an immanent female who is possessed of a demonic rage, and that renunciation of ambition is the only defence against its destructive potential. The alternative is typified by women poets from Christina Rossetti to Emily Dickinson. According to Gilbert and Gubar, the constraints of GENRE are such that, whilst women novelists can write about madwomen and their demonic doubles, women poets *become* madwomen who die melodramatically at the crossroads where tradition and genre, art and society, meet.

The three volumes of *No Man's Land* describe the period from the mid-nineteenth century to the present as a contested battlefield (hence the title) in which men and women clash in a conflict born of the rise of FEMINISM and the lingering legacy of the Victorian femininity embodied in the 'angel of the house', and explore topics as diverse as reactions to the emergence of the New Woman, the sexual imagery of imperialism in popular fiction, the Harlem Renaissance and the literary effects of the emergence of modern FEMINISM.

Gilbert and Gubar insist (especially in their preface to the first volume of *No Man's Land*) that MODERNISM and similar cultural shifts are not experienced in the same manner by men and women, and that a study of the territory of literature must involve a study of marriage, the family, education and so on. The working assumption is that there is a knowable history and that texts are authored by individuals affected by material historical factors. This implies a challenge both to the theorists of the DEATH OF THE AUTHOR and to those who, like WHITE, claim that historiography is a form of narrative fiction. According to Gilbert and Gubar, such theories erase the reality of GENDER and of the engendered experience recorded in literature by making it impossible to trace the shifting dynamics of the conflict-ridden sexual relations that are the basic subject-matter of literature in the nineteenth and twentieth centuries. This does not imply a naïve return to the traditional notion of authorship: if the author is viewed as a gendered human, and a text as a reflection of cultural conditions, individual narratives can be collated to produce a metanarrative or a story about stories of gender strife in a given period.

Ginzburg, Carlo (1939–) Italian historian specializing in the study of sixteenth- and seventeenth-century religious radicals, witchcraft and folklore. Most of his work draws on surviving transcripts of interrogations carried out by the Inquisition, and is remarkable for the technical skills the author brings to bear on his archival material as he explores the collective mental structures of the early modern period. His work has much in common with both that of the *ANNALES* historians and that of the British practitioners of HISTORY FROM BELOW.

Ginzburg's first major book (1966) dealt with the Benandanti, a group of northern Italian peasants who believed that on certain nights their souls left their bodies and rode away on the backs of animals to fight witches. Moving between summaries of the trials in which they were accused of witchcraft (even though they claimed to be fighting witches) and interpretative commentary, Ginzburg explores the relationship between the official and print culture of the Inquisition and the survivals of older fertility cults. Similar concerns inform the better known *The Cheese and the Worms* (1976), which reconstructs the strange cosmogony elaborated by Menocchio, a Friulian miller who was burned at the stake as a heretic in 1599. He believed that an original chaos of earth, fire, air and water solidified into a mass in the same way that milk solidifies into cheese, and that God was created out of that mass. Worms then appeared in the cheese and became angels. As in the earlier study, Ginzburg argues that this vision is the result of the interaction between the official culture of the Church and oral memories of older beliefs. More generally, the eradication of heresy is analysed as a process of exclusion designed to root out and destroy popular oral cultures. Like Le Roy Ladurie, Ginzburg exploits official documents and trial reports to produce a vivid reconstruction of an alien culture.

READING: Anderson (1990); Schutte (1976)

Glissant, Édouard (1928–) Martiniquan poet, novelist and essayist. His essays (1981, 1990) anticipate the themes of CREOLENESS. In his writings on what he terms 'Antilleanity', Glissant gives a bitter account of the cultural effects of Martinique's dependency on France, which has led to the virtual destruction of local culture and sapped its people's political will. For Glissant, the solution does not lie in the NEGRITUDE of CÉSAIRE or in the reclamation of a lost African identity, but in the creation of a creole culture that will insert Martinique into an open network of cultural exchanges spanning the whole of the Caribbean archipelago and combining creole, French, Spanish and Anglo-American influences. His vision of this hybrid culture of the future is broadly similar to Derek WALCOTT's vision of transforming the 'shipwreck of fragments' that is the Caribbean into a synthetic culture with a single literature written in a variety of different languages (1982).

In his powerful poetry and fiction, Glissant explores the history and cultures of Martinique from the days of slavery to the present and demonstrates that, despite its official status as an overseas *département*, the island is by no means a mere outpost of metropolitan France. His best known novel is *La Lézarde* (1958), which has been translated as *The Ripening*.

READING: Dash (1995)

Goldmann, Lucien (1913–70) Romanian-born French literary theorist. Goldmann's early study of Pascal and seventeenth-century French tragedy (1959) is greatly influenced by LUKÁCS's writings on the historical novel, but replaces the traditional notion of the individual author with that of a collective subject. Analysing the theology of Jansenism, Goldmann demonstrates that it embodies the IDEOLOGY or world-view of a class which is doomed to historical extinction and unable to realize the absolute values it seeks in a contingent world. Unable to prove the existence of God by rational means, Jansenism is obliged to wager that God does exist and formulates an ethics of worldly renunciation. The resultant tragic vision finds its finest aesthetic expression in the structures of the tragedies of Racine.

In his later work on the sociology of literature (1965), Goldmann abandons the notion of a world-view and concentrates on the 'structural homology' that exists between literary texts and social forms and ideologies. The impersonal descriptions typical of the French *NOUVEAU ROMAN* are described as homologous with the ideology of a society dominated by commodities and characterized by ALIENATION and REIFICATION.

Politically, Goldmann was sympathetic to the Workers' Councils tradition of self-governing communities. In his later writings, which have not been collected, he contends that the mass-education needs of modern capitalism will create a new collective revolutionary subject by producing a highly skilled workforce that will become frustrated by the contradiction between its aspirations and the authoritarianism of both industry and educational establishments. Goldmann's rejection of MARXISM's traditional emphasis on the leading role of the industrial working class reflects his sympathy for the student revolt of May 1968 and for the claim that educated young people and the new middle class had become the revolutionary vanguard.

READING: Cohen (1994)

Gombrich, Sir Ernst Hans Josef (1909–) Viennese-born British art historian. Gombrich is unusual amongst art historians in that his work spans the full range from specialist studies of Renaissance art (1966, 1972) to the popularizing *Story of Art* (1950), which has been continuously in print since publication, and major contributions to the psychology of pictorial representation (1960, 1982) and of decorative art (1979).

Gombrich's history of art is a fairly conventional, if immensely erudite, study in the classification and description of stylistic change from the age of Egyptian and Greek art onwards, but his theory of perception and representation is a novel combination of psychology and historical insight. He borrows from the GESTALT psychology of Wolfgang Köhler (1947) to explore how the interplay between figure and ground informs the human perception of the complex patterns of decorative art, which is seen as being guided by an innate or inbuilt sense of order. This psychology of perception goes far beyond the usual parameters of art history, taking in (1982) such topics as cartography, commercial art and advertising.

The other main component of Gombrich's psychology derives from POPPER. Far from imitating reality or painting what he sees, in Gombrich's view, the artist does not start by observing reality but by constructing models which are gradually modified in the light of the viewer's reaction until they come to 'match reality'. The artist works, that is, with conventional concepts that make up a mental set and not with an external observable reality. Artistic experiments and innovations are akin to the scientific hypotheses that are tested against the principle of FALSIFIABILITY. By comparing the styles of the past, which easily become suffocating 'prisons', and the tentative projects of the future the artist experiments to see how far nature can be represented in images. The role of the viewer is to collaborate with the artist's transformation of a piece of coloured canvas into a likeness of the visible world. The Popperian strand in Gombrich's work makes him highly critical of the HISTORICISM which tries to find in the history of art a series of organic unities or world-views. He is also suspicious of relativist warnings about the dangers of parochial pride and of seeing Western culture as superior to others. Gombrich describes himself (1982) as an 'unrepentant parochial' who remains convinced that Greek culture and the rise of science have given the Western tradition tools that others lack. The absence of any discussion of women artists in *The Story of Art* was a factor in stimulating the feminist intervention into art history (Parker and Pollock 1981).

grammatology The study or history of writing, scripts and alphabets. The word derives from the Greek *gramma*, meaning 'letter'. Defined in the strictest of senses, grammatology borders on the impossible as the very notion of history implies the existence of lasting written records, and the history of writing therefore cannot be extended backwards into a hypothetical pre-linguistic or pre-grammatological past. Grammatology is more commonly viewed as relating to the deciphering of hitherto incomprehensible forms of writing such as Mayan scripts or the hieroglyphs on the Rosetta Stone. Traditional grammatology usually assumes that the evolution of writing is a gradual transition from the concrete to the abstract, as in the sequence 'hieroglyph', 'pictogram', 'ideogram', 'phonetic character'. That assumption is contested by all schools of modern linguistics. A much broader definition of grammatology is given by Gelb's *Study of Writing* (1952), which links the study of writing to that of other semiotic activities and of the principles and techniques of writing. Gelb's grammatology provides the starting-point for DERRIDA's critique of the PHONOCENTRISM and LOGOCENTRISM (1967a) which has, throughout the history of Western philosophy, privileged the spoken or phonic element in linguistic communication to the detriment of the written or graphic element.

Gramsci, Antonio (1891–1937) Italian Marxist thinker and one of the principal representatives of WESTERN MARXISM. Active in the Italian Socialist Party and then the Italian Communist Party, Gramsci was arrested by Mussolini's police in late 1928 and spent the rest of his life in prison. During Gramsci's trial the public prosecutor famously remarked: 'For twenty years we must stop this brain from functioning.' The brain did not stop functioning, but produced the thirty-three notebooks (*Quaderni*) on which Gramsci's posthumous reputation is based. The prison notebooks have a chequered publication history and it was not until 1975 that a good edition was established; only a selection, made from earlier Italian editions, is available in English (1971). Together with his letters from prison (1965; a selection in English 1988), they are a remarkable testimony to the intellectual work that can be done in the most difficult of circumstances. Two volumes of selected political writings are available in translation (1977, 1978), as is a selection of Gramsci's writings on cultural topics (1985).

Although it contains some interesting comments on the arts – Gramsci was one of the first to realize the importance of Luigi Pirandello's theatre – Gramsci's early political journalism is mainly taken up with a discussion of the workers' council movement that emerged during and after the First World War (for the context see Quintin Hoare's introduction to Gramsci 1971 and Clark 1977). Established in the great industrial factories of Milan and especially Turin – which allowed Gramsci to identify the new phenomenon of FORDISM – workers' councils were autonomous organizations and not affiliated to the trades union movement. According to Gramsci, they were the Italian equivalent of the Soviets that emerged during the Russian Revolution of 1917 and he held that they could provide the basis for a true workers' democracy. He argued in the left-wing press that, rather than trying to obtain higher wages or better working conditions, the councils should take full control of production in the factories and thus pose a direct challenge to the capitalist system. In March 1920 the factories of Turin were occupied by striking workers and a general strike was called. What appeared to be an insurrectionary movement was defeated when the PSI withdrew its support; two years later Mussolini's fascist party seized power.

The *Prison Notebooks* cover an immense range of topics, ranging from the experience of the workers' councils to popular serial novels, and cannot be said to represent a systematic or even coherent body of thought. They include plans for a history of Italian intellectuals from the nineteenth century onwards, for a comparative study of HISTORICAL MATERIALISM and the philosophy of Benedetto Croce and the history of the Risorgimento, the movement that led to the reestablishment of a unified Italian state in the nineteenth century. Although a detailed study of the *Notebooks* requires a high degree of knowledge of Italian history, politics and literature, their broad themes have had a huge influence on Western Marxism and particularly on the theory of IDEOLOGY. By concentrating on the notions of HEGEMONY, or the manufacture of spontaneous consent to the ideas of the ruling classes, and of the ORGANIC INTELLECTUALS who are related to rising classes or groups, Gramsci adds a new dimension to MARXISM's understanding of ideology and stresses the importance of the struggles within CIVIL SOCIETY that are essential to the establishment of a socialist hegemony.

One of the most intriguing sections of the *Prison Notebooks* is entitled 'The Modern Prince' and is devoted to a discussion of Machiavelli's *The Prince* and *Discourses on Livy*. According to Gramsci's analysis, Machiavelli's treatise of statecraft is in fact an argument in favour of the creation of a national state that can take on a popular dimension thanks to the existence of a citizen militia which will draw the peasantry into national life. Machiavelli's Prince is the precursor of both the Jacobins of the French Revolution and the communists of the twentieth century. For Gramsci, the 'modern prince' is the revolutionary party, or the organism in which a collective will begins to assert itself in concrete form before becoming universal and total and combining force with consent, and authority with hegemony. The reference to a citizen militia that draws in the peasantry alludes to the 'southern question', which is one of Gramsci's recurrent themes. The 'southern question' refers to the CONTRADICTION between the industrial North and a rural South or *mezzogiorno* which was seen by even militant workers in the North as the ball and chain that was holding back Italy's development. For Gramsci, the southern peasantry was a potential reservoir of strength for the industrial North, and the failure to establish the requisite alliance between the two was one of the reasons for the defeat of 1920 and all that followed.

Gramsci has been the most important single influence on the development of Italian communism in the postwar period. Outside Italy his influence spread more slowly. Perry Anderson remarks (1976b) that, whereas Gramsci was still unfamiliar in England in the mid-1960s, by 1973–5 Gramscian themes were ubiquitous. The popularization of the ideas of hegemony and organic intellectuals resulted from developments within the NEW LEFT and CULTURAL STUDIES and from discussions of ideology that tried to move away from the BASE/SUPERSTRUCTURE model but rarely took account of the specifically Italian dimension to Gramsci's work.

READING: Buci-Glucksmann (1975); Fiori (1965)

grand narratives or **metanarratives** LYOTARD's term for narratives which make forms of knowledge legitimate by supplying them with a validating philosophy of history (1977, 1979a). In the ENLIGHTENMENT grand narrative, the hero of knowledge strives after the ethical-political goal of universal peace; the metanarrative of MARXISM is the story of the heroic people's march towards socialism. Metanarratives claim to have a universal status, and to be able to explain all other narratives. They therefore attempt to translate alternative accounts into their own language and to suppress all objections to what they themselves are saying. Grand narratives organize and legitimate politics and culture by positing an origin (God) or an end (universal emancipation) that can supposedly organize a story without becoming part of it. According to the Enlightenment narrative, reason will free the world from superstition and produce a universal knowledge. Democracy will make the people the subject of the universal history of humanity, and Marxism will free the proletariat through revolution. According to Lyotard, grand narratives are a feature of the period of MODERNITY; POSTMODERNITY's attitude towards metanarratives and universals is, in contrast, one of incredulity. The grand narratives of the past therefore have to be rejected in favour of 'little narratives' or cultural representations of local or minority subjects. Like the LANGUAGE GAMES of WITTGENSTEIN, no little narrative has any privileged status or power. No one can speak all these languages, and few, it is claimed, feel any nostalgia for the lost metanarrative. Now that the energy of the universalizing Enlightenment has been exhausted, legitimation springs from localized practices and culture.

It can obviously be argued that the story of the collapse of grand narratives is itself a new grand narrative. It has also been argued that this is as Eurocentric as the metanarratives it supposedly subverts (Gilroy 1993a), and that it excludes the black cultures that are producing a historical memory and a narrative of emancipation as they struggle against racism.

Greenberg, Clement (1909–) American art critic. In numerous articles published in *Partisan Review*, *The Nation* and elsewhere from the 1940s and 1950s onwards (collections 1986a, 1986b, 1993a, 1993b), Greenberg elaborates one of the most influential accounts of modern art. His early articles effectively launched the international careers of Jackson Pollock, Arshile Gorky and William de Kooning and made their Abstract Expressionism (comprehensively surveyed in Seitz 1985, though this volume does not cover Pollock himself) synonymous with AVANT-GARDE. The major themes of Greenberg's prolific writings (see in particular 1961, 1964) are outlined in his famous article 'Avant-Garde and Kitsch' (1941). The avant-garde is characterized in terms of an ABSTRACTION that begins when the artist turns away from the subject-matter and concentrates on the medium of art itself. The very processes and disciplines that were once used to imitate or represent external reality now become the subject-matter of art; MIMESIS becomes the representation of mimesis. Painting now exists in its medium. For Greenberg, the avant-garde represents the only living culture and the only defence against KITSCH, viewed as a pseudo-artistic activity which takes as its raw material the debased and academicized simulacra of genuine culture and exploits them to produce vicarious experience and faked sensations.

In his later writings Greenberg celebrates a rarefied, purified abstraction for which there are only two norms or conventions: flatness and the delimitation of flatness that underlines the painting's existence as a two-dimensional object. This rarefication represents a search for the absolute, for something that is valid purely in its own terms, and which exists independently of meaning or representation. Greenberg's championing of abstraction often borders on the dogmatic. SURREALISM, for example, is criticized (1944) for seeking inspiration in dreams or automatic doodlings, and not in the medium itself.

Greer, Germaine (1939–) Australian feminist and cultural critic. Like Kate MILLETT's *Sexual Politics* and FIRESTONE's *Dialectic of Sex*, Greer's bestselling *The Female Eunuch* (1970) is one of the classics of the early WOMEN'S LIBERATION movement. Her subsequent work covers a wide range of subject-matter, ranging from a study of the problems facing women artists (1979) to a polemical and controversial discussion of the issue of overpopulation (1984).

Angry, witty and at times extremely funny, *The Female Eunuch* is a powerful manifesto calling for the liberation of womanpower, or the self-determination of women and, ultimately, the overthrow of PATRIARCHY. The eunuch of the title is the 'castrated' woman whose sexuality has been repressed and denied by a woman-hating society whose fear and loathing of women is typified by the widespread use of synonyms for the female genitals as a term of abuse. In this society, woman has been economically marginalized and exploited, confined within a social system that transforms mothers into the 'dead heart' of the nuclear family, and turned into a sex-object by all-pervasive male fantasies. Greer is at her polemical best, and her funniest, in the scathing discussions of the cult of romantic love and of the romantic fiction that promotes it.

Although Greer's name became synonymous with women's liberation, or the 'women's lib' that was so mocked in the popular media, her concerns depart from those of the broader movement in a number of ways. Her extreme individualism is at variance with the collectivist values of many women's groups, and she displays little sense of sisterhood or solidarity with other women. Her favourable references to avant-garde sexual morality are a reminder that Greer was at this time an enthusiastic participant in the counter-culture and a contributor to underground magazines like *Oz* and the explicitly titled *Suck*, whilst her argument that the chief means of liberating women is the promotion of the pleasure principle owes less to FREUD than to a fellow-Australian's manifesto of hippiedom and individual hedonism

(Neville 1970). Greer's individualism surfaces again in her essay on the menopause (1991), which combines a bitter attack on what she calls ANOPHOBIA with a rather self-indulgent portrait of the author as wise old woman. In 1970 relatively few British feminists were convinced by the argument that the organic extended families of the southern Mediterranean countries offered women and their children a positive alternative to the nuclear family. That argument reappears at length in *Sex and Destiny* (1984), where Greer also contends that the Western concern with overpopulation expresses a deep loathing of children and women's fertility.

Greer's background is in English literature (her doctoral thesis was on Shakespeare's early comedies and she has coedited an anthology of seventeenth-century women's verse (Greer, Hastings, Medoff and Sansone 1989)), but she has published relatively little on literature. In her detailed historical study of women's poetry (1995), she argues against those who attempt to expand the CANON to include more women on the grounds that much 'she-poetry' is in fact poor, and that the doomed and suicidal figure of the poetess is a myth created by the multiple factors that have always excluded women from full participation in literary culture. As a critic has remarked (Pollock 1988) of Greer's study of women artists, this argument tends to reduce women's poetry to the role of illustrating the oppression of women, to perpetuate the idea that creativity is masculine, and to suggest that the woman artist or poet can never be anything more than a female eunuch. Greer's heavily promoted *The Whole Woman* (1999) marked a return to the anger of 1970, argued strongly that the new FEMINISM (Walter 1998) has lost its liberationist edge, but also provided further evidence of its author's extreme individualism.

Greimas, Algirdas Julien (1917–92) Lithuanian-French specialist in SEMIOTICS, NARRATOLOGY and POETICS, defined in the broadest possible sense as a linguistic description of poetic communication and as an explanation of the structural features of any given poetic object.

Greimas's work draws heavily on that of PROPP on the morphology of the folk-tale and LÉVI-STRAUSS's analysis of mythology, and is designed to produce a general theory of action which will be scientific in that it is coherent, systematic and simple. The theory supposedly applies to all meaningful phenomena from narrative to the theory of the passions (Greimas and Fontanille 1991). In the case of the passions, the goal is to elaborate a theory of SUBJECTS as acting cognitive beings endowed with character and temperament. The central element in Greimas's analysis of semantics (1966a), meaning (1970) and narrative (1976) is the notion of the ACTANT, defined as a functional unit which *does* something. Typical narrative actants include the sender and its binary opposite, the receiver. Greimas's other major innovation is the semiotic square, which groups actants or semiotic units into groups of binary oppositions. The notion of binary opposition used here derives ultimately from SAUSSURE's insight that it is because they are different that signs are meaningful, and from JAKOBSON's analysis which demonstrates that PHONEMES form a system of minimal differential units of meaning. The paired relations are designated relations of contradiction (A and A), contrariety (A and non-A) and presupposition (non-A and A), arranged into the square:

The category of being can be articulated as

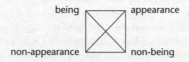

According to Greimas, this deep structure, which is never 'visible' in the narrative on the page, is basic to all phenomena, and generates all DISCOURSE. The semiotic square generates the successive situations in which the hero of a quest narrative chooses between the options open to him, and thus opens up further possibilities and impossibilities. It can also be used to describe and explain (1966a) the existence of possible sexual relations within a human community: marital relations, normal relations, abnormal relations and extramarital relations, governed respectively by rules of prescription, taboo, non-prescription and non-taboo. The categories do not designate actual behaviour, but rather the logical possibilities available to any human community.

READING: Schleifer (1987)

group-in-fusion The term is used by SARTRE (1960) to describe the sudden transformation that comes about when a number of individuals existing in the mode of SERIALITY are suddenly and spontaneously united by a common purpose or PRAXIS. The emergence of the group-in-fusion transcends the ALIENATION of seriality and allows individuals to overcome their isolation through their participation in a collective project. Individuals no longer see one another as Others and potential rivals or competitors, and can realize their potential freedom in praxis. A group-in-fusion begins to emerge when a queue waiting outside a baker's in a time of scarcity explodes into a spontaneous riot as a collective fear that no one will have bread overcomes the worry that the first person in the serial will deprive others of bread. Sartre's primary example of the group-in-fusion is that of the crowd of Parisians who stormed the Bastille on 14 July 1789. They are united by the almost anonymous cries to 'To arms' and 'To the Bastille' that emanate from the group-in-fusion rather than from identifiable individuals. At one level, the existence of the group-in-fusion is temporary and apocalyptic, as it will lapse back into seriality once its goal (the destruction of the Bastille) has been accomplished. At a second level, it transcends its own temporary existence: once the Bastille has been stormed, Paris can never again be the Paris of June 1789. The relationship between seriality and the group-in-fusion illustrates in miniature the broader DIALECTIC between the PRACTICO-INERT and PRACTICE.

Guattari, Félix (1930–92) French psychiatrist, psychoanalyst and political activist, closely associated with DELEUZE. The partnership between Deleuze and Guattari, which began with *Anti-Oedipus* (1972) and culminated with the publication of *What is Philosophy?* (1991), was remarkably productive but has tended to obscure the interest of Guattari's own work. All too often, he is reduced to being 'merely' Deleuze's partner and is subsumed into the cumbersome adjective 'Deleuzo-Guattarian'. His work is based firmly in his practice as a psychiatrist working mainly with schizophrenics and is broadly similar to, but also critical of, the British ANTI-PSYCHIATRY of Laing, and constantly tries to find humane forms of treatment that can be used in an institutional setting. Although Guattari trained as a psychoanalyst and was a member of LACAN'S ÉCOLE FREUDIENNE DE PARIS from 1964 until its dissolution in 1980, he is bitterly critical of PSYCHOANALYSIS's reliance on and reproduction of Oedipal structures that reduce everything to 'papa-mama-me'.

A tireless political activist, Guattari was active on many fronts and the materials collected (as Guattari 1984 and in Genosko 1996) trace the trajectory that took him from the student protests of 1968 to GAY activism, campaigns for free community radio stations, the politics and philosophy of DESIRE and eventually the Green Party. In 1973 Guattari faced obscenity charges and was condemned to pay a fine of 600 francs when his journal *Recherches* (Research) published a 'Great Encyclopedia of Homosexualities' with the provocative subtitle 'Three Billion Perverts' (the notes he prepared for his defence are included in Genosko 1996), which can be seen as an early version of QUEER theory. He liked to boast that he never paid the fine.

READING: Bogue (1989)

gynocritics Expression introduced by Elaine SHOWALTER to describe the sustained investigation of women's writing exemplified by her study of British women novelists from Brontë to Lessing (1977).

Showalter (1979, 1981) makes a distinction between feminist criticism and gynocritics. Feminist criticism tends to concentrate on the investigation of the ideological assumptions of both literature and literary criticism and their representation of women. It is often a form of REVISIONISM to the extent that it queries the adequacy of conventional conceptual structures and invokes the need to revise or expand the CANON to include women writers who have been neglected by a male tradition. Gynocritics seeks, in contrast, to construct a female framework for the analysis of new models based upon the study of female experience, which is described in anthropological terms by Showalter as a subculture in which the status ascribed to women and internalized images of femininity interact with their experience and changing self-awareness. The study of the history and themes of writings by women is combined with detailed readings of specific texts, and with investigations into the psychodynamics of female creativity. Gynocritics further seeks to establish the existence of a continuous female experience which can easily become invisible or mute if it is confined within the diagrams of structuralists or the class conflicts of Marxists.

Although Showalter's concept of gynocritics is very influential within women's studies programmes, it has been heavily criticized by feminists who are closer to

STRUCTURALISM and the concerns of theorists such as KRISTEVA and CIXOUS. Toril Moi, for instance (1985), criticizes Showalter for her concentration on 'experience' which, she argues, has always been a feature of the humanist tradition which reduces texts to a transparent image of a pure reality. According to such critics, the creation of a female canon would merely reproduce the structure in which the student listens while her 'mistress' functions as the voice of an 'authentic tradition' embodied in 'great works'.

Habermas, Jürgen (1929–) German philosopher, and the foremost contemporary representative of the CRITICAL THEORY associated with the FRANKFURT SCHOOL. Habermas's work can be divided into two main phases. His earlier work (1968, 1971) is Marxist-oriented and offers a theory of crises and of the emergence of the sciences, but from *Legitimation Crisis* (1973) onwards he develops a theory of COMMUNICATIVE ACTION that is heavily influenced by SPEECH ACT theory and hermeneutics. He finally develops a theory of 'discourse ethics' (1991b, 1992) which he regards as contributing to a critical defence of constitutional democracy (1983, 1997).

Perhaps more so than any other thinker associated with the Frankfurt School, Habermas stresses that, insofar as it is a CRITIQUE of political economy that helps to analyse the crises of capitalism, MARXISM can be seen as a continuation of the ENLIGHTENMENT tradition, which he later describes as the philosophical discourse of modernity (1985). Marxism is, that is, a critique of IDEOLOGY that offers a potential experience of emancipation by supplying critical insights into relations of power (1971). Critical theory and its Marxist component are, for Habermas, guided by their interest in the future and in the realization of a truly rational society in which 'men make their own history with will and consciousness' (1973). Habermas habitually makes Marxism synonymous with HISTORICAL MATERIALISM and stresses the importance of the sequence of MODES OF PRODUCTION that it identifies (Rockmore 1989), but is highly critical of the tendency to transform DIALECTICAL MATERIALISM into a philosophy of nature or even a natural science; this transforms Marxism into a form of POSITIVISM or SCIENTISM. Positivism is criticized for its lack of self-reflective criticism and for the way it reduces EPISTEMOLOGY to a crudely mechanical methodology. At the same time, Habermas accepts that traditional METAPHYSICS has been discredited and denies that philosophy has any privileged claim to knowledge or truth; philosophy is a form of critique and does have an emancipatory potential, but is now in competition with other forms of knowledge. Philosophy's newly restricted role reflects the evolution of society as a whole; in an advanced capitalist society, research, technology, production and administration are condensed into a system whose parts are functionally interdependent, but which it is difficult to perceive as a whole. At the same time, according to Habermas (1971), repression no longer works at the economic level of the labour market, but through the sociopsychological mechanisms of the leisure market.

Here Habermas's argument echoes Adorno's caustic comments on the CULTURE INDUSTRY.

Throughout the 1970s, Habermas gradually elaborates the theory of 'communicative action' that culminates in his two-volume *magnum opus* (1981, 1987). The theory relies upon a two-tier model of society. Drawing on HUSSERL, Habermas describes the world of everyday action and beliefs as the 'lifeworld' (*Lebenswelt*) and broadly identifies it with the public sphere and CIVIL SOCIETY. The division of labour, the development of the productive forces and the accumulation of knowledge result in the emergence of a number of 'systems' with either a 'steering' (decision-making), or an 'institutional' role. Systems are free from all moral constraints and act in accordance with the ends and means logic of strategic action, or what ADORNO and HORKHEIMER call 'instrumental reason'. Systems tend to evolve into an alienated pseudo-nature against which there is no appeal and constantly threaten to invade or colonize the lifeworld; the role of critical thought is to defend the latter against their encroachments by mediating between the two tiers of social existence and by supplying a link between 'expert knowledges' and everyday action. The sphere of the lifeworld is dominated by language, which is the agency for both socialization and the intersubjective recognition that enables individuals to relate to one another. For Habermas, the basic unit of linguistic meaning is the speech act and the intersubjectivity it implies. Speech acts provide the potential basis for the consensus agreement that founds Habermas's discourse ethics. The answer to the basic ethical question 'What must I do?' is supplied not by a prescriptive ethics, but by agreement as to what constitutes the good. Habermas acknowledges that his theory implies the existence of an idea-speech situation in which free individuals rationally discuss alternative possibilities without being coerced, and in which critical philosophy can act as a mediator. Constitutional democracy offers a potential space for such discussions, but the 'democratic deficit' signalled by bureaucratic non-accountability and non-participation on the part of citizens greatly restricts its potential. Discourse ethics is an ideal to be realized in the future rather than a political reality.

Habermas's continued attachment to the ideal of rational enlightenment and of modernity, viewed as an incomplete project (1980), makes him very critical of POSTMODERNISM and even the notion of POSTMODERNITY. FOUCAULT is criticized (1988) for his extreme relativism and for severing every link between truth and the philosophy of history. More generally, postmodernism is attacked because it makes the necessary critique of an incomplete modernity quite independent of scientific analysis and thus retreats into the irrational. Habermas's major criticism of HEIDEGGER is reminiscent of Adorno's remarks in *Negative Dialectics* (1966); Heidegger is accused of renouncing all questions that can be handled in argumentative form and of rejecting in advance the very possibility of consensus.

Although Habermas's books are characterized by a high level of abstraction (and by a style of writing that can only be described as laboured) and rarely make reference to contemporary events, he has long been a frequent contributor to newspapers and magazines and an active participant in the defence of civil society and its lifeworld. His comments on the so-called historians' debate (*HISTORIKER-*

STREIT) are an important contribution to the discussion of German REVISIONISM (1986b, 1989), whilst his discussion of the problems of German reunification is notable for its critical lucidity (1991a).

READING: Geuss (1981); McCarthy (1984)

habitus A Latin word meaning style of dress and disposition, attitude or character, introduced into the vocabulary of sociology by BOURDIEU. The term is originally used by Bourdieu in his studies of French peasant culture (1962) and of the notion of honour in the Kabyle society of Algeria (1965). It is used here to designate an 'attitudinal disposition' and is related to *hexis*, derived from the Greek and meaning 'physical deportment'. In Bourdieu's later work, habitus is used more broadly to describe any form of bodily disposition or comportment that encodes a certain cultural understanding. At a very basic level, a habitus consists of the forms of behaviour – beginning with bodily posture – appropriate to a given social context that are inculcated into a child as it learns, for example, to defer to others. In more general terms, Bourdieu uses the term to describe the unconscious internalization of objective social structures which appear spontaneous and natural, but which are in fact socially conditioned.

READING: Robbins (1991)

Hall, Stuart (1932–) Jamaican-born cultural critic. It would be difficult to overestimate the importance of Hall's role in the creation and development of British CULTURAL STUDIES. As one of Britain's leading black intellectuals and in his successive roles as a founding editor of *NEW LEFT REVIEW*, as cofounder and then Director of Birmingham University's Centre for Contemporary Cultural Studies (1967–79) and as Professor of Sociology at the Open University until his retirement in 1997, he has played a central part in the creation and development of a discipline which he neatly defines (1997b) as the study of the organization of power and cultural power. Hall's role has mainly been that of editor and facilitator, usually working in collaboration with others. The collective studies of GRAMSCI and IDEOLOGY (Hall, Lumley and McLennan 1977) and of racial stereotyping (Hall et al. 1979) helped to make the issues of race and GENDER central to cultural studies. In the 1980s Hall was a central figure in the debates over Thatcherism (the body of policies associated with Margaret Thatcher's premiership between 1979 and 1990), when he argued persuasively that the left could learn from her ability to think in terms of a long-term strategic perspective, and that it should not lapse back into support for outdated socialist policies: Britain was living in 'New Times' and the left had to adjust accordingly if it was to be able to respond to Thatcher's 'authoritarian populism' (1988). In 1995 Hall was one of the cofounders of *Soundings*, a journal of culture and politics that explicitly attempts to restore a continuity with the cultural politics of the original NEW LEFT (1995).

Hall's contribution to cultural theory is not expounded in any single book, and is dispersed across a host of articles, interviews and collaborative projects. Many of his essays on identity and ethnicity have been collected, together with interviews with Hall and critical contributions by others, in *Stuart Hall: Critical Dialogues in*

Cultural Studies (Morley and Kuan-Hsing 1996); the interview given to Peter Osborne and Lynne Segal in 1977 (Hall 1977b) provides a good overview of his main concerns.

hate speech The expression is used in American English (and more rarely in the UK) to describe intimidating, harassing or abusive forms of speech that promote or encourage hatred, discrimination and violence. In the 1980s many American colleges adopted so-called speech codes designed to outlaw the use of sexist language and to prevent derogatory remarks being addressed to ethnic and other minorities. Whilst attempts to promote POLITICALLY CORRECT modes of address have enjoyed some success, US courts have repeatedly ruled that hate speech is protected under the free speech provision of the First Amendment to the Constitution. The dilemma facing liberals is encapsulated by the terms of the International Covenant on Civil and Political Rights. Whilst Article 19 guarantees that 'everyone shall have the right to freedom of expression', Article 20 recommends the prohibition of all advocacy of national, racial or religious hatred that can be construed as an incitement to discrimination, hostility or violence. In Britain, incitement to racial hatred is an offence under the terms of the Race Relations Acts of 1965 and 1975.

The related 'hate crime' is used to describe offences motivated by racism, sexism or HOMOPHOBIA. In 1999 West Yorkshire Police (UK) officially launched an initiative called PACT (Positive Action Against Hate Crime) to increase the level of reporting of hate crime, broadly defined as any incident that appears to either the victim or the investigating officer to be motivated by racism or homophobia.

READING: Owen (1998)

hegemony The term derives from the Greek *hegemon*, meaning leader, prominent power or dominant state or person, and is widely used to denote political dominance. A more specific and sophisticated concept of hegemony is elaborated by Antonio GRAMSCI in his *Prison Notebooks* (1971). In Britain the Gramscian concept has been popularized and widely disseminated by the work on popular culture undertaken by the Open University (see section four of Bennett, Martin, Mercer and Woolacott 1981) and Birmingham University's Centre for Contemporary Cultural Studies (Hall, Lumley and McLennan 1977).

Gramsci's notion of hegemony makes an important contribution to the theory of IDEOLOGY, particularly insofar as it offers an alternative to the BASE/SUPERSTRUCTURE model. Gramsci makes a fundamental distinction between the two superstructural levels of political society, or the state and its agencies, and CIVIL SOCIETY, or that set of organs usually assumed to belong to the private realm. Whereas the state establishes and reproduces the dominance of a ruling group or class through direct forms of domination ranging from legislation to coercion, civil society reproduces its hegemony by ensuring that the mass of the population 'spontaneously' consents to the general direction imposed upon social life by the ruling group. Within civil society, dominance is manifested by the intellectual and moral leadership conferred upon a ruling group by its dominance in the realm of economic production. A conception of the world becomes hegemonic when it is no longer confined to professional philosophers or the intelligentsia, but comes to belong to a popular culture that permeates the whole of civil society. The establishment of a hegemony is the task of the ORGANIC INTELLECTUALS of the ruling class. At the highest level, they create philosophy, the sciences and the arts; at a lower level, they administer an existing body of knowledge and ideology through their work in the educational system, cultural institutions and the media. Hegemony is not simply an expression of dominance, but also its precondition: a social group or class cannot take governmental power unless it has already established its ideological hegemony over society. Nor is the establishment of a hegemony simply a matter of imposing an ideology. A potentially hegemonic group always attempts to absorb and transform the ideologies of allied and even rival groups. The hegemonic group establishes and maintains its dominance by creating a 'historical bloc' in which there is an organic cohesion between leaders and led, and in which the 'feelings' of the population are completely imbued with its dominant view of the world.

Heidegger, Martin (1889–1976) German philosopher. Heidegger is one of the key figures in the history of CONTINENTAL PHILOSOPHY and his *Being and Time* (1927) is one of the most significant books of the twentieth century. In his early work Heidegger takes his inspiration from HUSSERL'S PHENOMENOLOGY and provides, in turn, the theoretical basis for EXISTENTIALISM, even though he is at pains to distance himself from the variant proposed by SARTRE (Heidegger 1946), and his influence on twentieth-century French philosophy is all-pervasive (Rockmore 1995). Many of the theses associated with DECONSTRUCTION can be traced back to Heidegger.

Heidegger's prolific output – and the fact that English translations have appeared in a rather haphazard order – makes him difficult to approach. Still incomplete, the collected edition published in Frankfurt by Vittorio Klosterman already runs around eighty volumes, many of them consisting of posthumously published lectures. Heidegger's style provides a further obstacle. The constant reliance on Greek and German etymologies, which reflects Heidegger's conviction that Greek and German are *the* philosophical languages, makes his work extremely difficult to translate; most English versions come festooned with explanatory translators' notes. The anthology of *Basic Writings* edited by Krell (1977) is the best introduction to Heidegger, whilst the fourteen essays collected as *Pathmarks* (Heidegger 1976) supply an overview of his career as a whole.

In the 'Postscript' to *What is Metaphysics?* (originally published in 1929; the postscript, now in *Pathmarks*, is from 1949), Heidegger remarks that 'Of all beings, only the human being . . . experiences the wonder of wonder: *that* things *are*', and 'being' (*Sein*) is the central theme of the early Heidegger, who holds that 'being is the proper and sole theme of philosophy' (1975a). It is, he insists, also a theme that has been forgotten or eclipsed by the history of METAPHYSICS from Plato and Aristotle onwards; the history of philosophy has been that of 'forgetfulness of being', and Heidegger's goal is to return to the very beginnings of Western philosophy in order to make 'the wonder *that* things *are*' its main theme. It is this insistence on beginning that explains Heidegger's concern with etymology: the Ancient Greek words bring the thinker into contact with 'the thing itself' (1958).

The central category of Heidegger's analysis in *Being and Time* and related works like the 1927 lectures published as *The Basic Problems of Phenomenology* (1975a) is DASEIN, literally meaning 'being there'. This is a specifically human attribute, and it is contrasted with the being-at-hand (*Vorhandensein*) of things, which are 'at hand' or 'to hand' in that they are there to be used by Dasein. Dasein is the mode of human beings' being (*Seiende*) in the world, and is often described as 'thrownness' (*Geworfenheit*) in that Dasein is literally cast or thrown into a world of contingency or FACTICITY and must therefore strive towards AUTHENTICITY rather than fall back (*verfallen*) into the apparent familiarity of the world or the idle chatter that distracts it from the understanding of its situation. Existence has, that is, no fixed or predetermined meaning: Dasein must choose between authenticity or determination by others and the forgetfulness of its own self that Sartre will describe as BAD FAITH. Dasein's mode of being is spatial in that it is thrown into a three-dimensional world, but it is also temporal. Dasein does not exist within time; its being is, rather, time itself. Here Heidegger departs considerably from Husserl's phenomenology, which captures only the 'temporal mode of the present' (1936), by insisting that Dasein is characterized by the fact that it has been in the past and will be in the future. Its temporal horizon is imposed by its finitude or the prospect of ceasing to be: Dasein is being-towards-death. The care (*Sorge*) and anxiety (*Angst*) induced by the prospect of being-towards-death can be overcome only by 'resoluteness' and striving towards authenticity.

It is conventional to make a distinction between an 'early' and a 'late' Heidegger, and he himself describes his work as being characterized by a change of direction or 'turning' (1977). The concern with being now gives way to a concern with HERMENEUTICS and language, described by Heidegger and followers such as GADAMER as 'the house of being' (Heidegger 1959). Increasingly, thought is identified with poetic language, and particularly poetry, as Heidegger repeats (1951) that 'poetically man dwells' (a quotation from Hölderlin) and identifies thinking (*Denken*) with writing (*Dichten*) in a poetic mode. The concentration on poetic language is in part an attempt to escape the technological world in which things are 'enframed' (1955) and dehumanized, and to allow poetic being to reveal itself through the process of *aletheia* (the Greek term for 'disclosure' or 'unconcealment'). As early as 1935 Heidegger was speaking of 'the spiritual decline of the earth', and his vision of the history of philosophy is also one of decline. In his later work the concentration on the house of being is viewed as a means of arresting that decline and effecting a return to the origins of both language and thought.

Heidegger's reputation has long been surrounded by political controversy. Although many accounts suggest that the controversy erupted after the publication of the biographical studies (Farias 1987; Ott 1988) which revealed the extent of the philosopher's involvement with Nazism, doubts about the nature of Heidegger's politics were already being voiced in France in the 1930s (Birchall 1998). Heidegger's remarks in *An Introduction to Metaphysics* (1935), where he speaks of Europe (or in other words Germany) being 'squeezed' between the technological societies of the United States and the Soviet Union, are a typical expression of the conservative thought of the 1930s, and anticipate the anti-technological theses of the late Heidegger (1955). The speech made on being elected Rector of Freiburg University in 1933 (now included, with other materials from this period, in Wolin 1993) is more disturbing in that Hitler's Third Reich is identified with the spiritual rebirth and destiny of Germany, and in that Heidegger invokes the 'Führer principle' as the model for the reorganization of the University. Heidegger quickly resigned from the rectorship, claiming to have moved into opposition to Nazism, but quietly retained his party membership. Whether or not his support for Nazism invalidates or detracts from his work as a philosopher is still a matter of bitter controversy (see, *inter alios*, Derrida 1987; Rockmore and Margolis 1992; Young 1997).

READING: Dreyfus (1991); Dreyfus and Hall (1992); Guignon (1993)

heritage industry Term used from the mid-1970s onwards to describe, often in pejorative terms, the preservation of sites of natural beauty or historical interest which are assumed to enshrine some aspect of the British national heritage. It is also applied to the creation of industrial museums that bring the past to life through the use of reconstructed environments, costumed attendants, visual displays and participatory activities. The re-enactment of Civil War battles, the reopening of steam railways and the application of preservation orders to Victorian suburbs can all be described as aspects of the heritage industry. The industry can be seen either as an expression of a popular, if nostalgic, conception of history, or as a transformation of British history into a Disneyfied theme park. Paradoxically, the heritage industry often seems to deny the historicity of history, and does not shrink from oxymoronic references (OXYMORON) to the 'timelessness' of the historical relics it preserves.

The National Heritage Acts of 1980 and 1983 provided for the preservation of a range of properties, including a large proportion of country houses, and for the provision of public access. The heritage of the past was thus put on display and made available for consumption. For the heritage industry, it is axiomatic that traces of an important cultural patrimony are under threat and in need of preservation. The semantic choice of 'heritage' places the emphasis on a pattern of inheritance associated with the family, thus reinforcing the sense of belonging to what Benedict ANDERSON calls an 'imagined community'.

For its critics (Wright 1985, 1991), the effect of the heritage industry is to redeploy existing images of the past, many of them rural and utopian, and to turn a history that has been purged of political tensions into a spectacle of a unified nation. More sympathetic observers take the view that such 'heritage-baiting' (Samuel 1994) is an expression of a condescending aesthetic snobbery and insist that 'heritage' has a large and genuine public popularity. All parties agree that the heritage industry relies heavily upon INVENTED TRADITIONS; any given stretch of the National Heritage Coast is likely to have at least one 'smuggler's cave'.

hermeneutics The art or science of interpretation. The term is supposedly derived from the name of 'Hermes' who was the fleet-footed messenger of the Greek gods, but also the patron of travellers, robbers and interpreters. Hermeneutics has a very long history which stretches from Antiquity to the postmodern period; it has been claimed (Vattimo 1987) that it is the common idiom of the latter period. Although the modern hermeneutics of HEIDEGGER, GADAMER and RICOEUR is generally secular in its inspiration, the art of interpretation was for centuries associated with the study of scripture and has always been a vital aspect of the three great monotheisms, all of which rely for their authority upon the interpretation of a sacred text. Christianity, Judaism and Islam all have distinct but related hermeneutic traditions. Frank Kermode's *Genesis of Secrecy* (Kermode 1979) is an elegant late example of scriptural hermeneutics. The Jewish hermeneutic tradition of *Midrash* is particularly rich, with multiple layers of meaning ascribed to every word, and even every consonant of the Books of the Law (which are written without vowels). Hermeneutics takes a slightly different form in the Islamic tradition, in which the Koran (which means 'recitation') is held to be the literal word of God, as handed down by oral tradition prior to the establishment of a written text; the Koran itself warns against excessive interpretation, and hermeneutics tends therefore to take the form of attempts to reconcile the divine text with a *sunna* (tradition) made up of *hadiths* (sayings and actions attributed to the Prophet) and the texts of the law (*sharia*).

In Antiquity, hermeneutics was closely associated with the study of Homer in the various academies and with the codification of RHETORIC that was such an important part of the Greek conception of education. Linguistic knowledge and detailed textual analysis were combined in an attempt to establish and evaluate an authentic text. The degree to which that tradition is perpetuated in early Christianity is evident from Book II of St Augustine's *On Christian Teaching*, which deals with the correct reading of Scripture and in doing so outlines both a classic study in rhetoric and an early theory of the linguistic SIGN. Hermeneutics played a central role in the establishment of the CANONS of the three monotheisms and in the shaping of the Christian and Hebrew scriptures, as well as of the Koran. As in Classical Antiquity, comparative textual variations and the elimination of scribal errors were the means used to establish the true text of scriptural revelation, and hermeneutics also provides a defence against incorrect readings and corrupt texts. The process whereby the commentaries of interpreters were themselves incorporated into the sacred texts gradually gave rise to the medieval bibles in which the text itself was literally hemmed in by commentaries, and then commentaries on commentaries (some Italian editions of Dante are so cluttered with explanatory notes that they still look like this). Scripture was held to have a fourfold nature, and to contain both literal and historical meanings (revealed by grammatical interpretation) and mystical and spiritual meanings revealed by contemplating and communing with the divinely inspired text. Throughout early and medieval Christianity, ALLEGORY played an important role in hermeneutics, particularly when it came to deciding which parts of the Old Testament foretold the New.

The rise of modern hermeneutics is influenced primarily by developments in German thought. Luther's great slogan of *scriptura sola* ('by Scripture alone') represents both a rejection of centuries of papal authority and a return to studying the letter of the scriptural text. In 1513–14 Luther taught a course on the Psalms at Wittenberg University, and had printed an edition of the text in which wide margins and white space replaced the accumulated glosses of the Church Fathers. After this symbolic act, the work of interpretation could begin anew with the belief that

Scripture was its own best interpreter and that the plain meaning of the text would emerge if the reader surrendered to the text itself rather than to traditional authorities.

The greatest single influence on the development of modern hermeneutics is the work of the Protestant theologian Friedrich Schleiermacher (1768–1834), who is also a significant figure in the rise of HISTORICISM. Schleiermacher's *Elements of Grammar, Hermeneutics and Criticism* (1808) combines the resources of grammar, comparative PHILOLOGY and textual criticism to produce a science of interpretation that can, in theory, be applied to any linguistic utterance, and not to Scripture alone. Schleiermacher can be seen as the source of the two main strands in contemporary hermeneutics: the quasi-psychological strand associated with his biographer Dilthey, and the more strictly linguistic tradition associated with GADAMER. The classic description of Schleiermacher's methods and goals is in fact supplied by Dilthey (1900), who states that an understanding (*Verstehen*) of Leonardo implies a global interpretation of his actions, paintings, sketches and written works as a single unified and homogeneous progress or project. Philology, grammar and historical interpretation combine to produce an understanding that is actually a re-experiencing (*Nachfühlen*) of the whole of the work on the basis of individual fragments, and a reconstruction of the spiritual leanings of the author on the basis of the whole work. The goal of the hermeneutic process is, concludes Dilthey, 'to understand the author better than he understood himself'. Under the influence of Dilthey, hermeneutics moves from being an interpretation of a text to being a historicist interpretation of the situation of the author himself.

As modern philosophy makes its LINGUISTIC TURN, hermeneutics takes on a new importance, but many of the old certainties are lost as the notion of a true or final interpretation becomes ever more problematic. For HEIDEGGER, hermeneutics is no longer a matter of textual interpretation, but an interpretative mode of being in the world and orientating oneself to it. Perhaps the most important single influence of contemporary hermeneutics from RICOEUR to DE MAN is, however, the adage in fragment 181 of NIETZSCHE's *The Will to Power* (1901), where the 'positivism which halts at phenomena' is refuted in the proclamation: 'No, facts is precisely what there is not, only interpretations.'

The paradox of any form of hermeneutics is that it is inevitably a circular process: there is no possibility of escaping the need to have already understood a verse of scripture before attempting to explain the process of understanding that verse. The detail is understood within the whole, and the whole from the detail. This is referred to as 'the hermeneutic circle', and it is impossible to step outside it. Meaning cannot be grasped from 'outside', precisely because 'there are only interpretations'.

READING: Bowie (1997); Bruns (1992); Hamilton (1996); Ricoeur (1969)

herstory Feminist coinage from the early 1970s, formed by analogy with the pseudo-etymological transformation of 'history' into 'his story', and stressing that the historical experience of women is often ignored or suppressed by conventional historiography.

heuristic In philosophy the term usually applies to a thesis or proposition that serves to discover something, or that is conducive to understanding or explaining it. It is also applied to the 'trial and error' method of problem-solving. In educational theory heurism refers to the training of pupils to find things out for themselves.

Hill, Christopher (1912–) British historian, specializing in the seventeenth century. Like HOBSBAWM and THOMPSON, he was a member of the COMMUNIST PARTY HISTORIANS' GROUP (Samuel 1980; Kaye 1984) and, whilst his work has always been oriented by MARXISM, like his colleagues he is careful to avoid the crude BASE/SUPERSTRUCTURE model that tends to make everything a simple expression of economic relations. At the opposite extreme, he also rejects Trevelyan's notorious definition of social history as 'the history of a people with the politics left out' (Trevelyan 1949–52) and concentrates on the interconnections between the social, the economic, the political and the intellectual.

Hill's first study of the English Revolution of the mid-seventeenth century appeared in 1940 and he has continued to explore that period in a series of major studies (including 1940, 1958, 1965, 1974) published over more than fifty years. For Hill, the Civil War period in England is that of the first European revolution and marks the beginning of the process that, thanks to the abolition of feudal structures of property ownership, the creation of a national identity and the spread of religious tolerance, would eventually allow England to emerge as the first industrial nation; his volume in the 'Pelican Economic History of Britain' series (1969) provides a good summary of his main themes. According to Hill, the Civil War period was marked by the emergence of the distinctively English radicalism associated with religious dissent, and the millenarian politics of the Diggers, Levellers and Ranters and the other representatives of a radical revolution was suppressed by the so-called Glorious Revolution that restored a protocapitalist order in 1688. Such movements are the subject of some of his most attractive books (1972; the late essays collected in 1996; etc). Like Thompson's studies in later working-class history, these make an important contribution to HISTORY FROM BELOW; whereas Thompson speaks of rescuing popular radicalism from 'the enormous condescension of posterity' (1963), Hill has described his aim as being to 'rescue the landless peasantry from posterity's enormous silence' (1996). The history of the radicalism of the landless peasantry is interwoven with that of the intellectual developments associated with the spread of the Protestantism and Puritanism that put an end to a quasi-magical world-view (1965, 1993) to provide a remarkable picture of a world-view that is alien to the modern temperament, but which must be imaginatively reconstructed if this important period is to be understood. For Hill, the historian's basic questions are 'Why here?' and 'Why now?' (1967) and the historian's task is to trace how elements of the new emerge from the old. His basic HISTORICISM is illustrated by a programmatic remark in his major study of the importance of the English translation of the Bible in seventeenth-century culture (1993): 'To say that the English Revolution was about religion is tautologous; it took place in the seventeenth century.'

histoire événementielle French phrase, often translated as 'factual history', though 'event-bound history' is a better, if cumbersome, rendition. It is widely used by the French historians of the *ANNALES* school as a pejorative description of the reduction of historiography to a superficial recording of events.

The expression derives from the work of the economist François Simiand in the 1930s, but was given much wider currency by BRAUDEL's preface to his study of the Mediterranean in the age of Philip I (1949), where events are described as the surface waves caused by the effect of a deep tidal movement. In his inaugural lecture to the Collège de France (1950), Braudel likens events to a swarm of phosphorescent fireflies which flicker and then disappear without doing anything to dispel the surrounding darkness. The darkness is, in this metaphor, the domain of the *LONGUE DURÉE* or of the slow and almost imperceptible time that passes unnoticed by individuals (Braudel 1958). A concentration on the *longue durée* and the dismissal of *histoire événementielle* are characteristic features of *Annales* historiography.

READING: Burke (1990)

historical materialism The theory of social development and CONTRADICTION outlined in the historical writings of Marx and Engels and, together with DIALECT-ICAL MATERIALISM, the theoretical core of MARXISM. No one text by either author is devoted exclusively to an exposition of historical materialism, but Marx's *Contribution to a Critique of Political Economy* (1859) and the first volume of *Capital* (1867), together with Engels's *The Origins of the Family, Private Property and the State* (1884), can be regarded as the classic expositions of the theory.

The basic premise of historical materialism is that human life is not determined by consciousness but by its material and social conditions of existence. Historical materialism asserts that all human history is the product of an antagonistic struggle between social classes and of the DIALECTIC between the forces of production, or forms of ownership and control of industry and commerce, and the relations of production, or the social, legal and ideological forms that determine how classes with conflicting interests coexist within a given society. Social development is ultimately determined by the growth of the productive forces, a process typified by the rise of large-scale industry during the British industrial revolution. The rise of industry dislocates and destroys the social relations typical of the early stage of feudalism; the relationship between lord and vassal, which implies both servility on the part of the vassal and obligations on the part of the lord, thus gives way to social relations based upon the exchange of labour-power for a wage. When the productive forces of society come into conflict with the existing relations of production or property relations, a period of social revolutions ensues. Historical development can thus be described in terms of the emergence of a sequence of MODES OF PRODUCTION. Marx identifies (1859) a sequence of Asiatic, ancient, feudal and bourgeois or capitalist modes which mark or punctuate the economic development of society. Each is described as having a specific form of social organization corresponding to the manner in which slaves, land or industry are owned and to the mode in which an economic surplus is extracted. In a slave society, a surplus is extracted by the direct exploitation of a servile class of men who are literally elements in production; in a capitalist society the surplus takes the form of the surplus-value produced by the wage-labourer who has reproduced the cost of his wages and then produces the surplus that is appropriated by the capitalist. The sequence of modes of production is assumed to end with the emergence of the socialism and communism that will finally abolish private property and the existence of antagonistic classes. For ALTHUSSER, historical materialism is a science established by the EPISTEMOLOGICAL BREAK it makes with political economy.

historicism The term is so widely used by so many authors in so many senses as to have become confusing, particularly as it can be defined in both positive and negative terms. In very general terms, it can be defined as the belief or conviction that historical phenomena are situated and defined by their specific context and are therefore to be explained in terms of the contingent factors that gave rise to them.

Perhaps best defined as a trend or mood rather than as a specific school of thought, historicism is usually associated with those developments in the German Romantic philosophy of the late eighteenth and early nineteenth centuries that are linked to the rise of HERMENEUTICS (see Meinenke 1936; White 1973; Hamilton 1996). Turning away from the abstract universalism of the ENLIGHTENMENT, major works such as Herder's *Essay on the Origins of Language* (1772), which argues that a people's culture and thought are accessible only through its language, and Ranke's *Histories of the Latin and German Nations* (1824) begin to look at national languages and nations themselves as particular expressions of human existence and introduce a new sense of relativism into linguistic and historical studies. The sense of relativism or comparativism is further promoted by the developments in comparative religion and comparative PHILOLOGY that inspired the hermeneutics of Schleiermacher's *Elements of Grammar, Hermeneutics and Criticism* (1808). As a result of the convergent effects of comparativism and hermeneutics, both history and linguistics begin to focus on the unique circumstances of individual examples rather than on the universal histories of the Enlightenment. Historians such as Ranke begin to attempt to stand aside from their own eras and cultures, to think in terms of the consciousness of the age they are studying, and to reproduce the way in which the world appeared to its contemporaries. A similar approach informs the history of MENTALITIES or collective beliefs associated with the French *ANNALES* school. An early (and by no means universally accepted) example of that version of historicism is supplied by Lucien Febvre's study of the religion of Rabelais (1942), which reconstructs the mental world of the sixteenth century in order to demonstrate that the modern notion of atheism was quite literally unthinkable in the world-view of that period.

In his discussions of literary realism LUKÁCS equates historicism with 'the conception of history as the destiny of the people', but also with the writer's 'historical fidelity' or faithful reproduction of the great collisions, the great crises and the great turning-points of history (1937). Ernst BLOCH, in stark contrast, describes historicism as the enemy of novelty, as the 'plundering and desecration of the past', and as the falsification of pedigree that allows the Nazi Party to pervert the medieval millenarian belief in the coming of a Third Reich, or the Kingdom of the Holy Spirit, into the nightmare of the totalitarian 'Thousand-Year-Reich' of Hitler (Bloch 1959, 1988; cf. Geoghegan 1996). Perhaps the most famous critic of historicism in the twentieth century is Karl POPPER whose *Poverty of Historicism* (1957) describes it as an approach to the social sciences which assumes that the discovery of the rhythms, patterns or laws that underlie the evolution of history will allow future developments to be predicted with scientific accuracy. This approach, Popper contends, is based upon false analogies with the natural sciences, upon a failure to realize that the 'laws of nature' are in fact hypotheses. History, according to Popper, is characterized by an interest in actual, singular and specific events rather than laws and generalizations. As the title of his polemic – which alludes to Marx's *Poverty of Philosophy* (1847) – makes clear, Popper's main target is MARXISM, which he views as a variety of fatalism and as a major threat to the open society of liberal democracy (Popper 1945).

That Marxism is a form of historicism is widely accepted, but that view is vehemently rejected by ALTHUSSER (Althusser and Balibar 1965). For Althusser, historicism is a characteristic of the nineteenth-century political economy which, for ideological reasons, cannot transcend its own presence or contemporaneity and cannot see beyond its own categories. Marxism makes an EPISTEMOLOGICAL BREAK with political economy by establishing itself as both a distinctive science of history (HISTORICAL MATERIALISM) and a theoretical science (DIALECTICAL MATERIALISM) which, unlike IDEOLOGY, is not constrained by the BASE/SUPERSTRUCTURE model. Althusser also uses the term 'historicism' to refer to the many 'deviations' from scientific Marxist theory which ignore the problem of OVER-DETERMINATION and argue that history can be understood by taking or cutting an 'essential section' through the social formation and reducing all contradictions to the expression of an essence. GRAMSCI, Lucio Colletti, Galvano Della Volpe and SARTRE are all accused by Althusser of succumbing to historicism.

In architecture, 'historicism' is sometimes used to describe the introduction of stylistic or decorative features that 'quote from' the styles of the past.

READING: Hamilton (1996); Meinenke (1936); White (1973)

Historikerstreit The 'Historians' Debate', which took place mainly in the pages of the daily *Frankfurter Allgemeine Zeitung* in 1985–6, centres on the 'normalization' of the Nazi period in German history, and is a major instance of REVISIONISM. An existing controversy was exacerbated in 1985 when Germany's Chancellor Kohl and US President Reagan took part in a wreath-laying ceremony at a military cemetery in Bitburg. The intended spirit of reconciliation was soured when it was revealed that some of the war victims buried there were SS troops.

In what was to become a notorious article, the conservative historian Ernst Nolte advanced the view (1985) that, leaving aside the 'technical procedure of gassing', all the atrocities claimed to be unique features of the Nazi regime had already been committed by the Soviet regime. It was also argued that the Nazi regime behaved as it did because it saw itself as the actual or potential victim of an 'Asiatic deed' and was in effect acting in self-defence. HABERMAS and other opponents of the revisionists argued for the need to emphasize the exceptional nature of the

Holocaust, and pointed to the dangers inherent in dissolving it into the broader and ahistorical category of totalitarianism (Habermas 1986b).

history from below An important strand in contemporary historiography, often associated with the labour movement and its historians and typified by the journal *HISTORY WORKSHOP*. History from below usually takes the form of a reaction against the 'noble' history of kings, queens, politicians and treaties and attempts to rescue the poor and working classes from what E. P. THOMPSON famously called 'the enormous condescension of posterity' (1963). In Britain the gradual emergence of history from below can be traced back to the early studies of social conditions in the late nineteenth and early twentieth centuries written by the Hammonds (1911, 1917, 1919) and to the work on the transition to capitalism and industrial society undertaken by the members of the COMMUNIST PARTY HISTORIANS' GROUP, as well as to Cole and Postgate's history of the 'common people' (1938). Eric HOBSBAWM's studies of primitive forms of political rebellion (1959a) and of banditry (1969) are also major influences. Carlo GINZBURG's studies of peasant heretics provide a parallel in Italy, as do some aspects of the work of the *ANNALES* school in France.

History from below is not always written by professionals, and amateur groups of local historians have also made important contributions. This form of historiography typically relies on sources of two kinds. Archives such as parish registers can be used to study the demography of marriage and patterns of birth-control, whilst local archives can be exploited to produce histories of the day-to-day activities of trade unions. The use of tape-recorders facilitates the recording of oral history, one of the most successful and compelling examples being Ronald Fraser's account (1979) of the experience of civil war in Spain between 1936 and 1939. The concept of a history from below has also made a major contribution to feminist history which records a female experience that was long 'hidden from history' as Sheila ROW-BOTHAM puts it (1973a).

History Workshop A collective of British historians founded by Raphaël SAMUEL and others in 1967; *History Workshop Journal* has been published biannually since 1976. The emphasis has always been on working-class history, oral history and HISTORY FROM BELOW.

History Workshop is dedicated to making history a democratic activity and to providing a broad context for its study, both in order to counter the scholastic fragmentation of the subject and to make it accessible to a wider and non-professional audience. Mature students and trade-unionists have always played an important role in its activities. History, it is argued, is too important to be left to the professionals, and should provide not only a means of interpreting the past but also a critical viewpoint from which to view the present. Both the members of the collective and the journal's readership have always had personal and institutional links with the broad NEW LEFT and the feminist and GAY movements.

The first of History Workshop's annual conferences was held at Ruskin College, Oxford in March 1967 and took as its title 'A Day with the Chartists'. Subsequent topics have included 'Children in History: Children's Liberation' in 1972, 'People's History and

Socialist Theory' in 1979, and 'Speaking for Ourselves?' in 1987. In 1970 the publication of a successful series of 'History Workshop Pamphlets' began with Frank McKenna's *A Glossary of Railwaymen's Talk* and Sally Alexander's *St Giles Fair 1830–1914*.

Although the first issue of *History Workshop Journal* included a plea for an autonomous feminist history, it was simply subtitled 'A Journal of Socialist Historians', and calls for a feminist input were greeted with derisive laughter at early conferences. It was not until the thirteenth issue (Spring 1982) that it officially became a 'journal of socialist and feminist historians'.

READING: Samuel (1992)

Hobsbawm, Eric John (1917–) British historian specializing in the history of nineteenth-century Europe (1962). Hobsbawm has also made major contributions to British labour history (1964) and to the study of preindustrial peasant rebellions in both Europe and Latin America (1959a), and can be regarded as one of the pioneers of HISTORY FROM BELOW. He is a prolific writer, and is probably best known for his trilogy of 'Ages' – *The Age of Revolution* (1962), *The Age of Capital* (1975) and *The Age of Empire* (1987) – which paints a panoramic picture of nineteenth-century Britain and Europe. In 1994 this was complemented by *The Age of Extremes*, a panoptic survey of a 'short' twentieth century spanning the period between the First World War and the collapse of communism at the beginning of the 1990s.

Hobsbawm was the only member of the COMMUNIST PARTY HISTORIANS' GROUP not to resign from the Party in 1956, when he argued that there was still a need for a strong organizational party, and he continues to contend that Marx's materialism is a good guide to history, and especially to the history of industrialization. His MARXISM has never been of the dogmatic variety. Even though he remained in the Communist Party of Great Britain, his books were never translated into Russian during the Soviet period. Hobsbawm is not, by his own admission, the most philosophically inclined of historians but his collection of essays on history (1997) reveals him to be a sophisticated and skilled craftsman who is highly sceptical of claims that history is merely another narrative to be judged in literary-rhetorical terms (WHITE); he insists that the object of historical inquiry consists of real facts.

The Age of Extremes attracted controversy by claiming that the Second World War was won by an alliance between liberal capitalism and Soviet communism (Mann 1995; Nairn 1995; Therborn 1995). For Hobsbawm, the central paradox of the twentieth century is that the Russian Revolution, whose goal was the abolition of world capitalism, actually saved its antagonist and, because of the fear it inspired in the West, provided capitalism with the incentive to introduce the reforms that produced a golden age that ended only with the global crisis of the 1970s. According to his critics, Hobsbawm is an apologist for the Soviet experiment which cost millions of lives.

Between 1955 and 1965 Hobsbawm was the weekly *NEW STATESMAN*'s jazz critic, writing under the name 'Francis Newton', which was borrowed from the trumpeter Frankie Newton (1906–54). 'Francis Newton's' informative guide to jazz (1959b) – seen as a form of cultural resistance – was reissued under Hobsbawm's own name in 1989.

READING: Kaye (1984); Samuel (1980)

Hoggart, Richard (1918–) British cultural critic, cofounder with Stuart HALL of Birmingham University's Centre for Contemporary Cultural Studies in 1964, and sometime Assistant Director of UNESCO.

Hoggart's immensely popular and influential *The Uses of Literacy* (1957) is a powerful study of 'the quality of working class life' in the Hunslet area of Leeds. A vivid picture emerges from this hybrid text, which is in part an autobiography and in part a study in phenomenological sociology. The first volume of Hoggart's autobiography (1988) makes it clear that the account of the trajectory or *BILDUNGS-ROMAN* of the 'scholarship boy' who is promoted out of his class of origin is a self-portrait.

Just as ORWELL makes a virtue of 'ordinary decency', Hoggart is primarily concerned with the remnants of a 'decent, local, personal and communal way of life' that has survived despite the Americanization of British culture and the inroads that have been made by what he calls chain-store modernism. His great regret is that working people are exchanging their birthright for a mass of pin-ups. Pulp fiction, cheap glossy magazines and advertisements are dissected with a scorn that is akin to the stern moralism of LEAVIS.

Hoggart's work can be read as a major expression of what has been called the 'Welfare State culture' (Mulhern 1996), and as a defence of the values embodied in Lord Reith's BBC, the adult education sector where Hoggart began his teaching career, and Allen Lane's Penguin Books. Published some forty years after *The Uses of Literacy*, *The Way We Live Now* (1995) is self-consciously written in the 'condition of England' tradition of Elizabeth Gaskell, Disraeli and Dickens, and defines democracy as a thoughtful society besieged on both left and right by a relativism that deliberately avoids all judgements of value in deference to either market forces or POLITICAL CORRECTNESS. Hoggart does not always succeed in avoiding a self-indulgent and even self-deluding nostalgia for his own past; Hunslet is still evoked as a touchstone and a source of values, but most of the area has in fact been demolished.

homophobia Pathological fear and loathing of lesbians and gay men. Expressions of homophobia can range from verbal abuse and the use of HATE SPEECH to physical violence and even murder. It can also find expression in legal judgments, as when a British judge sentenced a man to five years' imprisonment for manslaughter rather than life for murder on the grounds that he had been provoked to violence by the homosexual approaches allegedly made by his victim (Toolis 1995). In 1999 the British Association of Chief Police Officers officially described homophobia as 'animosity towards lesbians or gay men', and classified homophobic incidents as hate crimes (HATE SPEECH).

hooks, bell (1953–) Black American feminist. bell hooks is the pseudonym of Gloria Watkins, who writes under the name of her maternal grandmother; the lower case is intended to emphasize that the message is more important than the messenger, whilst the use of the pseudonym is designed to differentiate between the writer and the ego of Watkins herself (hooks 1997).

hooks's initial message is contained in *Ain't I a Woman* (1981) and states unequivocally that, from the days of the struggles for the abolition of slavery and for women's suffrage to the black liberation and WOMEN'S LIBERATION of the 1960s and 1970s, black liberation has been interpreted as the liberation of black *men*, and feminism as the liberation of *white* women. hooks argues that black liberationists such as Eldridge Cleaver (1935–88) demanded the establishment of a black patriarchy and the subservience of black women (Cleaver 1969), whereas white women have appropriated feminism to facilitate their own entry into mainstream capitalist society. This interpretation of black and women's liberation allows black men to shrug off accusations of sexism by appealing to the oppression they experience as blacks, but takes no account of the plight of the majority of black women. hooks's choice of title inscribes her book within a tradition of resistance on the part of black women. It is a quotation from the famous speech made in 1852 by Sojourner Truth, one of the first feminists to draw attention to the lot of black slave women. When told by a white man at a public meeting that women should not have equal rights because their physical inferiority made them unable to perform their share of labour, she famously replied: 'Look at my arm . . . I have plowed, and planted, and gathered into barns, and no man could head me – and ain't I a woman?' (cited hooks 1981).

hooks is a prolific writer, and the autobiographical *Wounds of Passion* (1997) is her sixteenth book. Her later work is mainly about the representation of race and gender, especially in the popular media (1992). She is also concerned with the need to record and preserve black popular culture and the values of the tight community in which she grew up in rural Kentucky (1996). Yet whilst she emphasizes the enormous importance of a 'homeplace' as a refuge and place for self-renewal created mainly by women, she is very careful not to lapse into the essentialism that sees all African-American experience as an expression of 'soul' (1990) and stresses the multiple and complex nature of black experiences. For hooks, the struggle against racism and sexism as such is inseparable from the struggle against racism *within* feminism and the struggle against sexism *within* black liberation movements.

Horkheimer, Max (1895–1973) German philosopher. In 1930 Horkheimer became Director of the Institut für Sozialforschung (Institute for Social Research) and, together with ADORNO and MARCUSE, he is one of the most significant figures to have been associated with the so-called FRANKFURT SCHOOL. He is now best known for his collaborative work with Adorno on the DIALECTIC OF ENLIGHTENMENT (1947).

Horkheimer's inaugural address to the Institut (1931) broadly outlines the programme for the Frankfurt School's CRITICAL THEORY, and stresses the need for an interdisciplinary mode of thought drawing on philosophy, economics, sociology and history in order to explore the dialectical relationship between the individual and society. In his well known paper 'Traditional and Critical Theory' (1937), he describes critical theory as a human activity that takes society itself as its object; its objective is to transcend the tensions between individual purposefulness and spontaneity, and the work-process relationships upon which society is founded. Until such time as those tensions are resolved, human beings will be in conflict with themselves, or in a state of ALIENATION.

Although the early Horkheimer could be described as a Marxist (see the essays in the collections of 1972 and 1993), his MARXISM, like that of the Frankfurt School as a whole, is highly intellectualized and does not imply either allegiance to the Communist Party or support for the Soviet Union. In many respects, Horkheimer is an heir to the ENLIGHTENMENT tradition, which he views as the self-consciousness of a revolutionary bourgeoisie, and to Kant in particular. His loyalty to that tradition is not, however, unambivalent and reflects his view that enlightenment and progress are themselves ambiguous, and that advances in the technical facilitation of enlightenment always go hand in hand with an increased dehumanization of the world (1947). Their ambiguity, he argues, stems from the relationship between the categories of objective and subjective or instrumental reason. The objective reason characteristic of the great philosophical systems seeks to establish a comprehensive system or a hierarchy of all beings, including human beings and their projects; subjective reason shows little concern for the ends of human actions, and assumes that they are reasonable if they serve the individual or collective subject's interest in self-preservation. Objective and subjective reason were divorced during the Enlightenment, when philosophers attacked religion in the name of reason. What they destroyed was not in fact the churches, but METAPHYSICS and the objective content of religion itself. The contention that instrumental reason has invaded the world and has replaced ends by means is the basis for Horkheimer's scathing critique of the LOGICAL POSITIVISM of the VIENNA CIRCLE, which he describes as a philosophical technocracy that makes no distinction between the production of mathematical formulae and their instrumental application in industry and technology.

In his early writings Horkheimer argues, in quasi-Marxist terms, that only a planned economy can solve the economic and political problem of exploitation; in his later, deeply pessimistic essays (1967), he takes the view that Soviet communism poses as great a threat as Nazism once did and contends that China's experiment with communism represents a descent into pure barbarism. Horkheimer's opposition to the totalitarianism of both left and right does not make him an apologist for liberalism. Liberalism and the mass society it has created are, like authoritarian societies, governed by instrumental reason and characterized by the decay of individual expressiveness.

READING: Benhabib, Bonss and McCabe (1993); Held (1980); Jay (1973); Stirk (1992)

human sciences Although widely used, the expression does not figure in the *New Shorter OED* of 1993. The term can be used very broadly, as in Smith's major history of the human sciences (1997), to refer to all those modes of knowledge from philology to neuroscience that attempt to comprehend what it means to be human. It is more usually used in a narrower sense to refer generically to anthropology, history, psychology, sociology and linguistics. In that sense, the idea of the human or cultural sciences derives from the German concept of *Geisteswissenschaften* or sciences of the mind (as opposed to the *Naturwissenschaften* or natural sciences), which was elaborated in the context of the rise of both HERMENEUTICS and HISTORICISM. The French equivalent is *sciences humaines*, which was given wider currency by the subtitle of FOUCAULT's *The Order of Things* (1966): 'an archaeology of the human sciences'.

Husserl, Edmund (1859–1938) German philosopher and founder of PHENOMEN-OLOGY. Husserl has had an immense influence on HEIDEGGER, who was his student, SARTRE, MERLEAU-PONTY and RICOEUR. His voluminous writings, collected under the general title *Husserliana* (twenty-three volumes published between 1950 and 1989), are highly technical exercises in philosophy; the 1907 lectures on the idea of phenomenology (posthumously published in 1950) provide one of the clearest introductions to his work (see also Kockelman 1967).

Husserl's early work was on logic and arithmetic (1887, 1891) and is heavily influenced by Franz Brentano (1838–1917) and the thesis that logical axioms are psychological laws. At this stage Husserl takes the view that psychology is the science that will clarify the foundations of logic and mathematics. The psychologism of *Philosophy of Arithmetic* (1891) was heavily criticized by FREGE; Husserl accepted the criticism and subsequently took the view that numbers and logical axioms were mind-independent concepts or ideal entities. *Logical Investigations* (the first part published in 1900 and the second in 1913) is largely taken up with a CRITIQUE of psychologism and is best seen as marking the transition from psychologism to the pure phenomenology of *Ideas* (1913) and the *Cartesian Meditations* (1931). The *Logical Investigations* inaugurate Husserl's repeated attempts to provide new foundations for a pure logic and epistemology which will be quite independent of all psychology; the preface to the first English edition of *Ideas* also speaks of the need to establish 'a new science' and the 'radical beginning of a philosophy'. Husserl's 'pure' phenomenology is intended to provide an objective description of the experiences of thinking and knowing. Whereas later phenomenologists like Heidegger and Sartre display little interest in the natural sciences, Husserl holds that philosophy supplements the achievements of natural scientists and mathematicians by supplying a perfect and genuine theoretical knowledge and promoting the synthetic unity of all the sciences. Both scientific knowledge and pure phenomenology are 'grounded' forms of knowledge which understand the necessity of their own nature and existence, as well as that of their objects. Pure logic and phenomenology are not concerned with the facts and appearances that are perceived when a natural stance towards the world is adopted, but with ideal entities or essences.

For Husserl, philosophy itself must be grounded in a radical reflection upon its own nature and activity, and must therefore take possession of 'an absolute ground of pure preconceptual experience' (1913). Grounding philosophy implies resorting to the technique of the EPOCHE, or the bracketing out of all conceptual presuppositions and assumptions in order to arrive at a pure intuitive perception of essences. The goal of the *epoche* is to bracket out the world that is actually given to perception, or the LIFEWORLD, and to arrive at a mathematically situated world of idealities. The same technique can be applied to consciousness, and reveals that consciousness is characterized by its INTENTIONALITY, or the fact of being directed towards an object; being conscious means being conscious *of* something, including the fact of being conscious. Husserl's *epoche* is obviously reminiscent of the process of methodical doubt employed by Descartes – hence the title *Cartesian Meditations* – to establish the certainty of his own existence through the *cogito* ('I am thinking, therefore I am', 1637). For Husserl, Descartes was the first modern philosopher in that he was the first to arrive at the idea that a rational science can systematically master a rational but infinite totality of being. Like Descartes before him, Husserl finds it difficult to refute the charge of SOLIPSISM; it is difficult, on this basis, to establish the existence of others. A further difficulty arises in that Husserl's phenomenological perception of the world gives only 'the temporal mode of the present', or a perception of a 'flowing-static now' (1936). Heidegger attempts to resolve this difficulty by introducing a temporal dimension into phenomenology.

Husserl's last great work, *The Crisis of European Sciences and Transcendental Phenomenology* (1936), which supplies his most extensive description of the lifeworld, was written against the background of the rise of Fascism and speaks pessimistically of the sickness affecting the nations of Europe. Speaking in terms reminiscent of HORKHEIMER and ADORNO'S DIALECTIC OF ENLIGHTENMENT, Husserl now describes how the use of reason has been perverted into irrationalism and a perverted rationalism. For Husserl, the rebirth of Europe will be impossible without a renewal of the spirit of a rigorous philosophy that can once more undertake the task of unifying all the modern sciences as members of the philosophical universe.

hybridity Literally, the term refers to the characteristics of plants or animals that are the offspring of individuals belonging to different species. The term is widely used in POSTCOLONIAL THEORY to describe the newness of the many different forms of migrant or minority DISCOURSES that flourish in the DIASPORAS of the modern and postmodern periods. For BHABHA, who is one of its main theorists, hybridity is the margin where cultural differences come into contact and conflict, and unsettle all the stable identities that are constructed around oppositions such as past and present, inside and outside, or inclusion or exclusion (1994). Hybridity offers a possible release from the singular identities that are constructed when class, race or gender are used as primary categories. Bhabha celebrates the 'in-between spaces' created and inhabited by hybrids, and holds that all cultures are now caught up in a continuous process of hybridization. The idea of hybridity can be compared with that of CREOLENESS and with GLISSANT's notion of 'Antilleanity'.

hyperbole In RHETORIC, the use of deliberate exaggeration or overstatement in order to express strong feelings or to produce a powerful impact on the listener. Hyperbole is a very common feature of everyday speech, as in 'If I've told you once, I've told you a thousand times not to tease the cat.'

hyperreality A term used by ECO (1975) in an essay on the culture of those American museums and theme parks where an illusion of absolute reality is created by holographs, dioramas and detailed reproductions of original works of art. They represent a hyperreal dimension in which the American imagination demands the real thing and, in order to attain it, fabricates the absolute fake. With cynical amusement, Eco describes the facsimile of the bill of sale of Manhattan to be found in museum shops. It looks old, feels old and even smells old. It is almost real. But,

Eco points out, its pseudo-antique characters are written in English whereas the original was in Dutch. Hyperreality is the defining characteristic of amusement cities such as Las Vegas or Disneyland; they are real fakes. They are also more real than the real. The real crocodile in the zoo may be asleep or hiding, but Disneyland's fake-real crocodiles never fail to appear on cue. BAUDRILLARD also describes Disneyland in these terms, and is fascinated by the way in which it causes the aesthetic to disappear into KITSCH and hyperreality (1986). Whilst the notion of hyperreality obviously stems from an encounter between European intellectuals and American culture, hyperreality itself is now more familiar thanks to Eurodisney and the Centerparc holiday resorts which reproduce a semi-tropical climate inside domes in the English countryside.

In the visual arts, the term 'hyperrealism' is often used as a synonym for 'photo-realism' or 'superrealism', and refers to a major trend in the art of the 1970s (Battcock 1975). A typical hyperrealist painting is a large-scale reproduction of a photograph of a car or street sign, often made using an air brush that leaves no traces of the artist's work on the smooth surface. Made from polyester and fibreglass, Duane Hanson's freestanding life-size figures of shoppers and tourists are the very disturbing sculptural equivalent. Here too, the dividing line between hyperrealism and kitsch is a very fine one. As Eco notes, the reality of such works is so real that they proclaim their own artificiality.

READING: Battcock (1975); Baudrillard (1986); Eco (1975)

hypertext Term used by GENETTE to describe a 'second-degree' literature made up of works which allude to, derive from or relate to an earlier work or hypotext. Joyce's *Ulysses* (1922) and Derek WALCOTT's *Omeros* (1990) are both hypertexts which use the Homeric EPIC as a hypotext; Thomas Mann's *Dr Faustus* uses both Goethe and the traditional Faust story in the same way. Together, a hypertext and its hypotext make up a multilayered PALIMPSEST. Hypertexts take a wide variety of forms, ranging from imitation to parody and pastiche (such as Henry Fielding's *Shamela*, which satirizes Samuel Richardson's *Pamela* by depicting its virtuous heroine as a cynical adventuress), and from transposition (the many rewritings of *Robinson Crusoe*, *Don Quixote* or *The Tempest*) to the 'continuation' of unfinished texts (such as Dickens's *Mystery of Edwin Drood*).

In computing and information technology, 'hypertext' refers to a machine-readable text that links together information in a mixture of media (text, video, sound, graphics); related items of information are connected by threads or links known as 'hyperlinks'.

hysteria A form of NEUROSIS for which no physical diagnosis can be found and in which the symptoms presented are expressive of an unconscious conflict. In conversion hysteria, the symptoms usually take a somatic form (hysterical paralysis, irritation of the throat, coughs); in anxiety hysteria or phobia, the cause of the anxiety is a particular external object. Hysteria has been explained in many different ways over the centuries; the most influential aetiology or causal explanation to have been put forward in the twentieth century is that supplied by FREUD'S PSYCHOANALYSIS.

The word hysteria derives from *hystera*, the Greek word for 'uterus', and the etymological association explains why the condition was for centuries viewed as being specific to women. It was only in the nineteenth century that the phenomenon of 'railway spine' (a psychosomatic syndrome observed in the victims of the frequent railway accidents of the 1880s) led to the recognition that men too could suffer from hysteria. The incidence of shell shock or 'war neurosis' during the First World War then confirmed the existence of male hysteria on a mass scale.

Greek medicine inherited from the Egyptians the view that the womb was a migratory organ or even a living creature in its own right. Plato summarizes the Greek theory in the *Timaeus*, where he describes the womb as a living creature which longs to have children. If left unfertilized, it strays around the body, blocking air-passages and causing 'acute distress and disorder of all kinds'. The womb was thought to possess a sense of smell, and could therefore be attracted back to its rightful place if sweet-smelling herbs were worn around the waist. Most Classical accounts of hysteria are variants on this description, but Galen (AD 129–99) held that the condition resulted from the retention of the female equivalent of sperm and thus began to hint at the existence of a sexual explanation. During the medieval period, hysterical phenomena were usually explained in terms of bewitchment or diabolic possession, but the Classical theory was revived during the Renaissance by authors such as Rabelais. Although the 'wandering womb' thesis was discredited by advances in anatomy and gradually replaced by the view that the seat of hysteria was in the brain or mind, elements of the old theory survived in the expression 'the vapours', widely used throughout the eighteenth and nineteenth centuries to describe a wide variety of complaints with no apparent physical cause; originally, the vapours were seen as emanations from the displaced and frustrated womb.

Nineteenth-century medical literature abounds in accounts of 'nervous' women suffering from the 'female malady' (Showalter 1985a), and they reflect prevailing views about the supposed frailty of women, as well as the social conditions that made them potential invalids. Probably the most important figure in this period is the French neurologist Jean Martin Charcot (1825–93), the so-called Napoleon of the neuroses whose work at the Salpêtrière hospital in Paris so impressed Freud. Charcot argued that hysteria was a physical condition resulting from trauma and taking the form of quasi-epileptic attacks. His observations of hundreds of patients led him to the conviction that the same symptoms occurred in the same manner in the same patient, and that they could be reproduced under hypnosis (but failed to realize that his patients might be responding to suggestion by acting as expected). He recorded the classic stages of the major hysterical attack in volumes of photographs which later became part of the iconography of SURREALISM. Charcot's therapeutic methods were traditional and designed to neutralize the original trauma and he insisted on the need for a moral environment that separated his patients from other hysterics, but the discovery that the symptoms of hysteria could be reproduced was an essential step to the psychoanalytic discovery that its causes could be reproduced, recovered and treated. Although the vast majority of Charcot's patients were women, he was also one of the first to realize that men too could be hysterics.

Freud's initial thesis (1896) was the so-called SEDUCTION THEORY which held that hysteria and the other neuroses originate in an experience of actual sexual abuse that has been repressed, but which can be recovered. Like Charcot, Freud initially used hypnosis to recover these memories, but abandoned it in favour of what Anna O. so felicitously termed the TALKING CURE of PSYCHOANALYSIS (Freud and Breuer 1893–5). Freud subsequently revised his original seduction theory in the course of a long correspondence with his collaborator Fliess (Freud 1985) and argued that hysteria stemmed from unconscious fantasies about incest that were bound up with the OEDIPUS COMPLEX, though he never denied either the existence or the pathogenic effects of real abuse (1938). The rejection of the seduction thesis is still the subject of intense controversy (see Masson 1984), and the question of the aetiology of hysteria now tends to merge into the bitter debate between the defenders of FALSE MEMORY SYNDROME and the supporters of the RECOVERED MEMORY (see Crews 1997).

Although psychoanalysis contradicts the old view that hysteria is a 'female malady', the feminist writers associated with ÉCRITURE FÉMININE tend in some ways to revert to the earlier theory and to argue that Dora's hysteria is a form of mute protest against PATRIARCHY (see Cixous 1976). Such claims derive from the Lacanian contention (LACAN) that it is the question of sexual identity that is at stake in hysteria, and that the female hysteric is actually asking the question 'Who am I? Am I a man or a woman?' (Lacan 1975a). Other feminist writers, such as SHOWALTER (1997), have suggested that the concept of hysteria should be broadened to include such recent phenomena as Gulf War syndrome and even accounts of abduction by aliens.

READING: Ellenberger (1970), Veith (1965)

hysteron proteron A Greek expression meaning 'latter [put] first'. It is used in RHETORIC to describe a figure of speech in which words that should, in terms of their meaning, come later, come first: 'O, for a fresh of breath air' (James Joyce, *Ulysses*). In the variant known as a Spoonerism (from the name of the English academic W. A. Spooner, 1844–1930) the initial sounds or other parts of words are transposed as in 'You have tasted the worm and hissed your mystery exams' ('You have wasted the term and missed your history exams').

icon Word derived from the Greek *eikon*, meaning 'likeness' or 'image'. In the SEMIOTICS elaborated by PEIRCE, an icon is a type of REPRESENTAMEN or SIGN in which the relationship between the signans and signatum (or signifier and signified, to use SAUSSURE's more familiar terminology) is one of factual similarity. A picture of a lion is an icon because of the factual resemblance between it and the real animal it depicts.

Icons are the sacred images of saints or holy personages that are venerated in the Eastern Orthodox Churches. The cult of icons is influenced by the neo-Platonic belief that a visible image can demonstrate an invisible religious truth. This meaning has been transferred to persons or things that are regarded as particularly representative of a given place, mood or period. In that sense, James Dean can be said to be an icon of teenage rebellion.

iconography Traditionally defined in art history as the identification of the subjects of portraits, and especially those featured on coins. It has also come to mean the identification and analysis of conventional images, stories and allegories, and the description and classification of those pictorial motifs. The iconographical approach to art history was largely pioneered by the French historian Louis Mâle (1862–1954) in his studies of the religious art of the Gothic period (1902), which contend that the art of the Middle Ages was primarily a form of 'sacred writing' whose characters had to be learned by every artist. An iconographic study of Dutch GENRE painting would read a still life depicting musical instruments, songbooks and precious metalware as an icon of *vanitas*, or of the vanity of life in a world where all is destined to perish. A woman standing by a map would be read as an image of 'Lady World', who is the personification of worldliness.

In his studies of the Renaissance, PANOFSKY (1939) introduces an important distinction between iconography and iconology. Whereas iconography simply classifies the images used by a pictorial tradition, iconology looks for and interprets symbolic meanings of which the individual artists may not be fully conscious. It treats the work of art as a historical document providing insights into how, in different historical conditions, essential tendencies of the human mind can be expressed through specific terms and relationships between terms. The erudite essays that make up Panofsky's *Meaning in the Visual Arts* (1955) demonstrate iconology to be an interdisciplinary mode of interpretation that relies upon a deep understanding of literary and philosophical traditions as well as of the history of pictorial motifs.

id A translation of the German *das Es* (literally 'the it'), introduced into the vocabulary of PSYCHOANALYSIS by FREUD (1923a). Freud borrows the term from the German psychiatrist Georg Groddeck, who held that 'man is animated by the Unknown' and that 'Man is lived by the It' (Groddeck 1923). The origins of the word can be traced back to Nietzsche, who remarks in *Beyond Good and Evil* that 'a thought comes when "it" wants, not when "I" want . . . *it* thinks' (1886).

The id is one of the three agencies of the psyche described in Freud's second or structural TOPOGRAPHY, the others being the EGO and the SUPEREGO, and tends to replace the UNCONSCIOUS of the first topography. Sometimes described by Freud as a reservoir of LIBIDO, the id is the instinctual pole of the personality and its contents are an expression of the DRIVES. There is no clear boundary between the ego and the id. Part of the ego merges into the id, and it draws energy from it thanks to the process of SUBLIMATION.

The French equivalent to *das Es* is *le ça*. LACAN frequently uses expressions such as *ça parle* ('It/id speaks'), playing upon a very familiar register of everyday French (*Ça va?* means 'How are things?' or 'How's it going?', and *Ça ne fait rien* 'It doesn't matter') to capture the radical impersonality of the id. For Lacan the id is not, however, the locus of uncontrollable biological or instinctual forces. *Ça nous parle* can be interpreted as meaning that 'id speaks through us' or that 'we are spoken by it', or in other words that human beings are not fully in command of the language that speaks through them and constitutes them as SUBJECTS.

identity politics Increasingly important from the 1970s onwards, identity politics is based upon the contention that collectivities and individuals defined by criteria of ethnicity, religion, GENDER or sexual orientation have interests that are not or cannot be promoted or defended by broader agencies such as class or a constitutional state. Identity politics usually takes the form of a demand for the right to be different, and for that difference to be recognized as legitimate. This form of politics can be viewed either as a celebration of cultural diversity and a defence of minority rights, or as a betrayal of the universalist values of the ENLIGHTENMENT. For its critics, it is a form of ESSENTIALISM which assumes that politics is a direct and unmediated expression of personal or collective experience. In their various ways, QUEER theory, CREOLENESS and the idea of HYBRIDITY all question the assumptions of identity politics, and raise the issue of whether the notion of a fixed identity is in itself desirable.

ideological state apparatus MARXISM has traditionally emphasized the role played by the repressive agencies of the state (the army, police and courts) in ensuring the maintenance of the social order. Just as GRAMSCI recognized that consent is as important as coercion if a HEGEMONY is to be established and maintained, ALTHUSSER (1970) stresses that repression alone cannot reproduce the existing social relations of production and that IDEOLOGY also has a crucial role to play. His category of ideological state apparatuses includes the educational system, the

family and the media; their function is to reproduce the social relations of production by producing individual SUBJECTS who recognize themselves in the dominant ideology, and therefore acquiesce to it.

ideology The term is very widely used in both the Marxist tradition and in the
social sciences as a whole to describe a distorted or illusory form of thought which
departs from a criterion of objectivity. It is also used to describe, usually in negative
terms, the world-view or collective beliefs and attitudes of a class or social group.
Whilst there are many competing definitions of ideology, they share a common
core that is well captured by GEERTZ's parodic PARADIGM: 'I have a social philosophy,
you have political opinions, he has an ideology' (1973). That paradigm is particularly
pertinent to debates about the 'end of ideology' thesis associated with Daniel BELL
and others who identify ideology with fanatical totalitarianism in general and
Marxist totalitarianism in particular (Bell 1960). Defined in this sense, ideology is
the antithesis of both empiricism and liberalism. The predictable Marxist reply that
liberalism is itself an ideology indicates how difficult it can be to arrive at a satisfactory definition of this elusively slippery concept.

The French term *idéologie* was coined in 1796 and immediately entered the English
language. The original *idéologues* were the French philosophers Destut de Tracy,
Cabanis and Constant, who described ideology as the study of ideas, their origins
and their laws and who, in accordance with the sensualist EMPIRICISM of Locke and
Condillac, believed that all ideas derived from physical sense-perceptions. Ideology
was meant to be an analytical social science of ideas (Destut de Tracy 1803–18).
Clauzade's critical anthology of the writings of the *idéologues* (1998) is an invaluable
source of information. The reluctance of the *idéologues* to become servile members
of the Napoleonic nobility provoked Napoleon into using the word as a term
of abuse (Hayward 1991). By 1813, 'ideology' had come to mean ideal or abstract
speculation.

All theories of ideology elaborated within the Marxist tradition derive to some
extent from the critique made of German idealism by Marx and Engels in Part I of
The German Ideology (1845–6), or from the slightly different BASE/SUPERSTRUCTURE
model elaborated by Marx in his *Contribution to the Critique of Political Economy*
(1859). *The German Ideology* describes ideology as a *camera obscura* in which social
relations are perceived in an inverted form. Ideologies such as morality, religion
and metaphysics are 'phantoms formed in the brain' or 'sublimates' of social
relations. The ALIENATION characteristic of capitalist society gives them a semblance
of independence and transforms them into an alien power which enslaves them.
The 'world spirit' which, in the Hegelian tradition, governs history proves on
examination to be the development of the world market. The existence of ideology
must be explained as originating in material practice, meaning the sum of the
productive forces, capital and social forms of existence. The Marxist theory of
ideology is closely bound up with the thesis that history is the product of class
conflict; in any given period, the ideas of the ruling class are the ruling intellectual
force or the dominant ideology. In a society divided into antagonistic classes,
ideology both derives from and masks real social relations and thus legitimizes class

domination by making it appear natural and ahistorical. The dominant ideology of a ruling class cannot be transformed by a philosophical critique, but only by the revolutionary action that overthrows the existing relations of production and transforms the material conditions of social existence. Communism, or the abolition of classes, will result in the disappearance of ideology.

Later Marxist theories of ideology range from LUKÁCS's description of bourgeois ideology as a form of false consciousness, as opposed to the true class consciousness of the proletariat, which is the true subject of history, to GRAMSCI's investigations into the organic ideologies or world-views of social classes, which give much more weight to cultural factors. The most sophisticated of the Marxist theories is that elaborated by ALTHUSSER. Whilst Althusser retains a science/ideology distinction and continues to define the latter as an IMAGINARY relationship with reality, he argues that ideology is an essential feature of the reproduction of social relations in all societies (including communist societies) and that it is its mechanism of INTERPELLATION that constitutes individuals as SUBJECTS. In adopting this argument, Althusser comes close to identifying ideology with a broader notion of culture, or even with a Durkheimian collective consciousness (see Macey 1994).

illocutionary act Defined by AUSTIN's theory of the SPEECH ACT (1962a) as the performance of an act in saying something, as opposed to the act of saying something. Asking questions, giving information, assurances and warnings are illocutionary acts. For SEARLE (1969, 1979), 'illocutionary act' is synonymous with 'speech act'.

imaginary A translation of the French *imaginaire*, which can be used both as an adjective and as a substantive. The term is used by both LACAN and SARTRE, though the latter's translator has confused the issue by rendering it as 'imagination'. It is also used by BACHELARD in his studies in POETICS. In all cases, the immediate connotation is 'image' rather than 'fictional' or 'unreal'. For Bachelard (1942), the measure of an image's value is the extent of its imaginary halo. The imaginary is not synonymous with the imagination, or the capacity to form images; it is the imaginary that frees the imagination and gives the psyche the experience of openness and novelty. The imaginary is the element of both daydreaming and poetic creation.

In his early work (1940), Sartre argues that an image is not a linguistic or mental picture of an object with an objective external existence, but a form of consciousness characterized by INTENTIONALITY. The image is produced by an imagining consciousness in a magical act that makes apparent the object or person we are thinking about or the thing that we desire.

For Lacan, the imaginary is one of the three orders that structure human existence, the others being the SYMBOLIC and the REAL. In his earliest papers (1936), Lacan writes that 'psychology is the domain of the imaginary', but makes the latter term synonymous with 'illusory'. The paper on the MIRROR-PHASE (1949) sets the stage for the theory of the order of the imaginary, even though the term is not used there, and it is frequently discussed by Lacan from the early 1950s onwards. The seventh chapter of Lacan's 1953–4 Seminar on *Freud's Papers on Technique* (1975) provides a clear exposition of the concept.

In the mirror-phase stage, the child identifies with its specular image, and this inaugurates the series of identifications that will construct the EGO. The child is literally captivated by a specular other thanks to an identification which is also an alienation. The imaginary is thus the realm in which self and other merge, and in which identity is grounded in a mere semblance of unity. The imaginary is not a stage which is overcome or transcended, and is a constant presence in the lives of human SUBJECTS and in the stories they tell themselves and others about what they are.

The relationship between the Sartrean and Lacanian theories of the imaginary is far from clear, but they do have features in common. In her valuable discussion of their respective theories, Howells (1992) cites Sartre as accepting that his description of Flaubert's *moi* corresponded to Lacan's definition of the ego as an imaginary construction, a fiction with which one identifies retrospectively. She adds that Sartre first took that view in his early essay on the transcendence of the ego (1936).

imago The Latin noun means 'portrait' or 'statue', but also 'the shade or ghost of a dead person', and was introduced into the vocabulary of PSYCHOANALYSIS by JUNG, who speaks of paternal, maternal and fraternal imagos (1911). The word is commonly used to refer to unconscious prototypical figures constructed on the basis of real or imagined relationships within the family as the individual learns to situate him or herself with respect to other family members.

Although the term is widely used within ANALYTIC PSYCHOLOGY and psychoanalysis, particularly by Kleinians (KLEIN), it is very rarely employed by FREUD himself. He does, however, occasionally use it to describe the series of prototypes and stereotypical images into which the imago of the analyst is woven during the TRANSFERENCE (1912a), and the parental images that linger in the unconscious as the maturing child becomes increasingly detached from his or her progenitors (1924b).

The term 'imago' appears in the earliest writings of LACAN, but he makes no further use of it after the 1950s. In an early essay on the family, Lacan attributes the ills of modern society to the declining importance of the paternal imago (1938), but in subsequent texts (1946) the imago is described as part of an imaginary spatio-temporal complex within which the SUBJECT identifies with the image of the other. Identification with an imago is thus seen as the beginning of a process of ALIENATION. In subsequent texts, the reference to the imago is replaced by the broader concept of the IMAGINARY.

implied reader An essential feature of Wolfgang ISER's phenomenological theory of aesthetic response or *Wirkungstheorie* (1974). Unlike the 'real' reader, whose responses to a text can be known from his or her documented reactions, the implied reader designates a HEURISTIC concept grounded in the structure of the text. The concept of the implied reader designates a network of response-inviting structures, such as patterns, points of view and blanks in the text, which impel the actual reader to grasp the text. Insofar as it is a transcendental model, the implied reader denotes the role of the reader, as defined by the textual structure and the structured acts inherent in reading, and makes it possible to describe the effects of literary texts. For Iser, the concept of the implied reader makes it possible to describe how textual structures are transformed through ideation, or the formation of ideas and mental images, into personal experiences.

Independent Group A loose coalition of British artists active between 1952 and 1955 and based mainly at London's Institute of Contemporary Arts. Its leading members were Richard Hamilton, Eduardo Paolozzi, Nigel Henderson and William Turnbull. The most successful group exhibition was *This is Tomorrow* (Whitechapel Gallery, London, 1956). The Independent Group played an important role in the redefinition of MODERNISM in British art by reacting both against the neo-Romanticism which was officially promoted as an indigenous art celebrating a quintessential Englishness at the time of the 1951 Festival of Britain, and against the European-centred modernism promoted by Herbert Read (see *Herbert Read: A British Vision of World Art*, 1993) and the original founders of the Institute of Contemporary Arts. Rather than looking, like Read, to SURREALISM and Bauhaus architecture for a modernist PARADIGM, the Independent Group began to break down the high/low culture divide by incorporating images culled from the pop culture and the mass media (and especially American comics and science fiction magazines) into their work. Its members have often been described as the fathers of Pop Art (Lippard 1966); some (Jencks 1996) also describe them as the harbingers of POSTMODERNISM.

In PSYCHOANALYSIS, the term 'Independent Group' refers to the majority tendency within British psychoanalysis which emerged after the near-schism caused by the differences between the Kleinians and the followers of ANNA FREUD. Although a number of different tendencies coexist within the group, the theory of OBJECT-RELATIONS is the dominant trend.

READING: Kohon (1986); Massey (1995); Rayner (1991)

index In the SEMIOTICS developed by PEIRCE (1932, 1934), an index is defined as a REPRESENTAMEN in which the relationship between signans and signatum is one of factual or existential contiguity. Smoke, for example, is an index of fire. When Robinson Crusoe finds a footprint on the beach he finds an index that allows him to infer the presence of another human being on the island.

in-itself/for-itself The terms correspond to the French *en-soi* and *pour-soi* and the German *an sich* and *für sich*, and refer in PHENOMENOLOGY to two contrasting modes of being. They are used both as absolute nouns and as parts of compounds. Sartre, for example, speaks both of the in-itself and of being-in-itself (1943a). Being-in-itself is the mode of being of non-conscious objects such as tables or trees which are simply what they are. Existence-for-itself, in contrast, is the dimension of human freedom; a human being is not a human being in the sense that a stone is a stone. The for-itself arises when it negates the in-itself and rushes into the future, as when a human subject strives towards AUTHENTICITY by assuming a SITUATION and the possibility of freedom that it affords. In striving towards authenticity, the for-itself is or becomes what it is not, and negates what it was. The subject's existence-in-itself is always a project rather than a stable state, as there is always a temptation to avoid freedom and the anxiety it induces by lapsing into BAD FAITH and inauthenticity, or by attempting to be a person in the way that a stone is a stone. Sartre also speaks of a hypothetical in-itself-for-itself mode of being. This, however, could only be the attribute of a deity. It would imply a total but free coincidence of the self with the self and an absence of the negation that actually produces the self. Ultimately, human existence is futile to the extent that it seeks to reach this impossible state.

intentional fallacy In very general terms, the confusion of an author's intended meaning with the actual meaning of the text. The intentional fallacy is a major concern for NEW CRITICISM, and the classic description is given by Wimsatt and Beardsley, first in an encyclopedia article (1942) and then in a longer essay (1954a). They argue that the author's design or intention is neither available for study nor desirable as a standard for judging the success of a work of literary art. The intentional fallacy is a Romantic illusion which confuses the poem with its origins, attempts to derive a standard of criticism from the psychological cause, and ends in either biography or relativism. Like the AFFECTIVE FALLACY, the intentional fallacy causes the poem, defined as an object of specifically critical judgement, to disappear as psychological speculation replaces objective criticism.

The expression 'the intentional fallacy' is modelled on the more familiar 'pathetic fallacy', first used by John Ruskin in his *Modern Painters* (1856) to describe the illusory attribution of human feelings or responses to inanimate objects.

intentionality One of the main themes of the PHENOMENOLOGY of HUSSERL (1900, 1913) and SARTRE (1939, 1943a). In this context 'intentional' is not synonymous with 'willed' or 'purposeful', but refers to the fact that all consciousness is a consciousness *of something* or is directed *towards something*. Intentionality is not confined to the pure perception of an object; fearing, hating and loving are all forms of intentionality or ways of being conscious of another person or thing.

The term derives from the Latin *intentio*, which was used in medieval scholastic philosophy to refer to representations of things that are formed in or by the mind. As SEARLE points out (1999), the term can be a source of confusion in English as it may be misunderstood as meaning 'purpose' or 'goal'. Husserl's term is *Intentionalität*, which is unlikely to be confused with *Absicht*, meaning 'design' or 'purpose'.

international style The style of modernist architecture associated with Walter Gropius (1883–1969), Le Corbusier (1887–1965) and above all the German-American architect Ludwig Mies van der Rohe (1886–1969). The expression derives from the title of an exhibition on modern American architecture held at New York's Museum of Modern Art in 1932 (Hitchcock and Johnson 1932). In the postwar period the style became truly international in that it was used throughout the world with little regard for local styles and traditions. It follows the general principles of FUNCTIONALISM; Le Corbusier famously defined a house as a machine for living.

The main principles of the international style are an emphasis on architecture as volume, formal regularity and the avoidance of applied decoration. The characteristic building is constructed from concrete, steel and glass, with skeletal columns or pillars allowing great flexibility and creating an impression of weightlessness. In aesthetic terms, the style has a lot in common with *NEUE SACHLICHKEIT* and the regular grids of Piet Mondrian's neo-plasticist paintings (see Fauchereau 1994). Familiar examples include the UNESCO building in Paris, New York's Rockefeller Center and, on a smaller scale, the Penguin Pool in London Zoo.

The critique of the international style put forward in the 1970s (see in particular Venturi, Scott and Izenour 1977) argues that its rationalism is both authoritarian and oppressive, introduces the idea of a postmodernist architecture and provides one of the starting-points for the more general debate over POSTMODERNISM.

READING: Khan (1998)

interpellation In ALTHUSSER's theory of IDEOLOGY, interpellation is the mechanism that produces SUBJECTS in such a way that they recognize their own existence in terms of the dominant ideology of the society in which they live (1970). The French *interpellation* is commonly used to mean 'being taken in by the police for questioning'; it also means the 'questioning' of a minister in parliament. Althusser's basic illustration of the mechanism exploits this sense of 'questioning' or 'hailing'. An individual walking down the street is hailed by a police officer – 'Hey, you there!' – and turns round to recognize the fact that he is being addressed. In doing so, that individual is constituted as subject. According to Althusser, the idea of interpellation demonstrates that subjects are always and already the products of ideology, and thus subverts the idealist thesis that subjectivity is primary or self-founding.

A similar notion of interpellation can be found in VANEIGEM's contribution to the theory of SITUATIONISM (1967). Confronted by the flow of signs and images that constitute DEBORD's 'society of the spectacle', individuals are constantly interpellated by posters, advertisements and stereotypes offering universal images in which they are invited to recognize themselves. The function of interpellation is to block spontaneous creativity.

Whether or not there is any direct connection between the two notions of interpellation remains unclear.

interpretive community A central notion in the version of READER-RESPONSE theory developed by Stanley FISH (1980). An interpretive community is made up of readers who are agreed as to what constitutes literature and who have internalized the structures of understanding and the practices deemed relevant to reading literary texts. Such readers display a literary competence comparable to the linguistic COMPETENCE described by CHOMSKY. They are sufficiently experienced to have internalized the community's definition of the properties of literary discourse, and can thus respond appropriately to individual texts that they have not previously encountered.

intertextuality Term coined by Julia KRISTEVA in her study of BAKHTIN's work on dialogue and carnival (1969a). The basic premise of the theory of intertextuality is that any text is essentially a mosaic of references to or quotations from other texts; a text is not a closed system and does not exist in isolation. It is always involved in a dialogue with other texts, just as Joyce's *Ulysses* is involved in a dialogue with Homeric epics and other texts. Intertextuality is not simply a matter of influences which pass from one author to another, but of the multiple and complex relations that exist between texts in both synchronic and diachronic terms. 'Influence' is simply one mode of intertextuality.

Although the term 'intertextuality' is Kristeva's, Harold BLOOM's notion of literary REVISIONISM and of the ANXIETY OF INFLUENCE is broadly similar in that it stresses that it is the relationship between existing poems that creates new poems. GENETTE's concepts of the PALIMPSEST and of HYPERTEXT also supply a theory of intertextuality.

READING: Worton and Still (1990)

introjection Term introduced into the vocabulary of psychoanalysis by the Hungarian analyst Sándor Ferenczi, who uses it as the opposite of PROJECTION (1909). It denotes a mechanism that permits the absorption into the EGO of those parts of the outside world that can be used as sources of pleasure. In the writings of FREUD himself, it is not always easy to grasp the distinction between introjection, incorporation and identification.

Freud uses the conception of introjection to analyse aspects of mourning and melancholia (1917b). The loved OBJECT was once absorbed or introjected into the ego, thus effectively becoming a part of it. When the object is lost or dies, its shadow falls upon the ego; in mourning the loss of a loved one, the ego is also mourning the loss of part of itself. Freud also describes introjection as a form of regression to the oral stage in which the child literally seeks to devour the objects that afford it pleasure (1923a). For Klein, the interaction between introjection and projection helps to constitute the ego and the SUPEREGO and to lay the foundations for the OEDIPUS COMPLEX (1946).

invented tradition Described by HOBSBAWM as a set of practices, usually of a symbolic or ritual nature, designed to inculcate values and norms through repetition and to establish a sense of continuity with a past which may be either real or imaginary (Hobsbawm and Ranger 1983). Invented traditions can serve to establish and legitimize social cohesion and to legitimize relations of authority. They can also promote socialization by inculcating beliefs, value-systems and conventions of behaviour.

The invention of traditions is a widespread phenomenon. The distinctive Highland costumes and clan tartans of Scotland are less traditional than they seem, having been created in the eighteenth and nineteenth centuries and popularized by the Romantic novels of Walter Scott (1771–1823). Many of the 'centuries-old traditions' surrounding the British monarchy are surprisingly recent inventions and were often designed with television coverage in mind. Some of the horse-drawn carriages that took heads of state to the coronation of Elizabeth II in a 'traditional' procession in 1953 were props on loan from a film company; cars had been used in earlier coronations and there was in fact no tradition to perpetuate. In June 1999, a whole new tradition was invented when Elizabeth II made Prince Edward 'Earl of

Wessex'. The last Earl of Wessex died at the Battle of Hastings in 1066, and as a geographical entity Wessex exists only in the novels of Thomas Hardy. Invented traditions are an important feature of the modern HERITAGE INDUSTRY. They are also part of everyday life; the traditional figure of Father Christmas in his fur-trimmed red robe first appeared in an advertisement for Coca-Cola.

Irigaray, Luce (1932–) Belgian-born psychoanalyst and feminist philosopher.

Irigaray's earliest work (1973) is on the linguistic disturbances associated with senile dementia and attempts to establish a grammar of dementia which owes a lot to LACAN's thesis that the UNCONSCIOUS is structured like a language. The concentration on the language patterns associated with psychic states later develops into an investigation into gender differences in language and to the contention that speech is never neutral, but always marked by sexual difference (1985). Irigaray's writing on the theory of sexual difference offers a powerful, if controversial, critique of PSYCHOANALYSIS.

In 1974 Irigaray was expelled from the ÉCOLE FREUDIENNE DE PARIS following the publication of her *Speculum* (1974), in which she argues that, because FREUD always takes a boy as his PARADIGM of psychosexual development, girls and women are reduced to being inferior males and are excluded from the SYMBOLIC. In the course of a detailed reading of Freud and of Plato, she demonstrates that psychoanalysis is deeply rooted in a Western philosophical tradition which has constructed a monosexual culture in which the masculine is always taken as the norm and in which women are simply exchanged as commodities. Freud's observation that the little boy becomes aware of castration when he sees that a girl does not possess a penis is typical of a male scopic economy focused on the visibility of the penis and reflecting the morphology of the male body. This economy actively constructs femininity as something invisible, and therefore unknowable, and thus renders itself incapable of accounting for or coming to terms with women's desire. This is a culture in which the line of descent goes from father to son, and its symbolic takes no account of the mother-daughter line. Within it, women do not exist as women, but only as mothers subordinated to a patriarchal order, and preferably as the mothers of sons.

In her *This Sex Which is Not One* (1977a), Irigaray begins to map out a possible female IMAGINARY and a different sexual economy which can speak of and to women's desire. The title plays on the two senses of 'one': women are not a sex because they are demoted to being nothing more than inferior men and do not exist in their own right, and their sex is not *one* because it is not reducible to one organ. Irigaray posits a countervailing imagery of multiplicity and describes women's sexuality as always involving two pairs of lips in permanent contact: the lips of the mouth and the labia. Her imagery has led to her being accused, particularly in Britain, of being either a biological essentialist who reduces women's sexuality to anatomy (Sayers 1982) or a psychic essentialist who believes in the existence of a specifically female LIBIDO and thus perpetuates the myth of the eternal feminine (Segal 1987). It is in fact difficult to determine whether Irigaray is speaking literally or whether her 'two lips' are metaphors. A more positive reading suggests that the image both describes a reduction to the biological brought about by a monosexual culture and looks forward to a woman-to-woman mode of speech that takes a positive view of women's sexual difference from men (Whitford 1991b).

Most of Irigaray's later work (1984, 1989, 1990) is an exploration of the possibility of producing a female imaginary that will allow women to speak as women (and not as lesser men), and incorporates utopian speculations about a possible ethics of sexual difference. The latter implies a recognition of distinct male and female psychosexual economies that can coexist without one being reduced to the other.

Irigaray is not easy to read as she constantly moves, often with little or no explanatory transition, from psychoanalysis to philosophy and makes few concessions to her readers. She can, on the other hand, write, as in those sections of *This Sex* which celebrate female sexuality, with an extraordinary and quasi-poetic lyricism, and her talent for polemic (see especially 1977b) makes for invigorating reading.

READING: Whitford (1991a)

irony The term is used widely and in a number of related senses in RHETORIC and literary theory. The basic rhetorical definition of irony is a figure of speech in which the intended meaning is the antithesis of the literal meaning of the words used. Thus, words of praise can be used to convey contempt for someone or something. This inversion of meaning is also characteristic of more extended forms of irony, as in Jonathan Swift's *Modest Proposal* (1729), in which it is suggested that poverty in Ireland could be alleviated by fattening up children and selling them to the rich as delicacies for the dinner-table. Socratic irony refers to the strategy adopted in Plato's *Dialogues* by Socrates, who feigns ignorance or lack of knowledge and goes on asking questions which gradually undermine the certainties of the self-professed expert against whom he is arguing. Dramatic irony arises when readers or spectators know in advance what is about to happen, and when the characters do not. The most famous example occurs in *Oedipus Rex*, in which Oedipus pursues the murderer of his father Laius without knowing that he himself is the killer.

The term 'irony' can also be used in looser senses. RICHARDS defines it as 'the bringing in of the opposite' and speculates that irony may be a characteristic of poetry of the highest order (1924). His speculation influences the NEW CRITICISM's tendency to define 'mature' poetry in terms of its ironic complexity or allusiveness. In FRYE's archetypal criticism, irony or satire is the defining characteristic of the pregeneric plots or *mythoi* of the cycle of winter.

Iser, Wolfgang (1926–) German literary theorist and specialist in English literature. Iser's theory of aesthetic response (*Wirkungstheorie*) and concept of the IMPLIED READER are major contributions to READER-RESPONSE THEORY (1974, 1976). Iser's description of the act of reading draws heavily upon the tradition of PHENOMEN-OLOGY and GESTALT psychology. Like FISH and other reader-response theorists, Iser argues that the meaning of a text is not something that is contained within it or that can be extracted from it, but rather the product of the interaction between author, text and reader. Reading is described as being centred on an author-reader/

artistic-aesthetic polarity: the artistic element comprises the text created by the author, whereas the aesthetic response is the realization of the text accomplished by the reader. A literary text exists, that is, only when it is read. A second polarity of meaning and significance is then introduced. Meaning designates the referential totality that is assembled in the course of reading, and significance the reader's absorption of that meaning into his own experience.

Iser uses Henry James's short story 'The Figure in the Carpet' (1896) as a paradigmatic example (PARADIGM) of the inevitable failure of attempts to extract a hidden meaning, be it the spirit of the age, social conditions or the NEUROSIS of the author; as in James's story, the critic who is intent on a hidden meaning is incapable of seeing anything simply because the text does not offer a detachable message. Texts do not relate to contingent reality as such, but to models or concepts of reality in which the contingencies and complexities of the empirical world are reduced to meaningful structures or world-pictures. Such models, and the social norms and literary allusions from which they are constructed, make up the repertoire of the text. The role of the actual reader, which is partly defined by the response-inviting structure described as the implied reader, is to decode the repertoire and to create a virtual text through the act of reading. Given that the act of reading is a temporal process, the virtual text is constantly modified as the reader reassesses his existing reading in the light of the new information and changing viewpoints that emerge as the reading proceeds, and as the text stimulates the formation of new images. It is the constant play of decoding, modification and revision that explains the inexhaustibility of the literary text, which has no one meaning but an almost infinite number of potential meanings. The creative role of the reader is typified by the very common experience of seeing a cinematic adaptation of a novel and being disappointed because the hero does not correspond to one's imagined picture of him. Literary texts do not simply simulate or copy a familiar reality; their function is to enable the reader to see that reality with new eyes. There is an obvious parallel here between Iser's theory of reading and aesthetic response and RUSSIAN FORMALISM's concept of defamiliarization or *OSTRANENIE*. A more ludic note is struck when Iser cites Sterne's *Life and Opinions of Tristram Shandy* (1759–67) to demonstrate that the literary text is an arena in which reader and author participate in a game of the imagination.

The Fictive and the Imaginary (1991) further explores the above themes in the broader context of a discussion of the use of fictions in philosophy and of a fascinating analysis of the notions of fancy, fantasy, the IMAGINARY and imagination from the English Renaissance to the era of SARTRE. The analysis establishes a threefold distinction between the real (the thought systems and world-pictures that make up the text's repertoire), the fictive (an intentional act that, by convention, relieves fiction from the burden of saying *what* fiction is) and the imaginary. Fictionality, or the quality of being fictive, is not literature; fictionality is what makes literature possible. The GENRE of Renaissance pastorale is taken as a paradigm of the act of fictionalizing: the conventional shepherds of pastorale act out their fictional imitation of the shepherds of an older literary tradition, and their ritualized game of the singing competition becomes the subject-matter of poetry.

J

Jakobson, Roman (1896–1982) Russian-American linguist. The Russian epitaph on Jakobson's grave reads simply 'Roman Jakobson: Russian Philologist' and gives little indication of his immense importance and influence. He was a cofounder of both OPOYAZ and the MOSCOW LINGUISTIC CIRCLE and a long-term associate of the PRAGUE CIRCLE, and has had a crucial influence on the development of modern POETICS. His 'Closing Statement: Linguistics and Poetics', made to the 'Conference on Style' held at Indiana University in 1958 (Jakobson 1960), is one of the great manifestos of modern STRUCTURALISM, whilst the analysis of Baudelaire's poem '*Les Chats*' made in collaboration with LÉVI-STRAUSS (1962) is a classic example of structural analysis. Addressing a conference of anthropologists and linguists in 1952 and paraphrasing the Latin writer Terence, Jakobson (1952) defined his field of research thus: '*Linguista sum: linguistici nihil a me alienum puto*' ('I am a linguist: I regard nothing linguistic as alien to me'). Jakobson published some 650 books and papers dealing with philology, poetics, linguistics, folklore and Slavic studies. His *Selected Writings* have been published in eight volumes (1962–88); two posthumously published collections (1985, 1987) provide convenient introductions to this immense body of work. A full bibliography has been compiled by Stephen Rudy (1984).

In his youth, Jakobson was close to both the linguists associated with RUSSIAN FORMALISM and the poets of FUTURISM. Futurist poetry was the subject of his first articles (1914, 1919), and his tribute to the poet Mayakovsky (1930), who committed suicide in 1930, is a powerful evocation of the intellectual climate that gave birth to both movements. It was in this context that Jakobson first read SAUSSURE and discovered the *LANGUE/PAROLE* distinction and the theory of the SIGN that are so basic to all forms of structuralism. At the same time, the formalist emphasis on devices such as FOREGROUNDING and *OSTRANENIE*, or those techniques that stress the poetic function of literature rather than its communicative function, was eventually to provide the basis for the very influential CODE/MESSAGE model of linguistic communication elaborated in the 1950s (1956, 1960).

Written in collaboration with the Russian Jurij Tynjanov [Yury Tynyanov] (1894–1948) in 1928, the so-called 'Jakobson-Tynjanov theses' (Jakobson and Tynjanov 1928) outlined the programme for a lifetime's work. Stressing the need for a precise theoretical programme for Russian literary and linguistic science, they reject 'naïve psychologism' and characterize the history of literature as the history of a complex network of specific structural laws. The basis for Jakobson's later work on poetics was laid with the contention that the analysis of the structural laws of language and literature would allow the identification of a limited series of actually existing structural types; the study of such systems required an analysis of their internal laws.

In the 1930s Jakobson began to work on two related topics that would shape much of his later work. Together with Nikolai Trubetzkoy (1890–1938), who was also a member of the Prague Circle, he worked extensively on sound-patterns and phonology. The result of this work was the theory that PHONEMES are not physical entities but abstract and differential features of a language which can be identified on the basis of their contrastive or distinctive features: the word 'pig' is identified as being different from the word 'fig' because of the differences between the phonemes /p/ and /f/ (see Trubetzkoy 1939 and Jakobson and Halle 1956). In Jakobson's view, the existence of a minimal number of phonemes – he suggests the figure twelve – with distinctive features (voiced/unvoiced, and so on) and organized into binary oppositions, is enough to explain the workings of the most complex natural language. Once the distinctive features of a language's phonemes have been identified, phonology can be linked to Saussure's thesis that a language is a system of differential SIGNS.

At roughly the same time, Jakobson was also working on the topics of APHASIA, or the loss of the speech-function, and the acquisition of language in childhood (1941 and, more succinctly, Jakobson and Halle 1956). He observed that aphasia and language-acquisition were mirror images of one another, and that two basic patterns or types of mechanism could be observed. Individuals suffering from contiguity disorder could not combine simple linguistic units into higher and more complex units; individuals suffering from similarity disorder had difficulty in selecting the appropriate unit and would substitute 'knife' for 'fork'. Jakobson maps these disorders onto the major figures of RHETORIC and identifies them with METAPHOR/METONYMY respectively. Metaphor and metonymy are redefined as the fundamental aspects or poles of language, and are further identified with the basic literary modes of poetry (metaphor) and prose (metonymy). An individual's use of language, a system of differences and similarities, is described in terms of the selection of items from the metaphoric or paradigmatic dimension (PARADIGM) and their combination in a metonymic SYNTAGM.

The importance of Jakobson's model of a language functioning on two great axes and with a minimal number of basic elements can scarcely be overstated. It virtually defines the French form of structuralism that became dominant in the 1950s and 1960s and provides the theoretical starting-point for much of BARTHES' work on SEMIOLOGY as well as for the linguistic rereading of FREUD that allowed Lacan to conclude that the UNCONSCIOUS is 'structured like a language'.

READING: Bradford (1994)

Jarry, Alfred (1873–1907) French dramatist, novelist, founder of 'PATAPHYSICS or the science of imaginary solutions, and a major influence on both DADA and SURREALISM. Jarry is best remembered for his black farce *Ubu Roi*, which provoked riots when it was first performed in Paris in 1896. The tale of the rise and fall of a grotesquely murderous tyrant, it is widely regarded as one of the founding texts of the THEATRE OF THE ABSURD (Esslin 1968).

jouissance The French noun means 'enjoyment' in both the sense of pleasure and in the sense in which one speaks of the enjoyment of rights and privileges. It can also mean orgasm, and the cognate verb *jouir* is commonly used to mean 'to come'. The use of the noun in English has been promoted by translations of LACAN and others, but it is commonly treated as a French word and italicized accordingly. *Jouissance* can in fact be found in the *Shorter OED*, where it is defined simply as 'enjoyment' and flagged as obsolete.

Lacan begins to use the term *jouissance* in his seminars of 1953–4 where it refers to KOJÈVE's version of the master–slave dialectic, in which the work of the slave provides objects for the master's enjoyment. The term's meaning gradually shifts and acquires more sexual connotations from the early 1960s onwards (particularly in Lacan 1960). The most sustained discussion will be found in the seminar of 1969–70 (Lacan 1991).

For Lacan, *jouissance* is not simply synonymous with orgasm. Orgasms are quantifiable, but *jouissance* is always used in the singular and is always accompanied by the singular definite article. It evokes an eroticized DEATH-DRIVE and a degree of intensity which takes the SUBJECT beyond the PLEASURE PRINCIPLE. Pleasure is described as an obstacle to *jouissance* in that it always leads to a reduction in tension and to a return to homoeostasis, or a dynamically stable state; *jouissance*, in contrast, takes the subject to that extreme point where the erotic borders upon death. Lacan's later comments on *jouissance*, and in particular his speculations as to the existence of a specifically female *jouissance*, are greatly influenced by BATAILLE's explorations of the relationship between eroticism, death and mysticism. Significantly, both the first edition of Bataille's *Eroticism* (1957) and the twentieth volume of Lacan's seminar (1975) are illustrated with reproductions of Bernini's representation of St Teresa, which depicts the saint at the moment of her 'transverberation' or penetration by the word of God. By way of commentary, Lacan remarks: 'She's coming, no doubt about it.' He goes on to speculate that St Teresa is experiencing a female *jouissance* that goes beyond the PHALLUS. This, he argues, is a *jouissance* that women can experience without being able to speak of it. The argument overlooks the fact that the historical St Teresa has a great deal to say about her experience (Teresa of Avila 1588).

Kristeva works with a broadly similar concept of *jouissance*, but makes a distinction between a phallic *jouissance* which mobilizes the clitoris and involves competition and identification with the symbolic power of the male partner, and an 'other' specifically female *jouissance* involving the whole of the body and the whole of psychical space (1987a).

Barthes invokes the distinction between pleasure and *jouissance* to describe the delight afforded by the mastery of regular forms, and the asocial and potentially disorienting experience generated by avant-garde texts that bring the reader into contact with a level corresponding to Kristeva's SEMIOTIC (Barthes 1973a). The distinction between *jouissance* and pleasure corresponds to that contained in the concept WRITERLY AND READERLY TEXTS (Barthes 1970a).

Jung, Carl Gustav (1875–1961) Swiss psychiatrist and founder of the school of analytical psychology, which provides both a metapsychology or a theory of the workings of the psyche, and a theory of psychotherapy. Jung's analytical psychology and FREUD'S PSYCHOANALYSIS have had an immense influence on all aspects of twentieth-century thought. Although both originate in nineteenth-century philosophy, a major historian of psychiatry notes (Ellenberger 1970) that whereas Freud is heir to its positivistic, scientific and Darwinian strands, Jung reverts to a more subjectivist and Romantic tradition and claims to be exploring a realm of the human soul that exists midway between religion and psychology.

Jung's early work on schizophrenia and word associations (1904–07; included in *Collected Works*, vol. 2), which revealed the existence of meaningful COMPLEXes or nuclei of unconscious ideas and AFFECTS, led to an exchange of publications with Freud. The relationship that ensued, which can be traced in detail through the fascinating Freud–Jung correspondence (1974), followed the pattern of close collaboration and then estrangement that marked Freud's relationships with many of his colleagues. Freud at one point regarded Jung as his heir apparent, and Jung did become the first president of the International Psychoanalytic Association in 1910, but the publication of the latter's *Symbols of Transformation* (1912) led to a complete break between the two. From this point onwards, psychoanalysis and analytical psychology developed along very different lines.

The initial disagreements between Freud and Jung centred on the LIBIDO theory, with Jung contending that it gave too great an importance to the role of sexuality, and especially of incestuous wishes, in the aetiology of NEUROSIS. Jung gradually elaborates a much broader and less sexualized notion of 'psychic energy', which can be transmitted or communicated to any field of human activity, and argues that the sexual aspects of neurosis are secondary. Psychic energy is described in very broad terms, and might be compared to the notion of *élan vital* associated with the French philosopher Henri Bergson (1859–1941) or even with the many theories that speak of a primal 'life-force'. Whereas Freud speaks of *libidinal* types (1931b), Jung speaks of *character* types, and his essay on that topic (1921) is the source of the familiar distinction between extroverted and introverted personality types. The concept of the UNCONSCIOUS also undergoes important modifications in Jungian theory. A distinction is made between a personal unconscious, which is specific to the individual, and a deeper COLLECTIVE UNCONSCIOUS which is described as being common to the entire human race and as containing universal ARCHETYPES. Dreams are thus regarded as pertaining to archetypal or fixed symbols rather than to the repressed wishes described by Freud. The concept of a collective unconscious whose effects can be observed in both an individual's complexes and in the great religions is at the source of Jung's passionate interest in religion, and especially primitive religion, spiritualism, alchemy and the occult. In a sense, Jung reverts to the etymological sense of 'psychology' (the study of the psyche or soul) and employs psyche in a quasi-religious sense (1933).

A theory of archetypes is also applied by Jung to the personal history of the individual who goes through a series of stages in a life-cycle going from birth to death. In the course of that cycle, the individual obviously goes through a sequence of archetypal experiences and incorporates them into his or her personal life. The gradual piecing together of archetypal and personal experiences and of conscious and unconscious aspects of the personality is referred to as 'individuation'. True individuation usually begins in mid to later life, when the individual has acquired sufficient maturity to come to terms with life and his or her experiences. It is therefore also described as the process of 'becoming what one is'. Like the enlightenment of Eastern religions, true individuation can be a difficult and even painful process, as it involves coming to terms with one's PERSONA and with 'the shadow'. The latter term is Jung's designation for the darker and more dangerous side of the personality that exists in the shadowland of the personal unconscious. Jung describes his own experience of the process of individuation, which can be likened to the heroic questions of legends and myths, in his *Memories, Dreams, Reflections* (1963).

Although Jungian therapy is very widely practised throughout the world and although his theory of archetypes has been adopted and modified by literary theorists such as BACHELARD and FRYE, Jung's theories have not really become part of the orthodoxy of THEORY in the way that Freud's have, perhaps because they so often appear to recommend a flight into irrationalism and even mysticism. Jung's works are collected in twenty volumes (1953–83). The published abstracts of the collected works are a valuable introduction to their extremely varied contents (Rothgeb 1991), whilst the *Critical Dictionary of Jungian Analysis* (Samuels, Shorter and Plaut 1968) is a standard guide to Jung's conceptual terminology.

READING: Fordham (1953); Stevens (1990)

K

Kitchen Sink School The expression is widely used to describe art, and particularly film and drama, dealing with domestic reality, usually in its more sordid forms. It was originally applied by the British art critic David Sylvester (1954) to the work of the painters John Bratby, Jack Smith and Paul Rebeyrolle, whose domestic interiors signalled a move away from the traditional 'artist's studio' theme and depicted 'a very ordinary kitchen lived in by a very ordinary family'. The term was then used by G. Wilson Knight (1963) to describe characteristic British plays of the 1950s; his examples included John Osborne's *Look Back in Anger* (1956), Arnold Wesker's *Roots* trilogy (*Chicken Soup with Barley*, 1958; *Roots*, 1959; and *I'm Talking About Jerusalem*, 1960) and Shelagh Delaney's *A Taste of Honey* (1957), 'since it is remarkable how many of these plays contain a sink or some equivalent.'

kitsch The German word, which can be used as both a noun and an adjective, means 'worthless trash', 'rubbish', 'gaudy' and 'trashy'. It has been used in English since the 1920s to describe the tasteless products of commercial advertising, gaudy tourist souvenirs and works of art that pander to bad taste. Although it is often used pejoratively, kitsch can also refer to a knowingly ironic enjoyment and celebration of bad art and bad taste (Dorfles 1969). The work of the American artist Jeff Koons (1950–) is kitsch in the extreme. It includes mixed-media tableaux of the artist having sexual intercourse with Italian porn-star Cicciolina and a larger-than-life ceramic sculpture of pop star Michael Jackson and his pet chimpanzee Bubbles (reproduced in Muthesios 1992). The aesthetic theory of Clement GREENBERG is based mainly upon the contention that the only defence against the invasion of kitsch is the ABSTRACTION of the AVANT-GARDE (1941).

Klein, Melanie (1882–1960) Austrian-born psychoanalyst. A pioneer of child analysis, Klein is, together with ANNA FREUD, one of the most important influences on the OBJECT-RELATIONS school of PSYCHOANALYSIS (Rayner 1991). Her collected writings have been published in four volumes (1975a–d).

Klein's earliest papers, written in 1921–3 (and collected in Klein 1975a) are based upon the direct observation and analysis of her own children, and provide the theoretical basis for the play technique she developed in Vienna and Berlin and then perfected after her move to London in 1931. The technique is described at great length in her narrative account of the psychoanalysis of a ten-year-old boy (1975d;

see also 1955). Their relative lack of verbal sophistication means that it is not possible to analyse young children by using the classic technique of FREE ASSOCIATION on the couch. Klein's great insight is that free play can be an equivalent to free association. The manipulation of small toys, water and paper is a symbolic activity in the course of which the child reproduces unconscious fantasies and impulses, and thus reveals how it relates to its OBJECTS. The play technique gives the analyst access to the child's unconscious inner world, and Klein claimed to be able to analyse children as young as three. The technique is purely therapeutic and has no educational content or goal.

Klein's work with young children led her to conclude (1928) that the effects of the OEDIPUS COMPLEX are observable in the second year of life; FREUD and his more orthodox followers argue that true Oedipal feelings begin to emerge between the ages of three and five. Observing that even very young children can experience the remorse and guilt which Freud attributes to the post-Oedipal internalization of the SUPEREGO, Klein argues (1933) that that agency in fact consists of a number of internal objects, and not simply of internalized parental figures. According to Klein, the origins of the superego lie in an early deflection of the DEATH-DRIVE. The issue of the dating of the Oedipus complex and of the origins of the superego are the source of major disagreements between Kleinians and the followers of Anna Freud.

Klein's concentration on the child's objects results in a number of other departures from Freudian orthodoxy. Whereas Freud, and LACAN after him, attach great importance to the role played in a child's early development by the father, Klein tends to emphasize the maternal function. Rather than tracing the stages of a linear libidinal development through the oral, anal and genital stages, she describes a series of positions which overlap and fluctuate in early childhood and which may be reactivated in later life. In the early paranoid-schizoid position, the child uses splitting mechanisms as a defence against the AMBIVALENCE it feels towards the maternal part-object (Klein 1946). Typically, love is projected onto a fantasized 'good breast' which provides nourishment, and hate or aggression is projected onto a 'bad breast' which, in the child's FANTASY, has been withheld or withdrawn. Development is largely a matter of integrating part-objects into a whole, but the gradual perception of the mother as a complete object with both good and bad qualities also leads to the realization that she might be lost completely or be damaged beyond repair. The child therefore moves into the depressive position (Klein 1935, 1940). Ambivalence towards the object now gives rise to feelings of guilt, and then to attempts to make reparation to it. The attempt to make reparation represents a further stage in the integration of the object, but the underlying feelings of guilt can be reactivated in mourning or depression.

Klein's work has been enormously influential, but it remains controversial. Her interpretation of children's play can seem very reductive. Lacan, for instance, comments sharply on her readiness to interpret a four-year-old boy's game with a toy train and station with a 'brutal verbalization of the Oedipus myth . . . *You are the little train, you want to fuck your mother*' (1975a; the reference is to Klein 1930, and Klein actually interprets the game as 'The station is mummy; Dick is going into mummy'). Less outspoken critics tend to remark that the unconscious operations and symbolism described by Klein imply an improbably high level of intellectual ability in very young children.

READING: Grosskurth (1986); Hinshelwood (1989); Segal (1979).

Kojève, Alexandre (1902–68) Russian-born French philosopher. Although he never held a full-time academic position, Kojève's intellectual influence has been enormous. The lectures he gave on Hegel's *Phenomenology of Mind* in Paris between 1933 and 1939 (published 1947) had a major impact on BATAILLE and LACAN, and prepared the ground for the renaissance in French Hegelian studies of the immediate postwar period (see Butler 1987; Kelly 1992). In the United States, his influence can be seen in the work of Allan BLOOM and, more recently, Francis FUKUYAMA. Kojève's later writings, which are much less well known than his work on Hegel, include a three-volume study of 'pagan philosophy' from the pre-Socratics to the neo-Platonists (1968, 1972, 1973a), an essay on Kant (1973b) and an incomplete phenomenology of right (1982).

Kojève's reading of Hegel's *Phenomenology* is notable for its concentration on the violence of the struggle or DIALECTIC between the master and the slave. The two are involved in a struggle for prestige and for the recognition of their existence. The master's desire for recognition is greater than his fear of death, whereas the slave opts for life and submits to the master. The paradox is that the master's quest for recognition and self-mastery ends in failure; having lost his independence, the slave cannot give the recognition the master desires. At the same time, the master becomes dependent on the slave who fulfils his life needs, and who thus learns self-awareness. For Kojève, the true hero is the sage who achieves a full self-consciousness of his own finitude, rises above the passions and acquires an almost superhuman status.

Kojève uses the master-slave dialectic as a model of intersubjectivity in which self-consciousness exists only insofar as it exists for another self-consciousness, and only insofar as it is recognized by that other self-consciousness. The dialectic centres on the DESIRE for recognition, and the object of desire (recognition) is always in the possession of the OTHER. Human desire is therefore a 'desire for the desire of the other' (Hyppolite 1947). This was a very common theme in French philosophy in the late 1940s and 1950s, and is the starting-point of Lacan's 'dialectic of desire' (1960).

Kojève is also closely associated with the 'end of history' thesis revived by Fukuyama in his celebration of the alleged worldwide triumph of liberal democracy (1992). At the beginning of the Cold War, Kojève claimed that the end of history had been reached, that a world culture was being created by the United States, that Russia was no more than an impoverished America, and that the future lay in capitalism and not communism. After the Second World War, Kojève worked for the French government and played an important role in the politics of early European unification. He was clearly convinced that the unification of Europe would lead to the emergence of a supranational state ruled by bureaucrats advised by sages. Kojève's almost aristocratic contempt for the passions of the modern world is typified by his comment on the French student revolt of May 1968: nothing had happened because 'no one died.'

READING: Auffret (1990); Drury (1994); *Parallax 4: Kojève's Paris/Now Bataille* (1997)

Koyré, Alexandre (1882–1964) Russian-French philosopher and historian of science. Koyré's extensive writings include an interesting early study of Slavophiles and Westernizers in nineteenth-century Russia (1929), but he is best known for his work on the scientific revolution of the seventeenth century, centring on the history of astronomy and related topics (1961) and including major studies of Galilean (1939) and Newtonian science (1965). For Koyré the COPERNICAN REVOLUTION inaugurates a century of innovative thought which destroys the notion of the cosmos that was dominant from Antiquity to the Renaissance and makes the intellectual transition from a closed world to an open, even infinite universe (1957). As a result of this scientific revolution, the universe can be viewed not as a closed world united by its internal structure, but as an infinite geometrical space united only by the identity of its fundamental contents and laws. Koyré's history of the sciences is broadly similar to that of BACHELARD and CANGUILHEM in that it stresses the importance of theoretical advances rather than empirical discoveries (1971). For this version of historical EPISTEMOLOGY, experimental science is not the source but the result of the applications of theoretical approaches to the natural world. Koyré's intellectualism and his claims that the social structures of seventeenth-century England could not explain Newton provoked an angry reaction from the British historian Christopher HILL, who argues the contrary contextualist case (1967). Even though Koyré spent much of his career in the United States, FOUCAULT claims (1978) that his work is part of the distinct tradition of a French 'philosophy of concepts' that includes Bachelard, Canguilhem and ALTHUSSER.

Koyré made a vital, if almost accidental, contribution to the history of French philosophy by ensuring that KOJÈVE took over his seminar on Hegel when he left Paris for Cairo in 1933. The published text of Kojève's seminar on the *Phenomenology of Mind* (1947) was a crucial influence on the Hegelian revival in postwar France.

Kracauer, Siegfried (1899–1966) German cultural critic and associate of the FRANKFURT SCHOOL. Kracauer is still best known for his history of the German cinema of the 1920s and 1930s (1947) and his *Theory of Film* (1960), both of which were written in English after he sought exile in the United States during the Second World War and which have obscured the importance of his earlier work; it was until recently largely forgotten in Germany too, as Kracauer disappeared from the German intellectual scene by becoming an American citizen and resident. Although his film studies have been described as the work of a 'naïve realist' (Andrew 1976), that view is in need of revision. Kracauer does view photography and cinema as 'realist' forms, but when he remarks (1960) that films alienate us from our environment by exposing it for what it is, he is closer to RUSSIAN FORMALISM than naïve realism.

Kracauer worked mainly as a journalist, contributing some two thousand articles (catalogued in Levin 1989) to the daily *Frankfurter Zeitung* between 1921 and 1933, but it was only in 1963 that a selection (made by the author) was republished in book form. Kracauer produced a vast number of film reviews, and his other articles cover topics as varied as the architecture of cinemas, the circus, dance halls, bestsellers and the arcades of Berlin. His prolific literary output also included a posthumously published study of detective novels (1922–5). All his writings testify to his belief that the nature of a historical period can best be understood by looking at its 'inconspicuous surface-level expressions' rather than by examining its judgements about itself. His essays strive to find the universal in the particular by studying the ephemeral productions of contemporary life, and provide a vivid picture of the culture of pre-Nazi Germany. Rather than working with great theoretical abstractions, Kracauer presents small-scale images in such a way that they speak for themselves in an almost phenomenological sense; the similarity with his friend BENJAMIN's 'thinking in images' (*Bilddenken*) is startling. The role of the critic is to question the abstract rationality (*Ratio*) that has come to dominate the modern world by introducing an element of disenchantment or disillusion that will promote reason or critical understanding (*Vernunft*). Whilst the *Ratio/Vernunft* opposition anticipates HORKHEIMER and ADORNO'S DIALECTIC OF ENLIGHTENMENT, Kracauer's notion of disenchantment also has something in common with BARTHES' approach to his MYTHOLOGIES. The influence of the abstract *Ratio* can be seen in the blank objectivity of *NEUE SACHLICHKEIT* painting, which he describes as a false façade that conceals nothing (1930), but also in the geometrical patterns made by the dancers of the Tiller Girls troupe, whose bodies form the 'mass ornament' that gives the 1963 collection its title.

Borrowing a phrase from LUKÁCS's early study of the novel (1920), Kracauer describes the modern world as displaying a 'transcendental homelessness' induced by the collapse of great ideological systems and values. The void is typified by the empty hotel lobby or the lonely city street, and it is filled by the dreams sold by the cult of distraction, by the emergence and distribution of a mass culture that is so calculated that all spectators will have the same response because they have been reduced to standard social types. The consumer society sees to it that the demand for cultural needs is met by products that do not lead to a critical reflection on that society. The parallel with Adorno's scathing critique of the CULTURE INDUSTRY is obvious, but Kracauer's critique is not so harsh, being based on the belief that it is still possible for *Vernunft* to overcome *Ratio*. He also displays a definite, if melancholy, sympathy with the pleasures of mass culture, and does not contrast it with the austerity of high MODERNISM. As Adorno remarks (1974), Kracauer seems to smile at the 'little shopgirls' as they go to the movies because he shares something of their naïve pleasure (1927). It is difficult to imagine Adorno smiling at them.

Although there are elements of MARXISM in Kracauer's work, which often relies on a BASE/SUPERSTRUCTURE model, he is no orthodox Marxist and studies the salaried white-collar workers (*Angestellung*) of Berlin rather than the industrial working class. The 'salaried masses' were a product of the economic climate of the late 1920s, a metaphorically homeless and homogenized mass employed in banks, offices and department stores and entertained by the cult of distraction in the 'pleasure barracks' of the great cinemas and dance-halls of Berlin. Kracauer's short but trenchant study of the salaried masses (1930) is an extraordinarily vivid document made up of direct quotations and observations which are not examples of theory but 'exemplary instances of reality'. The most memorable 'exemplary instance' is the quotation from the store manager who states that a precondition for employment in his shop is the possession of 'a morally pink complexion'.

READING: *New German Critique* (1991)

Kristeva, Julia (1941–) Bulgarian-born French theorist of language and literature, psychoanalyst and member of the TEL QUEL group. Kristeva's work is extremely wide-ranging and demanding, but the twenty-three interviews collected in English translation (Guberman 1996) provide a remarkably lucid and sympathetic introduction to her writings. She is also the author of a helpful introduction to linguistics (first published under her married name, Joyaux 1969, republished as Kristeva 1981). Although Kristeva has always worked at the crossroads where linguistics, psychoanalysis, philosophy and literature meet, the emphasis changes as the scientific ambitions of STRUCTURALISM give way to a psychoanalytically inspired exploration of subjectivity, and as the early conceptual borrowings from the mathematical sciences give way to the study of monotheism. Although Kristeva's work is immensely sophisticated and innovatory, it can also be surprisingly traditional. In her study of love (1983), she remarks, for instance, that literature gives a more public account of the essence of loving relationships than her patients, and thus returns to one of the more traditional themes of PSYCHOANALYTIC CRITICISM.

Perhaps the most important of Kristeva's early essays is the study of BAKHTIN (1969a) that allowed her to elaborate the very influential concept of INTERTEXTUALITY. In a major series of related essays (collected 1969b), she begins to work out a theory of 'semanalysis' (from 'SEMIOTICS' and 'PSYCHOANALYSIS') which studies the SUBJECT in relation to the archaic DRIVES and the prelinguistic elements that circulate in the *CHORA* and the SEMIOTIC. Semanalysis concentrates on the limits of language to the extent that it studies the child at a prelinguistic stage in which desires and drives are not yet subject to the laws of the SYMBOLIC and to the breakdown of language in PSYCHOSIS. For Kristeva, this level of language corresponds to the practice of AVANT-GARDE writing which contests established meanings and brings the writer into a potentially dangerous proximity to the semiotic. This relationship is explored in the doctoral thesis (1974a) on the revolution in poetic language associated with the avant-gardes of the late nineteenth century, and especially with Lautréamont and Mallarmé. Here Kristeva contends that these writers, together with ARTAUD and BATAILLE, bring into play the relationship between the speaking body and society. They are described as making a violent critique of the state, family and religion; at the same time, their critique inaugurates a linguistic rebellion that disrupts the structure of language by allowing the semiotic to traverse their literary productions. The implicit equating of avant-garde literary production with revolutionary politics, or even the substitution of one for the other, is in keeping with the politics of *Tel quel* in the 1970s.

In the trilogy of studies that look, respectively, at ABJECTION (1980), love (1983) and depression (1987a), Kristeva gradually elaborates a history of subjectivity in Western thought and increasingly uses religious discourse as her point of reference. The traditional figure of the Virgin with Child now becomes the prototypical image of love, whilst psychoanalysis is described as confirming and amplifying the truths enshrined in Jewish and Christian monotheism. The Christian vision of love, in particular, is said to be at once paternal, maternal and narcissistic and to supply the richest mosaic of words that human beings could wish to hear.

Although Kristeva has written extensively on femininity and sexual difference, her relationship with FEMINISM is both complex and difficult. The relationship with the mother is central to her psychoanalysis, but she tends to view feminism as involving women in a 'phallic competition' with men and has described (1983) feminism as 'our last religion' or the religion of the woman of authority. In her *New Maladies of the Soul* (1987b) she speaks of the need for a 'civilized' feminism which will put an end to the war between the sexes and give a new value to motherhood, viewed as woman's most important civilizational vocation.

In general terms, Kristeva's political evolution follows the same trajectory as the rest of the *Tel quel* group. Her visit to China with the rest of the group in 1974 inspired an idealistic and highly utopian picture of Chinese society, and particularly the position of Chinese women (1974b), which typifies *Tel quel*'s Maoist period. In stark contrast, her later study of the role and image of 'the foreigner' celebrates the republican virtues and universalism of the France of Montesquieu and De Gaulle (1988). Her most recent writings are dominated by a deep pessimism, and Kristeva likens (1994) our epoch to 'the fall of the Roman Empire, but without the promise of a new religion'. The pessimism stems in part from the changing symptoms presented by her psychoanalytic patients (see 1987b in particular), who no longer suffer from HYSTERIA or the classic neuroses observed by FREUD, but from an ill-defined depression and a lack of any sense of direction. According to Kristeva, their depression is an expression of a generalized social distress, and she likens France itself to a depressed patient (1998); national confidence has to be restored in the same way that the narcissism of a patient must be restored before the real analysis of his or her resistances can begin. Psychoanalysis tends, in Kristeva's later writings, to take on an exemplary social role (notably in 1988). Thus, the psychoanalytic recognition that the OTHER exists within everyone in the form of the unconscious provides a model for a new cosmopolitanism; just as the presence of the other within the psyche has to be recognized, so the presence within the nation of 'others' (immigrants and foreigners) must be recognized and accepted because we are all strangers to ourselves.

READING: Moi (1986); Oliver (1997)

Kuhn, Thomas Samuel (1922–96) American historian and philosopher of science. His *Structure of Scientific Revolutions* (1962) is one of the most influential books in its field and has given the notions of 'PARADIGM' and 'paradigm shift' an extremely wide currency.

Kuhn's best-known book originated in a science course designed for arts under-graduates at Harvard University and in its author's realization, on reading Aristotle's *Physics*, that Aristotelian physics was not simply a false or incomplete version of Newtonian physics, but was simply different and had its own conceptual coherence and intellectual unity. That realization forced him to abandon his earlier conviction that the history of science was a gradual and linear accumulation of knowledge.

Kuhn now began to describe scientific history as consisting of long peaceful inter-ludes, which he described as periods of NORMAL SCIENCE, punctuated by the intel-lectual revolutions brought about by paradigm shifts. He saw the transition from Newtonian to Einsteinian mechanics as a particularly clear example of how a scientific revolution displaces the entire conceptual network through which the scientific community views the world.

For Kuhn, the task of the historian of science is twofold: to determine when and by whom a given scientific fact or theory was discovered, and to describe the errors, myths and superstitions that inhibited a more rapid accumulation of the constituent elements of modern science. The close historical study of the state of a science at any given time discloses a set of recurrent and almost standard illustrations of a number of theories. These are the paradigms of the normal science of a scientific community. Further study of these paradigms reveals how they were finally aban-doned, not because they were inherently false or untrue, but because they could not answer all the questions they themselves raised. The failure of existing rules is therefore the prelude to the quest for new rules. Kuhn notes (1962) that the shift from Ptolemaic to Copernican astronomy began with the growing realization that, whilst the former could predict the position of the stars and planets, it was unable to predict the precession of the equinoxes.

L

Lacan, Jacques (1901–81) French psychoanalyst. The most controversial psychoanalyst since FREUD himself, Lacan has had an immense influence on literary theory, philosophy and, more controversially, feminism (PSYCHOANALYSIS AND FEMINISM), as well as on PSYCHOANALYSIS itself. Despite the notorious difficulties posed by his prose style, Lacan's work has done more than that of any other analyst to make psychoanalysis a central reference to a whole field of disciplines within the HUMAN SCIENCES.

Lacan's most important papers are collected in his *Écrits* (1966); fewer than one-third of them are included in the English *Écrits: A Selection* (1977). Until the publication of *Écrits*, the main vector for the dissemination of his ideas was the weekly seminar that began in 1953 and continued until shortly before his death. Edited transcripts of the seminar began to be published during his lifetime (1975b), and twenty-six volumes are planned. The quality of the editing is a matter for controversy (Roudinesco 1993); no notes have been appended to the eleven volumes to have been published to date and they are not indexed. Paradoxically, it is easier to work with the annotated English translations (1975a, 1978, 1981) than with the originals. Dylan Evans's *Introductory Dictionary of Lacanian Psychoanalysis* (1996) provides an invaluable guide to Lacan's terminology and concepts.

Lacan's career was dogged by controversy and regularly punctuated by conflicts with the psychoanalytic establishment, most of them focusing on his refusal to follow the conventions of the 'analytic hour' and his insistence on using short sessions of varying length during training analyses. In 1953 Lacan and others resigned from the Société Psychanalytique de Paris (SPP) to found the Société Psychanalytique de France (SPF); Lacan's continued use of short sessions ensured that the latter was never recognized as a competent society by the International Psychoanalytic Association (IPA). In 1963, similar issues led to a split in the new association and to the foundation of the ÉCOLE FREUDIENNE DE PARIS (Psychoanalytic School of Paris), which was unilaterally dissolved by Lacan himself in 1980.

Lacan's original training was in medicine and psychiatry, and his prepsychoanalytic early work was on paranoia. The publication of his doctoral thesis, which dealt mainly with a woman patient suffering from a PSYCHOSIS that led her to attempt to murder an actress (1932), won him the admiration of BRETON and the surrealist group, with which he was briefly associated. Lacan's writings are steeped in allusions to SURREALISM, and it is probable that surrealist experiments with language (and particularly automatic writing) and speculations about the relationship between forms of language and different psychical states had a long-term influence on his famous contention that the unconscious is structured like a language. His notion of the FRAGMENTED BODY is one of the clearest indications of his debt to surrealism (Bowie 1991). The association with surrealism is less surprising than it might seem; the surrealists, to Freud's irritation, were much more sympathetic to his ideas than the French medical establishment.

Lacan began his analysis with Rudolph Lowenstein in 1934, and was elected to the SPP in the same year. Ironically, Lowenstein was one of the pioneers of the EGO-PSYCHOLOGY that Lacan came to loathe so much. Lacan's first contribution to psychoanalysis was made in 1936, when he presented his paper on the MIRROR-STAGE to the Marienbad Conference of the IPA. For reasons that have never been clearly explained, it has never been published; the version included in *Écrits* was written thirteen years later (1949). In the late 1940s Lacan began to use the idea of the mirror-stage to elaborate a theory of subjectivity that views the EGO as a largely IMAGINARY construct based upon an alienating identification with the mirror-image of the SUBJECT. At the intersubjective level, the subject is drawn at a very early age into a DIALECTIC of identification with an aggression towards the OTHER (1948). Originally based upon the findings of child psychology and primate ethology (from which Lacan adopts the thesis that a child, unlike a young chimpanzee, recognizes its own image in a mirror), the theory of subjectivity is subsequently recast in terms of a dialectic of DESIRE (see in particular Lacan 1960). The influence of KOJÈVE's seminar on Hegel's *Phenomenology of Mind* (1947) is crucial here; Lacan was an assiduous attender, and all his numerous allusions to Hegel should in fact be read as allusions to Kojève.

The paper on language and speech in psychoanalysis (1953) read to the founding congress of the SPF in Rome in 1953 (and therefore often referred to as the 'Rome Discourse') is the first great manifesto of Lacanian psychoanalysis. Lacan calls for a 'return to Freud', stressing the pressing need to read Freud in detail (and preferably in German) and denouncing the dominant tendencies within contemporary psychoanalysis (ego-psychology, Kleinian analysis – KLEIN – and OBJECT-RELATIONS theory) as so many forms of revisionism. At the same time he elaborates an immensely broad synthetic vision in which psychoanalysis appropriates the findings of philosophy (notably Kojève and HEIDEGGER), the structural anthropology of LÉVI-STRAUSS and the linguistics of SAUSSURE. This vision is consistent with the thesis that psychoanalysis is indeed a TALKING CURE, with speech and language as its only media, but it also allows Lacan to develop a universalist theory of the origins of human subjectivity. Lévi-Strauss's accounts of the non-conscious structures of kinship and alliance, and of the crucial transition from nature to culture, allow Lacan to describe the OEDIPUS COMPLEX as a structural moment that integrates the child into a preexisting SYMBOLIC order by obliging it to recognize the NAME-OF-THE-FATHER and to abandon its claim to being the sole object of the mother's desire (PHALLUS).

Although the 1953 paper abounds in reference to language and linguistics, it is only in his paper on the agency of the letter (1957) that Lacan truly begins to explore and appropriate the legacy of Saussure. At the same time he also relies heavily on JAKOBSON's work of PHONEME analysis and on METAPHOR/METONYMY, which are likened to the mechanisms of CONDENSATION and DISPLACEMENT. Language is now defined as a synchronic system of SIGNS which generate meaning through their interaction; meaning insists in and through a chain of signifiers, and does not reside in any one element. The structural isomorphism between the workings of language and the unconscious mechanisms of the DREAM-WORK allows Lacan to conclude that the unconscious is structured like a language. For Lacan there is never any direct correspondence between signifier and signified, and meaning is therefore always in danger of sliding or slipping out of control. An element of stability is, he argues, provided by privileged signifiers such as the phallus and the name-of-the-father, and it is this claim that exposes him to DERRIDA's accusations of LOGOCEN-TRISM and PHALLOGOCENTRISM.

Lacan's early use of linguistics anticipates a distinctive feature of his later work in that he makes use of quasi-mathematical formulae to illustrate the workings of metaphor and metonymy (1957). The initial formulae are no doubt little more than pedagogic devices, but they gradually develop into a so-called Lacanian algebra (which is clearly described by Evans) and a set of MATHEMES designed to ensure that psychoanalytic theory can be subjected to a FORMALIZATION and to guarantee its integral transmission. The major influence here is the historical EPISTEMOLOGY of BACHELARD, CANGUILHEM and KOYRÉ.

READING: Macey (1988); Roudinesco (1982, 1986); Turkle (1978); Weber (1990)

language-games Notion introduced by WITTGENSTEIN in notes dictated in 1933–4 and in the draft for what eventually became his *Philosophical Investigations* (1953). Known respectively as the 'Blue' and 'Brown' Books, the notes and draft were published posthumously (1958).

Wittgenstein defines a language-game as a way of using signs that is simpler than that in which the signs of everyday language are used, and contends both that language-games are the forms of language with which children first make use of words and that they are primitive forms of language. In philosophical terms the study of such simplified languages has a therapeutic goal and is designed to clarify our thinking about language, and to clear up the problems created by linguistic confusion as to the meanings of categories such as 'true' and 'false'. Language, that is, is viewed as a matter of practical convention or actual use in which usage determines meaning, and Wittgenstein challenges the conventional view that it is an expression of preexisting mental images. The introduction of the notion of language-games thus breaks with the so-called 'picture theory' of the earlier *Tractatus Logico-Philosophicus* (1921) which, under the influence of FREGE's logic, held that truth depended upon the resemblance between a sentence and that of which it was a picture.

Wittgenstein proposes a number of hypothetical games of growing complexity that display a family resemblance. He invites, for instance, the reader to imagine a language in which the sentence-form 'the water in the glass' does not exist. A more complex game consists of the words 'cube', 'brick', 'slab' and 'column' and is used to illustrate how a language is learned. A builder calls out one of these words, and his labourer brings a stone of a certain shape. Language-acquisition is reduced to a demonstrative process (pointing to the stone) based on a pattern of stimulus and response. The contrast between 'cube' and 'brick' exists solely at the level of the language-game, and is not necessarily present in the mind of either the builder or the labourer when these words are uttered or heard. Although Wittgenstein's language-games are said to be purely descriptive and demonstrative constructs, their status is ambiguous; it is unclear whether they are fragments of natural languages or complete in themselves.

LYOTARD borrows the notion of language-games in his account of the collapse of GRAND NARRATIVES (1979, 1983), and uses it to stress that the little narratives that replace them are singular language-games, each with its own rules and conventions, or 'truth-regime'. There is therefore no one principle that can act as a criterion for evaluation, and language-games are always incommensurable. Speakers involved in different games literally cannot understand one another and cannot appeal to any higher principle to resolve their 'differend' (Lyotard 1983). They can reach agreement only by proceeding on a case to case basis, inventing the rules as they go and refraining from importing criteria of judgement from other language-games.

langue/parole An important distinction in SAUSSURE's linguistics (1916) which poses considerable translation problems. Unlike English, French has two terms that can both mean 'language': *langage* and *langue*, as in *la langue française* (the French language or tongue) or *les langues vivantes* (modern languages). *Langage* tends, in contrast, to be used of the human faculty of language in the abstract philosophical sense, and not of specific natural languages. *Parole* can be translated as both 'speech' and 'word'. Because it is so difficult to find strict equivalents in English, it has become conventional to use the French terms.

Saussure follows the norms of French usage in using *langage* to refer to the phenomenon of language insofar as it is a human attribute. *Langue*, in contrast, is defined as the social aspect of language. It has little to do with individuals, and can be described as the product of a linguistic contact between all members of a community. *Langue* consists of SIGNS organized into a system and expressive of ideas. As the signs constituting it are arbitrary and purely conventional, it is the differences between them that confer meaning upon them. *Langue* can therefore be said to be an organized system of differences. *Langue* is the object of SEMIOLOGY, or the science that studies the life of signs within society.

Parole, in contrast, refers to the individual aspect of language, or to the actual manifestations of *langue* in individual SPEECH ACTS. The relationship between *langue* and *parole* takes the form of a DIALECTIC: at the level of *parole* individuals are creative agents whose linguistic innovations can modify *langue*, but only by becoming impersonal elements of a system over which individuals have no control. The dialectic between the two aspects of language is the motor-force behind linguistic evolution.

READING: Culler (1976); Gadet (1986)

Leavis, Frank Raymond (1895–1978) and **Leavis, Queenie Dorothy** (1906–81) British literary critics. The influence of Leavis and his wife on the development of English as an academic discipline has been so great that it might be claimed that anyone who has studied English literature in Britain is an unwitting Leavisite without necessarily having read a word of their works. Together with the PRACTICAL CRITICISM of RICHARDS and EMPSON's practice of close reading, the Leavises' recommendation of attention to the text played an immensely important role in turning English into a serious and disciplined mode of study rather than a 'gentlemanly' conversation about books. The network of connections centred on the journal *SCRUTINY* extended their influence throughout schools and colleges and shaped the literary education of more than one generation of students, whilst the insistence from the 1930s to the 1970s on the distinctive discipline of University English is the major single factor that has made English literature the hegemonic discipline within the English education system (see for example Leavis 1975). In major studies of both poetry (1936) and general studies of prose (1948, 1952), as well as of individual novelists such as Lawrence (1955) and Dickens (1970), the Leavises helped to shape the modern CANON of English literature. *The Great Tradition* (1948) opens with the characteristic and influential statement: 'The great English novelists are Jane Austen, George Eliot, Henry James, and Joseph Conrad.'

Although her husband was always the dominant partner, Q. D. Leavis is generally regarded as having played an important part in the writing of his books. Her early study of fiction and the reading public (1932) helped to define the terms of the later debates by establishing distinctions between 'fiction' and 'literature', and mere 'novel-reading' and 'serious reading'. 'Seriousness' or 'moral seriousness' is the hallmark of Leavisite criticism, and an apprenticeship in the 'labour of reading' is viewed as a defence against the mass culture born of industrialization. Although Leavisite criticism is quite open about its attachment to a high culture, it also made possible the study of popular culture and thus had an influence on early developments in CULTURAL STUDIES. In a short book intended for use in schools, F. R. Leavis and Denys Thompson (1942) recommended the training of critical awareness through the study of advertisements, films and newspapers. Studying mass culture's 'exploitation of the cheapest emotional responses' and applying the method of practical criticism to advertisements was a way of developing a critical sense of just how exploitative they were, and hence of promoting an enhanced moral seriousness and sense of discrimination. This simultaneous disdain for and interest in mass or popular culture can be seen in HOGGART's very influential *Uses of Literacy* (1957), with its nostalgia for the working-class communities of Leeds and its loathing of the Americanization of their culture. Nostalgia for an 'organic' or 'common' culture that has been lost to industrialization is an important strand in the work of the Leavises and all those they have influenced, whilst the contention that it continues to exist within the literary tradition alone provides the main rationale for the defence of the tradition. The preservation of tradition goes hand in hand with a celebration of the life-force that once sustained the sturdy communities of sixteenth-century England (see in particular Q. D. Leavis 1932), and which survives in the capacity for experience, the reverent openness towards life and the moral seriousness that typify the great novelists. Organic METAPHORS of physical health are constant throughout Leavisite criticism. James's *Portrait of a Lady*, *Washington Square* and *The Bostonians* are described as having 'the abundant full-blooded life of well-nourished organisms', whilst the same author's later works are condemned for their unhealthy undernourishment and etiolation (Leavis 1948). D. H. Lawrence gradually emerges as the quintessential Leavisite novelist whose work is characterized by a deep interest in life, and a preoccupation with the unconscious forces that well up within human beings.

In the preface to his most important study of English poetry, *Revaluation* (1936), Leavis defines the task and duty of the critic as being to perceive for himself, to make the finest and sharpest discriminations possible and to state his findings as responsibly, clearly and forcibly as he can. Leavisite 'discriminations' can be forceful indeed. In 1932 Q. D. Leavis criticizes Charlotte Brontë for the indulgence in undisciplined emotion that makes her a 'schoolgirl of genius' and unfavourably compares her genius with the 'well-regulated minds' of Jane Austen and Maria Edgeworth, whilst F. R. Leavis complains (1936) that Milton's habit of writing Latin verse forces him to exhibit in *Samson Agonistes* a loss of 'all feeling for his native English'. The most notorious 'discrimination' concerns George Eliot's last novel; Leavis argues (1948) that a 'good' novel entitled *Gwendolen Harleth* could (and should) be extricated from *Daniel Deronda* by cutting away the 'bad part', or in other words the passages dealing with Judaism and Zionism.

Leavis's preferred method of analysis – displayed to best advantage in his studies of poetry – is a close reading of short passages and he was happiest when working in a classroom with an open text before him. Like the theorists of practical criticism, he holds that literary analysis should contain nothing that cannot be produced from, or related back to, the text itself. In a rare discussion of philosophy and literary criticism (1937) he argues that the critic must guard against extrapolating from the text under analysis, and refrain from all premature or irrelevant generalizations. His refusal to theorize or philosophize about what he is doing is based upon the conviction that the authority of the mature and experienced critic or reader is based upon the immediate sense of values instilled by a training in the labour of reading.

READING: MacKillop (1995); Mulhern (1979, 1990)

lesbian feminism   A minority tendency within modern FEMINISM and the WOMEN'S LIBERATION movement which argues that the interests of lesbians are not necessarily identical with those of heterosexual women, and that they should therefore organize and work separately. The emergence of a specifically lesbian feminism originates from the recognition that lesbians could be silenced and ignored even within women's organizations, and was influenced by RADICAL FEMINISM's argument that political lesbianism was a logical choice for women whose sense of identity was grounded in their existence as women and in an antagonistic relationship with heterosexuality. Although it can be argued that it originates in the old tradition of 'romantic friendship' between women (Faderman 1981), organized lesbian feminism is, like the GAY movement, very much a product of the early 1970s. The first National Lesbian Conference to be held in Britain took place in Canterbury in April 1974, and in 1975 the National Coordinating Committee of the Women's Liberation Movement called for an end to all discrimination against lesbians. In the United States the National Organization of Women adopted a resolution supporting lesbians in 1971.

READING: Abelove, Barale and Halperin (1993); Cruikshank (1992)

Lévi-Strauss, Claude (1908–) French anthropologist and one of the most important figures in the development of STRUCTURALISM. The publication of *Structural Anthropology* (1957) was a declaration of war against the subjectivism of Sartrean EXISTENTIALISM (see also SARTRE) and marked the emergence of structuralism as the school of thought that was to dominate French intellectual life until the 1970s. In the course of an academic career spanning fifty years, Lévi-Strauss, often described as one of the giants of twentieth-century thought, has written extensively on art, music and literature as well as on the anthropology of kinship systems and mythology. Music, 'the great mystery of the human sciences' (1964), is a constant theme in the four volumes of *Mythologiques* (1964, 1967, 1968, 1971); he returns to it with an elegant essay which combines studies of Rameau, Poussin and Proust (1993).

Although linguistics provides the theoretical foundations for Lévi-Strauss's structural anthropology, it also draws on philosophy and sociology. Jean-Jacques Rousseau's *Discourse on the Origin of Inequality* (1755) is viewed by Lévi-Strauss (1962a) as one of anthropology's founding texts because it poses the basic anthropological issue of the transition from nature to society. The title of his all-important study of the elementary structures of kinship (1949) contains a transparent allusion to that of Emile Durkheim's sociology of the elementary forms of the religious life (1912; for a comprehensive account of Durkheim, see Lukes 1973). Durkheim is the source of the thesis that human behaviour and culture form a coherent and logical system made up of sets of subsystems, and that individuals are not truly conscious of the rules that govern their behaviour. Marcel Mauss's description (1923) of how the exchange of gifts in archaic societies establishes binding links of reciprocity also makes an important contribution to Lévi-Strauss's theory of symbolic exchange (see in particular Lévi-Strauss 1950).

Lévi-Strauss's original fieldwork was carried out in Brazil and provided the material for the early study of the social and family life of the Nambikwara (1948) and then *The Elementary Structures of Kinship* (1949), which, more so than any other book, can rightly be regarded as the text that founds French structuralism. In it Lévi-Strauss applies to the study of kinship the lessons to be learned from what he calls, in the preface to a later collection of essays (1983), the COPERNICAN REVOLUTION brought about in the human sciences by structural linguistics. For Lévi-Strauss, 'structural linguistics' means the entire post-Saussurean tradition (SAUSSURE), but especially the work done on PHONEMES by JAKOBSON and Trubetzkoy (Trubetzkoy 1939). Their analysis of phonemes had demonstrated that vast systems can be constructed with a minimal number of elementary units of meaning, and that relations between terms are more important than the terms themselves. By concentrating on the intelligible relations between terms, it is possible to pursue anthropology's ultimate goal of identifying the invariant forms and consistent laws that lie behind the empirical diversity of human societies. The knots in the web of the social fabric take logical priority over the lines. The invariants regulate how human societies deal with religion, marriage, the incest taboo and the burial of the dead. In the later *Mythologiques* series Lévi-Strauss applies the same methodology to the myths of pre-Columbian America, breaking them down into their component MYTHEMES and demonstrating that, far from being picturesque stories, myths are a way of understanding the world by classifying it in terms of categories based on binary oppositions between air and water or day and night. One of Lévi-Strauss's greatest achievements has been to show that the 'savage mind' (1962a) is neither savage nor primitive, and that tribal peoples assemble myths by using the materials to hand via the same process of BRICOLAGE that is used in all cultural and intellectual production.

The application of the lessons of structural linguistics to kinship structure reveal that, whatever form it may take, the institution of marriage is an invariant structure of human societies. Lévi-Strauss's principal theses on kinship structures are expounded at length in *The Elementary Structures*; an essay on the family written in 1956 (and revised for inclusion in Lévi-Strauss 1983) provides a conveniently succinct account. Whatever the individuals involved may think or believe, marriage is a matter of relations between groups rather than between individual partners. Marriage enables groups to form alliances: they give daughters and receive wives in exchange. The basic mechanism is supplied by the taboo that prohibits incest between fathers and daughters or mothers and sons: it establishes an interdependence between biological families by making them produce the new families that alone can allow the social group to reproduce itself. As though to forestall feminist objections that this analysis reduces women to commodities, Lévi-Strauss adds for the benefit of 'women readers' that the rules of the game would remain unchanged if the opposite convention were adopted and women exchanged men.

The existence of structured matrimonial exchanges that are unconscious to the degree that the parties involved are never fully aware of them is a basic feature of the transition from nature to culture that is the hallmark of human societies which have gone from eating raw food to eating cooked food (1964). Order and classification replace chaos and meaninglessness, and instinctual disorder gives way to symbolic order. It is on the basis of this anthropology of kinship that LACAN (1953) is able to construct his theory of the SYMBOLIC and make the OEDIPUS COMPLEX symbolized by the NAME-OF-THE-FATHER its universal key.

Lévi-Strauss is one of the most elegant of French writers and his most elegant book is the autobiographical *Tristes Tropiques* (1955a). It is in part a celebration of the brotherhood of man and of the revelation that we can find in the life of the poorest tribe a confirmation of our own image, and in part a melancholy realization that the New World of Brazil has already been destroyed or even that, like Rousseau's state of nature, it existed only in the imagination. Dispirited with the progress and rationalization that have destroyed the savour of life, the great anthropologist seeks consolation in the contemplation of minerals more beautiful than any human creation, or in the brief glance, 'heavy with patience, serenity and mutual forgiveness that, through some involuntary understanding, one can sometimes exchange with a cat'.

READING: Charbonnier (1961); Hayes and Hayes (1970); Leach (1970)

Levinas, Emmanuel (1905–95) Lithuanian-born French philosopher. His work is influenced by both the PHENOMENOLOGY of HUSSERL and HEIDEGGER and the rabbinical tradition of Talmudic studies. Levinas did not regard himself as 'a Jewish philosopher', but as a Jew who was a philosopher. Significantly, his Talmudic studies (1968, 1983, 1995) and his phenomenological essays were entrusted to different publishing houses. Although his early study of Husserl (1930) played a major role in making phenomenology a major current in French thought and had a great influence on the young SARTRE, Levinas remained a fairly obscure figure for much of his career, partly no doubt because he taught mainly in private Jewish institutions and did not take up a university post until 1961. A major essay on his work by DERRIDA (1965) helped to gain him a wider public audience, and at the time of his death almost all his major works were available in cheap paperback editions. The long interview with Poirié is an excellent introduction to his work (Poirié 1987).

For Levinas, philosophy has no real subject-matter of its own, and must therefore feed on the prephilosophical. In his own case, the 'prephilosophical' means primarily the Bible or in other words the Old Testament, as interpreted by the rabbinical tradition, and the metaphysical fictions of Dostoyevsky and the other Russian classics. His work is also deeply influenced by the experience of being exiled from the (now vanished) rich Judaic culture of his childhood, and by the memory of the Holocaust: one of his major books (1974) is dedicated to the millions who were killed in the name of 'hatred of the other man'.

The central theme of Levinas's philosophy is that of the obligation to care for that other man. His version of phenomenology is unusual in that, unlike Sartre in particular, he does not analyse the relationship between the SUBJECT and the OTHER in terms of an inevitable alienation or antagonism. In arguing that we are always responsible for and to the other, he is following the biblical tradition that makes all human beings responsible before the Law and pronounces the injunction 'Thou shalt not kill', but he grounds that tradition in a rigorous phenomenological ethics. For Levinas, ethics is not secondary to EPISTEMOLOGY and nor is it simply a 'branch' of philosophy; ethics, and not metaphysics or epistemology, is 'first philosophy'. He defines subjectivity itself as hospitality and as the welcome that must be given to the other (see in particular 1961, 1972). The immediate relationship with the other is, for Levinas, inaugurated by the simple greeting *Bonjour*, which recognizes the existence of the other as fellow, as another subjectivity to be welcomed and cared for. The face-to-face encounter with the other is the primal moment from which all language and communication spring. 'Face-to-face' is to be understood in the most literal of senses; it is the face of the other that pronounces the imperative we must obey in order to live by the Law. The face of the other demands that we care for others because it establishes a basic I-thou relationship. For Levinas, this recognition of and care for the other is the basis for resistance to the 'inexpiable damnation' wreaked by the Holocaust and the other genocides of the twentieth century, and to the reduction of human others to the status of commodities to be transported to their death in cattle-trucks. To look into the face of the other is to hear the injunction not to kill.

READING: Hand (1989)

libido From the Latin word for 'desire' or 'lust', and used in PSYCHOANALYSIS to describe the mental energy generated by the stimulation of erogenous zones such as the mouth, the breasts, the anus or the genitals. Libido is a specifically sexual energy, and a distinction is made by FREUD between the sexual or libidinal DRIVES and the self-preservation or ego drives. One of the major sources of the disagreements between FREUD and JUNG is the latter's tendency to desexualize the concept of libido and to dissolve it into a more general category of mental energy.

Freud often employs metaphors from the science of hydraulics to describe libido. It is said to be quantifiable, plastic and adhesive, and can be attached to or withdrawn from OBJECTS thanks to the mechanism of CATHEXIS. It can also be desexualized or used in SUBLIMATION. Libido is also described by Freud as being active and masculine; some contributions to the debate between PSYCHOANALYSIS AND FEMINISM respond to this claim by arguing that there is also a specifically feminine libido (Irigaray 1977a). Although Freud refers to libido throughout his work, he rarely defines the concept with any great precision. The clearest discussions are to be found in his *Three Essays on the Theory of Sexuality* (1905a), chapter 26 of the *Introductory Lectures on Psychoanalysis* (1916–17) and the second of the 'Two Encyclopedia Articles' (1922c).

LACAN uses the term 'libido' very sparingly, and tends to discuss sexuality in terms of DESIRE and *JOUISSANCE*.

lifeworld The usual translation of the German *Lebenswelt*, used by HUSSERL to describe the world of human activity and everyday sociability. The lifeworld is a prescientific realm that is ever-present, taken for granted and always/already there as a background to other dimensions of life (Husserl 1936). The concept of the lifeworld is an important element in the phenomenological tradition, where it influences Alfred Schutz's notion of 'familiarity' (1953) or a world that is taken for granted, and especially in HABERMAS's theory of COMMUNICATIVE ACTION (1981 and particularly 1987). For Habermas, the lifeworld, as opposed to the world of 'systems' governed by the logic of instrumental reason, is a realm of shared intersubjectivity bounded by all those interpretations of the world that are presupposed by its members and provide a shared background knowledge. It gives the horizon for all the processes of reaching a common understanding and coordination through communicative action.

linguistic criticism A mode of textual analysis, associated mainly with the British linguist Roger Fowler, which concentrates on the relationship between language-use and the social world (Fowler 1970, 1981). Texts are viewed as the medium of DISCOURSE and as objects to be analysed by using a precise terminology and concepts, as opposed to the often vague analytic notions invoked by so many advocates of close reading and PRACTICAL CRITICISM, Brooks's repeated use of the phrase 'shifts of tone' (1947) being a case in point. Linguistic codes are said to interpret, organize and classify topics of discourse in such a way as to embody theories of how the world is organized, or ideologies. The task of linguistic criticism, which has a lot in common with BARTHES' analyses in his *MYTHOLOGIES*, is to unravel such codes. Fowler draws here on the idea of *OSTRANENIE* or defamiliarization elaborated by RUSSIAN FORMAL-ISM. Whereas language appears to have a natural tendency to degenerate into fixed or fossilized meanings, the task of linguistic criticism is to make these appear new, unfamiliar and non-naturalized by returning them to the historical and political dimension of social life. The task is defined in explicitly political terms: a training in linguistic criticism will equip individuals to resist familiar ideological meanings and constructs and then to question the structures of a society that benefits from its members' lack of critical consciousness.

In principle, any form of text is open to linguistic criticism and the method has been successfully applied (Fowler 1991) to the analysis of newspaper reports. Fowler argues that the way in which newspaper headlines are constructed is not essentially different from the mode of construction used in Pope's *Rape of the Lock*, and he has little sympathy with those who argue that literature is a special or autonomous form of discourse. Arguing strongly against the NEW CRITICISM's insistence on 'the poem itself', linguistic criticism stresses the need to bring historical and documentary knowledge to bear on the text. By doing so, linguistic criticism can reactivate for modern readers patterns of language that may have lost their force because of historical changes in the language or because the text itself has become overfamiliar. One example (Fowler 1986) is a careful analysis of the shifting use of *you* and *thou* in *King Lear* I.ii. The historical sociolinguistic analysis of the way the pronouns are used reveals relations of power that would have been obvious to Shakespeare's contemporaries, but which are less apparent to an audience speaking a form of English in which the *you/thou* distinction has become blurred.

linguistic turn The term is generally applied to those tendencies in Western philosophy that lead to the conclusion that language or discourse represents the limit to philosophical investigations into truth, or that there is nothing outside language. As Wittgenstein puts it in his *Tractatus Logico-Philosophicus*: 'The limits of my language are the limits of my world' (1921), or as DERRIDA argues: 'There is nothing outside the text' (1967a). In their various ways, the debates over ORDINARY LANGUAGE and DECONSTRUCTION and Derrida are illustrative of the linguistic turn. The expression itself was greatly popularized by the title of a collection of essays in philosophical theory edited by RORTY (1967).

lipogram A text in which one or more letters of the alphabet is or are omitted throughout (Perec 1973). The technique, also known as 'letter-dropping', is one of those favoured by OULIPO and the most sustained example is George Perec's novel *La Disparition* (Disappearance, 1969), which was written without using the letter 'e', even though it is the most frequently used letter in the French alphabet.

literaturnost' The Russian term is normally translated as 'literariness', and is a key term in the vocabulary and discourse of RUSSIAN FORMALISM. Writing in 1921,

JAKOBSON argued in very militant terms that the object of study in literary study is not literature but 'literariness', or the body of qualities that make a work a *literary* work. Describing the quality or nature of literariness was viewed as an essential stage in the production of an autonomous science of literature by concentrating on how formal devices such as OSTRANENIE or 'making strange', and the foregrounding of the signifying function of literariness to the detriment of its referential function (REFERENT), contributed to a poetic effect. The study of such devices would, it was held by formalists like Eikhenbaum, help to transform literary science into a science of the specific features of literary objects that make them distinct from all other objects (Eikhenbaum 1926).

litotes Term used in RHETORIC to describe a form of ironical understatement, as in the expression 'no small achievement' or as in St Paul's description of himself as 'a Jew of Tarsus, a city in Cilicia, a citizen of no mean city' (Acts xxi.39).

locutionary act Defined by AUSTIN'S theory of the SPEECH ACT (1962a) as the act of saying something in the sense of uttering words in a certain construction, with a certain sense and a certain reference.

logical positivism An important strand within twentieth-century philosophy, sometimes referred to as 'logical empiricism' and associated primarily with the philosophers, logicians and scientists of the VIENNA CIRCLE. The major proponent of logical positivism in Britain was A. J. Ayer (1910–89), whose *Language, Truth and Logic* (1936) is perhaps the classic statement in English of the theory. The influence of logical positivism was at its height in the late 1940s and the 1950s, and it is widely agreed that it has been on the wane since the 1960s.

Logical positivism was seen by its original theorists as a new philosophy based upon science and logic which could either absorb the whole of existing philosophy or eliminate much of it as irrelevant. Like the thinkers associated with ORDINARY LANGUAGE PHILOSOPHY, logical positivists such as Moritz Schlick (1882–1936), Friedrich Waismann (1896–1959) and Rudolf Carnap (1891–1970) hold that the problems of philosophy, and especially those of METAPHYSICS, are mainly problems of language but, being heavily influenced by FREGE, they look to logic rather than everyday usage to resolve the questions 'What is meaning?' or 'What kinds of statements have meaning?' Philosophy's task is to reduce statements to their empirical components and to verify their truth-claims, or in other words to ascertain whether they are true or false, according to the principle known as the 'verification principle' (or the 'verifiability principle' in Ayer's version). Often attributed to WITTGENSTEIN (see Ayer 1985), the verification principle states that the meaning of a statement is the method of its verification. The statement 'I believe in God' cannot be verified because it is predicated upon the assertion of the existence of a God who is, by definition, not available for empirical observation. It is neither false nor true: 'I believe in God' is an unverifiable and therefore meaningless or 'metaphysical' statement. Waismann provides a clear example of what is meant by the verification principle (1965, cited in Hanfling 1981). The statement 'If it rained yesterday, the earth is moist today' is an empirical statement; its truth can be asserted but does not determine its meaning. The statement 'If the metal ball is charged with electricity, the leaves of the electroscope will diverge' gives a rule of inference, and thus makes the meaning of the sentence dependent upon the method of its verification.

logocentrism The Greek *logos* has a wide range of meanings, and designates both a rational or intelligible principle and a structure or order that provides phenomena with an origin, or that explains their nature. Hence the common use of the suffix 'ology' to designate a branch of study or knowledge, as in 'psychology', literally meaning 'the study of the soul'. The related verb *legein* means 'say', 'tell' or 'count'. Aristotle uses *logos* to mean the rational principle or element of the soul, as opposed to the irrational principle of DESIRE (*Nicomachean Ethics* I.13). In Christian theology, the *logos* becomes the Word that was with God and that was made flesh when it was incarnated in Christ. The opening verse of the fourth Gospel provides the most sublime example of logocentrism: 'In the beginning was the Word, and the Word was with God, and the Word was God' (John ii.1).

The critique of logocentrism is a central feature of DERRIDA'S DECONSTRUCTION. According to Derrida (1967a), Western philosophy from Plato onwards has always been logocentric in that it makes speech, or the *logos*, the origin and site of truth, and privileges the phonic aspect of language at the expense of the graphic aspect of WRITING. Speech, that is, is assumed to be the spontaneous and complete means of expression available to a SUBJECT who is self-present in the sense of being self-transparent, self-conscious and self-sufficiently rational. Logocentrism assumes that spoken language is an adequate expression of preexisting ideas and that writing is merely a secondary or even parasitic SUPPLEMENT to speech. The Saussurean theology of the SIGN (see also SAUSSURE) is a classic instance of logocentrism which locates meaning in the perfect coincidence between a sound (signifier) and an idea or image (signified). Ultimately, such a theory is a return to the biblical thesis that 'In the beginning was the Word', and it implies the existence of a primal or transcendental signifier which is the origin of all meaning. According to Derrida, logocentrism, and the related PHONOCENTRISM, is a form of ETHNOCENTRISM, or even the original and most powerful form of ethnocentrism, because it privileges Western phonetic alphabets over all other forms of writing and makes Western reason (*logos*) the sole criterion for knowledge. The related term PHALLOGOCENTRISM is employed in Derrida's critique of LACAN (1975) which insists that his privileging of the role of the PHALLUS and the NAME-OF-THE-FATHER in the subject's accession to the SYMBOLIC is merely another form of logocentrism.

longue durée The French expression means 'long duration' or 'long term' and was introduced into the historiography of the *ANNALES* school by BRAUDEL (1949, 1950, 1958). Discussions in English tend to use the original French term. The concentration on the long-term is a characteristic feature of the *Annales* historians, and reflects Braudel's dismissive attitude towards historical studies based upon the transient and often insignificant 'facts' recorded by *HISTOIRE ÉVÉNEMENTIELLE*.

Historical studies of the *longue durée* tend to concentrate upon slow processes of historical change that are almost imperceptible to the individuals who live through them. In economic history, the *longue durée* is studied by looking at the evolution of grain prices, demographic growth rates and the long trade cycles examined by Braudel in his study of the Mediterranean world (1949). Statistically based and quantitative studies, sometimes described as 'serial' history (Chaunu 1978), of the history of climate (Le Roy Ladurie 1967) or of mortality rates emphasize the slow changes that take place in a time that seems to be almost immobile, but which structure the environment in which human beings live. The history of MENTALITIES also places great emphasis on the underlying structural dimension revealed by the study of the *longue durée*.

READING: Burke (1990)

Lukács, Georg (1885–1971) Hungarian philosopher and literary theorist, best known for his contributions to a Marxist theory of IDEOLOGY and for his theory of literary realism.

Lukács's earliest work is heavily influenced by Hegelian idealism, and is typified by his *Theory of the Novel* (1920) in which a contrast between the world of Ancient Greek epic and the modern world allows him to describe the novel as the epic of an age in which the unified totality of the Greeks has been lost. For the Greeks, there was no rift between the self and the world, or between the inner and the outer, and the divine heroes of the epic testified through their actions to its unity. The novel emerges from a world in which that unity no longer exists, and its hero is a product of his estrangement or ALIENATION; he is a problematic individual moving through a contingent world, seeking adventures in order to test himself and to find his own essence. His destiny no longer has any cosmic meaning, and the novel itself becomes a private memoir describing how he becomes reconciled to living in a degraded world. At this stage, Lukács regards Cervantes' *Don Quixote* as the archetypal novel.

Lukács's main studies of the novel were written from the 1930s onwards and reflect both his political activity as Commissar for Education in Béla Kun's short-lived Communist government of 1919 and his discovery of Marx's *Economic and Philosophical Manuscripts* (1844), which were first published in 1932. It was in the 1920s that he made his main contribution to the theory of ideology with *History and Class Consciousness* (1923). Here he describes the proletariat as a potentially universal class which is both the product of the CONTRADICTIONS of history, of a crisis affecting the totality of society, and the instrument of the tendencies that produce the crisis. The proletariat is itself history as consciousness or the embodiment of history, and it will perfect itself by abolishing itself as it creates a classless society. Unlike the consciousness of the bourgeoisie, which is subjective and partial, that of the proletariat is potentially universal. Lukács also makes a crucial distinction between the 'ascribed' and actual consciousness of the proletariat. The latter is out of step with the ascribed consciousness that should be able to grasp a total vision of its role in destroying capitalist society; the higher ascribed consciousness is embodied in the revolutionary party whose every action is justified by its historic mission.

The new theory of the novel elaborated by Lukács in the 1930s (mainly in 1937 and the contemporary essays collected in 1950 and 1970) relies implicitly on the same vision of history and the contention that the exhaustion of bourgeois culture leaves the proletariat and its party as the only true agents of history. Thus the classical period of bourgeois ideology was marked by the struggle against feudalism; it enters a long and supposedly terminal period of crisis when the revolutions of 1848 usher in the battle between the bourgeoisie and the proletariat, which now enters Hegel's world-historical stage. This vision of history is grafted onto the 'reflection theory' which holds that the role of great art is to reflect and portray the great historical forces at work in a given historical moment. Walter Scott, for example, is described as translating the new elements of economic and social change that occur during the decline of feudalism into the social fate and changing psychology of his characters. Like Balzac and Tolstoy, who are the other exemplars of Lukácsian historical realism, Scott derives individual but typical characters from the historical peculiarity of their age. The HISTORICITY of the great novelists lies in their faithful artistic reproduction of the great causes and turning-points of history.

Lukács's insistence that bourgeois culture entered a period of crisis and decline from 1848 onwards produces a negative evaluation of all forms of MODERNISM and particularly of EXPRESSIONISM (*The Historical Novel*, 1937). Given that the bourgeoisie is no longer a universal class, its artists can no longer perceive or portray the totality of the process of social development, and concentrate on surface details and immediate impressions, and on form at the expense of content. Hence the somewhat dogmatic contrast between the realism of Balzac, with its grasp of deep historical processes, and the alleged superficiality of Zola's naturalism. As writers are increasingly alienated from popular life, they find it increasingly difficult to see into the 'inner active forces' of capitalist society and cannot portray it as a totality. Historical realism thus fragments into biographical trivia and superficiality. Lukács's studies of realism were mainly written against the background of the Popular Front movement of the 1930s, and he describes realism as a struggle between democratic humanism and fascist irrationalism. Although he does not use the term in *The Historical Novel*, the repeated argument that democratic humanists such as André Gide cannot, despite their best efforts, either perceive or portray reality in depth, strongly suggests that the solution to their dilemmas lies in some form of SOCIALIST REALISM. The main problem with Lukács's theory, and with that of his disciple GOLDMANN, is, however, that the exclusive focus on the novel as GENRE and great historical trends makes it difficult to analyse individual novels in any detail or to look seriously at modernist literature without condemning it as formalist or decadent.

Lyotard, Jean-François (1924–98) French philosopher, best known for his *Postmodern Condition* (1979a) which, together with his later writings (1983, 1988), has done much to set the terms of the debate about POSTMODERNITY. The attention focused on *The Postmodern Condition* has the unfortunate effect of obscuring Lyotard's complex evolution and the sheer variety of the twenty-seven books published in his lifetime. It tends, for instance, to be forgotten that his first major publication was – and remains – an excellent introduction to PHENOMENOLOGY (1954). He has also written powerfully on the visual arts, evoking the classical notion of the SUBLIME to describe avant-garde works which challenge the rules of representation by simply *being there* and 'saying' nothing (Lyotard 1973c, 1984a).

According to Lyotard (1979a, 1988), postmodernity is not a historical period that simply occurs 'after' modernity (if it were, it would be no more than a new modernity), but rather a shift of mood or perception brought about by changes in the organization of knowledge since the late nineteenth century. As the traditional importance of labour declines in a postindustrial society dominated by the production of knowledge rather than physical commodities, knowledge itself becomes a commodity to be bought and sold. The prestige of the traditional intellectual fades, and the world becomes increasingly incredulous about the GRAND NARRATIVES that spoke of the ENLIGHTENMENT project or of the inevitable march towards socialism; they are seen as narratives which legitimate the authority of institutions that claim to have a monopoly on truth and which suppress dissent, and DESIRE, in its name.

Faced with the decline of GRAND NARRATIVES, Lyotard does not propose a new grand narrative, but rather a multiplicity of 'little narratives' and, in a later development, LANGUAGE GAMES (1979b, 1983), which subvert the dominant narrative and focus on local developments rather than universals. Little narratives are discontinuous and fragmentary, and therefore cannot be incorporated into larger narrative units. The grandiose theories professed by the 'priests' of philosophy and science (ALTHUSSER is a major target here) are rejected in the name of a 'paganism' that recognizes no overarching authorities or truths, and contested in the name of the flows of desire that emerge in marginal groups and temporary political alliances (1973a, 1973b, 1974). Lyotard's own distrust of grand narratives is grounded in suspicions about the nature of narrative and history itself: narrative history is a story told by dominant classes and groups in a bid to legitimate and 'naturalize' their power. He therefore contrasts history with the events that, like the explosion of May 1968, disrupt its flow. For Lyotard, an event is not part of a chronological sequence, but the fact that something happens and changes everything, or rather the fact of something happening and introducing a break in the space–time continuum. A parallel might be drawn between his notion of the event and his writings on aesthetics, in which the experience of the sublime is described as disrupting the tranquillity of representational art, and the emergence of the FIGURE as subverting the linear continuity of discursive knowledge and art.

Lyotard often uses a somewhat idiosyncratic vocabulary. Thus the term 'immemorial' is used to refer to something that can neither be remembered by being represented in or for consciousness nor be forgotten. Just as the figure returns, like the repressed, to disrupt discursive rationality, the immemorial returns to disrupt history. The classic example is 'Auschwitz', which obliges us to speak so that its horror is neither forgotten as something that did not happen, nor represented in such a way that its specific horror is dissolved into representative narrative history (see in particular Lyotard 1980), but the Algerian war is sometimes discussed in similar terms (see the introductory note to Lyotard 1993). The task of anamnesis or 'not forgetting' is not one for narrative or representational discourse; so unimaginable is the immemorial that its recording is a matter for the figural. Elsewhere, elements of standard French vocabulary are forced to serve particular strategies. *Différend* (which has somewhat unfortunately been 'translated' simply by retaining the original French) is, for instance, a normal term meaning 'difference of opinion' or 'controversy'; Lyotard uses it (1983 for example) to mean a dispute which cannot be resolved through consensus as the parties involved speak radically heterogeneous languages. To paraphrase or translate the terms of such a dispute would therefore prejudge the issue for one party. Such disputes cannot really be solved because there is no external point of view from which the respective claims being put forward can be judged. When successive French governments declared that Algeria was part of France, they created a *différend* between that statement and the Algerian demand for independence that could not be met or judged valid by French justice, and the outcome was war (see the introduction to Lyotard 1993). A *différend* cannot be resolved; at best, a partial resolution can be negotiated.

In political terms Lyotard was greatly influenced by the two years he spent in Algeria at the beginning of the 1950s, when he saw at first hand the oppressive realities of colonialism, and by his membership of Socialisme ou barbarie ('Socialism or Barbarism') between 1952 and 1963. Socialisme ou barbarie was a small group of intellectuals (including Cornelius Castoriadis, the political philosopher Claude Lefort and the psychoanalyst Jean Laplanche) and workers, most of whom had belonged to the Trotskyist Fourth International, but who had become increasingly critical of the bureaucratization of Trotskyist as well as Stalinist organizations and rejected the leading role given to the party by most forms of MARXISM. 'Pious Stalinism' and 'vague reformism' were both rejected in favour of autonomous self-organization and workers' control. Many of the themes associated with Socialisme ou barbarie reemerged during the French student revolt of May 1968 and in the discourse of the small gay, feminist and 'autonomist' (or quasi-anarchist) groups that flourished in the 1970s, and which were strongly supported by Lyotard in his 'philosophy of desire' period. Although Lyotard wrote in favour of Algerian independence, he was also highly critical of the bureaucratic tendencies within the Front de libération nationale, and never subscribed to the widespread view that independence would lead to socialism. His writings on Algeria and other political issues have now been collected in English translation (1993).

READING: Benjamin (1989); Bennington (1988); Readings (1991)

M

MacKinnon-Dworkin model law A legislative model for the suppression of pornography, drafted in 1983 by Andrea DWORKIN and Professor of Law Catherine A. MacKinnon (MacKinnon 1994). Drawing heavily on Dworkin's study of pornography (Dworkin 1981), the draft law states that pornography is a practice of sex discrimination, defined as the graphic and sexually explicit subordination of women through the use of pictures and/or words. Under its terms, civil actions for damages could be brought for the offences of trafficking in pornography, coercion into pornography, forcing pornography on a person, and assault due to pornography. The logic behind the model law hinges on the argument that pornography functions as a PERFORMATIVE. Pornography does not, that is, 'depict' sexual degradation; it *is* sexual degradation. It is a form of action and not a form of speech, and therefore cannot be protected by the freedom of speech guaranteed by the First Amendment to the US Constitution.

In 1983, the model law was adopted by Minneapolis City Council, and the precedent was followed by the States of Minnesota and Indiana. In 1984 the Supreme Court ruled that the law was unconstitutional. In 1992 the Canadian Supreme Court incorporated the model into Canada's existing obscenity laws.

Opponents of the MacKinnon-Dworkin model law, including the American Civil Liberties Union and anti-censorship feminists (Strossen 1995), argue that it reflects a deep distrust or even loathing of sexuality itself, that it could be used to suppress information that is essential to women's equality and self-expression, and that it could lead to the censorship of gay and lesbian art, as has reportedly been the case in Canada. For her part, BUTLER argues that the model law reproduces a pedagogical version of what it is seeking to suppress and claims that QUEERing (QUEER) terms of abuse would be more effective (Butler 1997).

magic realism Popularly applied to Salman Rushdie's *Midnight's Children* (1981) and *The Satanic Verses* (1988) and other novels which combine realism with elements of fantasy, the term originates in discussions of the Latin American novel. The best known example of Latin American magic realism is Gabriel García Marquez's *One Hundred Years of Solitude* (1967).

In an early and influential article on the topic (1955), Angel Flores traces many of the characteristic features of magic realism – the blend of history, myth and fantasy – back to the sense of wonderment and exoticism experienced by the Europeans who first colonized Latin America, and suggests that it was also influenced by the modernism of writers like Kafka and artists like Chirico. In his view, the founding texts of magic realism are Jorge Luis Borges's *Universal History of Infamy* (1935) and the same author's *The Garden of Forking Paths* (1941, and subsequently included in Borges 1962).

Other historians and commentators (including Gonzalez-Echevarría 1977 and contributors to King 1987) suggest that the starting-point for this distinctly Latin American style is the reference to '*lo real-maravilloso*' (the marvellous-real) in the Cuban novelist Alejo Carpentier's prologue to his *The Kingdom of This World* (1949). Related to SURREALISM's notion of the 'marvellous', Carpentier's *real-maravilloso* describes his response to the fantastic and brutal history, culture and landscape of Haiti. Carpentier argues that the marvellous is a feature of everyday life in Latin America and the Caribbean, that the continent's reality cannot be captured by the realism of a Balzac or a Dickens, and that it demands the creation of a new and magic realism. It is also sometimes claimed that magical realism derives in part from the picaresque tradition in the Spanish novel.

manifest/latent content In the psychoanalytic theory of dreams (Freud 1900), the expression 'manifest content' refers to the dream that is recounted by the patient in the course of an analytic session. It is a product of the DREAM-WORK and has been shaped by the mechanisms of CONDENSATION and DISPLACEMENT and by the censorship of the EGO. The latent content of a dream is not actually recounted, but is uncovered through the analysis of the manifest content and the interpretation of the patient's free associations. Freud often describes the manifest content as a fragmentary and impoverished translation of the latent content.

Marcuse, Herbert (1898–1979) German-American philosopher. Although he was initially attracted to the PHENOMENOLOGY of HEIDEGGER, Marcuse became a member of the FRANKFURT SCHOOL in 1933 and made important contributions to its CRITICAL THEORY. Unlike ADORNO and HORKHEIMER, he remained in the United States when the school relocated back to Germany after the Second World War and became a revered figure for the NEW LEFT, particularly in the 1960s when his concepts of REPRESSIVE TOLERANCE and REPRESSIVE DESUBLIMATION enjoyed great popularity and influence. Together with the writings of REICH, his *Eros and Civilization* (1955), which argued that the liberation, rather than the SUBLIMATION, of the DRIVES would have an emancipatory effect, was an important point of reference for the advocates of sexual liberation.

Although Marcuse's thought evolves through a number of different stages, his basic themes remain remarkably constant. In an early article published in the Frankfurt School's *Zeitschrift für Sozialforschung*, he argues (1937) in characteristic terms that, whilst bourgeois society liberates individuals from the chains of the past, it does so on condition that they keep themselves in check, and that the prohibition of pleasure is a precondition for their illusory freedom. Culture and the arts are used to pacify rebellious desire and to inculcate a toleration of the unfreedom of social existence. In his major study of Hegel, Marcuse argues (1941) that the

Hegelian strand in MARXISM is much more important than the Soviet version of HISTORICAL and DIALECTICAL MATERIALISM would allow. He stresses the importance of Marx's early work, and particularly the 'Economic and Philosophical Manuscripts' (1844), which he uses to elaborate a critical theory of ALIENATION and REIFICATION.

In an epilogue added to his study of Hegel (1941) in 1954, Marcuse remarks that the defeat of Fascism had not arrested the drift towards totalitarianism and that freedom was still on the retreat. His remarks outline the themes that would dominate his later work: the enslavement of man by the growth in productivity that should have liberated him, the repressive mastery of nature, the manufacture of consent to and acceptance of the status quo, and the development of human potential within a framework of domination. *One-Dimensional Man* (1964) is the classic expression of these themes. Here a deeply pessimistic Marcuse describes an advanced industrial society in which the total administration of human beings is both necessary and possible. People are efficiently manipulated and organized, and the mechanisms of REPRESSIVE TOLERANCE ensure that even rebellion is tolerated, recuperated and turned into a repressive force. In such a society every need is catered for but they are all false needs planned to meet the requirements of the system of production rather than those of individuals. The very possibility of rebellion or even opposition appears to have been extinguished. The upsurge of student rebellion in the late 1960s and the rise of THIRD WORLD radicalism in Vietnam and Cuba did lead Marcuse to the more optimistic view that a new culture was emerging and that it would fulfil the promise of emancipation that had been betrayed by both traditional culture and the totally administered society (1969), but the optimism was short-lived. In his last published work, Marcuse (1977) argues that it is only the aesthetic realm that preserves both the memory of a happier existence and the hope for a future emancipation.

Marinetti, Filippo Tommaso (1876–1944) Italian poet and principal spokesman for FUTURISM. Marinetti's writings celebrate speed, machines and violence, and he captures the spirit of futurism in his famous declaration that a speeding motor car is more beautiful than the Victory of Samothrace. The title of an English-language version of his selected writings is a good indication of his violent rejection of traditional poetry: *Let's Murder the Moonshine* (1971).

Marxism The body of thought associated with and inspired by the works of Karl Marx (1818–83) and Friedrich Engels (1820–95), comprising a system of political economy, a theory of politics and a materialist philosophy of history and nature. It was one of the most influential intellectual forces of the twentieth century. After the Russian Revolution of 1917, Marxism, now also known as Marxism-Leninism, became the official political IDEOLOGY of the Soviet Union and, subsequently, of the so-called 'People's Democracies' of Eastern Europe and China. Paradoxically, Marxism has always flourished best under non-Marxist regimes and the many variants of WESTERN MARXISM are much more sophisticated than anything developed in the 'socialist' countries. A similar paradox can be noted outside the 'socialist' bloc, where Communist parties usually developed a reductive and mechanistic form of Marxism, and where the most creative developments have been the work of relatively marginal organizations and individuals. This suggests that Marxism may outlive the collapse of communism in the East.

Although Marxism takes many different forms, its core concepts derive from two main sources. On the one hand, the political economy elaborated by British writers such as Adam Smith (*The Wealth of Nations*, 1776) and David Ricardo (*Principles of Political Economy*, 1817) is developed and transformed into the critical account of the capitalist economy advanced in the three volumes of Marx's unfinished *Capital* (1867, 1885, 1894) and in numerous shorter texts such as the *Contribution to the Critique of Political Economy* (1859) and 'Wages, Price and Profit' (1865). In parallel to this, a philosophy of history (HISTORICAL MATERIALISM) centred on the idea that history is driven by a DIALECTIC of conflict between social classes is derived from the Hegelian tradition. This is expressed most clearly in Marx's political writings, many of which deal with the history and politics of nineteenth-century France, and especially in the programmatic *Communist Manifesto* (Marx and Engels, 1847–8), which, together with Marx's lapidary 'Theses on Feuerbach' (1845), is certainly the most widely read of all Marxist texts. The former provided the international movement with its most rousing slogan: 'The proletarians have nothing to lose but their chains. They have a world to win. Working men of all countries, unite!' The last of the eleven 'Theses' neatly summarizes Marxism's philosophical-political ambitions: 'The philosophers have only *interpreted* the world, in various ways; the point is to *change* it.' The elaboration of DIALECTICAL MATERIALISM as a philosophy of nature and science is largely the work of Engels (1875–82, 1878).

The most significant of Marx's early writings are the so-called 'Economic and Philosophical Manuscripts' (1844). These were not intended for publication, and did not appear in print until 1932, when, together with *The German Ideology* (Marx and Engels 1845–6), they were found to contain a theory of ALIENATION and IDEOLOGY which explains human consciousness in terms of the material reality of human existence. Whereas the earlier Hegelian tradition had viewed history as the product of the development of ideas and consciousness, Marx contended that consciousness was determined by social existence and that the alienation and COMMODITY FETISHISM characteristic of capitalist society were effects of the property relations that estranged men from the product of their own labour. Although these early writings are dismissed by ALTHUSSER as deriving from a Hegelian PROBLEMATIC and as being 'pre-Marxist', they provide the basis for the many varieties of Marxist humanism and for the earliest work of the NEW LEFT.

Marxist economics centres on the analysis of the commodity, defined as an object that satisfies a human need, or as having a use-value. Commodities also have an exchange-value to the extent that they can be exchanged for other commodities. The common property that makes it possible for commodities to be exchange-values is the quantity of human labour-power or value contained in them. The value of a commodity is determined by the quantity of labour-time required to produce it, and therefore by historical and social variations in the productivity of labour. The value of labour-power itself is determined by the value of the necessities required to reproduce it, or in other words to sustain the wage-labourer or proletarian. Under capitalism, according to Marxist economic theory, the wage-labourer does not, however, simply reproduce the value of his wage. He also produces surplus-value, or value in excess of the cost of reproducing his wages; this is the source of the capitalist profit without which the system cannot work. The ratio between the time spent on reproducing the value of labour-power and the time spent on producing surplus-value is referred to as the rate of surplus-value. The rate of surplus-value is variable, and is the subject of both negotiations and conflict between workers and capitalists, but surplus-value must always be produced. Whilst working conditions can be improved up to a point, the need to extract surplus-value means that the traditional demand for a 'fair day's wage for a fair day's work' is meaningless; under capitalism, wages are always paid on an 'unfair basis'. Ultimately, the system cannot be reformed for the benefit of the wage-earning proletarian, and must be overthrown.

The Communist Manifesto proclaims that the history of all society hitherto has been the history of class struggles in which classes defined by economic relations of production come into conflict and either reconstitute society through revolution or destroy one another. In the age of capitalism, the struggle is one between the bourgeoisie, which owns the means of production, and the proletariat, which has nothing but the labour-power it is forced to sell in order to survive. By creating the modern capitalist system, or capitalist MODE OF PRODUCTION, and the proletariat exploited by that system, the bourgeoisie has created the means of its own destruction. At the same time, it has reduced the whole of human existence to naked self-interest and the cash nexus that destroys human relations. Being the product of the capitalist mode of production, the proletariat is both its enemy and its heir; the continued development of modern industry threatens to reduce the working classes to extreme poverty, and it is therefore in their interests to abolish classes by abolishing the private ownership of property and capitalist relations of production and establishing a dictatorship of the proletariat. Only then will it be possible to establish an association of citizens in which 'the free development of each is the condition for the free development of all.'

Marxist economics provides the basis for the analysis of culture, ideology and politics in accordance with the BASE/SUPERSTRUCTURE model. This is notoriously Marxism's weak point; it has a marked tendency to reduce all phenomena from ideological service to the state (classically seen as the agency for the political dictatorship of an economic class) to mere expressions or reflections of the economic base and to deny them any real autonomy.

Marxist criticism Although the writings of Marx and Engels abound in literary references and allusions, the founders of MARXISM cannot really be said to have elaborated a theory of literature. Their scattered and fragmented comments on literature have, however, often been anthologized; the anthology compiled by Baxandall and Morawski is one of the most useful (Marx and Engels 1973). In his preface to *A Contribution to the Critique of Political Economy* (1859), Marx generically describes the legal, political, religious or philosophical forms through which men become conscious of social conflict as 'ideological', and there is a marked tendency within many forms of Marxist criticism to reduce literature or art to IDEOLOGY and to analyse it in terms of the BASE/SUPERSTRUCTURE model. Although Engels insists in his letter of 1890 to Joseph Bloch (in Marx and Engels 1965) that whilst ideological forms are ultimately determined by the economic production and reproduction of real life, the economic element is not the only one, it has always been difficult for Marxists to escape the base/superstructure model.

In a typical product of the Marxism of the 1930s, the English poet and critic Christopher Caudwell (i.e. Christopher St John Sprigg, 1907–37) traces the history of the 'movement of bourgeois poetry' by establishing a series of economic periods characterized by both 'general characteristics' and 'technical characteristics' (1937). The Elizabethan Age is thus said to be a period of primitive accumulation in which the dynamic force of individuality is realized in poetry; the technical device of the iambic pentameter indicates the boundless development of the personal will. Although Caudwell's formulation is crude, it typifies the way in which Marxist criticism uses literary texts to identify values and ideologies associated with social classes and economic developments. The infinitely more sophisticated EAGLETON (1988) describes David Lodge's campus novel *Small World* (1984) as symptomatic of a liberal humanism which has fallen on hard times since its Victorian heyday. To parody SARTRE's remark that Paul Valéry is a petty bourgeois intellectual but not all petty bourgeois intellectuals are Paul Valéry (1960), it has to be said in Lodge's defence that not all symptoms of liberal humanism are as funny as *Small World*.

In a letter to the novelist Margaret Harkness (in Marx and Engels 1965) Engels makes a further crucial contribution to Marxist aesthetics when he defines realism in terms of both 'truth of detail' and 'truth in the reproduction of typical characters under typical circumstances', and thus lays the foundations for both LUKÁCS's aesthetic of Balzacian realism and SOCIALIST REALISM. The stress on 'typicality' is indicative of Marxism's insistence on the need for MIMESIS and for a realist depiction of the social relations obtaining in any given period, whilst the debate between BLOCH and Lukács over German EXPRESSIONISM in the 1930s illustrates how difficult Marxists find it to come to terms with the many forms of MODERNISM, ADORNO being one of the more notable exceptions.

Following the Russian Revolution of 1917, Marxism coexisted uneasily with very different currents such as RUSSIAN FORMALISM and the work of BAKHTIN, but the growing emphasis on the 'social command' inevitably resulted in the political utilitarianism exemplified by the argument that 'the incomplete acceptance of the revolution, insistence upon inessential details, superficiality, empty eloquence and sketchiness prevent completeness of socialist realism' (Kirpotin 1933). Not surprisingly, what is now recognized as Marxist criticism is a product of Western Marxism and not of the former 'socialist' countries. The most important contributors to the development of Marxist criticism include Lukács and his follower GOLDMANN, BENJAMIN, Adorno, WILLIAMS and Eagleton. Marxist criticism obviously does not develop in isolation, and many of its most sophisticated products have been born of an interaction between forms of Marxism and such currents as PSYCHOANALYSIS and STRUCTURALISM.

ALTHUSSER'S comments on literature and art (1962b, 1966a, 1966b) are laconic but influential. He argues that 'real art' is not to be ranked among the ideologies, even though it inevitably uses ideology as its raw material. The claim that the function of 'real art' is to reveal the workings and effects of ideology, together with the theory of SYMPTOMATIC READING, provides the theoretical basis for the important work of his student Pierre Macherey (1966; see also Eagleton 1976). For Macherey, what the literary text says is less important than what it does; literature is a form of intellectual production that works ideological raw material into literary texts, and in doing so transforms the raw material. Jules Verne's *The Mysterious Island* reworks the Robinson Crusoe myth (which Marx so often uses to mock political economists who ignore economic realities in their celebrations of the individual hero) in an attempt to show that science and industry can flourish in conditions of isolation, but undermines the Crusoe myth by making it obvious that the island is not uninhabited. Captain Nemo's submarine is based beneath it, and he supplies Verne's castaways with their needs; no island is isolated in the age of imperialism. The point is not that Verne is aware of the contradictions of his story, but that a symptomatic reading can reveal them. Macherey's later work (1990), which overlaps with a more general exploration of the history of materialist philosophy, explores similar themes and comes to the conclusion that the role of literature is to say what a period thinks of itself without necessarily understanding itself.

Perhaps the most sophisticated of contemporary Marxist critics is the American Frederic Jameson, who argues that whilst history is not a text, it is inaccessible to us except in textual terms (1974, 1981, 1988a, 1988b). He writes under the programmatic slogan 'always historicize' (1981) and asserts that, although organic life may be absurd, history itself is meaningful and that the task of the critic is to recover its meaning. Accepting that the MODE OF PRODUCTION is the ultimate determinant of literary forms, Jameson argues that all literature must be read as a symbolic mediation of the destiny of community. Rather like Macherey, Jameson holds that ideology is literature's raw material; it supplies the inherited narrative PARADIGMS (referred to as 'ideologemes' – the term is modelled on PHONEME and MYTHEME) with which the novel works and which it transforms into individual texts which function as individual utterances of the broader system of class discourse. The model here is the *LANGUE/PAROLE* distinction of SAUSSURE, with text corresponding to *parole*, discourse to *langue*. The borrowing from Saussure is symptomatic of Jameson's belief that a Marxist HERMENEUTICS can subsume other critical methods into a greater whole because it permits the coordination of a formal analysis of the individual text with the twin diachronic perspective of the history of forms and the evolution of social life. The sophistication of Jameson's HISTORICISM is not to be denied, but he has been criticized (Young 1990) for the 'relentless synthesizing' with which he incorporates everyone from PROPP and LÉVI-STRAUSS to GREIMAS into an extremely rich brew. Yet even Jameson reverts to a version of the base/superstructure model when he describes POSTMODERNISM as an effect of the transition to Mandel's 'late capitalism' (1988c, 1991) and claims (1981) that the DEATH OF MAN, DERRIDA'S 'dissemination' and LYOTARD'S *DÉRIVE* are all symptoms of a modification of the experience of the subject in consumer or late monopoly capitalism.

masquerade The notion that femininity is a masquerade, or a matter of acting out a role, was originally advanced by the British psychoanalyst Joan Rivière in her paper 'Womanliness as Masquerade' published in 1929. The idea of a masquerade is not uncommon in feminist theory, and is often invoked in protests against the compulsion to conform to masculine stereotypes of femininity. Germaine GREER, for instance, writes: 'I am sick of the masquerade . . . I'm sick of belying my own intelligence, my own will, my own sex' (1970).

Observing the behaviour of 'a particular type of intellectual woman', Rivière notes that, although such women hold positions that are conventionally described as 'masculine', they habitually seek approval from father-figures by adopting an exaggeratedly feminine or even flirtatious mode of behaviour. The deliberate display of femininity is interpreted as a propitiatory ploy designed to ward off aggression and retribution from men who sense that such women have usurped a masculine role thanks to a symbolic castration of their fathers. For the women in question, it is a way of overcoming the fear that the father will take his revenge.

Rivière's short paper is highly ambiguous. Although she uses 'masculine' and 'feminine' in a purely conventional sense and suggests that GENDER is reducible to biological characteristics, she also refuses to make any distinction between 'genuine womanliness' and the 'masquerade' and moves from a description of a 'particular type' of woman to 'womanliness' as such. She thus hints both that the behaviour she describes is a general phenomenon, and, more importantly, that there is no true femininity that exists behind or prior to the masquerade. BUTLER argues (1990) that Rivière's paper implies that gender is always a matter of performance, and that it is therefore to be understood as a cultural construct and not as an expression of a biological reality.

The early work of the American artist Cindy Sherman (1954–) explores the theme of the masquerade, and the related theme of the GAZE, in a series of 'untitled film stills' (reproduced in Krauss 1993). The sixty-five black and white photographs made between 1977 and 1980 appear to show the artist in stills from Hollywood or *NOUVELLE VAGUE* films; acting out a variety of female roles, she appears as the plucky Hitchcock heroine, the woman detective and so on, but the scenes are staged. Like BAUDRILLARD'S SIMULACRUM, the untitled stills are reproductions without an original or excerpts from a masquerade that conceals no reality. They tell us nothing about Sherman herself.

matheme Neologism coined by LACAN in the early 1970s. Formed by derivation from 'mathematics' and by analogy with PHONEME and LÉVI-STRAUSS'S MYTHEME, the term is an equivalent to 'mathematical sign'. It is not used in conventional mathematics.

Lacan begins to use a variety of graphs and 'schemata' at an early stage in his work. Originally used as teaching aids, these range from the relatively simple 'schema L' illustrating the imaginary function of the EGO in the 1955 paper on

PSYCHOSIS (1957–8) to the complex chart of the workings of desire (1960). Perhaps the most familiar is the 'algorithm' which in 1957 replaces SAUSSURE's simple diagram of the SIGN

$$\overline{\text{arbor}}$$

with the notation

$$\frac{S}{s}$$

This is to be understood as demonstrating that the signifier is above the signified, and that the two are separated by a bar that resists signification and forces the signifier to slide endlessly (Lacan 1957).

The graphs and schemata gradually become more complex, and are eventually replaced by an 'algebra' of 'little letters' or mathemes in which, for instance, 'P' is the symbolic father, and 'M' the symbolic mother (a very helpful tabulation can be found in Evans 1996). The function of the FORMALIZATION that results in the emergence of the matheme is said by Lacan (1975b) to be the integral transmission of his teachings on psychoanalysis.

McLuhan, Herbert Marshall (1911–80) Canadian pioneer of media studies. McLuhan was originally a specialist in English literature, but he is best known for the work on the mass media he carried out at the University of Toronto's Center for Culture and Technology. His theories are expounded in *The Gutenberg Galaxy* (1962), *Understanding Media* (1964), and in more popular presentations such as *The Medium is the Massage* (1967) and *War and Peace in the Global Village* (1968).

McLuhan's basic theses are that technologies are extensions of the body, and that societies are shaped by their media. The book – the organizing factor in the 'Gutenberg era', which McLuhan names after the inventor of printing (1400–68) – was an extension of the eye; the electrical and electronic media are an extension of the central nervous system and will abolish the old linear conception of time and space. They usher in the age of the global village in which space is abolished by immediate communications. McLuhan's version of technological determinism is extreme: the emergence of the entire European feudal system is explained (1968) in terms of the invention of the stirrup, which made it possible to mount a heavily armoured man on a horse and thus brought about the rise of a military-feudal aristocracy. The most striking feature of his studies of the media is their total failure to discuss the ownership and control of means of communication.

Ironically, the books that proclaim the end of the print media (1967, 1968) are, thanks to the graphic design of Quentin Fiore, striking collages of photographs, drawings and innovatory typography that now look like the design-classics of their day. McLuhan is often said to have prophesied the digital age, but his prophetic gifts failed him badly when he wrote (1968) that the pace of the game was such that 'English' (sic) cricket would be a failure on television.

mentalities, history of An important concept in the French school of historiography associated with the journal *ANNALES*. Mentalities are described as collective mental experiences with their own rhythms and causation. They are the product of a form of COLLECTIVE UNCONSCIOUS defined not in JUNG's sense, but simply in the sense that they are not fully present to the individual awareness. To that extent, mentalities are similar to ideologies but the expression does not have the negative associations of IDEOLOGY (Vovelle 1990). Examples of the history of mentalities include the history of religious sensibility, or the slow changes in attitudes towards death that are studied by Philippe Ariès (1985). Sources for the history of such attitudes include wills, funerary monuments, and the iconography, architecture and archaeology of religious artefacts, as well as long series of demographic statistics.

The idea of a history of mentalities derives from the idea of a 'collective consciousness' associated with the sociology of Emile Durkheim (see Lukes 1973), but can also be compared with Raymond WILLIAMS's notion of a STRUCTURE OF FEELING.

Merleau-Ponty, Maurice (1908–61) French philosopher and, together with SARTRE, the most important representative of French PHENOMENOLOGY. Merleau-Ponty's work is strikingly incomplete and some of his most significant works were published posthumously, like the long essay on the prose of the world, abandoned in 1952 and not published until 1969, and that on the visible and the invisible, largely reconstructed on the basis of an incomplete manuscript (1964b). It is therefore difficult to reconstruct the development of his thought, and matters are made more complex still by the recent publication of the 1952 lectures on the idea of nature (1995) and a collection of essays and occasional pieces written between 1935 and 1951 (1997). The starting-point for most of Merleau-Ponty's work is the HUSSERL of *Ideas* (1913) and *The Crisis of European Sciences and Transcendental Phenomenology* (1936), but he is the first philosopher writing in the phenomenological tradition to incorporate SAUSSURE into his work (1960, 1964a) and can therefore be seen as a major figure in the transition from phenomenology to STRUCTURALISM (see Schmidt 1985). He is also unusual in that he combines the findings of phenomenology and those of clinical and GESTALT psychology to an unprecedented degree.

Merleau-Ponty outlines a philosophy of consciousness and perception which has much in common with Sartre. Like Sartre, he is critical of PSYCHOANALYSIS, arguing that all the phenomena noted by FREUD can be explained in terms of a fragmented consciousness which does not always have the same meaning; there is no need for the hypothesis of the UNCONSCIOUS (1942). Consciousness is an attribute of human beings, and one of only two possible modes of being, the other being that of things; it is characterized by its INTENTIONALITY and by its ability to transcend or overcome its FACTICITY in a movement into the future. Consciousness is therefore at once freedom and certitude as it strives to overcome or escape from all the facticity that threatens to drag it back to the in-itself existence of things.

In the last essay he completed before his premature death (1964a), Merleau-Ponty remarks that the world is 'round me, not in front of me' and the attempt to capture that immediate 'aroundness' is a constant throughout his work. In his great study of the phenomenology of perception (1945), he describes the primary philosophical act as a return to the lived world that exists before it is objectified by science or metaphysics. It is this conception of the philosophical task that leads him to reject all dualisms that introduce a separation between subject and object, and even Sartre's distinction between being-in-itself and being-for-others on the grounds that it is 'too antithetical' and introduces a divorce into what should be viewed as a continuum of existence in which I exist alongside others (1945, 1948). For the same reasons, in his early study of the structure of behaviour (1942), Merleau-Ponty rejects all theories that attempt to break down perception or behaviour into component parts: the functioning of the body is not a mechanism made up of mutually independent behavioural mechanisms because it exists and functions as a whole. Perception is not merely a matter of the registration of objective data: consciousness of something implies that something shows or reveals itself as a phenomenon. Neither the phenomenon nor the act of cognition exists prior to perception, which is the primal modality of consciousness.

Merleau-Ponty's emphasis on the body is one of the characteristic themes that distinguishes his work from that of Husserl, HEIDEGGER and Sartre, all of whom tend to describe a disembodied consciousness. For Merleau-Ponty, in contrast, the physical body is not only the seat of perception, but the vehicle for the being-in-the-world or being-in-SITUATION of an embodied consciousness. The body is not something that simply *is* in space and time; it inhabits space and time in a truly physical sense and the individual perceives it by constructing a bodily schema out of memories and perceptions. The body is a way of having a world, but it can only be understood as being 'already born' and 'still alive'; no one can know his or her own birth or death. In his later work (e.g. 1964b), Merleau-Ponty replaces the notion of the body with that of 'flesh', which he describes as an element in the sense that earth and water were once described as the elements that made up the world.

Merleau-Ponty gradually came to view his early phenomenological studies as merely the introduction to a much more general study, provisionally entitled 'The Origin of Truth', which would eventually provide a link between the analysis of the perceptual world and a philosophy of history drawing on Marx and Weber as well as Saussure, the wayward aspect of his understanding of the latter being that he saw Saussurean linguistics as providing a new philosophy of history that could integrate the speaking subject into a broader history.

Merleau-Ponty's political views are characterized by a rather strained dialogue with MARXISM. He was active in the Resistance and, in the early postwar years at least, sympathetic to the French Communist Party. In the introduction to his essay on humanism and terror (1947), he argues in terms very reminiscent of Sartre that one can be neither communist nor anti-communist. Most of the essay itself is taken up with a discussion of the show trial of Bukharin and of Arthur Koestler's novel *Darkness at Noon* (1940), and comes close to providing an awkward and embarrassed apologia for Stalinism. The later *Adventures of the Dialectic* (1955) is much more critical of dogmatic Marxism and its truth-claims and argues the case for a non-communist left. It was Sartre's continued, if critical, support for the French Communist Party that led to the final split between two of the original founders of *LES TEMPS MODERNES*.

READING: Schmidt (1985)

metahistory The term was originally used by Northrop FRYE (1963) as a synonym for 'a speculative philosophy of history' such as the universal system of history elaborated by Hegel, but has been given much wider currency by Hayden WHITE's major studies in historiography (1973, 1978). The idea of metahistory has had a considerable influence on POSTCOLONIAL THEORY and NEW HISTORICISM.

White argues that it is a methodological error to make a clear-cut distinction between history, or the narrative form which describes what has happened in history, and the philosophy of history, or the interpretive schema or theory that legitimizes the narrative. The writing of history, which inevitably takes a narrative form, necessarily involves the tacit adoption of a philosophy which seeks to justify the particular narrative form adopted. Metahistory designates the common ground where both narrative history and the philosophy of history originate in their attempt to make sense of what has happened. The historical text is to be regarded as a literary artefact, and is to be analysed as such. Metahistory asks questions about the structure of historical consciousness, about the epistemological status of historical explanations, as compared with other explanations of the same data, and about the forms of historical representation. It asks, for example, what is at stake when THOMPSON describes his *Making of the English Working Class* (1963) as 'a biography of the English working class from its adolesence to its early manhood', and assumes both that 'biography' is a neutral or natural literary form, and that 'adolescence' and 'manhood' are ahistorical categories rather than culturally determined metaphors.

The goal or ambition of White's metahistory is to reestablish the dignity of historical studies, not by producing a 'scientific history' – which he regards as a contradiction in terms – but by making history a much more self-conscious and self-critical discipline. It suggests that whilst history cannot provide scientific knowledge in the sense that biology can, it can offer forms of knowledge similar to those proposed by art and literature.

metalanguage In linguistics, a technical or second-order language used to describe and analyse a natural or first-order language, or a set of propositions about other propositions. More generally, any descriptive DISCOURSE such as literary criticism can be said to function as a metalanguage. According to JAKOBSON, the process of acquiring or learning a language involves many metalinguistic operations. He also argues (1960) that all speakers of a language also use a metalanguage without realizing it in order to ensure that they are using the same code as their interlocutors.

Although linguists accept the need for metalanguage, the very possibility of a metalinguistic dimension is denied by many of the thinkers associated with POSTSTRUCTURALISM, POSTMODERNISM and DECONSTRUCTION. LACAN, for example, flatly denies the existence of any metalanguage (1960), basing his claim on HEIDEGGER's contention that language is the 'house of being' and that it is impossible to step outside it (1959). In Heidegger's view, any metalanguage is a METAPHYSICS and a 'technicalization' that destroys the experience of language. Most of the philosophers associated with the LINGUISTIC TURN take a similar view and argue, like WITTGENSTEIN, that there can be no metalinguistic or extralinguistic dimension because 'the limits of my language are the limits of my world' (1921) or, like DERRIDA, that 'there is nothing outside the text' (1967).

metalepsis In RHETORIC, the metonymical substitution of one word for another that is itself figurative; more generally, an inversion of cause and effect. RICOEUR has shown (1990) that the exploitation of metalepsis is basic to Nietzsche's onslaughts on the convention that the 'I' is a cause rather than an effect of its effects. In *Beyond Good and Evil* (1886) Nietzsche argues that it is a falsification to say 'the subject "I" is the condition of the predicate of "thinks"'; in Fragment 479 of *The Will to Power* (1901) he further contends that 'In the phenomenalism of the "inner world" we invert the chronological order of cause and effect' and, in Fragment 483, that the claim that the 'I' is the given cause of thought is a further inversion of cause and effect, that it is the effect and not the origin of thought.

metaphor/metonymy Common figures of speech and important categories in RHETORIC. Metaphor transfers the meaning of a name or descriptive phrase to an object by analogy or substitution, and is typified by the elision of the comparison ('as', 'like') characteristic of a simile. In his 'Elegie: To his Mistress Going to Bed', John Donne metaphorically addresses his mistress as 'Oh my America, my new found lande'. In metonymy, which is closely related to the figure SYNECDOCHE, an attribute of a thing stands for the thing itself ('the deep' for 'the sea'); according to other definitions, the part is made to stand for the whole, as when 'four tails' is used to signify 'four cats'.

Drawing on psychopathological studies of APHASIA, JAKOBSON demonstrates (1956) that metaphor and metonymy represent fundamental poles or aspects of language and that they are essential to the primary operations of selecting and combining basic linguistic units in order to form higher and more complex units. An individual suffering from similarity disorder or an inability to construct metaphors has difficulty in selecting appropriate terms and typically employs very general terms such as 'thing' or 'what's it'. The term 'bachelors' will be replaced by 'unmarried people', and the individual will be unable to supply a more precise definition. Individuals suffering from contiguity disorder have difficulties with the combinatory or metonymic dimension of language and speak in a telegraphic and agrammatical style as they have lost any sense of linguistic hierarchy. Jakobson also uses the basic opposition between metaphor and metonymy to construct a basic literary typology. Romantic and symbolist poetry is described as being predominantly metaphoric, whilst Tolstoy's concentration on Anna's handbag in the suicide scene in *Anna Karenina* is said to exemplify the metonymic nature of realist fiction.

Jakobson describes both the DREAM-WORK's mechanisms of CONDENSATION and DISPLACEMENT (Freud 1900) as metonymic processes; and he also describes symbolism of dreams as a metaphoric process. LACAN identifies them with, respectively, metaphor and metonymy in order to demonstrate that the UNCONSCIOUS functions in accordance with rhetorical principles and is structured like a language.

metaphysics Traditionally defined as that branch of philosophy which deals with the most general and abstract questions, such as those pertaining to the nature of existence, the categories of space and time, the existence of God or the immortality of the human soul. Metaphysics seeks to provide a comprehensive account of the world that is proof against the uncertainties of experience.

The term supposedly derives from the Greek *ta meta ta physica*, meaning 'the work after the physics', or in other words the treatise by Aristotle that was catalogued after his *Physics* in some lost library. Aristotle's *Metaphysics* (fourth century BC) – which he himself called 'first philosophy' – is one of the earliest treatises on the subject and has had immense influence on the entire history of Western philosophy. It might also be said to come 'after the physics' in that it offers a systematic account of the categories employed by physics, defined as the study of *phusis* or 'nature'. In that sense, metaphysics is to physics as METALANGUAGE is to language.

Although it was long considered to be the most noble branch of philosophy, metaphysics has come under attack from a variety of quarters in the twentieth century, and its very existence has been called into question. On the one hand, developments in the natural sciences mean that questions pertaining to space and time are now a matter for mathematicians and theoretical physicists rather than speculative philosophers. Developments within philosophy itself, and especially the so-called LINGUISTIC TURN, mean, on the other hand, that the traditional concerns of metaphysics are often viewed as problems that arise from the misuse of language. For the logical positivists of the VIENNA CIRCLE, 'metaphysics' is a derogatory term to be applied to speculative or unverifiable statements (such as 'God exists'); for many of the theorists associated with ANALYTIC PHILOSOPHY and ORDINARY LANGUAGE philosophy, metaphysical problems are simply a product of the ambiguities of language. The task of philosophy is therefore to arrive at a better undertanding of concepts through a better understanding of language that will rid philosophy of metaphysical pseudo-problems. DERRIDA and the practitioners of DECONSTRUCTION tend to use the term 'metaphysics' or 'Western metaphysics' as a synonym for philosophy itself, and hold that it is the most dangerous manifestation of LOGOCENTRISM.

Metz, Christian (1941–) French film theorist. Metz's influential writings on cinema can be divided into two temporal groups. His earlier works (1966, 1968, 1971) represent an attempt to establish a SEMIOTICS of cinema based upon the linguistic model that was so important to the STRUCTURALISM of the 1960s and early 1970s. In the mid-1970s, Metz's work changes direction considerably as, largely under the influence of LACAN, he begins to elaborate a psychoanalytic theory of film (1977). His later work has greatly influenced the discussions of the GAZE, and particularly of the male gaze in feminist studies of cinema and visual perception (see Mulvey 1975; Kuhn 1982; Rose 1986).

Metz's early writings represent an attempt to go beyond metaphorical talk of the 'cinematic language' by actually elaborating a semiotics of cinema. It rapidly becomes apparent that the linguistic model cannot be applied to cinema in any simple sense. Film is, writes Metz, a form of *PAROLE* without a *LANGUE*. Unlike a natural language, it is a one-way process of communication without a return channel that allows the viewer to communicate with the film or the film-maker. The second major difference is that cinema does not really use a paradigmatic axis (PARADIGM); a film is made up of a syntagmatic axis (SYNTAGM) that moves from single images to sequences and finally filmic narratives. A semiotics of cinema must therefore concentrate, rather like the NARRATOLOGY that is its literary equivalent, on identifying the minimal units that combine to produce meaning in cinema. By doing so, it can elaborate a grammar of cinema. The grammar consists of sets of codes and subcodes, defined as the analytic constructs that account for the production of signification in a set of filmic messages. One of the main codes is described by Metz (1966) as *la grande syntagmatique*, and it consists of six 'segments': the scene (a small piece of action), the sequence (a chase), alternating syntagm (parallel montage or cutting between scenes), frequentative syntagm (a walk across a desert using fade-ins and fade-outs which show a complete set of actions in a way that can never be done in the theatre), descriptive syntagm (a succession of images of spatio-temporal coexistence) and the autonomous shot (inserts, close-ups).

In his later work Metz expands on his early distinction between film and cinema, describing the latter as the extra-filmic apparatus of an industry, but also all the psychological forces that make an audience wish to watch a film. The cinema is described as including cinematic writing and history, or the sum total of discourses about it as well as its actual institutions. The imaginary dimension of film now comes to the fore in analyses of processes of identification with characters and with the camera itself as Metz incorporates Lacan's notion of a scopic drive, or 'urge to look', into his analysis. Psychoanalysis is further invoked to promote an analysis of IDEOLOGY in film. Thus Howard Hawks's classic Western *Red River* (1948) can be seen as a defence of private property, and as an instance of misogynist male homosexuality, but those themes are not visible in the film. They are revealed by analysis, rather as though they were the UNCONSCIOUS of the film.

READING: Andrew (1976); Heath (1973); *Screen* (1973)

Millett, Kate (1934–) American feminist critic and artist. Her *Sexual Politics* (1969) is one of the early classics of the WOMEN'S LIBERATION movement. This hugely successful and influential study, which makes a significant contribution to FEMINIST CRITICISM, was followed by a short collection of sympathetic interviews with prostitutes (1971), in which the author called for the decriminalization of prostitution. Millett's subsequent work has been much more subjective, and includes a novel based on her affair with an older woman (1977) and an explicit autobiographical memoir of her life after the publication of *Sexual Politics* (1974). Her *The Loony Bin Trip* (1990) is a grimly moving account of her mental breakdown, of the subsequent diagnosis of manic depression and of her period of incarceration in an Irish mental hospital.

Millett understands politics as meaning the power-structured relationships in which one group controls another, and sexual politics as meaning the power relations inherent in PATRIARCHY that subordinate women to men, perpetuate their economic exploitation and justify their sexual oppression. *Sexual Politics* is therefore a call for a sexual revolution that will abolish patriarchy and male supremacy, and lead to a profound reexamination of masculine and feminine social roles. There can be no resolution of the conflicts of sexual politics within marriage, and the sexual revolution therefore implies its abolition. Millett traces the origins of the sexual revolution to the suffrage movements and the New Women of the early twentieth century, but concentrates mainly on the effects of the counter-revolution against it. Like FRIEDAN before her and her contemporary FIRESTONE, Millett is bitterly critical of FREUD's role in the counter-revolution. Although she acknowledges the importance of the discovery of infantile sexuality and of the inherent bisexuality of human beings, she insists that the idea of penis envy ignores the social aspects of women's subordination and their protests against it, arguing that it is not the penis that is envied by the little girl, but the social status and power that are associated with it. Such arguments are not untypical of the early stages of the stormy debate between FEMINISM AND PSYCHOANALYSIS; later contributors such as Juliet MITCHELL (1974) argue that they rest upon a naïve confusion of reality with fantasy.

Millett's academic background is in English literature, and major sections of *Sexual Politics* are devoted to examining literary representations of the power relations between men and women. Her detailed readings of the stereotyping involved are largely thematic, and owe nothing to the more sophisticated modes of analysis elaborated in the wake of STRUCTURALISM, but they remain powerful in their own terms. The book opens with analyses of sexually explicit passages from Henry Miller and Norman Mailer, including the notorious passage from the latter's *An American Dream* (1965) in which the male protagonist, having murdered his wife, forcibly sodomizes his maid. These are used to demonstrate that what is at stake is power rather than sexuality as such, and are contrasted with the more 'honest' depictions of sexual hierarchies to be found in the fiction and plays of Jean Genet. In the long final section, Millett returns to literary reflections of sexual politics with a detailed reading of D. H. Lawrence, Miller, Mailer and, by way of contrast, Jean Genet. The choice of authors is significant: in the 1950s and 1960s, Lawrence, Miller and Mailer were commonly viewed as heralds of sexual liberation (the *Lady Chatterley's Lover* trial of 1960 and the defence argument that it was not PORNOGRAPHY supposedly helped to usher in a more liberal sexual era), but Millett argues convincingly that their depictions of sexuality are deeply rooted in a fear of femininity and express a murderous urge to suppress it; that Miller, in particular, displays a puritan revulsion from sexuality by equating orgasm with defecation and women's sexuality with defilement; and that, given that women are defiled by sexuality and therefore a source of defilement, the logical response is to defile women who consent to sexuality as completely as possible.

Although *Sexual Politics* is widely regarded as a path-breaking book, Millett's career has not been a success. By 1998, when no American publisher would reprint *Sexual Politics* on the grounds that it was 'obsolete', she was living in poverty, unable to obtain an academic post, and making a living by selling Christmas trees (Millett 1998).

mimesis The concept of mimesis (the Greek word means imitation) is a fundamental issue in all discussions of the representational nature of the arts, and particularly in discussions of realism.

Debates about mimesis begin with the Greeks, and the issues involved are illustrated by the differences of opinion expressed in Aristotle's *Poetics* and Book III of Plato's *Republic*. Plato adopts a very broad definition: all the arts, the sciences and all forms of discourse are mimetic to the extent that they imitate the ideal objects (ideas) described in the famous fable of the cave in which men dimly perceive the shadows of the ideal. For Aristotle, mimesis is more narrowly defined as a characteristic of the poetry (above all, epic and tragic poetry and drama) that represents men in action, or men actually doing things. Unlike RHETORIC, whose function is to persuade, and unlike DIALECTIC which establishes truth, mimesis is, at one level, a representation of human actions that founds the possibility of both history and what would now be termed realist fiction. At the same time, it is said by Aristotle to be an expression of an inherent instinct for imitation that is a source of both knowledge and pleasure. For Plato, in contrast, mimetic imitation is a potential source of danger and he contrasts it unfavourably with DIEGESIS. It is not simply that 'true reality' is to be preferred to 'mere appearances' or that the poets are sophists who tell lies (and who should therefore be excluded from the ideal republic); mimesis implies a threat to the social order because, if any individual can mimic a carpenter, a doctor or a soldier, the boundary lines that define a society in which everyone has his or her place will dissolve, and society will collapse. The inescapable paradox is that Plato himself is speaking mimetically: he imitates Socrates and thus forsakes what he himself describes as the virtues of 'speaking in one's own name' or diegesis (for a deconstructive reading of the many paradoxes and APORIA involved here, see Derrida 1968).

Debates about the nature of mimesis continue throughout modern philosophy and critical theory. When LUKÁCS defines HISTORICISM as the writer's 'fidelity to history' or as a faithful reproduction of the past (1937), he is invoking a mimetic theory of both history and literature; when RORTY attacks the traditional view that philosophy is the 'mirror of nature' (1980), he is openly calling into question the whole notion of mimesis, and indeed its epistemological utility.

The association between mimetic realism and the novel is a very common one, exemplified by AUERBACH's great study in comparative literature (1946) and, in the case of English literature, by Ian Watt's classic study of the rise of the novel (1957; on the French realist tradition, see Prendergast 1986, the first two chapters of which provide a very helpful discussion of mimesis in general), even though the term 'realism' originates, significantly, in French debates about the visual arts (Nochlin 1971). The metaphors of 'windows', 'mirrors' and 'pictures' that abound in so many discussions of realism can be traced back to Plato's dialogue *Cratylus*, where Socrates describes how Zeuxis painted grapes so realistically that the birds tried to eat them. That anecdote points to a further paradox about mimesis: an imitation exists only if we can in some sense perceive the difference between it and the original. If that difference does not exist, it is a replica like the famous grapes. The theory of mimesis thus opens up the question of VERISIMILITUDE, or 'seeming-to-be-real'.

In the twentieth century, mimesis has come under attack on a number of grounds. BRECHT tries to undermine mimetic realism in the theatre by introducing an ALIENATION-EFFECT that distances spectators from the theatrical illusion and asks them to be critical of it in a directly political sense. RUSSIAN FORMALISM destroys the realist illusion by demonstrating that any text is made up of formal devices that have no representational function in the traditional sense, whilst the NEW CRITI-CISM defines poetry in such terms as to make it refer to nothing but itself. The 'verbal icon' does not represent anything: it simply *is* (Wimsatt 1954). In much broader terms, the entire thrust of post-Saussurean linguistics (SAUSSURE), and the literary theories derived from it, is to provide powerful arguments against mimesis by stressing the arbitrary nature of the SIGN. The sign does not imitate an external reality; it alludes in a purely conventional way to a REFERENT. The structural analyses of BARTHES and others demonstrate that, far from being a reflection of reality, a 'realist' text sustains an illusion of reality by creating a REALITY-EFFECT. Barthes' (1957) MYTHOLOGIES demonstrate that the most 'natural' images are constructed by the mechanisms of an ideologically motivated system of connotation; here realism is effectively equated with 'bourgeois IDEOLOGY'. In his study of a short story by Balzac (1970a), the same critic describes mimesis as inducing a sense of nausea.

Mimesis remains, despite all the attacks, a central category of both aesthetic experience and everyday life. Any child will use 'realistic' as a term to praise a film, television programme or video game and whilst the painters of HYPERREALITY take the debate about mimesis to a new and ironic level, its basic terms remain remarkably constant and are still broadly defined by Plato and Aristotle.

mirror-phase (or **-stage**) LACAN's description of the mirror-phase was his first major contribution to the theory of PSYCHOANALYSIS. It is of central importance to his theory of the origins of subjectivity and provides the basis for his critique of EGO-PSYCHOLOGY. Although Lacan first described the mirror-phase in a paper read to the Marienbad Conference of the International Psychoanalytic Association in 1936, he did not publish his findings until the late 1940s (1948, 1949, 1951b).

The notion of a mirror-phase derives from two main sources, and also alludes to the reflection image that inspires FREUD's notion of NARCISSISM. Lacan draws on the studies of child psychology carried out by Henri Wallon in the 1930s, which describe the reactions of very young children on seeing their reflection in a mirror (Wallon 1947). The perception of a mirror-image is described by Wallon as an essential stage in self-perception and the development of a sense of selfhood. Lacan also draws on studies in primate ethology which claim to demonstrate that a young chimpanzee confronted with a mirror does not behave in the same way as a human infant and takes no interest in its own reflection.

The mirror-phase is a vital moment in the constitution of a human SUBJECT and typically occurs at the age of between six and eighteen months. A child which is still helpless, unable to speak and without any control over its motor activities is confronted with the image of its own body in a mirror or some equivalent. Its immediate reaction is one of jubilation, as the image shows it a functional unity it has yet to achieve. The child thus identifies with an image of what it will become, but that image is illusory and the child's identification signals the beginning of a dialectic in which recognition is simultaneously a form of misrecognition: a child is not an image in a mirror. For Lacan, the element of recognition signals that the

EGO is a product of the IMAGINARY or an illusory structure in which the subject becomes trapped into ALIENATION.

The mirror-phrase is associated with the threatening fantasy of the FRAGMENTED BODY, which expresses the fear that the unity perceived in the mirror will disintegrate or be torn apart. A child in the mirror-phase often displays a characteristic pattern of behaviour described as 'transitivity'. It identifies so strongly with the image of the other that it cries when it sees another child fall; a child who strikes another will claim to have been struck. Transitivism is an interpersonal instance of the play of recognition and misrecognition initiated by the recognition of the self in an illusory image.

mise-en-abyme French expression originally used in heraldry to describe a small shield set within a larger shield bearing the same device. In English the smaller shield is said to be 'set in escutcheon'; the expression is used only in heraldry. Equivalent formal devices have long been used in both literature and the visual arts, the obvious examples being the play within a play in *Hamlet* and Velázquez's *Las Meninas*, which depicts the artist painting the court scene shown on the canvas. The expression *mise-en-abyme* was given a new currency by the French novelist André Gide (1869–1951), who defined it as the representation within a work of art of that work's structure. Gide often uses the device in his novels, especially in *The Vatican Cellars* (1925). *Mise-en-abyme* is frequently used by the writers associated with the *NOUVEAU ROMAN*, and a similar self-reflexivity is typical of much postmodernist fiction. The opening of Italo CALVINO's *If on a Winter's Night a Traveller* (1979) is a particularly fine example.

READING: Dällenbach (1977)

Mitchell, Juliet (1940–) British feminist and psychoanalyst, born in New Zealand.

Originally published in *New Left Review*, Mitchell's influential article 'Women: The Longest Revolution' (1966; reprinted 1984) is one of the earliest statements of modern British FEMINISM and argues that the situation of women is different from that of any other social group in that women are at once fundamental to the human condition, but exploited and marginalized in their economic, social and political roles. Widely circulated, often in pirate form, in the years following the emergence of an organized WOMEN'S LIBERATION Movement in 1970, it was expanded to form the basis of *Women's Estate* (1971), which remains a classic text of the feminist movement. The title of the original article is a direct allusion to RAYMOND WILLIAMS's *The Long Revolution* (1961).

Mitchell's interest in how IDEOLOGY constructs representations of women led to a study of psychoanalysis. Her *Psychoanalysis and Feminism* (1974) attacks feminist critics of psychoanalysis such as GREER and FRIEDAN, arguing that psychoanalysis is not, as they supposed, a recommendation for a patriarchal society, but an analysis of one. It follows that a rejection of psychoanalysis is fatal for feminism. Mitchell's criticisms of the neo-Freudianism of FROMM and REICH and of the ANTI-PSYCHIATRY of Laing begin to open up a new and important dialogue between psychoanalysis and feminism in which FREUD and LACAN become the crucial figures. The importance of

Lacan was subsequently underlined when Mitchell produced an edited collection of Lacanian writing on female sexuality in collaboration with Jacqueline Rose (1982).

After publishing *Psychoanalysis and Feminism*, Mitchell trained as a psychoanalyst. Despite the important role she played in introducing Lacan to readers in Britain, she trained with the Independent Group in the British Psychoanalytic Association and her subsequent work on psychoanalysis (see, for example, 1984) is closer to the OBJECT-RELATIONS school than to Lacan.

READING: *New Formations* 26 (1995)

mode of production Term used in MARXISM and HISTORICAL MATERIALISM to characterize the articulation, within a given historical period, of social relations and forms of production, and forces of production. The social relations and forms of production are the modes in which surplus labour (that labour which does more than merely reproduce the work force and its physical requirements) is appropriated and the ways in which it is distributed. The forces of production are the forms in which nature and raw materials are appropriated and used in the labour process. In a feudal mode of production, the relations of production are the social relations that allow dues or rents to be collected, or which provide for the supply of corvée labour on an estate once the vassals have produced the food and other material requirements needed to reproduce a vassal class. The forces of production are the land and plant such as mills, and their use is subject to political and social controls.

Classic Marxist texts such as Marx's *Contribution to the Critique of Political Economy* (1859) and the first volume of *Capital* (1867) and Engels's *Origins of the Family, Private Property and the State* (1884) describe a historical sequence of modes of production that succeed one another in accordance with the laws of the DIALECTIC. They range from hypothetical primitive communism, in which private property does not exist, to the slave modes of Classical Antiquity, the feudal mode of production and then capitalism, which will, it is claimed, give way to socialism. Marx also speaks almost in passing (1853, 1867) of an Asiatic mode of production characterized by the despotic state's construction of hydraulic works and supposedly reflecting the 'unchangingness of Asiatic societies'. Karl August Wittfogel (1896–1941), who was associated with the FRANKFURT SCHOOL, uses the idea of an Asiatic mode of production to argue that there are two paths of historical development leading, respectively, to the pluralism of the West and to oriental despotism (1955). The argument is not widely accepted by Marxists (Anderson 1974b).

According to ALTHUSSER, historical materialism is a 'science of modes of production'; the most sophisticated exposition of this science is contained in Étienne Balibar's contribution to *Reading 'Capital'* (Althusser and Balibar 1965).

modernism The term is widely used to describe a variety of tendencies within the European, and especially Anglo-American, literature of the early twentieth century.

Virginia Woolf captures something of the essential experience of modernism when she remarks (1924) that 'in or about December 1910, human character changed'. Many would agree that something, if not human character itself, changed in the first decades of the twentieth century but some would proclaim 1922 – which saw the publication of *The Waste Land, Ulysses* and Virginia Woolf's *Jacob's Room* – as 'the year of modernism'. Modernism is in fact a surprisingly elusive term, not least in that there are so many national variations in its meaning. Whilst the adjective 'modern' can in some sense be applied to an enormously wide variety of movements from FUTURISM to SURREALISM, the Anglo-American tradition usually understands modernism as meaning the literary production of novelists and poets such as James Joyce, Gertrude Stein, T. S. Eliot, Wallace Stevens and Ezra Pound. In his study of 'the imaginative literature of 1870–1930', which played an important role in defining modernism – even though he does not actually use that term – Edmund Wilson (1931) discusses Yeats, Valéry, Eliot, Proust, Joyce and Stein. The inclusion of French authors, who also figure prominently in Cyril Connolly's popular *The Modern Movement* (1965), is paradoxical in that, even though the French *art moderne* is a highly significant term in the history of MODERNITY, French does not use *modernisme* in the Anglo-American sense. *Modernisme* refers primarily to the attempt to modernize the doctrine of the Catholic Church by incorporating into it the findings of modern historical criticism and to bring it more into line with contemporary culture in general. Modernism was condemned by Pope Pius X in the encyclical *Pascendi* of 1907. The Italian term *modernismo* has a similar sense, as does the German *Modernismus*; one of the opponents of theological modernism was a very young Martin HEIDEGGER (Ott 1988). *Der Moderne* ('the modern') was, in contrast, widely used from the 1880s onwards to describe virtually anything that challenged 'the old-fashioned'. In Spanish-speaking Latin America, *modernismo* was applied from the 1890s onwards to a variety of poetic and literary movements, including ARIELISM, which adapted French Romanticism and symbolism to local conditions in a bid for cultural independence from Spain; in Brazil *modernismo* refers to the attempts made from the 1920s onwards to destroy the culture of the past and to give Brazil a leading role in the creation of that of the future (Franco 1970).

Whilst it would be very difficult to identify modernism with any one style, the use of techniques such as STREAM OF CONSCIOUSNESS, *vers libre* or 'free verse' which eschews rhyme, the stanza form and obvious rhythmical patterns, and equivalents to Gide's *MISE-EN-ABYME* are its most common literary devices. Modernism in the visual arts is usually identified with the process of ABSTRACTION associated with cubism and other manifestations of the AVANT-GARDE, and it has been argued that cubism provides the paradigm for the fragmentation and juxtaposition of images characteristic of the literary modernism of Pound's *Cantos*, Stein and even Eliot's *The Waste Land* (Macleod 1999). GREENBERG remarks (1960) that, whereas naturalistic art dissembles the medium, modernist art calls attention to its artfulness, and this concentration on the medium is characteristic of modernism as a whole. Self-referentiality and a stress on the brittleness of the self-contained work of art are typical of much modern painting, but also feature in such devices as Eliot's addition of footnotes to *The Waste Land* or Joyce's parodic anthology of English prose styles in the 'Oxen of the Sun' chapter of *Ulysses*. This literary introversion represents a rejection of most forms of nineteenth-century realism, but also a withdrawal from the public sphere; modernist poets do not aspire to being Shelley's 'unacknowledged legislators'. Self-referentiality or reflexivity can be accompanied by a note of high aesthetic or moral seriousness (hence the common complaint that modernism is 'difficult'), as well as a certain hostility towards the emerging mass culture of an increasingly industrialized society. Greenberg's argument that the abstraction of modernism is the only real defence against the KITSCH of mass culture appears to be anticipated in the fourth ('Calypso') chapter of *Ulysses* when Bloom uses a sheet from the popular magazine *Tit Bits* as toilet paper. The aesthetic introversion that leads to the accusation of elitism and the distrust of popular culture are perhaps symptomatic of the darker side of modernism typified by Eliot's anti-Semitic remarks in *After Strange Gods* or Pound's apologias for Italian Fascism.

Despite the presence in the modernist CANON of Woolf and Stein, modernism often appears to be a very masculine affair, but Scott's *Gender of Modernism* anthology (1990) does much to correct the GENDER imbalance. Sara Blair's suggestion (1999) that the Harlem Renaissance should figure in any serious discussion of modernism is also to be welcomed.

In architecture, modernism is effectively synonymous with the INTERNATIONAL STYLE associated with Gropius, Le Corbusier and Mies van der Rohe, and it was the critique of modernist architecture that first gave currency to the idea of POSTMOD-ERNISM. Standard accounts of modernism (Bradbury and McFarlane 1976; Levenson 1999) do not usually extend the discussion of music beyond passing mentions of Stravinsky's *Rite of Spring* (1913). A more interesting line of inquiry might begin with the so-called 'New Vienna School' of Arnold Schoenberg, Anton Webern and Alban Berg, whose experiments with atonality from about 1908 onwards have inspired so many developments in contemporary music (Adorno 1949).

modernity The period or quality of the modern. 'Modern' derives from the late Latin *modernus*, formed from the earlier *modo* ('recently') by analogy with the adjective *hodiernus*, meaning 'of or pertaining to today' (*hodie* = today). Although it takes a variety of forms, the idea of modernity always implies that of a break with or departure from something earlier, and 'modern' is often used as the opposite of 'traditional'. For centuries, the modern implied a break with Classical Antiquity, or a consciousness of a complex and differential relationship with that epoch. In the fifth century, *modernus* was used to distinguish the Christian 'present' from the pagan past of Greek and Roman Antiquity (Habermas 1980). The civilization of the European Renaissance (rebirth) is often understood as a form of modernity in that it establishes a new relationship with classical learning and art (Panofsky 1965). The so-called 'quarrel of the ancients and the moderns' in seventeenth-century France centred on the question of the respective merits of classical and contemporary literature, as does Jonathan Swift's *Battle of the Books* of 1704. Something of the classical/modern distinction survives in the phrase 'modern languages', originally used to distinguish between the living languages of the present and the dead languages of Antiquity.

The contemporary understanding of modernity is influenced by a number of other conceptions ranging from philosophy to sociology and aesthetics. In terms of the history of philosophy, modernity is sometimes seen, as in HUSSERL, as being inaugurated by Descartes' vision of a philosophy and science that would make men the masters and possessors of nature (1637), but is usually made synonymous with the ENLIGHTENMENT project and its belief that the light of reason and the natural sciences would eventually dispel the shadows and darkness of superstition, religion and political tyranny. HABERMAS, for example, takes the latter view and argues that modernity has proved to be an unfinished project whose emancipatory potential has yet to be realized (1985); his main objection to the idea of POSTMODERNITY is that it is an irrational anti-modernism which turns against the heritage of the Enlightenment. More pessimistic members of the FRANKFURT SCHOOL tend to view modernity as a double-edged DIALECTIC OF ENLIGHTENMENT that has both positive and negative effects.

The classic sociological accounts of the phenomenon of modernity, which they relate to industrialization, are equally ambivalent. The German sociologist Tönnies (1855–1936) describes the emergence of modern society as a transition from community (*Gemeinschaft*) to society (*Gesellschaft*), or from a social organization based upon customary relations, religion and common property to one based upon status, legal contract, freedom of thought, but also the individual ownership of property (1887). A similar dichotomy can be seen in Durkheim's distinction (1893) between organic and mechanical solidarity, or between a social system based upon a similitude of consciousness and a set of common beliefs, and a system in which legal rules backed by the threat of coercion impose a uniformity of beliefs in a society dominated by an increasingly sharp division of labour. For Weber (1904–05), modernization means the 'disenchantment of the world' as traditional beliefs and the unified complex of religion, metaphysics and superstition collapse under the impact of a substantive reason or the instrumental rationality which subordinates means to ends. Politics, public life, private life and religion become separate spheres of existence as reason itself divides into the distinct realms of science, morality and art. Whilst modernity emancipates individuals, it also threatens to imprison them in the 'iron cage' of a coldly impersonal rationality. For the Marx of *The Communist Manifesto* (1847–8), modernity is an experience of tumultuous and rapid change in which capitalism unleashes the might of the productive forces, creates wonders, but also expands the realm of COMMODITY FETISHISM and of an ALIENATION that can be overcome only by the revolution that will lead to the classless society of communism. Fittingly, Marx's most striking description of this period of change – 'all that is solid melts into air' – has been used as the title of one of the finest studies of the experience of modernity (Berman 1982).

Contemporary discussions of aesthetic modernity have been greatly influenced by BENJAMIN's reading of Baudelaire (1939a) and his image of Paris as the capital of the nineteenth century (Benjamin 1939b). For Benjamin, following Baudelaire, the characteristic figure of modernity is the *FLÂNEUR* who wanders through the great city as both observer and consumer. Baudelaire's archetypal *flâneur* is 'the painter of modern life' (1863), namely Constantin Guys (1805–92), best known for his GENRE drawings of the everyday life of the Paris of the Second Empire (see Geoffrey 1920; many of Guys' drawings are held in the Musée Carnavalet, Paris). Baudelaire praises Guys for his ability to capture the ephemeral but irreversible changes brought about by fashion and the proliferation of new commodities in the arcades frequented by the *flâneur*. Once more, the image of modernity is profoundly ambiguous. Change is so rapid that it becomes a form of changelessness; as Benjamin puts it, 'the new' becomes the 'almost the same'. Baudelaire himself expresses this view in starker terms in the final poem in the augmented edition of *Les Fleurs du mal* (1861) when he calls upon death to raise the anchor and to 'plunge into the depths of the unknown in order to find something *new*'.

Guys' drawings make a radical break with the conventionally academic history painting that dominated French art in the nineteenth century and in many respects anticipate the themes of the 'tradition of the new' inaugurated by Manet (Hanson 1977). The tradition of the new is continued by the various AVANT-GARDES and MODERNISMS that punctuate the history of modern art – a term that, like 'modern life' (*la vie moderne*) first became current in the France of the 1850s – from Impressionism to FUTURISM and SURREALISM.

Moscow Linguistic Circle Founded at Moscow University in 1915 by Roman JAKOBSON and others, the Circle was, along with OPOYAZ, the main centre for the development of RUSSIAN FORMALISM and brought together linguists, dialecticians and folklorists with an interest in the formal properties of poetic language. More oriented towards linguistics than the poets and literary historians of OPOYAZ, the Circle followed Jakobson in arguing that poetics was an integral part of linguistics. From 1924–5 onwards, the Moscow Circle came under increasingly severe attacks from the dogmatic Marxists for whom 'formalism' was a term of abuse and who promoted the doctrine of SOCIALIST REALISM.

READING: Erlich (1965)

Movement An unsigned article in the weekly *Spectator*'s issue of 1 October 1954 entitled 'In the Movement' first spoke of the Movement as consisting of a generation of poets who were bored by the despair of the 1940s, impatient of poetic sensibility, 'Little Magazines' and experimental writing. They were, continued the anonymous author (who was in fact the magazine's literary editor J. D. Scott), anti-phoney, anti-wet, robust and ironic. The only names mentioned were Donald Davie, Kingsley Amis, John Wain and Iris Murdoch. The Movement issued no manifestos, and represents a mood rather than a movement, but two anthologies gave it a more concrete existence. D. J. Enright's *Poets of the 1950s* (1955) which, oddly enough, was published only in Japan, anthologized a Movement made up of Amis, Robert Conquest, Davie, John Holloway, Elizabeth Jennings, Philip Larkin and Wain. Robert Conquest's *New Lines* anthology (1956) added Thom Gunn to the rollcall.

Although most of the Movement poets were influenced by LEAVIS's idea of a university-based and professionally trained audience, they tended to be provincial, politically neutral, anti-intellectual, sceptical of the obscurity of modernism and, like Philip Larkin, deeply suspicious of 'abroad' and all it stood for. In general, the poetic tone is that of a chatty familiarity that assumes that the reader automatically shares the poet's tastes and interests. Two novels accurately capture the atmosphere: Kingsley Amis's *Lucky Jim* (1954) and John Wain's *Hurry on Down* (1955).

READING: Hewison (1988); Morrison (1980); Motion (1993)

mytheme Neologism coined by LÉVI-STRAUSS by analogy with PHONEME, and used to describe the elementary units employed in the structural analysis of myths (Lévi-Strauss 1955, 1956). Like SAUSSURE's signs, mythemes are created by binary or ternary oppositions and are analogous with the functions identified by PROPP in his morphology of the folk tale. Mythemes are to be identified with functions, and not with the characters of mythical tales. Thus, in Native American tales and myths, the role of the trickster can be taken by the raven, the coyote or the mink but the underlying mytheme or function remains constant, despite the different characteristics of the individual creatures.

Mythologies The general title of a series of short essays by BARTHES, mainly published in *Les Lettres françaises* between 1954 and 1956 and then republished in book form and supplemented by a long essay entitled 'Myth Today' (1957). A selection of the essays appeared in English translation in 1973, and most of the remainder in 1979.

The essays cover an immense range of everyday topics and rank amongst Barthes' most charming and amusing texts. Descriptions of all-in wrestling matches and their excessive 'rhetorical violence', analyses of the way in which a plate of steak and chips comes to signify a certain idea of France and Frenchness (*francité*) and of the advertising of detergents combine to produce an ideological critique of so-called mass culture and an initial semiological analysis of that language. The essays are contemporary with a number of others on BRECHT and Barthes is attempting to demystify his myths by producing a semiological equivalent to the dramatist's ALIENATION-EFFECT (see, for example, Barthes 1956). The effect of the mythologies studied by Barthes is to transform ideology into nature; the intended effect of the critique is to reverse it as semiology becomes what Barthes, with a typical neologism, calls 'semioclasm'. The essay 'Myth Today' illustrates the transformation of history into nature by analysing, *inter alia*, a magazine cover showing a black soldier saluting the French flag. The sign composed of the soldier and the flag is made to signify that France has an Empire, that all its subjects are loyal to it, and that all are equal and untouched by racial discrimination. The zeal with which the soldier salutes the flag answers the criticisms of those who criticize France for its colonial policies; it effectively says: 'The black soldier is loyal to France.' A second level of signification, or a second semiological system (a certain idea of the military and of France), is thus grafted onto the first level at which the initial sign (the photograph of the soldier) existed, and connotation replaces denotation. The second mythical level contains nothing of the history that led a black soldier to volunteer for (or be conscripted into) the French army. The object of Barthes' semioclasm is to destroy the obviousness of the myth by reintroducing a historical and political dimension.

Barthes describes the myth as having an imperative or interpellatory character; like an advertisement, the picture of the soldier speaks directly to the viewer. It speaks directly to the viewer as a magical object appearing in the present, without any trace of the history that produced it. Given the importance that has been ascribed to INTER-PELLATION in the theory of IDEOLOGY elaborated by ALTHUSSER in the late 1960s, it is interesting to note that Barthes was working with similar notions a decade earlier.

N

name-of-the-father Originally used by LACAN (1953) to describe the castrating father of the OEDIPUS COMPLEX who personifies the taboo on incest, the expression is at once a semi-humorous religious allusion (*In nomine patris*) and a play on the near-homonyms *non* and *nom*: the name-of-the-father (*nom-du-père*) is also the father's 'no' (*non-du-père*) to the child's incestuous desire for its mother. In Lacan's 1955–6 seminar on the psychoses (published 1981), the name-of-the-father is described as the fundamental signifier that both confers identity on human subjects by situating them in a lineage and the SYMBOLIC order, and reiterates the prohibition on incest. The FORECLOSURE of the name-of-the-father, or its expulsion from the subject's symbolic universe, is said by Lacan to be the mechanism that triggers PSYCHOSIS.

narcissism Love of one's own image. In Book II of his *Metamorphoses*, Ovid retells the Greek legend of the beautiful youth Narcissus who, ignoring the charms of the nymph Echo, falls in love with his own reflection. Nemesis punishes him for his cruelty to Echo by so paralysing him that Narcissus perpetually contemplates the image of his own face reflected in a pool of water. Narcissus pines away and dies; after his death he is transformed into the spring flower that bears his name.

FREUD borrows the term 'narcissism' from Havelock Ellis (1859–1939) and the tradition of sexology, in which it was used to describe auto-eroticism or the solitary practice of gaining sexual satisfaction from one's own body. Freud initially uses the term to explain OBJECT-choice in male homosexuals who love young men who resemble them, and whom they can love as their mothers once loved them (Freud 1910c). Although the suggestion that narcissism is a specific feature of male homosexuality is quickly rejected, the idea of recovering a lost object (the mother) is present throughout Freud's discussions of the topic. According to the classic formulation (Freud 1914a), narcissism is a state in which LIBIDO is withdrawn from the outside world and directed towards the EGO. At one level, narcissism is a libidinal complement to the egoism of the self-preservative instincts, but it also reproduces the hypothetical stage of primary narcissism, in which the child takes itself as a love-object. That stage is said to correspond to the child's magical belief in the omnipotence of its thoughts. According to Freud, all narcissists display something of the very young child's self-contentment and inaccessibility. As well as loving what he was, a narcissist may also love what he would like to be, and narcissism thus provides the libidinal basis for an identification with ideal figures. The reappearance of primary narcissism is an important aspect of the FANTASY lives of parents, who project their own lost ideals onto their children's future lives.

LACAN's theory of the MIRROR-PHASE explicitly invokes the Greek legend. Like Narcissus, the child literally falls in love with its own image and thus enters into the dimension of the IMAGINARY.

narratee A translation of the French *narrataire*, which is modelled on *destinataire*, the French term for the 'addressee' in JAKOBSON'S CODE-MESSAGE model of linguistic communication. The term is used in some forms of NARRATOLOGY to describe the agent (BREMOND) or ACTANT (GREIMAS) who is addressed by a narrator. The narratee may be extradiegetic or 'outside' the story, and is then addressed directly by the narrator. Examples include the Sultan who is told stories by Scheherazade in the *Arabian Nights*, but who never appears in the stories, or the sailors who listen to Marlow's story in Conrad's *Heart of Darkness*. The narratee may also appear in the story. The play between narrator and narratee is at its most complex in epistolary novels such as Richardson's *Pamela* or Laclos' *Les Liaisons dangeureuses*; here characters alternate between the two positions as they write and read the letters they exchange.

READING: Prince (1973a, 1973b); Rimmon-Kenan (1983)

narratology Whilst narratology can be broadly defined as the study of narrative, it is perhaps best described as the structuralist study of narrative plots. One of the most significant developments in narratology was the publication in 1966 of the eighth issue of *Communications*, the journal of the Centre for the Study of Mass Communications at the École Pratique des Hautes Études, which was for a long time the main bastion of French STRUCTURALISM. Prefaced by an introduction to the structural analysis of narrative by BARTHES (1966a), it included major contributions by the main theorists of narratology: GREIMAS, BREMOND, METZ, TODOROV and GENETTE; and Umberto ECO's essay on the narrative structures of Ian Fleming's James Bond novels provided a timely reminder that structuralist analysis *can* be entertaining.

Narratology draws on two main sources. It owes much to LÉVI-STRAUSS's application of linguistic principles to the analysis of myths (especially 1957) and to the thesis that apparently disparate myths are in fact variants on more basic themes that express underlying and constant universal structures. Those structures can be revealed by breaking down mythical narratives into a finite number of component MYTHEMES. The second major source is the POETICS of RUSSIAN FORMALISM and PROPP's morphological analysis of Russian folk-tales, which demonstrates that a limited number of narrative elements ('functions') and roles can be combined in different ways to generate an almost infinite number of stories. Using these models, the contributors to *Communications* attempt to formulate what Bremond terms a 'logic of narrative' and what Todorov describes (1969) as a 'grammar' which can provide a formal description of narrative possibilities. The structures observable in narratives are held to be analogous to those found in natural language, and are therefore, as Barthes in particular argues, considered to be amenable to the kind of analysis practised in linguistics. The notion of a narrative grammar or logic implies that any given set of narrative structures will display recurrent features that can be identified as distinctive regularities. The grammar is constructed on the basis of such regularities; it consists of a limited number of principles (such as Propp's functions, or Greimas's ACTANTS) and functional rules which generate the production of narratives. Narrative grammar is not visibly present in any given folk-tale or novel. Just as the speaker of a natural language is not consciously aware of CHOMSKY's deep structures, neither the reader nor the writer of a story is truly aware of the grammar on which it depends. Genette demonstrates this (1972) by extending the STORY/PLOT distinction and differentiating between 'story' (*histoire*), 'text' (*récit*) and 'narration' (*narration*). The story is a sequence of events, and the text the discourse which tells of them. 'Narration' is at once the grammar that makes the text and its story possible, and the abstraction produced by the theory of narratology. We read a text telling a story, but the narration that generates them is not spontaneously available to us as we read.

Narratology deals with narrative at the level of METALANGUAGE: narratives are the 'natural language' of which it speaks. It is not a form of literary criticism and does not seek to evaluate texts by making value-judgements. Its underlying thesis is that the same mode of analysis can be applied to Fleming's 'Bond' novels and Boccaccio's *Decameron* (Todorov 1969); at the narratological level, the distinction between 'good' and 'bad' is strictly non-pertinent.

READING: Rimmon-Kenan (1983)

negritude   French noun, now current in English, designating the francophone Afro-Caribbean cultural movement associated with CÉSAIRE, DAMAS, SENGHOR and the journal *PRÉSENCE AFRICAINE*.

The word was first used by Aimé Césaire in his great prose poem *Notebook of a Return to my Native Land* (1939). It encapsulates a defiant sense of identity ('Accommodate me. I'm not going to accommodate you') which is linked to a sense of history by the allusion to the Haitian insurrection of 1791 ('Haiti, where negritude stood up for the first time and said that it believed in its humanity'). Césaire's neologism is also an appropriation of *nègre* – which can mean either 'negro' or 'nigger' – that gives a positive sense to a potentially pejorative word. Negritude is in part a positive celebration of a black culture that had been dismissed as primitive barbarism. His fellow Martiniquan FANON remarks (1952b) that it was only with the appearance of Césaire that negritude or blackness became a condition that would be assumed with pride by a French West Indian.

Although it is influenced by the Black American writers of the Harlem Renaissance, the true origins of negritude lie in the publications of small surrealist-influenced groups of African and West Indian students active in Paris in the 1930s (see Mireille Rosello's introduction to the English translation of Césaire 1939; many of the relevant texts are now collected in Richardson 1996). Its full influence was not felt until the late 1940s and 1950s, and coincided with the beginnings of French decolonization. The idea of negritude was given a much wider currency and acquired a more philosophical dimension when SARTRE prefaced Senghor's anthology of negritude poetry (1948), claimed that it was the only revolutionary poetry of the day and spoke of negritude as a salutary 'anti-racist racism'. Adapting Senghor's argument that negritude is 'the collective personality of black peoples', Sartre described it as 'a certain quality common to the thought and behaviour of black people' or a black mode of being-in-the-world.

The cultural geography of negritude centres on the triangle made up by Paris, the French Caribbean and Senegal. The reclamation of a lost African identity and heritage is a major theme in Césaire's *Notebook*, but Senghor in particular tends to equate negritude with an essentialist celebration of an inherently African affectivity and personality (see the essays collected in Senghor 1964a).

Negritude was the major theme of the international congresses organized by the journal *Présence africaine* in 1956 and 1959, but there was little agreement as to its political content. In Césaire's native Martinique there is now a tendency to reject and criticize his negritude in favour of CREOLENESS.

READING: Corzani (1978); Kennedy (1975)

neorealism The Italian *neorealismo* was first coined in the 1920s to translate the German *NEUE SACHLICHKEIT*, but applies more specifically to the films and novels produced in the decade following the fall of Mussolini in 1943. The first film to be described as 'neorealist' was Luchino Visconti's *Obsession*, made in 1942 and adapted from James Caine's novel *The Postman Always Rings Twice* (1934). The acknowledged classics of neorealist cinema include Roberto Rossellini's *Rome Open City* (*Roma, città aperta*, 1945), *Paisan* (1946) and *Germany Year Zero* (1947), which deal with the end and aftermath of the war in Italy and Germany, Vittorio de Sica's *Bicycle Thieves* (1948), which paints a sympathetic portrait of the precarious life of the Roman poor, and Visconti's *The Earth Trembles* (*La terra trema*, 1947), a powerful and tragic portrayal of Sicilian fishermen.

Neorealist cinema is characterized by its naturalistic depiction of the lives of ordinary people and breaks decisively with the conventions of the historical costume dramas made during the fascist period. Most films were shot on location and on low budgets, often using non-professional actors. Rossellini in particular introduces into fictional films many of the techniques normally associated with documentary; it is difficult to believe at first that the outdoor sequences in *Rome Open City* are in fact reconstructions and not documentary footage. The so-called 'poetic realism' of the French cinema of the 1930s, and especially of Jean Renoir (1894–1979), is also a significant influence. Although widely regarded as classics of world cinema, not all neorealist films were immediately successful on release in Italian. *The Earth Trembles*, for example, was not a success, partly because its uncompromising use of Sicilian dialect meant that it had to be subtitled for exhibition in mainland Italy.

Neorealist literature is less well known outside Italy. It draws on the *verismo* tradition associated with Giovanni Verga (whose *I Malavoglia* of 1881 provided the inspiration for *The Earth Trembles*); in Italian, the term *verismo* is often used in preference to *neorealismo*. It is also heavily influenced by SARTRE's theory of

COMMITTED LITERATURE, which was popularized by the translations published in Elio Vittorini's journal *Il Politecnico* (1945–7). The dominant themes are drawn from the struggle of the Resistance against Mussolini and then the German occupation forces, the best-known examples being Vasco Pratolini's *Chronicles of Poor Lovers* (1947) and Elio Vittorini's *Men and Not Men* (1945). The early fiction of CALVINO is also close to the aesthetic of neorealism; see his 1964 preface to his first novel *The Path to the Nest of Spiders* (1947).

In political terms, neorealist cinema and fiction are based upon an appeal to freedom and the hope that the ideals of the wartime resistance movement would lead to a national renewal grounded in the values of 'the people', a rather vague category including the urban working classes, the rural poor of the regions and their intellectual-artistic allies. Neorealism declined as the unity of the wartime resistance gave way to a harsh polarization between an increasingly dogmatic Communist Party and the dominant Christian Democrats. It has also been argued that Fellini's *The Road* (*La Strada*, 1954) signalled the demise of neorealist cinema by indulging in a sentimentalized poetry of poverty.

READING: Armes (1972); Re (1990)

Neue Sachlichkeit 'New objectivity' is a major trend within art and photography in the Germany of the 1920s and early 1930s. Unusually for a twentieth-century AVANT-GARDE movement, *Neue Sachlichkeit* did not produce any manifestos or theoretical statements. It represents a retreat from both the excesses of DADA and EXPRESSIONISM, and a return to a more conventional figurative art, but retains elements of Dada's bitter condemnation of the First World War and its aftermath. The expression was first coined in 1923 in the publicity material for a collective exhibition to be held in Mannheim. It did not in fact open until 1925, and featured work by Max Beckmann, Otto Dix and George Grosz. Although there are obvious stylistic differences between the artists grouped together under the *Neue Sachlichkeit* label, there are also constants. The influence of the Italian De Chirico's 'metaphysical paintings' of 1910–17 is apparent in the sober depiction of almost empty architectural spaces in which human figures are dwarfed by alien artefacts. Firm lines replace the blur of abstraction and banal, everyday objects are painted with a sobriety that makes them unfamiliar in a way that recalls both the Russian formalist notion of OSTRANENIE and BRECHT'S ALIENATION-EFFECT. For its detractors, *Neue Sachlichkeit* was 'a façade concealing nothing' and a mere simulation of profundity (Kracauer 1930). The movement came to an end in 1933, when the ruling Nazi Party condemned *Neue Sachlichkeit* as a form of ENTARTETE KUNST or degenerate art.

READING: *Neue Sachlichkeit and German Realism of the Twenties* (1979)

neurosis A pathological mental condition in which there are no observable lesions in the neuropsychological system (as there are in, for instance, epilepsy). The patient is normally aware of the morbidity of his or her condition and a neurosis can, unlike a PSYCHOSIS, be treated with the patient's consent. Although a neurosis can have long-term effects, they are rarely incapacitating. In current usage, neurosis is usually understood in the sense in which it is defined by PSYCHOANALYSIS, that is as a condition such as HYSTERIA in which somatic symptoms are an expression of a psychical conflict originating in childhood. Modern psychoanalysis describes patients presenting obsessional, phobic or hysterical symptoms as neurotic.

The word 'neurosis' derives from the Greek term for 'nerve', and it is generally accepted that it was first used in 1792 by the Scottish doctor William Cullen, who made it synonymous with 'nervous disease'. Throughout most of the nineteenth century, both neurosis and hysteria were thought of as specifically female conditions or aspects of 'the female malady' (Showalter 1985a). FREUD inherits from nineteenth-century German and French psychiatry the crucial distinction between neurosis and psychosis, describing neurosis as the outcome of a conflict between the EGO and the ID, and psychosis as the outcome of a disturbance in the relationship between the ego and the outside world (Freud 1924c, 1924d). A further distinction is made between actual neuroses, which stem from problems at the somatic level of sexuality, and psychoneuroses, in which mental conflict is the determinant factor. A neurosis such as hysteria originates in the ego's refusal to accept an impulse or desire that comes from the id, and in the attempt to repress that impulse. Neurotic symptoms are the expression of the compromise that is reached by the ego and the id; a psychical conflict has been translated into physical symptoms which Freud describes as the result of an act of repression that has failed. The symptoms usually relate to sexualized memories or fantasies that are unacceptable to the ego; the sore throat and nervous cough that plague Freud's patient 'Dora' are, for example, expressions of her unconscious fantasies about fellatio (Freud 1905c).

For Freud, the distinction between normal and neurotic life is quantitative and not qualitative, and neurosis is therefore a curable condition (1900). For LACAN, the absence of any structural distinction between normality and neurosis means that neurosis is a permanent structure resulting from the splitting of the SUBJECT (1981). The goal of psychoanalytic treatment is therefore not the restoration of a supposed normality, but the repositioning of the subject with respect to an inescapable condition. In Lacan's view, the hysteric is constantly asking basic questions about sexual identity; in her dreams Dora is asking: 'What does it mean to be a woman?'

READING: Ellenberger (1970); Laplanche and Pontalis (1967); Veith (1965)

New Criticism The term, borrowed from the title of John Crowe Ransom's major essay on poetry (1941), applies to the dominant tendency within American literary criticism in the 1930s and 1940s. The main figures associated with the New Criticism, which, whilst vastly influential, was not really cohesive enough to be described as a 'school', were Ransom (1888–1974), Cleanth Brooks (1906–94), Kenneth Burke (1897–1973), Allen Tate (1899–1979) and William Kurtz Wimsatt (1907–75).

The New Criticism was largely a reaction to the historical-philological approach to literature that was dominant in American universities in the first decades of the century and, as in the case of RICHARDS and EMPSON with their characteristic emphasis on the close reading of individual texts, its main concern was to establish the irreducibility of the literary text, and particularly the poem. The poem is treated as a self-contained and self-sustaining unit of meaning which does not have to be explained in terms of its author's personality or biography, or in terms of historical and social factors. The task of the critic is therefore to make 'the closest possible examination of what the poem says as poem' (Brooks 1947). Such close examinations preclude the possibility of paraphrase; the New Critics are scathing about the 'common-sense' view that a poem contains a 'prose meaning' that can be extracted or paraphrased. Brooks, for instance, is highly critical of Empson's insistence on trying to extract a latent political meaning from Gray's *Elegy Written in a Country Churchyard* and sternly denounces 'the heresy of paraphrase'. For their part, Wimsatt and Beardsley warn critics of the dangers of the AFFECTIVE FALLACY and the INTEN-TIONAL FALLACY in two essays (1954a, 1954b) that guard the approaches to Wimsatt's *The Verbal Icon* (1954) like forbidding watchdogs.

In *Modern Poetry and the Tradition* (1939), Cleanth Brooks speaks of the need for 'a critical revolution of the order of the Romantic Revolt'. Such a revolt is necessary because of the 'difficulty' of modern poets such as Yeats, Eliot, Auden, Frost and MacLeish, but it also corresponds to the needs of a generation that was rediscovering John Donne and the Metaphysical Poets as well as Pope and Dryden. The frequency with which the moderns rely on shifts of tone, IRONY and indirect rather than direct statement – to use the characteristic terminology of all the New Critics – is an indication of how deeply rooted their work is in a tradition that places such emphasis on 'wit' and 'conceits'. Hence the New Critics' stress upon paradox and, above all, METAPHOR. For Brooks, the language of poetry is the language of paradox; for Wimsatt, metaphor is the structure most characteristic of concentrated poetry. The appreciation of difficult or concentrated poetry is primarily a matter of sympathetic intuition, and the New Criticism is profoundly anti-scientific and opposed to the stasis of scientific language, especially when applied to poetry.

The self-sufficiency ascribed to the poem by the New Criticism is well described by Brooks (1947). The characteristic unity of a poem lies in the unification of the tensions it creates through its use of propositions, metaphors, symbols and paradoxes. The unification that is brought about is not logical, but dramatic and emotive. It relies upon the crucial relationship between each element that makes up the whole; the essential structure relates to the complex of attitudes portrayed in the poem. Two images encapsulate the aesthetics of the New Criticism. For Wimsatt (1954), a verbal composition is supercharged with significance and has the character of a stone statue or porcelain vase. It possesses an iconic solidity which means that it simply *is*. For Brooks, the perfect metaphor for poetry is Keats's 'Grecian Urn' (that 'still unravish'd bride of quietness'); the title of his best-known book alludes both to Keats's urn and the 'storied urn' in Gray's *Elegy Written in a Country Churchyard*.

The usual criticism addressed to the New Criticism is that, as Brooks admits, it relies on the near-tautology which insists that the meaning of the poem is what the poem says as poem. As Christopher Norris has noted (1978), the poem confirms the poetry, whilst the theory confirms the poem by closing it off within its own formal limits. Advocates of a strict LINGUISTIC CRITICISM note that the stress of close reading is somewhat at odds with the terminological vagueness of Brooks's refer-ences to 'shifts of tone' and 'complexes of attitudes'. Others, like SAID, are critical of the New Criticism's 'fierce parochialism' (1983), whilst FRYE complains that it denies the importance of documentary criticism and pays too little attention to GENRE (1971). Whilst the New Criticism can look very introverted, its defenders argue that its close attention to language offers a defence against the 'spiritual gangrene' that may spread from the 'dying flesh of language' in a mass consumer society (Brooks 1971).

The French term *la nouvelle critique* (which can be translated as 'new criticism') was often applied to the STRUCTURALISM of BARTHES and others in the 1960s (Picard 1965; Doubrovsky 1966).

READING: Brooks (1963); Burke (1966); Lee (1970); Ransom (1955); Tate (1958); Wellek (1986)

New German Critique An interdisciplinary journal of German studies published quarterly since 1973 by the University of Wisconsin-Milwaukee. A product of the NEW LEFT, the journal was originally an expression of a critical but sympathetic stance towards the then German Democratic Republic, whose culture and literature was often neglected by the German departments of British and American universities. It has developed into one of the major journals in its field; the special issues on BENJAMIN, KRACAUER and others are important works of reference.

new historicism A style of literary analysis developed mainly in the United States from the 1980s onwards which challenges the dominance of DECONSTRUCTION and the legacy of NEW CRITICISM by attempting to produce a 'cultural poetics' and reintroducing a historical dimension to literary studies. It is often seen as the American equivalent to the CULTURAL MATERIALISM of Raymond WILLIAMS, as further developed by Dollimore and Sinfield's collection of essays on 'political Shakespeare' (1985). There is a certain overlap between new historicism and QUEER theory. The expression 'new historicism' is generally accepted as having been coined by Stephen Greenblatt in his preface to an important collection of essays on English Renaissance literature (1982), and Renaissance and Shakespeare studies are its privileged field of application (Greenblatt 1980; Tennenhouse 1986), whilst journals like *Representations, New Literary History* and *English Literary History* are its main institutional supports. Greenblatt initially defined new historicism as the study of the collective making of cultural practices and an inquiry into the relations among those practices.

New historicism might be more accurately described as a set of preoccupations rather than a fully fledged theory. Influences range from FOUCAULT to GEERTZ'S notion of THICK DESCRIPTION and the METAHISTORY of Hayden WHITE, as well as strands within WESTERN MARXISM. The invocation of a historical framework does not mark a return to the traditional view that history is a stable or unified body of facts or a neutral 'background' to the literary text; it is a constituent part of both the 'facts' and the 'text'. Montrose, for example (1989), speaks of 'the historicity of texts and the textuality of history' (cf. Montrose 1986). The general assumptions that reappear throughout the various forms of new historicism have been conveniently summarized by Veeser in his key anthology (1989). All expressive acts are embedded in a network of material practices which means that literary and non-literary texts circulate inseparably and penetrate one another. No DISCOURSE gives access to unchanging truths or to an inalterable human nature. Every act of criticism and opposition necessarily employs the tools it is criticizing; as White puts it, history itself is a text made up of TROPES, and it is inescapable. Finally, a critical method that describes cultural production in a capitalist society is part of the economy it describes.

new left Although the term is often associated with the widespread student revolts of the late 1960s (see, for example, Caute 1988), the founding editor of *NEW LEFT REVIEW* notes that it dates back to the 1950s and is a translation of the French *la nouvelle gauche*, which was applied to the independent socialists associated with *France-Observateur* (the forerunner of the weekly *Le Nouvel Observateur*) who were critical of both Stalinism and conventional social democracy (Hall 1989).

In Britain it is common to make a somewhat sweeping distinction between a 'first' new left which emerged in 1956 when communist dissidents, including prominent members of the COMMUNIST PARTY HISTORIANS' GROUP, left the Party in protest at the Soviet invasion of Hungary, and a 'second' new left associated with Perry ANDERSON and the editorial board that took over *New Left Review* in 1962. Whereas the first new left, whose members included E. P. THOMPSON, Raymond WILLIAMS and Stuart HALL, took a broadly culturalist view influenced by HOGGART and a socialist reading of LEAVIS, the second generation was more oriented towards WESTERN MARXISM and at times very critical of Thompson's defence of a quintessentially English tradition of radicalism (Anderson 1980). Both generations were critical of the Western Communist parties and of the institutional politics of the British Labour Party, particularly when its leadership supported American intervention in Vietnam, and had links with the Campaign for Nuclear Disarmament and a wide variety of social movements.

Although the new left has been enormously influential, and although the first generation in effect set the agenda for British CULTURAL STUDIES, it never succeeded in transforming a sophisticated intellectual culture into a political organization. As a result, it could not really survive the economic crises of the 1970s. The weaknesses of the new left included a lack of concern with the natural sciences and a surprising lack of serious interest in economics. It is widely accepted that the underrepresentation of women in the new left was a major factor in the emergence of the WOMEN'S LIBERATION movement in the early 1970s.

READING: Archer et al. (1989); Lin Chun (1993).

New Left Review British political journal, published on a bi-monthly basis since 1960. Originally edited by Stuart HALL, *New Left Review* emerged from the crises within the British communist movement after the Soviet invasion of 1956 and the revelation that forced-labour camps did indeed exist in the Soviet Union (Khrushchev 1956). As the title indicates, it was founded as the flagship of the British NEW LEFT and was dedicated to the creation of a humane and democratic socialism. Early contributors included Raymond WILLIAMS and E. P. THOMPSON. *New Left Review* has been dogged by political splits and quarrels throughout its history. These began in

1962, when Perry Anderson became editor and when the journal became more oriented towards the philosophical tradition of WESTERN MARXISM. The result was a bitter quarrel over the so-called Nairn-ANDERSON Theses (Nairn 1964; Anderson 1964, 1966, 1968a) which, to the dismay of Thompson (1965), rejected the weak version of EMPIRICISM in the name of what came to be known simply as THEORY. After 1968 the Leninist-Trotskyist positions adopted by the editorial board led to the frequent accusations that they were acting as the leaders of an embryonic but dogmatic political party and not as the editors of a journal. In the early 1990s the editorial committee was greatly expanded, partly in order to achieve a better generational and gender balance in an aging organization in which women have always been unrepresented. When in 1992 control was handed to a new shareholders' trust, the majority of the committee resigned in protest (Wright 1993).

New Left Review and the associated publishing house of New Left Books (launched in 1970, and subsequently relaunched as Verso) have played an immensely important role in making continental authors such as ALTHUSSER and GRAMSCI available in English translation. Verso's more recent editorial policy has become much more open and less confined to the classic tradition of Western Marxism as a result of the decision to publish the work of postmodernists such as BAUDRILLARD and Slavoj Zizek (1989).

READING: Lin Chun (1993)

New Philosophers   The *nouveaux philosophes* were a group of young French philosophers whose criticisms of MARXISM and socialism attracted much attention in the mid-1970s. The most conspicuous members of the loosely-knit group were Bernard-Henri Lévy (1948–) and André Glucksmann (1937–); most had been involved in the student revolt of May 1968 or had been associated with the militant Maoism of the early 1970s. Influenced both by the fragmentation and decay of French leftism (see Khilnani 1993) and by the appearance in 1974 of a French translation of Solzhenitsyn's *The Gulag Archipelago*, they argued (Lévy 1977; Glucksmann 1975, 1977) that the totalitarianism of the gulag's labour camps was the ultimate truth of the entire Hegelian-Marxist tradition. The New Philosophers were widely criticized for the facile nature of their arguments and for their manipulation of the media for self-promotion (Dews 1980).

Newspeak   The official language of Oceania, the totalitarian state described by George Orwell in his dystopian novel *Nineteen Eighty-Four* (1949); its principles are outlined in the appendix to the novel. Designed to meet the needs of Ingsoc or English Socialism and to supersede Oldspeak (Standard English), Newspeak is also intended to make it impossible to think outside the IDEOLOGY it promotes. The language is a simplified English which makes extensive use of OXYMORON, as in the famous slogans 'War is peace', 'Freedom is slavery' and 'Ignorance is strength'.

'Newspeak' is widely used as a disparaging way of describing official pronouncements or propaganda. A good example of real Newspeak is the remark attributed to a US military spokesman during the Vietnam war: 'In order to save the village, it was necessary to destroy it.'

Ngugi wa Thiong'o (1938–) Kenyan novelist, playwright and critic. His best-known novel is *Petals of Blood* (1977), which traces the evolution of a small town from precolonial self-sufficiency to a source of cheap labour in the colonial period and then a postcolonial boom town in which people are worse off than ever. Ngugi's reflections on the novel and drama, and on the language issue in newly independent countries, make him an important reference in POSTCOLONIAL THEORY and in criticisms of the notion of COMMONWEALTH LITERATURE.

For Ngugi, colonialism was a matter of cultural violence as well as physical violence; the night of military conquest was followed by the morning of the psychological violence of the classroom that colonized the mind. Language, or the imposition of the English language, was a means of spiritual subjugation. The struggle against colonialism is therefore also a struggle to decolonize the mind, and that struggle continues long after formal independence has been attained, not least because postcolonial elites follow the example set by English colonizers in downgrading and marginalizing vernacular languages. Ngugi first wrote in English, but soon became critical of what he calls the Afro-European novel (typified by the titles published in Heinemann's 'African Writers' series) on the grounds that it had failed to revitalize the African tradition. In 1968 Ngugi called for the abolition of Nairobi University's English Department, asking why African literature should not be at the centre and rejecting the primacy accorded to English literature and culture. This call was not indicative of a narrow cultural nationalism; on the contrary, Ngugi stressed the need for a compulsory knowledge of Swahili, English and French.

In 1976 Ngugi's concern with the creation of a popular national culture led to his deep involvement in a rural drama project which attempted to reconnect with the broken roots of African civilization and its traditional theatre by producing plays dealing with the role played by the people, 'the true makers of history'. It was this experience, and the realization that a truly African theatre cannot use English, that led him to write in Gikuyu, a decision that he describes as 'an epistemological break' with his past (1984a). Written in Gikuyu in 1980, *Devil on the Cross* returns to the oral tradition of story-telling and actually became part of that tradition. Difficulties in distributing the novel in rural areas were overcome by developing a network of professional readers who read it aloud in bars and were encouraged to go on reading by being bought beer (see Ngugi 1984a).

The community theatre centre at which Ngugi worked was destroyed by the Kenyan government in 1982. Ngugi was detained without trial in 1978 and has lived in exile since the publication of *Detained: A Writer's Prison Diary* (1981).

READING: Cook and Okenimkpe (1997)

Nietzsche, Friedrich (1844–1900) German philosopher. Few figures in the history of modern thought are more ambiguous than Nietzsche, whose work has been interpreted in an astonishing number of different ways. His name has been associated with German militarism and the ideology of Nazism, even though he himself speaks frequently of the 'lunacy of nationality' and is scathing about German culture. The association with Nazism, from which Nietzsche has been rehabilitated by Walter Kaufman, who is one of his main translators (Kaufman 1950), is widely viewed as having been promoted by his sister Elizabeth Förster, whose tendentious contributions to early editions of the posthumously published *Will to Power* (1901) were conducive to a pro-Nazi and anti-Semitic reading. Nietzsche continues to be invoked in very different ways. For the conservative Allan BLOOM, his description of the decadent society of 'last men' in which 'Everyone wants the same thing, everyone is the same' (Nietzsche 1892) is a fitting comment on the state of universities that have been distracted from their true vocation by calls for democracy and affirmative action (Bloom 1987). Yet the Nietzsche who contends that there are no facts, but only interpretations (1901) has become the patron saint of DECONSTRUC-TION and contemporary HERMENEUTICS, as well as a powerful influence on DELEUZE, FOUCAULT and DERRIDA, who praises him for his mistrust of metaphysics and values and for his ability to deconstruct the history of philosophy by asking it rhetorical and philological questions (Derrida 1972a). These are the very trends and figures that are denounced by Bloom.

Nietzsche's academic background was not in philosophy but in classical PHILOLOGY, and his first book (1872) is a study of the origins and decline of Greek tragedy. Although conventional in form, it anticipates the concerns of the later works by proposing to 'take down' the elaborate edifice of Apollonian culture and to show that the apparent sense of order of the Greeks is based on a tension between the Apollonian stress on order and individuation, and the Dionysiac rapture, violence and destruction of individuality that underlies it. Far from reflecting an inner sense of order and calm, Greek culture is based upon a SUBLIMATION of an awareness of the horrors of existence; it is the sublimation of fear and violence that creates the bright pantheon of gods.

In the *Untimely Meditations* of 1874, Nietzsche continues to use the conventional essay form, but in *Human, All Too Human* (1878) he begins to perfect the aphoristic style that makes his later works both so attractive and so deceptively easy to read but so difficult to summarize. It is clear from this transitional text that the pithy style – 'The will to overcome an emotion is ultimately only the will of another emotion or of several others' (1886) – owes much to the French moralist La Rochefoucauld (1613–80), in whose view 'The heart has reasons of which reason knows nothing.' The use of highly polished aphorisms, many of which are reworked and used in different contexts, is basic to Nietzsche's inversion of values and especially to his onslaughts on the 'prejudices of philosophers' in *Beyond Good and Evil* (1886). Here he demonstrates that it is not the 'I' that thinks: a thought comes when 'it' wants, not when I think. (*Das Id* is the origin of FREUD's ID.) Elsewhere Nietzsche contends that the 'subject I' is not the condition of the predicate of 'thinks', but rather its effect; the I is the effect of thought and not its cause (1901). It is this strategy of inversion or reversal which, as Ricoeur has pointed out (1990), exploits the rhetorical properties of METALEPSIS that so recommends Nietzsche to deconstructionists like Derrida and DE MAN. The strategy is consistent with Nietzsche's use of etymological and philological methods to 'take down' edifices like Apollonian culture and conventional values by demonstrating their inconsistencies.

Although much of Nietzsche's work consists of the criticism of prevailing views – he describes this as philosophizing with a hammer – it does also contain a systematic body of thought. In *The Genealogy of Morals* (1887) he remarks that the 'human polity' began with a 'pack of savages' and a 'race of conquerors', and his world-view is characterized by its stress on the conflict between the two groups. The conflict is an expression of the will to power, as life itself is a struggle in which instinctual drives strive for their continued survival and for power over other drives. The notion that the will is a creative source of values derives in part from Arthur Schopenhauer's *The World as Will and Idea* (1818), which greatly influenced the young Nietzsche before he became critical of Schopenhauer's unrelieved pessimism. The world itself is 'a monster of energy, without beginning and without end, a sea of forces' (1901). Any individual, creature or force that loses the will to power lapses into decadence, but 'power' is not an object to be possessed. It is, rather, a permanently contested balance of power and forces; here Nietzsche provides the basis for FOUCAULT's theses on the nature of power. The conflict between savages and conquerors, or slaves and masters, gives rise to equally conflicting values. A 'master morality' is generated by dominant groups which have acquired power and project their own values as 'the good'. In projecting their own sense of the good, they eventually come to see dominated groups as 'bad' rather than simply as inferior. Conversely, dominated groups see themselves as helpless victims, lose their potential will to power, and come to regard the values of masters as 'evil'. The ultimate example of the slave morality is, in Nietzsche's eyes, the Christian religion. The evil master morality comes to be viewed as the cause of the slave's helplessness, rather than as an effect of the slave's situation; once more, the cause is mistaken for the effect as the 'doer' is added to the 'deed' by the imagination (1887). Conceptions of morality do not originate in abstract notions of good and evil, but in the impersonal structures of power that impose standards in the name of the will to power.

In his earlier writings, Nietzsche speaks in very positive terms of the 'free spirits' who defy convention and its imposed values (1878) and thus acquire a joyful or gay wisdom (*fröhliche Wissenschaft*). In his later writings they become the 'superman' or higher man (*Übermensch*) who is celebrated in the most extraordinary of all Nietzsche's works. *Thus Spoke Zarathustra* (1892) is a combination of lyrical poetry and philosophical speculation that heralds the transformation and enhancement of man by a figure who will be to man what man is to the apes. Nietzsche proclaims the death of God and the demise of the Christian slave morality; the death of God also announces the 'overcoming' of man and the appearance of higher men who, possessed by their joyful wisdom, will at last learn to laugh and to overcome the decadence and NIHILISM of European culture.

nihilism Derived from the Latin *nihil*, the term literally means 'belief in nothing' or a refusal to believe in any values, and particularly ethical values. It derives from Ivan Turgenev's characterization of the younger generation of Russian intellectuals of the mid-nineteenth century in his novel *Fathers and Sons* (1861). The protagonist Bazarov is described as a nihilist, 'a person who does not take any principle for granted, however much that principle may be revered'. NIETZSCHE is often said to be a nihilist, but the opening section of *The Will to Power* (1901), which describes the nihilism that stands at the door like the 'uncanniest of all guests', is in fact a plea for the overcoming of nihilism and for the adoption of the new values of the superman.

Nochlin, Linda (1931–) American art historian and critic, specializing in nineteenth-century European art. Her major study of realism in the visual arts (1971a) examines the political upheavals of mid-nineteenth-century Europe and the related desire for democracy in art that led to the rise of a new and contemporary style of realism in the art of Courbet, Degas, Manet and other European and American realists. Her many articles (collected 1989, 1991) deal with related issues, but concentrate primarily on the representation of women. Her frequent examinations of the representation of work and leisure in Impressionist painting are particularly fine.

Nochlin's 'Why Have There Been No Great Women Artists?' (1971b) is widely regarded as one of the pioneering studies to apply the principles of an emergent FEMINIST CRITICISM to the visual arts. Like Griselda Pollock (1988), Nochlin regards the search for undiscovered or forgotten women artists (Nochlin and Harris 1976) as an important aspect of the feminist intervention into art history, but concedes that it is only a starting-point. Whereas standard histories of modern art concentrate on form and a heroic sequence of AVANT-GARDES (see Pollock 1998), feminist criticism must examine the social forces and ideologies that create the woman artist and assign her a specific position in the artistic hierarchy. There are, for instance, no great women history painters quite simply because throughout the nineteenth century women were excluded from the nude life class which provided the essential apprenticeship in figure painting. Women became flower painters and painters of mother and child portraits not because of some innate femininity, but because the artistic equivalent of FRIEDAN's feminine mystique confined them to such minor GENRES. Here Nochlin's crucial essay anticipates Parker and Pollock's study (1981) of how embroidery, once regarded as an important art form, was reduced to the status of a minor women's craft thanks to the workings of the IDEOLOGY that redefined women's social roles.

normal science The activity characteristic of those long periods in the history of a science when research is based upon past achievements that are accepted by a scientific community as supplying the foundations for their future practice (Kuhn 1962). In such periods scientists can take for granted the PARADIGMs that govern their normal science, and do not have to start from first principles in order to justify the use of every concept they invoke. The description and justification of first principles are tasks for the writers of textbooks.

Periods of normal science are punctuated by the recognition of anomalies that cannot be explained by the existing paradigms, and by crises culminating in the scientific revolutions brought about by paradigm shifts.

nouveau roman French phrase meaning 'new novel', and used as a generic description of a loose grouping of novelists who came to prominence in the 1950s, even though certain of them had, like Nathalie Sarraute, first been published before the Second World War (*The Age of Suspicion*, 1939). The most prominent are Alain

Robbe-Grillet (*The Erasers*, 1953), Claude Simon (*The Word*, 1957) and Michel Butor (*Passing Time*, 1957).

The term *le nouveau roman* was first used in a special issue of the monthly *Esprit* in July–August 1958, and helped to create the impression that these very different authors were embarked upon a joint project. The polemical essays collected in Robbe-Grillet's *Towards a New Novel* (1963) helped to strengthen that impression, even though it was clear that his was a very individual voice. As most of the 'new novelists' were published by Éditions de Minuit ('Midnight Editions'), reference was also made to a so-called Minuit School; the first serious discussion in English described the new novelists as 'Midnight Novelists' (*Yale French Studies* 1959).

The essays published in *Esprit* in 1958 define the *nouveau roman* in almost purely negative terms. The authors concerned are described as rejecting traditional forms of narration and as degrading human beings. Their impersonal style and concentration of description (best exemplified by Robbe-Grillet's hypnotic description of physical objects) and the almost complete absence of traditional characters and psychology led to accusations of formalism and aridity. *Esprit* thus establishes the criteria that allow Marxist critics like GOLDMANN to claim that the new novel is a product of ALIENATION and a reflection of the impersonality of the consumer society. The alternative view is that the *nouveau roman* introduces a self-conscious and sophisticated practice of writing which explores and reveals the formal devices inherent in any form of fiction and thus demonstrates the dominant style of realism to be an IDEOLOGY (Heath 1972).

Although it is difficult to generalize or to draw out similarities between Robbe-Grillet's objectivism, Sarraute's exquisitely delicate explorations of the automatic tropisms that subtend conversations, Simon's baroque studies of obsessive memories, and Butor's multiple narratives, some common features do emerge. The rejection of conventional realism, characters and psychology (exemplified by Robbe-Grillet's attacks on the anecdotal nature of Balzacian realism), and the FORE-GROUNDING of devices such as *MISE-EN-ABYME*, point to the artificiality of all narrative activity. The constant reminder that we are reading a linguistic construct, and not a reproduction of events that exist outside or prior to the text, can be a source of considerable intellectual pleasure.

Although it was originally a specifically French phenomenon, the *nouveau roman* clearly has its equivalent in other languages. Obvious examples include CALVINO's *If on a Winter's Night a Traveller* (1979), the fiction of the Algerian novelist Rachid Boudjedra, who adds a political dimension to what is usually seen as an apolitical style (1975), and the work of the British novelist Christine Brooke-Rose, who exploits the ludic and even comic potential of a new practice of writing (see the four novels collected as Brooke-Rose 1986). Viewed in a wider historical perspective, the *nouveau roman* can be seen as a continuation of the long tradition of novels that ironically recount their own genesis or describe the writer's inability to tell the story he is supposed to be narrating. The obvious predecessors include Sterne's *Tristram Shandy*, Diderot's *Jacques le fataliste* and Cervantes's *Don Quixote*.

Nouvelle Vague French term meaning 'new wave', widely applied to any artistic tendency that appears to make a radical break with the past. In the 1950s and 1960s, the Impulse record label used the slogan 'The New Wave of Jazz is on Impulse' to promote the music of Eric Dolphy, Gil Evans, John Coltrane and others.

The expression '*la nouvelle vague*' was first used as the title of an article about a survey of the attitudes and opinions of young French people published in the weekly *L'Express* on 5 December 1957. It was then used by *L'Express*'s Françoise Giroud (1958) as the title of her study of the ALIENATION experienced by the generation born between the two world wars. *La Nouvelle Vague* soon became a generic description of the group of young film directors associated with CAHIERS DU CINÉMA. In 1958–9, Jean-Luc Godard (*Breathless*), Claude Chabrol (*Le Beau Serge* – Handsome Serge), François Truffaut (*The Four Hundred Blows*) and Jacques Rivette (*Paris Belongs to Us*) suddenly emerged as a new generation of independent film-makers, heavily influenced by Hollywood and AUTEUR THEORY, and impatient with the literary and theatrical conventions of the French cinema of the day. In terms of film history, they are still the original *Nouvelle Vague*.

Nouvelle Vague films are characterized by their use of location shooting (facilitated by new and lightweight equipment), fast cutting, and knowing references to and quotations from the entire cinematic tradition, with special reference to the Hollywood 'authors' identified by *Cahiers du cinéma*. With its witty performance as a charming but amoral gangster from Jean-Paul Belmondo and its shots of Jean Seberg selling the *International Herald Tribune* on the Champs-Elysées, Godard's *Breathless* is the archetypal *Nouvelle Vague* film.

READING: *Cahiers du cinéma* (1985); Graham (1968)

O

object The term is employed in PSYCHOANALYSIS in the sense in which one speaks of the object of someone's affection or attentions. No distinction is made between persons and inanimate things: individuals, parts of the body and the satisfaction of needs can all be objects. It is the theory of objects that provides the intellectual basis for the OBJECT-RELATIONS school of psychoanalysis.

The notion of an object originates in FREUD's discussion of the DRIVES (1905a), where 'object' is defined as that which allows a drive to achieve its aim. The sexual object of a drive may, for instance, be a person; its aim, or the act towards which the drive tends, may be sexual intercourse with that person (1915a). The object of a drive is contingent and is not defined by any natural or predetermined purpose; sexual object-choice is determined by the individual's life-history, and primarily by experiences in childhood.

It is clear from Freud's account, and especially from his remarks on FETISHISM (1927c), that the object of a drive is not necessarily a whole person and that it may be a part of the body or part-object, such as the penis or the breast. Although Karl Abraham speaks of 'partial incorporation of the object' and of 'partial object-love' (1924), it is KLEIN who really develops the theory of part-objects. Part-objects are essential features of the fantasy world constructed by the child, and are endowed with 'good' and 'bad' qualities thanks to the mechanism of PROJECTION. Projecting the AMBIVALENCE it feels towards its mother, a child typically fantasizes the existence of a good breast which offers comfort and nourishment, and a bad breast which denies or withdraws the instinctual satisfaction it seeks (Klein 1935, 1936).

object relations Generally used in PSYCHOANALYSIS to refer to the individual's interaction with the OBJECTs and part-objects that constitute his or her environment. Object-relations theory attempts to avoid FREUD's tendency to speak of the subject in isolation and to introduce an interpersonal dimension into psychoanalysis. The so-called 'object-relations school' is the majority tendency within British psychoanalysis (Kohon 1986; Rayner 1991). Strongly influenced by KLEIN, WINNICOTT and Michael Balint (1952), as well as by ANNA FREUD, it gives primary importance to the early relationship between mother and child rather than the father-child relationship that is so important in Freud's own writings, and has helped to produce a 'mother-centred psychoanalysis' (Sayers 1991). Object-relations analysts use a number of different approaches and, whilst they share similar conceptions, do not really subscribe to a fixed body of theoretical principles. In historical terms, the group, sometimes described as the INDEPENDENT GROUP, developed out of the need to find a working compromise between the followers of Anna Freud and those of Klein.

objet (petit) a Although the term could obviously be translated as 'object (small) a', it is normally left in the French at LACAN's insistence. He argues that it thus acquires 'the status of an algebraic sign' (see the translator's note to Lacan 1977). This is an early instance of Lacan's tendency, especially in his later writings, to use quasi-algebraic signs or 'MATHEMES'. This FORMALIZATION is intended to guarantee the 'integral transmission' of psychoanalytic theory.

The concept of *objet (petit) a* derives from FREUD's theory of the OBJECT and from Lacan's own meditations on the theme of the OTHER; there are some similarities between it and both KLEIN's part-objects and WINNICOTT's transitional object. The '*a*' stands for '*autre*' ('other'), and the use of the lower case marks the distinction between this object and the 'Big Other' symbolized by the capital *A[utre]*. Unlike the 'Big Other', *object (petit) a* exists within a relationship with the EGO and is described as belonging to the order of the IMAGINARY. The earliest references to '*a*' appear in the 1950s, and it initially designates the ego, with '*a*' designating the specular image of the MIRROR-PHASE and '*A*' the unconscious or the discourse of the Other (Lacan 1957–8). '*a*' is imagined by the SUBJECT to be an object that can be separated from the body in such a way as to take on an existence of its own. From the 1960s onwards, *objet (petit) a* comes to mean an object of DESIRE that can never actually be attained. To that extent, it can be viewed as the cause of desire rather than a concrete object that is actually sought by the DRIVES. Lacan later describes it (1973) as an 'object-cause', defined as any object of desire that sets the drives in motion. It can be a source of anxiety as well as a promise of pleasure. Rather than seeking to attain or possess it, the drives endlessly circle around it.

READING: Green (1966)

Oedipus complex One of the cornerstones of the theory of PSYCHOANALYSIS, the idea of the Oedipus complex derives from the Greek legend that tells how Oedipus unwittingly killed his father Laius and married his mother Jocasta. When he finally learns what he has done, he blinds himself. The existence of the Oedipus complex explains the child's sexual attraction towards the parent of the opposite sex and jealousy of the parent of the same sex. Although the Oedipus complex is absolutely central to FREUD's theory of human development, no one paper is devoted to it. In Lacanian terms (LACAN), the Oedipus complex marks the transition from a dual and potentially incestuous relationship with the mother to a triadic relationship in which the role and authority of the father or the NAME-OF-THE-FATHER are recognized. Failure to negotiate this transition is held by all schools of psychoanalysis to be the primary cause of NEUROSIS. Freudians normally date the Oedipus complex to the ages of three to five years; according to KLEIN, it occurs much earlier.

References to the Oedipus story can be found in some of Freud's earliest writings.

In a letter to Fliess dated 17 October 1897, he remarks that Sophocles's *Oedipus Rex* has such 'gripping power' because being in love with one's mother and jealous of one's father is 'a universal event in early childhood' (Freud 1985), but the canonical expression 'the Oedipus complex' is not used until 1910 (1910c). It initially refers to the boy's perception of his mother as a sexual OBJECT and of his father as a rival, but Freud's description of this 'universal phenomenon' becomes more complicated as he integrates the findings of his studies of the 'sexual theories of children' (1908a). These theories are attempts to explain the phenomenon of sexual difference, and assume the existence of a primal state in which only maleness exists; the fact that a girl does not have male genitals is therefore the result of her castration (1923b), castration being an equivalent to the blinding of Oedipus. A girl may believe that she has been castrated by a jealous mother who resents her sexual feelings for her father, whilst the boy fears that he might be castrated by a jealous father. As he comes both to accept the reality of that threat and to identify with his father, the Oedipus complex begins to dissolve. For the girl, matters are more difficult. The dissolution of her Oedipus complex requires her to adopt a 'feminine attitude' towards her father, and to displace her desire to regain the penis she has lost onto the desire to have a baby (1924b).

Although Lacan follows Freud in making the Oedipus complex the crucial moment in human development, he modifies the concept in a number of ways, both by introducing the idea of a symbolic PHALLUS which is distinct from the biological penis, and by mapping it onto the transition from nature to culture described by LÉVI-STRAUSS. A successful negotiation of the Oedipal triangle is a precondition for entry into the human SYMBOLIC order.

OPOYAZ Russian acronym standing for *Obshchevsto po izucheniyu poeticheskogo yazyka* (Society for the Study of Poetic Language). Founded in 1916 in St Petersburg (then Petrograd), OPOYAZ, together with the MOSCOW LINGUISTIC CIRCLE, was the main centre for the development of RUSSIAN FORMALISM and was closely associated with FUTURISM. Its main members were Viktor SHKLOVSKY, L. Yakubinsky and E. Polivanov and it was chaired by the poet Osip Brik. Whereas the Moscow Linguistic Circle consisted mainly of linguisticians, OPOYAZ brought together literary historians, folklorists and poets who were united by the conviction that the study of literature must be based upon the close analysis of texts, particularly at the phonetic level, and on the systematic description of literary facts. In 1923 OPOYAZ disbanded and merged with the Moscow Linguistic Circle.

READING: Erlich (1965); Shklovsky (1940)

ordinary language philosophy An important strand within British ANALYTIC PHILOSOPHY, associated mainly with AUSTIN and to some degree WITTGENSTEIN, and a good example of the results of the LINGUISTIC TURN. It is sometimes referred to as 'linguistic philosophy', but has little to do with linguistics in the conventional or technical sense.

The underlying argument is that, unlike the sciences, philosophy has no real subject-matter of its own except in the sense that its subject-matter consists of the propositions it advances. Many of the problems of philosophy stem not from epistemology, but from misunderstandings about or misuse of language. Ordinary language, according to Austin (1962a, 1962b), is much richer and much subtler than philosophers have realized, and a careful examination of the wealth of meanings it contains is therefore a precondition for any philosophical thinking. Whereas philosophers often proceed on the assumption that they can simply assign meanings to words, they should begin by examining their actual meaning. A sharpened awareness of the meaning of words will result in a sharpened, but not complete, awareness of phenomena. SEARLE, for example, argues (1969) that 'troublesome' concepts such as knowledge or memory can be analysed by looking carefully at how the words are actually used.

Although the careful dissection of meaning recommended by Austin can be a source of clarification, critics argue that the 'ordinary language' argument is a trivialization of philosophy. One of its most trenchant critics contends (Gellner 1959) that it relies upon the argument from impotence: 'What else – other than the study of words and our uses of them – *could* philosophy be?'

READING: Chappell (1964); Hacker (1996a)

organic intellectual In the short section of his *Prison Notebooks* (1971) devoted to the formation of intellectuals, GRAMSCI notes that all men are intellectuals in the sense that all human activity involves at least some creative and intellectual activity, but immediately adds that not all men have the social function of intellectuals. It is therefore an error to concentrate on the intrinsic nature of intellectual activity rather than on the system of relations that permit intellectual activity. Gramsci then goes on to outline a typology of 'traditional' and 'organic' intellectuals. Traditional intellectuals, such as priests, teachers and administrators, can be likened to subaltern officers in an army; they articulate the relationship between their superiors and the rank and file, but have no innovative or creative role and repeat their tasks over and over again. Organic intellectuals, in contrast, are directly related to the rising classes or groups which use them to innovate and to establish a new HEGEMONY. The capitalist entrepreneur, that is, creates the industrial technician, the specialist in political economy and the designer of the new legal system. Every fundamental social group or class has its stratum of organic intellectuals, and the role of the state or party representing that group is to weld organic and traditional intellectuals together so as to form a hegemonic bloc. Gramsci's distinction between organic and traditional intellectuals parallels his distinction between urban and rural society, and he speculates that the increasing role played by science and technology in an increasingly complex society will create a new type of organic intellectuals. These remarks have often been interpreted (by, for instance, Said 1994) as foreshadowing the increasingly important role of the knowledge industries in the late twentieth century, when the production and administration of knowledge became at least as important as the physical production of commodities.

Orientalism In its most general sense, Orientalism can be defined as the academic discipline that studies the languages and culture of the Orient, usually understood as meaning the Islamic countries of the Near and Middle East. The term has come to be associated mainly with the work of Edward W. SAID, whose *Orientalism* (1978) is one of the founding texts of POSTCOLONIAL THEORY.

Orientalism is analysed by Said in terms reminiscent of FOUCAULT as a DISCURSIVE FORMATION originating in the work of British and French scholars from the late eighteenth century onwards. The development of Orientalism both coincides with and justifies the expansion of European colonialism, and studies of the languages, anthropology, geography and religions of the Orient combine to form a system of knowledge or a grid that filters the East into the consciousness of the West. Orientalism is predicated upon an unquestioned belief in Western superiority and upon the conviction that, as the East cannot understand itself, the West must interpret it for both East and West. It is therefore a project designed to produce what GRAMSCI terms a HEGEMONY, or a Western mode of thought which can dominate, structure and have authority over the East. This is a system of representations forced upon the East by a set of references that deny it any history, culture or identity of its own, and that inscribe it within Western ideological constructs. The master text of French Orientalism is provided by the twenty-three volumes of the *Description de l'Égypte* produced by the scholars and scientists who accompanied Napoleon's army on the unsuccessful Egyptian expedition of 1793. Their exhaustive studies and surveys of the country indicate an almost intuitive realization that military conquest alone does not guarantee dominance; it must be consolidated by knowledge, which is in itself a form of power.

The almost mythical Orient constructed by Orientalism is a geographical space populated by individuals and races who display essentialist characteristics and behavioural patterns that can be explained in terms of such notions as 'the Arab mind' or 'Muslim culture'. Said's study of Orientalism is no exercise in neutral historiogaphy. He argues convincingly that both commonplace racist stereotypes and policy-making decisions assume the existence of an 'Arab psychology' or 'Arab mentality' and are still influenced by the discourse of Orientalism.

In art history, 'Orientalism' refers to a school of nineteenth-century French painting associated mainly with Jean Léon Gérôme (1824–1904) and Eugène Delacroix (1798–1863). The key work is the latter's *Women of Algiers in their Apartment* (1833, Musée du Louvre, Paris), which depicts a group of women in a luxuriously furnished harem; for the white male artist, the fascination of the subject is that he has the privilege of gazing for the first time at unveiled Algerian women who normally live in seclusion. Delacroix's brief visit to Algiers took place in 1832, or two years after the beginning of the French conquest of Algeria. The careful depiction of the rich fabrics in the room recalls the imagery of the sado-erotic *Death of Sardanapalus* (1827–8, Musée du Louvre, Paris), which was painted before the Algiers trip; the women of Algiers are inscribed in a preexisting dream of the Orient. Said does not discuss Orientalist painting; see Nochlin's comments in 'The Imaginary Orient' (in Nochlin 1991) and the Algerian novelist Assia Djebar's discussion of Delacroix (1980).

READING: Stevens (1984)

Orwell, George (1903–50) Pseudonym of Eric Blair, British cultural critic and novelist.

Orwell is something of a paradox. Although disillusioned with organized social-ism by his experiences in the Spanish Civil War (1938), he remained a socialist in a sense but was always scathing about bearded, sandal-wearing socialists, and is perhaps best remembered for his *Animal Farm* (1945), which uses the old convention of an ALLEGORY, with animals representing humans, to satirize Stalinism. His numerous essays include the celebrated readings of boys' magazines (1939), English leisure occupations ('The Lion and the Unicorn', 1941) and the 'saucy' postcards of Donald McGill (1942; such postcards are still part of the British seaside experience), which might be compared with HOGGART's sympathetic analysis of working-class culture. They are part of a tradition of investigating 'what it means to be English' and should be seen as harbingers of what has come to be known as CULTURAL STUDIES. Consciously written in the tradition of Cobbett's *Rural Rides* (1830), but also contesting its optimism, *The Road to Wigan Pier* (1937) is an unforgettable picture of poverty and depression. It has helped to establish a form of reportage which has produced some fine writing on contemporary Britain, such as Danziger's account of his travels in the urban badlands (1996) and Hudson's extraordinary account of a year in a mining village in East Durham (1994). The feminist Beatrix Campbell (1984) is scornful of Orwell's elevation of the miner to heroic status, and scathing about his failure to note that there were more women working in the mills around Wigan than there were men in the mines, but cannot escape the Orwellian model or tone in her account of poverty in the 1980s.

ostranenie The Russian term can be translated as 'making strange' or 'defamiliar-ization', and is an important feature of the poetics of RUSSIAN FORMALISM. It is especially associated with Viktor SHKLOVSKY (1917, 1925).

Ostranenie denotes the poetic use of devices such as disrupted metrical patterns, long descriptive passages, METAPHORS and other figures of RHETORIC to produce a semantic shift which makes the habitual appear strangely unfamiliar, rather as though it were being perceived for the first time. The distortion of form produced by the poetic device destabilizes the relationship between the perceiving subject and the object of perception, slowing down the act of perception and making it more difficult. It thus serves the poetic function of promoting seeing, as opposed to recognizing something that is already familiar and known. Shklovsky (1940) takes the example of Tolstoy's description of dusting his room in his diaries to demon-strate how the writer uses newly discovered words to restore a perception of everyday life by destroying the conventional logic of verbal associations. In doing so, he makes everday life 'more perceptible' and thus underlines the artificiality of his own description.

Although Shklovsky's notion of making strange is intimately bound up with the poetics of formalism and FUTURISM, it is not difficult to relate it to BRECHT's ALIENATION-EFFECT or to the analysis of mythologies undertaken by BARTHES in the 1950s. In all three cases, there is an implicit contrast between the AVANT-GARDE or experimental work of art which challenges received perceptions by forcing the reader or viewer to perceive its formality or artificiality, and the conventional work in which the formal devices are concealed in such a way as to make it appear natural and ahistorical.

READING: Erlich (1965); Sherwood (1973)

other The notion of the other is widely used in a variety of disciplines ranging from philosophy, and especially PHENOMENOLOGY, to PSYCHOANALYSIS and POST-COLONIAL THEORY. Although the meaning of the term varies considerably, it refers, at its most general level, to one pole of the relationship between a SUBJECT and a person or thing defined or constituted as a non-self that is different or other.

Following HUSSERL, both SARTRE (1943a) and MERLEAU-PONTY (1945) see the other as the source of a threat to the autonomy and freedom of the subject or the 'I'. Whilst the subject exists both in-itself and for-itself (IN-ITSELF/FOR-ITSELF), it does not exist in isolation but alongside other subjectivities, and therefore has a third mode of existence, described as 'being-for-others' (*être-pour-autrui*). The classic description of being-for-others is to be found in Sartre's phenomenological account of the GAZE (1943a) with which the other reduces the for-itself existence of the subject to a thing-like in-itself existence, takes away its autonomy and denies it its freedom. For Sartre in particular, the relationship with the other is always conflict-ridden and antagonistic as it is based upon a dialectic in which the only possibilities are being dominated or being dominant. No real solution to this dilemma is offered in *Being and Nothingness* and it is only in his later Marxist writings that Sartre begins to outline a theory of collectivity that breaks with the individualism or even SOLIPSISM of his early work. For LEVINAS, in contrast, the encounter with the other, and more specifically the face of the other, is positive in that, by challenging the subject's feeling of self-assurance and self-containment, it inaugurates the possibility of an ethics. For Levinas, the naked face of the other appeals to the subject in a way that cannot be ignored or forgotten; it is an appeal for the subject to go towards, to welcome and to take responsibility for the other (1961, 1972). In this perspective, the identity of the subject is dependent upon an otherness that is always and already present before the subject is constituted, and it is founded by the ethical demand to take responsibility for the other.

Perhaps the most influential account of the other is that advanced by LACAN and it too originates in a phenomenological tradition. In his enormously influential reading of Hegel's *Phenomenology of Mind*, KOJÈVE (1947) contends that self-consciousness exists only to the extent that it exists for another self-consciousness, and only to the extent that it is recognized by the other as existing. The paradigm for this relationship is the dialectic between the master and the slave, in which both parties strive for recognition in the eyes of their other. This relationship inaugurates a dialectic of DESIRE, in which the subject strives after an object that is always in the possession of the other. Lacan will therefore say that man's desire is the desire of the other (see in particular 1960), and the formula is now so closely associated with him that it is easy to forget that it enjoyed a very wide currency in the France of the later 1940s and 1950s (Hyppolite 1947 is a typical instance).

In the quasi-algebraic formulae that are the source of his concept of the MATHEME,

Lacan frequently uses the notations '*a[autre]*' and '*A[autre]*' – 'o[ther]' and 'O[ther]' – to describe two modalities of otherness (1978). Although his usage is not entirely consistent, '*a*' tends to represent an other that is not truly 'other' but a projection or effect of the EGO, the prototype being the specular image with which the subject identifies in the alienation of the MIRROR-STAGE (1949). The alienation of the mirror-stage and the DECENTRING effects of the UNCONSCIOUS are such that Lacan can, like the poet Rimbaud, conclude (1978 and elsewhere) that 'I is an other' (*Je est un autre*). '*A*', or the 'big Other', refers, in contrast, to the SYMBOLIC and to language itself insofar as they are orders that are quite alien to and inassimilable by the subject, but into which the subject must be inserted or inscribed if it is to be able to speak and exist as a human being. Speech does not, according to Lacan, originate in the subject or the ego but in the Other; speech is outside the subject's control and it can thus be said that 'the unconscious is the discourse of the Other' (1955b). Here Lacan is also referring to the spatial metaphors of FREUD'S TOPOGRAPHY: the unconscious is *elsewhere* and performs on a different scene or in a different theatre (*ein anderer Schauplatz*), as Freud puts it in *The Interpretation of Dreams* (1900).

The conference held at Essex University entitled *Europe and its Others* (Barker 1985) is an indication that the other, defined in a slightly different but not unrelated sense, is also a major theme in POSTCOLONIAL THEORY. In this context the term refers to the discursive production of an other – a process typified by the way in which Europe produces an Orient-as-other through the discourse of the ORIENTALISM analysed by SAID. This has been described as 'othering' (Spivak 1985a). Europe, that is, functions as a subject, asserts its control over the means of communication and intepretation, and at the same time constitutes its colonial peoples and nations as 'other'. According to another theorist of postcolonialism (Bhabha 1984), the dominant discourse constructs otherness in an ambivalent manner. Whilst it attempts to construct the other as radically different from itself, it must, that is, also ascribe to the other an element of its identity in order to valorize or justify the control it exerts.

OULIPO The OUvroir de LIttérature POtentielle (Workshop on Potential Literature) is a small but influential research group founded in 1960 by the French novelist Raymond Queneau (1903–76) and the mathematician François Le Lionnais (1901–84) to explore the interaction between mathematics and literature. Many of the original members once belonged to the now dormant Collège des 'Pataphysiciens, which was established to promote 'PATAPHYSICS or the science of imaginary solutions. Members of OULIPO include Queneau, Italo CALVINO, Marcel Duchamp, Harry Matthews and Georges Perec; it should be noted that published lists of members make no distinction between the living and the dead. The group's title is a typical example of Queneau's sly humour: *un ouvroir* is a sewing room in a nunnery.

Most of OULIPO's activities are devoted to illustrating the thesis that all literature is a combination of inspiration and constraint, and to exploring how formal constraints can be used to generate literary texts. Examples of the formal constraints include LIPOGRAMS, acrostics, palindromes and the 'S + 7' method, in which every noun in a passage is replaced by the seventh noun to follow it in the dictionary.

Mathematical structures are also used to generate texts. The most sustained and successful examples of OULIPO's research are provided by Perec and Calvino. The chapter plan of the former's monumental novel (or novels, according to its subtitle) *Life: A User's Manual* (1978) mimics the 'knight's tour' problem in chess, in which the knight's moves are so plotted that the piece lands on every square of the board in a preordained sequence, whilst Calvino's *If On A Winter's Night A Traveller* (1979) explores a set of narrative options generated by GREIMAS's semiotic square. OULIPO has declared 2002 the 'Year of the Palindrome'.

READING: Mathews and Bratchie (1998); OULIPO (1973, 1981)

over-determination Also known as 'multiple determination'. In PSYCHOANALYSIS the term is used to indicate that an unconscious formation such as a dream or a symptom is not the result of a single causal factor. In the earliest psychoanalytic descriptions of the 'nucleus' of a symptom FREUD speaks of a ramifying system of associations that over-determine it (Freud and Breuer 1893–5). In a later and more generally accepted formulation, Freud (1900) states that the same element of a dream may be represented many times over in the dream-thoughts and in the patient's associations. Such over-determination is the result of the way the DREAM-WORK makes use of the mechanisms of CONDENSATION and DISPLACEMENT.

ALTHUSSER uses the term (1962a) to describe the manner in which the CONTRADICTIONS within the practices that make up a social formation affect that formation in its entirety. The contradiction between labour and capital is never a simple contradiction that exists at the economic level alone; it is over-determined by the specific historical form in which it exists, and that form is in its turn over-determined by political and ideological practices. Althusser's critique of HISTORICISM relies heavily on the concept of over-determination. Because every contradiction is over-determined, it is impossible to make an 'essential section' which demonstrates that the same essential contradiction runs through every aspect of society in the way that the same lettering runs through a stick of rock.

oxymoron A figure of RHETORIC in which contradictory images or words are juxtaposed in order to intensify a statement or to produce a heightened poetic effect, as in Milton's 'No light, but rather darkness visible' (*Paradise Lost* I. 63).

P

Paglia, Camille (1947–) Italian-American cultural critic. Although Paglia's background is in English literature, she is better known for her controversially polemical comments on FEMINISM (she has described academic feminists as 'feminazis') and the nature of male sexuality. Her reputation is based on her lengthy study of sexual personae from Nefertiti to Emily Dickinson (1990) and two volumes of essays (1992, 1994).

Paglia's notorious statements to the effect that 'there is no female Mozart because there is no female Jack the Ripper' and 'women are not sexual conceptualizers just as they are not lust-murderers' (1990) indicate the degree to which her work assumes the existence of unchanging sexual archetypes or even essences of masculinity and femininity. Male lust is the energizing force in culture, whereas the feminine tends to be equated with a destructive and self-destructive nature. Biology itself is seen by Paglia as conforming to this polarity: whereas the male body is contoured for invasion, the female body is a cave waiting to be penetrated (1992). Whilst Paglia concludes from the inherently aggressive nature of male sexuality that women who put themselves in dangerous situations that can lead to date-rape are acting irresponsibly and even argues that sex will be risk-free only in a totalitarian society, her many feminist critics argue that she is an apologist for male violence.

Paglia's polemical verve, her references to pop culture and stated enthusiasm for pornography tend to mask the traditional nature of her views on Western culture. The polemical rejection of French theorists and their American followers may be entertaining, but the uncritical reliance on sources such as Frazer's *The Golden Bough* (1890–1915) to construct a theory of sexual personae is deeply conservative. In her ambitious study of art and literature (1990), Paglia traces the history of a series of unchanging personae or archetypes (the beautiful boy, the androgyne, the *femme fatale* . . .) and concludes, rather like her mentor Harold BLOOM (who taught her at Yale), that the humanities are about great enduring human truths that never change and that the overall line of Western culture will never change.

READING: Phillips (1998)

palimpsest A paper or parchment on which the original text has been partly erased or effaced to allow a new text to be written, leaving fragments of the original still visible. The term is also used in geology to describe a rock formation displaying features produced in two or more distinct periods. It is used by GENETTE and others to describe a form of INTERTEXTUALITY. Genette (1966) initially uses the term to describe the style of Proust's *À la recherche du temps perdu*, which is made of up multiple superimposed impressions, none of which is ever truly eradicated and none of which in itself provides a 'true' image of a character or sign (Proust's text is also a palimpsest in the most literal of senses; to the immense frustration of his publisher, he rewrote it in the margins of the galley proofs). In his later work (1982a) Genette uses the term to describe a 'literature to the second degree' made up of HYPERTEXTS which derive from, imitate or refer to earlier hypotexts. Joyce's *Ulysses* and the hypotext of *The Odyssey* together make up a palimpsest, as do Thomas Mann's *Joseph and his Brothers* and the bibical story of Joseph. STEINER's anthology *Homer in English* (1996), which includes extracts of English versions of Homer from Chaucer's *Troilus and Cressida* to WALCOTT's *Omeros*, is a fine example of a modern palimpsest.

Panofsky, Erwin (1892–1968) German-American art historian. Most of his work deals with the art of Northern Europe, beginning with a monograph on Dürer (1943) and then studies of early Dutch painting (1953) and Gothic architecture (1957).

In the introduction to his classic study of the Renaissance (1939), Panofksy introduces the canonical (CANON) distinction between iconography, or the study of the conventional subject-matter of works of art, and ICONOLOGY or the study of its intrinsic meaning. Citing PEIRCE, he distinguishes between subject-matter and content, defined as 'that which a work betrays but does not parade'. Panofsky's primary concern is with meaning in the visual arts. Meaning is something that can be recovered by a combination of re-creative experience, in which the historian painstakingly reconstructs the meaning of works of art of the past, and archaeological research, using contemporary documentary evidence to confirm his re-creative experience. It is on the basis of this theory of meaning that LÉVI-STRAUSS (1965) describes Panofsky as a 'great structuralist' who finds in history both a source of irreplaceable information and a combinatory field in which the accuracy of his interpretations can be tested in thousands of ways. Panofsky's essays collected as *Meaning in the Visual Arts* (1955) are virtuoso displays of erudition which combine iconology, philology and the study of theories of perspective (as well as of the theories of optics that inform them) to demonstrate that the cosmos of a culture is always shaped by specific spatio-temporal structures: the date 1400 means different things in Rome and Venice, and the historian's task is to discover just what it means in either context.

Panofsky's major study of the Italian Renaissance (1965) argues that, despite the claims of historians who find earlier 'renascences' of classical art and culture in the Middle Ages, it is a highly specific period during which the linear perspective of medieval art and the medieval world is broken down and then recomposed so as to shape the world into forms amenable to scientific study, thanks mainly to a reformulation of the laws of perspective.

panopticism Expression formed from 'pan' and 'optic' ('all-seeing') and coined by FOUCAULT (1975) to describe a form of power which relies not upon overt repression but upon the constant surveillance of a population and 'discipline', or the regimentation of the body. Panopticism is an important feature of modern disciplinary societies. Foucault derives the notion of panopticism from the writings of the British utilitarian philosopher Jeremy Bentham (1748–1832; see the materials collected as Bentham 1996). Bentham's original 'panopticon' is a model prison. A tower stands at the centre of a hollow circular structure housing a number of individual cells. The tower, which is also circular, is pierced by windows that allow a supervisor to look into the cells without being seen. The individual prisoner never knows whether he is under surveillance or not, and therefore assumes that he is; he is trapped by his visibility.

For Foucault, the major effect of the panopticon is to induce in the inmate a feeling of conscious and permanent visibility that ensures the automatic functioning of a regime of silent discipline. He argues that panopticism is also a structural feature of mental hospitals, educational institutions and factories, and that it introduces a regime of power based upon visibility and silence. Foucault's study of panopticism and the origins of the modern prison system opens with a diptych contrasting the noisy spectacle of the public judicial torture of the Ancien Régime and the silent discipline of the contemporary prison.

paradigm In grammar, a list serving as a standard model or pattern. The inflections of the Latin verb *amare* (*amo*, *amas*, *amat* . . .) provide the paradigm for regular verbs of the first conjugation. The term is widely used in related senses in linguistics, the history of science and the social sciences.

In post-Saussurean linguistics (SAUSSURE), a paradigm is usually understood as a set from which lexical items are selected and then combined to form a SYNTAGM. The paradigmatic dimension of language is represented as a vertical set, as opposed to the horizontal dimension of the syntagm. BARTHES demonstrates how items are selected from a paradigmatic menu and combined to form a syntagmatic meal (1964a), and that items of clothing are selected from a paradigm of styles to produce the syntagm of an individual ensemble. Saussure himself does not use the term 'paradigm', but the 'associative relations' he describes in his *Course in General Linguistics* (1916) are often said to be paradigmatic. According to JAKOBSON (1956), paradigm and syntagm correspond respectively to the metaphoric and metonymic poles of language revealed in studies of APHASIA.

KUHN defines paradigms as the universally recognized scientific achievements which for a time provide a scientific community with model problems and solutions (1962). They provide the basis for the NORMAL SCIENCE that is the usual activity of most scientists. At the same time, a paradigm restricts the phenomenological field that is available for scientific investigation by blinding scientists to potentially important problems that are literally invisible to their normal science. As anomalies are recognized, normal science enters a period of crisis, and new and competing paradigms emerge. A paradigm gains status and acceptance because it is recognized as being better at solving acute problems than its competitors, and the resultant paradigm shift inaugurates a scientific revolution.

In Kuhn's own view, the theory of paradigms and paradigm shifts applies only to the natural sciences because no other discipline of knowledge has achieved the same degree of maturity. His views have been largely ignored, and the ideas of 'paradigm' and 'paradigm shift' are widely invoked in a variety of disciplines ranging from sociology to literary theory.

parapraxis In psychoanalytic theory, a bungled action such as a slip of the tongue whose goal is not achieved and which is replaced by another. Like symptoms, parapraxes are interpreted by FREUD as compromise formations resulting from a conflict between conscious intentions and repressed feelings or impulses. One of the many examples given by Freud (1901) is the story of the President of the Lower House of the Austrian Parliament who opened a sitting by noting the presence of a full quorum and therefore declared the sitting *closed* because he wished it were over.

paratext Modelled somewhat archly on 'paramilitary', the term is used by GENETTE (1982a) to describe the wide variety of devices, including titles, subtitles, prefaces, epigraphs and cover 'blurbs', which act upon the reader by raising expectations and creating a contract between reader and text. The paratext 'novel' creates expectations different from those created by the paratext 'collected poems'. The role of a paratext can be ambiguous. When James Joyce's *Ulysses* was first published in instalments, each section had a title ('Nausicaa', 'Penelope') indicating its origins in the HYPERTEXT supplied by *The Odyssey*; their non-inclusion in the final text raises the intriguing question of whether or not they should be considered part of *Ulysses*.

'pataphysics The science of imaginary solutions, as defined (and spelled) by Alfred JARRY in his novel *Gestes et opinions du Docteur Faustroll* (Deeds and opinions of Docto Faustroll, 1911). It is described by Jarry as extending as far beyond META-PHYSICS as the latter extends beyond physics. 'God is the tangent point of zero and infinity' is a typical 'pataphysical proposition. The deliberately mysterious Collège de 'pataphysique was founded in December 1948 and can be seen as one of the forebears of OULIPO. Its members included Ionesco and other writers associated with the THEATRE OF THE ABSURD and, although now difficult to obtain, its periodical *Cahiers* is an important source of information on both Jarry and the absurdists. The Collège went into voluntary '*occultation*' in 1975, but was due to reappear in 2000.

    BAUDRILLARD revives Jarry's 'pataphysics to describe the work of military planners and the inexorable build-up of sophisticated weapons-systems that are designed not to be used (1983). DELEUZE (1993) has suggested that his 'pataphysics makes Jarry an unrecognized precursor of HEIDEGGER.

patriarchy The term's literal meaning is 'rule of the father', but it is habitually used, particularly within FEMINISM, to mean 'male domination' in a much more general sense. One of the first writers to use it in that sense was Kate MILLETT, whose *Sexual Politics* (1969) outlines a sketch 'which might be described as "notes towards a theory of patriarchy"'. Millett argues that patriarchy's main institution is the family, 'a patriarchal unit within a patriarchal whole'. In historical terms, Millett's thesis can be seen as part of a broader debate. MARXISM and PSYCHOANALYSIS supply contradictory accounts of the origins of patriarchy and the modern family and, as Coward has shown (1983), they originate from within the nineteenth-century debates over the nature of 'primitive' society that gave rise to so much of the modern discipline of anthropology. Although the term 'patriarchy' is widely used, there is little agreement as to either its meaning or its relevance to contemporary debates about the social position of women.

The Marxist strand in the patriarchy debate is best summarized by ENGELS's *Origins of the Family, Private Property and the State* (1884) which relies heavily on Johann Jakob Bachofen's *Mutter-Recht* (Mother-right 1861; in Bachofen 1968) and Lewis Henry Morgan's *Ancient Society* (1877). On the basis of a study of Greek mythology and tragedy, Bachofen argues that patriarchy was preceded by a state of primitive promiscuity in which the principle, or even the nature, of paternity was unknown and in which the preference for the mother therefore prevailed. The discovery of the biological workings of paternity and procreation is represented as the great intellectual discovery that both inaugurates the dawn of a truly human history and abolishes mother-right, which is equated with the sensual, the material and the animal (a thesis with considerable appeal for Freudian revisionists such as FROMM), by establishing a father-right that can be equated with intellectuality. Engels argues against the 'primitive promiscuity' thesis, claiming that the earliest human societies were characterized by the existence of collective or group marriage, communal households and the common ownership of property (primitive communism). Patriarchy originates within the division of labour which, as agriculture and stock-rearing become more widespread, assigns different roles to men and women. He follows Bachofen in arguing that the establishment of father-right is a major historical and intellectual advance in that it promotes both economic and political development, but adds that 'the overthrow of mother-right was the world-historic defeat of the female sex'. Engels's account of the origins of patriarchy had an immense influence on socialist thinking in the twentieth century and contributes to the argument that WOMEN'S LIBERATION can become a reality only through the socialist revolution that abolishes classes and private property. This is still an important argument within SOCIALIST FEMINISM.

FREUD's hypothetical account of patriarchy (1913, 1939) derives from his attempts to explain the prohibition of incest and the OEDIPUS COMPLEX by establishing an evolutionary parallel between the structure of the UNCONSCIOUS and the history of the human race. In stark contrast with Bachofen, he speculates that the earliest human societies were dominated by a male horde under the despotic control of a father whose monopoly on all the females in the group inspired such jealousy in his sons that they banded together to kill and eat him in a primal totemic meal. The murder of the father inaugurated a lengthy period of maternal dominance or matriarchy which was ended when the brothers realized the folly and destructiveness of fighting amongst themselves over their father's heritage (namely their mother and sisters) and formed an alliance, recognized their mutual obligations and renounced their incestuous instinctual demands. Matriarchy, and the concomitant importance of goddess-figures, thus ends with the reestablishment of patriarchy.

The major problem with both Bachofen's and Freud's theories is that, whilst matrilinear societies in which the line of legitimate descent is traced through the mother (as in Judaism) are by no means unknown, no anthropologist has discovered a truly matriarchal society. Few contemporary psychoanalysts would accept Freud's anthropological speculations at face value, but most would argue that they do contain a symbolic or metaphorical truth that helps to explain the universal taboo on incest and the universality of the Oedipus complex. Perhaps the greatest innovation of LACAN's rereading of Freud in the light of the structural anthropology and linguistics of LÉVI-STRAUSS (Lacan 1953) is the abandonment of the evolutionary perspective. The prevalence of the Oedipus complex is now explained in terms of the child's need to renounce a potentially incestuous relationship with the mother and to accept that a symbolic submission to the NAME-OF-THE-FATHER is the precondition for accession to the SYMBOLIC and culture. Much of the debate between PSYCHOANALYSIS AND FEMINISM centres on whether Freudian, and subsequently Lacanian theory, supplies a historical or structural explanation of the origins of patriarchy, as MITCHELL would argue (1974), or whether, as FRIEDAN or MILLETT contend, it justifies the continued existence and reproduction of women's subordination. The Lacanian theory of the name-of-the-father is equally controversial and has been seriously challenged by writers such as IRIGARAY.

Pêcheux, Michel (1938–83) French philosopher, linguist and specialist in DIS-COURSE analysis. He himself (1975) describes his work as taking place under the sign of a 'Triple Alliance' concluded in the 1960s between ALTHUSSER, LACAN and SAUSSURE, but it is also heavily influenced by BACHELARD and CANGUILHEM.

For Pêcheux, language and discourses are to be regarded as social practices, and their analysis therefore merges with that of the nature of IDEOLOGY and the constitution of the SUBJECT. His work on discourse analysis is intended to promote an EPISTEMOLOGICAL BREAK that will wrest the social sciences away from bourgeois IDEOLOGY by identifying the conditions of their production thanks to a process of FORMALIZATION and eventually computerization. Discourses are broken down into elementary utterances resembling Z. S. Harris's 'kernel sentences' (see Harris 1970); when broken down in this way, they become the formal input of a process of analysis whose output is an understanding of the political production of meaning. The best introduction to this ambitious and difficult project is provided by the essays by Pêcheux and his collaborators and the introductory materials included in a collection published twelve years after his premature death (1995).

Peirce, Charles Sanders (1839–1914) American philosopher, best known as the founder of pragmaticism and SEMIOTICS (see also SEMIOLOGY/SEMIOTICS). Although he lectured on logic at Harvard in the 1860s and at Johns Hopkins in 1879–84, Peirce did not enjoy a successful academic career and never published a book expounding his complex theories, even though he wrote widely on mathematics, logic and the sciences. His numerous essays – which originally appeared in such journals as *Popular Science Monthly* – and voluminous unpublished writings are collected in the eight-volume *Collected Writings* published by Harvard University

Press between 1931 and 1958. *Selected Philosophical Writings* (1955) provides a comprehensive introduction to his work.

Peirce's pragmaticism stems from his distrust of METAPHYSICS – regularly dismissed by him as 'moonshine' – and his conviction that logic and science alone will allow us to know what we think and to be masters of our own thinking. Together, they will sweep away dogma and belief, or ingrained habits of thinking; what will remain are those problems that are capable of investigation by the observational method of the sciences. Logic is described by Peirce as the theory of self-controlled or deliberate thought, but he holds that even logic cannot overcome the problem of 'fallibilism' or the fact that we cannot obtain absolute certainty concerning questions of fact. Pragmaticism itself is defined simply as a method of ascertaining the meaning of 'hard words and abstract concepts'. Any theory that goes beyond this and that cannot be at least approximately defined through further discussion is dismissed as 'metaphysical gabble'.

In his PHENOMENOLOGY, which is not an equivalent to HUSSERL's 'pure phenomenology' but rather a descriptive classification of modes of being, Peirce establishes a hierarchy of 'Firstness', 'Secondness' and 'Thirdness'. Firstness denotes the raw qualities of a subject's being precisely what it is, and is not amenable to observation. Firstness is the quality of 'redness' before any red exists in the world. Secondness is a mode of being in which one thing consists in how a second object is; this category of being corresponds to the actual fact of the existence of objects that exist alongside others and are defined by their relationship with them. Thirdness denotes a mode of being in which the future fact of secondness will take on a determinate general character: this is the level of thought and of the establishment of patterns and laws.

Thirdness is a matter of interpretation, logic and semiotics, defined as a quasi-necessary or formal doctrine of signs. Although Peirce's semiotics was elaborated at much the same time as SAUSSURE's semiology, there are major differences between their theories. Whereas Saussure tends to work with dyads such as the signifier and signified that together constitute a SIGN, Peirce works with a triadic structure. The sign or REPRESENTAMEN is something which stands *to* somebody *for* something; it addresses someone and creates in his or her mind an equivalent sign. This is the 'interpretant' of the first sign, and it too stands for something, namely the object or 'idea' of that first sign. All communication is therefore the result of the interplay between representamen, interpretant and idea. Peirce goes on, especially in volumes 2 and 4 of the *Collected Writings*, to establish an extremely complex typology of ten classes of signs, such as the 'qualisign' (a quality such as the 'feeling of red' insofar as it is a sign) and the 'iconic sinsign' (an individual diagram) and the 'dicent sinsign' (a weathercock or any sign that affords information about its object). The system of classification is so complex, and Peirce's terminology so arcane, that it has never been widely accepted in its original form. The most familiar of Peirce's categories are the ICON, the INDEX and the SYMBOL (described in an article in *Collected Papers* II), which JAKOBSON incorporates into his study of APHASIA (1956).

READING: Feibleman (1960)

performative A form of speech in which the issuing of the utterance is also the performance of an action, as in the biblical 'Let there be light: and there was light' (Genesis i.3). Standard examples include the utterances 'I do [take this woman to be my lawful wedded wife]' and 'I name this ship . . .' in, respectively, the context of the marriage ceremony and that of the ceremonial breaking of a champagne bottle against the ship's stern. Unlike a CONSTATIVE, a performative is neither true nor false.

The performative was first described by the British philosopher AUSTIN in a radio talk on 'performative utterances' given in 1956 (and published posthumously in Austin 1970). In his later work (1962a), Austin modifies his theory slightly, and now speaks of LOCUTIONARY ACTS, ILLOCUTIONARY ACTS and PERLOCUTIONARY ACTS, which are viewed as the component parts of a SPEECH ACT. Austin's performative is an essential element in speech-act theory, and has also been applied in other forms of discourse analysis. The thesis that pornography is not a form of speech but a performative equivalent to an act of sexual degradation provides the theoretical basis for the MACKINNON-DWORKIN LAW. Judith BUTLER applies the theory of the performative to the production of GENDER, arguing that gendering is a reiterated performative process that begins when someone says of the neonate: 'It's a girl.'

perlocutionary act In a modification of his first description of the form of utterance known as the PERFORMATIVE, AUSTIN describes the perlocutionary act as an utterance which has consequential effects on the feelings, thoughts or actions of either the audience or the speaker. Convincing, persuading and deterring are perlocutionary acts.

persona The term is used in JUNG's analytical psychology to describe the social mask or role behind which most people live. A form of compromise between the individual and what society requires that individual to be, the persona is a collective phenomenon, or a socially acceptable 'packaging' or presentation of the EGO. As Jung remarks (1953), society expects a man who is a parson to play the role of 'the parson' as flawlessly as possible, and most parsons do precisely that. Failure to adopt an appropriate persona may make individuals seem gauche or clumsy; the adoption of too rigid a persona, on the other hand, may lead to a denial of other aspects of the personality. The term is borrowed from the Latin word for the masks worn by the actors of Antiquity to indicate which role they were playing.

petitio principii A Latin phrase literally meaning 'begging of the principle' and often rendered as 'begging the question'. It describes the logical fallacy in which the conclusion is taken for granted in the premise or in which the validity of a mode of argument is established through its use.

phallocentrism The tendency to focus all discussion of sexual difference on the primacy of the PHALLUS.

The adjective 'phallo-centric' was coined by the British psychoanalyst Ernest Jones in a discussion of the early development of female sexuality (1927) that brought him into conflict with FREUD over the question of the phallic phase, in which children believe that the penis is the sole sexual organ and that femininity is the result of castration. Jones argues that the girl does have an awareness of her own sexual organs, but also that masculinity and femininity are innate and absolute polarities. He contends that discussions of the development of sexuality have been dominated by the 'unduly phallo-centric views' of male analysts and that the importance of the female organs has been 'correspondingly underestimated'. The possible protofeminist implications of his claims are immediately undermined when Jones goes on to add that women have compounded the problem by adopting what he calls 'a secretive attitude towards their own genitals' and by showing 'a hardly disguised preference for interest in the male organ'.

In contemporary usage, 'phallocentrism' tends to refer to the Lacanian theory of the phallus (LACAN). The accusation of phallocentrism is crucial to IRIGARAY's critique of PSYCHOANALYSIS (1974).

phallogocentrism A condensation of PHALLOCENTRISM and LOGOCENTRISM coined by DERRIDA (1975) to describe how LACAN perpetuates the traditional philosophical view that the word or *logos* is the site of truth by making the PHALLUS the key signifier that both governs access to the SYMBOLIC, or language, and determines sexual difference.

phallus The term is rarely used by FREUD but is central to LACAN's reorientation of psychoanalytic theory. For Lacan the concept of the phallus refers primarily to the imaginary and symbolic value taken on by the biological penis in the course of the SUBJECT's accession to language and the SYMBOLIC.

Although he often refers to the existence of the phallic stage in which children believe the penis to be the sole sexual organ and explain femininity in terms of castration (1905a, 1908a), Freud normally uses the noun 'phallus' to refer to the ancient symbol of royal power (1923b). Lacanians often attempt to find a phallus/penis distinction in Freud's writings, but he himself usually uses the two words as synonyms and rarely makes a clear distinction between the two (Macey 1988).

Lacan's theory of the phallus was elaborated in the 1950s. In the 1955–6 seminar on the psychoses (published 1981), the phallus is described as the mediating element in the castration complex and as an imaginary object which the child finally recognizes as being in the possession of its father. In Lacan's major paper on the significance of the phallus (1958), it is redefined as a privileged signifier which facilitates the articulation of DESIRE and the *logos*, and as the symbol of sexual difference itself. The phallus is the OBJECT of the mother's desire, and the child identifies with it in an attempt to satisfy both the mother's desire and its own desire for the mother. In this recasting of Freud's description of the OEDIPUS COMPLEX, the subject's insertion into language and the symbolic is a form of castration which obliges the child to recognize that it cannot possess the phallus because it is not an attribute of an individual, but a symbol. It is the symbol of sexual difference in that there is no corresponding female symbol or signifier; both male and female subjects are constituted as male and female with reference to it. Elsewhere Lacan describes the phallus as appearing in place of the lack of the signifier in the other (the mother) and as the signifier of DESIRE itself (1991).

The theory of the phallus is one of the most controversial aspects of Lacan's work and it has triggered important debates relating to the fraught relationship between PSYCHOANALYSIS AND FEMINISM. It has been argued (Mitchell 1974; Mitchell and Rose 1982) that the introduction of the concept of the phallus allows sexual difference to be understood in symbolic and non-biological terms and that it renders obsolete the criticisms of psychoanalysis that focus on the notorious issue of penis envy (Millett 1970). Conversely, it has also been said (Grosz 1990) that the symbolic function ascribed to the phallus valorizes the biological penis by making it a sign of masculine privilege, and thus naturalizes male dominance. For DERRIDA (1975), the notion of a 'privileged signifier' is unsatisfactory in that it contradicts SAUSSURE's basic thesis that signifiers acquire value and meaning only because they are different from other signifiers. The idea of a privileged signifier implies the existence of a transcendental point of origin for language as a whole, and reproduces the META-PHYSICS of LOGOCENTRISM in the form of PHALLOGOCENTRISM.

phatic function Defined by JAKOBSON (1960), following Malinowski (1923), as any element in the CODE/MESSAGE system that serves primarily to establish, prolong or interrupt the communication of a message rather than to impart information. The ritual 'Hello, can you hear me?' of a telephone conversation is an everyday example. The phatic function can give rise to a complex exchange of ritualized formulae or even to whole dialogues designed solely to prolong a conversation or to ensure that communication is still taking place. The term 'phatic' derives from the Greek *phatos*, 'spoken'.

phenomenology A major strand within twentieth-century CONTINENTAL PHIL-OSOPHY, originating in the work of HUSSERL. Its primary representatives are Husserl himself, HEIDEGGER, SARTRE, MERLEAU-PONTY and LEVINAS. It is conventional to distinguish between the 'pure' phenomenology of Husserl and the existential phenomenology (or EXISTENTIALISM) of Heidegger and Sartre, but differences of opinion between the latter two mean that the distinction is not as clear-cut as it might seem.

The term 'phenomenology' derives from the Greek words *phainomenon*, a participial form of *phainein* ('to show'), and *logos* ('reason' or 'study'), and literally means 'the study of things shown'. From Plato onwards, a distinction has traditionally been made between that which can be seen and that which is intelligible; Kant (1787) famously divides all objects into 'phenomena' (the actual objects of sensuous experience and perception) and 'noumena' (intelligible existences which are cogitated by the intellect alone, and which can never be perceived as things in themselves). Phenomenology can thus be described as a superficial description of appearances that does not provide an understanding of the higher category of noumena. The modern meaning of phenomenology is greatly influenced by Hegel's *Phenomenology of Mind* (1807), which traces the emergence and development of the self-consciousness of mind or spirit (*Geist*), and equates phenomena with the 'element of immediate positive existence'. Hegel's later *Philosophy of Mind* (1830) refers to phenomenology as 'the study of consciousness as such', and to consciousness as 'the appearance [or 'phenomenon'] of mind'.

For Husserl, phenomenology is a scientific project designed to produce a fundamental description of the phenomena that present themselves to the human consciousness. It is further described as being designed to establish knowledge of essences, defined not as occult qualities concealed within 'phenomena' but as the ideal form of that which exists here and now in *this* time-spot. The slogan 'Back to the things themselves' captures something of the immediacy of the entire project. The starting-point for knowledge is experience, or the 'lived experience' of the human consciousness. Consciousness itself is defined by its INTENTIONALITY, or by the fact that consciousness is always consciousness *of* something. Phenomena are therefore said to exist *for* consciousness; conversely, consciousness is nothing outside its relationship with the world of phenomena and exists within an *Umwelt* or environment that is always/already there. The world is the sum-total of objects that can be known through experience.

If the intentionality of consciousness is the most basic theme of all phenomenology, equal importance has to be accorded to the notion of *EPOCHE*, or the 'bracketing out' of all preconceptions, assumptions and a priori ideas that might intervene with the immediate perception of phenomena. The process of bracketing out is obviously reminiscent of the process of methodical doubt that allows Descartes to call into question the very existence of the world in order to arrive at the *cogito* ('I am thinking, therefore I am') that permits him to establish beyond all doubt that he exists (1637), and phenomenology has often been described as a new Cartesianism. It does not in fact call into question the existence of the world, but does strive to bracket out all assumptions, including scientific assumptions, about the nature of that world, and its major appeal is that it promises direct knowledge of the here and the now. What remains after everything else has been bracketed out is pure consciousness itself, defined as a phenomenological residue. The emergence of this pure or transcendental consciousness and EGO provides the basis for a new beginning. The transcendental ego ignores all presuppositions about the world in order to arrive at a new and immediate knowledge of that world based upon streams of 'pure experience'; at the same time, it makes it difficult to demonstrate the existence of other streams of experience, other consciousnesses or even another ego. The problem of the existence or non-existence of others (SOLIPSISM) is never finally resolved by Husserl, and remains a difficult issue for all forms of phenomenology.

Although Heidegger and Sartre take Husserl as their starting-point, they also depart from him in a number of ways. Heidegger (1927) rejects the idea of the transcendental ego as the starting-point for a phenomenology, and prefers to speak of a Being (*Sein*) that is revealed or disclosed to human consciousness. He also introduces the idea of AUTHENTICITY, which is taken up by Sartre, and the all-important notion of the temporality of being; that human beings live in a temporal and finite world means that their existence is dominated by the inevitability of their demise, or by their being-towards-death. Sartre, for his part, stresses (1943a) that freedom is the fundamental dimension of human existence, and thus introduces the themes of commitment, responsibility and BAD FAITH, whilst MERLEAU-PONTY, unlike either Husserl or Heidegger, emphasizes that consciousness is always an embodied consciousness, and therefore accords much more importance to the physical body or 'the flesh' as he calls it in his later works.

READING: Bell (1990); Lyotard (1954); Pivcevic (1970)

philology A historical and descriptive theory of language development and of the relationships between languages, developed in the nineteenth century and associated, especially in Germany, with HERMENEUTICS and HISTORICISM. The starting-point for philology is the recognition of 'family resemblances' between the vocabulary of natural languages. Such resemblances, like that between the English 'mother' and the German *Mutter*, point to common origins in an earlier language. Most European and many Asian languages are held to originate from the hypothetical Indo-European language. Both English and German are said to belong to the Germanic branch or subfamily; other branches include Romance, Celtic and Slavonic. Philology traces linguistic change by recording sound-shifts thanks to a careful and etymological study of surviving texts, and codifying the laws that govern them. Exceptions to laws are usually explained in terms of borrowings from other languages.

This approach to the study of language provides the theoretical basis for the pedagogical argument that the study of modern English, French and German should go hand in hand with, or even be preceded by, the study of Anglo-Saxon, Old French and Middle High German. Modern linguistics has largely abandoned philology in favour of the study of the synchronic dimension of language. Although many of those who are obliged to study philology at university (usually as part of a degree in modern languages) regard it as a very dismal science, it should be recalled that the discipline did, along with a classical education in Latin and Greek, produce scholars of great erudition. Critics like AUERBACH and Spitzer owe their ability to range freely across so many languages to their background in Romance and German philology and, although he inaugurated the revolution against philology, SAUSSURE himself was a distinguished philologist.

phoneme In the linguistic FUNCTIONALISM of the PRAGUE SCHOOL and the work of JAKOBSON and André Martinet (1960), a phoneme is defined as a phonological unit with a distinctive function that cannot be broken down into smaller units with similar functions. A phoneme is defined by its distinctive features, such as its being voiced (/v/) or non-voiced (/f/). The list of phonemes making up any given language is a closed list; Castilian employs twenty-four phonemes.

As Jakobson remarks (1956), the Cheshire Cat in Lewis Carroll's *Alice in Wonderland* shows an intuitive grasp of phonematic analysis when it asks Alice: 'Did you say "fig" or "pig"?' In English there is a functional difference between /f/ and /p/, and it conveys the difference of meaning between 'pig' and 'fig'. Not all phonetic differences are functional: standard English employs both a 'clear' and a 'dark' /l/ – to use Lyons's terminology (1968) – employed respectively before consonants ('*leaf*') and at the end of words ('*feel*'). The substitution of one for the other would not constitute a significant error of pronunciation for any speaker or listener with a native COMPETENCE in English. Such variations are sometimes described as 'allophones'.

READING: Jones (1950); Lyons (1968); Trubetzkoy (1939)

phonocentrism A form of LOGOCENTRISM which prioritizes the acoustic or phonetic aspect of language over the graphic dimension of WRITING. According to DERRIDA (1967a), the insistence that it is only the acoustic differences between PHONEMES that make language a meaningful system of SIGNS means that all forms of modern linguistics and STRUCTURALISM are instances of phonocentrism. Derrida therefore contrasts phonocentrism with GRAMMATOLOGY.

pleasure principle According to FREUD (1911a), one of the two principles that govern mental or psychical activity, the other being the REALITY PRINCIPLE. All psychical activity is directed towards the procurement of pleasure and the avoidance of unpleasure. The latter results from increased excitation, and the pleasure principle therefore serves to reduce tension and to return the psyche to a state of equilibrium or constancy. Freud further suggests (1920a) that there is something 'beyond the pleasure principle', namely the DEATH DRIVES that attempt to reduce psychic tension to zero, and thus to return living beings to an inorganic state. For LACAN (1960, 1991) the pleasure principle is an obstacle to the *JOUISSANCE* that takes the SUBJECT to that extreme point where the erotic borders upon death and where subjectivity risks extinction.

poetics The word derives from the Greek adjective *poietikos*, related to the noun *poietes*, 'maker' or 'poet'. Its etymology can be a source of confusion as it can appear to imply that 'poetics' applies to poetry or verse alone; in its modern usage it applies to a very general descriptive theory of literature, as when TODOROV speaks of a 'poetics of prose' (1971).

The earliest theory of poetics is to be found in Aristotle's *Poetics*, which is primarily a study of the art of composing poems (synonymous with tragic drama). Here poetics is viewed as an integral part of MIMESIS (imitation of reality). It is a form of embellishment but, unlike RHETORIC, it is not intended to convince the reader or spectator of the probability or VERISIMILITUDE of the tragic poem. Its function is, rather, to promote the CATHARSIS or 'purging' of violent emotions that is the purpose of tragedy.

Modern theories of poetics are, like theories of NARRATOLOGY, mainly associated with STRUCTURALISM and fill out the basic Aristotelian notion of a GENRE-based description of literature by drawing on RUSSIAN FORMALISM and the work of PROPP. The formalist notion of literariness or LITERATURNOST' attempts to define and describe the distinctive properties of the literary as such, whilst PROPP's work on folk-tales demonstrates that any narrative is composed of functions or impersonal elements that serve to advance the story (the donor sets a narrative in motion by giving the hero a gift which may or may not be stolen from him). It thus becomes possible to establish a general typology or poetics of narrative. JAKOBSON's description of the 'poetic function' in his influential CODE/MESSAGE model of linguistic communication adds a further element: the FOREGROUNDING of the poetic function, which is inherent in all communication, detracts from the referential function (REFERENT) and draws attention to the formal devices that structure the message.

The poetics of BARTHES, TODOROV, GENETTE and others might be described as an attempt to elaborate categories that allow us to grasp both the unity and variety of all literary works. Individual works, such as a tragedy by Shakespeare, are 'illustrations' of the broad category or GENRE of tragedy. Todorov provides one of the clearest descriptions of this form of poetics (1971). It is not concerned with literature or poetry, and less still is it concerned with the critical evaluation of texts on a scale of 'good' and 'bad', but with their 'poeticity' or 'literariness'. Its object consists of the properties of literary DISCOURSE as such, and particular works are exemplars of those properties. As Todorov notes, Aristotle's concern was with tragedy and the epic, not a particular epic by Homer or a particular tragedy by Aeschylus. For Barthes (1966a), poetics is a hypothetical descriptive model which allows the analysis of how literary works are constructed. Just as the linguist cannot master all the sentences in a language, and therefore constructs an explanatory but hypothetical model to analyse the construction of sentences, so poetics constructs a model of the laws of literary structure. For Barthes, poetics is not a form of HERMENEUTICS and is not intended to find or recover a meaning in the text; it describes how meanings are generated by the text and how and why they are accepted as meaningful by readers. Poetics's concentration on the general and anonymous structures of literary texts is one of the reasons why Barthes was able to announce the DEATH OF THE AUTHOR (1968b).

READING: Culler (1975)

politically correct Conforming to liberal or radical opinion on social matters. Political correctness usually consists in the avoidance of the discriminatory and offensive language and behaviour associated with SEXISM and RACISM. A typical example is the use of 'chairperson' in preference to 'chairman'. In the United States, some universities have adopted formal speech codes which set out rules governing which terms may and may not be applied to persons of the opposite sex and of different ethnic groups. This has not been the case in Britain, but the National Association of Teachers in Further and Higher Education (NATFHE) has had an *Equal Opportunities Guide to Language* since 1993. It recommends, *inter alia*, the use of 'workforce' rather than 'manpower', and 'synthetic' rather than 'man-made'.

Political correctness, often abbreviated to PC, is frequently attacked and mocked, especially by the popular media, for being puritanical, repressive and humourless or even an expression of FUNDAMENTALISM. In December 1990 *Newsweek* published an article entitled 'Watch What You Say: There's A Politically Correct Way to Talk About RACE, Sex and Ideas' (Robbins 1991). Attacks on political correctness are often based upon misapprehensions and even myths. Thus the story, which circulated in the 1990s, that certain primary schools in London had banned the singing of 'Baa Baa Black Sheep' on the grounds that it was politically incorrect was widely reported in the British press, but had no basis in fact.

Although it is a commonplace to claim that the demand for political correctness indicates a dour lack of any sense of humour, there are indications that the reverse is true. The expression, and the related 'ideologically sound', may have originated in the FEMINISM of the 1970s, when badges saying 'I am a Humourless Feminist' enjoyed some popularity, and could be used in a self-mocking sense. A widely circulated postcard of the day reproduced a photomontage by Ray Lowry in which a man says to a woman: 'I could have made you so happy, Beryl . . .' A woman-friend replies on Beryl's behalf: 'She doesn't want to be happy, Graham. She wants to be ideologically correct . . .' Beryl adds 'Right on!'

Some politically correct euphemisms, such as 'vertically challenged' for 'short', do almost inevitably raise a smile, though one suspects that the more extreme examples are journalistic inventions. The underlying issue is, however, serious, and few people would like to see a return to forms of speech in which 'yid', 'nigger' and 'chick' were deemed to be acceptable expressions.

Popper, Sir Karl R. (1902–94) Austrian-born philosopher and historian of science, best known for his work on the EPISTEMOLOGY of science, his critique of HIS-TORICISM (1957) and his defence of the 'open' or democratic society (1945).

As a young man in prewar Austria, Popper was associated with the VIENNA CIRCLE and shared its interest in the science/non-science distinction. In later life he became highly critical of both LOGICAL POSITIVISM and linguistic or ORDINARY LANGUAGE philosophy, arguing (notably in the preface to the revised edition of *The Logic of Scientific Discovery*, 1934) that they had redefined philosophy in such a way that they could make no further contribution to knowledge of the world. His own understanding of philosophy was that it should centre on the problem of cosmology, or in other words the problem of understanding the world. That, he argued, implied understanding human beings and human knowledge as part of the world.

In his major study of 1934 and many related essays (e.g. 1963), Popper takes as his starting-point the 'induction problem', the classic formulation of which is to be found in Hume's *Enquiry Concerning Human Understanding* (1758). The problem centres on science's reliance upon the inference from particular to general statements. Induction, that is, does not provide a suitable criterion for the demarcation betwen scientific and non-scientific statements, even though science must consist of universal statements. Empirical sense-data constitute an inadequate criterion: we cannot infer from the fact that we have seen countless white swans that all swans are white. Popper's solution is to propose FALSIFIABILITY as a criterion of demarcation: scientific statements are not confirmed by verification, but are subject to potential falsification by subsequent and more accurate statements. A scientific theory does not, that is, seek or claim to explain everything or to predict all that can happen; it rules out what cannot happen and will itself be ruled out if what it has ruled out does in fact happen. For Popper (1934), scientific theories are nets which attempt to 'catch' the world, to explain, rationalize and master it. The goal of scientific endeavour is to make the mesh finer. This is, ultimately, an expression of a basic human characteristic. Human beings are problem-solving animals, but their knowledge is always provisional and they are therefore engaged in an unended quest, to use the title of Popper's autobiography (1976). Popper's notion of 'catching the world' has had a significant influence on GOMBRICH's account of stylistic change in the visual arts.

Popper's falsification criterion provides the basis for a critique of systems of knowledge that claim to be complete and therefore seek to confirm their own validity, PSYCHOANALYSIS and MARXISM being the prime examples. Marxism, condemned by Popper for its historicism, claims to be in possession of the irrefutable laws of history; psychoanalysts evade refutation by reformulating Freud's insights in ever more dogmatic terms.

The falsification criterion and the stress on provisional problem-solving are also basic to Popper's vision of the open society (1945). Whereas the emphasis on irrefutable forms of knowledge has, from Plato to Marx, always carried with it the implicit threat of authoritarianism or even totalitarianism, an open society is pluralistic, permits the expression of conflicting views and the pursuit of contradictory goals, and allows its members to criticize and replace its rulers.

READING: Magee (1973)

positivism A school of thought associated with the French philosopher Auguste Comte (1798–1857) and linked to the rise of sociology; the word *sociologie* was coined by Comte in 1830, and defined as meaning 'social physics'. The influence of positivism in the nineteenth century ranges from the lexicography of Émile Littré, whose monumental dictionary of the French language was published between 1863 and 1873, to the 'experimental medicine' of Claude Bernard (1865), which did much to define the modern conception of experimentation and scientific method.

Comte's positivism, also known as 'positive philosophy', is at once a theory of knowledge or EPISTEMOLOGY and an evolutionary philosophy of history governed by the Law of the Three States. Mankind and human knowledge both evolve through three distinct 'states'. In the theological state man progresses from primitive fetishism to polytheism and then to monotheism, and lives in a theocracy which is the most primitive stage of social life. In the metaphysical state, the human mind no longer looks for supernatural causes, but creates secular divinities such as 'properties' or 'powers' and evolves into a secular monotheism based upon a very general concept of 'nature'. In the positive state, humanity ceases to ask *why*, or to speculate about the inner being of phenomena, and looks at *how* things happen. Defined as a method, positivism seeks to discover the immutable universal laws that govern the universe by using observation, experimentation and calculation. The term 'knowledge' is reserved for the results of observations that are observable in nature and verifiable thanks to experimental method. The utopian strand in Comte's thought leads him to attempt to found a Religion of Humanity, complete with secular saints, which celebrates humanity's positive achievements. The principle of this religion is love; its basis is order and its goal is progress. The evolutionary schema is a classic expression of the assumptions of EUROCENTRISM; it is made quite clear that non-European societies are still living in the theological state. Comte's writings are voluminous and very repetitious. The four volumes of the *Système de politique positive* (1852–4) provide a comprehensive introduction to his thought.

Postivism remained a force in twentieth-century thought. WITTGENSTEIN, for instance, struck a positivist note when he remarked in *The Blue Book* that: 'The difficulty in philosophy is to say no more than we know' (1958). The LOGICAL POSITIVISM of the VIENNA CIRCLE openly laid claim to Comte's heritage. The emphasis today, however, tends to fall on the verifiability or otherwise of linguistic or scientific propositions rather than on Comte's rather crude notion of experimentalism, whilst the Religion of Humanity is viewed simply as an episode in the history of utopianism.

READING: Kolakowski (1966)

postcolonial theory A broad tendency in literary studies that has developed out of the earlier theories of COMMONWEALTH LITERATURE and of THIRD WORLD studies, and which seeks to analyse the global effects of European colonialism. Although SAID's *Orientalism* (1978) is widely regarded as one of the founding texts of postcolonial theory, both the term and the discipline are products of the late 1980s and the 1990s. The field, whose origins and terminology have been carefully traced by Mishra and Hodge (1991), has been broadly defined by *The Empire Writes Back* (Ashcroft, Griffiths and Tiffin 1989) and influential readers in postcolonial studies appeared in the mid-1990s (Williams and Chrisman 1994; Ashcroft, Griffiths and Tiffin 1995). The popularity of the discipline has been enhanced by the success of writers such as Salman Rushdie; the title of *The Empire Writes Back* is, significantly, borrowed from a newspaper article by Rushdie which makes playful allusion to *The Empire Fights Back*, the second film in the hugely successful *Star Wars* trilogy (Mishra and Hodge 1991).

The term 'postcolonial' can be slightly misleading. In general, it refers not, as might be expected, to the period following the independence of the former colonies, but to the period that began with colonization itself. In geographical terms, it refers to a vast spatial unity. Ashcroft, Griffiths and Tiffin describe the postcolonial as referring to 'all the cultures affected by the imperial process from the moment of colonization to the present day'. Postcolonial theory thus seeks to study the cultures and literatures of India as well as Africa, of Australia as well as Canada and New Zealand. Ashcroft, Griffiths and Tiffin further argue that the literature of the United States 'should also be placed in this category' on the grounds that nineteenth-century American literature was marked by an attempt to construct a CANON that was not dominated by the English classics. It has often been noted by critics that such a broad definition is very problematic, and the example of Canada is frequently mentioned (see, for instance, Moore-Gilbert 1997). Whilst Canada was a British dominion that sought to define its own literary identity, it is sometimes argued that it is now in danger of becoming an American colony. For the French-speaking population of Québec, however, it is the anglophone majority that is the colonizing force; in the 1960s Québecois separatists defined themselves in Fanonian terms as 'the wretched of the earth' (FANON) and 'the white niggers of America' (Vallières 1968); in the 1980s and 1990s the francophone Québecois were themselves accused of being colonialists by the Mohawks and other members of the First Nations as bitter disputes broke out over land rights. The First Nations do not speak French, and their rights are based upon negotiations with the federal government in Ottawa and not the francophone authorities of Quebec. When the separatists narrowly lost a referendum on independence in 1995, they blamed their defeat on the 'ethnic note', meaning the First Nations. Other critics point out that the aboriginal peoples of Australia and New Zealand are involved in anti-colonial struggles rather than a postcolonial culture (Rattansi 1997).

In methodological terms, postcolonial theory tends to be dominated by the theoretical discourses associated with POSTMODERNITY, or in other words DECON-STRUCTION, forms of Lacanian PSYCHOANALYSIS (LACAN) and forms of DISCOURSE ANALYSIS derived in part from FOUCAULT. The field is dominated by the names of BHABHA, SAID and SPIVAK and sceptics have expressed doubts about the promotion of 'name-brand theory' (Loomba 1998). More virulent critics complain that postcolonial theory ignores the economics of colonialism and imperialism, that it has depoliticized the major debates that took place about the nature of postcolonial states in the 1970s, or even that it is a postmodern attempt to recolonize non-European literatures and cultures which rename 'Third World literature' 'postcolonial literature' as the theoretical framework shifts from Third World nationalism to postmodernism (Ahmad 1992, 1995; Ahmad is referring to the debates sparked by Alavi 1972).

Postcolonial theory breaks with the ideology associated with COMMONWEALTH LITERATURE's unthinking claim that the cultural role of anglophone writers around the world is to enrich English literature, and has successfully demonstrated that the centre-periphery relationship is much more complex than such claims would suggest. In rather different ways, Said and Spivak have shown that 'the periphery' is in fact present in 'the centre': the wealth that built the Mansfield Park of Austen's quintessentially English novel is based on slavery in the West Indies (Said 1993); the emergence of Jane Eyre as the white individualist heroine requires the sacrifice of the mulatto woman, and may even evoke the Indian custom of suttee (Spivak 1985b). The profoundly ambivalent images of colonialism in Conrad's *Heart of Darkness* have been analysed so often that little remains of the classically 'English' Conrad promoted, or even created, by the Leavisite canon (LEAVIS). Much of the best work associated with postcolonial theory has followed the original thesis put forward by Said on how colonial conquests resulted in an attempt to know and administer colonial subjects which inagurated an othering (OTHER) generating the pervasive images of effeminate Indians, savage Africans and inscrutably sinister Orientals that are so common in the literature of Empire.

The hidden kinship with Commonwealth Literature is, however, apparent at an institutional level. Postcolonial theory has emerged in, or on the margins of, English departments and, despite references to 'all the cultures' affected by imperialism, has defined its field in almost exclusively anglophone terms. Thus although FANON is often evoked, there have been few attempts to extend the debate to the rich cultures of *FRANCOPHONIE* or Latin America. The concentration on the anglophone literature of the Indian subcontinent, as opposed to its vernacular literatures, has also been criticized, and it is to be hoped that Macmillan India's 1996 decision to launch an extensive series of 'Modern Indian Novels in Translation' will extend the debate (see Nayar 1998).

postmodernism The term is applied, often loosely, to a wide variety of cultural practices and theoretical discourses associated with the experience of POSTMODERNITY, and is usually contrasted with the MODERNISM of the earlier twentieth century. Postmodernism, together with DECONSTRUCTION, has become one of the main themes of POSTSTRUCTURALISM. Early references to postmodernism derive from discussions of the visual arts and literature (especially in the United States), and the debate subsequently incorporates discussions of developments within architecture. Elements of contemporary philosophy, mainly French, are then introduced into a very wide and hotly contested debate.

Although the postmodernist debate is mainly a product of the 1970s, the term 'postmodernism' itself is much older and has been traced (Anderson 1998) to an anthology of Spanish and Hispanic poetry from 1882 to 1932 (Onis 1934); here it is described as a reactionary tendency within modernism, and is contrasted with the *ultramodernismo* associated with Lorca, Borges and Neruda. Two decades later the term was being used by American poets such as Charles Olson and Robert Creeley, and then in the artistic circles where Pop Art was beginning to challenge the modernist abstraction championed by GREENBERG. In 1971 the journal *New Literary History* published a special issue on 'Modernism and Postmodernism' which included Ihab Hassan's influential 'paracritical bibliography' of postmodernism (1971), which both summarized and went beyond his earlier work on the 'literature of silence', defined as spanning the period marked by the names of Kafka and Beckett. Hassan (whose evolution is conveniently traced in Bertens 1995) now spoke of a 'change within modernism' and of a literature in search of itself. With an extraordinary eclecticism, Hassan names JARRY and his 'PATAPHYSICS, Andy Warhol, William Burroughs, MCLUHAN, John Barth's novel *Giles Goat Boy* (1966) and the music of John Cage as harbingers of postmodernism. Linda Hutcheon's much more substantial and reasoned survey of postmodernism in literature (1988) also cites Barth, along with Vonnegut, ECO and Salman Rushdie, as one of the exemplars of a postmodern or metafictional literature which deliberately and playfully employs paradox to display its own artificiality and contradictions, which plays with GENRE and its convention and alludes to both high and popular culture in such a way as to appeal to a very wide audience. An emphasis on the playful and popularity is a frequent theme in discussions of postmodernism, and a reminder that one of the objections to the modern has always been that it is 'difficult'. That the adjective 'postmodernist' can be alarmingly imprecise is noted by Barth himself (1995), who recalls that his novels *The Sot-Weed Factor* (1960), *Giles Goat Boy* (1966) and *Lost in the Fun House* (1968) were described as 'fabulist' before they became 'postmodernist', and that the latter term is now retrospectively applied to his earlier fiction, successively described in the past as 'provincial American existentialism', 'fabulism' or 'black humour'.

In architectural circles the idea of postmodernism – if not the term itself – was originally associated with the critique of the INTERNATIONAL STYLE initiated by Robert Venturi (1966) and expanded in the seminal *Learning from Las Vegas* (Venturi et al. 1972), which celebrated the neon signs and extraordinary palaces of the gambling strip in the desert which are so often dismissed as KITSCH. The populist architecture of the 'decorated shed', whose startling neon signs are constantly being altered and redesigned in a relentless quest for novelty, is contrasted with the alleged elitism, puritanism and sterility of international modernism. The first to speak of postmodernist architecture as such appears to have been Charles Jencks, who in a series of essays (1977, 1996) outlines the important theme of 'double coding' in his descriptions of buildings which allude to or quote from a variety of historical styles. The architectural examples cited by Jencks (1996) include the Byker Wall housing estate (Newcastle-upon-Tyne, 1974), where traditional and modern materials, dyed wood and concrete are combined to remarkable (and genuinely popular) effect, and the Neue Staatsgalerie (1977–84 Stuttgart), where the public descends a curved walkway leading into a sculpture whose style borrows from the Pantheon and Hadrian's Villa. Such knowing juxtapositions are the source of the much-abused term 'postmodernist irony'. A perfect example of what is actually meant by that term is provided by former pop artist Peter Blake's *The Meeting, or Have a Nice Day, Mr Hockney* (1981–3, Tate Gallery, London). It shows the artists Howard Hodgkin, David Hockney and Blake himself in a Venice, California that looks more like a Hockney painting than an actual cityscape, and mimics Gustave Courbet's *The Meeting, or Bonjour Monsieur Courbet* (1854, Musée Fabre, Montpellier), often described as inaugurating the age of heroic realism in European art (see Nochlin 1971a).

In philosophical terms, the key postmodernist text is LYOTARD's *La Condition postmoderne*, which alludes to Hassan's early notes on postmodernism as well as to the effects on human knowledge of computerization and the more general idea of a postindustrial society (Touraine 1969; Bell 1973, 1976), but associates the postmodern primarily with contemporary incredulity to the GRAND NARRATIVES of progress, socialism and the ENLIGHTENMENT. Like RORTY's rejection of FOUNDATIONALISM and VATTIMO's celebration of 'WEAK THOUGHT', Lyotard's rejection of grand narratives unsettles the stability of traditional notions of reason and rationality, whilst BAUDRILLARD's comment on the SIMULACRUM (1981) calls into question the existence of reality itself by pointing out (1986) that in some senses Disneyland is more real than the 'real' America in which it was built.

Criticisms of postmodernism come from many sources. Some black writers (Gilroy 1993b) and certain feminists (Lovibond 1990) object to the seeming complacency with which Lyotard announces the demise of grand narratives, pointing out that the grand narrative of *their* emancipation has by no means come to an end. HABERMAS (1980, 1985) argues that postmodernism is in fact an anti-modernism that betrays the promise of modernity by retreating into a wildly eclectic irrationalism, whilst the conservative Christopher Lasch (1979, 1995) holds that it is an expression of the rampant individualism of a 'culture of narcissism' which has lost all sense of values. For one of the most thorough historians of the idea of the postmodern, postmodernism represents the cultural logic of a period of late capitalism in which COMMODITY FETISHISM has become so extreme that it is the commodification process itself that is being consumed (Jameson 1991, 1998). Defenders of postmodernism, in contrast, tend to insist that it affords a liberation from a rationality that has indeed, in Weber's phrase (1904–05), become an 'iron cage', and is ushering in an era of relativism and a welcome pluralism.

postmodernity Although the debate about postmodernity and POSTMODERNISM is characterized by a degree of chronological and conceptual confusion, 'postmodernity' usually refers to a historical period subsequent to modernity, whilst 'postmodernism' tends to refer to the cultural and above all artistic manifestations of that period.

The transition from modernity to postmodernity, or the period of accelerated change that began after the Second World War, is usually assumed to be governed by some form of social or economic change and the postmodernist debate is – ironically, given that most participants would no longer consider classical MARXISM relevant to their concerns – often informed by a tacit appeal to the BASE/SUPER-STRUCTURE model which explains ideological phenomena in terms of an underlying economic structure. JAMESON, one of the few self-confessed Marxists to have contributed to the debate, bases his analysis of postmodernity (1991), described as embodying the cultural logic of late capitalism, on the Belgian economist Ernest Mandel's thesis (1972) that in the postwar period market capitalism and then monopoly capitalism have been superseded by a third technological revolution that gives rise to an era of *Spätkapitalismus* or late capitalism. This era is characterized, according to Mandel, by an unprecedented fusion of science, technology and production as the new technologies of nuclear energy and computers extend industrialization to all sectors of the economy and society. The importance of manual and physical labour declines as continuous flows of production and computerized control come to dominate industry and accord a new importance to intellectual workers such as scientists, laboratory workers and technicians.

Although Mandel himself denies it, his analysis does have something in common with the widespread argument that postmodernity is the era of a postindustrial society (Touraine 1969; Bell 1973, 1976) in which the production of commodities gives way to the production and manipulation of knowledge. Computerization is again accorded a major role in the transition to postmodernity; Touraine makes 'postindustrial society' synonymous with 'the programmed society', whilst LYOTARD also refers in his seminal account of the postmodern (1979a) to the hegemony of information technology as well as to the vaguely McLuhanite account of a global electronic revolution (MCLUHAN) invoked by Hassan (1971) in one of the early contributions to the postmodernity debate. A similar theory of technological modernization underpins BAUDRILLARD's vision of a postmodernity dominated by the accelerated circulation of signs and the new dominance of the SIMULACRUM, though it is also very reminiscent of DEBORD's theory of the society of the spectacle. The shift from modernity to postmodernity has also been explained in terms of a transition from FORDISM to POSTFORDISM (Harvey 1989), notably by those who, like Stuart HALL, argue that Britain began to live in 'new times' under the period of Conservative government that lasted from 1979 to 1997. The widespread feeling that modernity has in some sense come to an end is echoed by FUKUYAMA's reworking of KOJÈVE's thesis that history itself has come to an end and that we are living in a post-historical period (1992).

Most theorists regard postmodernity as marking a break with modernity and, in more general terms, the whole ENLIGHTENMENT project. HABERMAS (1980) argues that postmodernism represents an irrationalist reaction against a modernity which failed to supply the emancipation it promised, and that the project of modernity must therefore be continued. The more frequent argument, associated primarily with LYOTARD, is that postmodernity represents a liberation from the illusory GRAND NARRATIVES of the Enlightenment and its successors. BAUMAN, for his part, remarks (1992): 'modernity was a long march to prison', but also holds that, given that modernity's promise was never fulfilled, the task of the intellectual is to discover new forms of emancipation rather than surrendering to the seductions of postmodern consumerism.

READING: Bertens (1995); *Theory, Culture and Society* vol. 5 nos 2–3 (1988)

poststructuralism It might be argued that the idea of a 'poststructuralism' first emerged just as STRUCTURALISM reached its zenith at the international conference on 'The Languages of Criticism and the Sciences of Man' held at Johns Hopkins University in October 1966. In the discussion that followed his paper 'Structure, Sign and Play in the Discourse of the Human Sciences', Derrida described his DECONSTRUCTION as 'a criticism of structuralism' (1966; in Macksey and Donato 1972). And in their preface to the second (1972) edition of the published conference proceedings, Macksey and Donato remark: 'Today [November 1971] we may question the existence of structuralism as a meaningful concept.' BARTHES was already speaking (1971b) of his awakening from 'the dream of scientificity' he had associated with SEMIOLOGY and structuralism. Elsewhere, more political doubts about the value of structuralism were being voiced (see Macey 1994). When the Sorbonne was occupied by revolutionary students in May 1968, one item of graffiti proclaimed that 'Structures do not take to the streets', to which an anonymous hand added 'Nor does Barthes.' Another accused: '*Althusser à rien*' ('Althusser no good' or 'Al, you're useless' – '*Al, tu sers à rien*').

The term 'poststructuralism' is used very loosely and it is difficult to identify it with any specific school of thought. DERRIDA, BAUDRILLARD, DELEUZE, LYOTARD, RORTY and the later Barthes could all be described as poststructuralists; poststructuralism is often equated with deconstruction, also with POSTMODERNISM in general, but can also be seen as a strand within everything from NEW HISTORICISM to POSTCOLONIAL THEORY. If there is a common core to all the tendencies that have been described as poststructuralist, it lies in a reluctance to ground discourse in any theory of metaphysical origins, an insistence on the inevitable plurality and instability of meaning, a distrust of systematic scientificity, and the abandoning of the old ENLIGHTENMENT project.

practical criticism A mode of literary analysis centred on the intellectual exploration of the internal coherence of a short text or poem without making reference to external factors such as the author's biography or the historical context, and taking care to respect the liberty and autonomy of the text. The underlying assumption is that no poem can be judged by standards external to itself. Intimately associated with the close reading advocated by both LEAVIS and the NEW CRITICISM, the method originates in an experiment in the psychology of reading carried out by RICHARDS at Cambridge University in the 1920s (Richards 1929).

Having asked a group of students to read and comment on a set of poems whose author remained unidentified, Richards was struck by the lack of skill in reading revealed by their responses. He ascribed their misinterpretation of the poems to the difficulties inherent in reading, an inability to distinguish between levels of meaning, misapprehensions as to how METAPHOR works, sentimentality and spontaneous stock responses. The stated goal of practical criticism and of the privileging of the intensive rather than the extensive study of literary texts is to attain a finer, more precise and more discriminating form of communication. The theory of practical criticism is grounded in the psychology of reading outlined in I. A. Richards's *Principles of Literary Criticism* (1924), but it is also influenced by Richards's conviction that the First World War had ushered in a period of chaos in which cultural values were being standardized and levelled down by the mass media. In his view (1925), poetry was a repository of values and therefore a potential defence against chaos. Practical criticism of poetry in particular was intended by him to provide a means of climbing out of the trough of the cultural wave.

practico-inert SARTRE's term (1960) denoting the matter in which human PRAXIS is embodied. As the outcome of praxis is not predictable, the practico-inert may frustrate the original goal that defined its finality. One of Sartre's illustrations of the relationship between praxis and the practico-inert is his account of the Chinese peasants who cleared forests in order to create more arable land for food production. Their praxis did indeed create more cultivated land but, by stripping the mountains of their forest cover, it also resulted in erosion, a faster run-off of rainwater and therefore flooding which destroyed houses. The finality of expanding food production was achieved, but it was also frustrated by the counter-finality of flooding and destruction. It is because of the way that finality is so often turned into counter-finality that Sartre speaks of the 'hell' of the practico-inert. The DIALECTIC between the practico-inert and praxis is similar to that between the IN-ITSELF/ FOR-ITSELF aspects of being.

Prague School The Prague Linguistic Circle, often referred to simply as 'the Prague School', was founded in 1926 by a small group of Czech and Russian linguisticians. Like OPOYAZ and the MOSCOW LINGUISTIC CIRCLE, it played a vital role in the development of modern STRUCTURALISM. Although the Prague School is sometimes seen merely as an offshoot of RUSSIAN FORMALISM and although its work is often reduced to the PHONEME analysis of JAKOBSON and Trubetzkoy (1939), it in fact had a very broad agenda ranging from the study of folklore to aesthetics, the semiology of theatre and the semantic analysis of philosophical texts. Standard anthologies such as Vachek (1964) and Steiner (1982) give a good indication of the School's range of activities. The Prague Linguistic Circle was officially dissolved in 1950, but effectively died with the communist takeover of Czechoslovakia in 1948 and the subsequent imposition of a drab Marxist orthodoxy.

Prague linguistics draws on SAUSSURE, but tends to give more weight to SYNCHRONY and the historical dimension of language than many of his followers. The theses presented to the First Congress of Slavic Philologists in 1929 (reprinted in Steiner 1982) give a good indication of the Circle's main concerns and of its FUNCTIONALISM. Language is viewed in functional terms as a 'system of goal-oriented means of expression'; no linguistic phenomenon can be understood without reference to the system to which it belongs. Art, or rather the artistic system, is defined in terms very reminiscent of the Russian formalist notion of LITERATURNOST' or 'literariness'; the distinguishing feature of literary art is its orientation towards the sign rather than towards what it signifies. Writing on aesthetics and literary studies in 1941, Jan Mukarovsky (1891–1975), who was the group's main aesthetician, gives a representative account of the 'epistemological stance' of the Prague School: 'Structuralism sees the conceptual system of every discipline as internally correlated. Every concept in it determines all the others and is in turn determined by them.'

Praxis The Greek word meaning 'doing' is very widely used as a synonym for purposeful human activity. In his later Marxist-influenced work, SARTRE, for instance, defines praxis as practical action on the world, or as the practical transformation of the world in accordance with a desired end or finality (1960). Praxis is a specifically human activity; the dam-building of a beaver is not praxis because it is an instinctual and unchanging response to a natural environment, and because it implies neither the mastery of existing technology nor the development of new technical means. Beavers will always build dams in the same manner; human engineers will develop new ways of doing so. Although praxis is determined by a finality or goal, its outcome is not always predictable and it may be reversed into a counter-finality that frustrates the original intention. The outcome or material embodiment of praxis is referred to as the 'PRACTICO-INERT'; the relationship between the two is not dissimilar to that between the IN-ITSELF and the FOR-ITSELF.

In his *Prison Notebooks*, Gramsci (1971) uses the term 'philosophy of praxis' as a synonym for MARXISM.

Présence africaine Cultural and literary journal published in Paris and Dakar since 1947. 'Presénce africaine' is also the name of the associated publishing house, which specializes in francophone African literature, and its bookshop in Paris.

Founded by the Senegalese Alioune Diop (1910–80), *Présence africaine* is a product of the NEGRITUDE movement, and its original ambitions were to assert a black cultural presence and to implant African civilization in Europe. It has been a major vehicle for the promotion of Afrocentric writers such as DIOP and has done much to provide authors like CÉSAIRE and SENGHOR with a European audience. Although an English-language edition was produced for a while, the journal's focus has always been the triangle formed by France, francophone West Africa and the French-speaking Caribbean; North and Southern Africa have never been major concerns. *Présence africaine* has never been associated with any one political party or political line; its original programme was inseparable from the process of decolonization. The major Congresses of Black Writers and Artists organized in Paris (September 1956) and Rome (March/April 1959) have often been described as the cultural equivalent to the 1955 Bandung Conference of non-aligned Afro-Asian nations. Although it was held under the sign of black unity, the Paris Congress in particular was marked by difference of opinion between francophone Africans like Senghor and Americans like Richard Wright, who argued that the problems faced by Afro-Americans living in an industrial society were not the same as those faced by the population of France's African colonies. James Baldwin's 'Princes and Paupers' (1957) gives a good first-hand account of the Paris Congress. The first (November–December 1947) issue of *Présence africaine* and the issues that printed the proceedings of the two Congresses (nos 8–9–10, June–November 1956; nos 24–5, February–May 1959) were reprinted in facsimile in 1997.

Présence africaine originally spoke of 'bringing together men of colour', and its pages were male-dominated for a very long time; it was only in 1987 that an issue (no. 141) was devoted to women.

READING: Mudimbe (1992)

primal scene A scene of sexual intercourse between the parents and observed (or fantasized) by a child, who usually interprets it as an act of violent aggression on the part of the father. The memory of the primal scene feeds into most fantasies, and especially those of neurotics, the classic case history being that of FREUD's 'Wolf Man' patient (1918). The scene leads to the sexual arousal of the child, but at the same time induces castration anxiety and thus lays the foundations for the OEDIPUS COMPLEX. According to KLEIN, the child fantasizes that its parents are locked together in permanent intercourse; they merge to form the combined parent figure, and torment and destroy one another in the act of copulation. The combined parent figure is one of the most terrifying fantasies of early childhood (Klein 1932).

Whether or not the primal scene is an actual memory of a real event or a fantasy elaborated on the basis of fragmentary observations and suppositions is a question that is not really resolved by Freud.

problematic Derived from the historical EPISTEMOLOGY of BACHELARD and CANGUILHEM, the noun 'problematic' is used by ALTHUSSER (1965) to describe the system of unspoken or non-articulated questions governing the answers that a given text or discourse can and cannot answer. The problematic of a text determines the structural preconditions determining what it can and cannot perceive. A problematic is usually revealed by the gaps and contradictions that exist within the text, and is uncovered by the practice of SYMPTOMATIC READING.

problematization In the introduction to the second volume of his history of sexuality, FOUCAULT (1984a) speaks of his own work as an exercise in the history of problematization. In this context the expression refers to the way in which human sexuality becomes an object of concern, an element for reflection, and a material for stylization. Although he does not use the term 'problematization' until the 1970s (1976a), all Foucault's work can be described as a history of problematization in that it is an examination of how sets of DISCURSIVE FORMATIONS and practices constitute aspects of human behaviour as objects of knowledge, regulation and normalization. His early study of the history of madness (1961) looks, that is, at how a combination of institutional practices and a body of knowledge transforms the folly of old into the madness of the Classical period by problematizing it, whilst his history of sexuality explores how, in Classical Antiquity and the early Christian period, pleasures, desires and sexual behaviour in general come to be constituted as objects of knowledge and elements in an art of living (1984a, 1984b).

projection The term is widely used in both PSYCHOANALYSIS and clinical psychology to describe mechanisms that relocate elements of the psyche in the external world.

In psychoanalysis, projection is used to describe the process that enables the subject to expel feelings, qualities or OBJECTS it refuses to recognize in itself. Projection makes them appear to be external objects rather than internal parts of the psyche. For FREUD, projection is not a purely pathological phenomenon, but a normal feature of, for example, superstition and religious beliefs; demons and ghosts are projections of 'evil' unconscious desires and impulses. In so-called projective jealousy, the subject wards off his desire to be unfaithful by projecting jealousy onto his partner, and thus deflects attention away from his own unconscious desire (Freud 1922b). Projection is an important aspect of paranoia, and Freud's clearest descriptions of the phenomenon come from his account of the Schreber case (1911b). The statement 'I hate him' is transformed by projection into the statement 'He hates me and is persecuting me'; the paranoiac's initial impulse to hate can thus be justified as a rational defence against aggression. According to ANNA FREUD (1936), projection is one of the EGO's defence mechanisms. The projection of hatred characteristic of paranoia relieves, that is, the ego from the guilt it feels over its hatred of an OBJECT. Anna Freud thus assumes that the ego already knows the difference between 'inside' and 'outside'. The mechanism of projection is basic to the play-therapy technique developed by KLEIN: it allows the child to act out internal conflicts by projecting them onto the toys it has been given. In psychoanalytic terms, projection is the antithesis of INTROJECTION.

In clinical psychology, projective tests such as Rorschach tests and Thematic Aperception Tests are used to diagnose personality types. The patient is given an unstructured set of stimuli, such as visual images, that can trigger a wide range of responses. A correct interpretation of the stimuli is an indication of adaptation to reality; analysis of the fantasies and emotional responses that are simultaneously projected provides insight into the individual personality of the patient. The underlying thesis is that an individual's response to the outside world is governed by the state and structure of his or her inner world.

Propp, Vladimir (1895–1970) Russian folklorist. It might be said that Propp's *Morphology of the Folktale* (1928) is to modern NARRATOLOGY what SAUSSURE's *Course in General Linguistics* (1916) is to STRUCTURALISM.

Propp does not analyse the content of traditional Russian folk-tales, but their form or morphology, arguing that a rigorous synchronic description of their formal features is an essential preliminary to any study of their content or historical importance. The careful description of a broad corpus of tales reveals that, despite their apparent diversity, they in fact revolve around a small number of functions and roles which are constant throughout the corpus. These functions and roles form the grammar or deep structure of the tales, and they are assumed by Propp to be universal. Propp identifies thirty-one functions, each of which serves to advance the narrative development of the tale. The first three functions of a tale might be as follows: 1) A member of a family leaves home or sets out on a quest; 2) he or she is told not to do something ('Do not go into the woods . . .'); 3) he or she disobeys that injunction, and thus triggers a new development. Propp also identifies seven roles, which may be played by a wide variety of different characters but which always have the same narrative purpose. They are the villain, the hero, the donor, the helper, the princess and her father, the dispatcher and the hero. Not all roles and functions are present in every tale, but no tale can be told without using at least some of these basic units.

Propp was associated with RUSSIAN FORMALISM and his work, like that of other formalists, has had a crucial influence on modern structuralism and on the work of such narratologists and semioticians as GREIMAS and BREMOND.

READING: Lévi-Strauss (1960)

prosopopoeia In RHETORIC, a device whereby an imaginary or absent figure is represented as acting or speaking; more generally, the introduction into a speech or discourse of a pretended or imaginary figure.

psychanalyse et politique (psychoanalysis and politics).   An influential group within the French women's movement, founded by Antoinette Fouque, Monique WITTIG and others in 1969, and usually referred to as *psych et po*. Fouque soon proved to be the dominant figure, and she has often been accused by critics of promoting her own personality cult. *psych et po*'s influence was greatly extended by the establishment of the 'éditions des femmes' publishing house in 1973. 'des femmes' has long been associated with *ÉCRITURE FÉMININE*.

psych et po has always taken the view that, *pace* Simone de BEAUVOIR, women are born and not made, and celebrates the innate homosexuality of all women (though this is not necessarily synonymous with lesbianism) by emphasizing the need to use a modified psychoanalysis to recover a repressed woman-ness. The group has always refused to define itself as feminist, claiming like CIXOUS that FEMINISM is an inverted image of the dominant ideology of the PATRIARCHY and that feminists are mere reformists, if not ideological transvestites. Always controversial, the group was at the centre of a major scandal in 1979 when it registered the initials MLF (Mouvement de libération des femmes, Women's Liberation Movement) as a trademark and claimed exclusive rights to its use.

READING: Clément (1981); Marks and Courtivron (1979)

psychoanalysis In a lucid and non-specialist description of the discipline he founded, FREUD (1922c) describes psychoanalysis as comprising: 1) a discipline founded on a procedure for the investigation of mental processes that are otherwise inaccessible because they are UNCONSCIOUS; 2) a therapeutic method for the treatment of neurotic disorders; and 3) a body of psychological data evolving into a new scientific discipline. Freud's third and broadest category comprises his work on culture (which is based largely on the view that culture is a product of the diversion or SUBLIMATION of sexual energy) and art, which provides the starting-point for the many varieties of PSYCHOANALYTIC CRITICISM. The two series of *Introductory Lectures on Psychoanalysis* (1916–17, 1933) provide an excellent overview of Freudian theory; *The Language of Psychoanalysis* by Laplanche and Pontalis (1967) provides an essential guide to its concepts and terminology.

Although the history of psychoanalysis is inseparable from that of Freud's life and of the long self-analysis (see Anzieu 1975) which led him to write his great *Intepretation of Dreams* (1900), it is clear that his new science is rooted in the traditions of nineteenth-century psychology (Ellenberger 1970) and biology (Sulloway 1979). Freud's ventures into anthropology, which he views as an integral part of his new scientific discipline, are also influenced by nineteenth-century theories of evolution and by their attendant EUROCENTRISM; hence the analogy between the 'mental life of savages and neurotics' posited in *Totem and Taboo* (1913), and the argument that the life of an individual re-enacts or repeats the life of the species (see in particular the posthumously published article 1915d). It is also clear that Freud's descriptions of the workings of the unconscious, with its flows of energy, and of LIBIDO and its mechanisms of discharge, owe much to the physics and hydraulics of his age.

Freud constantly revises and reworks his theories, and all the modifications he introduces are closely related to developments at the clinical level as he gradually abandons the therapeutic technique of hypnosis and CATHARSIS in favour of the TALKING CURE, and moves from his early SEDUCTION THEORY of HYSTERIA to a theory of both neurosis and normal development that is based upon the discovery of the OEDIPUS COMPLEX and its vital importance in psychosexual development. Yet despite all the changes that are introduced, there is a constant emphasis on the unconscious and on sexuality, defined in such broad terms as to include the oral and anal dimensions and not merely the narrowly genital or procreative dimension. It is the emphasis on sexuality that leads to the major disagreements between Freud and JUNG, whom the former at one point regarded as his crown prince. Freud's theories are obviously not beyond criticism (see PSYCHOANALYSIS AND FEMINISM), but they have had an incalculable impact on the twentieth-century vision of sexuality, not least by insisting that children are not asexual and have a sexual life of their own (1905a, 1908a).

The best account of the gradual development of the technique of psychoanalysis is that provided by Freud himself in his correspondence with Wilhelm Fliess, the ear, nose and throat specialist with whom he collaborated in the 1890s (Freud 1985), in the studies on hysteria coauthored with Breuer (1893–5), and in the five published case histories (1905c, 1909b, 1911b, 1918, 1920b). The technique that evolved is still in use today, sometimes with certain modifications. The central element is the method of FREE ASSOCIATION, with the patient or analysand lying on a couch and with the analyst sitting slightly to the rear and out of eyeshot. The patient is required to tell everything and omit nothing; the analyst to listen to everything and to privilege nothing. Free association around dreams or memories allows unconscious chains of fantasies and wishes to be reconstructed and then interpreted so as to uncover underlying structures which, typically, relate to the Oedipus complex, FAMILY ROMANCES, and repressed childhood memories, usually with a sexual content. Although dreams are described by Freud as 'the royal road to the unconscious' (1900), it should be noted that the psychoanalyst's raw material is not the unconscious itself (which is by definition inaccessible), but material that has already been shaped by the DREAM-WORK. The central factor in the analytic treatment is the TRANSFERENCE that allows unconscious or repressed material to be reactualized in verbal form rather than reproduced in symptoms, and projected onto the analyst. In a classic Freudian psychoanalysis, the analysand has daily sessions of analysis, each lasting fifty minutes (the so-called 'analytic hour'); the payment of fees is held to have great symbolic importance. Freud never claimed that his method was a universal panacea, but once remarked with typically pessimistic wit that it could transform 'hysterical misery' into 'common unhappiness' (Freud and Breuer 1893–5).

Although psychoanalysis is widely practised and has had an important influence on related therapeutic methods, it has never been defined in either medical or legal terms. The profession is self-regulated and its standards of practice are defined by the various national associations recognized as competent by the International Psychoanalytic Association. The would-be psychoanalyst undertakes a personal analysis before embarking upon a rigorous training analysis designed to promote a recognition of the importance of transference and countertransference. Qualified analysts normally work under the supervision of their seniors, and usually undertake at least one 'second analysis'. The first generation of psychoanalysts were, like Freud himself, doctors of medicine, but suitably qualified non-medical or lay analysts were admitted to the profession from the 1920s onwards (Freud 1926a). The desirability or otherwise of medical qualifications is a matter for the various national associations. The question of the scientific nature of psychoanalysis remains controversial. The British Medical Association, for instance, has always argued that it is not competent to judge either its therapeutic or scientific value and therefore maintains a neutral stance on the matter. One of the more common philosophical criticisms of Freud and his followers is that they seek confirmation for their theories and do not test them by invoking the epistemological criterion of FALSIFIABILITY.

Freud's own career was punctuated by a series of breaks with colleagues to whom he had once been close, and the history of the psychoanalytic movement is one of splits and schisms as well as of international expansion. All the major tendencies within contemporary psychoanalysis claim a Freudian ancestry, but take as their starting-point different periods in his work or different aspects of his theories. Very schematically, the main post-Freudian currents within psychoanalysis are EGO-PSYCHOLOGY, Kleinian analysis (KLEIN), OBJECT-RELATIONS theory and Lacanian analysis (LACAN).

psychoanalysis and feminism The debate between psychoanalysis and feminism has been long and often acrimonious. Although it begins with the discussions of the so-called phallic stage of development that took place in the 1920s and 1930s (Jones 1927, 1933), it took on a new importance in the 1970s as questions of GENDER and its reproduction came to the fore and as feminists such as Juliet MITCHELL reacted against the anti-psychoanalytic stance taken by many of the early spokeswomen for WOMEN'S LIBERATION. The literature on feminism and psychoanalysis is now so extensive and the debate so far-reaching as to have become the subject of a valuable critical dictionary (Wright 1992).

In her pioneering *The Feminine Mystique*, FRIEDAN (1963) argued that psychoanalysis was one of the major sources of the mystique of her title, which persuaded women to collude in their own domination by men. BEAUVOIR, for her part, had already described (1947b) psychoanalysis as encouraging or even engineering a social conformity that was detrimental to women's interests. MILLETT, FIRESTONE and GREER were all agreed that psychoanalysis was part of the IDEOLOGY of PATRIARCHY. A major shift occurred when Mitchell began to contend (1974) that, far from being a prescription for patriarchy, psychoanalysis offered a theory of patriarchy and gender that could contribute to the liberation of women.

Precedents for both sides of the argument can be found in the writings of FREUD himself. On the one hand, he states quite baldly that 'anatomy is destiny' (1924b) and explains the little girl's 'sense of inferiority' in terms of the narcissistic wound inflicted by her realization that she does not have a penis (1925); elsewhere he argues that, whilst psychoanalysis cannot describe 'what a woman is', it can help to elucidate 'how she comes into being, how a woman develops out of a child with a bisexual disposition' (1933). Despite this claim, Freud's writings are full of metaphors of darkness and obscurity that help to turn femininity into a 'dark continent' (1926a) which is almost impossible to understand (see Macey 1988 chapter 5).

It was the references to a 'sense of inferiority' and the stress on penis envy which defined women as incomplete males that were so offensive to writers like Millett. The Freudian notion of penis envy was the central issue in the early debates over the phallic phase, or that stage in psychosexual development in which children of both genders believe in the existence of only one genital organ. The girl's realization that she does not have a penis leads her to conclude that she once had one but has been castrated, and she then embarks on the long process of feminization which will lead her to transform her wish for the penis into a wish for a child. Although Ernest Jones, Karen Horney and others argued that the girl did have an intuitive knowledge of her own genitals, the Freudian view prevailed. The authors of a standard work of reference – both eminent psychoanalysts – are quite firm: penis envy is the 'fundamental element in female sexuality and root of its dialectic' (Laplanche and Pontalis 1967).

Arguing that the psychoanalysis that so offended many feminists was in fact a vulgarized or revisionist version of Freud, Mitchell and others like Jacqueline Rose (see the essays collected in Rose 1986 and the introductions to Mitchell and Rose 1982) contend that LACAN's 'return to Freud' offered a solution. Others suggested that feminism was in danger of being seduced by psychoanalysis (Gallop 1982).

Lacan's main contributions to the debate are the concepts of the SYMBOLIC, the PHALLUS and the NAME-OF-THE-FATHER, which do move the discussion away from the biologism of Freud's remarks about anatomy and destiny. They also create new problems. It is difficult to find precedents for the use of 'phallus' rather than 'penis' in Freud, and the link that is established by Lacan between the phallus and access to the symbolic is vulnerable to DERRIDA's accusation of PHALLOGOCENTRISM. The importance ascribed to the name-of-the-father can, for its part, be seen as a rearguard

action against the greater emphasis that is placed on mothering by KLEIN, WINNIC-
OTT and Nancy Chodorov (1978). Whilst elements of Lacanian psychoanalysis have
become an essential part of certain forms of feminism, and certainly of some
FEMINIST CRITICISM, critics such as IRIGARAY argue that both its basic epistemology
and its practices are inherently masculinist.

psychoanalytic criticism Psychoanalytically based approaches to literature and
the other arts take a wide variety of forms, ranging from BETTELHEIM's thesis (1976)
that fairy-tales depict stages of psychic development and serve as metaphors for
unconscious conflicts to BLOOM's description of the ANXIETY OF INFLUENCE
(1973). FREUD's paper on FAMILY ROMANCE (1909a) has been used to formulate a
typological study of the novel (Robert 1972), whilst his essay on the UNCANNY (1919)
has inspired a more thematic approach (Kofman 1974). All are grounded or based
upon Freud's descriptions of the workings of the UNCONSCIOUS and they usually
claim to uncover or work with material that is not consciously present in the mind
of the author or artist in question. It would be erroneous, however, to speak of the
psychoanalysis *of* authors; psychoanalytic criticism is an application of Freudian
theory and not an equivalent to a TALKING CURE involving a direct encounter
between analyst and analysand. It cannot, by definition, have any therapeutic goal
or dimension.

Freud's writings abound in allusions and references to literature, usually in the
form of the German classical tradition, and he believes that the sources of literary
creativity and psychoanalysis are similar. Lacan makes a similar point when he
remarks (1965) of the French novelist Marguerite Duras that 'she knows without
me what I teach.' Literary models play an important role in the development of
psychoanalysis; the theory of the OEDIPUS COMPLEX originates in Freud's reading
of Sophocles and Greek mythology and his contention that *Oedipus Rex* encapsulates
a universal experience or memory. Yet Freud is less interested in aesthetics as such
than in the psychology and psychopathology of creativity; as he notes (1914b),
psychoanalysis therefore tends to move from the analysis of works of art to the
analysis of their creators. Literary examples are often used by Freud to illustrate or
confirm his theories. His interest in Jensen's *Gradiva*, a 'Pompeian fantasy' published
in 1905, appears to stem from the fact that it can be read as a study of the return of
the repressed rather than from its intrinsic value as a novel (1907). A similar note is
struck when Kristeva suggests (1987a) that the important thing about Dostoyevsky
is his ability to illustrate her own views on the dynamics of depression.

Freud devotes a number of papers to aesthetic and literary topics. The most
important are the study of Dostoyevsky (1927a), the essays on Leonardo da Vinci
(1910a) and Michelangelo (1914b), and the shorter and more general paper on creative
writing (1908b). In these papers, creative activity is usually described as the adult
equivalent to the fantasies of childhood. Fiction is seen as providing a form of
wish-fulfilment and a pleasurable exploration of imaginary identifications with
heroes and heroines. Freud's investigations into creativity make frequent reference
to his concept of SUBLIMATION: Leonardo's scientific curiosity, for example, is
analysed as a sublimated expression of his childhood curiosity about sexuality,

whilst the famous smile of the Mona Lisa is traced back to a childhood fantasy of suckling and passive oral intercourse.

The study of Leonardo, which is in fact flawed by Freud's reliance on inaccurate information, provides the prototype for psychobiography, which is the dominant mode of classic psychoanalytic criticism. In Marie Bonaparte's study of Edgar Allan Poe (1933), the *Tales* are grouped into cycles centred on maternal and paternal figures which are analysed as though they were the manifest content of a dream. Bonaparte's interpretation of their latent content is then integrated into the known biographical data to produce a psychobiography in which 'The Purloined Letter' is illustrative or expressive of Poe's nostalgia for the maternal phallus and of his hatred and fear of his father. There is thus a tendency to dissolve particular works by individual authors into a universal symbolism.

Like Freud before him, LACAN makes frequent use of literary and cultural allusions, often for illustrative or pedagogic purposes. His style is heavily influenced by his youthful association with SURREALISM, but his use of literature can be surprisingly conventional and even utilitarian, as when he describes *Hamlet* as illustrating a decadent form of the Oedipus complex (1958–9) or when he reads Poe's 'Purloined Letter' as an allegory of the workings of the signifer (1955b; this paper can also be read as a personal critique of Bonaparte, who was one of Lacan's many enemies).

Post-Lacanian psychoanalysis has developed into a highly literate, even literary style of reading and writing, perhaps because so many of those who have turned to Lacan have, especially outside France, backgrounds in the humanities and literary studies. As Lacanian psychoanalysis fuses with Derridean DECONSTRUCTION and HERMENEUTICS, the traditional divorce between 'theory' and 'fiction' becomes blurred by the emergence of 'theoretical fictions' (Kofman 1974; Felman 1977; Bowie 1987). The sophistication and erudition of such studies cannot be denied, but they are surely far removed from Freud's more positivistic ambitions and statements.

READING: Wright (1984); *Yale French Studies* (1977)

psychosis Defined in clinical psychiatry as a serious mental illness affecting the whole of the personality. Unlike a patient suffering from a NEUROSIS, the psychotic is not usually aware of the morbidity of his or her condition, cannot be treated on a consensual basis and may therefore have to be committed to a psychiatric institution.

The word *Psychose* has been current in German since the 1840s, but was originally used to refer to any form of mental illness (Laplanche and Pontalis 1967). The distinction between psychosis and neurosis was introduced and gradually refined in the course of the nineteenth century, and is basic to PSYCHOANALYSIS. In psychoanalysis, 'psychosis' is used to describe conditions such as hallucinatory confusion, paranoia and schizophrenia (which Freud, using an earlier terminology, tends to refer to as 'paraphrenia'). FREUD himself tended to take the neurosis/psychosis distinction for granted, but devoted relatively little attention to the latter, mainly because his theory of psychoanalysis was developed primarily with reference to neurosis. LACAN, in contrast, began his career by working with psychotics in psychiatric hospitals before he became a psychoanalyst (1932) and therefore elaborates a more specific theory of the origins of psychosis.

Contrasting neurosis and psychosis, Freud argues (1924c, 1924d) that, whilst both conditions originate in a conflict between the EGO and other agencies of the psyche, psychosis results from a disturbance in the ego's relationship with the external world, neurosis from a conflict between the ego and the ID. In psychosis the ego withdraws from some part or aspect of the real world, either failing to perceive it or being unaffected by its perception of it. In schizophrenia, for instance, there is no participation in the world. A rent appears in the relationship with the world, and it is 'patched' by delusions and hallucinations.

Lacan draws on Freud's comment, and especially his remarks (1911b) on the case of Daniel Paul Schreber, an appeal court judge who wrote an autobiographical account of his paranoid delusions, to elaborate the thesis that psychosis is triggered by the specific mechanism of FORECLOSURE (Lacan 1957–8, 1981). A key signifier such as the PHALLUS or the NAME-OF-THE-FATHER is expelled or foreclosed from the subject's symbolic world, and a hole or rent is left in its place. The foreclosed signifier is not integrated into the UNCONSCIOUS thanks to an act of repression, and therefore cannot return in the form of a neurotic signifier. It returns, rather, in the REAL, usually in the form of persecutory hallucinations and delusions.

queer Synonym for 'homosexual' or 'GAY'. The word has traditionally been used in a highly pejorative sense and has been seen as a classic expression of HOMOPHOBIA but, according to Green's authoritative dictionary of slang (1998), did not acquire negative connotations until c. 1925. It was reappropriated as a positive self-designation by gay or queer militants in the early 1990s. In the United States the militant Queer Nation organization was founded in 1990; the gay newspaper *The Advocate* proclaimed 1992 the 'Year of the Queer'. The change of terminology reflects both a growing unease with the gay IDENTITY POLITICS of the previous decades and the impact of the new and angry militancy provoked by the media panic over the spread of AIDS and media attempts to 'blame' gays for it (Watney 1987). Queer theory questions the early gay liberationist notion of a stable or core gay identity, pointing out that homosexuality is a category of knowledge rather than a tangible reality. It also attempts to broaden the definition of gay and lesbian politics to include a bisexuality that is often viewed with suspicion by gays and feminists alike (Phelan 1997).

Queer theory is largely a product of the 1990s and has been influential in literary studies, POSTCOLONIAL THEORY and some areas of sociology (Seidman 1996). A number of influences can be detected, but the starting-point for most queer theory is FOUCAULT's theses about regimes of sexuality and the epistemological shift brought about by the emergence of the category of 'the homosexual', when a taxonomy of acts (such as the remarkably vague notion of 'sodomy') was replaced by a typology of sexual identities (Foucault 1976a; see also Weeks 1977). One of the key texts in the development of queer theory describes those theses as 'axiomatic' (Sedgwick 1990). DERRIDA'S DECONSTRUCTION is frequently evoked in order to demonstrate the instability of binary oppositions such as male/female and hetero/homosexuality, as are Judith BUTLER's theses on GENDER as PERFORMATIVE (1990). Masculinity can be demonstrated to be an unstable cluster of fears about effeminacy and repressed homosexual or homosocial desires, rather than the 'simple' opposite of femininity. There is, for some, a considerable overlap between queer theory, NEW HISTORICISM, CULTURAL MATERIALISM and the theory of SUBCULTURES (Dollimore 1991; Sinfield 1994), and it is argued that it is part of a more general defence of minority cultures.

In literary terms, the most important fields for queer theory are the Renaissance and early modern periods (Sedgwick 1985; Greenblatt 1985; Traub 1992). In her important afterword to the anthology *Queering the Renaissance* (Goldberg 1994),

Margaret Hunt explains that Renaissance societies are sufficiently different from modern societies to destabilize received notions of gender, sexuality and identity because they did not, for example, have any psychological or medical model of homosexuality; at the same time, the Renaissance often provides models that are used to validate mainstream concepts of individuality. The literature of those societies thus makes it possible to chart the rise of modern Western social-political systems and the way they define gender in normative terms. In the same anthology Alan Bray examines the uncertain boundary between male friendship and homosexuality by looking at the ambiguous relationship between Edward and Gaveston in Marlowe's *Edward II*; what could be a sodomitical relationship is seemingly inscribed within the socially acceptable category of passionate male friendship, but the tension between the two categories is never resolved. Queer theory ultimately raises the question of whether the notion of fixed sexual identities is desirable or even tenable.

R

radical feminism A tendency within FEMINISM and the WOMEN'S LIBERATION movement, typified by FIRESTONE's *Dialectic of Sex* (1971), which defines women as forming a class in a quasi-Marxist sense and considers the sex-class division as the fundamental division within a society dominated by PATRIARCHY. Many of the earliest statements from the American women's movement were made from a radical feminist perspective (see the materials collected as Morgan 1970) and, although the British movement tended to be dominated by SOCIALIST FEMINISM, radical feminism was a powerful force in Britain from the early 1970s onwards.

Whilst not all its supporters would agree with Firestone that women's oppression is grounded in their biological role as potential mothers, most radical feminists would agree that all women are to be regarded as potential allies in a struggle for liberation that brings them into conflict with all men. The insistence that the primary struggle is one against men and PATRIARCHY, rather than against the social structures of capitalist society, leads radical feminists to be suspicious of the broader concerns of socialist feminism, which, they argue, subordinates women's interests to those of male-dominated political parties, trade unions and other organizations. Differences of opinion between socialist and radical feminists lay at the origins of many of the divisions within the women's liberation movement of the 1970s. The most extreme forms of radical feminism led to separatism, or a refusal to cooperate even with heterosexual women, to calls for male babies to be excluded from women's conferences, and to the argument that the logical choice for 'women-identified women' was political lesbianism.

READING: Coote and Campbell (1982)

Radical Philosophy British journal founded in 1972, initially published three times a year but appearing bimonthly since January 1995 (issue 69). *Radical Philosophy* is a product of the NEW LEFT, born of discontent with the complacency of traditional departments of philosophy and of impatience with the dominant tradition of ANALYTIC PHILOSOPHY. The journal has long been a major forum for the discussion of WESTERN MARXISM and strands of CONTINENTAL PHILOSOPHY. Although it is subtitled 'A Journal of Socialist and Feminist Philosophy', it was not until 1977 (issue 17) that 'women and philosophy' became one of its major concerns. Collectively edited, financially independent and accessible to non-professionals, *Radical*

Philosophy represents a remarkable achievement; very few products of the political radicalism of the early 1970s have survived for so long.

reader-response theory A theory of literature associated mainly with Stanley FISH and, in slightly different form, Wolfgang ISER. The central tenets of all varieties of reader-response theory are that meaning is not something that is contained within a text or that can be extracted from it, and that what a text does is more important than what it is. Far from being pregiven, meaning is produced by readers working in conjunction with the structures of the text, and in accordance with the reading strategies and interpretive conventions that bind readers together into INTERPRETIVE COMMUNITIES and put them in possession of an internalized literary COMPETENCE that allows them to respond appropriately to the texts they encounter. Reader-response theory is in many ways a response to the excesses of both the NEW CRITICISM, with its vision of the text as a self-contained monad, and STRUCTURALISM, with its stress on the impersonal laws and structures that govern texts.

In her remarkable study of ROMANCE and its readers, Radway (1984) combines a form of reader-response theory with a sociological inquiry based on the analysis of questionnaires to demonstrate that the readers and writers of romances form a loosely-knit community, mediated by the publishing industry and its marketing strategies, that is bound together by shared assumptions as to what constitutes a 'good' romance.

A variant on reader-response theory can be found in those theories of SUBCULTURE which stress that, far from responding passively to the mass culture distributed by the CULTURE INDUSTRIES, social groups actually use pop music and styles of dress to create meanings and identities.

READING: Tompkins (1980)

real In Lacanian (LACAN) PSYCHOANALYSIS, one of the three orders that structure human existence, the others being the IMAGINARY and the SYMBOLIC. Lacan's references to the real tend to be allusive, and he does not discuss it as fully as the other two orders. The fifth chapter of his seminar on the four fundamental concepts of psychoanalysis (1973) provides perhaps the clearest exposition.

The real is not simply synonymous with external reality, and nor is it simply the antonym of 'imaginary'. It exists outside or beyond the symbolic, is menacingly homogeneous, and is not composed of distinct and differential signifiers. The real is described as that which resists symbolization and signification, and is usually encountered in the context of trauma and PSYCHOSIS. If, for instance, the NAME-OF-THE-FATHER cannot be integrated into the subject's symbolic world, the mechanism of FORECLOSURE will ensure that it is expelled into the real and not repressed into the UNCONSCIOUS, thus triggering a PSYCHOSIS. The foreclosed signifier will then return in the real in the form of a persecutory image that cannot be mastered through verbal symbolization.

reality-effect (*effet de réel*) BARTHES' term for the effect produced by details that are, from a strictly structural point of view, redundant or superfluous in that they do nothing to advance the narrative and may in fact interrupt it (Barthes 1968a).

One of the examples given by Barthes is taken from Flaubert's 'A Simple Heart' (in Flaubert 1877): an old piano beneath a barometer with a pyramidal pile of boxes on top of it. None of these objects has any structural role in the economy of the narrative. They are an INDEX of atmosphere, and their function is to state 'we are real', and thus to signify the category of reality that underpins the VERISIMILITUDE of the narrative by guaranteeing that 'it happened.' The reality-effect is an essential feature of literary realism.

reality principle Together with the PLEASURE PRINCIPLE, the reality principle is, according to FREUD (1911a), one of the two principles governing the workings of the psyche. The reality principle modifies the pleasure principle by regulating the instinctive search for pleasure. Under its influence, the search for pleasure ceases to be immediate as momentary and uncertain pleasures are renounced in order to gain a more assured pleasure at a later stage (deferred gratification). The quest for pleasure is thus modified so as to make it conform to the conditions imposed by external realities. The religious doctrine which holds that those who renounce earthly pleasures can expect to be rewarded in the afterlife is viewed by Freud as a PROJECTION of the reality principle.

reality-testing Defined by FREUD (1917b) as a process which allows the individual to distinguish between external stimuli and internal stimuli from within the psyche, and to establish the vital inner/outer distinction. Reality-testing is a defence against hallucination and the confusion of what is actually perceived and what is imagined. Reality-testing is one of the major functions of the EGO.

recovered memory A memory, recovered during psychotherapy, of sexual abuse, usually at the hands of a father or other male relative, suffered during childhood. Recovered memory syndrome, in which adults discover during therapy that they were abused by their parents, became a highly controversial issue during the early 1990s, particularly in the United States. Critics refer to it as FALSE MEMORY SYNDROME and argue that the memories are actually 'induced' or even implanted during therapy. The bitter debates about recovered memory and false memory syndrome have led to renewed controversy about PSYCHOANALYSIS and especially the contentious issue of the SEDUCTION THEORY. In 1998 the British Royal College of Psychiatrists published a report concluding that 'recovered' memories of abuse were almost certainly unreliable (Brandon, Boakes, Glaser and Green 1998).

READING: Crews et al. (1997)

referent The real or extra-linguistic object designated by a SIGN. The referent is to be distinguished from the SIGNIFIED, which is described by SAUSSURE as a mental image, and not as a material object. The relationship between sign and referent is one of DENOTATION.

Reich, Wilhelm (1897–1957) Austrian-American psychoanalyst and apostle of sexual liberation. Reich enjoyed the unique distinction of being expelled from both the German Communist Party and the International Psychoanalytic Association.

Reich's main contribution to PSYCHOANALYSIS is his study of character analysis

(1933), in which he examines those defensive attitudes on the part of the patient which resist the analyst's attempts at interpretation and which persist despite the patient's verbalizations in FREE ASSOCIATION. In a character-NEUROSIS, defensive conflicts take the form of character traits or modes of behaviour rather than that of classic symptoms. They result in the formation of a 'character armour' typified by the physical rigidity of the body and an absence of emotional contact with others. In Reich's view, the development of character armour is a defence against the anti-sexual pressures exerted by the authoritarian family.

Reich departs from FREUD and psychoanalytic orthodoxy by reducing sexuality to a narrowly defined genital sexuality and by transforming the theory of DRIVES to the notion of a search for purely genital satisfaction. Neuroses are viewed as resulting from a disturbance in genital sexuality and a loss of 'orgastic' potency, defined as the capacity to achieve full sexual excitation and complete release in a full and uninhibited surrender to the flow of biological energy. The release of dammed-up energy is defined as the end-pleasure of the 'normal' (i.e. heterosexual) sex-act.

In the 1930s Reich was active in sexual politics in Vienna and then Berlin, where he helped to establish sex-hygiene clinics offering advice and contraception to young people in an attempt to promote a sexual revolution which, in the view of the Communist Party leadership, threatened to divert the energies of the young into sexual rather than political activity. Reich was one of the first to posit a link between psychoanalysis and MARXISM, arguing (1935) that psychoanalysis originates in an awareness of or resistance to sexual repression, just as Marxism's origins lay in the struggle against economic repression.

In 1933 Reich emigrated to the United States, where he spent the remainder of his life. His last years were devoted to an attempt to capture the blue cosmic energy he called 'orgone'. In 1952 he was imprisoned for renting out an orgone accumulator, described by the Food and Drug Administration as a fraudulent therapeutic device. Despite the eccentricity of his later theories, Reich was something of a cult figure in the 1960s, when his *The Function of the Orgasm* (1942) enjoyed widespread popularity. The emphasis placed on genitality and 'normal' sexuality makes his writings look distinctly problematic in a contemporary cultural climate influenced by FEMINISM and GAY politics.

READING: Robinson (1972); Rycroft (1971)

reification From the Latin *res* ('thing') and *facere* ('to make'): to make a thing, or to make into a thing. In MARXISM, the term is used to describe an extreme form of ALIENATION induced by COMMODITY FETISHISM. The classic formulation of the theory of reification is to be found in the chapter entitled 'Reification and the Consciousness of the Proletariat' in LUKÁCS's *History and Class Consciousness* (1923); it is an important theme in the writings of the FRANKFURT SCHOOL and in the work of many of the theorists associated with the NEW LEFT.

According to Lukács, the nature of a modern capitalist society is such that commodity fetishism extends to all fields of human activity, including consciousness itself. Human beings literally appear as things rather than the active agents of economic activity and historical change. As labour and the commodities in which it is embodied take on an illusory autonomy, human activity becomes passive or contemplative in the face of the apparently autonomous exchange of commodities that appear to have been divorced from the sociopolitical relations in which they are produced. The only form of consciousness that can escape and transcend reification is the active collective consciousness that is embodied in the revolutionary party of the proletariat.

representamen A key notion in the SEMIOTICS of PEIRCE (1932, 1934), and an equivalent to SAUSSURE'S SIGN. The representamen consists of a signans and a signatum, which correspond roughly to the more familiar signifier and signified. Unlike Saussure, Peirce elaborates a complex classification of types of signs defined by the nature of the relationship between signans and signatum. The most familiar are the ICON, the INDEX and the SYMBOL.

repression For FREUD the theory of repression (1915c), together with the assumption that unconscious processes exist and the appreciation of the importance of sexuality and of the OEDIPUS COMPLEX, is one of the cornerstones of PSYCHOANALYSIS (1922c). Repression occurs when impulses, wishes or memories, usually but not always of a sexual nature, that are bound up with the DRIVES, are denied access to the conscious mind by the ego because it regards them as a threat to its integrity or because they offend the ethical standards imposed upon it by the SUPEREGO. Such impulses and wishes are forced back into the UNCONSCIOUS but almost inevitably find other means of expression by using the mechanisms of CONDENSATION and DISPLACEMENT. The resultant conflict between the respective demands of the EGO and the UNCONSCIOUS results in the formation of symptoms, which are a form of substitute sexual satisfaction or wish-fulfilment. Repression is not a single act which occurs only once, but a continuous application of pressure in the direction of the unconscious. The theory of repression is the key to the psychoanalytic understanding of NEUROSIS and especially HYSTERIA. LACAN argues (1957–8) that the triggering of a PSYCHOSIS is governed by the different and specific process of FORECLOSURE.

The expression 'primal repression' is used by Freud to refer to a hypothetical process in which the unconscious is constituted through the formation and repression of unconscious ideas and representations (1926b). The result is the lasting fixation of the drive to one particular representation. 'Primal' is used here in the sense in which Freud speaks of the PRIMAL SCENE.

repressive desublimation A process described by MARCUSE in his *One-Dimensional Man* (1964) and related to his notion of REPRESSIVE TOLERANCE. Desublimation reverses the process of SUBLIMATION described by Freud, and offers the immediate gratification of instinctual desires rather than their mediated or deferred gratification. Repressive desublimation is a characteristic feature of advanced industrial-capitalist societies in which individuals are conditioned by the CULTURE INDUSTRY and other agencies to accept spontaneously whatever is offered them by society. Whereas sublimation produces true works of art, REPRESSIVE SUBLIMATION generates the eroticism and PORNOGRAPHY that offer only a hollow semblance of freedom and liberation. The mechanism absorbs the PLEASURE PRINCIPLE into the REALITY

PRINCIPLE, and sexuality, for example, is 'liberated' through forms of sexual activity that promote social cohesion. For Marcuse, unbridled forms of sexuality which should have an anti-authoritarian dimension are actually transformed into a new form of social conformism.

repressive hypothesis FOUCAULT's term for the widespread belief that, whereas a certain openness about sexuality prevailed until the end of the seventeenth century, the eighteenth century ushered in a period of repression that culminated in the Victorian era's silence about sex and in the imposition of the monogamous heterosexual model (Foucault 1976a). Foucault demonstrates that, on the contrary, the nineteenth century is characterized by a proliferation of DISCOURSES on sexuality and by the appearance of new 'perversions' as a *DISPOSITIF* of criminological, sexological and psychiatric theories produce new objects of knowledge ranging from masturbating children to hysterical women. The emergence of the category of homosexuality is another example. Although homosexual acts have always been performed, the late nineteenth century both produces the noun 'homosexual' and constructs homosexuality as a medical and legal category that defines a homosexual character-type.

Foucault's demolition of the repressive hypothesis was in part inspired by his reading of Steven Marcus's important study of Victorian pornography (Marcus 1966).

repressive tolerance According to Marcuse (1965), a form of absolute or pure tolerance characteristic of advanced industrial societies in which REPRESSIVE DESUBLIMATION, the CULTURE INDUSTRY and the tyranny of public opinion combine to create a mentality in which all values are predetermined to the extent that they are vital to the workings of the economy. It is argued on supposedly democratic grounds that nonsense and sense should both be tolerated on the grounds that no group or individual is in possession of the truth or capable of defining good and evil. In a society which has reached the point of total administration, the exercise of political rights of free speech or assembly is transformed into a confirmation of the existence of a democracy that has in fact lost the real content it once had. By the same criterion, tolerance comes to mean a refusal to take sides which makes it impossible to challenge the machinery of discrimination against minority groups or society's victims.

revisionism The term is widely used, in both a positive and a negative sense, to describe a challenge to a ruling orthodoxy and attempts to revise it. The original revisionists were the French intellectuals who, like Émile Zola, called for the revision or review of the case of Alfred Dreyfus, a Jewish artillery officer wrongly condemned for treason in 1894 (Chapman 1972). A group of American historians who contested the view that Germany bore full responsibility for the outbreak of the First World War subsequently described themselves as revisionists. Revisionism has a rather different and specific meaning within MARXISM. In 1908 Lenin condemned Edward Bernstein as a revisionist because he had tried to deny the doctrine of Marxism by arguing that parliamentary democracy and universal suffrage removed the need for class struggle; a decade later he described Karl Kautsky's pamphlet *The Dictatorship of the Proletariat* (1918) as 'revisionist' because it departed from the principles of Marxism by querying the need for the dictatorship of the proletariat. The term was subsequently used in the same sense by the Communist Party of China, which accused the Soviet Union of being revisionist on the grounds that it had abandoned the principles of Marxism in favour of peaceful coexistence with the West.

The term 'revisionist' (and sometimes 'negationist') is now regularly applied to those historians who try to deny that the Holocaust perpetrated by Nazi Germany actually occurred, or to attenuate its extent and importance, as in the so-called *HISTORIKERSTREIT*. Holocaust denial is a criminal offence in Germany.

In his studies of how poets struggle with their predecessors and try to overcome the ANXIETY OF INFLUENCE, Harold BLOOM (1982) uses 'revisionism' to describe the way they re-evaluate, re-vision and misread the strong poets of the past.

READING: Lipstadt (1993), Vidal-Naquet (1985)

rhetoric The art of persuasive communication and eloquence. Rhetoric originally developed as a discipline in fourth-century BC Athens, where the ability to speak effectively was an essential attribute for anyone who wished to play a part in public life, or who had to plead a case before a court of law. It played a similar role in the Roman Republic. Insofar as it is in part a study of a language-object (eloquence), rhetoric can be seen as a very early form of METALANGUAGE. Classical rhetoric is designed to sway an audience by appealing to both reason and the emotions, and treatises therefore include discussions of the psychology of the passions.

The teaching and study of rhetoric was a central element in European education from before the time of Plato to the late Romantic era. Eclipsed by logic and grammar during the Middle Ages, it enjoyed a new popularity during the Renaissance, when more books on rhetoric were published than at any other time. Rhetoric fell into decline as a result of the Romantic concentration on freedom of individual expression and creativity, whilst its institutional base was undermined by the educational reforms that did away with the rote learning of examples that had once been the standard practice of both the Jesuit colleges of Catholic Europe and the grammar schools of England. In France it was only at the end of the nineteenth century that the study of rhetoric was abolished in state schools and replaced by the study of literature. *Rhétorique* was the name of the highest and final class in a French *lycée*; in the Belgian system, pupils progressed through classes called *syntaxe*, *poésie* and finally *rhétorique*. In the twentieth century, STRUCTURALISM's concern with the invariants of language led to a renewed interest in rhetoric.

Classical treatises on logic such as Aristotle's *Art of Rhetoric* and Quintilian's *De institutione oratoria* (The education of an orator) normally divide rhetoric into three GENRES: judicial, deliberative and epideictic. The latter, in which the orator apportions blame or praise, was especially important at Roman funerals and was the dominant genre during the Renaissance. The composition of a speech is traditionally broken down into five stages: *inventio* (the discovery of valid arguments), *dispositio* (arrangement), *elecutio* (expression), *memoria* (memory) and *pronuntiatio* (delivery). *Elecutio* is the specific art of the orator, and rhetorical treatises devote much space to cataloguing the TROPES and FIGURES that allow him to deploy the most convincing arguments. An excessive concentration on *elecutio* is a characteristic feature of late rhetoric books, which are often little more than catalogues of tropes and figures; Giovanni Baptista Bernardi's *Thesaurus rhetoricae* of 1559 is an encyclopedic compilation containing definitions of some five thousand terms such as ANAPHORA, CHIASMUS, HYSTERON PROTON, LITOTES, METAPHOR/METONYMY, OXYMORON and ZEUGMA.

The central paradox of most theories of rhetoric is that whilst its figures and tropes are ornamental or stylized forms of speech that depart from a linguistic norm and that whilst orators must learn to use them, they are also spontaneously used by those who have no training in the art of persuasion. Both Aristotle and Quintilian were well aware that metaphors and metonyms feature in the gossip of the market-place as well as the oratory of the law court. It is the existence of this everyday rhetoric that leads STRUCTURALISM to see it as a universal feature of language and DISCOURSE. JAKOBSON (1956) goes so far as to claim that studies of APHASIA demonstrate that, far from being mere figures of speech, metaphor and metonymy are the fundamental poles or axes of all language. It is this thesis that allows LACAN to contend that the UNCONSCIOUS also uses figures of speech because it is structured like a language.

The noun 'rhetoric' is often used to mean artificial or insincere language, and criticisms of rhetoric are as old as the art itself. In Classical Antiquity its most forceful critic was Plato who, especially in the *Gorgias*, argues that rhetoric means pandering to the prejudices of the audience and flattering it with a standard repertoire of verbal tricks. For Plato rhetoric is not an art, and has the same base status as cookery. The standard explanation for Plato's hostility to rhetoric is that he saw it as an integral part of the political system that condemned Socrates to death; it was a technique as corrupt as the society that had produced it, and a perversion of justice and integrity. Plato's arguments inaugurate a long-standing and acrimonious quarrel between rhetoric and philosophy. Variants on his claim that whilst rhetoric may teach the plausible, philosophy alone can provide access to the truth can be found in texts as different as Locke's *Essay Concerning Human Understanding* (1690b) and Kant's *Critique of Judgement* (1790).

READING: Barthes (1970c); Vickers (1988)

Richard, Jean-Pierre (1922–) French literary critic. Richard's major thematic studies of Flaubert and Stendhal (1954) and of nineteenth-century French poetry (1955) are grounded in the tradition of PHENOMENOLOGY, and are influenced by BACHELARD's theory of the IMAGINARY. His later studies of Mallarmé (1961) and Proust (1974) show that, whilst the basic phenomenological framework remains intact, he has also incorporated the lessons of STRUCTURALISM and PSYCHO-ANALYSIS.

Richard's unit of analysis is the complete works of the author in question, and he traces the patterns of themes and motifs in order to demonstrate the shaping of the imaginary landscape of the text and its author. It is made up of visual and spatial themes, but also has tactile and sensory aspects; they combine to produce a thematic pattern, exemplified by the recurrence of the image of fading or a 'faded quality' in the poetry of Verlaine (1955). The imaginary landscape is an expression of the choices, desires and obsessions that lie at the heart of personal experience. Although Richard always stresses that literature is a form of experience, he does not lapse into a crude psychology of authors. His studies are an attempt to recreate the moment at which a literary work is born of the silence that precedes it or at which the 'speech' of the text allows the author to come into being. In that sense, both the author and the text are creations of the imaginary.

In a footnote to his study of Proust, Richard remarks that any form of criticism or literary analysis inevitably breaks up the text it studies, tears it apart and transforms it into a FRAGMENTED BODY, adding that the only way that it can be repaired is through the infinite and never-ending work of reading. In a sense, Richard is a reader rather than a critic and he is remarkably good at communicating his enthusiasm to his own readers. The compelling essay on Flaubert is an urgent invitation to read *Madame Bovary* and *The Temptation of St Anthony*, and it is extremely difficult to refuse it.

Richards, Ivor Armstrong (1893–1979) British literary critic. Richards's theory of PRACTICAL CRITICISM (1929), together with the work of EMPSON and LEAVIS and, in the United States, the NEW CRITICISM, is one of the contributing factors that made the study of English literature a serious academic discipline rather than a body of untheorized and subjective value-judgements, by emphasizing the importance of close textual reading. The theoretical presuppositions governing the theory of close reading are expounded in two earlier studies by Richards (1924, 1929).

The title of *Principles of Literary Criticism* (1924) is somewhat misleading in that it in fact offers a diagnosis of a crisis rather than protocols for reading. The crisis originates in the rise of science, which neutralizes nature and, by becoming an autonomous domain, destroys the older cultural patterns based upon religion and tradition. The emotive language of the arts, and of poetry in particular, becomes divorced from the objective language of the sciences. At the same time, the rise of commercialism and mass culture leads to a lowering of standards. The defence of values thus becomes a priority and assigns the critic the role of accounting for values and their communication. The critic defends, that is, the works of art that are our storehouse of recorded values. Richards is highly critical of theories that view the aesthetic as an independent realm of cultural life and that assume that beauty is a quality of artefacts rather than of our response to them. Works of art, for Richards, are no more than an extension of more ordinary realms of experience. But their value is such that bad taste is not just a flaw in the individual reader, it is the root evil from which other defects follow.

The great weakness of Richards's theory is that the crucial notion of value remains surprisingly vague, and is simply defined as existing 'prior to all explanation'. The underlying psychology is based on the behaviourist model of stimulus and reponse, and of what Richards calls 'appetencies and adversions'. The role of literature and the critic is to find a balance between the two, he writes in *Principles*, because 'No life can be excellent in which the elementary responses are disorganized and confused' and because 'the best life' is one in which the whole personality is engaged. The elitism implicit in Richards's view of the importance of criticism is captured by his remark (1924) that the rearguard of society cannot be extricated from the present crisis unless the vanguard has gone further.

Ricoeur, Paul (1913–) French philosopher. Ricoeur is perhaps the most international of French philosophers, and his work might be described as a triangular conversation between the French tradition of self-reflexive philosophy that begins with Descartes, German philosophy (primarily HERMENEUTICS, but also HEIDEGGER's ontology and HABERMAS'S COMMUNICATIVE ACTION) and the ANALYTICAL PHILOSOPHY that is dominant in the English-speaking world. There can be few other, if any, French philosophers capable of discussing American NEW CRITICISM in the same breath as the more familiar themes of CONTINENTAL PHILOSOPHY (Ricoeur 1975). Despite his prolific output, Ricoeur was for a long time relatively ignored in France, and he has spent long periods teaching in the United States. For most of the 1960s and 1970s he was eclipsed by ALTHUSSER, DERRIDA and others and his criticisms of STRUCTURALISM did not endear him to his compatriots. His main objection to structuralism is that it surrenders to a POSITIVISM which views the textual object as a closed entity which is independent of the subjectivity of both author and reader. Whereas LÉVI-STRAUSS finds in the myths he analyses nomenclatures and systems of classification, Ricoeur (1963) insists that the core of meaning of the Old Testament consists of founding events such as the deliverance from Egypt and the crossing of the Red Sea. It was not until 1988, when a major colloquium (Greisch and Kearney 1991) was devoted to his work, that Ricoeur was accorded any real recognition in France.

Ricoeur's work includes studies of Jaspers (1947, 1948), psychoanalysis (1965) and metaphor and rhetoric (1975), a three-volume study of time and narrative (1983–5), and numerous essays on hermeneutics (many collected 1969). His erudition is remarkable; his study of metaphor must be one of the most thorough to have been written, whilst his study of time and narration covers a field so vast as to encompass a detailed analysis of Aristotle on MIMESIS to readings of Proust and Woolf's *Mrs Dalloway*.

Despite the variety of topics covered in his writings, Ricoeur's philosophy can be described (1986) as centring on three main preoccupations: the narrative function (1983–5), metaphor (1975) and hermeneutic philosophy. He also decribes it as a self-reflexive philosophy in the tradition of Descartes and Kant, 'reflection' being defined as the act whereby a subject reflects, in a moment of intellectual clarity and ethical responsibility, upon the unifying principles that make him or her a subject.

Although Ricoeur is critical of structuralism, he does agree with the structuralist insistence that language is central and even essential to human experience, and that it must therefore be philosophy's central concern. He is, however, concerned less with the structures of language than with the linguistic activity of narrative and rhetoric. The act of narration is a founding moment of human societies. All societies are founded on or by the narratives in which they tell of their origins, and all human action constitutes a text. In his studies of the GENRE of narrative (defined as including both fictional and historical texts) and metaphor, Ricoeur contends that metaphor is a form of semantic innovation which redescribes reality and therefore works in parallel with mimesis or the imitation of reality. Together they create a world of meaning which is inhabitable by human beings. Because it necessarily has a temporal dimension, narrative also reflects the lives of subjects who live in time: life is lived, and history is recounted. The task of a hermeneutic philosophy is to reconstruct the internal dynamics of texts recounting actions so that those texts can be projected into the habitable world. It is to reconstruct how a text or narrative work arises out of the opacity of life, action and suffering, and is given by an author to readers who receive it and change their lives on the basis of what it teaches them about the world and themselves.

The self-reflexive aspects of Ricoeur's thought, which he describes as 'a hermeneutic variant' on HUSSERL's phenomenology, lead him to ask how it is that the subject can recognize itself as subject. This is the guiding theme of a dense but very rewarding essay on the hermeneutics of the self or of 'selfhood' (1990).

READING: Mongin (1998); Clark (1990)

risk society The expression derives from the title of the German sociologist Ulrich Beck's bestselling study (1986) of how risk, and the calculation of the probability of risk, has become an essential feature of modern societies. Heavily influenced by the FRANKFURT SCHOOL and the experience of the German Green Party, Beck argues that the drive towards the technological domination of the natural world has raised living standards but has also generated high-consequence risks which, whilst they have a low probability, would have catastrophic results if events actually occurred. Examples include global warming, chemical toxity, ecological catastrophe and nuclear accidents. More generally, modern societies are characterized as having no settled futures but, rather, an open field of both positive and negative consequences. Living with a calculative attitude to those possibilities, typified by the use of COUNTERFACTUALS predicated on the question 'What if?', becomes an essential feature of both individual and collective life.

The concept of risk society is one of the many symptoms of a growing unease about the ENLIGHTENMENT project of MODERNITY.

READING: Giddens (1991); Rustin (1994)

roman The French and German word for 'novel' is commonly used in English in compounds designating a number of subgenres (GENRE). A *roman à clef* (literally 'novel with a key') is a novel in which actual and identifiable people or events appear under fictitious names. A *roman à thèse* ('novel with a thesis') uses fiction as a way of promoting a theory or argument; the term is often used in a pejorative sense. The more unusual *roman-fleuve* ('river-novel') is used to describe a sequence of related but self-contained novels such as Trollope's 'Palliser' series. It can also be used to describe a very long novel dealing with several generations of the same family. The German *BILDUNGSROMAN* ('novel of education') is extensively used, in the widest sense; the rarer *Künstlerroman* is used of a novel about an artist or musician.

romance A literary GENRE with a long history going back to the Middle Ages. The term itself derives from the use of 'romance' to describe the vernacular languages that evolved out of the vulgar Latin of late Antiquity (French, Italian, Spanish, Portuguese and Romanian). Although the romances of the thirteenth century did inherit some themes from Classical literature, they deal primarily with tales of love and adventure associated with the legends of the court of King Arthur and with the adventures of Charlemagne. Originally written in Old French and Anglo-Norman, their popularity spread throughout Europe. The subgenre of the quest-romance, based upon the search for the Holy Grail or the cup used by Christ and his disciples at the Last Supper, is particularly important; its structures survive in many adventure stories and in popular films such as Steven Spielberg's *Indiana Jones* films.

The term 'romance' is still used in its original sense by medievalists, but its general meaning has changed considerably. By the late eighteenth century, a distinction was commonly made in English between the novel, defined in broadly realist terms, and the romance, which was defined as describing improbable events in highly-blown language. Later usage is strongly influenced by the shifting SEMAN-TICS of the word 'romantic', once used to designate a poetic tradition but increasingly synonymous with 'romantic love'.

In contemporary usage, 'romance' can be defined as a subgenre of popular fiction written primarily for a female audience, dealing with the emotional tribulations of a heroine, usually beautiful and virginal, and ending with her marriage to a hero who initially spurns her. The classic romance plot, which has obvious antecedents in Richardson's *Clarissa*, is exemplified by Jane Austen's *Pride and Prejudice*, Charlotte Brontë's *Jane Eyre* and Daphne du Maurier's *Rebecca* (1938). It traces the transformation of the hero from a distant, insensitive figure who is coldly superior to the heroine, into her tender lover. In some cases the hero's ill-treatment of the heroine may extend to sexual violence (hence the term 'bodice-ripper', derived from the scene in which he rips open her bodice) or even rape, but the goal of the narrative is always monogamous, heterosexual marriage. Romance easily blends with other genres, as in the historical romances of Georgette Heyer or the regional fiction of Catherine Cookson (set in industrial North-East England and inevitably featuring an element of romance).

The 'Harlequin' romances of North America and the Mills and Boon romances of Britain (and their equivalents elsewhere) come into a category of their own. Never reviewed in the mainstream press, not stocked by traditional bookshops, written to formula under pseudonyms and generally despised, they sell in immense quantities. In a fascinating study that combines READER-RESPONSE theory with sociological inquiry and a description of femininity derived from Nancy Chodorov (1978), Janice A. Radway (1984) explores the meaning of romance for a group of American women and demonstrates the existence of a loosely knit INTERPRETIVE COMMUNITY of readers and writers with a shared perception as to what constitutes a good romance. For Radway, reading romances is a form of escapism, both in the sense that their readers can participate in an exotic world of high passion and in the sense that it allows an escape from housework. The women readers whose experience was studied used romance to escape the role imposed on them by PATRIARCHY, but at the same time their reading-matter, with its stress on an ideal monogamous heterosexuality, made that very role appear desirable.

Rorty, Richard (1931–) American philosopher, originally trained in the tradition of ANALYTIC PHILOSOPHY, but now a trenchant critic of traditional EPISTEMOLOGY and FOUNDATIONALISM.

Rorty's *Philosophy and the Mirror of Nature* (1980) launches what he describes as an anti-Cartesian and anti-Kantian revolution designed to undermine both the belief in the philosophical category of 'mind' and the view that 'knowledge' is something with objective foundations which can be described by an epistemology or theory of knowledge. The book is in part a historical study of the emergence of the Kantian thesis that there exists a permanent and a historical framework for a theory of knowledge, and it has a therapeutic aim: just as the patient in psychotherapy must relive his past in order to understand his problems, so it is with philosophy.

The epistemological model is traced back to the emergence of modern philosophy in Locke and Descartes and to the underlying notion that knowledge is a set of non-material representations or ideas that faithfully mirror the external world of nature. Knowledge is to be judged in terms of the accuracy of its representations, and in accordance with foundational truths that exist prior to the sciences. It is guaranteed by moments of indisputable insights such as the *cogito* that allows Descartes to conclude: 'I am thinking, therefore I am' (1637). For Rorty, the epistemological model, and the presumption that objective truths exist, is simply a product of the metaphor of seeing that informs so much of Western philosophy (see Jay 1993). If philosophy is to progress, it must rid itself of its visual metaphors and accept that language is not a matter of representation, but of conversation. It is, as WITTGENSTEIN and HEIDEGGER argue, a tool and not a mirror.

Like VATTIMO, Rorty contrasts epistemology with those varieties of HERMEN-EUTICS according to which knowledge is a matter of understanding the social justification of belief rather than of the accuracy of representations. Knowledge, Rorty insists, is a matter of conversation and social practice, and philosophy should therefore abandon the illusory project of mirroring nature. The role of the philosopher is, rather, to attempt to prolong the conversation between various discourses whilst accepting that the absence of objective criteria of judgement makes it improbable that any final agreement will be reached.

Rorty's denial of the possibility of objective truth is controversial, and he is often accused by critics on both the left and the right of promoting an absolute relativism in which no value-judgements can be made about anything. He himself denies that this is the case, and is a self-professed liberal democrat who believes that American democracy is the best sort of society to have been invented. Bitterly hostile to Marxism and its claim that some views are objectively progressive whilst others are objectively reactionary, he is by his own admission a defender of democratic liberalism.

READING: Rorty (1991a, 1991b); Sayers (1997)

Rowbotham, Sheila (1943–) British feminist historian. A prominent figure in the WOMEN'S LIBERATION movement of the 1970s and a major contributor to HISTORY WORKSHOP, Rowbotham has long been an important practitioner of HISTORY FROM BELOW. Her *Women's Consciousness, Man's World* (1973b) is one of the classics of 'second-wave' FEMINISM and a vivid account of its concerns, whilst her *Women: Resistance and Revolution* (1972) and *Hidden from History* (1973a) are amongst the founding texts for feminist history in Britain. Her *Century of Women* (1997) combines oral history, archival research and the study of ephemera and fashion to provide an engrossing comparative history of women's experience in twentieth-century Britain and the United States. In an interview given in 1981 and published in MAHRO's *Visions of History* (1983), she traces her own intellectual and political history in a typically vivid style.

Russian formalism A vitally important trend within Russian criticism, Russian formalism originates in the work of OPOYAZ and the MOSCOW LINGUISTIC CIRCLE and is closely associated with the poetics of Russian FUTURISM. Although formalism was discredited by the rise of SOCIALIST REALISM during the Stalinist period, when 'formalist' became a term of abuse, it lays the foundations for the later work of the PRAGUE LINGUISTIC CIRCLE and thus inaugurates the tradition that eventually gives rise to STRUCTURALISM (see the introduction to TODOROV 1965). PROPP's work on the morphology of folk-tales can be seen as an extension of the original formalism of OPOYAZ and the Moscow Linguistic Circle. All subsequent forms of POETICS and NARRATOLOGY owe an incalculable debt to Russian formalism, which was one of the first schools to apply the methodology of linguistics to the study of literature. The most important figures associated with it are JAKOBSON, Boris Eikhenbaum, SHKLOVSKY and Yury Tynyanov.

Although the work of the Russian formalists covers a wide range of topics from folklore to dialectology, its main focus is on poetics. Formalism reacts against both the symbolism that came to dominate Russian poetry in the late nineteenth century and which promoted a quasi-religious or metaphysical idea of the poetic image by concentrating on the sound and syntax of poetry, and the subjectivist discussion of literature which Jakobson (1921) dismissed as a form of *causerie* which happily slipped from lyrical effusions on the elegance of poetic forms to anecdotes about the artist's life. As he and Tynyanov put in the so-called 'Jakobson-Tynyanov theses' (1928), the problems facing Russian literary and linguistic science demanded 'a precision of the theoretical platform'. Eikhenbaum's retrospective 'Theory of the Formal Method' (1926) describes the requisite 'precision' as the creation of an autonomous science that takes as its starting-point the intrinsic qualities of the literary text. Eikhenbaum makes it clear that there is a parallel here with WÖLFFLIN's vision of a history of styles, or of a history of art in which the names of individual artists do not appear because they are mere exemplars of a historical sequence of styles. For the Russian formalists, the task of literary and linguistic research was to study the style of the writer as a totality or a linguistic system. Eikhenbaum himself studies Gogol's tale *The Overcoat* as a play of styles, in which the poetic effect is created by an interplay between a comic narration and sentimentally pathetic declamations. The object of study is therefore not the individual literary text, but rather *LITERATURNOST'* or the 'literariness' that makes it a literary text and not a documentary report. The text is to be approached not as a representation of some external reality, but as a literary and linguistic object governed by intrinsic laws.

Extending this line of argument, Jakobson (1921) defines the history of literature as that of a literary 'series' of styles which exists alongside but independently of other 'series' of cultural artefacts. 'Realism' is no more than a series of styles, and its apparently transparent reflection of the external world is the product of formal conventions. The old form/content opposition is thus dissolved by the realization that form in fact 'creates' content.

Formalist studies of both poetry and prose concentrate on verbal forms, tropes, the phonetics of verse, parallelisms, patterns of repetition and the syntactic forms used. Literary composition is viewed as a process of arranging such 'devices' and images into an order which will have the maximum poetic effect. Devices and images are studied, that is, in terms of the 'function' they fulfil within the text and not in accordance with external criteria. According to Shklovsky (1917), the poetic use of the image differs from its practical use (in the communication of information) in that it brings about a semantic shift. The difficulty inherent in reading poetic language, which is compounded by the FOREGROUNDING of the devices it uses, transfers the object it describes to a different level and makes it appear 'strange', rather as though it had been perceived for the first time. The very difficulty of the text breaks down conventional and habitual associations and makes it possible to see or read it in all its newness. This notion of creative deformation, estrangement or *OSTRANENIE* is perhaps one of the most important to have been developed by the Russian formalists, anticipating as it does both the ALIENATION-EFFECT of BRECHT and the 'denaturalization' of the familiar that characterizes BARTHES' studies of the MYTHOLOGIES of the contemporary world.

READING: Erlich (1965); Jackson and Rudy (1985); Matejka and Pomorska (1971); Pomorska (1968)

S

Said, Edward William (1935–) Palestinian-American literary and cultural critic. His major study of ORIENTALISM (1978) is widely regarded as one of the founding texts of POSTCOLONIAL THEORY.

Said has described himself as a secular or worldly critic and he is critical of the undue emphasis on 'limitless interpretation' that has forced so many literary theorists to retreat into a labyrinth of textuality quite divorced from the world. He argues the case (1983) for a form of criticism that is life-enhancing, opposed to every form of tyranny, and that promotes non-coercive forms of knowledge that further the goals of human freedom. His own evolution might in fact be described as a gradual exit from the labyrinth of textuality. Said's first book was a study of Joseph Conrad (1966), an author to whom he returns again and again but in increasingly politicized ways, and whose *Heart of Darkness* eventually becomes (1993) a paradigmatic text (PARADIGM) of both imperialism and the uneasy sense that imperialism's knowledge and control of the dark continent is neither complete nor final. His important study of beginnings in both fiction and philosophy (1975), which contrasts the theological notion of 'origins' with a secular 'beginning' that allows a writer to work with a set of instruments and to begin a performance, takes the view that literary theory could be an insurrectional discourse and provides, almost in passing, an excellent introduction to STRUCTURALISM. In his later works, Said (1993) seems to take the more traditional erudition of AUERBACH and Leo Spitzer (1887–1960; see 1948a, 1948b) as a model for intellectual work, and is openly sceptical about the value of high theory.

Culture and Imperialism (1993) is in many ways a continuation and expansion of *Orientalism*. Like so many of the products of POSTCOLONIAL THEORY, it is relatively weak on the economics of colonialism and tends to blur the differences between forms of colonialism, equating French colonialism in Algeria with British colonialism in India in an oversimplified way. The book's great strength lies in Said's demonstration that novels, travel diaries and a host of other literary forms serve to naturalize imperialism by making it part of a common experience and both legitimizing the subordination of 'inferior peoples' and reproducing their subordination. The very hostile reactions he provoked by pointing out that the life of Jane Austen's *Mansfield Park* is materially supported by slavery on the Bertrams' plantations in Antigua indicate that he had indeed touched a sore point. Similarly, the insistence on the material conditions that allowed Verdi's *Aida* to be first performed in Cairo in 1872 has the salutary effect of grounding High Culture in a very secular world. Said's argument is not the reductive claim that culture reflects imperialist realities, still less that it causes them. It is, rather, that cultural forms appropriate space and time in such a way as to naturalize imperialism by monopolizing all the ways in which it can be represented. Kipling's *Kim*, for instance, represents an India in which the British can do or become literally anything by promoting a self-consciousness that understands both the country itself and how the mechanisms of control work.

Said has long been a defender of the Palestinian struggle for self-determination and a stern critic of US foreign policy in the Middle East, and is a very good analyst of how government statements and media presentations alike have constructed a mystifying image of a monolithic Islam whose very existence poses a threat to Western civilization (1981). From 1977 to 1991 he was an important member of the Palestinian National Council, but became increasingly critical of the Palestinian Liberation Organization (1994), partly on the grounds that it was corrupt but mainly on the grounds that its acceptance of the negotiated partial settlement with Israel under the 'land for peace' terms of the Oslo Accords of 1994 was a betrayal of the Palestinian cause. He was also very critical of the PLO's support for Iraq during the Gulf War of 1991. In September 1996 his books were banned in the PLO-controlled territories of Gaza and the West Bank. Whilst the Reith Lectures of 1993 provide a general description of what Said sees as the political responsibilities of the intellectual, they are also a poignant personal account of his own experience of national and political exile.

READING: Moore-Gilbert (1997)

Samuel, Raphaël (1934–96) British historian and cofounder, in 1967, of HISTORY WORKSHOP.

As the guiding spirit behind History Workshop, Samuel was one of the most important figures involved in the historiographical tradition associated with the British NEW LEFT and, as a tutor at Ruskin College, Oxford from 1962 to 1996, influenced generations of working-class mature students and trade-unionists attracted to the adult education movement. Born into a communist family in the East End of London and a very youthful member of the COMMUNIST PARTY HISTORIANS' GROUP, he left the Party in 1956, and was in 1960 one of the founders of *NEW LEFT REVIEW*. The long article on 'The Lost World of British Communism' published in four parts in *New Left Review* (1985–7) is a remarkable autobiographical document as well as a rich evocation of working-class life, politics and culture.

Samuel had little interest in theoretical discussions on the nature of history, and was primarily an empirical historian with a remarkable feel for the detail of place and time, especially in the case of his native East End. Although he was passionately committed to his work on people's history or HISTORY FROM BELOW, most of Samuel's remarkable energies went into editing *History Workshop Journal* and associated publications rather than writing and it was not until two years before his death that he published his first sole-authored book (1994; a second volume was posthumously published in 1998). A typical product of his endeavours was the oral autobiography – based upon many hours of tape-recordings – of an East End gangster that provides a rich picture of the culture and economy of the classic slums of East London (1981a, 1981b). Samuel's final book challenges critics of the so-called HERITAGE INDUSTRY, and argues that it reveals much about the culture of ordinary people and about the way the past is constantly reconstructed in the popular imagination. An attractively wide-ranging, if somewhat ill-organized book, it also exemplifies Samuel's great feel for detail; this was a historian for whom a Victorian house-brick was as important a document as the minutes of a union meeting.

READING: Hall, Rowbotham and Blackburn (1997)

Sartre, Jean-Paul (1905–80) French philosopher. Sartre was for a long time the principal French representative of EXISTENTIALISM, but his later philosophy is oriented towards MARXISM, which he came to see as 'the untranscendable philosophy of our time' (1960).

No other philosopher has ever dominated the intellectual and cultural life of a period in the way in which Sartre dominated the French intellectual scene from the 1940s to the 1960s, when STRUCTURALISM tended to eclipse his existentialism. His omnipresence is due in part to his mastery of so many GENRES. His first novel, *Nausea* (1938), remains one of the few great philosophical novels of the twentieth century, and combines social satire with a philosophical approach to the experience of the ABSURD to remarkable effect. In the postwar period Sartre used the theatre to popularize existentialism but, although they are still staged, his plays now appear more dated than the *Chemins de la liberté* (Roads to freedom) trilogy of novels (1945a, 1945b, 1949a) which exemplify the theory of COMMITTED LITERATURE outlined in *What Is Literature?* (1947c). The dominance was completed by popularizing lectures such as *Existentialism and Humanism* (1947b), whilst the success of the journal *TEMPS MODERNES* (Modern Times) gave Sartre a popularity and influence rarely enjoyed by a professional philosopher. Although Sartre's philosophy derives from the difficult tradition of HUSSERL and HEIDEGGER and although his terminology can be arcane, his gift for using concrete illustrations from everyday life to exemplify philosophical arguments is unrivalled. The structures of BAD FAITH are, for instance, complex, but few readers of *Being and Nothingness* (1943a) will ever forget the example of the waiter who attempts to *be* a waiter in the same way that a tree *is* a tree, and in so doing denies his freedom by lapsing into bad faith. The best guide to Sartre's enormous output is the critical bibliography prepared by Contat and Rybalka in 1970 and subsequently expanded for English publication (1973).

Sartre's earliest work was on the psychology of the imagination and the IMAGINARY, and has something in common with the early LACAN, Lacanian and post-structuralist attempts to dismiss him as a classically Cartesian philosopher notwithstanding (for a critical view of these attempts see Howells 1992), but it was with the publication of *Being and Nothingness* that he established himself as the leading philosopher of his generation. Sartre's philosophy is primarily a theory of consciousness, so much so that his EXISTENTIALIST PSYCHOANALYSIS denies the very existence of Freud's unconscious and replaces it with the idea of bad faith. Although the 1943 study in phenomenological ontology draws heavily on

Heidegger, the stress on human freedom strikes a distinctively new note. Freedom, for Sartre, is an essential feature of human existence, and it is grounded in the distinction between 'BEING-IN-ITSELF' and 'BEING-FOR-ITSELF'. Whilst the former category is characteristic of inanimate objects, the latter is an attribute of human beings who have no predetermined essence. Hence the oft-cited dictum that existence precedes essence. Human beings exist for themselves to the extent that they are forever in the process of becoming, forever choosing what to be in SITUATIONS that are not of their own making and which they negate. They are therefore what they are not, and are not what they are. Human beings are, that is, condemned to be free, and can escape their freedom only by denying their humanity. With his typical taste for paradox, Sartre can thus argue (1944a) that the French were never as free as they were under the German occupation of their country, when every gesture and word involved choices that could put their lives at stake. Being-for-onself is a process rather than a state; only at the moment of death will the for-itself coincide with the in-itself dimension: it is death that transforms a life into an irrevocable destiny. For the living human being, freedom is a matter of constant and renewed choice; the trilogy of novels provides ample examples of how the refusal of choice is itself a choice made in bad faith. The true dimension of freedom is thus AUTHENTICITY, or the lucid consciousness of choice and the concomitant lucid acceptance of responsibility.

Whilst human beings are condemned to be free, they are also condemned to live with other human beings, and the relationship between self and other is central to Sartre's analysis of the human condition. The central feature of that relationship is structured by the GAZE that turns the free human being into an objectified thing. A character in the play *Huis Clos* (1944b) typically concludes that 'hell is other people' and the early Sartre does not really offer a way out of the self-other antagonism, which constantly threatens to introduce an element of sadomasochism into interpersonal relations as the subject attempts to possess the other. The theory of literature may do so in that it establishes a circuit of communication between reader and writer.

In his prewar writings Sartre paints a very individualistic and apolitical picture of human existence. Both he and BEAUVOIR have stated that it was the war, and particularly the enforced, if temporary, experience of a collective existence in a German prison camp that helped to politicize him. Sartre's postwar politics and philosophy take the form of a highly critical engagement with socialism and of critical fellow-travelling with the PCF, and of the attempt to find a 'third way' that would avoid the traps of both capitalism and Soviet-style Stalinism (see Burnier 1966). The bitter opponent of France's war in Algeria, who prefaced FANON's incendiary *The Wretched of the Earth* (1961), subsequently became the champion of the radicalism of the 1960s and 1970s.

With his *Critique of Dialectical Reason* (1960), Sartre finally abandons the ahistorical individualism of his earlier philosophy and adopts a Marxist-orientated and collective approach to history and politics, with the new emphasis on the transition from SERIALITY to a GROUP-IN-FUSION and PRAXIS. Despite the change of orientation, there are continuities between the earlier work and the *Critique*. The new concept of the PRACTICO-INERT, for example, displays many of the characteristics of the in-itself, whilst the future-oriented project of TOTALIZATION has something in common with the for-itself's perpetual flight into the future.

As in the case of Beauvoir, the posthumous appearance of supposedly lost or unfinished material means that it is still difficult to make an overall assessment of Sartre's evolution or importance. The most important of the posthumous publications are the *Notebooks for an Ethics* (1983a), announced at the end of *Being and Nothingness* but never completed, the war diaries (1983b) and the incomplete second volume of the *Critique of Dialectical Reason* (1985).

READING: Aronson (1980); Cohen-Solal (1985); Hayman (1986); *Temps modernes* (1990)

Saussure, Ferdinand de (1857–1913) Swiss linguist, generally regarded as the founder of modern linguistics and the forefather of STRUCTURALISM and SEMIOLOGY.

During his lifetime Saussure's reputation was based upon his work on PHILOLOGY. He published only two books: a study of the vowel system of the Indo-European languages (1878) and a doctoral thesis on the use of the genitive in Sanskrit (1880). His celebrated *Course in General Linguistics* (1916) was published posthumously, having been reconstructed by Charles Bally and Albert Séchehaye on the basis of student notes taken during the lectures given by Saussure at the University of Geneva between 1907 and 1911. In Saussure's own view, those lectures were intended to clarify the issues facing linguists, and not to inaugurate a new approach to language. His central role in the modern human sciences is largely the product of the appropriation of his work by anthropologists (LÉVI-STRAUSS 1949), philosophers (MERLEAU-PONTY, whose idiosyncratic approach to Saussure is well described in Schmidt 1985) and psychoanalysts like LACAN.

Saussure inverts the SYNCHRONY/DIACHRONY relationship characteristic of the historical linguistics in which he was trained, demonstrating that although the noun *pas* ('footstep') and the negative particle *pas* ('not') share the same etymology, this is not relevant to their roles in modern French. They function as distinctive SIGNS operating within a system. The systematic dimension of natural language is described by Saussure as *langue*, as opposed to *langage*, which refers to the human faculty of language. *Parole* refers to individual manifestations or realizations of *langue*, both written and spoken. The translation of *langage*, *langue* and *parole* poses considerable difficulties; both *langage* and *langue* can be translated as 'language', whilst the latter term can also be rendered as 'tongue'; *parole* signifes both 'word' and 'speech' or 'speaking'. Most discussions of Saussure therefore retain the French *langue/parole* distinction; in more general terms 'language' tends to be used for both *langage* and *langue*, with the French terms inserted in brackets as appropriate. The basic unit of Saussurean linguistics is the SIGN, defined as a psychical entity consisting of a 'signifier' (an acoustic image) and a 'signified' (a concept). The sign is said to be arbitrary as there is no logical or necessary relationship between signifier and signified, or between a sign and its REFERENT (the extra-linguistic object to which it refers).

Saussure's emphasis on the synchronic and systematic dimension of *langue* implies that it is neither a matter of individual expression nor a nomenclature in which there is a natural relationship of designation between a sign and an object or REFERENT. The relationship between sign and referent is, like that between signifier and signified, arbitrary or purely conventional. There is no pregiven reason why the signifier 'cow' should designate a bovine quadruped. It is because they are different and mutually exclusive that signs have value and meaning. In post-Saussurean structuralism, there is a marked tendency to emphasize the importance of the signifer at the expense of the signified, largely as a result of Lacan's claim that the two never coincide because the signifier 'slides over' the signified in a never-ending chain of signification.

In a series of unpublished notebooks (selections have been published as Starobinski 1971), Saussure expounds his private theory that Latin poets concealed anagrams of proper names in their verse. The first thirteen lines of Lucretius's *De rerum natura* (The nature of the universe) are an invocation of the goddess Venus, and Saussure finds in them three anagrams of the name Aphrodite, who was her Greek equivalent. Unable to determine whether the presence of these cryptograms was the fortuitous product of coincidence or an intentional act on the part of the poets concerned, Saussure eventually abandoned his 'anagrams' project. It has been argued that the project reveals the existence of 'Two Saussures' (Starobinski 1971) and that one of the two was attempting to escape his own LOGOCENTRISM by reexamining the status of WRITING, which is subordinated to speech in the *Course*.

READING: Culler (1976); Gadet (1986)

school of resentment Harold BLOOM's dismissive term (1994) for the academic-journalistic network made up of all those who wish the overthrow of the literary CANON by developing a programme for social change. The object of their resentment is the power and influence of the canon. The school includes Marxists, feminists, Foucauldians, the theorists of NEW HISTORICISM and all those who attack the heritage of those they call DEAD WHITE EUROPEAN MALES in the name of the POLITICALLY CORRECT. Bloom also applies the term to those who wish to expand the canon to include texts that are conducive to social change and argues that, unlike canonical texts, such works cannot be read and reread precisely because they are designed to be rapidly ingested and then discarded.

scientism The belief that the natural sciences are the only valid mode of knowledge or that knowledge as such must be identified with the sciences. Scientism thus relegates the arts and philosophy to a secondary domain, or demands that they be reformulated in scientific terms. Scientism is typified by POSITIVISM's conviction that the meaning of knowledge is defined by what the sciences do and can be explained only in terms of an analysis of scientific procedures. LOGICAL POSITIVISM is often criticized for its scientism.

Screen British journal of film studies, published since 1969. *Screen* was originally the journal of the Society for Education in Film and Television, which was founded by the British Film Institute in 1950. SEFT was wound up in 1980, but *Screen* continues to be published by Oxford University Press on behalf of Glasgow University's John Logie Baird Centre.

Screen has had a number of different incarnations. The original bimonthly was relaunched as a quarterly in 1971 and almost immediately became a major conduit for the importation of so-called 'French theory'. The editorial published in spring 1971 (vol. 12 no. 1) described the emphasis on THEORY as crucial; *Screen's* role was to go beyond 'subjective taste-ridden criticism' and to produce a theory of cinema as a context for the teaching of film. As an educational and theoretical journal, *Screen* saw no need to indulge in the 'practical "reviewing"' engaged in by other journals' and rarely commented on contemporary commercial cinema. Over the next decade it concentrated on working on the SEMIOTICS of cinema, as defined by METZ, and on theories of representation drawing on both PSYCHOANALYSIS and the theory of IDEOLOGY elaborated by ALTHUSSER. RUSSIAN FORMALISM and BRECHT were also major interests. Although *Screen's* role in creating a climate conducive to a high level of theoretical debate cannot be underrated, it was also accused of promoting an intimidatory obscurantism that was at odds with its stated educational goals. The reliance upon Lacanian psychoanalysis (LACAN) in particular was frequently a cause for controversy.

It was partly in response to these criticisms that another relaunch and change of format attempted to broaden the journal's frame of reference to include all practices of representation, including the plastic arts, from 1980 onwards. After the demise of SEFT, *Screen* reverted to being a quarterly, and became a much more conventionally academic journal rather than a theoretical-political platform, and began to carry more reviews and 'reports and debates'.

screen memory In PSYCHOANALYSIS a screen memory is described as a memory of childhood characterized both by its exceptional sharpness and its apparently trivial or insignificant content (Freud 1899, 1901). Screen memories are not preserved because of their own content, but because of the way that their content relates to a content that has been subject to REPRESSION. They literally screen or mask repressed memories. The analysis of a screen memory leads to the discovery of indelible childhood experiences and unconscious fantasies, usually of a sexual nature.

Scrutiny British literary journal, published quarterly in Cambridge between 1932 and 1953 and the main organ for the propagation of the Leavisite view of literature (LEAVIS). The entire run of *Scrutiny* was republished in nineteen volumes by Cambridge University Press in 1963; the twentieth volume contains the index and Leavis's 'Retrospect', which evaluates the success of the *Scrutiny* project. A two-volume *Selection from 'Scrutiny'* edited by Leavis was issued by the same publisher in 1968. The main contributors to *Scrutiny* included F. R. and Q. D. Leavis, L. C. Knights, D. J. Enright and Denys Thompson.

Scrutiny represents a reaction against both the Good Taste of the belletrist school associated with Arthur Quiller-Couch (1863–1944), who was appointed Professor of English at Cambridge in 1912, and the effects of a mass culture which was allegedly leading to a general lowering of standards. Q. D. Leavis diagnoses the problem addressed by the journal in her *Fiction and the Reading Public* (1932), where she deplores the supremacy of 'fiction', as opposed to great literature, and the 'neglect of serious reading'. The solution is to foster a 'missionary spirit' and to train 'a picked few who would go out into the world equipped for the work of forming and organising a conscious minority'. *Scrutiny* was to become the mouthpiece for that picked few. Criticism was viewed as a serious professional activity and not as an entertainment for aesthetes and the journal was characterized by its moral and literary severity. The 'Manifesto' published in the first issue spoke of the need for reviews that combined the criticism of literature with the criticism of extra-literary, and particularly educational activities, and took it as axiomatic that there exists 'a necessary relationship between the quality of the individual's response to art and his general fitness for a humane existence'.

With a print-run of only 750 in the 1930s and at most 1,500 in the 1950s, *Scrutiny* was never a large-circulation journal, but its influence on the teaching of English literature has been almost incalculable; most people who have studied English at school or universities in Britain have almost unconsciously absorbed its values. The National Association of Teachers of English was founded by *Scrutiny* associates, as were most of the contributors to the influential seven-volume *Pelican Guide to English Literature* edited by Boris Ford in the 1950s. The stated purpose of the *Guide* is 'to re-establish . . . a sense of literary tradition and to define the high standards that this tradition implies.'

READING: Mulhern (1979)

SCUM Manifesto The founding manifesto of the Society for Cutting Up Men (Solanas 1967) takes it as given that it is now technically possible for women to reproduce without help from men and that all males should be exterminated. No aspect of modern society is of relevance to women, and it is therefore in their interest to overthrow the government, eliminate the money system and destroy the male sex. Although obsessed with sex and prepared to do anything to achieve sexual intercourse, the male is in genetic terms an incomplete female. Maleness is a deficiency disease and all men are emotional cripples.

SCUM's only member was its founder Valerie Solanas (1936–88). In 1969 she was imprisoned for shooting and seriously wounding the artist Andy Warhol. Released in 1971, she spent the rest of her life in obscurity.

Searle, John Rogers (1932–) American philosopher working in the tradition of ANALYTIC PHILOSOPHY and best known for his development (1969, 1979) of AUSTIN's theory of SPEECH ACTS. Searle identifies five categories of PERFORMATIVE or ILLOCU-TIONARY ACTS: assertives (either true or false), directives (which oblige the listener to act), commissives (which commit the speaker), expressives (revelatory of the speaker's psychological state) and declaratives (which cause something to happen). For Searle, performatives play an important role in the constitution of social reality (1995). The performative inscribed on a bank note ('I promise to pay the bearer on demand') is, that is, an act that constitutes it as legal tender rather than a mere piece of paper.

Searle has also written on INTENTIONALITY (1983), and argues that whilst the mind is certainly a biological phenomenon, it is not reducible to a biological entity because it is characterized by intentionality or the fact that consciousness is directed towards objects and therefore creates their social reality. A chair is a physical object made up of molecules, but it is human consciousness that makes it an object designed, used and perceived as a chair.

Searle is intolerant of DECONSTRUCTION and POSTMODERNISM, and the barbed exchange with DERRIDA (centred on the interpretation of Austin, and initiated by Derrida 1971 and Searle 1977) is a good illustration of the gulf that divides analytic and CONTINENTAL philosophy.

Searle's lucidly written *Mind, Language and Society* (1999) provides an excellent and non-technical introduction to his work.

seduction theory The term is not used by FREUD himself but is commonly employed to describe his first theory of the origins of NEUROSIS (1896), which holds that all neuroses can be traced back to repressed memories of sexual traumas experienced in early childhood. In his earliest papers, Freud variously describes these 'infantile sexual scenes' as 'rape', 'assault', 'aggression' and 'seduction'. Throughout his long correspondence with his associate Wilhelm Fliess (Freud 1985), Freud discusses the viability of his seduction theory and eventually comes to suspect that it implies an improbably high incidence of sexual abuse and of incest on the part of fathers. The theory is finally abandoned in favour of the thesis that what appear to be memories of 'seduction' are in fact fantasies related to the OEDIPUS COMPLEX and that they are an expression of the child's unconscious desire to seduce its father. Freud does not, however, deny that the sexual abuse of children takes place, and remarks in one of his last publications that it is 'common enough' (1938).

The research he undertook in connection with the publication of the Freud-Fliess correspondence led Jeffrey Moussaieff Masson, who had been employed by the Sigmund Freud Archives, to the conclusion that Freud's 'intellectual cowardice' had led him to suppress the truth about the reality and extent of the sexual abuse of children and to falsify his own theory (Masson 1984). Masson was promptly removed from his position as Projects Director (see the account in Malcolm 1984). The so-called suppression of the seduction theory continues to arouse controversy, especially in the wake of the bitter debates over FALSE MEMORY SYNDROME and RECOVERED MEMORY treatment. Critics such as Alice Miller, the Swiss analyst who gave up her analytic career in 1988 as a result of her studies of abuse, argue that Freud's revision of the seduction theory implies that children are naturally wicked (i.e. sexualized) and therefore have to be disciplined and punished (Miller 1988). For such critics, the revision of the theory invalidates psychoanalysis in both theoretical and practical terms because it locks the doors to our awareness of the sexual abuse of children.

semantic field A set of words or lexical items whose meanings have certain elements in common. The terminology of kinship provides obvious examples. The broad field of terms such as 'father', 'grandfather', 'cousin' and so on is defined by the common elements of 'humanity', 'relatedness' and 'animate'. A subfield of terms designating female relatives can then be defined: 'mother', 'sister', 'niece', 'granddaughter' and so on. The term 'semantic field' was introduced by the German linguist Trier, who also demonstrated that the meaning of words is created by a play of relatedness and difference, and who described the vocabulary of a language as a set of semantic fields that define and delineate one another without overlapping (1931).

SAUSSURE comes close to the notion of semantic fields when he describes how meaning arises out of a play of differences and similarities between SIGNS, and when he discusses 'associative relations' in Part Two of his *Course in General Linguistics* (1916). Such relations are created by a process of mental association. In the series *enseignement* ('teaching'), *enseigner* ('to teach'), *enseignons* ('we teach'), the radical is common to every term; further series of associations may be constructed on the basis of the suffix *-ment* (*enseignement, changement*), the concept that is signified (*instruction, éducation*), or the similarity of the sound-image (*justement*, 'precisely').

That semantic fields, like COLLOCATIONS, are specific to different natural languages is the source of many of the problems facing translators. Unlike English, French has two words for 'river'; *un fleuve* runs into the sea, but *une rivière* does not. Similarly, there is no single French equivalent to 'a loaf of bread'. Bilingual dictionaries often claim that the closest equivalent is *un pain*, but that term actually designates a type of bread that is neither *une baguette* (the familiar 'French stick'), *une ficelle* (a smaller form of *baguette*), nor *une miche* nor *une boule* (types of round loaf).

Works of reference such as Roget's *Thesaurus* (first published in 1852) use the idea of a semantic field as an organizing principle.

semiology/semiotics Defined by SAUSSURE (1916) as the science of SIGNS or the study of the life of signs within social life. According to Saussure, a true semiology has yet to be developed, but the future science of semiology will discover what constitutes a sign and the laws that govern the use of signs. Linguistics will eventually be no more than one subdiscipline within a general semiology.

During the heroic phase of STRUCTURALISM, BARTHES inverts Saussure's original definition and argues that semiology is part of the linguistic study of the great signifying units of DISCOURSE. Barthes (1964) broadens the definition to include all sign-systems, including images, gestures and melodic sounds. Everything from the menu that is used to select and combine the items that make up a meal to the fashion system that operates in women's magazines can be studied in semiological terms (Barthes 1967).

The Anglo-American tradition that derives from the work of PEIRCE tends to speak of SEMIOTICS rather than semiology but the terminological distinction has little practical importance.

In medicine semiology is used as a synonym for symptomatology, defined as the study and classification of symptoms.

READING: Eco (1976); Sebeok (1994)

semiotic The term is derived by KRISTEVA from the Greek *semeion* meaning 'distinctive mark', 'trace' or 'sign', and is contrasted with the SYMBOLIC described by LACAN (Kristeva 1974a, 1987a).

The semiotic is a dimension of language arising from the continued contact with the maternal body that is repressed by the symbolic. It is characterized by the features of FREUD's unconscious primary processes (DISPLACEMENT, CONDENSATION) and by alliteration and vocal and gestural rhythmicality. Supported by the biophysiological rhythms of the transmission of excitation and by discharges of energy structured in relation to the primal mother, the semiotic is a pre-linguistic level that exists prior to or 'beneath' the logical and grammatical structures of the symbolic, but a minimal and provisional degree of articulation and stability is introduced by the *CHORA*. The existence of the semiotic implies that the unconscious is structured not like a language, but like the archaic and preverbal traces of a narcissistic relationship with the mother. At the cultural level, the semiotic preserves and expresses a multifarious libidinal DESIRE that subverts the symbolic law. Expressed primarily in poetic and AVANT-GARDE texts characterized by their multiple or polysemic meanings and their subversion of grammar and syntax, the semiotic represents a challenge to the NAME-OF-THE-FATHER and remains in contact with the maternal and female element. The actual gender of the writers concerned is held by Kristeva to be irrelevant; in practice they are inevitably male (Joyce, Mallarmé, Lautréamont, Céline, ARTAUD . . .) and figure prominently in the pantheon of marginal and avant-garde authors celebrated by *TEL QUEL*.

Senghor, Léopold Sédar (1906–) Senegalese poet and politician. Together with CÉSAIRE and DAMAS, Senghor is one of the founding fathers of NEGRITUDE and his major anthology of negritude poetry (1948) is one of the movement's literary landmarks. For Senghor, negritude is at once a universalist humanism and an expression of an African personality and of an essentially African culture based upon an intellectual and moral equilibrium between man and the natural environment. His poetry (collected as 1964b) combines Afrocentric themes with a lyricism that owes much to the French Romantic tradition, and especially to Baudelaire and Rimbaud. His political theory of 'African socialism' defines the future of Africa in terms of both a fidelity to the culture of negritude and the exploitation of advanced technological and organizational forms borrowed from the West. It is widely regarded as a vague formulation that cannot provide concrete solutions to the problems of underdevelopment.

During the colonial period, Senghor represented Senegal in the French Assemblée Nationale from 1946 onwards. From 1961 until his resignation in 1980, he was President of Senegal. In 1984 Senghor, who had by then retired to live in Normandy, was elected to the Académié Française. He was the first black African to be so honoured.

READING: Vaillant (1990)

seriality The term is used by SARTRE (1960) to describe the mode of being of individuals who, although defined by their common PRAXIS, are not integrated into an organized group by labour, struggle or some other collective undertaking, and who therefore constitute themselves as others who are alien to one another. Sartre's illustrative example is that of a queue waiting for a bus on the Place Saint-Germain in Paris. It consists of a serial of individuals united by the common goal (praxis) of getting on the bus, but they have no collective purpose; they wait *as individuals* and are potentially in competition with one another as the bus can take only a limited number of passengers. From the bus-driver's point of view, they are quite interchangeable. Seriality is a form of ALIENATION that can also be observed on the assembly-line of a factory, where workers are brought together by the common praxis of industrial production but serialized by their working conditions and by the workings of mass media such as radio. The radio broadcaster, that is, speaks to a mass of undifferentiated individuals who are not able to communicate with one another. The serial is not necessarily a permanent phenomenon. A group of women waiting outside a baker's during a time of scarcity, such as the period of the French Revolution (which supplies most of the historical examples used by Sartre to illustrate the theses of the *Critique of Dialectical Reason*), forms a classic serial but also has the potential to become the nucleus of a bread riot. If that occurs, the serial is suddenly transformed into a GROUP-IN-FUSION.

sexism The assumption that one sex (inevitably the female) is inferior, or discrimination based upon presuppositions based on a fixed notion of GENDER. The term was formed by analogy with racism and dates from the early 1970s. Images that degrade women or turn them into sex-objects for the gratification of men are commonly said to be sexist. The issue of sexism in language is an important aspect of debates about the POLITICALLY CORRECT and centres on the contention that the use of masculine forms as universals ('the subject . . . he') works to the detriment of women (Spender 1980). Thus 'chairperson' will be used in preference to 'chairman', and 'humanity' or 'humankind' in preference to 'mankind'. Coinages such as HERSTORY attempt to counter the effects of sexist language. 'Sexism' has given rise to many other coinages such as 'SPECIESISM' and 'ageism'.

shifter A term borrowed by JAKOBSON from the Danish linguist Jens Otto Henry Jespersen (1860–1943), who uses it (1922) to describe a class of words whose meaning varies according to their situation or whose reference varies. For Jakobson, a shifter is a term whose meaning cannot be determined without referring to the message that is being communicated between a sender and a receiver (1957). Personal pronouns are shifters: the word 'I' designates both the speaker or sender who says 'I' and the 'I' contained in the message that is sent. Shifters are often referred to as 'DEICTICS'.

Shklovsky, Viktor Borisovich (1893–1984) Russian literary theorist, critic, writer and founder-member of OPOYAZ. Shklovsky is best known for his innovative work on the POETICS of prose fiction (1925).

Shklovsky's earliest writings are a good illustration of the close relationship between FUTURISM and RUSSIAN FORMALISM. His 'Resurrection of the Word' (1914) describes futurism's aim as the 'resurrection of things' and 'the return to man of the sensation of the world'. The words of conventional poetry are said to be dead, and must be replaced by new and innovative words. Shklovsky's emphasis on the need for an innovative language, and his insistence that poetry's concern is with language and not external reality, recalls the conclusion of the collective futurist manifesto 'A Slap in the Face of Public Taste' (1912), which rejects both common sense and good taste and looks forward to 'the summer lightnings of the New-Coming Beauty of the Self-sufficient (self-centred) Word' (cited Markov 1969). Shklovsky's distinction between the true perception associated with innovative art and the recognition promoted by dead or dying art forms, for its part, prefigures the introduction of the concept of estrangement or defamiliarization (OSTRANENIE) in 'Art as Technique' (1917), which is rightly regarded as the great manifesto of Russian formalism. Here the FOREGROUNDING of poetic devices such as repetition and parallelism is described as making the text difficult or strange, and thus inducing a new perception of both language and the world.

In his writings on the poetics of prose, Shklovsky anticipates later developments in NARRATOLOGY and POETICS by making a distinction between 'motif' (*motiv*) and 'plot' (*syuzhet*), defined respectively as basic narrative units which cannot be broken down into smaller units, and narrative situations (*motivy*) are woven together to form a linear narrative or a story made up of motifs that have been so combined as to have a causal and temporal logic. There is an obvious similarity here with PROPP's morphological approach, which breaks down complex folk-tales into smaller units and functions, but Shklovsky also anticipates STRUCTURALISM's concern with universals, as exemplified by LÉVI-STRAUSS's analysis of mythologies and kinship systems. The universality of the 'abduction of wives' motif, which appears in stories and legends from all over the world and from all periods, derives, in Shklovsky's view, from history and social customs rather than from the structures of the mind, but his work does lay the foundations for a more sophisticated approach to narrative analysis and to the STORY/PLOT distinction.

The theory of estrangement is well illustrated by Shklovsky's semi-autobiographical works (1923a, 1923b) and especially by his fascinating account of Mayakovsky and his circle (1940), which provides a good account of the heady climate that produced both futurism and Russian formalism.

READING: Sherwood (1973); Todorov (1971b)

Showalter, Elaine (1941–) American critic and theorist of GYNOCRITICS. Showalter is one of the most influential of feminist literary critics, and her anthology of 'new feminist' critical essays is an important work of reference (1985b). Originally a specialist in nineteenth-century English literature, Showalter has devoted her most recent books to the history of madness and psychiatry, with particular reference to women's experience. The link between these apparently disparate disciplines is supplied by the theme of the 'madwoman in the attic' in the English novel (see GILBERT AND GUBAR).

Showalter's study of British women novelists (1977) is a good example of her gynocritics, and establishes the existence of a distinct female tradition that constitutes a subculture within the wider society. She identifies three stages in its history:

an initial stage characterized by the imitation and internalization of the prevailing modes of the dominant literary culture; a phase of protest in which those modes are contested by the assertion of minority rights; and a final phase of self-discovery and of the assertion of identity. The three stages are described respectively as 'feminine', 'feminist' and 'female'.

Showalter's concentration on women's experience leads her to contrast experience with THEORY, and she tends to describe all literary theory as male-oriented. Whilst feminists such as Moi (1985) are very critical of this tendency within gynocritics, it is difficult to deny the cogency of the argument (in Showalter 1977) that BLOOM's account of the ANXIETY OF INFLUENCE relies so heavily upon an Oedipal struggle between fathers and sons that it can scarcely apply to women writers whose predecessor is the powerful George Eliot. This reading, however, is at odds with that of Gilbert and Gubar (1979a).

Showalter's important study of the 'female malady' of HYSTERIA (1985a) examines the history of psychiatry from the reforms of the Victorian period to the ANTI-PSYCHIATRY of Laing. Looking at both clinical and literary material, she argues that the relationship between women and psychiatry is dominated by a dual imagery. On the one hand, madness is one of the wrongs of women (the allusion is to an unfinished novel by Mary Wollstonecraft, 1797); on the other, it is an essential female nature which unveils itself before scientific male rationality. Psychiatry is thus an important factor in the characterization of women as irrational, silent, natural and corporeal, as opposed to men who are rational, cultured and intellectual. Showalter's *Hystories* (1997) further explores the issue of hysteria, but expands the discussion beyond women's experience and argues, very controversially, that late twentieth-century phenomena as diverse as panics over alien abduction, chronic fatigue syndrome (ME) and Gulf War syndrome all have psychological origins and can be viewed as new forms of hysteria. Similar but less controversial parallels between the two fins de siècle were also drawn in the earlier and highly entertaining *Sexual Anarchy* (1991), which ranges across a wide variety of topics from male bonding in nineteenth-century fiction and contemporary cinema to Victorian perceptions of syphilis and modern representations of AIDS.

sign Reflections upon how meaning is constituted by the relationship between what is signified and what signifies it are probably as old as human thinking about language, and the notion of the sign can be traced back to Classical Antiquity. The modern concept of the sign is largely defined by the theory elaborated by SAUSSURE in his posthumously published *Course in General Linguistics* (1916).

Many early theories of the sign are bound up with speculations about the origins of human language, and the sign is often viewed as an automatic or natural expression of emotional states. Writing in c. 55 BC, Lucretius, for instance, speculates that, just as wild animals utter distinct sounds when gripped by fear or pain, men are driven by nature to utter similar sounds that give a form to the names of different objects. Those forms, which might be described as rudimentary signs, are in a sense both natural and conventional. In AD 427 St Augustine writes in his *De doctrina christiana* (On Christian teaching) that a sign is 'a thing which in itself makes some other thing come to mind, besides the impression that it presents' to the mind. Augustine distinguishes between natural signs, such as smoke which signifies fire, and given signs, which human beings and other living things 'give' to one another to demonstrate their emotions or something they have felt or learnt. Although Augustine's speculations are linked to his reflections on the nature of the divine word or *logos* that created the world and on the sacred signs to be read in Scripture, the notion that a sign is an expression of some pre-linguistic reality remains a commonplace until the ENLIGHTENMENT. In his *Essay Concerning Human Understanding* (1690b) Locke, for example, explores the expressive link between ideas and the words that express them, whilst Condillac's *Essai sur l'origine des connaissances humaines* (Essay on the origin of human knowledge, 1746) describes words as 'instituted signs' which give human beings control over their thoughts. It is only with the emergence of modern linguistics and the thesis that language is a system in its own right, and not an expression of a pre-linguistic reality or emotional state, that the contemporary theory of the sign develops.

With Saussurean linguistics, the sign becomes the basic unit of the analysis of language. A sign is defined as a psychical entity consisting of a SIGNIFIER (an acoustic image) and a SIGNIFIED (a concept). A sign is not a combination of an object and a name for that object, and language therefore cannot be regarded as a nomenclature or a list of names for things. The nature of the sign is said to be arbitrary, as there is nothing logical or necessary about the relationship between signifier and signified, or between the sign and its extra-linguistic REFERENT. There is, that is, no necessary connection between the acoustic image evoked by the signifer /cat/ and the concept of a domestic quadruped which purrs. Saussure does, however, make a distinction between sign and SYMBOL, arguing that a symbol is not entirely arbitrary and that there is a rudimentary link between its signifier and its signified. The scales are a quasi-natural symbol of justice, and cannot be replaced by a cart.

The value or distinctiveness of a sign is determined by the phonic differences that allow it to be differentiated from all other signs; those differences are both syntagmatic and paradigmatic (SYNTAGM, PARADIGM). As Jakobson remarks (1956), the Cheshire Cat in Lewis Carroll's *Alice in Wonderland* illustrates the basic principle by asking Alice, 'Did you say pig or fig?' It is the play of differences and similarities between signs that constitutes language as a meaningful system centred upon the LANGUE/PAROLE system.

A rather different theory of the sign or REPRESENTAMEN is elaborated by PEIRCE in his work on semiotics. According to PEIRCE, the representamen addresses someone and creates an equivalent sign in that person's mind; this is the interpretant of the first sign, and it stands for an idea or object. Unlike Saussure, Peirce also elaborates a very complex typology of signs, the most familiar being the ICON, the INDEX and the SYMBOL.

Signs A major interdisciplinary journal of feminist scholarship published quarterly by the University of Chicago Press since 1975, and subtitled 'Journal of Women in Culture and Society'. The editorial to the first (autumn 1975) issue describes *Signs'* purpose as being 'to publish the new scholarship about women from both the

United States and other countries'. That scholarship is described as a 'means to the end of an accurate understanding of men and women, of sex and gender, of large patterns of human behavior, institutions, ideologies and art'.

simulacrum In Latin this word denoted a material representation or image, usually of a deity. The term has been given a new importance by BAUDRILLARD's account of POSTMODERNITY. A discussion of the role of the simulacrum in Greek and Roman theories of representation can be found in the Appendices to DELEUZE's *Logic of Sense* (1969). Baudrillard's most systematic expositions of his theory of simulacra are to be found in his *Symbolic Exchange and Death* (1976) and *Simulacra and Simulations* (1981).

For Baudrillard, a simulacrum is a reproduction of an object or event characteristic of a specific stage in the history of the image or SIGN. He traces a series of stages in its emergence. Whereas the image was once a reflection of a basic reality, as in the feudal order in which signs were clear indications of hierarchical status, it came to mask or pervert a basic reality when, in the baroque period that privileged artifice and counterfeit over natural signs, arbitrary or artificial signs began to proliferate. Such signs are described as first order simulacra. With the mass production of industrial objects in BENJAMIN's 'era of mechanical reproduction', second order simulacra predominated as 'originals' lost their mystic AURA; such simulacra signal the absence of a basic reality. The third order simulacra of POSTMODERNITY have no relation to reality whatsoever, and are their own pure simulacra or imitations of imitations. The ultimate simulacrum is Disneyland. According to Baudrillard, Disneyland is presented as imaginary – or simulates its own imaginary nature – in order to make us believe that the rest of America is real rather than something belonging to the order of simulation and HYPERREALITY.

The early work of the American artist Cindy Sherman (1954–) represents an exemplary exploration of the simulacrum, and can also be seen as a comment on femininity as MASQUERADE. A good selection of her work has been reproduced in Rosalind Krauss's important study (1993). The series of sixty-five black and white 'untitled film stills' produced between 1977 and 1980 are carefully staged photographs in which the artist appears in what seem to be scenes from Hollywood or *NOUVELLE VAGUE* films from the 1950s. The grain of the photographs and even the depth of focus are so calculated as to look like actual stills from real films and appear disturbingly familiar, but everything is staged by Sherman, who acted as her own director, photographer and actress, appearing as female detective, potential crime-victim and typical Hitchcock heroine. The stills are simulacra, or reproductions of originals that never existed.

singular universal The notion of the singular universal is the great leitmotiv of SARTRE's monumental study of the novelist Gustave Flaubert (1821–80) and the methodological culmination of his earlier exercises in EXISTENTIALIST PSYCHOAN-ALYSIS. The three volumes of Sartre's *The Idiot of the Family* (1971–2) are described by their author as the sequel to the *Search for a Method* that introduced the *Critique of Dialectical Materialism*, and as an attempt to answer the question 'What can we know of a man today?' They, and the question they pose, are a further attempt to overcome the HEURISTIC inadequacy of a MARXISM that can say of the Professor of Poetry at the Collège de France: 'Paul Valéry is a petty-bourgeois intellectual', but fail to explain why 'Not every petty-bourgeois intellectual is Paul Valéry' (Sartre 1960).

According to Sartre, Flaubert is not merely an individual, but an individual instance of the universal. In typically paradoxical terms, he describes his subject as universal in terms of the singular universality of human history, and singular in terms of the universal singularity of the project that defines him. Flaubert's words as a novelist reveal his individual socialization and background, which are determined by the entire culture that shaped him, but they are always mediated through the way in which he internalizes, interprets and transcends the roles available to him in the society in which he lives. Flaubert, like any individual, shapes and internalizes those roles in a way that is unique to him alone. He is a singular universal who is universalized by his era, but who then reproduces that era in his singularity.

situation The term is used by SARTRE (1943a) to describe the individual's being-in-the-world, or the fact that individuals are always and already situated in relation to others, time and space, the inevitability of death and their own FACTICITY. Whilst the situation restricts and conditions the basic freedom of human beings, it is also a precondition for that freedom insofar as their for-itself (IN-ITSELF/FOR ITSELF) realizes its freedom in the conscious and responsible action that transcends the situation. Sartre can thus argue (1944a) that the French had never been so free as they were during the German occupation of their country; a situation that denied them their freedom also allowed them to reassert it through resistance.

The issue of the relationship between situation, freedom and responsibility lends itself well to dramatic and fictional treatment. It is the major theme of Sartre's plays and novels, and is explored with great skill in the novels that make up the *Roads to Freedom* trilogy (1945a, 1945b, 1949b).

situationism A political ideology combining elements of MARXISM with avant-garde artistic practices in the tradition of DADA; its main spokesmen are Guy DEBORD (1931–94) and Raoul VANEIGEM (1935–). Founded in 1957, the Situationist International was a small but influential group based in Paris and with members in Holland, Germany and Belgium; one of the few British members was the Scottish novelist Alexander Trocchi (1925–84; see Scott 1991). The organization survived in one form or another until 1972. The journal *Internationale Situationiste* was published in Paris between 1958 and 1969, and has been reprinted many times.

The Situationist International (SI) developed out of a number of small groups of artists whose ambition was to use both artistic and more practical activity to shape a SITUATION (defined in quasi-Sartrean terms) designed to unleash a free and spontaneous creativity leading to a revolution in everyday life. Favoured activities included the aimless locomotion of the *DÉRIVE* and *détournement*. The latter term means 'diversion', but also 'subversion' and 'corruption', and refers to the techniques of creative plagiarism and altering the words of posters and comic strips to give them an unexpectedly political slant. The SI is often credited with having inspired the French student revolt of 1968, and many of the slogans and graffiti of the period are situationist-inspired: 'It is forbidden to forbid' and 'Take your desires for reality.'

Situationism's main critique of contemporary society is encapsulated in the phrase 'the society of the spectacle', which is the title of Debord's main contribution to its theory (1967). The society of the spectacle is a society in which the accumulation of images has become more important than the accumulation of commodities, and in which rapidly circulating signs transform individuals into actors who play out artificial roles that suffocate their subjectivity. Even acts of rebellion against the consumer society can be recuperated to become elements in the never-ending and ever-changing spectacle. According to this theory of ALIENATION, which is heavily influenced by LUKÁCS, modern society caters for no real needs, and acts on the principle of 'to each in accordance with his or her artificial needs'. In organizational terms, situationism is distantly related to the tradition of 'workers' council' or 'self-management' socialism, and its supporters have always been deeply suspicious of organized political parties.

The SI was always divided by the tensions between its artistic heritage and its political ambitions, and these have often been seen as resulting from conflicts between a 'spontaneous' Vaneigem and a 'theoretical' Debord. The conspiratorial organization was always plagued with internal quarrels and its history is largely the history of the denunciation and expulsion of its own members. It is a measure of the SI's collective talent for polemic and invective that one account of its history (Raspaud and Voyer 1972) includes an 'index of those insulted' in the pages of its journal. A typical entry reads: 'Sartre, Jean-Paul: stupid, liar, idiot, damaged goods, corpse in an advanced state of decay, nonentity, unspeakable.'

READING: Plant (1992); Wollen (1989)

soap opera Narrative GENRE characterized by the use of open-ended multiple plots with a large number of characters. Originally developed for radio, soap operas are now one the mainstays of television. Shown several times a week in prime-time slots, they typically deal with the everyday lives of 'ordinary people' and often have a street, a workplace, a school or some other centre of collective life as a setting. Soap operas are serial in nature, and have much in common with the serial narratives, often melodramatic, that began to be featured in newspapers in the nineteenth century. Like their predecessors, they are often structured around cliffhanger endings that leave a major character at a moment of indecision or danger that will be resolved in a coming episode, and are constructed around the implicit question 'What will happen next?'

The expression 'soap opera' dates from the 1930s, when serials (also known as 'washboard weepies') sponsored by – and sometimes even produced by – detergent manufacturers began to be broadcast on US radio. The first British equivalent was *Mrs Dale's Diary* (later retitled *The Dales*), broadcast twice daily by the BBC between 1948 and 1969. Successful soaps can have extraordinarily long runs; *Coronation Street* has been showing on British commercial television since 1960, and the highly popular *East Enders* was first broadcast in 1985.

The early radio soap operas were designed with a specific audience in mind: women at home during the day. Some were little more than ill-disguised vehicles for advertising soap powders and other household products, and all were punctuated by advertisements from their sponsors. Narratives tended to be constructed around 'women's issues' such as love, the breakdown of relationships and the themes of traditional ROMANCE, but these could be seen to be subverted by the presence of strong and assertive female characters. Anyone who watched the early *Coronation Street* will still have memories of the fearsome Ena Sharples; no feminist, but certainly a strong woman. The association between soap opera and a predominantly female audience is still strong, but shifting GENDER roles have weakened it somewhat. Positive accounts of modern soap operas suggest that they provide a convenient and popular medium for sexual and gender issues, and soaps such as *East Enders* can deal with AIDS, homosexuality and sexual violence against women in a remarkably responsible manner.

Whilst British soap operas at least do not feature direct advertising, worries are sometimes expressed about 'product placement'. Soap opera is a realist genre and therefore makes great use of the REALITY-EFFECT created by the inclusion of recognizable products and commodities: the juke box in the bar plays the hits of the day, characters drink from recognizable cans and bottles, and so on. Whilst this is essential if the reality-effect is to be sustained, it can also be argued that it reinforces the viewer's 'product awareness'.

Traditional critical approaches to television criticism, which were modelled on film and even theatre criticism, tended to be dismissive of soap opera. Raymond WILLIAMS's important study of television has, for example, almost nothing to say about the genre. One of the problems they pose for traditional approaches is that of authorship. Soaps are written by teams of writers working on various storylines and might almost be said to be written by no one in particular. Very few viewers could name the director of an individual episode of their favourite soap opera. It is really only with the emergence of CULTURAL STUDIES that soap opera becomes an object of serious study. In many such studies (see, for example, Brown 1994) it is argued that soap operas still appeal to a predominantly female audience and that they sustain an oral women's SUBCULTURE founded upon discussion of their content.

READING: Geraghty (1991); Hobson (1982)

socialist feminism A very broad tendency within modern FEMINISM with a general commitment to socialism, but also to the transformation of existing socialist organizations in order to make them more responsive to and representative of women's interests. There has never been any single manifesto of socialist feminism and it can take many different forms, but most of those involved argue for some combination of the socialist and feminist traditions. Whilst RADICAL FEMINISM tends to view all men as the main enemy of all women and to operate with a biological definition of both masculinity and femininity, most forms of socialist feminism look to social structures and ideologies to explain the existence of a male-dominated society. The existence of mass socialist organizations, and the fact that many involved in the early WOMEN'S LIBERATION movement came from the NEW LEFT, made socialist feminism much more important in Britain and Europe than in the United States. One of the classic statements of socialist feminism is BEAUVOIR's *The Second Sex* (1949), but by the 1970s few agreed with her surprisingly traditionalist claim that socialism would automatically lead to the liberation of women. In Britain, Juliet Mitchell's pioneering article 'Women – The Longest Revolution' (1966) is widely regarded as one of the founding statements of both socialist feminism and the women's movement itself. In their significant *Beyond the Fragments* (1979), Sheila Rowbotham, Lynne Segal and Hilary Wainwright provide an eloquent account of the difficulties faced by women working in or with male-dominated socialist organizations.

READING: Coote and Campbell (1982)

socialist realism The dominant style in official Soviet literature and art from 1934 onwards, characterized by its heroic depiction of labour and glorification of the ruling Communist Party. In 1934 it was defined by the statutes of the Union of Writers as the basic method of Soviet literature and as requiring from writers and artists a truthful portrayal of realities in their revolutionary development and a commitment to the ideological remoulding of the people in the spirit of socialism. The writer was defined as 'the engineer of the human soul'; the expression is often attributed to Stalin himself. The optimism of socialist realism was habitually contrasted with what ZHDANOV (1950) called 'the riot of mysticism, religious mania and pornography' that supposedly characterized the decaying culture of Western capitalism. Similar literary policies were adopted by Western Communist parties. The adoption of socialist realism as an official doctrine put an end to the earlier period of debates about the relationship between literature and politics within the Soviet Union. In the visual arts, stereotypical and heroic images glorifying industrial and agricultural labour (often caricatured as the 'boy meets tractor' school) quickly replaced the experiments of the futurists and constructivists.

The notion of socialist realism is usually regarded as originating in Engels's comments in his letter of April 1888 to the novelist Margaret Harkness (in Marx and Engels 1965), where he defines realism as both 'truth of detail' and 'truth in reproduction of typical characters under typical circumstances'. 'Typicality' is an important element in the theory of realism developed by LUKÁCS, and he duly gave the notion of socialist realism his somewhat guarded approval (1937). One of the more readable examples of socialist realism to have been produced in English is John Sommerfield's *May Day* (1936), but in his note to the 1984 reprint the author retrospectively described it as 'early 30s communist romanticism'.

READING: *Socialist Realism in Literature and Art* (1971); *Soviet Socialist Realist Painting 1930–1960* (1992)

Sokal, Alan (1955–) American physicist. In 1996 Sokal published an article on the 'transformative hermeneutics of quantum gravity' in the prestigious journal *Social*

Text (reprinted in Sokal 1998). It took the form of an attack on the dogma imposed by the 'long post-Enlightenment hegemony on Western intellectual thought', the dogma that stated that there exists an external world with law-governed properties that exist independently of individual human beings, and that objective knowledge of those properties is possible. Sokal went on to demolish that dogma with the help of extensive quotations from the French philosophers of POSTMODERNITY and their Anglo-American followers. That the article, with its 107 footnotes and impressive bibliography, was a spoof which did not actually make any scientific sense went quite unnoticed by *Social Text*'s editorial board. When the scandal broke, Sokal's article became the subject of very wide press coverage, and in 1997 he expanded his underlying thesis into a highly controversial book (written in French) coauthored with a Belgian professor of theoretical physics (Sokal and Bricmont 1997); the authors subsequently produced a slightly different English-language version (1998).

Sokal's original article was born of his distress at the repeated abuse of scientific concepts and terminology he had observed in the work of so many French intellectuals and at the extreme epistemic relativism promoted by a reading of KUHN'S history of science that spoke of incommensurable PARADIGMs and of the irreconcilable and mutually incomprehensible LANGUAGE GAMES described by LYOTARD and others. Such theories can come close, he was convinced, to a dangerous and potentially anti-scientific irrationalism.

There are two main strands to Sokal's argument. He contends that many French thinkers borrow from mathematics and physics without really understanding the concepts they invoke, and that they do so in order to impress and intimidate readers with little or no scientific knowledge. He has little difficulty in demonstrating that, from a strictly mathematical point of view, LACAN'S quasi-algebraic formulae and MATHEMES are virtually meaningless and that his use of mathematical topography is based upon a very poor understanding of that subject. Similarly, it is pointed out that KRISTEVA'S use of set theory, particularly in her *Semiotiké* (1969b), is seriously flawed, and that it is improbable in the extreme that Lautréamont (1846–70) could have used a theorem associated with the set theory developed by Gödel and Bernays between 1937 and 1947. A similar absurdity is noted in Irigaray's contention (1987) that 'If the identity of the human subject is defined in the work of Freud by a *Spaltung*, this is also the word used for nuclear fission'; as Sokal remarks, this is not an argument, and if it were, it appears to lead to no conclusion. Comparable weaknesses and misunderstandings are found in the writings of BAUDRILLARD, DELEUZE, GUATTARI, Lyotard and others.

The second strand in Sokal's argument is a defence of scientific method and scientific realism against a relativism that draws on KUHN and on FEYERABEND'S claim that 'anything goes' in scientific research in such a way as to promote an irrationalism that can flourish alongside creationism and New Age mysticism. Science is not, maintains Sokal, 'just another discourse' and nor is it merely a reservoir of metaphors for use in the human sciences. Postmodernism stands accused of encouraging obscurantism and of using pseudo-scientific arguments to pervert the very ideas of justice and progress. Although Sokal's polemic can look like a conservative attack on an intellectual avant-garde, he claims to be 'an unabashed Old Leftist' who is demystifying a dangerous dominant discourse. Sokal and Bricmont are also very careful to restrict their criticisms to the use and abuse of mathematics and physics; they have nothing to say about Lacan's psychoanalysis or Kristeva's theory of poetics as such.

solipsism Derived from the Latin words *solus* ('only') and *ipse* ('self'), the term is sometimes used as a synonym for 'selfishness' or 'egotism'. In philosophy it is used more strictly to describe the thesis that only the self exists. All philosophies that, like the Cartesian *cogito* ('I am thinking, therefore I am', 1637), take as their starting-point the immediate experience of an individual consciouness tend to lapse into solipsism as they have difficulty in establishing the existence of other conscious-nesses. Both HUSSERL's pure PHENOMENOLOGY and the EXISTENTIALISM of the early SARTRE have been criticized for their alleged solipsism.

Sollers, Philippe (1936–) French critic, novelist, cofounder in 1960 of *TEL QUEL* and, from 1983 onwards, editor of its successor *L'Infini*. 'Sollers' is the pseudonym of Philippe Joyaux; he himself has explained his choice of name on a number of occasions (1973, 1994). It derives from the Latin, and he glosses it as meaning 'possessed of an art or skill', 'clever' and 'adroit'.

Sollers' first novel, *Une Curieuse Solitude* (1958), a tale of sexual initiation which he subsequently disowned, was praised by both the Catholic novelist François Mauriac and the veteran communist Aragon, and its author quipped that his career was launched with the help of both the Vatican and the Kremlin. His subsequent and very successful career is indissociable from the evolution of *Tel quel* as it moves from admiration of the *NOUVEAU ROMAN* to Marxism and even Maoism, and then to admiration for Solzhenitsyn and the Soviet dissidents. His many novels follow a similar trajectory and evolve through a phase of 'textual writing' (1973) which deliberately blurs the boundaries between theory and fiction and insists that a text is a self-productive system with no external REFERENT, and finally to a return to what Sollers calls 'figurative' novels such as *Women* (1983). The latter, and the related *Portrait du joueur* (Portrait of the player 1994), is in part an entertaining *ROMAN-à-clef*, in part a satire on Parisian intellectual life (with particular reference to the alleged conspiracy of feminists who want to establish a matriarchal dictator-ship), and in part a highly controlled and contrived portrait of the author as libertine. It also contains a warm and thinly disguised portrait of Sollers' wife Julia KRISTEVA.

Despite all the changes and shifts of direction, there are constants in Sollers' work as both theorist and novelist. The novel is viewed as a way of exploring and even anticipating the theoretical developments associated with psychoanalysis or Marxism, and as 'the continuation of thought by other means' (1996). The interest in eroticism (which goes hand in hand with the contention that sexual difference is irreducible and that men and women are strangers to one another) and in mysticism, madness and the baroque are constants, as is the reference to *Tel quel's* pantheon of authors (Céline, Lautréamont, Sade, Artaud, Bataille, Joyce . . .). It is clear from the essays and prefaces collected in *La Guerre du goût* (The war of taste,

1996) that Sollers is convinced that literature and art are, ultimately, the only civilizing values and the sole source of creative freedom.

Sontag, Susan (1933–) American literary critic, cultural commentator and novelist. Although her reputation in academic circles has always been slight, Sontag is an influential critic whose essays and reviews (mostly collected 1966, 1969, 1980) have done much to introduce European modernism to an American audience. Her editions of ARTAUD (Artaud 1976) and BARTHES (Barthes 1981b) have been particularly influential, and she has written with elegance on authors such as BENJAMIN Sarraute and LUKÁCS and on film-makers like Bresson, Resnais and Godard. She is also a shrewd commentator on the aesthetics of photography (1977), and on social phenomena such as the 'camp' vision of the world in terms of style, with its exploration of a refined sexuality 'going against the grain of one's own sex'.

Sontag's programmatic slogan of 'Against interpretation' (1966) is a plea for the work of art to be 'left alone' and an attack on the kind of criticism that represents the intellect's revenge on art. It does not, however, imply an anti-intellectualism; on the contrary, 'intelligence' is the central term of praise in Sontag's aesthetic. The combination of will and intelligence are more important to Sontag than the expression of fully worked out ideas. In general terms, she takes the modernist view that art is a statement of self-awareness and a testimony to the disharmony between the artist and his or her community.

Sontag's essays on illness as metaphor (1978b) and metaphorical representations of AIDS (1989) apply the 'against interpretation' strategy to human suffering. The metaphors of war and invasion that are so often applied to cancer and AIDS are a form of mystification which actively discourages sufferers from seeking scientific treatment, and which promotes myths, including the belief that certain character types are more liable than others to be affected by cancer. A person suffering from cancer has not been invaded by a military force, and he or she will not benefit from miracle diets or psychotherapy; cancer is quite simply a disease to be treated as such. Arguing in terms reminiscent of FOUCAULT, Sontag claims that societies appear to need some illness that can be characterized as evil and that cancer and AIDS are now being described in terms that were once applied to leprosy and syphilis. The introduction of metaphors of evil, contagion or invasion stigmatizes the ills and disempowers them.

Sontag's fiction tends to centre on the amoral, affectless characters who are so typical of European modernism, and the protagonist of her first novel (1967) appears to be directly descended from the Lafcadio figure in Gide's *The Vatican Cellars* (1925). That Sontag's real gift is for the short, even fragmentary, essay may explain why her short stories (1978a) are rather more successful than her novels.

READING: Sayres (1990)

speciesism The belief that the human species enjoys an innate superiority over all other species and is therefore justified in exploiting them. The main argument against speciesism is that if it is justifiable to assume that human beings feel pain, there is no reason to suppose that other species do not (Singer 1976). This is the major thesis of the supporters of animal liberation, who argue that all species are equal and have a right to life. The logical conclusion of the argument is a plea for universal vegetarianism.

speech act A form of verbal utterance which constitutes an action, as in 'And God said, Let there be light: and there was light' (Genesis i:3). Modern speech act theory derives from AUSTIN's work on the PERFORMATIVE and the ILLOCUTIONARY ACT; its main advocate is John R. SEARLE, who was Austin's student. Searle's theory of the speech act (1969, 1979) is underpinned by the thesis that both the mind and language are intentional, or that any linguistic act is an attempt to communicate with a listener by getting that listener to recognize the speaker's intention to communicate just what he is saying. Conversely, understanding an utterance implies the assumption that it was produced by a being with a certain intention. For Searle, the principle of expressivity implies that whatever can be meant can be said. Speaking a language is a complex rule-governed form of behaviour; the fact that natural languages are intertranslatable implies that the rules are universal and that different languages are merely different conventional realizations of those rules. Convention alone dictates that French uses *pain*, and English 'bread'. The unit of linguistic communication is neither the symbol, the word nor the sentence, but their production in the performance of a speech act. Speech acts or illocutionary acts include making statements, giving commands, asking questions, making promises, referring and predicating. All are rule-governed: a request involves a future act, the ability to perform it and the belief on the part of the speaker that it will be done. It is also an attempt to make the listener do something. An order has the additional preparatory rule that the speaker must be in a position of authority over the listener.

Although Searle's theory is an important contribution to ANALYTIC PHILOSOPHY and can be viewed as an extension of ORDINARY LANGUAGE PHILOSOPHY, his emphasis on the combination of convention and intentionality marks a departure from WITTGENSTEIN's argument that 'meaning is use.'

Spivak, Gayatri Chakravorty (1942–) Bengali cultural-literary critic and exponent of a feminist DECONSTRUCTION. Spivak first came to prominence in 1977 as the translator of DERRIDA's *Of Grammatology* (1967a) and has subsequently emerged as one of the most influential figures in POSTCOLONIAL THEORY. Although she works mainly in the United States, she is closely associated with the Delhi-based SUBALTERN STUDIES group.

Spivak is not, by her own admission (1986), 'a book writer', and her considerable reputation is therefore based on her numerous articles, lectures and conference papers (mainly collected 1987, 1990, 1993). She also confesses (1986) to writing 'with great difficulty in both Bengali and English' and her style has to be described as difficult. Spivak makes extensive use of figures such as CATACHRESIS, frequently coins neologisms and often relies upon unexpected juxapositions of images and ideas. Her exclusive use of the essay-lecture mode also means that there is much repetition across her prolific output.

Spivak's texts are often deeply personal, and she writes with a certain humour –

and, critics would add, a certain narcissism – of her anomalous position as a THIRD WORLD woman working in the prestigious universities of the West, stressing the need to 'unlearn' the privileges (here she might be compared with Bhattacharyya, who gives – 1996 – a witty and wry account of how a black woman teacher can be so easily cast in the role of the 'race lady'). She is also deeply suspicious of essentialist categories such as 'Third World' and 'woman', stressing in typical deconstructionist fashion that they are based upon artificial and unstable binary oppositions, and highly critical of the inverted racism that assumes that all Third World writing is by definition of great value. Such essential categories do not found, and are not based upon, stable identities. The name 'Indian' or 'Asian' is itself a product of colonial discourse and has been constructed in a violent encounter between colonialism and the 'subjects' it produces through what Spivak calls 'epistemic violence', or the violence involved in the production and acquisition of knowledge of the OTHER. The discursive production of the 'savage Indian' is also described as 'othering'. Yet whilst she resists essentialism and criticizes the assumption that the 'sovereign SUBJECT' is the source of meaning and authority, Spivak also stresses (particularly in 1985b) that there is a need for a moment of 'strategic essentialism' when it becomes necessary to speak 'as a woman' or 'as an Asian' in order to challenge the HEGEMONY of colonial discourse.

Spivak's essay on Charlotte Brontë's *Jane Eyre* (1985c) provides a good example of her strategies of reading. Like SAID's reading of *Mansfield Park*, it stresses from the outset that nineteenth-century English literature played an important role in the construction of the cultural representation of Britain, and that imperialism, or Britain's self-appointed social mission, is part of that representation and self-representation. That mission can also influence how Marxists and feminists read literary texts. In his reading of *Jane Eyre*, the Marxist Terry EAGLETON stresses (1975a) Jane's class position as a governess, whilst the feminists GILBERT AND GUBAR (1979a) concentrate on her relationship with the 'madwoman in the attic' and contend that Bertha Mason is Jane's 'dark double'; Spivak emphasizes that Mason is a creole from Jamaica whose role is to blur the boundary between the human and the animal. Her narrative function is to set fire to the house and kill herself in order to allow Jane Eyre to become the feminist individual heroine of British literature. Her individuality requires the death of the other in a metaphoric depiction of the epistemic violence of the colonialism that allowed Thornfield Hall to be built. Turning to Jean Rhys's *Wide Sargasso Sea* (1965), Spivak reads it as a novel which rewrites the canonical *Jane Eyre* (CANON) in the interests of the creole woman, but which, because it is bound by the conventions of the European novel, cannot allow the black Christophine (the housemaid) to speak the truth of slavery and makes her the absolute other.

READING: Loomba (1998); Moore-Gilbert (1997)

Stanislavsky, Konstantin Sergeyevich (1863–1938) Russian theatre director and cofounder, in 1898, of the Moscow Arts Theatre, where his productions were characterized by an extraordinary attention to naturalistic detail. In a series of books (especially 1926), Stanislavsky elaborates a 'system' of actor-training which has had an enormous impact and still provides the pedagogic model used in drama schools throughout the world. The System, which includes physical exercises and improvisations as well as psychological methods of training and preparation, is designed to help the actor to identify with and effectively reproduce the whole life of the character he is playing by concentrating on the inner elements of characterization and unleashing his own creative and emotional capacities. The actor is trained to 'get into character', or to believe in the reality of the imaginary character he has created as strongly as a little girl believes in the reality of her doll. Transposed to America by Lee Strasberg (1902–82), who cofounded the Actors Studio in 1947, Stanislavsky's System came to be known as the 'Method' and Method acting soon became the dominant style in both the theatre and the cinema. The Actors Studio's famous graduates include Marlon Brando, James Dean and Paul Newman. The psychological realism of Stanislavsky's System is the antithesis of the style of acting BRECHT sought to promote through the ALIENATION-EFFECT.

READING: Magarshack (1961)

Steiner, George (1929–) American literary critic. Although his is one of the most distinctive voices in modern criticism, Steiner has always displayed what he terms 'a distrust of theory' (1997) and is as sceptical about the claims of DECONSTRUCTION as he was once distrustful of the 'shimmering technical obscurities' of the NEW CRITICISM (1962). 'THEORY', for Steiner, represents a failure of nerve in the face of the prestige of the sciences, a doomed attempt to introduce a scientific veneer into a literary realm in which verification and FALSIFIABILITY have no place. His deeply personal vision and commitment to a sense of values has something in common with the famous seriousness of LEAVIS, whom he greatly admires, but his multilingualism and polymathy owe much to his background as a Jewish exile from Europe.

Voiced in many books and essays written throughout his life – among them *Tolstoy or Dostoyevsky* (1960), *The Death of Tragedy* (1961), *Language and Silence* (1967), *In Bluebeard's Castle* (1971), *Real Presences* (1989), *After Babel* (1992) and the autobiographical memoir *Errata* (1997) – Steiner's main preoccupation is with the defence of what he calls a 'humane literacy' (1963). Here the role of the critic is defined in almost messianic terms. The critic is the custodian of 'that great discourse with the living that we call reading', the mediator between past and present, and between languages, but he also 'feels ahead', looking over the horizon and preparing the context for the recognition of the literature of the future. The critic's concern is with language, and the health of language is essential to the health and survival of a living society. In Steiner's view, the totalitarianism of Nazism, the jargon of the mass media and the 'monotony' of pornography are all major threats to the health of language, and he is an unapologetic defender of 'high' cultural values in both literature and the arts. It is clear that, in his own view, Steiner's criticism is dominated by a sense that language died, or that words failed in the face of the inhumanity of the Holocaust and totalitarianism. Born in Paris into a multilingual Jewish family that fled Nazi-occupied Europe for the United States, he is, he writes (1965), a 'kind of survivor'. In the moving *Errata*, he describes 'an unforgiving childhood, an enormity of history, pressed on us'. Steiner's work is best seen as a constant effort to resist that enormity, to ward off the death of language and the political oblivion imposed upon Europe by Nazism.

story/plot The distinction between story and plot is a feature of most forms of NARRATOLOGY from RUSSIAN FORMALISM onwards. SHKLOVSKY, for instance, distinguishes between 'motif' (*motiv*) and 'plot' (*syuzhet*), defined respectively as the basic building-blocks of narrative ('The king died'), and as the manner in which motifs are combined to make a plot which is coherent in both logical and temporal terms (1925). Tomashevsky (1925) modifies the original schema by introducing the term 'fable' (*fabula*) to describe the combination of the basic units into a consistent narrative. The phrase 'unrolling the subject' is used by Shklovsky to describe the way in which the whole narrative is presented to the reader. Unrolling the subject is often a matter of delaying or retarding the exposition of the series of motifs, and is a good instance of what Shklovsky calls 'estrangement' or 'defamiliarization' (*OSTRANENIE*). The making strange or defamiliarization of the plot as the basic narrative is interrupted or delayed by the introduction of digressions and other devices is one of the sources of the pleasure in reading that Shklovsky illustrates by referring to the endless digressions of Sterne's *Tristram Shandy*. It is the distinction between story and plot that allows PROPP to analyse the morphology of folk-tales by breaking them down into functional units, and in doing so to lay the foundation for the later work of narratologists such as BREMOND and GENETTE.

stream-of-consciousness A mode of narration characteristic of early literary MODERNISM in which a character's thought and sense-impressions are presented directly, without conventional dialogue or description and, in many cases, without punctuation. The term is derived from a passage in William James's *Principles of Psychology* (1890), but the technique was first employed in European literature by the Russian writer Vsevolod Garshin in his short story 'Four days' (1877). Reviewing a novel by Dorothy Richardson (1873–1957), Virginia Woolf remarks that, when perfected, the technique should 'make us feel ourselves seated at the centre of another mind' (1919).

Woolf herself uses the stream-of-consciousness to great effect, especially in *Mrs Dalloway* (1922). The most famous example of stream-of-consciousness is probably Molly Bloom's monologue in the final chapter of James Joyce's *Ulysses* (1922), but the most sustained is surely the twelve-volume sequence of semi-autobiographical novels that makes up Dorothy Richardson's *Pilgrimage* (1915–38 and (posthumous) 1967).

structuralism One of the most influential movements in twentieth-century thought, and especially French thought, structuralism appeared to reach its apotheosis in the mid-1960s, with the appearance of major collective studies of NARRATOLOGY (*Communications* 1966), the *Écrits* (Writings) of Jacques LACAN (1966), FOUCAULT's *The Order of Things* (1966), following ALTHUSSER's *For Marx* (1965) and *Reading 'Capital'* (Althusser and Balibar 1965). The appearance in 1968 of a collection of four essays on structuralism in PSYCHOANALYSIS, anthropology, linguistics and POETICS edited by Ducrot both provided a general introduction to the so-called sciences of the SIGN and established structuralism as the dominant discourse of the moment. The publication of an important issue of *Yale French Studies* (1966) and the proceedings of the Johns Hopkins' Conference on *The Languages of Criticism and the Sciences of Man* (Macksey and Donato 1972) marked structuralism's American moment of triumph, though it is also clear in retrospect that the conference, and more especially DERRIDA's contribution (1966), also inaugurated the beginnings of a critique of structuralism and of POSTSTRUCTURALISM.

Structuralism can be defined in very broad terms as an attempt to unify the HUMAN SCIENCES by applying a single methodology (Barthes 1964a; Eco 1976) derived from the model supplied by Saussurean linguistics (SAUSSURE). In Barthes' case, the overall project was to develop a universal SEMIOLOGY or a theory of signs applicable to all areas of human activity. Structuralism also draws on a number of other sources ranging from RUSSIAN FORMALISM (Todorov 1965) and the work of the PRAGUE SCHOOL to the all-important analyses of APHASIA and PHONEMES elaborated by JAKOBSON, who draws heavily on the work of the Prague School. PROPP's work on the morphology of the folk-tale provides an important methodological model for structuralist POETICS and NARRATOLOGY. Structuralism also overlaps in France in the 1960s with the broader theme of 'theoretical anti-humanism' or the general revolt against the humanism associated with SARTRE that gives rise to the notions of the DEATH OF MAN and the DEATH OF THE AUTHOR. It is this overlap that allows theorists such as Althusser and Foucault, who rarely apply a strictly linguistic model, to be classified by some as structuralists. (For a discussion of humanism and anti-humanism, see Soper 1986.)

The general linguistic model derives from Saussure's insight that a language (*LANGUE/PAROLE*) is not a nomenclature or a list of names of things, but a system of SIGNS consisting of a 'signifier' (an acoustic image) and a 'signified' (a concept). Signs do not designate an external reality (or REFERENT) and are meaningful only because of the similarities and differences that exist between them. Saussure also displaces the study of language away from the historical dimension of PHILOLOGY and towards the study of its synchronic dimension (SYNCHRONY/DIACHRONY). It has often been pointed out that the structuralist reading of Saussure (common to Barthes, Jakobson and Lacan) is a highly selective reading, which overlooks the fact that much of his *Course in General Linguistics* (1916) is taken up with a discussion of philology and historical linguistics. The linguistics of the Prague School makes a crucial contribution to the development of structuralism by introducing the idea of FUNCTIONALISM, or the idea that the 'meaning' of linguistic units is the function they perform with the system of a language. The emerging structuralist model is completed by Jakobson, whose work on phonemes demonstrates, drawing on Trubetzkoy (1939), that an underlying system of minimal differences or binary oppositions between elementary units (/f/, /p/) can explain all the observable features of a natural language. Jakobson's studies of aphasia and language-acquisition further led him to conclude that any language is organized around the axes or poles of METAPHOR and METONYMY, and that these can be mapped onto the dimensions of PARADIGM and SYNTAGM respectively. The linguistic model that emerges is that of an unconscious system made up of differences and oppositions, and existing independently of the observer. Language is no longer seen as a means of expression at the disposal of a speaking SUBJECT; language, or the SYMBOLIC in Lacanian terms, is not an instrument of thought, but the precondition for both thought and social existence.

By the late 1940s, LÉVI-STRAUSS was applying the lessons of what he called the COPERNICAN REVOLUTION brought about by structural linguistics (1983) to the analysis of both kinship systems (1949) and mythology (1958). His analysis of both is based upon the classically structuralist thesis that the relations *between* observable phenomena are more important that the phenomena themselves. By concentrating on the knots in the web of the social fabric rather than the lines, he demonstrates that the lives of social subjects are governed by laws of which they are not fully conscious. All human societies give away daughters and receive wives in return, even though their members are not aware of the laws that structure their exchange. Myths are demonstrated to consist of elementary units or MYTHEMES which permit a conceptual understanding of the world by ordering it in terms of opposition between day and night, inside and outside, male and female and so on. It is Lévi-Strauss's structural anthropology that provides the model for the great synthesis of linguistics and anthropology that enables Lacan to reformulate FREUD's OEDIPUS COMPLEX as a universal structure grounded in a transition from nature to culture and to argue that the UNCONSCIOUS is 'structured like a language' in that the basic processes of CONDENSATION and DISPLACEMENT can be likened to metaphor and metonymy (see in particular Lacan 1953).

In the literary domain, structuralism has been a very productive theory but its exponents, who include TODOROV, BARTHES, GENETTE, GREIMAS and BREMOND, have rarely been concerned with the critical evaluation of individual texts. Authorial intentions are largely ignored in favour of an approach which highlights the formal and poetic devices used in the text (Barthes 1963, 1966a, 1970a), whilst Todorov's study of the fantastic (1970) is a major contribution to the theory of GENRE. At a more general level still, the structuralist theory of literature is concerned mainly with the elaboration of broad typologies of narratives or narrative grammars which seek to explore and classify the workings of literature; individual texts tend to be evoked as examples of broader categories and are rarely studied in their own right (Todorov 1969; Bremond 1973).

READING: Culler (1975); Hawkes (1977); Merquior (1986); Pavel (1989)

structure of feeling The term is first used by Raymond WILLIAMS in the co-authored *Preface to Film* (Williams and Orram 1954) but takes on a central function in the analysis of culture made in *The Long Revolution* (1961) and later works such as *Marxism and Literature* (1977).

In its broadest sense, a structure of feeling describes the actual living sense of a culture in a particular historical period or in the experience of a particular generation. It is the area in which the official consciousness of a period, as codified in legislation and doctrine, interacts with the lived experience of that period, and defines the set of perceptions and values common to a generation. The structure of feeling of an epoch operates in the most delicate and least tangible realms of human activity, and is not uniform throughout society, being most evident in the dominant social group. It is a matter of feeling rather than of thought, and supplies values that are communicated between individuals without being taught in any direct way. The privileged area for the study of structures of feeling are literary and dramatic texts which, without being directly related to or influenced by one another, display common patterns or impulses and tones. The classic examples studied by Williams include the British industrial novels of the 1840s, in which plots and themes are structured, as in Elizabeth Gaskell's *Mary Barton* (1848), by an oscillation between sympathy for an oppressed working class and fear of its potential violence. Williams also suggests (1979) that texts as apparently disparate as Webster's *The White Devil* (1612) and Thomas Hobbes's *Leviathan* (1651) have in common a 'very precise structure of feeling' centred upon the premise that the initial human condition is one in which every man is at war against every other man.

Subaltern Studies The title of a series of volumes of historical-political essays edited by Ranajit Guha, published annually since 1982 and representing an important strand in South Asian studies and, more generally, POSTCOLONIAL THEORY.

The title alludes to the dictionary definition of subaltern as 'of inferior rank', but also to the reference to 'subaltern social groups' in GRAMSCI'S 'Notes on Italian History' (in Gramsci 1971), where the Italian Marxist speaks of the need to study the formation of subaltern groups which are not united and which cannot unite until they become a 'state'. He goes on to recommend the study of the origins and transformations of such groups, their affiliation to dominant groups, and their ability to put forward claims of a partial and limited nature and to assert their autonomy. In the South Asian context, 'subaltern' is very broadly defined as comprising all those groups that have been made subordinate in terms of class, caste, age, gender, office or 'in any other way'. The subaltern is seen as one of the constitutive terms of a binary relationship in which subaltern groups, even when they rise up and rebel, are subject to the activity of dominant groups.

The need to produce subaltern studies that record the role played by the urban poor and the peasantry in resisting British rule and shaping Indian nationalism arises from the very nature of Indian historiography. The latter is viewed as an ideological form produced by British rule which has outlived the transfer of power in 1947 and which takes the form of an elitist neocolonialist discourse in Britain, and an elitist bourgeois-nationalist discourse in India itself. Both deny and suppress the role of the subaltern, who remains hidden from history. The aim of the collective that produces *Subaltern Studies* is therefore to fill in the missing part of the picture, and to stress the role played by subaltern groups as they interact with both colonialism and the nationalism of elite groups.

READING: Guha (1982); Guha and Spivak (1988); Spivak (1985b); *Subaltern Studies* (1982–)

subculture The study of subcultures has long been an important aspect of British CULTURAL STUDIES. Two of the founding studies were Phil Cohen's account (1972) of how working-class youths in the East End of London used symbolic structures signalled by styles of dress and a strong sense of territoriality to create a sense of identity that at once demarcated them from their parents and reproduced elements of the 'parent culture', and Paul Willis's study of motorcycle gangs (1972). An important issue of *Working Papers in Cultural Studies* (published by Birmingham University's Centre for Contemporary Cultural Studies) devoted to *Resistance through Rituals* (1975) further consolidated the discipline by examining how groups of young people used music, dress and symbolic activities to create meanings and an identity. As the title indicates, the creation of subcultures centred on distinctive activities, patterns of consumption and 'focal concerns', and was seen as a form of resistance that helped to contest the HEGEMONY of the wider society and its values. The subcultures studied were those of mods, teddy boys, skinheads, drug-users and Rastafarians. Two women contributors were quick to point out that subcultures were being viewed in very masculinist terms that paid little or no attention to the role of girls or even suggested that specifically female subcultures do not really exist (McRobbie and Garber 1975).

There are obvious precedents for subcultural studies in ORWELL and in HOGGART's classic study of working-class life *The Uses of Literacy* (1957), as well as in much earlier studies of the London poor by Mayhew (1851) and Booth (see the selection in Booth 1969). It could also be argued that Colin MacInnes's novels offer a fictional prototype: his *City of Spades* (1957) deals with the subculture of London's black immigrants whilst *Absolute Beginners* (1959) is one of the first novels to look at the then new phenomenon of 'the teenager'. Methodological inputs to subcultural studies come from participant-observer sociology and from the sociology of deviancy typified by Young's study of the recreational use of drugs (1972). Hebdige's study of the social meaning of style (1979) is one of the classics of subcultural studies, whilst Savage's definitive account of the punk rock subculture of the late 1970s (1991) combines subcultural theory with musicology to remarkable effect.

Whilst subcultural theory, with its stress on the active creation of meanings, is a good antidote to more pessimistic theories that tend to view, say, the CULTURE INDUSTRY as all-powerful and monolithic, its practitioners do not always avoid the trap of voyeurism or that of a vicarious identification with their subjects.

subject Few terms are more ubiquitous in the contemporary HUMAN SCIENCES than 'the subject', and few are more elusive. It is typically used in work deriving from CONTINENTAL PHILOSOPHY, the psychoanalysis of LACAN and the MARXISM of ALTHUSSER, and from all those descriptions of DECENTRING that displace the source of meaning away from the individual (often described as the 'Cartesian subject') and towards structures, impersonal or unconscious processes and IDEOLOGY. For most theories of the subject, the 'individual' is a product rather than a source of meaning. The concept of the subject is thus frequently invoked to undermine the notion that an innate sense of 'self' can provide a stable personal identity or be the focus of experience. The goal of much writing on the subject is to subvert that sense of immediate identity. When KRISTEVA, for instance, writes (1973) of '*un sujet en procès*' she is playing on the double meaning of *en procès*: the subject is both involved in or produced by a process, and on trial. The inherent ambiguity of the term goes some way to explaining its popularity and productivity. It is both a grammatical term ('the subject of a sentence') and a political-legal category ('a British subject'), and at once active ('subject of') and passive ('subject' or 'subjected to'). The term 'the subject' is not used in the PHENOMENOLOGY of SARTRE (who uses it only in critical discussions of structuralism, e.g. 1966) or MERLEAU-PONTY, but nor is it a standard expression in all forms of STRUCTURALISM; LÉVI-STRAUSS very rarely employs it.

Lacan refers to 'the subject' in his very first publications but when he refers in his thesis (1932) to 'the psychosis of our subject', he is simply following the conventional medical-psychiatric usage that speaks of 'the subject of an experiment' or of 'the subject under examination'. In his other prewar writings Lacan refers to the analysand, or the patient in analysis, as 'the subject' (1936); this too appears to be a variant on traditional usage. It is in the 1950s that Lacan introduces the crucial distinction between ego and subject (1953). The EGO is now described as a product of the MIRROR-STAGE and as belonging to the order of the IMAGINARY, whilst the subject is understood to mean 'the subject of the unconscious'. In a typical display of wordplay, Lacan makes his point by stressing the homophony between the initial letter of the word *sujet* and the German *Es* (the ID). The true subject of human behaviour is to be found, that is, in the unconscious. The entry of the subject into the dimension of the SYMBOLIC produces a further splitting or decentring of the subject by subordinating (subjecting) it to the laws of language and to the unavoidable difference between the subject of the utterance (*énoncé*) and the subject of the enunciation (*énonciation*): the 'I' that speaks does not coincide with the 'I' that appears in the message it sends.

Lacan uses the related expression 'the subject who is supposed to know' ('*le sujet supposé savoir*') to describe an important dimension of the TRANSFERENCE (1973). Thus it is the analysand's supposition that the analyst knows the meaning of his words or has a privileged insight into his behaviour that sets in motion the transference.

Althusser uses 'subject' in a broadly similar sense to Lacan in his theory of IDEOLOGY and in his description of its fundamental mechanism of INTERPELLATION (1970): the subject does not exist prior to its interpellation, but is summoned into being by it. For Althusser, the existence of OVER-DETERMINATION means that the social totality has no essence or single focus, and therefore no subject. It follows that history is a process without a subject (Althusser 1969c) and that individuals are no more than the 'supports' for a subjectless DIALECTIC.

sublimation In chemistry, the vaporization of a solid without the intermediate formation of a liquid. The term is used in a derivative sense in PSYCHOANALYSIS to describe the diversion of a DRIVE towards a non-sexual aim or a socially valued OBJECT (Freud 1933), and in an analogous sense by NIETZSCHE when he claims (1872) that the Apollonian culture of Greece is a sublimation of the violence on which it is founded.

The term is widely used in PSYCHOANALYTIC CRITICISM to describe the conversion of sexual drives and energies into creative and intellectual activity, and this usage appears to be influenced by the aesthetics of the SUBLIME. In his study of Leonardo da Vinci, Freud uses 'sublimation' in this sense (1910a) to describe the transformation of the young Leonardo's sexual curiosity into a spirit of intellectual inquiry. Whilst this produced great works of art, the sublimation of LIBIDO into a general urge to know meant that a smaller quota of Leonardo's sexual energy was directed towards sexual aims, and resulted in a stunted adult sexuality. Elsewhere (1931a) Freud suggests that a mature woman's capacity to pursue an intellectual profession may be a sublimated expression of her childhood desire to acquire a penis. Although the term 'sublimation' is one of the most familiar terms in the vocabulary of psychoanalysis, Freud does not devote any one paper to the topic and cannot be said to have developed a truly coherent theory of sublimation.

sublime Although the idea of sublimity (the Greek *hypsos*) can be traced back to the discussion of the 'elevation' and the 'uplifting of the soul' associated with great works of art combining an exalted style and excellence of expression in Longinus's treatise *On the Sublime* (first or second century AD), a rather different version of the sublime emerges in the late eighteenth century, when a distinction begins to be made between 'the beautiful' and the 'sublime'. It finds its classic expression in Burke's *Philosophical Enquiry into the Origin of our Idea of the Sublime and the Beautiful* (1756), where the 'sublime' refers to the mingled terror and pleasure inspired by the ruins, Alpine passes and storms that became the standard imagery of the Gothic novel. In a short reply to Burke (1757) and then in Book II of *The Critique of Judgement* (1790), Kant also contrasts 'the beautiful', which is characterized by its use of form, with 'the sublime'. The sublime is not a matter of form, but is found in formless and limitless phenomena such as the interstellar spaces or storms at sea; it is a representation of limitlessness that cannot be contained in any sensuous form.

The Kantian idea of the sublime has been revived by LYOTARD (1973b) in his writings on the abstract AVANT-GARDE art of the American Barnet Newman (1905–70), whose work is usually regarded as a form of Abstract Expressionism. According to Lyotard, Newman's monochrome canvases emancipate the work of art from both the classical role of imitation or MIMESIS and the canon of the beautiful. The art object no longer bends itself to models and no longer testifies to a truth that can be conceptualized. The only possible reaction is a surprised 'Ah' as the viewer encounters a canvas which does not represent anything, which is simply *there* and which says simply: 'Here I am. I am Yours. Be mine.' Although Lyotard's comments are confined to Newman, they could easily apply to the nine *Black on Maroon* and *Red on Maroon* canvases by Mark Rothko (1958–9, Tate Gallery, London). The sublime has always been associated with the sacred and the mystical, and there is a significant element of quasi-religious mysticism in the work and pronouncements of both Barnet and Rothko.

superego One of the three agencies described by FREUD's second TOPOGRAPHY of the psyche, the others being the EGO and the ID. Freud introduces the concept of the superego in 1923 (1923a). The superego begins to take shape as the child emerges from the OEDIPUS COMPLEX, renounces its incestuous desire for the parent of the opposite sex and internalizes the paternal prohibitions that make that desire taboo. Freud therefore describes the superego as the 'heir to the Oedipus complex' (1933) and sees it as an internal conscience. It gradually becomes more refined and sophisticated as the ideals conveyed by education, morality and religion are internalized and fuse with the internalized parental images. In keeping with her views on the 'early' Oedipus complex, KLEIN holds (1933) that the effects of the superego are observable in very early stages of childhood.

supplement An important feature of DERRIDA'S DECONSTRUCTION and of his critique of LOGOCENTRISM's neglect of WRITING, as typified by the Western tradition from Plato to SAUSSURE and LÉVI-STRAUSS. Like *DIFFÉRANCE*, the expression is deliberately ambiguous; *suppléer* can mean either 'to supplement' or 'to supplant'. Derrida adopts (1967a) the term 'supplement' from Jean-Jacques Rousseau, who argues in his essay on the origins of language that writing is no more than a supplement to, or a parasite on, a natural spoken language, and who notes in his *Confessions* that masturbation is a 'dangerous supplement' to normal sexual intercourse. Derrida contends that, if speech has to be supplemented or supplanted by writing, it cannot be naturally self-sufficient and must therefore be characterized by an absence or gap, which he describes as an 'originary ("*originaire*") lack'. Language does not, that is, originate in a natural state of completion as there is no extra-linguistic point of origin, but merely the 'originary lack'. It is the logic of supplementarity that makes nature or speech appear to be the prior term; at the same time, the chain of supplements or substitutions (equated by Derrida with DIFFÉRANCE) reveals the lack within it. Any attempt to find a pure point of origin, such as HUSSERL's attempt to ground PHENOMENOLOGY in pure perception, can be shown to follow the same logic and to mistake a supplement for an origin (Derrida 1967c). Masturbation is a supplement, but if it is to function as such, it must resemble what it replaces; it may be a form of autoeroticism, but it still focuses on the imagined OBJECT that can never be possessed.

READING: Culler (1983a); Hobson (1998)

surrealism One of the major artistic and poetic movements of the twentieth century, founded in 1924 by the French poet André BRETON. The death of 'historic surrealism' was announced by Jean Schuster in an article published in *Le Monde* on 4 October 1969, but it is almost universally accepted that the influence of surrealism is still an integral part of the modern sensibility. Breton had been associated with Paris DADA, and surrealism always retained something of that movement's destructive energy but was much more organized and coherent. With its numerous manifestos and tracts, its repeated attempts to create a pantheon or CANON of exemplary authors from the past, and its highly personalized quarrels and schisms (which are wickedly satirized in Raymond Queneau's novel *Odile*, 1937), the surrealist movement established a pattern that would be followed by many of the twentieth century's AVANT-GARDE movements from SITUATIONISM to the *TEL QUEL* group. Breton was always the prime mover, and is often described as 'the pope' of surrealism. The history of surrealism can be written as the history of his quarrels with

Aragon, ARTAUD, BATAILLE and, not least, Salvador Dali, commonly regarded as the quintessential surrealist painter, but contemptuously dismissed by Breton as 'Avida Dollars' when he began to create surrealist window displays for New York stores.

The adjective *surréal* ('super-' or 'supra-real') was coined by the poet Guillaume Apollinaire in 1917 to describe his burlesque play *The Breasts of Tiresias*. The noun 'surrealism' was coined by Breton in 1924 and defined as a pure psychical automatism designed to express the real workings of thought in the absence of any controls exercised by reason, and as pure non-conformism. The second surrealist manifesto (Breton 1929) described surrealist activity as an attempt to reach an intellectual point at which life and death, real and imaginary, past and future, the communicable and the incommunicable, and up and down, all cease to be seen as contradictory. In both manifestos, surrealism is described as a revolt against all forms of realism and even rationality, and as an attempt to unleash unconscious creative forces. Their interest in the unconscious led the surrealists to champion FREUD'S PSYCHOANALY-SIS at a time when the French medical profession was deeply suspicious of that 'German science', and surrealism had a major and lasting effect on the young LACAN even though it was viewed with incomprehending indifference by Freud himself (see Macey 1988). The revolt against realism inspired a deep suspicion of the novel – in Breton's *Nadja* (1928a) photographs take the place of conventional descriptive passages – and Anatole France (1844–1924), one of the most respected novelists of the 1920s, was described as a 'corpse'. Poetry and painting are the preferred modes of expression.

A variety of techniques were employed to capture the true workings of thought, including automatic writing, or the immediate transcription of whatever came into the mind, self-induced trances, and word games like *le cadavre exquis* (the French equivalent to the game known in English as 'consequences'). The aesthetics of surrealist poetry centres upon the production of a startling image through the juxtaposition of unrelated words or phrases, the classic model being borrowed from Lautréamont's *The Songs of Maldoror* (1869): 'As beautiful as the chance encounter of an umbrella and a sewing machine on a dissecting table.' Surrealist painters like Max Ernst use techniques such as *frottage* (placing a sheet of paper on a rough surface, rubbing it so as to acquire the properties of the surface and then taking the resultant image as a stimulus to the imagination), collage and the random juxtaposition of objects and images (see Matthews 1973); others, like Dali, Paul Delvaux (see Scott 1992) and René Magritte employ an almost hyperrealist style to depict obsessive dream-images.

Surrealist poetry and art are intended to be unsettling and to produce a frisson of excitement as the artist and reader come into sudden contact with the marvellous. As Breton puts it in the last lines of *Nadja* (1928a), 'Beauty will be convulsive, or it will not be.' The quest for the marvellous and for convulsive beauty promotes an interest in African and other forms of non-European 'primitive' art (particularly Mexican), which had begun to be celebrated by Picasso and the cubists, and a fascination with the occult, but it also leads to a new and disturbing vision of the city, and especially Paris. In *Nadja* Breton repeatedly encounters a mysterious young woman, who is in fact mentally ill. Their nocturnal wanderings through Paris represent Breton's classic image of the theme of 'mad love' (1937), or the pursuit of irrational passion, but they are also a FLÂNEUR-like exploration of a city full of UNCONSCIOUS associations. Together with Aragon's *Paris Peasant* (1926) which had a significant influence on BENJAMIN (Cohen 1993), *Nadja* is one of the most haunting evocations of Paris.

Politically, surrealism is a movement of the non-conformist left. Attempts to come to a rapprochement with the French Communist Party in the mid-1920s ended in a bitter disillusionment with organized politics and to the break between Breton and Aragon, who became the Party's poet laureate and a convert to SOCIALIST REALISM. Breton's own sympathies tended to lie with Trotsky, but like most surrealists, he was temperamentally unsuited to the discipline of conventional political activity.

Eroticism was a major surrealist preoccupation, and the discussions of sexuality and personal sexual preferences were published in *La Révolution surréaliste* in 1928–32 (republished as Pierre 1990). The original surrealist group was all male, and it is often argued that surrealism is a misogynist movement which exploits women as muses, and makes them the object of a voyeuristic or even sadistic male gaze (see Gauthier 1971). Hans Bellmer's dismembered dolls of 1936 (which can be seen as the source for LACAN's fantasy of the FRAGMENTED BODY; they are reproduced in Chadwick 1985), in particular, have been denounced as being offensive to women. Recent reassessments (Chadwick 1985; Conley 1996) have concentrated more on the work of women artists such as Leonora Carrington and Meret Oppenheim, who came to be associated with the group in the 1930s, and suggest that surrealism did in fact open up areas that allowed a specifically female creativity to emerge.

Although surrealism is primarily a French phenomenon, it had international repercussions. In 1936 the International Surrealist Exhibition at London's New Burlington Galleries attracted an astonishing 25,000 visitors in three weeks and convincingly demonstrated the popular appeal of surrealism. Its history in Britain is traced in the exhibition catalogue *Surrealism in Britain in the Thirties* (1986), and Edward B. Germain (1978) has edited a comprehensive anthology of surrealist poetry from Britain and America.

READING: *Dada and Surrealism Reviewed* (1978); Polizzotti (1995)

symbol In the SEMIOTICS of Peirce (1932, 1934), a symbol is a type of REPRESENTA-MEN in which the relationship between signans and signatum (or signifier and signified, in the more familiar teminology of SAUSSURE) is a learned or imputed contiguity. Unlike an ICON or INDEX, a symbol, such as the scales that symbolize justice, requires the interpreter to know and understand the conventional code governing its meaning.

symbolic In Lacanian psychoanalysis (LACAN), one of the three orders that structure human existence, the others being the IMAGINARY and the REAL.

The adjectival 'symbolic' is often used by Lacan in a fairly conventional sense, but in the 1950s he begins to use the word as a substantive, and it rapidly becomes the cornerstone of his theory: the subject's relationship with the symbolic is the heart of psychoanalysis. As can be clearly seen from the rich synthesis effected in

Lacan's 'Rome Discourse' (1953), the change in usage reflects his incorporation into psychoanalysis of the linguistics of SAUSSURE and the anthropology of MAUSS and LÉVI-STRAUSS. In his work on kinship (1949, 1950) and in his introduction to a modern edition of Mauss (1923), Lévi-Strauss argues that any culture can be seen as a set of symbolic structures such as the rules governing kinship and alliance, language and art. He also demonstrates that in primitive societies the ritual exchange of gifts has an important role in the creation and perpetuation of social stability. The application of Saussure's theory of the SIGN allows these structures and exchanges to be analysed as exchange of signifiers. The emergence of symbolic structures is an essential feature of the human transition from nature to culture.

Adapting Lévi-Strauss's study of how kinship rules and exogamy govern exchanges between human groups to the field of psychoanalysis, Lacan now describes the OEDIPUS COMPLEX as a process which imposes symbolic structures on sexuality and allows the SUBJECT to emerge. Pre-Oedipal sexuality is likened to a state of nature and unbridled sexuality; the role of the NAME-OF-THE-FATHER is to disrupt the dual relationship in which the child tries to fuse with the mother in an incestuous union, and to establish a legitimate line of descent ('son of . . .', 'daughter of . . .'). Culture and the symbolic are thus imposed upon nature. The subject gains access to the symbolic, to a name and a lineage, but does so at the cost of a symbolic castration. Although the exchange of signifiers in speech is an obvious example of symbolic exchange, Lacan's symbolic is not simply synonymous with language, and should be understood as comprising the entire domain of culture.

symptomatic reading The practice of reading described by ALTHUSSER in his attempt to demonstrate that the PROBLEMATIC of Marx is divorced by an EPISTEMO-LOGICAL BREAK from that of the classical political economy of Adam Smith and David Ricardo (Althusser and Balibar 1965). A symptomatic reading concentrates not on the obvious features of the text itself, but on the silences, gaps and contradictions that reveal its problematic. Symptomatic reading is held by Althusser to be analogous to the evenly suspended or poised attention with which a psychoanalyst listens to a patient's FREE ASSOCIATIONS. A very similar concept of symptomatic reading underpins Macherey's contribution to MARXIST CRITICISM (1966).

synchrony/diachrony An opposition introduced by SAUSSURE to describe two aspects of language and two contrasting approaches to linguistics. The synchronic approach studies the state of a language at a given stage of its evolution and facilitates the analysis of the system of internal relations that constitutes it as a language. The diachronic approach typical of PHILOLOGY traces the historical evolution of a language through time by recording the changes that have taken place in it. Most schools of modern linguistics can be described as synchronic.

synecdoche A figure of RHETORIC in which the whole is made to stand for the part, or vice versa, distinguishing it from METONYMY (see METAPHOR/METONYMY). In the sentence 'France beat England at rugby', the whole (France, England) replaces the part (the English rugby team, the French rugby team); in the sentence 'There were new faces at the meeting', the part (faces) stands for the whole (people).

syntagm From the Greek *suntagma*, which derives from the verb *suntassein* meaning 'to put together', this term is used to describe a combination of linguistic elements or units. A sentence is a syntagm. A syntagm is formed by selecting units, such as PHONEMES, from a set or PARADIGM and combining them to form a higher meaningful unit. Paradigmatic relations are said to exist *in absentia*, as one element is used instead of an alternative that could be used; syntagmatic relations *in praesentia* – the elements involved are, that is, simultaneously present. In SEMIOLOGY and STRUCTURALISM, the syntagmatic dimension of language is said to be horizontal, whilst the paradigmatic dimension is vertical.

T

talking cure An expression coined by 'Fräulein Anna O' (Bertha van Pappenheim), a patient of Freud's early associate Joseph Breuer, to describe her treatment under hypnosis (Freud and Breuer 1893–5). It is widely used as a synonym for PSYCHOAN-ALYSIS as it indicates that it has only one medium: the speech that conveys the patient's FREE ASSOCIATIONS (Lacan 1953).

teleology The noun derives from the Greek *telos*, meaning 'aim', 'goal' or 'purpose', and was originally used to describe a branch of philosophy dealing with final causes. It also describes the belief, still widespread in the age of the Enlightenment, that nature reveals signs of a divine or cosmic providence or intention, or that things have an innate and God-given purpose. That view is satirized by Voltaire in his philosophical tale *Candide* (1759), in which a believer in teleology argues that noses were designed to facilitate the wearing of spectacles. The teleological view of history holds that a sequence of historical events necessarily leads to a *telos* such as the rule of God on earth or the classless society.

Tel quel French literary-philosopical journal. Ninety-four issues were published in Paris between 1960 and 1983. One of the major monuments in the history of modern French literary theory, *Tel quel* served at various times as a platform for BARTHES, DERRIDA, FOUCAULT and KRISTEVA. Although it was a collective venture, it was strongly influenced by the personality and tastes of its principal editor, Philippe Sollers. The title (literally meaning 'as such') derived from that of a collection of aphorisms published by the poet Paul Valéry in 1941.

When it began publication in 1960, *Tel quel* was, according to its manifesto-declaration, dedicated to the promotion and defence of 'literary quality', which was regarded as being under threat from ideological demagogues, the main culprits being SARTRE and the other theorists of COMMITTED LITERATURE. Despite the journal's hyperpoliticization, this literary aestheticism remains a constant, and formal experimentation was always a major concern. For most of its life, *Tel quel* promoted a 'textual writing' in which the linguistic or material reality of the text, or the painting (Pleynet 1977), took precedence over the representation of an external reality filtered through a narrative or authorial consciousness. The boundary between theoretical and fictional writing became blurred as the experimental novel was explored as an interrogation of the very possibility of meaning. Sollers' novel

H (1973) is a good example of the style. Even the previous generation of writers associated with the *NOUVEAU ROMAN* were attacked for restricting their experiments to the level of narrative and representation, and for failing to undertake a more radical exploration of subjectivity and meaning. The journal was also greatly influenced by the enormous theoretical importance ascribed in France to MARXISM and PSYCHOANALYSIS from the mid-1960s onwards. *Tel quel's* position was influenced by ALTHUSSER's insistence that the understanding of abstract theoretical objects is a necessary precondition for the understanding of real concrete objects. The psychoanalytic description of the DREAM-WORK was appropriated to promote the view that the literary text is a self-productive system. The result was perhaps the most exquisite of the many varieties of 'French THEORY'.

The history of *Tel quel* was punctuated by the adoption of extreme political positions and the publication of provocative manifestos, though this rarely led to any direct political involvement: the desired revolution was always a textual one. In 1968 the journal entered into a tactical alliance with representatives of the French Communist Party, but this soon gave way to a 'Maoist' period lasting from 1971 to 1977. Maoism in turn gave way to a fascination with the new intellectual model supplied by Solzhenitsyn and the Soviet dissidents (Kristeva 1977) and to a rapprochement with the *NOUVEAUX PHILOSOPHES*. By 1978 the United States was being described as a positive site of plurality. The final years of the journal's history were dominated by a new interest in religion and the symbolic origins and structures of society.

Despite all the political changes and shifts of emphasis, *Tel quel's* pantheon or CANON of exemplary authors remains remarkably constant, and includes ARTAUD, Lautréamont, Sade, BATAILLE, Joyce, Hölderlin and Céline. The canon has been described as one of sacrifice; *Tel quel's* canonical authors sacrifice themselves to their texts and, like ARTAUD, to the alienating effects of a language that speaks to and through the body.

When *Tel quel* ceased publication in 1983, it was replaced by *L'Infini* (meaning both 'the unfinished' and 'the infinite'). Much less theoretical and intimidatory than its predecessor, *L'Infini* has, under Sollers' editorship, effected a return to a defence of the 'literary quality' defended by the early *Tel quel*.

READING: Ffrench (1995); Ffrench and Lack (1998)

Temps modernes French political and cultural journal founded by SARTRE, BEAUVOIR and others, published monthly since October 1945. The title is a playful allusion to Charlie Chaplin's film *Modern Times* (1936).

Les Temps modernes played a vital role in making Sartre the dominant intellectual figure in the decade following the Second World War. In his editorial to the first issue, Sartre (1945c) gives a clear account of his theory of COMMITTED LITERATURE and argues that, given that every element in the contemporary world is meaningful and relates to every other element, the journal must take a synthetic anthropological approach in its attempt to discover meaning in everything.

In political terms, the journal has always been on the left, but has never been affiliated to any party and has often been highly critical of both the Socialist and

Communist parties. During the Algerian War (1954–62), it was one of the few journals to lend whole-hearted support to the cause of Algerian independence. Although the influence of *Les Temps modernes* has waned in recent years, its special issues on such varied topics as Algeria (July–August 1982) and French detective fiction (November 1997) remain important points of reference. The double issue *Témoins de Sartre* (Witnesses to Sartre) published in 1990 is a major contribution to both Sartre studies and French intellectual history.

READING: Davies (1987)

theatre of the absurd A generic term used to describe a trend within the theatre of the 1950s, and usually understood as applying to Samuel Beckett, Eugène Ionesco, Jean Genet and the early Harold Pinter. There was no organized 'school' of the absurd and, in retrospect, the differences between the authors invoked are greater than the similarities.

The notion of the ABSURD involved is broadly similar to that associated with Albert Camus and describes the futile search for meaning in a godless world that is by definition meaningless. The disintegration of language is a characteristic theme. The prototypical absurdist drama is Ionesco's *The Bald Prima Donna*, first staged in Paris in 1950 and described by its author as an 'anti-play'. Two couples, the Smiths and the Martins, mouth clichés and truisms (borrowed by Ionesco from a 'teach-yourself' English phrase-book) until language dissolves in a demonstration of the futility of all verbal communication. There is of course no prima donna, bald or otherwise.

In historical terms, the theatre of the absurd is a reaction against realism and the conventions of the well-made play. Most absurdist authors are resolutely non-political, and Ionesco in particular was violently critical of BRECHT's views on theatre. The origins of this style of drama can be traced back to a variety of sources and traditions ranging from Kafka to JARRY and 'PATAPHYSICS, and from DADA and SURREALISM to the music-hall comedy that seems to inspire the 'routines' of Beckett's *Waiting for Godot*.

READING: Esslin (1968)

theatre of cruelty In two manifestos originally published in 1932 and 1934 and a series of related articles, the French poet and actor Antonin ARTAUD (1938) outlines a theatrical aesthetic which departs radically from all forms of naturalism and psychological naturalism. Inspired by the troupe of Balinese dancers he saw at the Colonial Exhibition of 1931, Artaud speaks of the need to create a new language that is midway between gesture and thought. The theatre of the future must be based upon a metaphysics combining speech, gesture and physical expression, and will use physical objects to create new forms of expression. Abandoning the conventions of the proscenium theatre, the actors and musicians will circulate amongst the audience so as to break down all barriers between them. The text is much less important than the production; Artaud's vision is basically a vision of the theatrical performance as all-engulfing event. 'Cruelty' is not synonymous with sadism or even violence, but with a passionate and convulsive conception of life and with a cosmic experience of the darkness that surrounds it.

Artaud's projects included plays based on the story of Bluebeard, the fall of Jerusalem and the conquest of Mexico, and an adaptation of a story by Sade. None came to fruition, but he did succeed in staging a version of Shelley's tragedy *The Cenci* in 1935. Artaud's influence has been immense. Widely regarded as a precursor of the THEATRE OF THE ABSURD, he had a major impact on the ritualistic forms of theatre that emerged in the 1960s, and especially America's Living Theatre Company. The British director Peter Brook, who regards Artaud (1968) as the creator of a 'Holy Theatre' that has an effect comparable to intoxication or an outbreak of the plague, organized a 'Theatre of Cruelty' season in London in 1963, and acknowledges Artaud's influence on his own production of *King Lear* (1962) and Peter Weiss's *Marat/Sade* (1964).

READING: Hayman (1977)

theory In one of his many essays on POSTMODERNISM, the American critic Frederic Jameson notes that, whereas 'a generation ago' there was still a technical discourse of philosophy, as distinct from the discourses of other academic disciplines such as sociology, there is now a single discourse called 'theory' which is at once all or none of those things (1988; see also chapter 7 of Jameson 1991). It is noticeable that students in departments of literary studies and CULTURAL STUDIES are increasingly required to read 'theory' rather than what was once termed 'literary criticism' or even 'theory of literature'. Jameson suggests that the new usage indicates the effacement of the older categories of GENRE and discourse characteristic of postmodernism itself; is, for instance, the work of FOUCAULT to be categorized as philosophy, history, social theory or political science? The generic term 'French theory', an expression that is not always used with kindly intent, dates from the mid-1970s but the still broader 'theory' has a longer history.

Whilst the opposition between theory and practice is as old as Western philosophy itself, 'theory' begins to take on a distinct meaning in the England of the 1950s and 1960s. In 1958 the philosopher and novelist Iris Murdoch was demanding 'a house of theory' that could provide an alternative to the English tradition of scepticism and empiricism; in the 1960s the so-called Nairn-ANDERSON theses (Nairn 1964; Anderson 1964) castigated British culture for its reliance on empiricism and its failure to produce either an indigenous MARXISM or a classic sociology. This stimulated a further demand for theory in the form of WESTERN MARXISM and CRITICAL THEORY, but it was probably ALTHUSSER who most influenced the shift in usage when he redefined Marxist philosophy as 'Theory'. Significantly, an editorial in the spring 1971 issue of *SCREEN*, then heavily influenced by Althusser and 'French theory', spoke both of '*theories* of film study' and of a crucial emphasis on *theory*. In English studies, 'theory' soon came to refer to the blend of Marxism, PSYCHOANALYSIS and STRUCTURALISM to which a younger generation appealed in a struggle against the lingering effects of Leavisite criticism (LEAVIS; Hoyles 1982).

Despite the wide agreement as to the need for theory, there is no real consensus as to its content or even meaning. In December 1984, London's Institute of Contemporary Arts hosted a conference on the legacy of French theory; it focused mainly on the literary theory of BARTHES, Foucault and Althusserian Marxism (proceedings published as Appignanesi 1985). Had it been held a decade later, it is probable that BAUDRILLARD and DERRIDA would have been on the menu rather than Althusser.

thick description A term coined by the British philosopher Gilbert Ryle (1966–7, 1968) and given much wider currency by the anthropologist Clifford GEERTZ (1973). Thick description moves beyond neutral observation in order to capture the layers of meaning and implication inherent in a speech or gesture.

In one of his examples, Ryle asks (1968): 'What is Rodin's *The Thinker* doing?' A thin description would say that the figure is murmuring syllables under his breath. A thicker description will arise when we ask what he is trying to do as he murmurs those syllables. The description thickens as we ask if he is trying to find out something, if he has rejected some syllables in favour of others, and what made them seem inadequate. For Geertz, thick description is an attempt to capture a stratified structure of meaningful structures, or the accumulated structures of inference and implication that the anthropologist encounters in the field. He is faced with multiple and complex conceptual structures and stories which are always superimposed upon deeper structures. The anthropologist's role is to analyse them and make them meaningful through layers of thickening description.

Third World A literal translation of the French *tiers monde*, very commonly used as a generic description of the developing and underdeveloped countries. The expression was first used by the French economist Alfred Sauvy in an article published in the *Observateur* magazine on 14 August 1952. It is modelled on *le tiers état*, referring to the Third Estate (the common people) of prerevolutionary France; the First and Second Estates were, respectively, the nobility and the clergy. Remarking on how concentration on the two worlds of the Soviet and Western blocs tended to obscure the existence of a Third World, Sauvy noted that, although, like the Third Estate, it was ignored, exploited and despised, it too wanted to be something. His article's title is a reworking of that of the famous pamplet *Qu'est-ce que le Tiers État?* (What is the Third Estate?, 1789), in which Abbé Sieyès argued that the Third Estate which had been 'nothing' must become 'something', or in other words take charge of France's destiny. Held in the Indonesian city of Bandung in 1955, the first conference of Afro-Asian nations gave further credibility to the idea of a cohesive Third World that was at once opposed to colonialism and aligned with neither East nor West.

In the 1960s the Chinese Communist Party elaborated an apocalyptic but immensely influential theory of Three Worlds. The superpowers, or the United States and a Soviet Union which had abandoned Marxism for REVISIONISM, were contrasted with a second world of capitalist countries and an exploited Third World led by China which would bring about revolution by surrounding the first two worlds, just as the People's Liberation Army had surrounded the cities from the countryside during the Chinese Revolution of 1949.

Thompson, Edward Palmer (1924–93) British historian specializing in the eighteenth and nineteenth centuries, and political activist. Originally a member of the COMMUNIST PARTY HISTORIANS' GROUP, Thompson resigned from the Party in 1956 in revulsion against the revelations of Khrushchev's secret speech to the Twentieth Congress of the Communist Party of the Soviet Union, in which the nature of Stalin's terror was first discussed in communist circles. As the cofounder and editor of *The Reasoner*, a 'journal of socialist humanism' published 1957–9 and a predecessor of *NEW LEFT REVIEW*, he became one of the most significant figures associated with the NEW LEFT (Blackburn 1993). In the 1980s he was an important spokesman for the European Nuclear Disarmament movement, which demanded a nuclear-free Europe from the Atlantic to the Urals. There is no collected edition of Thompson's numerous essays and occasional writings, but the selected writings included in such volumes as *Writing by Candelight* (1980a) and *Persons and Polemics* (1983) provide good introductions to both his historiography and his politics.

Thompson's main concerns as a historian are to demonstrate the existence of a distinctively English socialist radicalism and to recover the memory of working-class experience. His first book was a major study of William Morris (1955), but it was his *Making of the English Working Class* (1963) that truly established his reputation as a radical historian. Typically, it was originally intended to be a chapter in a textbook; similarly, the lengthy study of the legislation introduced to suppress poaching in the eighteenth century (1975) was meant to be a contribution to a book of essays. The key sentence from the preface to *The Making* gives the flavour of Thompson's work and explains his enormous influence on the many researchers who subsequently sought to write HISTORY FROM BELOW: 'I am seeking to rescue the poor stockinger, the "obsolete" hand-loom weaver and even the deluded follower of Joanna Southcott, from the enormous condescension of posterity.' Although Thompson's inspiration is broadly Marxist, he rejects the economistic and sociological determinism that sees classes as mere effects of relations of production, and stresses that a class comes into being when a common experience allows men to feel that they have interests in common that oppose them to other groups. He uses the term 'class consciousness' to describe the manner in which that experience is expressed in cultural terms, and embodied in traditions, value-systems and ideas. For Thompson, the English working class was not made in the period 1780–1832 in the sense that an object is made; it had a considerable hand in its own making.

Thompson's emphasis on 'experience', which, given its importance in his thinking, always remains remarkably ill-defined, and his deeply humanist socialism led him to reject the more theoretically abstract varieties of WESTERN MARXISM imported by *New Left Review* and to a bitter polemic (1965) over the Nairn-ANDERSON theses and a later and still more violent polemic (1978) against ALTHUSSER, whose Marxism was memorably dismissed as a 'freak' and likened to such 'merely-ideological formations' as theology and even astrology.

The contemporary importance of the historical theme of an English radicalism that can be traced back to the freethinkers of the eighteenth century and to writers like Morris and Blake, and of the image of the free-born Briton, can be seen in Thompson's polemical pamphlets and essays of the 1980s (1980a, 1980b, 1983), which are consciously written in the tradition studied by the historian. Written at a time when nuclear war once more seemed a real possibility and when new weapons-systems seemed to many to pose the threat of mass destruction or of what Thompson called exterminism (1980b), they continue a much older tradition of political polemic.

Thompson has often been criticized for his failure to take the question of gender seriously, but a feminist historian such as Sheila ROWBOTHAM can still acknowledge (1974) that her history of women (1973a), whom she describes as being hidden from history, is in part inspired by his work.

READING: Kaye and McClelland (1990)

Todorov, Tzvetan (1939–) A Bulgarian-born naturalized French citizen, Todorov is a key figure in the history of STRUCTURALISM, POETICS and NARRATOLOGY. One of his first publications was the pathbreaking anthology of French translations of texts by important representatives of RUSSIAN FORMALISM (1965). The dictionary of linguistic science coauthored with Oswald Ducrot (Ducrot and Todorov 1972) is a standard work of reference, whilst his study of the symbol (1972) is one of the most complete studies of that subject and covers an immense field ranging from classical RHETORIC to FREUD's theory of dream symbolism. In his more recent work Todorov moves away from the purely literary domain and begins to elaborate a political ethics, but his concern with the production and control of meaning remains constant.

In the essays written between 1964 and 1969 (collected 1971a) and in his major study of the *Decameron* (1969), Todorov, like GREIMAS, posits the existence of a universal grammar of narrative which generates the individual stories that make up the body of literature. Language is fundamental to human existence and the schema of language, as described by SAUSSURE and his followers, can therefore be found in all human activities, including narrative. Drawing on a very sophisticated version of PROPP's narrative functions and on the formalist concept of *LITERATURNOST'*, Todorov contends that the goal of poetics is a scientific description of the workings of the literary system, and not the evaluative study of individual texts. Poetics is concerned with the structures of literature in general rather than with the interpretation of meaning. Given that poetics does not make value-judgements, 'structuralist criticism' is a contradiction in terms. In his analysis of Boccaccio and the related essay on poetics (1968), Todorov identifies three dimensions of narrative. The semantic or thematic dimension defines its content; the syntactical dimension combines structural units into a narrative order and corresponds to what was once called composition, whilst the verbal dimension manipulates the words and phrases with which the story is told. For Todorov, the syntactic dimension is the most important, and it can be broken down into 'propositions' that are combined into 'sequences'. A proposition is an action performed by an agent, or what Greimas calls an ACTANT: while her husband is away, a married woman is visited by her lover. This action can generate a number of possibilities: either her husband will return and find her *in flagrante delicto*, or her adultery will remain undetected. If her husband does return, he may punish her or be humiliated, and so on. Such sequences or strings of proposition-actions are the basis of all narratives.

The concentration on description rather than evaluation is characteristic of

Todorov's important contribution to the theory of GENRE, which he describes (especially 1971a) as the elaboration of a descriptive apparatus. A genre is a structure, a configuration or set of literary possibilities and an inventory of possibilities, but to identify a given text as belonging to a genre tells us nothing about its meaning. Genre criticism is concerned with the identification of the textual features that constitute the structural and functional categories of the narrative. Detective fiction can thus be described in terms of its double structure: the narrative of the investigation of the murder reproduces and explains the narrative of how and why the murder was committed. In the case of the fantastic, structural features such as the use of first-person narration combine to produce a moment of hesitation for both the narrator and the reader: the reader of James's *The Turn of the Screw* cannot tell if the governess sees ghosts or is hallucinating.

Todorov contends that story-telling is an indispensable feature of all civilizations and although his later works deal with topics as diverse as the Spanish conquest of the New World (1982), nationalism in French thought (1989), the Holocaust (1991), and Dutch genre painting (very attractively, 1993), they all centre on the production of meaning through forms of narration and the importance of communications. Thus the Spanish conquest of Mexico is explained not solely in military terms, but in terms of the Spaniards' ability to control communications, to establish contact with the Indian population and to manipulate how they saw and understood what was happening to them. A very personal narrative also emerges as Todorov describes a childhood and youth spent in communist Bulgaria (especially 1991) and the development of his almost visceral attachment to the democratic ideal (see the preface to *On Human Diversity*, 1989).

The major theme to emerge in Todorov's later work is that of the relationship with the OTHER. Todorov's study of the literature of the Holocaust, inspired by a visit to Warsaw, examines the moral responses of human beings to the extreme situation of the concentration camps and Nazism. Contrasting the insurrection staged by the Polish Home Army in 1944 and the Jewish ghetto uprising of the previous year, Todorov makes a distinction between the heroic virtues the Home Army dedicated to an abstract national ideal, and the everyday virtues that survived in the Warsaw Ghetto. The primary everyday virtue is described as a 'care for the other' that is manifested in a personal sympathy for the individual subject to whom it is directed. As in the conclusion to his study of the conquest of America, Todorov outlines an ethics based upon a relationship that strives to recognize the other as a subject and to reconcile the registration of otherness with a recognition of subjectivity. The model is supplied by the most basic linguistic exchange between an 'I' and a 'you'. To recognize the other as 'you' is to overcome the impersonality of the anonymous 'he/she' that denies the individuality of the other in the discourse of racism and prejudice. Although his elementary ethics is based in the analysis of a linguistic relationship and not in phenomenology, Todorov reaches conclusions similar to those of LEVINAS in his description of how the encounter with the face of the other brings with it the injunction to welcome and care for the other.

READING: Culler (1975); Hawkes (1977)

topography Literally, the representation on a map of the physical features of a landscape. In PSYCHOANALYSIS the term is used to describe the differentiation of the mind or psyche into subsystems with specific functions and characteristics.

FREUD's topographies of the psyche owe much to nineteenth-century theories of cerebral localization, which ascribe different mental functions to different areas of the brain, and especially to the psychophysics elaborated by Gustav Theodor Fechner in the 1860s (see Ellenberger 1970). It was the study of dreams that led Freud to the conclusion (1900) that unconscious activities such as dreaming are quite divorced from the conscious mind and literally take place on *ein anderer Schauplatz* (another stage or theatre).

Freud evolved two distinct topographies. The first, elaborated between 1900 and 1915, describes an apparatus comprising UNCONSCIOUS, preconscious and conscious systems, with mechanisms of censorship to prevent ideas from moving between them. Considerations of representability and the other mechanisms of the DREAM-WORK filter or censor the content of dreams and fantasies before allowing them to enter the conscious mind, usually because their sexual content is unacceptable to conscious thought-processes. The second or 'structural' topography, elaborated from 1920 onwards (1920a, 1923a), describes a structure of three agencies known respectively as the ID, the EGO and the SUPEREGO. The characteristics of the three agencies are very clearly described in the chapter on the 'dissection of the psychical personality' in the *New Introductory Lectures on Psychoanalysis* (1933).

topos (plural: topoi) The Greek word for 'place', used in RHETORIC to describe a set of conventional or stereotypical themes and images (commonplaces) used by an orator to structure an argument. To use the image of a carefully tended garden as an analogy of civilization is to use a topos. The usage derives from the Aristotelian argument that, if we are to be able to remember things, we must be familiar with the place or topos where they are kept. A topos is thus both a conventional association of ideas and a mnemonic or a system for improving the memory.

The description and classification of topoi can become a form of thematic criticism. The essays included in one collection of studies of topoi (Hunter 1991) comprise, for example, analyses of the topos of the *locus amenus* ('pleasant place') from Chaucer to Spenser, and of the topos of sight in *Macbeth*.

transference The actualization of unconscious wishes during psychoanalytic treatment. Prototypes, memories and desires are transferred by PROJECTION onto the analyst, who is often identified with an important or significant figure from the patient's childhood. The term is also used more generally to refer to all aspects of the patient's relationship with the analyst. The analyst's unconscious reactions to the patient – and to the transference itself – are described as the 'counter-transference'.

Freud initially took the view that transference was a DISPLACEMENT of existing AFFECTS or emotional charges, and that it was a facsimile of old emotions or something to be analysed like any other symptom. The transference was an obstacle because it induced repetitions and blocked the emergence of new FREE ASSOCI-

ATIONS. In his account of the 'Dora' case, Freud concluded that his inability to complete the analysis was the result of his failure to analyse the transference (1905c). Later (1912a), Freud still views transference as an obstacle to analysis, but also accepts that without it the actualization of repressed emotions would be impossible.

LACAN initially (1951a) refers to transference as a dialectic of identification; in later formulations (1977) it is said to be associated with the fantasy of the 'subject presumed to know'. The possession of knowledge is, that is, ascribed by the analysand to an OTHER who can understand his or her innermost thoughts. According to Lacan, any pedagogic relationship is underpinned by a similar fantasy.

trope Defined in RHETORIC as a device involving a change or transference of meaning, and working, unlike a FIGURE, at a conceptual level. The recognition and appreciation of tropes such as METAPHOR/METONYMY implies an intellectual effort on the part of speaker and listener alike.

U

uncanny Freud's short essay on the uncanny (1919) is an important landmark in the history of PSYCHOANALYTIC CRITICISM, not least in that it moves away from the analysis of authors and introduces a thematic reading of works of literature that provoke a sense of dread, unease or horror in the reader.

In this essay Freud explores Hoffmann's stories 'The Sandman' and 'The Devil's Elixir', concentrating on those themes that can be related to the fear of castration: severed limbs, the children's eyes that are magically removed by the sandman to feed his own children. He interprets them as an expression of the male conviction that there is something uncanny or threatening about the female genitals; the same theme is explored in the essay on Medusa's head (1922a). According to Freud, the feeling of dread arises because the uncanny (*unheimlich*) is also familiar or homely (*heimlich*); Hoffmann's stories evoke something that was once familiar, but which has been made unfamiliar and uncanny by REPRESSION. The *unheimlich* is the entrance – the maternal genitals – to the original human home or *Heimat*.

Freud's argument is underpinned by the philological theory that certain primal words have antithetical meanings and by the observation that dreams often use a single image to express contraries. Following the philologist Karl Abel, Freud claims (1910b) that the seeming antonyms *heimlich* and *unheimlich* are in fact synonyms and that they prove that primitive elements still survive in the UNCONSCIOUS. The encounter with the uncanny thus relates to the rediscovery of something that is very ancient in both individual and historical terms.

READING: Kofman (1974)

unconscious The adjective is very widely used to refer to any element of mental activity that is not present within the field of the conscious mind at a given moment. The noun-form is now usually used in the psychoanalytic sense, and refers to the unconscious system described by FREUD's first TOPOGRAPHY of the psyche. In the second topography, the unconscious system is replaced by the agency of the ID, but Freud continues to use 'unconscious' as an adjective. Although Freud is often credited with the discovery of the unconscious, it is clear that the notion of a non-conscious part of the mind has a long history in both philosophy – as in NIETZSCHE, whose descriptions of the logic of dreams (1901) are strikingly close to Freud's – and the psychological sciences (see Ellenberger 1970). A distinction has to be made between the Freudian unconscious and JUNG's concept of a COLLECTIVE UNCONSCIOUS.

Freud's initial descriptions of the unconscious are based upon his analysis of dreams (1900). Dreams are described as the royal road to the unconscious because they represent the fulfilment of unconscious wishes that are inadmissible to the preconscious-conscious system, usually because of their sexual nature. Further confirmation of the existence of an unconscious system is provided by Freud's study of phenomena such as PARAPRAXES (1901) and jokes (1905b); everyday phenomena such as slips of the tongue, bungled actions, lapses of memory and the inability to recall names all point to the existence of the unconscious.

The contents of the unconscious are described as representatives of the DRIVES and as unconscious wishes and desires that are organized into imaginary scenarios and narratives. Many of these elements have been subjected to REPRESSION or have been refused entry to the conscious mind. Others relate to fantasies or memories relating to the PRIMAL SCENE or the OEDIPUS COMPLEX. At times, Freud further speculates that the unconscious also contains elements of a phylogenetic heritage made up of residual elements of the vicissitudes of human history (1915d).

Insofar as it is a system, the unconscious is described by Freud (1915b) as having a number of special characteristics. It is governed by the primary processes of the free circulation of energy and LIBIDO, and characterized by the mobility of CATHEXIS. The unconscious is timeless, indifferent to external reality, oblivious to the notions of negation and doubt, and obeys only the PLEASURE PRINCIPLE.

Virtually all post-Freudian psychoanalysis may be regarded as contributing to an understanding of the unconscious, but the most extensive reworking of the concept is that propounded by LACAN. In his celebrated 'Rome Discourse' on the field and function of language and speech in psychoanalysis (1953), Lacan describes the unconscious as the censored chapter in the history of the individual subject. The truth of this censored chapter can, however, be found elsewhere; it exists in the form of 'monuments' such as the nuclei of a NEUROSIS, the symptoms that can be read like some strange language. It can be found in the 'documents' of infantile memories, in the individual's character traits, and in the fragments that link the censored chapter to the chapters that precede and follow it. Lacan remarks that psychoanalysis is quite literally a TALKING CURE, with speech as its sole medium, and goes on to describe the unconscious as being structured like a language (1957). Drawing on the linguistics of SAUSSURE and JAKOBSON's work on APHASIA, Lacan argues that symptoms and unconscious formations such as the DREAM-WORK display the same formal properties as the rhetorical devices of METAPHOR/METONYMY, which he likens to the mechanisms of CONDENSATION and DISPLACEMENT.

unreliable narrator A reliable narrator can be defined as one whose rendering of a story, and commentary on it, can be taken by the reader to be authoritative. An unreliable narrator is one whose account is suspect because he or she proves to have a limited knowledge of the events recounted either because his or her personal involvement in those events introduces bias, or because his or her values are in conflict with those of the narrative itself. Unreliable narrators do not necessarily lie, and may simply be mistaken about their own qualities. One of the great literary enigmas centres on the reliability or otherwise of the governess-narrator in James's

The Turn of the Screw: is she reliably reporting what she has seen, or is her unreliability a product of her neurosis? One of the most unreliable of modern narrators is Jean-Baptiste Clamence in Camus' *The Fall* (1956); he constantly contradicts himself as he strips away all his pretences to virtue by gradually revealing that he once failed to prevent a suicide by drowning, but in doing so traps the reader into having to recognize his own moral failings. Clamence's unreliable self-portrait becomes a portrait of his reader.

Section D of the bibliography appended to Booth's *The Rhetoric of Fiction* (1961) forms 'A Gallery of Unreliable Narrators and Reflectors'.

Vaneigem, Raoul (1935–) Belgian situationist; his *Revolution of Everyday Life* (1967) is one the classics of SITUATIONISM, alongside DEBORD's *Society of the Spectacle* (1967). Much less philosophically abstract and closer to the anarchist tradition than Debord, Vaneigem predicts a revolution in everyday life that will be brought about by a spontaneous explosion of poetic creativity and the founding of small self-governing communities that will unleash a free human creativity. His vision of poetic creativity is strongly influenced by the tradition of DADA; in Vaneigem's view, riots and vandalism are forms of spontaneous poetry. His vision of sexual revolution is decidedly prefeminist and owes a lot to REICH's views of the emancipatory function of the orgasm. His comments on the manner in which advertisements influence consumers through a mechanism of INTERPELLATION are intriguingly similar to ALTHUSSER's theses on IDEOLOGY.

Vaneigem's polemical denunciation of the society of the spectacle comprises a powerful and often witty description of the kaleidoscopic flow of signs which, by using the mechanism of interpellation, transforms individuals into actors who play out alienating roles. The function of the ideological, artistic and cultural spectacle is to transform the wolves of spontaneity into the shepherds of knowledge and beauty. Although he broke with what was left of the Situationist International in 1972, Vaneigem continues to write in a recognizably situationist style (1995).

READING: Plant (1992)

Vattimo, Gianni (1936–) Italian philosopher of POSTMODERNITY and exponent of WEAK THOUGHT. Vattimo has written extensively on HEIDEGGER (1981) and NIETZSCHE (1985) and is the Italian translator of GADAMER's *Truth and Method* (1960).

Vattimo's main concern is with the exhaustion or end of a modernity that was dominated by the idea of a progressive enlightenment which gradually strengthened and reinforced its own rational foundations. The modern era was the first historical era in which 'being modern' became a positive value in itself, or even the fundamental value, but it was also an era in which the new rapidly grew old and was immediately replaced by something still newer in an endless process that both demanded further creativity and made it impossible. Postmodernity first becomes visible in the arts, as they attempt to free themselves from this constant process of overcoming and reject the idea of constant progress. History experiences a similar crisis as writers such as Hayden WHITE realize that historical narratives display the same features as fictional narratives and challenge their claim to objective truth. In philosophy, Nietzsche's proclamation of the death of God demonstrates that there is no need for the excessively strong foundations demanded by traditional FOUNDA-TIONALISM and is thus a liberation from the metaphysical violence it implies, whilst science and technology remove the causes of the terror in the face of the unknown experienced by early eras.

Taking his inspiration from the NIHILISM of NIETZSCHE or absolute relativism, and from the hermeneutics of the later HEIDEGGER, Vattimo argues that hermeneutics is now the common idiom of a philosophy that has abandoned the quest for absolute knowledge and rejected the need for foundations. That claim in itself is an instance of Vattimo's weak thought; it describes a climate or a body of shared feelings rather than adherence to a common core of strong beliefs or principles. Nietzsche's nihilism describes a situation in which the human subject recognizes that the lack of foundations (metaphorically transformed into the death of God) is a part of its very condition. Rhetoric and aesthetic experience now replace epistemology as the model for the experience of truth. Rather like RORTY, Vattimo argues that postmodernity implies a recognition that there is no longer any single unifying language and that, rather than trying to appropriate the language of others, we should be attempting to translate it. He compares hermeneutics to the process of getting to know a person and contrasts it with the rational-epistemological model which tries to develop logically constructed and irrefutable demonstrations. In his *Beyond Interpretation* (1994), Vattimo compares modern man's experience of truth to that of the readers in Borges's short story about the library of Babel (1941). It begins: 'The universe (which others call the Library) is composed of an indefinite, perhaps an infinite, number of hexagonal galleries . . .' The library is infinite and the books in it always refer to one another rather than to an external authority. Here, as Vattimo puts it following Nietzsche, there are no facts but an infinity of interpretations.

Veblen, Thorstein Bunde (1857–1929) American economist and sociologist, best known for his *Theory of the Leisure Class* (1899).

Veblen's work is uneven and difficult to evaluate, and it has been said that there is no consensus as to either its value or even its meaning (Tilman 1992), but it contains some surprising insights. In his study of business enterprise, Veblen strikes, for instance, a very modern note in claiming that the search for profit inevitably leads companies to indulge in the 'irrational behaviour' that surrounds marketing and advertising and actually distracts them from their proper concerns. His expression 'conspicuous consumption' has passed into the English language, but at the cost of a change in its meaning. Whilst contemporary usage might describe the purchase of a luxury car as a form of conspicuous consumption that is designed to impress others, Veblen uses the term to describe forms of expenditure that are a waste, and which have to be counted as a loss. Examples of conspicuous consumption would include the squandering of wealth on parties, alcohol, narcotics or gaming. Such consumption is designed to confer prestige on the consumer by demonstrating that he can bear the losses involved. The previous leisure classes of priestly or feudal societies were conspicuously uninvolved in the productive process and their actual wealth remained largely invisible, but in late nineteenth-century America, the leisure class flaunted not its idleness, but its ability to consume valuable and exotic commodities as a way of demonstrating its social superiority. Although Veblen presents his thesis as a critique of American high society in general, it is widely recognized to be a satirical attack on the Vanderbilts and other nouveaux riches. A French critic has compared it with Proust's unforgiving analysis of snobbery in *Á la Recherche du temps perdu* (Revel 1960); in more general terms, Veblen's description of conspicuous consumption might perhaps be compared to the excess expenditure and destruction of wealth described in BATAILLE's 'general economy'.

READING: Dorfman (1934)

verisimilitude In chapter 9 of his *Poetics*, Aristotle establishes a fundamental distinction between the historical truth of Herodotus and poetic truth by arguing that one tells of what has happened, and the other of the kinds of things that might happen. Both are forms of MIMESIS, as 'what has happened' and 'what might happen' are both recounted in narratives that tell of the actions of men. The tragic poet, for example, retains the names of 'real people' because 'what is possible is credible'. The establishment of credibility or verisimilitude (seeming-to-be-true) is crucial to the representation of what might have happened. In a tragedy with a complex plot, every action should develop out of the very structure of the plot, so that each is the 'inevitable or probable consequence' of what has gone before.

The debate over the nature of verisimilitude (the French term *le vraisemblable* is sometimes used in English) has been going ever since Aristotle's day, and its repercussions are visible in the most banal conversations about the 'likelihood' of a character in a book or film acting in this or that manner. The manner in which verisimilitude is established is an important question for all the theories which, from RUSSIAN FORMALISM to STRUCTURALISM, hold that discourses are not governed by a correspondence with a REFERENT but by their own internal and intrinsic rules. At one level, verisimilitude can be established by the REALITY-EFFECT produced by the introduction into a narrative of details that do nothing to advance the narrative, and which are therefore redundant in structural terms, but which 'say' to the reader 'We are real', and thus guarantee the verisimilitude of the narrative as a whole. A similar effect can be produced by what Russian formalism calls 'motivation', or the concealment of the arbitrary character of the linguistic SIGN by giving narrative elements an appearance of causal determination, whereas their position is in fact determined by the form of the narrative.

Given that discourses refer not to the referent, but to other discourses, verisimilitude can be described as a form of conformity to a discourse which guarantees the seeming-to-be-real of the text. From Aristotle onwards, that guarantor-discourse has often been described as 'public opinion' or 'what is generally believed to be possible'; modern criticism would describe it as conformity to the dominant IDEOLOGY or the cultural conventions of a given society and period. Such conformity can override historical truth; Shakepeare's audience apparently had no difficulty in accepting as 'credible' that clock that strikes in *Julius Caesar* II.i and that for Racine's *Phèdre* found it credible that a Greek queen should wear seventeenth-century court dress.

Verisimilitude is also largely a matter of GENRE conventions which have been so internalized by readers as to become part of their literary COMPETENCE. As Aristotle knew, what is credible in comedy may not be credible in tragedy. The reader of a detective story, a horror story or a work of science fiction has learned what is credible within the terms of those genres. Within the genre of the British detective story, a very high incidence of murder in country villages (to say nothing of the high number of amateur detectives) is credible or even necessary, but outside that genre it would offend against the rules of verisimilitude.

READING: *Communications* (1968)

Vienna Circle Group of scientists and philosophers active in Austria in the 1920s and 1930s and responsible for the development of LOGICAL POSITIVISM. Although the origins of the Circle can be traced back to the early years of the twentieth century, it really began to flourish when Moritz Schlick (1882–1936) was appointed professor of the history and philosophy of the inductive sciences in 1922. The Vienna Circle was officially disbanded in 1938, when most of its members went into exile. The principal members were Schlick, Rudolf Carnap (1891–1970), Otto Neurath (1882–1945), Kurt Gödel (1906–78), and Friedrich Waismann (1896–1959). A. J. Ayer was associated with the group in 1932–3, and his *Language, Truth and Logic* (1936) is one of the classic accounts of logical positivism.

The scientific philosophy of the Vienna Circle is characterized by its total rejection of metaphysics, which is equated with a claim to knowledge that is inaccessible to empirical science, and its reliance on the verification principle or the criterion of FALSIFIABILITY popularized by POPPER. Traditional philosophical problems can be clarified in such a way as to demonstrate that they are either pseudo-problems to be relegated to the domain of metaphysics, or genuine problems that can be transformed into empirical problems to be subjected to the verification process. There are therefore no insoluble problems. Existing philosophy had, according to the Circle, to be replaced by the logic of science, which was equated with the logical syntax of the language of science (Carnap 1934). Heavily influenced by FREGE and WITTGENSTEIN and the thesis that conceptual knowledge is a simplifed form of language obtained through FORMALIZATION, the circle argued that what Neurath called the unity of science lay in its formal logic and not in empirical reality. The Vienna Circle's project was the publication of a twenty-six-volume *Encyclopedia of Unified Science* but, although a number of international conferences were held on the unity of science, it was never fully completed. A shorter encyclopedia was, however, published (Neurath, Carnap and Morris 1938). The lasting influence of the Vienna Circle is felt mainly within logic and in some strands within ANALYTICAL PHILOSOPHY.

READING: Hacker (1996a); Hanfling (1981); Kraft (1953)

Walcott, Derek (1930–) St Lucian poet, dramatist and winner of the 1990 Nobel Prize for Literature. Walcott is probably best known for his EPIC *Omeros* (1990), which majestically reworks themes from Homer in the context of the Caribbean, and for the large body of his collected poems (1992). His volume of essays (1998) also reveals him to be a sensitive critic of writers ranging from Hemingway to Ted Hughes and C. L. R. James, as well as an unexpectedly enthusiastic admirer of Philip Larkin, usually seen as the bard of a particularly grim English provincialism. In both his poetry and his essays (the most important dating from 1974 and 1982) Walcott makes an important contribution to the cultural politics of the Caribbean. Scathingly sardonic about the debasement of the region's folk arts into 'an adjunct of the tourist industry', he is also very critical of Caribbean writers' servitude to the muse of history, which has produced either a literature of recrimination and despair, or a literature of revenge written by the descendants of slaves, or a literature of remorse written by the descendants of masters. In his view, the great poets of the New World, whose number includes Argentina's Jorge Luis Borges, Chile's Pablo Neruda and Martinique's Aimé CÉSAIRE, have always viewed Latin America and the Caribbean as an awesomely new and virgin land. For Walcott, the culture of the Caribbean itself is a 'shipwreck of fragments'; the task of its poets and writers is to restore the shattered histories and the shards of vocabulary into a synthetic or hybrid culture. He looks forward to the future flowering of a single literature written in several 'imperial' languages (French, English and Spanish). In his poems, and especially in *Omeros*, Walcott describes the small islands of the eastern Caribbean not as small and enclosed communities, but as communities which open out onto the vast spaces of the archipelago. Far from being a barrier, the sea is a means of communication. His vision has much in common with that of GLISSANT and the younger theorists of CREOLENESS, and his essay on the Martiniquan novelist Patrick Chamoiseau (1997) is a fine introduction to their concerns.

Warner, Marina (1946–) British cultural critic and historian specializing in the study of the myths and ICONOGRAPHY that define representations and perceptions of women. Her work spans disciplines ranging from classical studies to the history of religion and the modern myths enshrined in video games and horror films. In 1994 she was the second woman to be invited to give the prestigious annual Reith Lectures on BBC radio (1994b).

Warner's first major study in cultural history (1976) originated in a personal investigation into just what she had been worshipping when she loved the Virgin Mary during her Catholic girlhood, and reveals the cult of the Virgin to be the instrument of a dynamic argument utilized by the Catholic Church to shape the structure of society and to define a role for women that is presented as God-given. Ultimately, that role is oppressively ambiguous. As the mother of Christ, she establishes maternity as the destiny of women, but avoids the sexual intercourse without which there can be no human reproduction; the female role established by the myth is thus simultaneously devalued. Warner's study of the changing mythologies surrounding Joan of Arc (1981) is a further investigation into how a particular icon has been fitted into an emotional tradition of thought concerning women. It also introduces a theme that distinguishes her work from more formalist approaches to such topics by insisting that when a story is told, it is told in accordance with the perception of its hearers; the teller must supply points of reference to make it culturally intelligible. Whilst formalists like PROPP stress the continuity of the content of tales, Warner stresses the changing role of their tellers.

In her major study of the allegorical iconography of the female form (1985) Warner examines the sculpted figures of women that are so common, and so frequently ignored, in Western cities. That a sculpture of a woman can represent so many things – virtue, democracy, or even telecommunications – is an effect of the anonymity imposed upon real women. If, argues Warner, women had had a voice, it would have been much more difficult to make a woman known only as 'Marianne' the abstract symbol of the French Republic. The origins of this imposed anonymity are traced back to the Greek myth of Pandora and to the biblical story of the creation of Eve: woman is man's creation and is easily confused with the work of art itself. In both mythology and art, men act as individuals, whilst women and their images become abstract and idealized forms onto which cultural meanings can be projected. In her monumental and beautifully illustrated study of fairy-tales (1994a), Warner places great emphasis on what happens when the stories that were once told by women begin, in the seventeenth and eighteenth centuries, to be written down by men and when their origins in a female tradition are forgotten. She argues that the archetypal teller of tales is the female Sibyl who speaks with a claim to truth, or the pagan prophetess who foretold the birth of Christ. The knowledge possessed by familiar figures like Mother Goose once pertained to sexuality and an outspoken female desire, and the transformation of traditional stories into tales told only to children has taken away some of their emotional force. The history of fairy-tales is also the history of changing attitudes towards the voices of women who have a claim to a store of knowledge that was once exchanged in predominantly female gatherings. Warner is critical of the archetypal approach to fairy-tales adopted by BETTELHEIM, arguing that it confines 'male' and 'female' within stock definitions and ignores the element of subversive transformation inherent in the genre. Like BARTHES, she argues that the function of myth is to turn history into nature and to naturalize IDEOLOGY, but she also stresses that the old stories can be reworked and transformed by new tellers, citing the British novelist Angela Carter's wicked reworkings of traditional fairy-tales (1979) as a modern example.

Warner's erudition and scholarship can at times be overwhelming or even intimidating, as in her exhaustive treatment (1985) of the Greek and Roman myths that supply so much statuary with its allegorical themes. In her 1994 Reith Lectures, in contrast, the application of her erudition to everything from Spielberg's film *Jurassic Park* to the gendered nature of computer games results in a sparkling display of wit in which telling insights into popular culture merge seamlessly with the barbed comments on the Conservative government of the day.

weak thought A translation of the Italian *pensiero debole*, which is used by VATTIMO to describe the results of his HERMENEUTICS (1994). In rather the same way that RORTY questions the need for FOUNDATIONALISM in philosophy, and that LYOTARD rejects the GRAND NARRATIVES of the Enlightenment, Vattimo, following Nietzsche, argues that the world is in effect no more than a conflict of interpretations and that truth therefore cannot be founded upon a correspondence between a proposition and a thing. The mode of thought he recommends is weak in that it does not need the strong foundations traditionally sought by Western metaphysics and science. Vattimo also contends that his own hypothesis that hermeneutics has become the common idiom of philosophy is in itself a weak hypothesis in that it does not try to demonstrate that thinkers such as Rorty, GADAMER, NIETZSCHE and HEIDEGGER share a great many precise philosophical beliefs, but rather that they share a general sensibility or write under the influence of a general climate.

Wellek, René (1903–) Austrian-born American literary critic and theorist and specialist in comparative literature. Wellek's great achievement is the work on the history of criticism and literary theory that culminates in his monumental five-volume *History of Modern Criticism* (1955–91; see also 1963). Clearly written and authoritative, the *History* is an essential work of reference for anyone concerned with literary theory.

Wellek's general approach to literature is expounded in the less specialist *Theory of Literature* coauthored with Austin Warren (1949); Wellek is the author of thirteen of the nineteen chapters. Here literature is defined as a specific field which cannot be identified with civilization or culture in general. The study of literature is not reducible to the study of the biography and psychology of authors, or to the compilation of lists of great books. The literary work is a many-layered whole with its own system of norms, and the task of literary analysis is a concern with its specific mode of existence. Warren's basic approach is broadly Kantian, and views the experience of the aesthetic as one of 'purposiveness without purpose' or the disinterested appreciation of the accord between aesthetic form and a universally valid sense of delight (Kant 1790). Wellek and Warren's *Theory of Literature* is an eloquent plea for the development of an *organon* or systematic set of methods for literary analysis; for the authors, that is the great need of literary scholarship. Their text provides an impressive account of prestructuralist modes of criticism.

Western Marxism Originally coined by MERLEAU-PONTY (1955) in the context of a discussion of LUKÁCS's *History and Class-Consciousness* (1923), the expression is usually applied to tendencies that emerged within MARXISM from the end of the

First World War onwards. The major representatives of Western Marxism are Lukács, Korsch (1923), BENJAMIN and others associated with the FRANKFURT SCHOOL, and GRAMSCI. In his comments on Lukács, Merleau-Ponty spoke of a conflict between Marxism and Marxism-Leninism, with the latter term applying to the institutionalized Marxism that had become a state IDEOLOGY in a Soviet Union where DIALECTICAL MATERIALISM had been reduced to a set of formulaic laws.

Although most of the thinkers associated with Western Marxism worked independently of one another, a number of common themes or concerns can be identified. Western Marxism emerged in the wake of the defeat of revolutionary working-class movements in Germany, Austria, Italy and Hungary, and is therefore forced to question Marxism's basic tenet that the proletariat is the revolutionary force that will overthrow capitalism. As a result, a new emphasis is placed upon the role of the intellectual or, in the case of the Frankfurt School in particular, upon the radical potential of reason itself. Rather than being a theory of the economic, Marxism becomes more philosophically-oriented and turns to a critical examination of IDEOLOGY, culture and aesthetics. If Marxism can be seen as a theory grounded in both the German philosophical tradition and political economy, Western Marxism stresses the philosophical heritage; significantly, it has produced no major economists. Western Marxism had little or no influence in the former Soviet Union, and its major figures worked on the fringes (or outside) the Communist parties of the West. The rediscovery of this rich tradition was the major intellectual achievement of the NEW LEFT and of *NEW LEFT REVIEW* in particular. Its best historians are Frederic Jameson (1974) and Perry ANDERSON (1976a).

White, Hayden V. (1928–) American historian and theorist of METAHISTORY. Like LYOTARD's rejection of GRAND NARRATIVES and VATTIMO's notion of WEAK THOUGHT, White's elaboration of a metahistory (1973, 1978) is an important contribution to the questioning of traditional forms of historical thinking that characterizes POSTMODERNITY.

White's basic insight is that, their 'scientific' and 'objective' pretensions notwithstanding, historical narratives are verbal fictions supported by philosophical theories of history that seek to validate their 'plots'. The sequences of events they record are selected from the historical data, and plot structures are imposed upon them to transform them into a comprehensible narrative which is told as a particular kind of story. In the introduction to his *Making of the English Working Class* (1963), THOMPSON can, for example, describe the story he is telling as that class's biography; his unthinking assumption that biography is a natural or neutral category, rather than a narrative GENRE with rules, leads him to tell a story that justifies his selection of the events that make it up. The style of any given historiographer can be described in terms of the linguistic-poetic protocols he uses to shape his historical field by bringing together the explanatory strategies he uses to shape a story out of the jumbled 'chronicle' of events that make up the historical record.

White borrows the term 'metahistory' from an essay by FRYE (1957) and his study of historiography is heavily influenced by the Canadian critic's archetypal theory of literary GENRE and the theory of pregeneric TROPES that underpins it, as well as by Mannheim's theory of IDEOLOGY (1929). In his immensely erudite study of the master-historians of the nineteenth century, White explores how the archetypal tropes of Romance, Tragedy, Comedy and Satire come to shape the narratives written by Michelet, de Tocqueville, Marx, Burckhardt, Ranke, Croce and others. To simplify greatly, Michelet's history of the French Revolution is read as a romance which uses the trope of METAPHOR to describe how the French people struggles against and transcends tyranny and internal divisions. In his *Democracy in America* (1835, 1840) and *The Ancien Régime and the French Revolution* (1856), de Tocqueville 'stands over' American and French society and judges them in a characteristically ironic mode, but also writes in the tragic mode to the extent that he concludes that the secret is no more than the story of man's eternal contest with himself. The eternal nature of that struggle determines his vision of history as an alternation between democratic and aristocratic states of society. Michelet, in contrast, sees history as a triumphal progression of events, whilst the German Ranke's *Histories of the Latin and Germanic Nations* (1824) provides a history in the comic mode which recommends, in a spirit of resolution and reconciliation, accommodation 'to things as they are'. Burckhardt's history of the Renaissance which, as White remarks, effectively creates the Renaissance we know, abandons the epic mode in favour of an ironic stance and produces a theory of history that is, in its own terms, both an accurate prediction of the rise of the future and a symptom of the illness that will bring it into being.

In White's view, there are no extra-ideological grounds for resolving the issue of the legitimacy or otherwise of narrative histories. Philosophies of history, typified by MARXISM, cannot lead to greater objectivity or 'scientificity' as they too are enmeshed in narrative strategies; the historiographical revolutions they seek to institute are born of a desire to change the sanctioned strategies that confer meaning on history, but they merely replace them with different narrative strategies. Disputes between, for example, Marxist and non-Marxist historians cannot be resolved by an appeal to the 'historical evidence'; it is precisely the question of what constitutes the historical evidence that is at issue in the dispute. The historical revolution initiated by NIETZSCHE with his notion of a Critical History that brings events to the bar of criticism, judges them and breaks them (Nietzsche 1874) is very close to White's own 'revolution' in that it demonstrates the folly of looking for some truth or subject *behind* events; the phenomena themselves are the subjects the historian is seeking, and there is nothing beyond or behind them.

White is convinced that history cannot reveal truth in the way that the natural sciences can; it will not reveal predictive or probable laws. Given that history is primarily a literary-narrative genre, it is to be studied from models derived from literary and rhetorical studies, and the truths it does reveal are of a literary or artistic order. Although there is no external point from which these truths can be judged, this does not imply that White's relativism is absolute. The choices that are made between historiographical models do influence our understanding of the present and our visions of the future, but they are to be made on aesthetic and ethical grounds.

Whorf/Sapir hypothesis A thesis associated with the American linguist Edmund Sapir (1884–1939) and his pupil Benjamin Lee Whorf (1897–1941) which contends that we dissect nature and reality along the lines laid down by the language we speak. In his introductory study of linguistics, Sapir remarks (1921) that language and our 'thought grooves' are so inextricably linked as to be almost one and the same. Whorf worked for a long time as an insurance agent and became convinced that language habits so influenced behaviour that workers who described oil drums as 'empty' would happily smoke beside them, even though they also knew that, whilst they contained no oil, they were full of flammable vapours. Whorf's subsequent study of American-Indian languages convinced him (1956) that categories as basic as those of space and time were modified, or even created, by natural languages and that the Hopi experience of space was therefore quite different from that of an English-speaker. Taken to its logical conclusion, the hypothesis would appear to imply that natural languages are as incommensurable as the LANGUAGE GAMES involved in LYOTARD's *différend*. If that were in fact the case, translation would be impossible as the translator would not be able to understand the mindset of the author or the author's text.

Williams, Raymond Henry (1921–88) British cultural and literary critic. A key figure of the British NEW LEFT (see Blackburn 1988), Williams has had an enormous influence on the development of English studies and on CULTURAL STUDIES. In the course of a long engagement with MARXISM and the BASE/SUPERSTRUCTURE model of IDEOLOGY, Williams gradually elaborates what he calls a theory of CULTURAL MATERIALISM (1973b, 1977, 1980), centred on the analysis of changing STRUCTURES OF FEELING. His writings deal with topics as diverse as drama (1954, 1966, 1968), television (1974), 'country-house' poetry (1973a) and the work of George ORWELL (1971). A posthumous collection of occasional pieces (1989) gives an indication of the breadth of his interests, and Williams himself gives a full picture of his intellectual and political development in a series of long interviews with the editorial board of *NEW LEFT REVIEW* (1979).

In a discussion of 'ideas of nature', Williams remarks that 'it is not ideas that have a history; it is society' (1972) and his work might be described as an exploration of the social history of ideas which constantly emphasizes the interaction between the social and the intellectual, between the life of intellectual traditions and the life of human communities. One of his characteristic working methods is to trace the shifting meaning of individual words: *Culture and Society* (1958) opens with a discussion of the changing meanings of *industry*, *democracy*, *class*, *art* and *culture*, all of which words acquired their current senses in the last decades of the eighteenth century and the first half of the nineteenth. This methodology would eventually culminate in a full lexicon or vocabulary of culture and society (1976; revised and expanded 1983). A study of the various senses of the key words identified in *Culture and Society* allows Williams to map the general shift in feelings and thought that takes place as Britain develops into an industrial country. The most important set of changes relates to the meaning of 'culture', and the history of the idea of culture provides a record of social reactions to the changing conditions of the common life of the nation. As industrialization proceeds, culture gradually comes to refer to a realm of values that exist independently of society and history. Defined in this way, culture is an ambiguous notion, which provides a defence against utilitarianism but which must also be defended against the emerging mass society. For Williams, the vision typified by Matthew Arnold's classic *Culture and Anarchy* (1869), which contrasts an elite culture with a non-culture, is the source of the important tradition that results in the Leavisite notion (LEAVIS) of a literary minority defending and keeping alive both a literature and the finest capacities of the English language.

Throughout his work, Williams contrasts the Arnoldian view with the ethnographic view that defines culture as a way of life or, as he puts it, a structure of feeling. Defined in this sense, culture is 'ordinary' in that it refers not to a 'high' culture but to the totality of practices and modes of communication that make up a way of life and a community. For Williams, the study of culture is the study of the relationships between all the elements that contribute to a way of life (this view is explored with particular clarity in Williams 1961). He therefore traces the growth of a reading public, and the corresponding changes in how books and newspapers are published, the emergence of 'standard English' as a national language, and, more generally, the interaction between patterns of understanding that have been learned, and the new patterns that are created in relationships, conventions and institutions.

The gradual process of industrialization, with its democratic and cultural effects as well as its anti-democratic and elitist aspects, is described by Williams as a long revolution that is still going on. Its culmination will be the participatory democracy that is the true heritage of men who are essentially learning, creating and communicating beings. The human energy that inspires the long revolution springs from the conviction that men can direct their own lives and break with old social forms by discovering new communal institutions. Williams was writing before the emergence of the new wave of FEMINISM and WOMEN'S LIBERATION and remained notoriously impervious to feminism, and it is the unthinking emphasis on 'men' that prompted Juliet MITCHELL (1966) to refer to 'the longest revolution', meaning women's liberation.

One of the central chapters of *Culture and Society* is devoted to the 'industrial novels' of the 1840s, regarded by Williams as an extension of Carlyle's 'Condition of England question' ('Is the condition of England so wrong that rational working men cannot rest quiet under it?'). He frequently returns to these novels and describes them (1970) as expressing the new sense that society is the bearer and creator of values, but also the destroyer of values and communities. The development of that 'new sense' is traced through a reading of the novel that takes Williams from the small-scale knowable community of Jane Austen to Eliot's *Felix Holt*, with its portrait of a lonely individual with a divided sense of belonging and non-belonging, and then on to the new image of 'the man alone in the street' in Joyce's *Ulysses*. For Williams, the novel is an essentially realist form, and he reads it in realist terms, speaking scornfully of critics who find in novels analogues, symbolic circumstances and abstract situations. The novel, he argues, is a privileged vehicle for social criticism in that it offers a way of seeing that is communicable to others.

Communication and community are the major themes of the English novel, as read by Williams; they are also the major themes of his best autobiographical novel (1960), which is not without a certain nostalgia for the Welsh border country in which he grew up, and of his broadly humanist vision of socialism.

READING: Blackburn (1988); Eldridge and Eldridge (1994); Inglis (1995)

Winnicott, Donald Woods (1896–1971) British child psychiatrist and psychoanalyst, greatly influenced by Melanie KLEIN and associated with the OBJECT-RELATIONS school. His major contributions to psychoanalytic theory are his *Collected Papers* (1958); the essays collected as *Playing and Reality* (1971) provide a good introduction to his work.

Winnicott liked to emphasize the importance of the facilitating environment provided by 'good enough' mothering by remarking that there is no such thing as a baby; the infant exists only within its relationship with a carer. The qualified 'good enough' helps to avoid an idealization of the maternal function that might inspire guilt or feelings of inadequacy in the mother. She should be 'good enough' but does not have to be perfect. Good-enough mothering and the 'holding' that provides a safe emotional environment permit a gradual move towards independence; their absence may lead the child to construct a protective but alienating false self.

Winnicott is noted for his introduction of the notion of a 'transitional object'. A transitional object is often a blanket or some other material object to which the child is emotionally attached. It is the child's first 'not-me possession' and permits a move away from the oral relationship with the mother and a step towards true object-relations, as well as establishing a first spatial distinction between the 'me' and the 'not-me'.

READING: Davis and Wallbridge (1980)

Wittgenstein, Ludwig (1889–1951) Austrian-born British philosopher. Wittgenstein is a key figure in the development of ANALYTIC PHILOSOPHY and an important influence on ORDINARY LANGUAGE philosophy. During his lifetime he published only one book, *Tractatus Logico-Philosophicus* (1921) and one article (1929) on philosophy; the many posthumous publications, the most important of which are *Philosophical Investigations* (1953), *The Blue and Brown Books* (1958) and *Philosophical Grammar* (1974), are based on either lectures or the voluminous notes which he kept and constantly rearranged. In all cases the titles are those supplied by his editors. The long silence that followed his first publication reflects both Wittgenstein's personal reticence and his deep ambivalence towards his own vocation. Between 1920 and 1926 he abandoned philosophy and taught in an Austrian primary school; his second book was a dictionary designed for school use. The secondary literature on Wittgenstein is now enormous; the *Philosophical Investigations* alone are the object of a four-volume commentary (Baker and Hacker 1980, 1985; Hacker 1990, 1996b).

Wittgenstein originally trained as an engineer and was drawn to philosophy, and particularly the philosophy of mathematics and logic, via his reading of FREGE and of Russell's work on mathematics. It has become almost conventional to make a distinction between the 'early' Wittgenstein of the *Tractatus Logico-Philosophicus* who is interested primarily in logic and a 'late' Wittgenstein who is concerned with language but, even though he subsequently took a very critical view of the *Tractatus*, it is more satisfactory to regard him as approaching the same issue of language from different angles. If there is one theme that is central to both the early and the late Wittgenstein, it is the claim that philosophy is primarily a critique of language, and it is this that makes him so important to analytic philosophy and to the VIENNA CIRCLE, with which he was closely associated in the late 1920s. For Wittgenstein and for the Circle, the task of philosophy is not to supply information about the universe in the sense that the sciences do, but to clarify the nature and workings of language.

The *Tractatus*, with its numbered propositions (ordered following a decimal principle in which 1.1 is a comment on or refinement of 1.0) and elliptical formulations, is one of the most elegant products of twentieth-century philosophy, but also one of the most forbidding. Its goal is stated in the Preface: 'to draw a limit to thought or rather the expression of thoughts.' That line can be drawn only in language, as it is language that establishes the limits of the world: '*The limits of my language* mean the limits of my world.' In such enigmatic phrases Wittgenstein is following Frege and the Russell and Whitehead of the *Principia Mathematica* (1910) in viewing the 'world' not as a sensible phenomenon, but as that body of propositions that makes it possible to speak of a world. The world is a totality of facts or factual propositions, and not of things. Such propositions can be broken down into atomistic logical propositions that must be true. It is on this basis that Wittgenstein elaborates his so-called 'picture theory' of language and reality. The expression can be misleading; Wittgenstein wrote in German, and *Bild* can mean 'model' as well as 'picture'. A proposition is a picture to the extent that it either represents existing phenomena or can be analysed or broken down into other propositions that do so. The goal of the *Tractatus* is to establish the limits of what can be said by such propositions. That, according to Wittgenstein, is all that philosophy can do. Hence the conclusion: 'What we cannot speak about we must pass over in silence.' To attempt to translate non-logical or non-scientific propositions into logical or scientific language would, in other words, distort both them and language. They therefore cannot be spoken of. The conclusion of the *Tractatus* explains Wittgenstein's appeal to the logical positivists of the Vienna Circle; it suggests that what cannot be 'spoken about' must be dismissed as METAPHYSICS because it cannot be subject to the principle of FALSIFIABILITY or verification (which is sometimes attributed to Wittgenstein). Wittgenstein himself is more circumspect and leaves open the question of what cannot be spoken about.

The *Tractatus* assumes that the limits of language are imposed by its logical or propositional structure and, although Wittgenstein does not in fact discuss natural languages such as German or English, implies that all languages have a common essence that can be revealed by logical analysis. With the *Blue and Brown Books*, so-called because of the colour of the paper in which they were bound, and *Philosophical Investigations* that derives from them, this assumption begins to change. Wittgenstein now introduces his LANGUAGE GAMES, which are simplified models of language designed to reveal both its workings and the process of language acquisition. The artificial models constructed by Wittgenstein – such as the 'language' that is gradually built up as a builder shouts instructions ('Slab', 'Brick') to his workmen – do not reveal a common logical essence, but a family resemblance with one another. The language games reveal two other vital features of language. On the one hand, no language is 'private' in that even one's most private thoughts can be expressed only in the language used by the other players involved in the game. The games also demonstrate that, contrary to the views expressed in the *Tractatus*, meaning is not primarily a matter of propositional logic: meaning is use.

READING: Anscombe (1959); Hacker (1996a, 1996b); Monk (1990); Pears (1971)

Wittig, Monique (1935–) French feminist, novelist and cofounder, in 1969, of *PSYCHANALYSE ET POLITIQUE*.

Wittig's claim (1981, 1996) that a lesbian is not a woman is based upon the argument that the category 'woman' exists only within the binary opposition of man/woman. That opposition both founds and perpetuates an oppressive and compulsory heterosexuality. The lesbian's rejection and refusal of heterosexuality places her beyond or outside the opposition, and she therefore cannot be described as a woman.

Wittig's novels (1969, 1973) owe something to the formal experimentation associated with the *NOUVEAU ROMAN*, but are seen by their author as weapons to be used in a war that will end with the creation of a new language and a new SYMBOLIC that exist outside heterosexuality and its linguistic system, which constantly represses the feminine voice. Her second novel, *The Lesbian Body* (1973), scrupulously avoids masculine pronouns, and turns the feminine plural *elles* into a new universal. Violent, erotic and lyrical, her fictional writings are a celebration of 'the lesbian body' and of a female community in which lesbian peoples can create a new utopia. The fictional world created in *Lesbian Peoples* (Wittig and Zeig 1979) provides a fascinating introduction to Wittig's version of LESBIAN FEMINISM.

Wölfflin, Heinrich (1864–1945) Swiss art historian. In his early studies of the differences between Renaissance and baroque art (1898, 1899), and then in the more general *Principles of Art History* (1915), Wölfflin argues that the history of art should be a history of styles and not a history of individual artists. Thus the stylistic qualities of baroque art – colossality, organic animation, and subordination of the parts to the dominant motif – are much more important than the biographies of the artists who produced it. Stylistic changes are an expression of an era's sense of feeling. Explaining a style means integrating it into the general history of an era and demonstrating that it 'says' the same thing as other manifestations of that period. Ultimately, styles relate to perceptions of the ideal human body: the elongated form of the Renaissance is contrasted with the massive 'Herculean' forms of the baroque. Such forms impose themselves on the figurative imagination of artists without their being consciously aware of them. Although Wölfflin's work, with its references to the states of the soul, seems dated in many respects, the emphasis on the need for a typology of styles does in some ways anticipate the impersonal typologies of NARRATOLOGY and STRUCTURALISM.

woman-identified woman   Term used in RADICAL FEMINISM to describe a woman who identifies her own interests as coinciding with those of all other women, and who rejects all loyalties to men. In 1972 the Radicalesbians group produced a paper entitled 'The Woman-Identified Woman', arguing that 'if we are male-identified in our heads, we cannot realise our autonomy as human beings'.

womanist   A woman who loves other women sexually and/or non-sexually and who is appreciative of the strength and emotional flexibility of women. The term is also synonymous with 'black feminist' or 'feminist of colour'. The term is used by the novelist Alice Walker, who derives it from the black American 'womanish', meaning 'like a woman' and as opposed to 'girlish' (frivolous). 'Womanist' connotes outrageous, audacious and above all wilful behaviour (Walker 1983). For Walker, womanist is to feminist as purple is to lavender. Walker's 'womanish' can be usefully contrasted with the boastful celebration of masculinity in Muddy Waters's classic blues song 'Mannish Boy'.

women's liberation   Often used as a synonym for FEMINISM, especially during the 1970s.

The first references to women's liberation are to be found in documents such as the 'Redstockings' Manifesto', published in New York in 1969 (and reprinted in Morgan 1970), which describes women as an oppressed class, exploited as sex-objects, breeders, domestic slaves and cheap labour. The agents of women's oppression are men, and the oppression of women is the oldest and most basic form of domination. The Women's Liberation Movement in the United States drew on the experience of the earlier black and chicano liberation movements, and fed on the anger fuelled by the marginalization of women within the movement to end the war in Vietnam. It quickly outflanked Betty FRIEDAN's National Organization of Women, and dismissed it as 'reformist' or 'bourgeois'.

In Britain, the organized Women's Liberation Movement emerged from the 1969 HISTORY WORKSHOP conference, during which Sheila ROWBOTHAM's attempt to argue the need for a GENDER-specific history of women was greeted with derisive laughter. Called for the end of February 1970, the first national Women's Liberation Conference was held at Ruskin College, Oxford and, to the astonishment of its organizers, brought together 600 women (and some men, most of whom were involved in running the crèche). The conference ended with the establishment of a National Coordinating Committee and with the formulation of four demands: equal pay; equal education and opportunity; twenty-four-hour nurseries; free contraception and abortion on demand. Accounts by a number of those present appear in Wandor (1990). Three further demands were later advanced: 'financial and legal independence' and 'an end to all discrimination against lesbians' in 1975, and 'freedom from violence and sexual coercion, regardless of marital status' in 1978. The last National Women's Liberation Conference was held in Birmingham in 1978, and was marked by bitter disagreements between the supporters of SOCIALIST FEMINISM and the supporters of RADICAL FEMINISM.

Although many different tendencies coexisted within the movement ranging from LESBIAN FEMINISM to socialist feminism, the broad consensus was that it was founded upon sisterhood, or the conviction that all women had common interests opposed to those of all men. The national organization coexisted with a host of smaller organizations, the most typical being small women's groups involved with local issues and often devoted to CONSCIOUSNESS-RAISING. Virtually all such groups were closed to men. More spectacular activities included the disruption of the Miss World competition in 1970, and the first national Women's Liberation Demonstration, held in the snow in London on International Women's Day (8 March 1971). Examples of the extraordinary range of publications produced after 1970 can be found in Wandor (1972) and Allen, Sanders and Wallis (1974); the classic American anthology is *Sisterhood is Powerful* (Morgan 1970). Bassnett (1986) discusses the emergence of the women's movement in Italy and the German Democratic Republic, as well as in the UK and the United States; important documents from the rather different French movement are reprinted in Duchen (1987).

For a younger generation of feminists, the heritage of women's liberation is an ambiguous bequest. Writers like Natasha Walter (1998) are highly critical of old slogans such as 'The personal is political' or 'Pornography is the theory; rape is the practice' and argue that the attempt to build a 'women's culture' is actually an obstacle to the achieving of economic equality with men.

Woolf, Virginia (1882–1941) British novelist and critic. One of the most significant figures in literary MODERNISM and a very sophisticated exponent of the STREAM-OF-CONSCIOUSNESS technique, Woolf is often regarded as a precursor of the so-called second wave of FEMINISM, though some feminists are critical of her. MILLETT, for example, dismisses her (1969) for 'glorifying two housewives', namely Mrs Dalloway and Mrs Ramsay (in *Mrs Dalloway* and *To the Lighthouse* respectively) and for recording the misery of Rhoda in *The Waves* without explaining it.

Whilst Woolf's many reviews and essays (collected in four volumes 1966–7) do not really constitute a full-fledged theory of literature, her writings on women and literature (edited by Michèle Barrett as Woolf 1979) can be read as anticipating the concerns of later feminist critics. Woolf's best known essays on women and writing are *A Room of One's Own* (1929) and the related *Three Guineas* (1938), in which she argues at length that independent minds need independent means. In the former essay Woolf tells the story of Shakespeare's fictitious sister Judith who, although as gifted as her brother, 'died young – alas, she never wrote a word. She lies buried where the omnibuses now stop, opposite the Elephant and Castle.' Judith Shakespeare did not write anything because, as a woman, she was denied an education and income. A woman who wishes to write fiction or poetry must have a room of her own, which she can lock, and an annual income of £500, but even with a room and money, she has other obstacles to overcome. In her essay 'Professions for Women' (1931) Woolf describes her own difficulties with the phantom known as the Angel in the House, who constantly interrupts her and wastes her time. The Angel is the embodiment of all the self-sacrificing and unselfish virtues ascribed to Victorian women by Coventry Patmore in his long poem *The Angel in the House* (1854); Woolf kills her in order to be able to write. She cannot, however, solve the second problem of 'telling the truth about my own experiences as a body'.

To the annoyance of some feminists, Woolf remarks (1929) that it is fatal for aspiring writers to think of their sex or for a woman to speak consciously as a woman. She recommends an intellectual androgyny as the only solution, and androgyny is the central theme of her novel *Orlando*. For SHOWALTER (1977), this flight into androgyny is symptomatic of Woolf's inability to come to terms with her own femininity or to tell the truth about her bodily experiences. Elsewhere Woolf does explore the possible existence of a specifically feminine aesthetic. In a discussion (1923) of the stream-of-consciousness techniques employed by Dorothy Richardson in her novel sequence *Pilgrimage* (twelve volumes published between 1915 and 1938), she describes the novelist as having written 'a woman's sentence'. More elastic than the traditional sentence, it is capable of 'suspending the frailest particles' of consciousness, and it is the work of a woman who is neither proud nor afraid of anything she may discover in the psychology of her sex.

writerly and readerly texts The usual translation of the French *textes scriptibles*, *textes lisibles*. A literal translation of the terms ('scriptable', 'readable') might be thought preferable; *scriptible* is one of the many neologisms coined by Barthes, whilst *lisible* is a conventional term which carries the same connotations as the English 'readable'. The distinction between two types of writing and reading is introduced by BARTHES in his extraordinarily detailed study of Balzac's short story 'Sarrasine' (Barthes 1970a). The study originated from the two-year-long seminar held at the École Pratique des Hautes Études in 1968 and 1969.

The readerly text is a product, and its ideological function is to make meaning appear natural and to make the story that is being told appear credible by following the codes that the reader expects to find in a well-made text. It restricts the polysemy or multiple meanings of the text by obscuring its formal structure, limiting its CONNOTATIONS and reducing the activity of reading to the passive and unthinking consumption or enjoyment of the story and the fate of its protagonists. The story has already been told, and the reader merely consumes it. The writerly text, in contrast, is a process which disrupts codes and turns the reader into a producer of meaning who experiences the enchantments of the SIGNIFIER in a never-ending present. Its overt polysemy means that a writerly text is never complete or closed. Barthes makes it clear from the outset that the writerly text is not a thing that exists, and that it is unlikely to be found in bookshops. It is in fact a utopian concept and its function is to subvert the obviousness and naturalness of the classic realist text, which is implicitly contrasted with the practices of representatives of the AVANT-GARDE such as Lautréamont and Joyce. The readerly/writerly distinction marks a transitional stage in Barthes' work. The readerly text, that is, has many of the features that Barthes previously ascribed to MYTHOLOGY and ideology in his quasi-Marxist period (1957), whilst the writerly text already displays the characteristics of the literary *JOUISSANCE* described in the more eroticized *Pleasure of the Text* of 1973.

writing An immensely important notion in French literary and philosophical theory from the 1950s onwards. Writing (*écriture*) is invoked in slightly different ways by BARTHES, DERRIDA, CIXOUS and the theorists of *ÉCRITURE FEMININE*, and the writers associated with *TEL QUEL* and the practice of 'textual writing'. The common element in these various invocations of writing is a rejection of the view that it is purely representational, or dedicated to the production of MIMESIS, and the insistence that language is not a transparent medium but a material substance in its own right. As Barthes puts it (1966c), 'to write' is an intransitive verb; the goal of writing is not to represent the world, but to use language.

Barthes' notion of writing is introduced in his first major publication (1953). Writing is defined not as an instrument of communication but as a function: writing is the relationship between creation and a literary language which has been transformed by its social 'destination'. Writing is not an expression of a writer's subjectivity, but the adoption of a position within a culture that is already loaded with meanings and representations. Those meanings include prior definitions of what literature and the literary text are or can be. In his subsequent work (e.g. 1964a), Barthes tends to refer to this adoption of a mode of writing as the adoption of a 'sociolect' defined by a culture's dominant DISCOURSE (in linguistics, a sociolect is more normally defined as a variety of language characteristic of the speaker's social background or status). Barthes then proceeds to outline a history of writings or modes of writing. The writing of MARXISM, for example, is characterized by its use of LITOTES: every word is a condensed reference to the entire set of concealed principles that supports it. Bourgeois writing, in contrast, has always been characterized by its use of the closed, asocial language that is the hallmark of the MYTHOLOGY of a 'natural' writing steeped in good taste. Modern writing, from Flaubert onwards, is characterized by an acute consciousness of the social constraints on language and writing and by the attempt to escape them. The 'writing degree zero' of Barthes' title refers to the blank or white style of Camus's *The Outsider* (1942b), in which the style of absence becomes an ideal absence of style.

This modern concept of writing goes against one of the oldest traditions in Western philosophy. In the final sections of the *Phaedrus*, Plato explicitly states that 'living and animate speech' is to be preferred to the 'written speech' which might be called its shadow. Socrates concedes that writing can, at best, be an aid to memory, but insists that 'spoken truths' are 'a man's legitimate sons'. As Derrida demonstrates at length in his study of GRAMMATOLOGY (1967a), the same LOGOCENTRISM and PHONOCENTRISM can be observed in Jean-Jacques Rousseau's thesis that writing is a SUPPLEMENT to speech, in SAUSSURE's insistence that writing 'veils' or obscures language (*langue*) and inevitably misrepresents it, and in modern STRUCTURALISM. Saussure's description (1916) of the 'illusory' importance that has been accorded to language typifies the logocentrist tradition: it is as though we believed that, if we wish to know someone, we should look at their photograph rather than their face. Derrida's DECONSTRUCTION is an attempt to subvert this entire tradition and to establish a broader and much more positive view of writing. Derrida adopts a very broad definition of writing which can be applied to literal, pictographic or ideogrammatic inscription, but also to cinematic, choreographic, musical and sculptural forms of writing. As he notes, both the logic of DNA and the science of cybernetics can be described as forms of writing. The concept of writing can be extended to include the whole field of linguistic signs and para-linguistic communication. But writing is not governed by the logic of the SIGN, which assumes that sound and image fuse into a unity reminiscent of the idea of divine *logos* that inspires the tradition of logocentrism. It is governed, rather, by the economy of *DIFFÉRANCE* and that of the SUPPLEMENT.

Z

zeugma A rhetorical device (RHETORIC) in which a single word is made to refer to two or more words in a sentence, often playing on their respective literal and metaphorical meanings, as in 'dressed in rags and misery'. The term derives from the Greek *zeugnunai* ('to yoke'). The same device is sometimes referred to as 'syllepsis' (another Greek word meaning a 'taking together' of several predicates following one subject).

Zhdanov, Andrey Aleksandrovich (1896–1948) Zhdanov first came to prominence during the Soviet purges of 1937–8, when the original Bolsheviks were eliminated and replaced by Stalin's henchmen, and rapidly became one of the dictator's closest associates. At the First All-Union Congress of Soviet Writers (1934), Zhdanov gave an influential speech on SOCIALIST REALISM. His postwar interventions at cultural congresses consisted mainly of attacks on formalism, 'cosmopolitanism' and the penetration of Russian culture by elements of 'bourgeois decay'. Shostakovich, Zoshchenko and Anna Akhmatova were particular targets. The posthumously published collection of essays on literature, music and philosophy (1950) is a classic example of Stalinist cultural IDEOLOGY.

Bibliography

Abelove, Henri, Barale, Michèle, Anna and Halperin, David, eds (1993), *The Gay and Lesbian Studies Reader*, London and New York: Routledge

Abraham, Karl (1924), 'A Short Study of the Development of the Libido, Viewed in the Light of Mental Disorders. Part II: Origin and Growth of Object-Love' in Abraham (1927)

—— (1927), *Selected Works*, London: The Hogarth Press

Abstraction: Towards a New Art. Painting 1910–1920, London: Tate Gallery, 1980

Ades, Dawn (1986), *Photomontage*, London: Thames and Hudson, rev. enlarged edn

Adler, Alfred (1913), 'New Leading Principles for the Practice of Individual Psychology' in Adler (1923)

—— (1923), *The Practice and Theory of Individual Psychology*, tr. P. Radin, London: Routledge & Kegan Paul, 1929, rev. edn

Adorno, Theodor W. (1931), 'The Actuality of Philosophy', *Telos* 31, 1977

—— (1949), *The Philosophy of Modern Music*, tr. Anne G. Mitchell and Wesley V. Blomster, New York: Seabury Press, 1973

—— (1951), *Minima Moralia: Reflections from Damaged Life*, tr. E. F. N. Jephcott, London: Verso, 1974

—— (1955), *Prisms*, tr. Samuel Shierry Weber, Cambridge, MA: MIT Press, 1981

—— (1957), 'The Stars Look Down: The *Los Angeles Times* Astrology Column: A Study in Secondary Superstition' in Adorno (1994)

—— (1965), *The Jargon of Authenticity*, tr. Knut Tarnowski and Frederic Will, London: Routledge, 1973

—— (1966), *Negative Dialectics*, tr. E. B. Ashton, London: Routledge, 1973

—— (1968), *Alban Berg: Master of the Smallest Link*, tr. Juliane Brand and Christopher Hailey, Cambridge: Cambridge University Press, 1991

—— (1970), *Aesthetic Theory*, ed. Gretel Adorno and Rolf Tiedermann, tr. Robert Hullot-Kentor, London: Athlone Press, 1997

—— (1970–86), *Gesammelte Schriften*, Frankfurt-am-Main: Suhrkamp, 23 vols

—— (1974), *Notes to Literature*, tr. Shierry Weber Nicholsen, New York: Columbia University Press, 1991–2, 2 vols

—— (1991), *The Culture Industry: Selected Essays on Mass Culture*, ed. with an introduction by J. M. Bernstein, London: Routledge

—— (1994), *The Stars Look Down and Other Essays on the Irrational in Culture*, ed. Stephen Crook, London: Routledge

—— et al. (1950), *The Authoritarian Personality*, New York: Harper and Brothers

Aglietta, Michel (1976), *A Theory of Economic Regulation: The US Experience*, tr. David Fernbach, London: New Left Books, 1979

Ahmad, Aijaz (1992), *In Theory: Classes, Nations, Literatures*, London: Verso

—— (1995), 'The Politics of Literary Postcoloniality', *Race and Class* vol. 36 no. 3

Alavi, Hanza (1972), 'The State in Post-Colonial Societies: Pakistan and Bangladesh', *New Left Review* 74

Al-Azmeh, Aziz (1993), *Islam and Modernities*, London: Verso

Ali, Tariq, ed. (1984), *The Stalinist Legacy: Its Impact on Twentieth-Century World Politics*, Harmondsworth: Penguin

Allen, Graham (1994), *Harold Bloom: A Poetics of Conflict*, Hemel Hempstead: Harvester Wheatsheaf

Allen, Sandra, Sanders, Lee and Wallis, Jan (1974), *Conditions of Illusion: Papers from the Women's Movement*, Leeds: Feminist Books

Althusser, Louis (1960), 'Feuerbach's Philosophical Manifestoes' in Althusser (1965)

—— (1961), 'On the Young Marx: Theoretical Questions' in Althusser (1965)

—— (1962a), 'Contradiction and Overdetermination' in Althusser (1965)

—— (1962b), 'The "Piccolo Teatro": Bertolazzi and Brecht' in Althusser (1965)

—— (1963), 'On the Materialist Dialectic' in Althusser (1965)

—— (1965), *For Marx*, tr. Ben Brewster, London: Allen Lane, 1969

—— (1966a), 'A Letter on Art in Reply to André Daspre' in Althusser (1971)

—— (1966b), 'Cremonini, Painter of the Abstract' in Althusser (1971)

—— (1967), 'Philosophy and the Spontaneous Philosophy of the Scientists', tr. Warren Montag, in Althusser (1990)

—— (1969a), 'Lenin and Philosophy' in Althusser (1971)

—— (1969b), 'Freud and Lacan' in Althusser (1971)

—— (1969c), 'Lenin Before Hegel' in Althusser (1971)

—— (1970), 'Ideology and Ideological State Apparatuses (Notes Towards an Investigation)' in Althusser (1971)

—— (1971), *Lenin and Philosophy and Other Essays*, tr. Ben Brewster, London: New Left Books

—— (1990), *Philosophy and the Spontaneous Philosophy of the Scientists and Other Essays*, London: Verso, 1990

—— (1992a), *'The Future Lasts A Long Time' and 'The Facts'*, tr. Richard Veasey, London: Chatto & Windus, 1993

—— (1992b), *Journal de captivité. Stalag XA 1940–1945*, Paris: Stock/IMEC

—— (1993), *Écrits sur la psychanalyse*, Paris: Stock/IMEC

—— (1994), *Écrits philosophiques et politiques I*, Paris: Stock/IMEC

—— (1995), *Écrits philosophiques et politiques II*, Paris: Stock/IMEC

—— (1998), *Lettres à Franca (1961–1973)*, Paris: Stock/IMEC

—— and Etienne Balibar (1965), *Reading 'Capital'*, tr. Ben Brewster, London: New Left Books, 1970

Ammerman, Robert R., ed. (1965), *Classics of Analytic Philosophy*, New York: McGraw Hill

Anderson, Benedict (1983), *Imagined Communities: Reflections on the Origin and Spread of Nationalism*, London: Verso

—— (1990), *Language and Power: Exploring Political Cultures in Indonesia*, Ithaca: Cornell University Press

Anderson, Perry (1964), 'Origins of the Present Crisis', *New Left Review* 23

—— (1966), 'Socialism and Pseudo-Empiricism', *New Left Review* 35

—— (1968a), 'Components of the National Culture' in Cockburn and Blackburn (1969)

—— (1968b), 'Introduction to Gramsci 1919–1920', *New Left Review* 51

—— (1974a), *Passages from Antiquity to Feudalism*, London: New Left Books

—— (1974b), *Lineages of the Absolute State*, London: New Left Books

—— (1976a), *Considerations on Western Marxism*, London: New Left Books

—— (1976b), 'The Antinomies of Antonio Gramsci', *New Left Review* 100

—— (1980), *Arguments Within English Marxism*, London: Verso

—— (1983), *In the Tracks of Historical Materialism*, London: Verso

—— (1990), 'Nocturnal Enquiry: Carlo Ginzburg' in Anderson (1992b)

—— (1991), 'Fernand Braudel and National Identity' in Anderson (1992b)

—— (1992a), *English Questions*, London: Verso

—— (1992b), *A Zone of Engagement*, London: Verso

—— (1998), *The Origins of Postmodernity*, London: Verso

André Breton: La Beauté convulsive, Paris: Centre Georges Pompidou, 1991

Andrew, D. (1976), *The Major Film Theories: An Introduction*, New York: Oxford University Press

—— and Truffaut, F. (1971), *André Bazin*, New York: Columbia University Press

Anscombe, G. E. M. (1959), *An Introduction to Wittgenstein's Tractatus*, London: Hutchinson

Anzieu, Didier (1975), *Freud's Self-Analysis*, tr. Peter Graham, London: Hogarth Press

Appignanesi, Lisa, ed. (1985), *Ideas from France: The Legacy of French Theory*, London: ICA

Aragon, Louis (1926), *Paris Peasant*, tr. Simon Watson Taylor, London: Cape, 1971

Archer, Robin, et al., eds (1989), *Out of Apathy: Voices of the New Left Thirty Years On*, London: Verso

Arendt, Hannah (1929), *Der Liebesbegriff bei Augustin*, Berlin: J. Springer

—— (1951), *The Origins of Totalitarianism*, New York: Harcourt, Brace

—— (1958), *The Human Condition*, Chicago: University of Chicago Press

—— (1961), *Between Past and Future: Six Exercises in Political Thought*, New York: Viking Press

—— (1963), *Eichmann in Jerusalem: A Report on the Banality of Evil*, Harmondsworth: Penguin, 1994, rev. enlarged edn

—— (1978a), *The Life of the Mind*, New York: Harcourt Brace Jovanovich, 2 vols

—— (1978b), *The Jew as Pariah: Jewish Identity and Politics in the Modern Age*, ed. R. H. Feldman, New York: Grove Press

Ariès, Philippe (1960), *Centuries of Childhood*, London: Jonathan Cape, 1962

—— (1985), *Images of Man and Death*, tr. Janet Lloyd, Cambridge, MA: Harvard University Press, 1985

Aristotle, *The Nicomachean Ethics*, tr. J. A. K. Thomson, Harmondsworth: Penguin, rev. edn, 2000

—— *The Art of Rhetoric*, tr. Hugh Lawson-Tancred, Harmondsworth: Penguin, 1991

—— *The Metaphysics*, tr. Hugh Lawson-Tancred, Harmondsworth: Penguin, 1998

Aristotle, Horace, Longinus, *Classical Literary Criticism*, tr. T. S. Dorsche, Harmondsworth: Penguin, 1965

Armes, Roy (1972), *Patterns of Realism: A Study of Italian Neo-Realism*, New York: Barnes

—— (1974), *Film and Reality: A Historical Survey*, Harmondsworth: Penguin

Arnold, James A. (1981), *Modernism and Negritude: The Poetry and Poetics of Aimé Césaire*, Cambridge, MA: Harvard University Press

Aronson, Ronald (1980), *Jean-Paul Sartre: Philosophy in the World*, London: Verso

Art in Revolution: Soviet Art and Design since 1917, London: Arts Council, 1971

Artaud, Antonin (1925a), 'Lettre aux recteurs des universités européennes' in Artaud (1970)

—— (1925b), 'Adresse au Pape' in Artaud (1970)

—— (1938), *The Theatre and its Double*, tr. Mary Caroline Richards, London: Calder & Boyars, 1988

—— (1947), 'Van Gogh, the Man Suicided by Society' in Hirschman (1965)

—— (1970), *Oeuvres complètes* I, Paris: Gallimard

—— (1976), *Selected Writings of Antonin Artaud*, ed. Susan Sontag, New York, Farrar, Straus & Giroux

Asante, Molefi Kete (1988), *Afrocentricity*, Trenton, NJ: Africa World Press, 3rd rev. edn

—— (1990), *Kemet, Afrocentricity and Knowledge*, Trenton, NJ: Africa World Press

Ashcroft, Bill et al. (1995), *The Post-Colonial Studies Reader*, New York and London: Routledge

Ashcroft, Bill, Griffiths, Gareth and Tiffin, Helen (1989), *The Empire Writes Back: Theory and Practice in Post-Colonial Literatures*, London: Routledge

——, eds (1995), *The Post-Colonial Studies Reader*, London: Routledge

Auerbach, Erich (1946), *Mimesis*, New York: Columbia University Press, 1968

Auffret, Dominique (1990), *Alexandre Kojève: Le Philosophe, l'état, la fin de l'histoire*, Paris: Grasset

Augustine, *On Christian Teaching*, tr. R. P. H. Green, Oxford: World's Classics, 1987

Austin, J. L. (1962a), *How To Do Things with Words*, ed. J. O. Ormson and Marina Shisà, Oxford: Clarendon Press

—— (1962b), *Sense and Sensibilia*, Oxford: Clarendon Press

—— (1970), *Philosophical Papers*, Oxford: Clarendon Press

Ayer, A. J. (1936), *Language, Truth and Logic*, London: Gollancz

—— (1940), *The Foundations of Empirical Knowledge*, London: Macmillan

—— (1985), *Ludwig Wittgenstein*, Harmondsworth: Penguin, 1986

Bachelard, Gaston (1928), *Essai sur la connaissance approchée*, Paris: Vrin

—— (1934), *The New Scientific Spirit*, tr. Arthur Goldhammer, Boston: Beacon Press, 1985

—— (1938a), *La Formation de l'esprit scientifique*, Paris: Vrin

—— (1938b), *The Psychoanalysis of Fire*, tr. A. C. M. Ross, Boston: Beacon Press, 1971

—— (1940), *The Philosophy of No: A Philosophy of the New Scientific Mind*, tr. C. Watson, New York: Orion Press, 1968

—— (1942), *L'Eau et les rêves*, Paris: Librairie José Corti

—— (1943), *Water and Dreams: An Essay on the Imagination of Matter*, tr. Edith R. Farsel, Dallas: Pegasus Foundation, 1983

—— (1948a), *La Terre et les rêveries du repos*, Paris: Librairie José Corti

—— (1948b), *La Terre et les rêveries de la volonté*, Paris: Librairie José Corti

—— (1953), *Le Matérialisme rationnel*, Paris: PUF

—— (1960), *The Poetics of Reverie*, tr. Daniel Russel, Boston: Beacon Press, 1971

—— (1961), *The Flame of a Candle*, tr. Joni Caldwell, Dallas: Dallas Institute of Humanities and Culture Publications, 1988

Bachofen, J. J. (1968), *Myth, Religion and Mother-Right*, tr. Ralph Mannheim, London: Routledge & Kegan Paul

Bair, Deirdre (1990), *Simone de Beauvoir: A Biography*, New York: Summit Books

Baker, G. P. and Hacker, P. M. S. (1980), *Wittgenstein: Understanding and Meaning: Volume 1 of an Analytical Commentary of the Philosophical Investigations*, Oxford: Blackwell

—— (1984), *Frege: Logical Excavations*, Oxford: Blackwell

—— (1985), *Wittgenstein: Rules, Grammar and Necessity: Volume 2 of an Analytical Commentary on the Philosophical Investigations*, Oxford: Blackwell

Baker, Houston A. Jr (1987), *Modernism and the Harlem Renaissance*, Chicago: University of Chicago Press

Bakhtin, Mikhail (1924), 'The Problem of Content, Material and Form in Verbal Artistic Creation' in Bakhtin (1990)

—— (1929), *Problems of Dostoievski's Poetics*, tr. C. Emerson, Minneapolis: University of Minnesota Press, 1984

—— (1934–5), 'Discourse in the Novel' in Bakhtin (1981)

—— (1936–8), 'The *Bildungsroman* and its Significance in the History of Realism (Towards a Historical Typology of the Novel)' in Bakhtin (1986)

—— (1952–3), 'The Problem of Speech Genes' in Bakhtin (1986)

—— (1965), *Rabelais and his World*, tr. Helene Iswolsky, Bloomington: Indiana University Press, 1984

—— (1981), *The Dialogic Imagination*, tr. Caryl Emerson and Michael Holquist, Austin: University of Texas Press, 1984

—— (1986), *Speech Genres and Other Late Essays*, tr. Caryl Emerson and Michael Holquist, Austin: University of Texas Press

—— and Medvedev, Pavel (1928), *The Formal Method in Literary Scholarship: A Critical Introduction to Sociological Poetics*, tr. Albert J. Wehrie, Cambridge, MA: Harvard University Press, 1978

—— and Voloshinov, Valentin (1929), *Marxism and the Philosophy of Language*, tr. Ladislav Matejka and I. R. Titunik, Cambridge, MA: Harvard University Press, 1986

Baldwin, James (1957), 'Princes and Paupers' in *Nobody Knows My Name: More Notes of a Native Son*, Harmondsworth: Penguin, 1991

Balint, Michael (1952), *Primary Love and Psychoanalytic Technique*, London: Tavistock

Bann, Stephen and Bowlt, John E. (1973), *Russian Formalism: A Collection of Articles and Texts in Translation*, Edinburgh: Scottish Academic Press

Barker, Francis et al., eds (1978), *1848. The Sociology of Literature. Proceedings of the Essex Conference on the Sociology of Literature, July 1978*, Colchester: University of Essex

—— (1985), *Europe and its Others*, Colchester: University of Essex

Barrett, Michèle and McIntosh, Mary (1982), *The Anti-Social Family*, London: Verso

Barsky, Robert F. (1997), *Noam Chomsky: A Life of Dissent*, Cambridge, MA: MIT Press

Barth, John (1966), *Giles Goat-Boy*, London: Secker & Warburg

—— (1995), *Further Fridays: Essays, Lectures and Other Non-Fiction*, Boston: Little, Brown

Barthes, Roland (1953), *Writing Degree Zero*, tr. Annette Lavers and Colin Smith, London: Cape, 1967

—— (1956), 'The Tasks of Brechtian Criticism' in Barthes (1964b)

—— (1957), *Mythologies*, tr. A. Lavers, London: Cape, 1972

—— (1963), *On Racine*, tr. Richard Howard, New York: Performing Arts Journal Publications, 1993

—— (1964a), *Elements of Semiology*, tr. Annette Lavers and Colin Smith, London: Cape, 1967

—— (1964b), *Critical Essays*, tr. Richard Howard, Evanston, IL: Northwestern University Press, 1976

—— (1966a), 'Introduction to the Structural Analysis of Narratives' in Barthes (1981b)

—— (1966b), *Criticism and Truth*, tr. Katrine Pilcher Keuneman, Minneapolis: University of Minnesota Press, 1987

—— (1966c), 'To Write – an Intransitive Verb' in Macksey and Donato (1970)

—— (1967), *The Fashion System*, tr. Matthew Ward and Richard Howard, London: Jonathan Cape, 1985

—— (1968a), 'L'Effet de réel' in Barthes (1984)

—— (1968b), 'The Death of the Author' in Barthes (1978)

—— (1969), 'Réflexions sur un manuel' in Barthes (1984)

—— (1970a), *S/Z*, tr. Richard Miller, Oxford: Blackwell, 1975

—— (1970b), *Empire of Signs*, tr. Richard Howard, London: Jonathan Cape, 1983

—— (1970c), 'The Old Rhetoric: An Aide-Mémoire' in Barthes (1980b)

—— (1971a), *Sade, Fourier, Loyola*, tr. Richard Miller, London: Cape, 1977

—— (1971b), 'Réponses', *Tel Quel* 47

—— (1973a), *The Pleasure of the Text*, tr. Richard Miller, London: Jonathan Cape, 1976

—— (1973b), *Mythologies*, tr. Annette Lavers, London: Cape

—— (1975), *Roland Barthes by Roland Barthes*, tr. Richard Howard, London: Macmillan, 1977

—— (1977), *A Lover's Discourse: Fragments*, tr. Richard Howard, London: Cape, 1982

—— (1978), *Image, Music, Text*, tr. Stephen Heath, New York: Noonday

—— (1979), *The Eiffel Tower and Other Mythologies*, tr. Richard Howard, New York: Hill and Wang

—— (1980), *Camera Lucida: Reflections on Photography*, tr. Richard Howard, London: Cape, 1982

—— (1981a), *The Grain of the Voice: Interviews 1962–1980*, tr. Linda Coverdale, London: Jonathan Cape, 1985

—— (1981b), *A Barthes Reader*, ed. Susan Sontag, London: Fontana

—— (1984), *Le Bruissement de la langue: Essais critiques* IV, Paris: Seuil

—— (1993–5), *Oeuvres complètes*, Paris; Seuil, 3 vols

Bassnett, Susan (1986), *Feminist Experiences: The Women's Movement in Four Cultures*, London: Allen & Unwin

Bataille, Georges (1928), *The Story of the Eye*, tr. Joachim Neugroschel, Harmondsworth: Penguin, 1982

—— (1941), *Madame Edwarda* in Bataille (1980)

—— (1949), *The Accursed Share*, tr. Robert Hurley, New York: Zone Books, 1988, 2 vols

—— (1955a), *Prehistoric Painting: Lascaux, or the Birth of Art*, tr. Austryn Wainhouse, London: Macmillan, 1980

—— (1955b), *Manet*, tr. Austryn Wainhouse and James Emmon, London: Macmillan, 1980

—— (1957), *Eroticism*, tr. Mary Dalwood, London: Calder & Boyars, 1962

—— (1973), *Theory of Religion*, tr. Robert Hurley, New York: Zone Books, 1988

—— (1980), *My Mother, Madame Edwarda and The Dead Man*, tr. Austryn Wainhouse, London: Marian Boyars

—— (1994), *The Absence of Myth: Writings on Surrealism*, tr. with an introduction by Michael Richardson, London: Verso

—— (1995), *Visions of Excess: Selected Writings 1927–1939*, tr. Alan Stoekl, Manchester: Manchester University Press

Bateson, Gregory (1972), *Steps Towards an Ecology of Mind*, Aylesbury: Intertext

—— et al. (1956), 'Toward a Theory of Schizophrenia', *Behavioural Science* 1, p. 251

Battcock, Gregory ed. (1975), *Super-Realism: A Critical Anthology*, New York: E. P. Dutton

Baudelaire, Charles (1863), *The Painter of Modern Life and Other Essays*, tr. and ed. Jonathan Mayne, New York: Da Capo Press, 1986

Baudrillard, Jean (1968), *The System of Objects*, tr. Chris Turner, London: Verso, 1996

—— (1970), *La Société de consommation: ses mythes, ses structures*, Paris: Denoël

—— (1976), *Symbolic Exchange and Death*, tr. Iain Hamilton Grant, London: Sage, 1993

—— (1979), *Seduction*, tr. Brian Singer, London: Macmillan, 1990

—— (1981), *Simulacra and Simulations*, tr. Paul Foss, Paul Patton and Philip Beitchmann, New York: Semiotext(e), 1983

—— (1983), *Fatal Strategies*, tr. Philip Beitchmann and W. G. J. Niesluchowski, ed. Jim Fleming, London: Pluto Press, 1990

—— (1986), *America*, tr. Chris Turner, London: Verso, 1988

—— (1987), *Cool Memories*, tr. Chris Turner, London: Verso, 1990

—— (1990), *Cool Memories II*, tr. Chris Turner, Cambridge: Polity Press, 1996

—— (1991), *The Gulf War Did Not Take Place*, tr. Paul Patton, Bloomington: Indiana University Press, 1995

—— (1995), *Fragments: Cool Memories 1990–1995*, Paris: Galilée

Bauman, Janina (1986), *Winter in the Morning: A Young Girl's Life in the Warsaw Ghetto and Beyond 1939–1945*, London: Virago

Bauman, Zigmunt (1956), *Soljalizm Brytjski*, Warsaw: PWN

—— (1982), *Memories of Class: The Pre-History and After-Life of Class*, London: Routledge & Kegan Paul

—— (1987), *Legislators and Interpreters*, Cambridge: Polity Press

—— (1989), *Modernity and the Holocaust*, Cambridge: Polity Press

—— (1992), *Intimations of Postmodernity*, London: Routledge

—— (1997), *Postmodernity and its Discontents*, Cambridge: Polity Press

Baxandal, Lee and Morawski, Stefan (1973), *Marx and Engels on Literature and Art*, St Louis: Telos Press

Bazin, André (1958–62), *What Is Cinema?*, tr. Hugh Gray, Berkeley: University of California Press, 1967, 1971, 2 vols

—— (1971), *Jean Renoir*, ed. François Truffaut, tr. W. W. Halsey and William Simon, New York: Delta

Beauvoir, Simone de (1944), *Pyrrhus et Cinéas*, Paris: Gallimard

—— (1947a), *The Ethics of Ambiguity*, New York: Philosophical Library, 1948

—— (1947b), *America Day By Day*, tr. Patrick Dudley, London: Duckworth

—— (1949), *The Second Sex*, tr. H. M. Parshley, Harmondsworth: Penguin, 1984

—— (1954), *The Mandarins*, tr. Leonard M. Friedman, London: Fontana, 1986

—— (1958), *Memoirs of a Dutiful Daughter*, tr. James Kirkup, Harmondsworth: Penguin, 1987

—— (1960), *The Prime of Life*, tr. Peter Green, Harmondsworth: Penguin, 1988

—— (1963), *Force of Circumstances*, tr. Richard Howard, Harmondsworth: Penguin, 1987

—— (1972), *All Said and Done*, tr. Patrick O'Brian, Harmondsworth: Penguin, 1987

—— (1990a), *Letters to Sartre*, tr. Quintin Hoare, London: Vintage, 1992

—— (1990b), *Journal de Guerre*, Paris: Gallimard

Beck, Ulrich (1986), *Risk Society: Towards a New Modernity*, tr. Mark Ritter, London: Sage, 1992

Bell, Daniel S. (1960), *The End of Ideology*, Glencoe, IL: Free Press

—— (1973), *The Coming of Post-Industrial Society*, New York: Basic Books

—— (1976), *The Cultural Contradictions of Capitalism*, London: Heinemann

Bell, David (1990), *Husserl*, London: Routledge

Bell, Stuart (1988), *When Salem Came to the Boro: The True Story of the Cleveland Child-Abuse Crisis*, London: Pan

Benhabib, Seyla, Bonss, Wolfgang and McCole, John, eds (1993), *On Max Horkheimer: New Perspectives*, Cambridge, MA: MIT Press

Benjamin, Andrew, ed. (1988), *Post-Structuralist Classics*, London: Routledge

——, ed. (1989), *The Lyotard Reader*, Oxford: Blackwell

Benjamin, Walter (1916), 'On Language as Such and on the Language of Man' in Benjamin (1996)

—— (1920), 'The Concept of Criticism in German Romanticism' in Benjamin (1996)

—— (1921), 'The Task of the Translator' in Benjamin (1996)

—— (1924), 'Naples' in Benjamin (1979)

—— (1924–5), 'Goethe's *Elective Affinities*' in Benjamin (1996)

—— (1928a), *The Origin of German Tragic Drama*, tr. John Osborne, London: Verso, 1977

—— (1928b), *One-Way Street* in Benjamin (1979)

—— (1928c), 'Marseille' in Benjamin (1979)

—— (1928d), 'Hashish in Marseille' in Benjamin (1979)

—— (1929), 'Surrealism' in Benjamin (1979)

—— (1931), 'A Small History of Photography' in Benjamin (1979)

—— (1932), 'Berlin Chronicle' in Benjamin (1979)

—— (1935), 'Paris: The Capital of the Nineteenth Century' in Benjamin (1973)

—— (1936), 'The Work of Art in the Age of Mechanical Reproduction', tr. Henry Zohn, in Benjamin (1969)

—— (1939a), 'The Paris of the Second Empire in Baudelaire' in Benjamin (1973)

—— (1939b), 'Some Motifs in Baudelaire' in Benjamin (1973)

—— (1940), 'Theses on the Philosophy of History' in Benjamin (1960)

—— (1966), *Understanding Brecht*, tr. Anya Bostock, London: New Left Books, 1973

—— (1969), *Illuminations*, ed. Hannah Arendt, New York: Schocken Books

—— (1972) *Über Haschisch: Novellistisches, Berichte, Materialien*, ed. Tillman Rexroth, Frankfurt-am-Main: Suhrkamp

—— (1973) *Charles Baudelaire: A Lyric Poet in the Age of High Capitalism*, tr. Quintin Hoare, London: New Left Books, 1973

—— (1974–89), *Gesammelte Schriften*, ed. Hermann Schueppenhäuser and Rolf Tiedermann, Frankfurt am Main: Suhrkamp, 7 vols

—— (1978), *Reflections: Essays, Aphorisms, Autobiographical Writings*, ed. Peter Demetz, tr. Edmund Jephcott, New York: Harcourt Brace Jovanovich

—— (1979) *One-Way Street and Other Writings*, tr. Edmund Jephcott and Kingsley Shorter, London: New Left Books

—— (1980), *The Correspondence of Walter Benjamin and Gershom Scholem, 1932–1940*, ed. Gershom Scholem, tr. Gary Smith and André Lefevere, introduction by Anson Rabinach, Cambridge, MA: Harvard University Press, 1992

—— (1982), *The Arcades Project*, tr. Howard Eiland and Kevin McLaughlin, Cambridge, MA: Harvard University Press, 1999

—— (1986), *Moscow Diary*, ed. Gary Smith, tr. Richard Sieburth, Cambridge, MA: Harvard University Press

—— (1996), *Selected Writings*. 1: *1913–1926*, ed. Marcus Bullock and Michael W. Jennings, Cambridge, MA: Harvard University Press

Bennett, Tony, Martin, Graham, Mercer, Colin and Woolacott, Janet (1981), *Culture, Ideology and Social Process: A Reader*, London: Batsford Academic and Educational in association with Open University Press

Bennington, Geoffrey (1988), *Lyotard: Writing the Event*, Manchester: Manchester University Press

—— and Derrida, Jacques (1991), *Jacques Derrida*, tr. Geoffrey Bennington, Chicago: University of Chicago Press

Bentham, Jeremy (1996), *The Panopticon Writings*, ed. and introduced by Miran Bozovic, London: Verso

Bentley, Eric, ed. (1968), *The Theory of the Modern Stage: An Introduction to Modern Theatre and Drama*, Harmondsworth: Penguin

Benveniste, Emile (1966), *Problems of General Linguistics*, tr. Mary E. Meek, Miami: Miami University Press, 1971

Benyon, Huw (1973), *Working for Ford*, Harmondsworth: Penguin

Berg, Barbara J. (1978), *The Remembered Gate: Origins of American Feminism. The Woman and the City 1800–1860*, New York: Oxford University Press

Berger, John (1965), *The Success and Failure of Picasso*, Harmondsworth: Penguin

—— (1972), *Ways of Seeing*, London and Harmondsworth: BBC and Penguin

Bergson, Henri (1896), *Matter and Memory*, tr. B. M. Pauland and W. S. Palmer, New York: Zone Books, 1991

Berke, Joseph and Barnes, Mary (1971), *Mary Barnes: Two Accounts of a Journey through Madness*, London: MacGibbon & Kee

Berman, Marshall (1982), *All That Is Solid Melts into Air: The Experience of Modernity*, London: Verso, 1983

Bernabé, Jean, Chamoiseau, Patrick and Confiant, Raphaël (1993), *Éloge de la créolité/ In Praise of Creoleness*, Paris: Gallimard, bilingual edn

Bernal, Martin (1976), *Chinese Socialism to 1907*, Ithaca: Cornell University Press

—— (1987), *Black Athena I: The Afroasiatic Roots of Classical Civilization*, London: Free Association Books

—— (1991), *Black Athena II: The Archaeological and Documentary Evidence*, London: Free Association Books

Bernard, Claude (1865), *Introduction to the Study of Experimental Medicine*, tr. Henry Copley Green, introduction by Lawrence J. Henderson, New York: Dover, 1957

Bernard-Donals, Michael F. (1994), *Mikhail Bakhtin: Between Phenomenology and Marxism*, Cambridge: Cambridge University Press

Bernauer, James W. (1990), *Michel Foucault's Force of Flight: Towards an Ethics for Thought*, Atlantic Highlands, NJ: Humanities Press

Bertens, Hans (1995), *The Idea of the Postmodern: A History*, London: Routledge

Bettelheim, Bruno (1960), *The Informed Heart*, Harmondsworth: Penguin, 1986

—— (1967), *The Empty Fortress: Infantile Autism and the Birth of the Self*, New York: Free Press

—— (1976), *The Uses of Enchantment: The Meaning and Importance of Fairy Tales*, Harmondsworth: Penguin, 1986

—— (1983), *Freud and Man's Soul*, London: Chatto & Windus

—— (1986), *Surviving the Holocaust*, London: Chatto & Windus

Bhabha, Homi K. (1984), 'Of Mimicry and Man: The Ambivalence of Colonial Discourse' in Bhabha (1994)

——, ed. (1990a), *Nations and Narration*, London and New York: Routledge

—— (1990b), 'Interrogating Identity: Frantz Fanon and the Postcolonial Prerogative' in Bhabha (1994)

—— (1994), *The Location of Culture*, London and New York: Routledge

Bhattacharyya, Gargi (1996), 'Black Skin/White Boards: Learning to be the "Race" Lady in British Higher Education', *Parallax* 2

Binswanger, Ludwig (1963), *Being in the World: Selected Papers with a Critical Introduction to his Existential Psychoanalysis by Jacob Needham*, New York: Basic Books

Birchall, Ian H. (1998), 'Prequel to the Heidegger Affair: Audry and Sartre', *Radical Philosophy* 88

Blackburn, Robin (1988), 'Raymond Williams and the Politics of the New Left', *New Left Review* 168

—— (1993), 'Edward Thompson and the New Left', *New Left Review* 201

Blair, Sara (1999), 'Modernism and the Politics of Culture' in Levenson (1999)

Blanche, Gertrude and Blanche, Robin (1974), *Ego-Psychology: Theory and Practice*, New York: Columbia University Press

Bloch, Ernst (1918), *Geist der Utopie*, Frankfurt am Main: Suhrkamp, 1964

—— (1921), *Thomas Münzer als Theologie der Revolution*, Frankfurt am Main: Suhrkamp, 1969

—— (1937), 'A Jubilee for Renegades', tr. D. Bathrisk and N. V. Schults, *New German Critique* 4, 1975

—— (1938), 'Discussing Expressionism', tr. Rodney Livingstone in Bloch et al. (1977)

—— (1959), *The Principle of Hope*, tr. Neville Plaice, Stephen Plaice and Paul Knight, Cambridge, MA: MIT Press, 1986, 3 vols

—— (1962), *Heritage of Our Times*, tr. Neville and Stephen Plaice, Cambridge: Polity Press, 1991

—— et al. (1977), *Aesthetics and Politics: Debates Between Ernst Bloch, Georg Lukács, Bertolt Brecht, Walter Benjamin, Theodor Adorno*, London: New Left Books

—— (1988), *The Utopian Function of Art and Literature*, tr. J. Zipes and F. Mecklenberg, Cambridge, MA: MIT Press

BLOCK Reader in Visual Culture, London and New York: Routledge, 1996

Bloom, Allan (1969), 'Preface' to Alexandre Kojève, *Introduction to the Reading of Hegel*, tr. James H. Nichols Jr, New York: Basic Books

—— (1987), *The Closing of the American Mind*, New York: Simon and Schuster

—— (1990), *Giants and Dwarves: Essays 1960–1990*, New York: Simon and Schuster

Bloom, Harold (1959), *Shelley's Mythmaking*, Ithaca: Cornell University Press

—— (1961), *The Visionary Company: A Reading of English Romantic Poetry*, Ithaca: Cornell University Press

—— (1973), *The Anxiety of Influence: A Theory of Poetry*, New York and Oxford: Oxford University Press

—— (1975a), *A Map of Misreading*, New York: Oxford University Press

—— (1975b), *Kabbalah and Criticism*, New York: Seabury Press

—— ed. (1979), *Deconstruction and Criticism*, New York: Seabury Press

—— (1982), *Agon: Towards a Theory of Revisionism*, New York: Oxford University Press

—— (1991), *The Book of J.*, tr. David Rosenberg, interpreted by Harold Bloom, London: Faber & Faber

—— (1994), *The Western Canon: The Books and the School of the Ages*, New York: Harcourt Brace

—— (1999), *Shakespeare: The Invention of the Human*, London: Fourth Estate

Bloomfield, Leonard (1923), *Language*, New York: Holt, Rinehart & Winston

Bogue, Roland (1989), *Deleuze and Guattari*, London and New York: Routledge

Bonaparte, Marie (1933), *The Life and Works of Edgar Allan Poe*, London: Imago, 1949

Booth, Charles (1969), *Charles Booth's London*, ed. Albert Fried and Richard Elman, London: Hutchinson

Booth, Wayne C. (1961), *The Rhetoric of Fiction*, Harmondsworth: Penguin, 1991, 2nd edn

Borde, Raymond and Chaumeton, Etienne (1955), *Panorama du film noir américain (1941–1953)*, Paris: Minuit

Borges, Jorge Luis (1962), *Fictions*, ed. with an introduction by Anthony Kerrigan, London: John Calder, 1965

Boudjedra, Rachid (1975), *Topographie idéale pour une aggression caractérisée*, Paris: Denoël

Bourdieu, Pierre (1958), *The Algerians*, tr. A. C. Ross, Boston: Beacon Press, 1962

—— (1962), 'Célibat et condition paysanne', *Études rurales* 5–6

—— (1965), 'The Sentiment of Honour in Kabyle Society', tr. P. Sherrard in Peristiany (1965)

—— (1966), 'Intellectual Field and Creative Project', tr. S. France, *Social Science Information* vol. 8 no. 2

—— (1979), *Distinction: A Social Critique of the Judgement of Taste*, tr. R. Nice, Cambridge, MA: Harvard University Press, 1984

—— (1982), 'Le Champ littéraire', *Actes de la recherche en sciences sociales*, September 1991

—— (1984a), *Homo Academicus*, tr. Peter Collier, Cambridge: Polity Press, 1990

—— (1984b), *The State Nobility: Grandes Écoles and Esprit de Corps*, tr. Lauretta C. Clough, Cambridge: Polity Press, 1996

—— (1992), *The Rules of Art: Genesis and Structure of the Literary Field*, tr. Susan Emanuel, Cambridge: Polity Press, 1996

—— (1993), *The Field of Cultural Production: Essays on Art and Literature*, ed. Randal Johnson, Cambridge: Polity Press

—— and Darbel, Alain and Schnapper, Dominique (1969), *The Love of Art: European Art Museums and their Public*, Cambridge: Polity Press, 1990

—— and Passeron, Jean-Claude (1964), *The Inheritors: French Students and their Relation to Culture*, tr. R. Nice, Chicago: University of Chicago Press, 1979

Boutang, Yann Moulier (1992), *Louis Althusser: Une Biographie* I: *La Formation du mythe*, Paris: Grasset

Bowie, Andrew (1997), *From Romanticism to Critical Theory: The Philosophy of German Literary Theory*, London and New York: Routledge

Bowie, Malcolm (1987), *Freud, Proust and Lacan: Theory as Fiction*, Cambridge: Cambridge University Press

—— (1991), *Lacan*, London: Fontana

Boyers, Robert and Orrill, Robert, eds (1971), *Laing and Anti-Psychiatry*, Harmondsworth: Penguin, 1972

Boyne, Roy and Rattansi, Ali (1990), *Postmodernism and Society*, London: Macmillan

Bradbury, Malcolm and McFarlane, James, eds (1976), *Modernism: A Guide to European Literature 1890–1930*, Harmondsworth: Penguin

Bradford, Richard (1994), *Roman Jakobson: Life, Language, Art*, London and New York: Routledge

Bradley, A. C. (1904), *Shakespearean Tragedy: Lectures on Hamlet, Othello, King Lear, Macbeth*, London: Macmillan, 1963

Brandon, S., Boakes, J., Glaser, D. and Green, R. (1998), 'Recovered Memories of Childhood Sexual Abuse: Implications for Clinical Practice', *British Journal of Psychiatry* 172

Braudel, Fernand (1949), *The Mediterranean and the Mediterranean World in the Age of Philip II*, tr. Sîan Reynolds, London: HarperCollins, 1972

—— (1950), 'The Situation of History in 1950' in Braudel (1969)

—— (1958), 'The Longue Durée' in Braudel (1969)

—— (1969), *On History*, tr. Sarah Matthews, Chicago: University of Chicago Press, 1980

—— (1975a), *Civilization and Capitalism* I: *The Structure of Everyday Life. The Limits of the Possible*, tr. Sîan Reynolds, London: HarperCollins, 1981

—— (1975b), *Civilization and Capitalism* II: *The Wheels of Commerce*, tr. Sîan Reynolds, London: HarperCollins, 1982

—— (1979), *Civilization and Capitalism* III: *The Perspective of the World*. tr. Sîan Reynolds, London: HarperCollins, 1984

—— (1986a), *The Identity of France* I: *History and Environment*, tr. Sîan Reynolds, London: HarperCollins, 1988

—— (1986b), *L'Identité de la France: Les Hommes et les choses*, Paris: Flammarion

Bray, Allan (1994), 'Homosexuality and Signs of Male Friendship in Elizabethan England' in Goldberg (1994)

Brecht, Bertolt (1918a), *Baal*, tr. Peter Tegel in *Plays* 1

—— (1918b), *Drums in the Night*, tr. John Willett in *Plays* 1

—— (1928), *The Threepenny Opera*, tr. Ralph Mannheim in *Plays* 2

—— (1929–31), *St Joan of the Stockyards*, tr. Frank Jones in *Plays* 2

—— (1934), *The Threepenny Novel*, tr. Desmond I. Vesey, verses tr. Christopher Isherwood, Harmondsworth: Penguin, 1963

—— (1939), *The Life of Galileo*, tr. J. and T. Stern with W. H. Auden in *Plays* 5

—— (1941), *Mother Courage and her Children*, tr. John Willett in *Plays* 7

—— (1945), *The Caucasian Chalk Circle*, tr. John Willett in *Plays* 7

—— (1949), 'A Short Organum for the Theatre' in Brecht (1964)

—— (1962), 'The Messingkauf Dialogues' in Brecht (1964)

—— (1964), *Brecht on Theatre*, ed. John Willett, New York: Hill & Wang, 1964

—— (1967a), 'Against Georg Lukács', tr. Stuart Hood in Bloch et al. (1977)

—— (1967b), *Gesammelte Werke*, Frankfurt am Main: Suhrkamp, 20 vols

—— (1994), *Plays*, London: Eyre Methuen, 7 vols

Bremond, Claude (1973), *Logique du récit*, Paris: Seuil

Breton, André (1924), 'Manifesto of Surrealism' in Breton (1969)

—— (1928a), *Nadja*, tr. Richard Howard, New York: Grove Press, 1960

—— (1928b), *Surrealism and Painting*, tr. Simon Watson Taylor, New York: Harper & Row, 1972

—— (1929), 'Second Manifesto of Surrealism' in Breton (1969)

—— (1937), 'Mad Love', tr. Mary Ann Caws, Lincoln: University of Nebraska Press, 1987

—— (1952), *Conversations: The Autobiography of Surrealism*, tr. Marc Polizzotti, New York: Paragon House, 1993

—— (1969), *Manifestoes of Surrealism*, tr. Richard Seavard and Helen R. Lane, Ann Arbor: University of Michigan Press, 1969

Brodersen, Momme (1990), *Walter Benjamin: A Biography*, tr. Malcolm R. Green and Ingrida Ligen, ed. Martina Dervis, London: Verso, 1996

Bronner, Stephen and Kellner, Douglas (1989), *Critical Theory and Society: A Reader*, New York and London: Routledge

Brook, Peter (1968), *The Empty Space*, London: MacGibbon & Kee

Brooke-Rose, Christine (1958), *A Grammar of Metaphor*, London: Martin Secker & Warburg

—— (1986), *The Christine Brooke-Rose Omnibus (Out, Such, Between, Thru)*, Manchester: Carcanet Press

Brooks, Cleanth (1939), *Modern Poetry and the Tradition*, Chapel Hill: University of North Carolina Press

—— (1947), *The Well-Wrought Urn: Studies in the Structure of Poetry*, London: Dennis Dobson, 1968, rev. edn

—— (1963), 'The Uses of Literature' in Brooks (1971)

—— (1971), *A Shaping Joy: Studies in the Writer's Craft*, London: Methuen

Brossard, Nicole (1989), *À Tout Regard*, Montréal: Bibliothèque Québecoise

Brown, Mary Ellen (1994), *Soap Opera and Women's Talk: The Pleasure of Resistance*, London: Sage

Bruns, Gerald L. (1992), *Hermeneutics Ancient and Modern*, New Haven: Yale University Press

Buci-Glucksmann, Christine (1975), *Gramsci and the State*, tr. David Fernbach, London: Lawrence & Wishart, 1980

Buck-Morss, Susan (1977), *The Origin of Negative Dialectics: Theodor W. Adorno, Walter Benjamin and the Frankfurt Institute*, Hassocks: Harvester Press

—— (1989), *The Dialectics of Seeing*, Cambridge, MA: MIT Press

Bürger, Peter (1980), *Theory of the Avant-Garde*, tr. Michael Shaw, introduction by Jochen Schulte-Sasse, Minneapolis: University of Minnesota Press, 1984

Burke, Edmund (1756), *A Philosophical Enquiry into the Origins of our Ideas of the Sublime and the Beautiful*, Oxford: World's Classics, 1990

Burke, Kenneth (1966), *Language as Symbolic Action*, Berkeley: University of California Press

Burke, Peter (1990), *The French Historical Revolution: The 'Annales' School 1929–89*, Cambridge: Polity Press

Burnier, Michel-Antoine (1966), *Les Existentialistes et la politique*, Paris: Gallimard

Butler, Judith P. (1987), *Subjects of Desire: Hegelian Reflections in Twentieth-Century France*, New York: Columbia University Press

—— (1990), *Gender Trouble: Feminism and the Subversion of Identity*, New York and London: Routledge

—— (1993), *Bodies that Matter: On the Discursive Limits of 'Sex'*, New York and London: Routledge

—— (1997), *Excitable Speech: A Politics of the Performative*, New York and London: Routledge

Butor, Michel (1957), *Passing Time*, tr. J. Stewart, London: John Calder, 1965

Cahiers du cinéma I. The 1950s: Neo-realism, Hollywood, New Wave, ed. Jim Hillier, London: Routledge, 1985

Cahiers du cinéma II. 1960–1968: New Wave, New Cinema, Re-evaluating Hollywood, ed. Jim Hillier, London: Routledge, 1986

Cahiers du cinéma III: The Politics of Representation, ed. Nick Browne, London: Routledge, 1990

Calvet, Louis-Jean (1990), *Roland Barthes: A Biography*, tr. Sarah Wykes, Cambridge: Polity Press, 1994

Calvino, Italo (1947), *The Path to the Nest of Spiders*, tr. Archibald Colquhoun, with a preface by the author (tr. William Weaver), Hopewell, NJ: Ecco Press, 1976

—— (1956), *Italian Folk Tales*, tr. George Martin, Harmondsworth: Penguin, 1986

—— (1969), 'Cybernetics and Ghosts' in Calvino (1982)

—— (1972), *Invisible Cities*, tr. William Weaver, London: Picador, 1978

—— (1979), *If on a Winter's Night a Traveller*, tr. William Weaver, London: Martin Secker & Warburg, 1981

—— (1982), *The Literature Machine: Essays*, tr. Patrick Creagh, London: Secker & Warburg, 1987

—— (1995), *Saggi 1945–1985*, ed. Mario Barenghi, Milan: Mondadori

Campbell, Beatrix (1984), *Wigan Pier Revisited: Poverty and Politics in the 80s*, London: Virago

—— (1988), *Unofficial Secrets: Child Sexual Abuse: The Cleveland Case*, London: Virago

Camus, Albert (1942a), *The Myth of Sisyphus*, tr. Justin O'Brien, London: Hamish Hamilton, 1955

—— (1942b), *The Outsider*, tr. Joseph Laredo, Harmondsworth: Penguin, 1983

—— (1956), *The Fall*, tr. J. O'Brien, Harmondsworth: Penguin, 1963

Canguilhem, Georges (1950), *On the Normal and the Pathological*, Boston: Reidel, 1978

—— (1952), 'La Pensée et le vivant' in Canguilhem (1989b)

—— (1955), *La Formation du concept de réflexe au XVII et XVIII siècles*, Paris: PUF

—— (1958a), 'Qu'est-ce que la psychologie?' in Canguilhem (1988)

—— (1958b), 'La Philosophie biologique d'Auguste Comte et son influence en France au XIXe siècle' in Canguilhem (1989a)

—— (1959), 'L'Idée de médicine expérimentale selon Claude Bernard' in Canguilhem (1989a)

—— (1960), 'L'Homme et l'animal du point de vue psychologique chez Charles Darwin' in Canguilhem (1989a)

—— (1962), 'L'Histoire des sciences dans l'oeuvre épistémologique de Gaston Bachelard' in Canguilhem (1989a)

—— (1970), 'Qu'est-ce qu'une idéologie scientifique' in Canguilhem (1988)

—— (1976), 'Le rôle de l'épitémologue dans l'historiographie scientifique contemporaine' in Canguilhem (1988)

—— (1988), *Idéologie et rationalité dans l'histoire des sciences de la vie. Nouvelles études d'histoire et de philosophie des sciences*, Paris: Vrin, rev. edn

—— (1989a), *Études d'histoire et de philosophie des sciences*, Paris: Librairie philosophique J. Vrin, 5th edn

—— (1989b), *La Connaissance de la vie*, Paris: Vrin, 2nd edn

—— (1993), *Georges Canguilhem: Philosophe, historien des sciences. Actes du colloque (6–7–8 décembre 1990)*, Paris: Albin Michel

—— (1994), *A Vital Rationalist: Selected Writings from Georges Canguilhem*, tr. Arthur

Goldhammer, ed. François Delaporte, with an introduction by Paul Rabinow, New York: Zone Books

Carmichael, Stokely and Hamilton, Charles V. (1967), *Black Power: The Politics of Liberation in America*, Harmondsworth: Penguin, 1969

Carnap, Rudolf (1934), *The Logical Syntax of Language*, London: Routledge & Kegan Paul

Carter, Angela (1979), *The Bloody Chamber and Other Stories*, London: Gollancz

Cassirer, Ernst (1932), *The Philosophy of the Enlightenment*, tr. Fritz C. A. Koelln and James P. Pettegrove, Princeton: Princeton University Press, 1951

Caudwell, Christopher (1937), *Illusion and Reality: A Study of the Source of Poetry*, London: Lawrence & Wishart, 1973

Caughie, John, ed. (1981), *Theories of Authorship*, London: Routledge & Kegan Paul

Caute, David (1988), *Sixty-Eight: The Year of the Barricades*, London: Hamish Hamilton

Césaire, Aimé (1939), *Notebook of a Return to my Native Land/Cahier d'un retour au pays natal*, tr. Mireille Rosello with Annie Pritchard, introduction by Mireille Rosello, Newcastle-upon-Tyne: Bloodaxe Books, 1996, bilingual edn

—— (1955), *Discours sur le colonialisme*, Paris and Dakar: Présence africaine

—— (1983), *The Collected Poetry*, tr. with an introduction and notes by Clayton Eshleman and Annette Smith, Berkeley, CA: University of California Press

Césaire, Suzanne (1942), 'Misère d'une poésie', *Tropiques* 4, facsimile reproduction, Paris: Jean-Michel Place, 1978

Chadwick, Whitney (1985), *Women Artists and the Surrealist Movement*, London: Thames & Hudson

—— (1990), *Women, Art, and Society*, London: Thames & Hudson

Chamoiseau, Patrick (1992), *Texaco*, tr. Rose-Myriam Réjouis and Val Vinokurov, London: Granta Books, 1997

Chapman, Guy (1972), *The Dreyfus Trials*, London: Batsford

Chappell, V. S. (1964), *Ordinary Language: Essays in Philosophical Method*, Englewood Cliffs, NJ: Prentice-Hall

Charbonnier, Georges (1961), *Conversations with Claude Lévi-Strauss*, tr. John and Doreen Weightman, London: Cape, 1969

Chartier, Jean-Pierre (1946), 'Les Américains aussi font des films noirs', *Revue du cinéma*, October

Chaunu, Pierre (1970), 'L'Histoire sérielle', *Revue historique* 243

Chodorov, Nancy Julia (1978), *The Reproduction of Mothering: Psychoanalysis and the Sociology of Gender*, Berkeley: University of California Press

Chomsky, Noam (1957), *Syntactic Structures*, The Hague: Mouton

—— (1959), 'Review of B. F. Skinner, *Verbal Behaviour*' in Fodor and Katz (1964)

—— (1965), *Aspects of the Theory of Syntax*, Cambridge, MA: MIT Press

—— (1966a), *Topics in the Theory of Generative Grammar*, The Hague: Mouton

—— (1966b), *Cartesian Linguistics: A Chapter in the History of Rationalist Thought*, New York and London: Harper & Row

—— (1968), *Language and Mind*, New York: Harcourt, Brace & World

—— (1969), *American Power and the New Mandarins*, Harmondsworth: Penguin

—— (1973), *For Reasons of State*, London: Fontana

—— (1996), *Power and Prospects: Reflections on Human Nature and the Social Order*, London: Pluto Press

Cixous, Hélène (1969a), *Inside*, tr. Carol Barka, New York: Schocken Books

—— (1969b), *The Exile of James Joyce*, tr. Sally A. J. Purcell, London: John Calder, 1976

—— (1973), *Neutre*, Paris: éditions des femmes

—— (1975), 'The Laugh of the Medusa', tr. K. Cohen and P. Cohen in Marks and Courtivron (1979)

—— (1976), *Portrait of Dora*, tr. Anita Barrows, *Gambit International Theatre Review* 8, 1977

—— (1977), 'Coming to Writing' in Cixous (1981)

—— (1981), *Coming to Writing and Other Essays*, ed. Deborah Jenson, tr. Sarah Cornell et al., Cambridge, MA: Harvard University Press

—— (1985), *The Terrible but Unfinished Story of Norodom Sihanouk, King of Cambodia*, tr. Janet Flower MacCannell, Judith Pike and Lollie Grath, Lincoln: University of Nebraska Press, 1994

—— (1987), *L'Indiade ou L'Inde de leurs rêves et quelques écrits sur le théâtre*, Vincennes: Théâtre du Soleil

—— (1997), *Or les lehres de mon père*, Paris: éditions des femmes

—— and Calle-Gruber, Mireille (1994), *Rootprints: Memory and Life Writing*, tr. Eric Prenowitz, London and New York: Routledge, 1997

—— and Clément, Catherine (1975), *The Newly-Born Woman*, tr. Betsy Wing, Minneapolis: Minnesota University Press

——, Gagnon, Madeleine and Leclerc, Annie (1975), *La Venue à l'écriture*, Paris: Union Générale d'Éditions

Clark, Martin (1977), *Antonio Gramsci and the Revolution that Failed*, New Haven: Yale University Press

Clark, S. H. (1990), *Paul Ricoeur*, London: Routledge

Clark, T. J. (1973a), *Image of the People: Gustave Courbet and the 1848 Revolution*, London: Thames & Hudson

—— (1973b), *The Absolute Bourgeois: Artists and Politics in France 1848–1851*, London: Thames & Hudson

Clauzade, Laurent (1998), *L'Idéologie ou la révolution de l'analyse*, Paris: Gallimard

Cleaver, Eldridge (1969), *Soul on Ice: Selected Essays*, London: Jonathan Cape

Clément, Catherine (1981), 'Interview with Antoinette Fouque' in Duchen (1987)

Cockburn, Alexander and Blackburn, Robin, eds (1969), *Student Power: Problems, Diagnosis, Action*, Harmondsworth: Penguin

Cohen, Margaret (1993), *Profane Illuminations: Walter Benjamin and the Paris of the Surrealist Revolution*, Berkeley: University of California Press

Cohen, Mitchell (1994), *The Wager of Lucien Goldmann: Tragedy, Dialectics and a Hidden God*, Princeton: Princeton University Press

Cohen, Phil (1972), 'Subcultural Conflict and Working-Class Community', *Working Papers in Cultural Studies* 2

Cohen-Solal, Annie (1985), *Sartre: A Life*, London: Heinemann, 1987

Cole, G. D. H. and Postgate, Raymond (1938), *The Common People*, London: Methuen

Colletti, Lucio (1974), 'Introduction', tr. Tom Nairn in Marx (1975)

Communications (1966) 8: *Recherches sémiologiques: L'Analyse structurale du récit*

Communications (1968) 11: *Le Vraisemblable*

Comte, Auguste (1852–4), *Système de politique positive, ou traité de sociologie instituant la religion de l'humanité*, Osnabrück: Zeller, 1961, 4 vols, facsimile edn

Confiant, Raphaël (1993), *Aimé Césaire: une traversée paradoxale du siècle*, Paris: Stock

Conley, Katherine (1996), *Automatic Woman: The Representation of Women in Surrealism*, Lincoln and London: University of Nebraska Press

Connolly, Cyril (1965), *The Modern Movement: One Hundred Key Books from England, France and America 1880–1950*, André Deutsch and Hamish Hamilton

Conquest, Robert (1956), *New Lines*, London: Macmillan

Contat, Michel and Rybalka, Michel (1973), *The Writings of Jean-Paul Sartre*, Evanston, IL: Northwestern University Press

Cook, David and Okenimkpe, Michael (1997), *Ngugi wa Thiong'o: An Exploration of his Writings*, Oxford, Nairobi and Portsmouth, NJ: James Currey, EAEP, Heinemann

Cooper, Douglas and Tinterow, Gary (1983), *The Essential Cubism 1907–1920*, London: Tate Gallery

Coote, Anna and Campbell, Beatrix (1982), *Sweet Freedom: The Struggle for Women's Liberation*, London: Picador

Copjec, Joan, ed. (1993), *Shades of Noir*, London: Verso

Corzani, Jacques (1978), *La Littérature des Antilles-Guyane Françaises*, Fort-de-France: Désormeaux

Coward, Rosalind (1983), *Patriarchal Precedents: Sexuality and Social Relations*, London: Routledge & Kegan Paul

Cresson, André and Deleuze, Gilles (1952), *David Hume, sa vie, son oeuvre*, Paris: PUF

Crews, Frederick, et al. (1997), *The Memory Wars: Freud's Legacy in Dispute*, London: Granta Books

Cruikshank, Margaret (1992), *The Gay and Lesbian Liberation Movement*, New York and London: Routledge

Culler, Jonathan (1975), *Structuralist Poetics: Structuralism, Linguistics and the Study of Literature*, London: Routledge & Kegan Paul

—— (1976), *Saussure*, London: Fontana

—— (1983a), *On Deconstruction: Thought and Criticism After Structuralism*, London: Routledge & Kegan Paul

—— (1983b), *Roland Barthes*, London: Fontana

Curthoys, Jean (1997), *Feminist Amnesia: The Wake of Women's Liberation*, London and New York: Routledge

D'Alembert, Jean Le Rond (1751), *Discours préliminaire de l'Encyclopédie*, Paris: Librairie Armand Colin, 1919

Dada and Surrealism Reviewed, London: Arts Council of Great Britain, 1978

D'Agostino, Fred (1986), *Chomsky's System of Ideas*, Oxford: Clarendon Press

Dällenbach, Lucien (1977), *The Mirror in the Text*, tr. J. Whitely and E. Hughes, Cambridge: Polity Press, 1989

Daly, Mary (1968), *The Church and the Second Sex*, Boston: Beacon Press

—— (1973), *Beyond God the Father: Towards a Philosophy of Women's Liberation*, Boston: Beacon Press

—— (1978), *Gyn/Ecology: The Metaethics of Radical Feminism, with a new Intergalactic Introduction by the Author*, London: The Women's Press, 1991

—— (1984), *Pure Lust: Elemental Feminist Philosophy*, London: The Women's Press

—— (1988), *Webster's First New Intergalactic Wickedary*, London: The Women's Press

Damas, Léon-Gontran (1972), *Pigments; Névralgies*, Paris and Dakar: Présence africaine

Dantziger, Nick (1996), *Dantziger's Britain: A Journey to the Edge*, London: Harper-Collins

Dash, Michael (1995), *Edouard Glissant*, Cambridge: Cambridge University Press

Davies, Howard (1987), *Sartre and 'Les Temps Modernes'*, Cambridge: Cambridge University Press

Davis, Madeleine and Wallbridge, David (1980), *Boundary and Space: An Introduction to the Work of Donald Winnicott*, Harmondsworth: Penguin

Debord, Guy (1967), *The Society of the Spectacle*, Detroit: Black and Red, 1977

—— (1989), *Panégyrique*, Paris: Gallimard

—— (1993), *'Cette mauvaise réputation . . .'*, Paris: Gallimard

Deleuze, Gilles (1962), *Nietzsche and Philosophy*, tr. Hugh Tomlinson, London: Athlone Press, 1997

—— (1963), *The Critical Philosophy of Kant*, tr. Hugh Tomlinson and Barbara Habberjam: Minneapolis: University of Minnesota Press, 1984

—— (1964), *Proust and Signs*, tr. Richard Howard, New York: George Braziller

—— (1966), *Bergsonism*, tr. Hugh Tomlinson and Barbara Habberjam, New York: Zone Books, 1991

—— (1967), *Masochism: An Interpretation of Coldness and Cruelty*, tr. Jean McNeil, New York: George Braziller, 1971

—— (1968), *Difference and Repetition*, tr. Paul Patton, New York: Columbia University Press, 1994

—— (1969), *Logic of Sense*, tr. M. Lester, London: Athlone Press, 1990

—— (1981), *Francis Bacon: Logique de la sensation*, Paris: Éditions de la différence

—— (1983), *Cinema I: The Movement-Image*, tr. Hugh Tomlinson and Barbara Habberjam, Minneapolis: University of Minnesota Press, 1986

—— (1985), *Cinema II: The Time-Image*, tr. Hugh Tomlinson and R. Galeta, Minneapolis: University of Minnesota Press, 1986

—— (1986), *Foucault*, tr. Sean Hand, Minneapolis: University of Minnesota Press, 1988

—— (1990), *Negotiations 1972–1980*, tr. Martin Joughlin, New York: Columbia University Press, 1995

—— (1993), *Essays, Critical and Clinical*, tr. Daniel W. Smith and Michael E. Greco, London: Verso, 1998

—— and Guattari, Félix (1972), *Anti-Oedipus: Capitalism and Schizophrenia*, tr. Robert Hurley, Mark Seem and Helen R. Lane, New York: Viking, 1983

—— (1976), *Rhizome: Introduction*, tr. Paul Foss and Paul Patton, *Ideology and Consciousness* 8, Spring 1981

—— (1980), *A Thousand Plateaus: Capitalism and Schizophrenia*, tr. Brian Massumi, London: Athlone Press, 1987

—— (1991), *What is Philosophy?*, tr. Hugh Tomlinson and Graham Burchell, New York: Columbia University Press

—— and Parnet, Claire (1977), *Dialogues*, tr. Hugh Tomlinson and Barbara Habberjam, London: Athlone Press, 1987

De Man, Paul (1971), *Blindness and Insight: Essays in the Rhetoric of Contemporary Criticism*, London: Methuen, 2nd edn, 1983

—— (1979), *Allegories of Reading: Figural Language in Rousseau, Nietzsche, Rilke and Proust*, New Haven: Yale University Press

—— (1984), *The Rhetoric of Romanticism*, New York: Columbia University Press

—— (1986), *The Resistance to Theory*, Minneapolis: University of Minnesota Press

—— (1988), *Wartime Journalism, 1939–1943*, ed. Werner Hamacher, Niel Herz and Thomas Kernan, Lincoln: University of Nebraska Press

—— (1989), *Critical Writings 1953–1978*, Minneapolis: University of Minnesota Press

—— (1996), *Aesthetic Ideology*, Minneapolis: University of Minnesota Press

Denham, Robert (1974), *Northrop Frye: An Enumerative Bibliography*, Metuchen, NJ: Scarecrow Press

—— (1978), *Northrop Frye and Critical Method*, University Park: Pennsylvania University Press

Derrida, Jacques (1962), *Edmund Husserl's 'Origin of Geometry'*, tr. J. P. Leavey, New York: Harvester Press, 1978

—— (1963), 'The Cogito and the History of Madness' in Derrida (1967b)

—— (1965), 'Violence and Metaphysics: An Essay on the Thought of Emmanuel Levinas' in Derrida (1967b)

—— (1966a), 'Structure, Sign and Play in the Discourse of the Human Sciences' in Macksey and Donato (1972)

—— (1966b), 'Freud and the Scene of Writing' in Derrida (1967b)

—— (1967a), *Of Grammatology*, tr. Gayatri Chakravorty Spivak, Baltimore: Johns Hopkins University Press, 1977

—— (1967b), *Writing and Difference*, tr. Alan Bass, London: Routledge & Kegal Paul, 1978

—— (1967c), *Speech and Phenomena*, tr. D. B. Allison, Evanston, IL: Northwestern University Press, 1973

—— (1968), 'Plato's Pharmacy' in Derrida (1972a)

—— (1971), 'Signature Event Context' in Derrida (1972b)

—— (1972a), *Dissemination*, tr. Barbara Johnson, London: Athlone Press, 1981

—— (1972b), *Margins of Philosophy*, tr. Alan Bass, Brighton: Harvester Press

—— (1972c), *Positions*, tr. Alan Bass, London: Athlone Press

—— (1974), *Glas*, tr. J. P. Leavey and R. Rand, Lincoln: University of Nebraska Press

—— (1975), 'The Purveyor of Truth' in Derrida (1987)

—— (1978a), *Signéponge/Signsponge*, tr. R. Rand, New York: Columbia University Press, 1984, bilingual edn

—— (1978b), *Nietzsche's Styles: Spurs*, tr. B. Harlow, Chicago: University of Chicago Press

—— (1979), *The Post Card: From Socrates to Freud*, tr. Alan Bass, Chicago: University of Chicago Press, 1987

—— (1987), *De L'Esprit: Heidegger et la question*, Paris: Galilée

—— (1990), *Le Problème de la génèse dans la philosophie de Husserl*, Paris: PUF

—— (1991), 'To do Justice to Freud. The History of Madness in the Age of Psychoanalysis', tr. Pascale-Anne Brault and Michael Naas in Dufresne (1996)

—— (1994), *Spectres of Marx: The State of Debt, the Work of Mourning and the New International*, tr. Peggy Kamuf, London: Routledge

—— (1995), *Points . . . Interviews 1977–1994*, ed. Elisabeth Weber, tr. Peggy Kamuf et al., Stanford: Stanford University Press

—— (1966), *Résistances à la psychanalyse*, Paris: Galilée

Descartes, René (1637), 'Discourse on the Method', tr. Roger Stoothof in *The Philosophical Writings of Descartes* I, Cambridge: Cambridge University Press, 1985

—— (1641), *Meditations on First Philosophy, with Selections from the Objections and Replies*, tr. John Cottingham with an introduction by Bernard Williams, Cambridge: Cambridge University Press, 1986

—— (1649), *The Passions of the Soul* in *Philosophical Writings* I

Descombes, Vincent (1983), *Objects of All Sorts: A Philosophical Grammar*, tr. Lorna Scott-Fox and Jeremy Harding, Oxford: Blackwell

Destut de Tracy, Antoine (1803–18), *Éléments d'idéologie*, Paris: Librairie philosophique J. Vrin, 1970, 2 vols

Dews, Peter (1980), 'The "New Philosophers" and the End of Leftism', *Radical Philosophy* 24

Dilthey, Wilhelm (1900), 'The Rise of Hermeneutics', tr. Frederic Jameson, *New Literary History* vol. 3, no. 2, 1972

Diop, Cheikh Anta (1954), *Nations nègres et culture*, Paris and Dakar: Présence africaine

—— (1974), *The African Origins of Civilization: Myth or Reality*, tr. M. Cook, New York: Laurence Hill

Djebar, Assia (1980), *Femmes d'Alger dans leur appartement*, Paris: éditions des femmes

Döblin, Alfred (1929), *Berlin Alexanderplatz: The Story of Franz Biberkopf*, tr. Eugene Jolas, Harmondsworth: Penguin, 1978

Dobson, Andrew (1993), *Jean-Paul Sartre and the Politics of Reason: A Theory of History*, Cambridge: Cambridge University Press

Dolamore, James, ed. (1998), *Making Connections: Essays in French Culture and Society in Honour of Philip Thody*, Bern: Peter Lang

Dollimore, Jonathan (1991), *Sexual Dissidence: Augustine to Wilde, Freud to Foucault*, Oxford: Clarendon Press

—— and Sinfield, Alan, eds (1985), *Political Shakespeare: New Essays in Cultural Materialism*, Manchester: Manchester University Press

Donoghue, Denis (1989), 'The Strange Case of Paul de Man', *New York Review of Books*, 29 June

Doray, Bernard (1981), *From Taylorism to Fordism: A Rational Madness*, tr. David Macey, London: Free Association Books, 1988

Dorfles, Gillo (1969), *Kitsch: The World of Bad Taste*, New York: Universe Books

Dorfman, Joseph (1934), *Thorstein Veblen and his America*, New York: Viking Press

Doubrovsky, Serge (1966), *Pourquoi la nouvelle critique? Critique et objectivité*, Paris: Mercure de France

Douglas, Mary (1966), *Purity and Danger: An Analysis of Concepts of Pollution and Taboo*, London: Routledge

Dreyfus, Hubert (1991), *Being-in-the-World: A Commentary on Heidegger's Being and Time, Division I*, Cambridge, MA: MIT Press

—— and Hall, H. (1992), *Heidegger: A Critical Reader*, Oxford: Blackwell

Drury, Shadia B. (1994), *Alexandre Kojève: The Roots of Postmodern Politics*, Basingstoke: Macmillan

Duberman, Martin (1993), *Stonewall*, New York: Dutton Signet

Du Bois, W. E. B. (1903), *The Souls of Black Folk*, Harmondsworth: Penguin, 1989

Duchen, Claire, ed. (1987), *French Connections: Voices from the Women's Movement in France*, London: Hutchinson

Ducrot, Oswald, ed. (1968), *Qu'est-ce que le structuralisme?*, Paris: Seuil

—— and Todorov, Tzvetan (1972), *Encyclopedic Dictionary of the Sciences of Language*, tr. Catherine Porter, Oxford: Blackwell, 1980

Dufresne, Todd, ed. (1996), *Returns of the 'French Freud': Freud, Lacan and Beyond*, London: Routledge

Dummet, Michael (1973), *Frege's Philosophy of Language*, London: Duckworth

—— (1978), *Truth and Other Enigmas*, London: Duckworth

During, Simon (1992), *Foucault and Literature: Towards a Genealogy of Writing*, London: Routledge

Durkheim, Emile (1893), *The Division of Labor in Society*, tr. W. D. Halls, New York: Free Press, 1984

—— (1912), *The Elementary Form of the Religious Life: A Study in Religious Sociology*, tr. J. W. Swain, London: Allen & Unwin, 1915

Dworkin, Andrea (1974), *Woman-Hating*, London: Women's Press

—— (1981), *Pornography: Men Possessing Women*, London: Women's Press

—— (1987), *Intercourse*, London: Martin Secker & Warburg

—— (1997), *Life and Death: Unapologetic Essays on the Continuing War Against Women*, London: Virago

Eagleton, Mary, ed. (1986), *Feminist Literary Theory: A Reader*, Oxford: Blackwell

Eagleton, Terry (1975a), *Myths of Power: A Marxist Study of the Brontës*, London: New Left Books

—— (1975b), 'Machery and Marxist Literary Theory' in Eagleton (1986)

—— (1976), *Criticism and Ideology*, London: New Left Books

—— (1981), *Walter Benjamin or Towards a Revolutionary Criticism*, London: New Left Books

—— (1983), *Literary Theory: An Introduction*, Oxford: Blackwell

—— (1984), *The Function of Criticism: From the Spectator to Post-Structuralism*, London: Verso

—— (1986), *Against the Grain: Selected Essays*, London: Verso

—— (1988), 'The Silences of David Lodge', *New Left Review* 172

—— (1991), *Ideology: An Introduction*, London: Verso

—— (1995), 'The Death of Self-Criticism', *Times Literary Supplement*, 24 November

—— (1996), *Heathcliff and the Great Hunger*, London: Verso

Eco, Umberto (1966), 'James Bond: une combinatoire narrative', *Communications* 8

—— (1975), 'Travels in Hyperreality' in Eco (1986)

—— (1976), *A Theory of Semiotics*, Bloomington: Indiana University Press, 1979

—— (1986), *Travels in Hyperreality*, tr. William Weaver, New York: Harcourt Brace Jovanovich

Economy and Society (1998) vol. 27 nos 2–3: *Society and the Life Sciences: In Honour of Georges Canguilhem*

Eikhenbaum, Boris M. (1926), 'The Theory of the Formal Method' in Matejka and Pomorska (1971)

Eisenstein, Hester (1984), *Contemporary Feminist Thought*, London: Unwin

Eisenstein, Sergei M. (1942), *The Film Sense*, tr. Jay Leyda, New York: Harcourt Brace Jovanovich

—— (1949), *Film Form*, tr. Jay Leyda, New York: Harcourt Brace Jovanovich

Eisner, Lotte H. (1965), *The Haunted Screen: Expressionism in the German Cinema and the Influence of Max Reinhardt*, tr. Roger Greaves, London: Secker & Warburg, 1973

Eldridge, John and Eldridge, Lizzie (1994), *Raymond Williams: Making Connections*, London: Routledge

Ellenberger, Henri F. (1970), *The Discovery of the Unconscious: The History and Evolution of Dynamic Psychiatry*, New York: Basic Books

Elliott, Gregory (1987), *Althusser: The Detour of Theory*, London: Verso

——, ed. (1994), *Althusser: A Critical Reader*, Oxford: Blackwell

—— (1995), 'Olympus Mislaid? A Profile of Perry Anderson', *Radical Philosophy* 71

Ellison, Ralph (1952), *Invisible Man*, Harmondsworth: Penguin, 1965

Empson, William (1930), *Seven Types of Ambiguity*, Harmondsworth: Penguin, 1995, 3rd edn

—— (1935), *Some Versions of Pastoral*, London: Chatto & Windus

—— (1951), *The Structure of Complex Words*, London: Chatto & Windus

—— (1955), *Collected Poems*, London: Chatto & Windus

—— (1961), *Milton's God*, London: Chatto & Windus

Engels, Frederick (1878), *Anti-Dühring (Herr Eugen Dühring's Revolution in Science)*, Beijing: Foreign Languages Press, 1976

—— (1875–82), *Dialectics of Nature*, New York: International Publishers, 1940

—— (1884), *The Origins of the Family, Private Property and the State*, Harmondsworth: Penguin, 1985

—— (1892), *Socialism: Utopian and Scientific*, New York: International Publishers, 1975

Enright, D. J. (1955), *Poets of the 1950s*, Tokyo: Kenkyska

Erlich, Victor (1965), *Russian Formalism: History – Doctrine*, The Hague: Mouton

Ernst, Anna-Sabine and Klinger, Gerwin (1997), 'Socialist Socrates: Ernst Bloch in the GDR', tr. Ulrike Kistner, *Radical Philosophy* 84

Esprit (1958): *Le Nouveau Roman*, July–August

Esslin, Martin (1968), *The Theatre of the Absurd*, Harmondsworth: Penguin, rev. and enlarged edn

—— (1980), *Brecht: A Choice of Evils. A Critical Study of the Man, his Work and his Opinions*, London: Eyre Methuen

Evans, Dylan (1996), *An Introductory Dictionary of Lacanian Psychoanalysis*, London: Routledge

Faderman, Lillian (1981), *Surpassing the Love of Men: Romantic Friendship and Love Between Women from the Renaissance to the Present*, New York: William Morrow

Fallaize, Elizabeth (1998), *Simone de Beauvoir: A Critical Reader*, Oxford: Blackwell

Faludi, Susan (1991), *Backlash: The Undeclared War Against American Women*, New York: Crown

Fanon, Frantz (1952a), *Black Skin, White Masks*, tr. Charles Lam Markmann, New York: Grove Press, 1965

—— (1952b), 'The North-African Syndrome' in Fanon (1964)

—— (1961), *The Wretched of the Earth*, tr. Constance Farringdon, London: MacGibbon and Kee, 1965

—— (1964), *Towards the African Revolution*, tr. Haakon Chevalier, New York: Grove Press, 1967

Farias, Victor (1987), *Heidegger and Nazism*, tr. Joseph Margolis and Tom Rockmore, Philadelphia: Temple University Press, 1989

Fauchereau, Serge (1994), *Mondrian and the Neo-Plasticist Utopia*, tr. David Macey, London: Academy Editions

Febvre, Lucien (1942), *The Problem of Unbelief in the Sixteenth Century: The Religion of Rabelais*, tr. Beatrice Gottlieb, Cambridge, MA: Harvard University Press, 1983

Feibleman, James K. (1960), *An Introduction to Peirce's Philosophy*, London: Allen & Unwin

Feigl, A. and Sellars, W., eds (1948), *Readings in Philosophical Analysis*, New York: Appleton-Century-Crofts

Felman, Shoshona (1977), 'Turning the Screw of Interpretation', *Yale French Studies* 55–6

Ferenczi, Sandor (1909), 'Introjection and Transference' in Ferenczi (1955)

—— (1955), *Final Contributions to Psycho-analysis*, London: Hogarth Press and the Institute of Psychoanalysis

Ferguson, Niall, ed. (1997), *Virtual History: Alternatives and Counterfactuals*, London: Picador

Feyerabend, Paul (1975), *Against Method*, London: Verso

—— (1981a), *Realism, Rationalism and Scientific Method (Philosophical Papers 1)*, Cambridge: Cambridge University Press

—— (1981b), *Problems of Empiricism (Philosophical Papers 2)*, Cambridge: Cambridge University Press

—— (1992), *Farewell to Reason*, London: Verso

—— (1995), *Killing Time: The Autobiography of Paul Feyerabend*, Chicago: University of Chicago Press

Ffrench, Patrick (1995), *The Time of Theory: A History of 'Tel Quel' (1960–1983)*, Oxford: Clarendon Press

—— and Lack, Roland-François, eds (1998), *The* Tel Quel *Reader*, London: Routledge

Fichte, Johann Gottlieb (1794), *Science of Knowledge*, ed. and tr. Peter Heath and John Lachs, Cambridge: Cambridge University Press, 1982

Fiori, Giuseppe (1965), *Antonio Gramsci: Life of a Revolutionary*, tr. Tom Nairn, London: New Left Books, 1970

Firestone, Shulamith (1971), *The Dialectic of Sex: The Case for Feminist Revolution*, London: Jonathan Cape

Firth, J. R. (1951), 'Modes of Meaning' in Firth (1964)

—— (1964), *Papers on Linguistics 1934–1951*, London: Oxford University Press

Fish, Stanley (1967), *Surprised by Sin: The Reader in Paradise Lost*, New York: St Martin's Press

—— (1980), *Is There a Text in this Class?: The Authority of Interpretive Communities*, Cambridge, MA: Harvard University Press

—— (1995), *Professional Correctness: Literary Studies and Political Change*, Oxford: Clarendon Press

Flaubert, Gustave (1857), *Madame Bovary*, tr. Alan Russell, Harmondsworth: Penguin, 1950

—— (1877), 'A Simple Heart' in *Three Tales*, tr. A. J. Krailsheimer, Oxford: World's Classics, 1991

—— (1881), *Bouvard and Pécuchet, with the Dictionary of Received Ideas*, tr. A. J. Krailsheimer, Harmondsworth: Penguin, 1976

Fletcher, Angus (1964), *Allegory: The Theory of a Symbolic Mode*, Ithaca: Cornell University Press

Flew, A. G. N. (1951), *Logic and Language*, Oxford: Blackwell

Flores, Angel (1955), 'Magical Realism in Spanish American Fiction', *Hispania* vol. 38 no. 2

Fodor, J. A. and Katz, J. J. (1964), *The Structure of Language: Readings in the Philosophy of Language*, Eagleton Cliffs, NJ: Prentice-Hall

Fordham, Frieda (1953), *An Introduction to Jung's Psychology*, Harmondsworth: Penguin, 1966, rev. edn

Forster, Penny and Sutton, Imogen (1989), *Daughters of de Beauvoir*, London: Women's Press

Foucault, Michel (1961), *Folie et déraison: Histoire de la folie à l'âge classique*, Paris: Plon

—— (1963a), *Birth of the Clinic*, tr. A. M. Sheridan, London: Tavistock, 1973

—— (1963b), *Death and the Labyrinth: The World of Raymond Roussel*, tr. Charles Ruas, London: Athlone Press, 1987

—— (1966), *The Order of Things*, London: Tavistock

—— (1967), *Madness and Civilization: A History of Insanity in the Age of Reason*, tr. Richard Howard, London: Tavistock

—— (1969a), *The Archaeology of Knowledge*, tr. A. M. Sheridan Smith, London: Tavistock, 1972

—— (1969b), 'What is an Author?', tr. Josué V. Harari in Foucault (1986)

—— (1971a), 'Nietzsche, Genealogy, History', tr. Donald F. Bouchard and Sherry Simon in Foucault (1986)

—— (1971b), 'Monstrosities in Criticism', tr. F. Durand-Bogaert, *Diacritics* vol. 1 no. 1, Autumn 1971

—— (1972), 'My Body, This Paper, This Fire', tr. Geoff Bennington, *Oxford Literary Review* vol. 4 no. 1, Autumn 1979

—— (1975), *Discipline and Punish: The Birth of the Prison*, tr. Alan Sheridan, London: Allen Lane, 1977

—— (1976a), *The History of Sexuality* I: *An Introduction*, tr. Robert Hurley, London: Allen Lane, 1979

—— (1976b), 'The Politics of Health in the Eighteenth Century' in Foucault (1980b)

—— (1977a), 'Le Jeu de Michel Foucault: sur *L'Histoire de la Sexualité*' in Foucault (1994) III

—— (1977b), 'Theatrum philosophicum' in Foucault (1980b)

—— (1978), Introduction to Canguilhem (1950)

—— (1979), 'Naissance de la biopolitique' in Foucault (1994) III

—— (1980a), Introduction to *Herculine Barbin: Being the Recently Discovered Memoirs of a Nineteenth-Century French Hermaphrodite*, tr. Richard MacDougal, Brighton: Harvester Press

—— (1980b), *Power/Knowledge: Selected Interviews and Other Writings 1972–1977*, ed. Colin Gordon, New York: Pantheon

—— (1984a), *The Use of Pleasure: The History of Sexuality* II, tr. Robert Hurley, Harmondsworth: Penguin, 1987

—— (1984b), *The Care of the Self: The History of Sexuality* III, tr. Robert Hurley, Harmondsworth: Penguin, 1987

—— (1984c), 'The Concern for Truth', tr. Alan Sheridan, in Foucault (1988)

—— (1986), *The Foucault Reader*, ed. Paul Rabinow, Harmondsworth: Penguin, 1986

—— (1988), *Politics, Philosophy, Culture: Interviews and Other Writings 1977–1984*, ed. Lawrence Kritzman, London: Routledge

—— (1994), *Dits et écrits 1954–1988*, ed. Daniel Defert and François Ewald, Paris: Gallimard, 4 vols

—— (1997), *The Essential Works. I: Ethics. Subjectivity and Truth*, ed. Paul Rabinow, London: Allen Lane

—— and Binswanger, Ludwig (1954), *Dream and Existence*, tr. Forest Williams and Jacob Needleman, ed. Keith Hoeller, Atlantic Highlands, NJ: Humanities Press, 1993

Fowler, Alistair (1982), *Kinds of Literature: An Introduction to the Theory of Genres and Modes*, Oxford: Clarendon Press

Fowler, Roger, ed. (1970), *Essays on Style and Language: Linguistic and Critical Approaches to Literary Style*, London: Routledge & Kegan Paul

—— (1981), *Literature as Social Discourse: The Practice of Linguistic Criticism*, London: Batsford

—— (1986), *Linguistic Criticism*, Oxford: Oxford University Press

—— (1991), *Language in the News*, London: Routledge

Franco, Jean (1970), *The Modern Culture of Latin America: Society and the Artist*, Harmondsworth: Penguin, rev. edn

Frank, Manfred (1977), *Das Individuelle-Allgemeine: Textstrukturierung und Interpretatione nach Schleiermacher*, Frankfurt-am-Main: Suhrkamp

—— (1980), 'The Infinite Text', *Glyph* 7

—— (1984), *What is Neo-Structuralism?*, tr. Richard Gray, Minneapolis: University of Minnesota Press

—— (1986), *Die Unhintergehbarkeit von Individualität, Reflexionen über Subjekt, Person und Individuum aus Anlass ihrer 'postmodernen' Totenklärung*, Frankfurt-am-Main: Suhrkamp

—— (1989), *Einführung in die frühromantischer Esthetik*, Frankfurt-am-Main: Suhrkamp

—— (1992a), *Stil in der Philosophie*, Stuttgart: Reclam

—— (1992b), 'Is self-consciousness a case of *présence à soi*? Towards a Metacritique of the Recent French Critique of Metaphysics', tr. Andrew Bowie in Wood (1992)

—— (1997), *The Subject and the Text: Essays on Literary Theory and Philosophy*, tr. Helen Atkins, ed. with an introduction by Andrew Bowie, Cambridge: Cambridge University Press

Frank, Nino (1946), 'Un Nouveau Genre "policier": l'aventure criminelle', *L'Écran français*, August

Fraser, Ronald (1979), *Blood of Spain: The Experience of Civil War 1936–1939*, London: Allen Lane

Frazer, George James (1890–1915), *The Golden Bough: A Study in Magic and Religion*, 12 vols, London: Macmillan

Frege, Gottlob (1879), 'Conceptual Notation and Related Articles', tr. and ed. Terrel Ward Byaum, Oxford: Clarendon Press, 1972

—— (1884), *The Foundations of Arithmetic: A Logico-Mathematical Inquiry into the Concept of Number*, tr. J. L. Austin, Oxford: Basil Blackwell, 1950

—— (1892a), 'On Sense and Meaning', tr. Max Black, in Frege (1952)

—— (1892b), 'On Concept and Object', tr. P. T. Geach, in Frege (1952)

—— (1893–1903), *The Basic Laws of Arithmetic: Exposition of the System*, tr. Montgomery Furth, Berkeley: University of California Press, 1964

—— (1952), *Translations from the Philosophical Writings of Gottlob Frege*, ed. Peter Geach and Max Black, Oxford: Basil Blackwell

Freud, Anna (1936), *The Ego and the Mechanisms of Defence*, London: Hogarth Press and the Institute of Psychoanalysis

—— (1966), *Normality and Pathology in Childhood: Assessment of Development*, Harmondsworth: Penguin, 1973

—— (1998), *Selected Writings*, ed. with an introduction by Richard Ekins and Ruth Freeman, Harmondsworth: Penguin

Freud, Sigmund (1895), 'Project for a Scientific Psychology', *Standard Edition* I

—— (1896), 'The Aetiology of Hysteria', *Standard Edition*, 1953–73, II

—— (1899), 'Screen Memories', *Standard Edition* III

—— (1900), *The Interpretation of Dreams, Standard Edition* IV–V; *Penguin Freud Library* IV

—— (1901), *The Psychopathology of Everyday Life, Standard Edition* VI; *Penguin Freud Library* V

—— (1905a), *Three Essays on the Theory of Sexuality, Standard Edition* VII; *Penguin Freud Library* VII

—— (1905b), *Jokes and their Relation to the Unconscious, Standard Edition* VIII; *Penguin Freud Library* VI

—— (1905c), 'Fragment of an Analysis of a Case of Hysteria', *Standard Edition* VII; *Penguin Freud Library* VIII

—— (1907), 'Delusions and Dreams in Jensen's *Gradiva*', *Standard Edition* XIX; *Penguin Freud Library* XIV

—— (1908a), 'On the Sexual Theories of Children', *Standard Edition* IX; *Penguin Freud Library* VII

—— (1908b), 'Creative Writers and Day-Dreaming', *Standard Edition* IX; *Penguin Freud Library* XIV

—— (1909a), 'Family Romances', *Standard Edition* IX; *Penguin Freud Library* VII

—— (1909b), 'Notes upon a Case of Obsessional Neurosis (The "Rat Man")', *Standard Edition* X; *Penguin Freud Library* XI

—— (1910a), 'Leonardo da Vinci and a Memory of his Childhood', *Standard Edition* XI; *Penguin Freud Library* XIV

—— (1910b), 'The Antithetical Meaning of Primal Words', *Standard Edition* XI

—— (1910c), 'A Special Type of Choice of Object Made by Men', *Standard Edition* XI; *Penguin Freud Library* VII

—— (1911a), 'Formulations on the Two Principles of Mental Functioning', *Standard Edition* XII; *Penguin Freud Library* XI

—— (1911b), 'Psycho-analytic Notes on an Autobiographical Account of a Case of Paranoia (Dementia Paranoides)', *Standard Edition* XII; *Penguin Freud Library* XI

—— (1912a), 'The Dynamics of Transference', *Standard Edition* XII

—— (1912b), 'Recommendations to Physicians Practising Psychoanalysis', *Standard Edition* XII

—— (1913), *Totem and Taboo*, *Standard Edition* XIII; *Penguin Freud Library* XII

—— (1914a), 'On Narcissism: An Introduction', *Standard Edition* XIV; *Penguin Freud Library* XI

—— (1914b), 'The Moses of Michelangelo', *Standard Edition* XII; *Penguin Freud Library* XIV

—— (1914c), 'Remembering, Repeating and Working Through [Further Recommendations on the Technique of Psychoanalysis]', *Standard Edition* XII

—— (1914d), 'On the History of the Psychoanalytic Movement', *Standard Edition* XIV; *Penguin Freud Library* XV

—— (1915a), 'Instincts and their Vicissitudes', *Standard Edition* XIV; *Penguin Freud Library* XI

—— (1915b), 'The Unconscious', *Standard Edition* XIV; *Penguin Freud Library* XI

—— (1915c), 'Repression', *Standard Edition* XIV; *Penguin Freud Library* XI

—— (1915d), 'A Phylogenetic Fantasy: Overview of the Transference Neuroses', tr. Alex Hoffer and Peter T. Hoffer, ed. Ilse Grumrich-Similis, New Haven: Harvard University Press, 1987

—— (1916–17), *Introductory Lectures on Psychoanalysis*, *Standard Edition* XV–XVI; *Penguin Freud Library* I

—— (1917a), 'A Metapsychological Supplement to the Theory of Dreams', *Standard Edition*, XIV; *Penguin Freud Library* XI

—— (1917b), 'Mourning and Melancholia', *Standard Edition* XIV; *Penguin Freud Library* XI

—— (1918), 'From the History of an Infantile Neurosis', *Standard Edition* XVII; *Penguin Freud Library* IX

—— (1919), 'The Uncanny', *Standard Edition* XVII; *Penguin Freud Library* XIV

—— (1920a), 'Beyond the Pleasure Principle', *Standard Edition* XVIII; *Penguin Freud Library* XI

—— (1920b), 'The Psychogenesis of a Case of Homosexuality in a Woman', *Standard Edition* XVIII; *Penguin Freud Library* IX

—— (1921), 'Group Psychology and the Analysis of the Ego', *Standard Edition* XVII; *Penguin Freud Library* XII

—— (1922a), 'Medusa's Head', *Standard Edition* XVIII

—— (1922b), 'Some Neurotic Symbols in Jealousy, Paranoia and Homosexuality', *Standard Edition* XVIII; *Penguin Freud Library* X

—— (1922c), 'Two Encyclopedia Articles', *Standard Edition* XVIII; *Penguin Freud Library* XV

—— (1923a), 'The Ego and the Id', *Standard Edition* XIX; *Penguin Freud Library* XI

—— (1923b), 'The Infantile Genital Organization: An Interpolation into the Theory of Sexuality', *Standard Edition* XIX; *Penguin Freud Library* VII

—— (1924a), 'The Economic Problem of Masochism', *Standard Edition* XIX

—— (1924b), 'The Dissolution of the Oedipus Complex', *Standard Edition* XIX; *Penguin Freud Library* VII

—— (1924c), 'The Loss of Reality in Neurosis and Psychosis', *Standard Edition* XIX; *Penguin Freud Library* X

—— (1924d), 'Neurosis and Psychosis', *Standard Edition* XIX; *Penguin Freud Library* X

—— (1925), 'Some Psychical Consequences of the Anatomical Distinction between the Sexes', *Standard Edition* XIX; *Penguin Freud Library* VII

—— (1926a), 'The Question of Lay Analysis', *Standard Edition* XX; *Penguin Freud Library* XV

—— (1926b), 'Inhibitions, Symptoms and Anxiety', *Standard Edition* XX; *Penguin Freud Library* X

—— (1927a), 'Dostoievsky and Parricide', *Standard Edition* XXI; *Penguin Freud Library* XIV

—— (1927b), *The Future of an Illusion*, *Standard Edition* XXI; *Penguin Freud Library* XII

—— (1927c), 'Fetishism', *Standard Edition* XXI; *Penguin Freud Library* VII

—— (1930), *Civilization and its Discontents*, *Standard Edition* XXI; *Penguin Freud Library* XII

—— (1931a), 'Female Sexuality', *Standard Edition* XXI; *Penguin Freud Library* VII

—— (1931b), 'Libidinal Types', *Standard Edition* XXI; *Penguin Freud Library* VII

—— (1933), *New Introductory Lectures on Psychoanalysis*, *Standard Edition* XXII; *Penguin Freud Library* II

—— (1938), 'An Outline of Psychoanalysis', *Standard Edition* XXIII; *Penguin Freud Library* XV

—— (1939), *Moses and Monotheism*, *Standard Edition* XXIII; *Penguin Freud Library* XIII

—— (1953–74), *The Standard Edition of the Complete Psychological Works of Sigmund Freud*, London: Hogarth Press and Institute of Psychoanalysis, 24 vols

—— (1974–86), *The Penguin Freud Library*, Harmondsworth: Penguin, 15 vols

—— (1985), *The Complete Letters of Sigmund Freud to Wilhelm Fliess 1887–1904*, tr. and ed. Jeffrey Moussaieff Masson, Cambridge, MA: The Belknap Press of Harvard University Press

—— and Breuer, Joseph (1893–5), *Studies on Hysteria*, *Penguin Freud Library* III

—— and Jung, Carl Gustav (1974), *The Freud/Jung Letters: The Correspondence between Sigmund Freud and C. G. Jung*, ed. William McGuire, tr. Ralph Mannheim and R. F. C. Hull, London: Hogarth Press and Routledge & Kegan Paul

Friedan, Betty (1963), *The Feminine Mystique*, New York: W. W. Norton

—— (1981), *The Second Stage*, London: Abacus

Fromm, Erich (1941), *Escape from Freedom*, New York: Farrar & Rinehart

—— (1956), *The Art of Loving*, New York: Harper & Row

—— (1963), *The Crisis of Psychoanalysis*, New York: Holt, Rinehart & Winston

—— (1985), *The Erich Fromm Reader: Readings Selected and Edited by Rainer Funk*, Atlantic Highlands, NJ: Humanities Press, 1994

Frye, Northrop (1947), *Fearful Symmetry: A Study of William Blake*, Princeton: Princeton University Press

—— (1957), *Anatomy of Criticism: Four Essays*, Princeton: Princeton University Press

—— (1963), *Fables of Identity: Studies in Poetic Mythology*, New York: Harcourt, Brace & World

—— (1965a), *A Natural Perspective: The Development of Shakespearean Comedy and Romance*, New York: Harcourt, Brace & World

—— (1965b), *The Return of Eden: Five Studies in Milton's Epics*, Toronto: University of Toronto Press

—— (1967), *Fools of Time: Studies in Shakespearean Tragedy*, Toronto: University of Toronto Press

—— (1970), *The Stubborn Structure: Essays on Criticism and Society*, London: Methuen

—— (1971), *The Critical Path: An Essay on the Social Context of Literary Criticism*, Indianapolis: Indiana University Press

—— (1982), *The Great Code: The Bible and Literature*, London: Routledge & Kegan Paul

Fukuyama, Francis (1989), 'The End of History?', *The National Interest* 16

—— (1992), *The End of History and the Last Man*, London: Hamish Hamilton

—— (1996), *Trust: The Social Virtues and the Creation of Prosperity*, London: Hamish Hamilton

—— (1997), *The End of Order*, London: Social Market Foundation

Futurismo 1909–1919: Exhibition of Italian Futurism, Newcastle-upon-Tyne and Edinburgh: Northern Arts and Scottish Arts Council, 1972

Gadamer, Hans-Georg (1960), *Truth and Method*, tr. rev. by Joel Weinsheimer and Donald G. Marshall, New York: Continuum, 1998

—— (1966a), 'The Universality of the Hermeneutical Problem' in Gadamer (1976)

—— (1966b), 'Man and Language' in Gadamer (1976)

—— (1968), *Platos dialektische Ethik*, Hamburg: Meiner, 2nd edn

—— (1976), *Philosophical Hermeneutics*, tr. and ed. David E. Linge, Berkeley: University of California Press

—— (1981), *Reason in the Age of Science*, tr. Frederick G. Lawrence, Cambridge, MA: MIT Press

Gadet, Françoise (1986), *Saussure and Contemporary Culture*, tr. Gregory Elliott, London: Hutchinson Radius, 1989

Gallop, Jane (1982), *Feminism and Psychoanalysis: The Daughter's Seduction*, London: Macmillan

Gane, Mike (1991a), *Baudrillard: Critical and Fatal Theory*, London: Routledge

—— (1991b), *Baudrillard's Bestiary: Baudrillard and Culture*, London: Routledge

——, ed. (1993), *Baudrillard Live: Selected Interviews*, London: Routledge

Garvey, Amy Jacques (1969), *The Philosophy and Opinions of Marcus Garvey*, New York: Atheneum

Garvi, Paul L., ed. (1964), *A Prague School Reader on Esthetics, Literary Structure and Style*, Washington, DC: Georgetown University Press

Gasché, Rodolphe (1998), *The Wild Card of Reading: On Paul de Man*, Cambridge, MA: Harvard University Press

Gates, Henry Louis Jr (1987), *Figures in Black: Words, Signs and the 'Racial' Self*, New York and Oxford: Oxford University Press

—— (1988), *The Signifying Monkey: A Theory of African-American Literary Criticism*, New York and Oxford: Oxford University Press

—— (1992), *Loose Canons: Notes on the Culture of Wars*, New York and Oxford: Oxford University Press

Gauthier, Xavière (1971), *Surréalisme et sexualité*, Paris: Gallimard

Gavron, Hannah (1966), *The Captive Wife: Conflicts of Housebound Mothers*, London: Routledge & Kegal Paul

Gay, Paul du, et al. (1997a), *Doing Cultural Studies: The Story of the Sony Walkman*, London: Sage

—— (1997b), *Production of Culture/Culture of Production*, London: Sage

Gay, Peter (1983), *Freud: A Life for our Times*, London: Dent

Gay Left Collective (1980), *Homosexuality: Power and Politics*, London: Allison & Busby

Geertz, Clifford James (1960), *The Religion of Java*, Glencoe, IL: Free Press

—— (1968), *Islam Observed: Religious Development in Morocco and Indonesia*, New Haven: Yale University Press

—— (1973), *The Interpretation of Cultures: Selected Essays*, New York: Basic Books

—— (1983), *Local Knowledge: Further Essays in Interpretive Anthropology*, New York: Basic Books

—— (1988), *Works and Lives: The Anthropologist as Author*, Cambridge: Polity Press

Gelb, I. J. (1952), *A Study of Writing: The Foundations of Grammatology*, Chicago: University of Chicago Press

Gellner, Ernst (1953), *Words and Things*, Harmondsworth: Penguin, 1968

—— (1983), *Nations and Nationalisms*, Oxford: Blackwell

—— (1994), *Conditions of Liberty: Civil Society and its Rivals*, Harmondsworth: Penguin, 1996

Genette, Gérard (1966a), 'Frontières du récit' in Genette (1972)

—— (1966b), *Figures* I, Paris: Seuil

—— (1966c), 'Raisons de la critique pure' in Genette (1969)

—— (1969), *Figures* II, Paris: Seuil

—— (1970), 'Rhetoric Restrained' in Genette (1982)

—— (1972), *Figures* III, Paris: Seuil

—— (1982a), *Palimpsestes: la littérature au second degré*, Paris: Seuil

—— (1982b), *Figures of Literary Discourse*, tr. Alan Sheridan, introduction by Marie Rose Logan, New York: Columbia University Press

—— (1987), *Paratexts: Thresholds of Interpretation*, tr. Jane Lewin, Cambridge: Cambridge University Press, 1998

Genosko, Gary, ed. (1996), *The Guattari Reader*, Oxford: Blackwell

Geoffrey, G. (1920), *Constantin Guys, l'historien du Second Empire*, Paris: Gallimard

Geoghegan, Vincent (1996), *Ernst Bloch*, London: Routledge

Geraghty, C. (1991), *Women and Soap Opera: A Study of Prime Time Soaps*, London: Sage

Germain, Edward B. (1978), *Surrealist Poetry in English*, Harmondsworth: Penguin

Gershman, Herbert S. (1969), *The Surrealist Revolution in France*, Ann Arbor: University of Michigan Press

Geuss, Raymond (1981), *The Idea of a Critical Theory: Habermas and the Frankfurt School*, Cambridge: Cambridge University Press

Giddens, Anthony (1991), *Modernity and Self-Identity: Self and Society in the Late Modern Age*, Cambridge: Polity Press

Gide, André (1925), *The Vatican Cellars*, tr. Dorothy Bussy, Harmondsworth: Penguin, 1989

Gilbert, Sandra M. and Gubar, Susan (1979a), *The Madwoman in the Attic: The Woman Writer and the Nineteenth-Century Literary Imagination*, New Haven: Yale University Press

——, eds (1979b), *Shakespeare's Sisters: Feminist Essays on Women Poets*, Bloomington: Indiana University Press

——, eds (1985), *The Norton Anthology of Literature by Women: The Tradition in English*, New York: W. W. Norton

——, eds (1986), *The Female Imagination and the Modernist Aesthetic*, New York: Gordon and Breech

—— (1987), *No Man's Land: The Place of the Woman Writer in the Twentieth Century* I: *The War of the Words*, New Haven: Yale University Press

—— (1988a), *No Man's Land: The Place of the Woman Writer in the Twentieth Century* II: *Sexchanges*, New Haven: Yale University Press

—— (1988b), *No Man's Land: The Place of the Woman Writer in the Twentieth Century* III: *Letters from the Front*, New Haven: Yale University Press

Gilbert, Stuart (1950), *James Joyce's Ulysses*, New York: Alfred A. Knopf

Gilroy, Paul (1987), *There Ain't No Black in the Union Jack*, London: Hutchinson

—— (1993a), *The Black Atlantic: Modernity and Double Consciousness*, London: Verso

—— (1993b), *Small Acts: Thoughts on the Politics of Black Cultures*, London: Serpent's Tail

Ginzburg, Carlo (1966), *I Benandanti: richerche sulla streganania et sui culti tra Cinquecento e Seicento*, Turin: Einaudi

—— (1976), *The Cheese and the Worms: The Cosmos of a Sixteenth-Century Miller*, tr. John and Anne Tedeschi, Baltimore: Johns Hopkins University Press, 1980

Giroud, Françoise (1958), *La Nouvelle Vague: Portraits de la jeunesse*, Paris: Gallimard

Glissant, Édouard (1958), *The Ripening*, tr. J. Michael Dash, London: Heinemann, 1985

—— (1981), *Caribbean Discourse*, tr. J. Michael Dash, Charlottesville: University of Virginia Press, 1989

—— (1990), *Poetics of Relation*, tr. Betsy Wing, Ann Arbor: University of Michigan Press, 1998

Glucksmann, André (1975), *La Cuisinière et le mangeur d'hommes: Essai sur l'État, le marxisme, les camps de concentration*, Paris: Seuil

—— (1977), *The Master-Thinkers*, tr. Brian Pearce, Brighton: Harvester Press

Goldberg, Jonathan, ed. (1994), *Queering the Renaissance*, Durham, NC and London: Duke University Press

Goldthorpe, Rhiannon (1984), *Sartre, Literature and Theatre*, Cambridge: Cambridge University Press

Goldmann, Lucien (1959), *The Hidden God: A Study of Tragic Vision in the 'Pensées' of Pascal and the Tragedies of Racine*, tr. Philip Thody, London: Routledge & Kegan Paul, 1964

—— (1965), *Towards a Sociology of the Novel*, tr. Alan Sheridan, London: Tavistock, 1975

Gombrich, Ernst Hans Josef (1950), *The Story of Art*, London: Phaidon

—— (1960), *Art and Illusion: A Study in the Psychology of Pictorial Representation*, London: Phaidon

—— (1966), *Norm and Form: Studies in the Art of the Renaissance* I, London: Phaidon

—— (1972), *Symbolic Images: Studies in the Art of the Renaissance* II, London: Phaidon

—— (1979), *The Sense of Order: A Study in the Psychology of Decorative Art*, Oxford: Phaidon

—— (1982), *The Image and the Eye: Further Studies in the Psychology of Pictorial Representation*, Oxford: Phaidon

Gonzalez-Echevarría, Roberto (1977), *Alejo Carpentier: The Pilgrim at Home*, Ithaca: Cornell University Press

Gordon, Colin (1990), 'Histoire de la folie; An Unknown Book by Michel Foucault', *History of the Human Sciences* vol. 3 no. 1

Gordon, Lewis R., Sharpley-Whiting, T. Denean and White, Renée T., eds (1996), *Fanon: A Critical Reader*, Oxford: Blackwell

Graham, Keith (1977), *J.-L. Austin: A Critique of Ordinary Language Philosophy*, Hassocks: Harvester Press

Graham, Peter, ed. (1968), *The New Wave: Critical Landmarks*, London: Secker & Warburg in association with the British Film Institute

Gramsci, Antonio (1965), *Lettere dal carcere*, ed. S. Caprioglio and E. Fubini, Turin: Einaudi

—— (1971), *Selections from the Prison Notebooks of Antonio Gramsci*, tr. and ed. Quintin Hoare and Geoffrey Nowell-Smith, London: Lawrence & Wishart

—— (1975), *Quaderni del carcere*, ed. Valentino Gerrantana, Turin: Einaudi, 4 vols

—— (1977), *Selections from Political Writings (1910–1920)*, sel. and ed. Quintin Hoare, tr. John Mathews, London: Lawrence & Wishart

—— (1978), *Selections from Political Writings (1921–1926)*, tr. and ed. Quintin Hoare, London: Lawrence & Wishart

—— (1985), *Selections from Cultural Writings*, ed. David Forgacs and Geoffrey Nowell-Smith, tr. William Boelhower, London: Lawrence & Wishart

—— (1988), *Gramsci's Prison Letters: Lettere dal Carcere. A Selection Translated and Introduced by Hamish Henderson*, London: Zwan and *Edinburgh Review*

Granta 8. Dirty Realism: New Writing from America

Green, André (1966), 'The Logic of Lacan's *objet a* and Freudian Theory: Convergences and Questions' in Smith and Kerrigan (1983)

—— (1977), 'Conceptions of Affect' in Green (1986)

—— (1986), *On Private Madness*, London: Hogarth Press and The Institute of Psychoanalysis

Green, Gayle and Khan, Coppélia, eds (1985), *Making a Difference: Feminist Literary Criticism*, London: Methuen

Green, Jonathan (1998), *The Cassell Dictionary of Slang*, London: Cassell

Green, Michael (1974), 'Raymond Williams and Cultural Studies', *Working Papers in Cultural Studies* 6

—— (1982), 'The Centre for Contemporary Cultural Studies' in Widdowson (1982)

Greenberg, Clement (1941), 'Avant-garde and Kitsch' in Greenberg (1986a)

—— (1944), 'Surrealist Painting' in Greenberg (1986a)

—— (1960), 'Modernist Painting' in Greenberg (1993b)

—— (1961), *Art and Culture*, Boston: Beacon Press

—— (1964), *Post-Painterly Abstraction*, Los Angeles: Los Angeles County Museum of Art

—— (1986a), *The Collected Essays and Criticism* I: *Perceptions and Judgements 1939–1944*, Chicago and London: University of Chicago Press

—— (1986b), *The Collected Essays and Criticism* II: *Arrogant Purpose, 1945–1949*, Chicago and London: University of Chicago Press

—— (1993a), *The Collected Essays and Criticism* III: *Affirmations and Refusals*, Chicago: University of Chicago Press

—— (1993b), *The Collected Essays and Criticism: Modernism with a Vengeance*, Chicago: University of Chicago Press

Greenblatt, Stephen (1980), *Renaissance Self-Fashioning: From More to Shakespeare*, Chicago: University of Chicago Press

—— (1982), 'Power and the Power of Form in the Renaissance', *Genre* vol. 15 nos 1–2

—— (1988), *Shakespearean Negotiations: The Circulation of Social Energy in Renaissance England*, London: Clarendon

Greer, Germaine (1970), *The Female Eunuch*, London: MacGibbon & Kee

—— (1979), *The Obstacle Race*, London: Weidenfeld & Nicolson

—— (1984), *Sex and Destiny: The Politics of Human Fertility*, New York: Harper & Row

—— (1991), *The Change: Women, Aging and the Menopause*, London: Hamish Hamilton

—— (1995), *Slip-Shod Sibyls: Recognition, Rejection and the Woman Poet*, Harmondsworth: Penguin, 1996

—— (1999), *The Whole Woman*, New York: Doubleday

——, Hastings, S., Medoff, J. and Sansone, M., eds (1989), *Kissing the Rod: An Anthology of Seventeenth-Century Women's Verse*, London: Virago

Greimas, A. J. (1966a), *Sémantique structurale: Recherche de méthode*, Paris: Larousse

—— (1966b), 'Élements pour une théorie de l'interpretation du récit mythique', *Communications* 8

—— (1970), *On Meaning: Selected Writings in Semiotic Theory*, tr. Paul Perron and Frank Collins, Minneapolis: Minnesota University Press, 1978

—— (1976), *Maupassant: La Sémiologie du texte*, Paris: Seuil

—— and Fontanille, Jacques (1991), *The Semiotics of Passions: From States of Affairs to States of Feeling*, tr. Paul Perron and Frank Collins, Minneapolis: University of Minnesota Press

Greisch, J. and Kearney, R., eds (1991), *Les Métamorphoses de la raison herméneutique*, Paris: Le Cerf

Grey, Camilla (1962), *The Russian Experiment in Art 1863–1922*, London: Thames & Hudson

Grimshaw, Jean (1988), 'Pure Lust: The Elemental Feminist Philosophy of Mary Daly', *Radical Philosophy* 49

Groddeck, Georg (1923), *The Book of the It: Psychoanalytic Letters to a Friend*, London: C. W. Daniel, 1935

Grosskurth, Phyllis (1986), *Melanie Klein: Her World and Her Work*, London: Maresfield Library

Grosz, Elizabeth (1990), *Jacques Lacan: A Feminist Introduction*, London: Routledge

Grosz, George (1971), *Love Above All and Other Drawings: Über alles die Liebe and die Gezeichneten*, New York: Dover

Guattari, Félix (1970), 'Franco Basaglio: Guerrilla Psychiatrist' in Genosko (1996)

—— (1971), 'Psychoanalysis and the Struggle of Desire' in Guattari (1984)

—— (1972a), *Psychanalyse et transversalité*, Paris: Maspero

—— (1972b), 'Anti-Psychiatry and Anti-Psychoanalysis' in Guattari (1984)

—— (1975a), 'A Liberation of Desire' in Genosko (1996)

—— (1975b), 'Institutional Practice and Politics' in Genosko (1996)

—— (1984), *Molecular Revolution: Psychiatry and Politics*, tr. Rosemary Sheed, introduction by David Cooper, Harmondsworth: Penguin

Guberman, Ross Mitchell, ed. (1996), *Julia Kristeva: Interviews*, New York: Columbia University Press

Guha, Ranajit (1982), 'On Some Aspects of the Historiography of Colonial India', *Subaltern Studies* 1

—— and Gayatri Chakravorty Spivak (1988), *Selected Subaltern Studies*, New York and Oxford: Oxford University Press

Guignon, C., ed. (1993), *The Cambridge Companion to Heidegger*, Cambridge: Cambridge University Press

Habermas, Jürgen (1968), *Knowledge and Human Interests*, tr. Jeremy J. Shapiro, London: Heinemann, 1972

—— (1971), *Theory and Practice*, tr. John Viertel, London: Heinemann, 1974

—— (1973), *Legitimation Crisis*, tr. Thomas McCarthy, London: Heinemann, 1976

—— (1980), 'Modernity versus Postmodernity', tr. Seyla Ben-Habi, *New German Critique* 22, Winter 1981

—— (1981), *The Theory of Communicative Action* I: *Reason and the Rationalization of Society*, tr. Thomas McCarthy, London: Heinemann

—— (1983), *Moral Consciousness and Communicative Action*, tr. Christian Lenhardt and Shierry Weber Nicholsen, Cambridge: Polity Press, 1990

—— (1984), 'A Philosophico-Political Profile' in Habermas (1986)

—— (1985), *The Philosophical Discourse of Modernity: Twelve Lectures*, tr. Frederick G. Lawrence, Cambridge: Polity Press, 1987

—— (1986a), *Autonomy and Solidarity: Interviews*, ed. and introduction by Peter Dews

—— (1986b), 'Apologetic Tendencies' in Habermas (1989)

—— (1987), *The Theory of Communicative Action* II: *Lifeworld and Style*, tr. Thomas McCarthy, Cambridge: Polity Press

—— (1988), *Postmetaphysical Thinking: Philosophical Essays*, tr. William Mark Hohengarten, Cambridge, MA: MIT Press, 1992

—— (1989), *The New Conservatism: Cultural Criticism and the Historians' Debate*, ed. and tr. Shierry Weber Nicholsen, Cambridge: Polity Press

—— (1991a), *The Past As Future*, tr. and ed. Max Pensky, Cambridge: Polity Press

—— (1991b), *Justification and Application: Remarks on Discourse Ethics*, tr. Ciaran Cronin, Cambridge: Polity Press, 1993

—— (1992), *Between Facts and Norms: Contribution to a Discourse Theory of Law and Democracy*, tr. William Rehg, Cambridge: Polity Press, 1996

—— (1997), *The Inclusion of the Other*, tr. Ciaran Cronin, ed. Ciaran Cronin and Pablo Greiff, Cambridge: Polity Press, 1998

Hacker, P. M. S. (1990), *Wittgenstein: Meaning and Mind: Volume 3 of an Analytical Commentary on the Philosophical Investigations*, Oxford: Blackwell

—— (1996a), *Wittgenstein's Place in Twentieth-Century Analytic Philosophy*, Oxford: Blackwell

—— (1996b), *Wittgenstein: Mind and Will: Volume 4 of an Analytical Commentary on the Philosophical Investigations*, Oxford: Blackwell

Hall, Stuart (1971), 'Introduction', *Working Papers in Cultural Studies* 1

—— et al. (1979), *Policing the Crisis: Mugging, the State and Law and Order*, London: Macmillan

—— (1988), *The Hard Road to Renewal: Thatcherism and the Crisis of the New Left*, London: Verso

—— (1989), 'The "First" New Left: Life and Times' in Archer et al. (1989)

——, ed. (1997a), *Representations: Cultural Representation and Signifying Practices*, London: Sage

—— (1997b), 'Culture and Power: Stuart Hall Interviewed by Peter Osborne and Lynne Segal', *Radical Philosophy* 86

——, Lumley, Bob and McLennan, Gregor, eds (1977), 'Politics and Ideology: Gramsci', *Working Papers in Cultural Studies* 10

——, Massey, Doreen and Rustin, Michael (1995), 'Editorial: Uncomfortable Times', *Soundings* 1

——, Rowbotham, Sheila and Blackburn, Robin (1997), 'Tributes to Raphael Samuel', *New Left Review* 221, January–February

Halliday, Fred (1992), 'An Encounter with Fukuyama', *New Left Review* 193

Halperin, David (1995), *Saint Foucault: Towards a Gay Hagiography*, New York: Oxford University Press

Hamacher, Werner, Hertz, Neil and Keenan, Thomas, eds (1988), *Responses: On Paul de Man's Wartime Journalism*, Lincoln: University of Nebraska Press

Hamilton, Paul (1996), *Historicism*, London: Routledge

Hammond, John Lawrence and Lucy, Barbara (1911), *The Village Labourer*, London: Longman, 1978

—— (1917), *The Town Labourer*, London: Longman, 1978

—— (1919), *The Skilled Labourer*, London: Longman, 1978

Hampson, Norman (1968), *The Enlightenment*, Harmondsworth: Penguin

Hand, Sean, ed. (1989), *The Levinas Reader*, Oxford: Blackwell

Hanfling, Oswald, ed. (1981), *Essential Readings in Logical Positivism*, Oxford: Basil Blackwell

Hanson, Anne Coffin (1977), *Manet and the Modern Tradition*, New Haven: Yale University Press

Harding, Sandra (1976), *The Science Question in Feminism*, Ithaca: Cornell University Press

Harris, Wilson (1960), *Palace of the Peacock*, London: Faber & Faber, 1998

Harris, Zellig S. (1951), *Methods in Structural Linguistics*, Chicago: University of Chicago Press

Hartmann, Geoffrey (1970), *Beyond Formalism*, New Haven: Yale University Press

——, ed. (1979), *Deconstruction and Criticism*, London: Routledge

Hartmann, Heinz (1939), *Ego Psychology and the Problem of Adaptation*, tr. David Rapoport, New York: International Universities Press, 1958

——, Kris, Ernst and Loewenstein, Rudolph (1946), 'Comments on the Formation of Psychic Structure', *Psychoanalytic Study of the Child* 2

Harvey, David (1989), *The Condition of Postmodernity: An Enquiry into the Origins of Cultural Change*, Oxford: Basil Blackwell

Haskell, Molly (1974), *From Reverence to Rape: The Treatment of Women in the Movies*, New York: Holt, Rinehart & Winston

Hassan, Ihab (1971), 'POSTMODERNISM: A Paracritical Bibliography', *New Literary History*, Autumn

Hawkes, Terence (1977), *Structuralism and Semiotics*, London: Methuen

Hayes, Nelson E. and Hayes, Tanya, eds (1970), *Claude Lévi-Strauss: The Anthropologist as Hero*, Cambridge, MA: MIT Press

Hayman, Ronald (1977), *Artaud and After*, Oxford: Oxford University Press

—— (1986), *Writing Against: A Biography of Sartre*, London: Weidenfeld & Nicolson

Hayward, Jack (1991), *After the French Revolution: Six Critics of Democracy and Nationalism*, Hemel Hempstead: Harvester Wheatsheaf

Heath, Stephen (1972), *The Nouveau Roman: A Study in the Practice of Writing*, London: Elek Books

—— (1973), 'The Work of Christian Metz', *Screen* vol. 14 no. 3

Hebdige, D. (1979), *Subculture: The Meaning of Style*, London: Routledge

Hegel, G. W. F. (1807), *The Phenomenology of Mind*, tr. J. B. Baillie, New York and Evanston: Harper Torchbooks, 1967

—— (1821), *Philosophy of Right*, tr. T. M. Knox, London: Oxford University Press, 1952

—— (1822), *The Philosophy of History*, New York: Dover, 1956

—— (1830), *Hegel's Philosophy of Mind, Being Part 3 of the Encyclopedia of the Philosophical Sciences*, tr. William Wallace, Oxford: Clarendon Press, 1971

—— (1837), *Reason in History: A General Introduction to the Philosophy of History*, tr. Robert S. Hartman, New York: Bobbs-Merrill, 1953

Heidegger, Martin (1927), *Being and Time*, tr. John MacQuarrie and Edward Robinson, Oxford: Basil Blackwell, 1962

—— (1929), *What is Metaphysics?*, tr. David Farrell Krell in Heidegger (1976)

—— (1935), *An Introduction to Metaphysics*, tr. Ralph Mannheim, New Haven: Yale University Press, 1959

—— (1946), 'Letter on "Humanism"', tr. Frank A. Capuzzi in Heidegger (1998)

—— (1951), 'Poetically Man Dwells' in Heidegger (1975)

—— (1955), 'The Question Concerning Technology' in Heidegger (1977)

—— (1958), *What is Philosophy?*, tr. William L. Klubach and Jean T. Wilde, New York: Vision Press

—— (1959), 'The Nature of Language' in Heidegger (1971)

—— (1971), *On the Way to Language*, tr. Peter D. Hertz, New York: Harper & Row

—— (1975a), *The Basic Problems of Phenomenology*, tr., introduction and lexicon by Albert Hofstadter, Bloomington and Indianapolis: Indiana University Press, 1982

—— (1975b), *Poetry, Language, Thought*, tr. Albert Hofstadter, New York: Harper & Row

—— (1975c, ongoing), *Gesamtausgabe*, Frankfurt-am-Main: Vittorio Klosterman

—— (1976), *Pathmarks*, ed. William McNeil, Cambridge: Cambridge University Press, 1998, rev. edn

—— (1977a), *The Question Concerning Technology and Other Essays*, tr. and introduction by William Lovitt, New York: Harper Torchbooks

—— (1977b), *Martin Heidegger: Basic Writings*, ed. D. E. Krell, New York: Harper & Row

Held, David (1980), *Introduction to Critical Theory: Horkheimer to Habermas*, London: Hutchinson

Herbert Read: A British Vision of World Art, Leeds: Leeds City Art Galleries in association with the Henry Moore Foundation and Lund Humphries, London, 1993

Herbert, Robert L. (1988), *Impressionism: Art, Leisure and Parisian Society*, New Haven and London: Yale University Press

Hewison, Robert (1988), *In Anger: Culture in the Cold War 1945–1960*, London: Methuen

Hill, Christopher (1940), *The English Revolution*, London: Lawrence & Wishart, 1955

—— (1958), *Puritanism and Revolution*, London: Martin Secker & Warburg

—— (1965), *Intellectual Origins of the English Revolution*, Oxford: Clarendon Press

—— (1967), 'Sir Isaac Newton and his Society' in Hill (1974)

—— (1969), *Reformation to Industrial Revolution*, Harmondsworth: Penguin

—— (1972), *The World Turned Upside Down: Radical Ideas During the English Revolution*, London: Temple Smith

—— (1974), *Change and Continuity in Seventeenth-Century England*, London: Weidenfeld & Nicolson

—— (1993), *The English Bible and the Seventeenth-Century Revolution*, London: Allen Lane

—— (1996), *Liberties Against the Law: Some Seventeenth-Century Controversies*, London: Allen Lane

Hinshelwood, R. D. (1989), *A Dictionary of Kleinian Thought*, London: Free Association Books

Hinton, William (1966), *Fanshen*, New York: Vintage Books

Hirsch, Marianne and Keller, Evelyn Fox (1990), *Conflicts in Feminism*, New York and London: Routledge

Hirschman, Jack, ed. (1965), *Artaud Anthology*, San Francisco: City Lights

Hitchcock, Henry Russell and Johnson, Philip (1932), *The International Style: Architecture since 1922*, New York: W. W. Norton

Hjemslev, Louis (1943), *Prolegomena to a Theory of Language*, tr. J. Whitfield, Madison: University of Wisconsin Press, 1961

Hobbes, Thomas (1651), *Leviathan*, ed. Richard Tuck, Cambridge: Cambridge University Press, 1991

Hobsbawm, E. J. (1959a), *Primitive Rebels*, London: Weidenfeld & Nicolson

—— ['Francis Newton'] (1959b), *The Jazz Scene*, London: Weidenfeld & Nicolson, 1989

—— (1962), *The Age of Revolution: Europe 1789–1848*, London: Weidenfeld & Nicolson

—— (1964), *Labouring Men: Studies in the History of Labour*, London: Weidenfeld & Nicolson

—— (1968), *Industry and Empire: An Economic History of Britain since 1750*, London: Weidenfeld & Nicolson

—— (1969), *Bandits*, London: Weidenfeld & Nicolson

—— (1975), *The Age of Capital 1848–1875*, London: Weidenfeld & Nicolson

—— (1987), *Age of Empire*, London: Weidenfeld & Nicolson

—— (1994), *Age of Extremes: The Short Twentieth Century 1914–1991*, London: Weidenfeld & Nicolson

—— (1997), *On History*, London: Weidenfeld & Nicolson

—— and Ranger, Terence, eds (1983), *The Invention of Tradition*, Cambridge: Cambridge University Press

Hobson, Dorothy (1982), *'Crossroads': The Drama of a Soap Opera*, London: Methuen

Hobson, Marian (1998), *Jacques Derrida: Opening Lines*, London and New York: Routledge

Hodges, Lucy (1996), 'Mother Church's Dissenting Daughter', *Times Higher Education Supplement*, 7 June

Hoggart, Richard (1957), *The Uses of Literacy: Aspects of Working-Class Life with Special Reference to Publications and Entertainment*, London: Chatto & Windus

—— (1988), *A Local Habitation (Life and Times I: 1918–1940)*, London: Chatto & Windus

—— (1995), *The Way We Live Now*, London: Chatto & Windus

Hollier, Denis, ed. (1979), *The College of Sociology 1937–39*, tr. Betsy Wing, Minneapolis: University of Minnesota Press, 1988

——, ed. (1989), *A New History of French Literature*, Cambridge, MA and London: Harvard University Press

Holtzmann, Harry and James, Martin S. (1987), *The New Art – The New Life: The Collected Writings of Piet Mondrian*, London: Thames & Hudson

hooks, bell (1981), *Ain't I a Woman?*, London: Pluto Press, 1982

—— (1990), *Yearning: Race, Gender and Cultural Politics*, Boston, MA: South End Press

—— (1992), *Black Looks: Race and Representation*, Boston, MA: South End Press

—— (1996), *Bone Black: Memories of Girlhood*, London: The Women's Press, 1997

—— (1997), *Wounds of Passion: A Writing Life*, London: The Women's Press, 1998

Horkheimer, Max (1931), 'The Present Situation of Social Philosophy and the Task of an Institute for Social Research' in Horkheimer (1993)

—— (1937), 'Traditional and Critical Theory' in Horkheimer (1972)

—— (1947), *The Eclipse of Reason*, New York: Seabury Press

—— (1967), *Critique of Instrumental Reason: Lectures and Essays since the End of World War II*, tr. Matthew J. O'Connell et al., New York: Seabury Press, 1974

—— (1972), *Critical Theory: Selected Essays*, tr. Matthew J. O'Connell et al., New York: Seabury Press

—— (1993), *Between Philosophy and Social Science: Selected Early Writings*, tr. G. Frederick Hunter, Matthew S. Kramer and John Turgy, Cambridge, MA: MIT Press

—— and Adorno, Theodor W. (1947), *Dialectic of Enlightenment*, London: Allen Lane, 1973

Horowitz, Daniel (1998), *Betty Friedan and the Making of the Feminine Mystique: The*

American Left, the Cold War and Modern Feminism, Ann Arbor: University of Massachusetts Press

Howe, Stephen (1998), *Afrocentrism*, London: Verso

Howells, Christine (1992), 'Conclusion: Sartre and the Deconstruction of the Subject' in Howells (1992)

——, ed. (1992), *The Cambridge Companion to Sartre*, Cambridge: Cambridge University Press

Hoyles, John (1982), 'Radical Critical Theory and English' in Widdowson (1982)

Hudson, Mark (1994), *Coming Back Brockens: A Year in a Mining Village*, London: Jonathan Cape

Huggins, Nathan Irvin (1971), *Harlem Renaissance*, New York: Oxford University Press

Hume, David (revised edn 1758), *An Enquiry concerning Human Understanding* in Ralph Cohen, ed., *Essential Works of David Hume*, New York: Bantam Books, 1965

Hunter, Lynette, ed. (1991), *Towards a Definition of Topos: Approaches to Analogical Reasoning*, Basingstoke: Macmillan

Huntington, Samuel S. (1996), *The Clash of Civilizations and the Remaking of World Order*, New York: Simon and Schuster

Hurston, Zora Neale (1934), *Jonah's Gourd Vine*, London: Virago, 1993

—— (1935), *Mules and Men*, New York: J. B. Lippincott

—— (1938), *Tell my Horse*, New York: J. B. Lippincott

Husserl, Edmund (1887), *On the Concept of Number: Psychological Analyses*, tr. D. Willard, *Philosophia Mathematica* 9, 1972; 10, 1973

—— (1891), *Philosophie der Arithmetik* in *Husserliana* XII, The Hague: Martinus Nijhoff, 1970

—— (1900, 1913 – two parts), *Logical Investigations*, tr. J. N. Findlay, London: Routledge & Kegan Paul, 1970

—— (1913), *Ideas: General Introduction to Pure Phenomenology*, tr. W. R. Boyce Gibson, New York: Macmillan, 1931

—— (1931), *Cartesian Meditations*, tr. Dorian Cairns, The Hague: Martinus Nijhoff, 1966

—— (1936), *The Crisis of European Sciences and Transcendental Phenomenology*, tr. D. Carr, Evanston, IL: Northwestern University Press, 1970

—— (1950), *The Idea of Phenomenology*, tr. William P. Alston and George Nakhnikian, The Hague: Martinus Nijhoff, 1964

Hutcheon, Linda (1988), *A Poetics of Postmodernism: History, Theory, Fiction*, London and New York: Routledge

Hyde, G. M. (1976), 'Russian Futurism' in Bradbury and McFarlane (1976)

Hyppolite, Jean (1947), 'Situation de l'homme dans la "phénoménologie" hégélienne' in Hyppolite (1971)

—— (1971), *Figures de la pensée philosophique*, Paris: PUF

Ibnifassi, Laïla and Hitchcott, Nikki (1996), *A Critical Introduction to African Francophone Writing*, Oxford: Berg

Information psychiatrique (1975): *Frantz Fanon à cinquante ans* vol. 51 no. 10

Inglis, Fred (1995), *Raymond Williams*, London: Routledge

Ionesco, Eugene (1950), *The Bald Prima Donna*, tr. Donald Watson in *Plays* 1, London: John Calder

Irigaray, Luce (1973), *Le Langage des déments*, The Hague: Mouton

—— (1974), *Speculum, of the Other Woman*, tr. Gillian C. Gill, Ithaca: Cornell University Press, 1985

—— (1977a), *This Sex which is not One*, tr. Catherine Porter with Carolyn Burke, Ithaca: Cornell University Press, 1985

—— (1977b), 'The Poverty of Psychoanalysis', tr. David Macey with Margaret Whitford in Whitford (1991a)

—— (1984), *An Ethics of Sexual Difference*, London: Athlone Press, 1993

—— (1985), *Speech is Never Neutral*, London: Athlone Press, 1989

—— (1987), 'A Chance for Life: Limits to the Concept of the Neuter and the Universal in Science and Other Disciplines' in Irigaray (1993)

—— (1989), *Thinking the Difference: For a Peaceful Revolution*, London: Athlone Press

—— (1990), *Je, tu, nous: Towards a Culture of Difference*, tr. A. Martin, London: Routledge, 1993

—— (1993), *Sexes and Genealogies*, tr. Gillian C. Gill, New York: Columbia University Press

Isaacson, Joel (1972), *Monet: 'Le Déjeuner sur l'herbe'*, London: Allen Lane

Iser, Wolfgang (1974), *The Implied Reader: Patterns in Communication in Prose Fiction from Bunyan to Beckett*, Baltimore: Johns Hopkins University Press

—— (1976), *The Act of Reading*, Baltimore and London: Johns Hopkins University Press, 1978

—— (1991), *The Fictive and the Imaginary: Charting Literary Anthropology*, tr. David Henry Wilson and the Author, Baltimore and London: Johns Hopkins University Press

Jack, Belinda (1996), *Francophone Literatures: An Introductory Survey*, Oxford: Oxford University Press

Jackson, R. and Rudy, S., eds (1985), *Russian Formalism: A Retrospective Glance*, New Haven: Yale University Press

Jackson, Stevi et al., eds (1993), *Women's Studies: A Reader*, Hemel Hempstead: Harvester Wheatsheaf

Jacobus, Mary (1979), *Women Writing and Writing About Women*, London: Croom-Helm

Jakobson, Roman (1914), 'The Newest Russian Poetry' in Jakobson (1987)

—— (1919a), 'Futurism' in Jakobson (1987)

—— (1919b) 'Modern Russian Poetry' in Jakobson (1987)

—— (1921), 'On Realism in Art' in Jakobson (1987)

—— (1930), 'A Generation that Squandered its Poets' in Jakobson (1987)

—— (1941), *Child Language, Aphasia and Phonological Universals*, The Hague and Paris: Mouton, 1968

—— (1952), 'Results of the Conference of Anthropologists and Linguists' in Jakobson (1971b)

—— (1956), 'Two Aspects of Language and Two Types of Aphasia' in Jakobson (1971a)

—— (1957), 'Shifters, Verbal Categories and the Russian Verb' in Jakobson (1971a)

—— (1960a), 'Closing Statement: Linguistics and Poetics' in Jakobson (1971b)

—— (1960b), 'Metalanguage as a Linguistic Problem' in Jakobson (1985d)

—— (1966), *Selected Writings* IV: *Slave Epic Studies*, The Hague: Mouton

—— (1971a), *Selected Writings* I: *Phonological Studies*, The Hague: Mouton

—— (1971b), *Selected Writings* II: *Word and Language*, The Hague: Mouton

—— (1979), *Selected Writings* V: *On Verse, Its Masters and Explorers*, The Hague: Mouton

—— (1981), *Selected Writings* III: *Poetry of Grammar and Grammar of Poetry*, The Hague: Mouton

—— (1985a), *Selected Writings* VI: *Early Slavic Paths and Crossroads*, Berlin: Mouton

—— (1985b), *Selected Writings* VII: *Contributions to Comparative Mythology. Studies in Linguistics and Philology, 1972–1982*, Berlin: Mouton

—— (1985c), *Selected Writings* VIII: *Completion* I: *Major Works 1976–1980*, Berlin: Mouton de Gruyer

—— (1985d), *Verbal Art, Verbal Sign, Verbal Time*, ed. Krystyna Pomorska and Stephen Rudy, Oxford: Basil Blackwell

—— (1987), *Language in Literature*, ed. Krystyna Pomorska and Stephen Rudy, New Haven: Harvard University Press

—— (1988), *Selected Works* VIII: *Major Works 1976–1980*, The Hague: Mouton

—— and Halle, Morris (1956), 'Fundamentals of Language', *Janua Lingarum* I

—— and Lévi-Strauss, Claude (1962), ' "Les Chats" de Charles Baudelaire' in Jakobson (1987)

—— and Tynjanov, Jurij (1928), 'Problems in the Study of Language and Literature' in Jakobson (1981)

James, William (1890), *Principles of Psychology*, New York: Holt, 2 vols

Jameson, Frederic (1974), *Marxism and Form*, Princeton: Princeton University Press

—— (1981), *The Political Unconscious: Narrative as a Socially Symbolic Act*, London: Methuen

—— (1988a), *The Ideologies of Theory. Essays 1971–1986* I: *Situations of Theory*, Minneapolis: University of Minnesota Press

—— (1988b), *The Ideologies of Theory. Essays 1971–1986* II: *Syntax of History*, Minneapolis: University of Minnesota Press

—— (1988c), 'Postmodernism and Consumer Society' in Jameson (1991)

—— (1991), *Postmodernism, or The Cultural Logic of Late Capitalism*, London: Verso

—— (1998), *The Cultural Turn: Selected Writings on the Postmodern 1983–1998*, London: Verso

Jarry, Alfred (1902), *The Supermale*, tr. Barbara Wright, London: Cape Editions, 1968

—— (1911), *Gestes et opinions du Docteur Faustroll*, Paris: Fasquelle, 1975

Jarvis, Simon (1998), *Adorno: A Critical Introduction*, Cambridge: Polity Press

Jay, Martin (1973), *The Dialectical Imagination: A History of the Frankfurt School and the Institute of Social Research, 1923–1950*, Boston: Little, Brown

—— (1993), *Downcast Eyes: The Denigration of Vision in Twentieth-Century French Thought*, Berkeley: University of California Press

Jencks, Charles (1977), *The Language of Post-Modern Architecture*, London: Academy Editions

—— (1996), *What is Post-Modernism?* London: Academy Editions

Jespersen, Otto (1922), *Language: Its Nature, Development and Origin*, London: Allen & Unwin

Johnson, Christopher (1993), *System and Writing in the Philosophy of Jacques Derrida*, Cambridge: Cambridge University Press

Johnson, Randal (1987), 'Tupy or not Tupy: Cannibalism and Nationalism in Contemporary Brazilian Literature and Culture' in King (1987)

Johnston, Claire, ed. (1973), *Notes on Women's Cinema*, London: Society for Education in Film and Television

Jones, Daniel (1950), *The Phoneme: Its Nature and Use*, Cambridge: Heffer

Jones, Ernest (1927), 'The Early Development of Female Sexuality', *International Journal of Psychoanalysis* vol. 8 pt 4

—— (1933), 'The Phallic Phase', *International Journal of Psychoanalysis* 13

Journal of Commonwealth Literature (1965) 1, September

Judge, Anne (1996), 'The Institutional Framework of *La Francophonie*' in Ibnifassi and Hitchcott (1996)

Jung, Carl Gustav (1911), 'Psychology of the Unconscious' in *Collected Works* V

—— (1912), *Symbols of Transformation*, *Collected Works* V

—— (1919), *Archetypes of the Collective Unconscious*, *Collected Works* VII

—— (1921), *Psychological Types*, *Collected Works* VI

—— (1933), *Modern Man in Search of a Soul*, London: Routledge & Kegan Paul

—— (1936), *The Concept of the Collective Unconscious*, *Collected Works* IX pt 1

—— (1953), *Two Essays on Analytical Psychology*, *Collected Works* VII

—— (1953–78), *The Collected Works of C. G. Jung*, London: Routledge & Kegan Paul, 18 vols

—— (1963), *Memories, Dreams, Reflections of C. G. Jung*, London: Routledge & Kegan Paul

Jung, Emma (1957), *Animus and Anima*, New York: Spring Publications

Kandinsky, Wassily (1912), *On the Spiritual in Art*, ed. Hilla Rebay, New York: Solomon R. Guggenheim Foundation, 1947

Kant, Immanuel (1757), *Observations on the Feeling of the Beautiful and the Sublime*, tr. John T. Goldthwait, Berkeley, CA: University of California Press, 1991

—— (1784), 'An Answer to the Question: "What is Enlightenment?" ' in Kant (1991)

—— (1787), *Critique of Pure Reason*, tr. J. D. D. Meiklejohn, London: Everyman, 1934

—— (1790), *Critique of Judgement*, tr. James Creed Meredith, Oxford: Clarendon Press, 1991

—— (1991), *Kant: Political Writings*, ed. Hans Reiss, Cambridge: Cambridge University Press

Kaplan, Cora (1986), *Sea Changes: Culture and Feminism*, London: Verso

Kaplan, E. Ann, ed. (1980), *Women in Film Noir*, London: British Film Institute

Kaplan, Sydney Janet (1985), 'Varieties of Feminist Criticism' in Green and Kuhn (1985)

Kaufman, Walter (1950), *Nietzsche: Philosopher, Psychologist, Anti-Christ*, Princeton, NJ: Princeton University Press

Kaye, Harvey J. (1984), *The British Marxist Historians: An Introductory Analysis*, Cambridge: Polity Press

—— and McClelland, Keith, eds (1990), *E. P. Thompson: Critical Perspectives*, Philadelphia: Temple University Press

Kellner, Douglas (1989), *Jean Baudrillard: From Marxism to Postmodernism and Beyond*, Cambridge: Polity Press

Kelly, Michael (1992), *Hegel in France*, Birmingham: Birmingham Modern Languages Association

Kennedy, Ellen Conroy, ed. (1975), *The Negritude Poets: An Anthology of Translations from the French*, New York: Viking Press

Kenny, Anthony (1995), *Frege*, Harmondsworth: Penguin

Kermode, Frank (1979), *The Genesis of Secrecy: On the Interpretation of Narrative*, Cambridge, MA: Harvard University Press

—— (1989), 'Paul de Man's Abyss', *London Review of Books*, 16 March

Khan, Hasan-Uddin (1998), *International Style: Modernist Architecture from 1925 to 1965*, Cologne: Taschen

Khilnani, Sunil (1993), *Arguing Revolution: The Intellectual Left in Postwar France*, New Haven and London: Yale University Press

Khrushchev, Nikita S. (1956), 'Secret Report to the 20th Party Congress of the CPSU' in Ali (1984)

King, John (1987), *Modern Latin American Fiction: A Survey*, London: Faber & Faber

King, Ursula (1989), *Women and Spirituality: Voices of Protest and Promise*, Basingstoke: Macmillan

King's Arcadia: Inigo Jones and the Stuart Court, London: Arts Council of Great Britain, 1973

Kirpotin, V. (1933), 'Fifteen Years of Socialist Realism', *International Literature* 1

Klein, Melanie (1928), 'Early Stages of the Oedipus Complex' in Klein (1975a)

—— (1930), 'The Importance of Symbol-Formation in the Development of the Ego' in Klein (1975a)

—— (1932), *The Psychoanalysis of Children* in Klein (1975b)

—— (1933), 'The Early Development of Conscience in Children' in Klein (1975a)

—— (1935), 'A Contribution to the Psychogenesis of Depressive States' in Klein (1975a)

—— (1936), 'Weaning' in Klein (1975a)

—— (1937), 'Love, Guilt and Reparation' in Klein (1975a)

—— (1940), 'Mourning and its Relation to Manic-Depressive States' in Klein (1975a)

—— (1946), 'Notes on Some Schizoid Mechanisms' in Klein (1975b)

—— (1955), 'The Psychoanalytic Play-Technique: Its History and Significance' in Klein (1975b)

—— (1975a), *The Writings of Melanie Klein* I: *'Love, Guilt and Reparation' and Other Works 1921–1945*, London: Hogarth Press and the Institute of Psychoanalysis

—— (1975b), *The Writings of Melanie Klein* II: *The Psychoanalysis of Children*, London: Hogarth Press and the Institute of Psychoanalysis

—— (1975c), *The Writings of Melanie Klein* III: *'Envy and Gratitude' and Other Works 1946–1963*, London: Hogarth Press and the Institute of Psychoanalysis

—— (1975d), *The Writings of Melanie Klein* IV: *Narrative of a Child Analysis*, London: Hogarth Press and the Institute of Psychoanalysis

Klossowski, Pierre (1967), *Sade my Neighbor*, tr. Alphonso Lingis, Evanston, IL: Northwestern University Press, 1991

Knight, Diana (1997), *Barthes and Utopia: Space, Travel, Writing*, Oxford: Clarendon Press

Knight, G. Wilson (1963), 'The Kitchen-Sink: On Recent Developments in Drama', *Encounter*, December

Koch, H. W., ed. (1986), *Aspects of the Third Reich*, New York: St Martin's Press

Kockelman, Joseph J., ed. (1967), *Phenomenology: The Philosophy of Edmund Husserl and its Interpretation*, Garden City, NY: Doubleday

Kofman, Sarah (1974), *Freud and Fiction*, tr. Sarah Wykes, Cambridge: Polity Press, 1991

—— (1983), 'Beyond Aporia?', tr. David Macey in Benjamin (1988)

Köhler, Wolfgang (1947), *Gestalt Psychology: An Introduction to New Concepts in Modern Psychology*, New York: Liveright Publishing Corporation

Kohon, Gregorio, ed. (1986), *The British School of Psychoanalysis: The Independent Tradition*, London: Free Association Books

Kojève, Alexandre (1947), *Introduction à la lecture de Hegel*, Paris: Gallimard

—— (1968), *Essai d'une histoire raisonnée de la philosophie païenne* I: *Les Présocratiques*, Paris: Gallimard

—— (1972), *Essai d'une histoire raisonnée de la philosophie païenne* II: *Platon–Aristote*, Paris: Gallimard

—— (1973a), *Essai d'une histoire raisonnée de la philosophie païenne* III: *La Philosophie hellénistique; Les néo-platoniciens*, Paris: Gallimard

—— (1973b), *Kant*, Paris: Gallimard

—— (1982), *Esquisse d'une phénoménologie du droit*, Paris: Gallimard

Kolakowski, Leszek (1966), *Positivist Philosophy: From Hume to the Vienna Circle*, tr. Norbert Guterman, Harmondsworth: Penguin, 1972

Korsch, Karl (1923), *Marxism and Philosophy*, tr. F. Halliday, London: New Left Books, 1970

Koyré, Alexandre (1929), *La Philosophie et le problème national en Russie au début du XIXe siècle*, Paris: Gallimard, 1976

—— (1939), *Galileo Studies*, tr. John Mepham, Atlantic Highlands, NJ: Humanities Press, 1978

—— (1957), *From the Closed World to the Infinite Universe*, Baltimore: Johns Hopkins University Press

—— (1961), *The Astronomical Revolution*, tr. R. E. W. Maddison, London: Methuen, 1973

—— (1965), *Newtonian Studies*, Chicago: University of Chicago Press

—— (1971), *Études d'histoire de la pensée philosophique*, Paris: Gallimard

Kracauer, Siegfried (1922–5), *Der Detektiv-Roman: Ein philosophischer Traktat* in *Schriften* I, Frankfurt-am-Main, 1971

—— (1927), 'The Little Shopgirls go to the Movies' in Kracauer (1963)

—— (1930), *The Salaried Masses: Duty and Distraction in Weimar Germany*, tr. Quintin Hoare, introduction by Inka Mülde-Bach, London: Verso, 1998

—— (1947), *From Caligari to Hitler: A Psychological History of the German Film*, London: Denis Dobson

—— (1960), *Theory of Film: The Redemption of Physical Reality*, New York: Oxford University Press, 1965

—— (1963), *The Mass Ornament: Weimar Essays*, tr., ed. and with an introduction by Thomas Y. Levin, Cambridge, MA: Harvard University Press, 1985

Kraft, Victor (1953), *The Vienna Circle: The Origins of Neo-Positivism*, New York: Philosophical Library

Kraniauskas, John (1998), 'Globalization is Ordinary: The Transnationalization of Cultural Studies', *Radical Philosophy* 90

Krauss, Rosalind (1993), *Cindy Sherman 1975–1993*, New York: Rizzoli

Krieger, Murray, ed. (1966), *Northrop Frye in Modern Criticism*, New York: Columbia University Press

Kris, Ernst (1951), 'Ego Psychology and Interpretation in Psychoanalytic Therapy', *Psychoanalytic Quarterly* 20

Kristeva, Julia (1969), 'Word, Dialogue and Novel', tr. Alice Jardine, Thomas Gora and Léon S. Roudiez in Moi (1986)

—— (1969b), *Semiotiké*, Paris: Seuil

—— (1973), 'The Subject in Process', tr. Patrick Ffrench in Ffrench and Lack (1998)

—— (1974a), *Revolution in Poetic Language*, tr. Léon S. Roudiez, New York: Columbia University Press, 1984

—— (1974b), *About Chinese Women*, tr. A. Barrows, London: Marion Boyars, 1986

—— (1977), 'A New Type of Intellectual: The Dissident', tr. Sean Hand in Moi (1986)

—— (1980), *Powers of Horror*, tr. Léon S. Roudiez, New York: Columbia University Press, 1982

—— (1981), *Language: The Unknown*, tr. Anne M. Menke, Hemel Hempstead: Harvester Wheatsheaf, 1989

—— (1983), *Tales of Love*, tr. Leon S. Roudiez, New York: Columbia University Press, 1992

—— (1987a), *Black Sun*, tr. Léon S. Roudiez, New York: Columbia University Press

—— (1987b), *New Maladies of the Soul*, tr. Leon S. Roudiez, New York: Columbia University Press, 1995

—— (1988), *Strangers to Ourselves*, tr. Leon S. Roudiez, Hemel Hempstead: Harvester Wheatsheaf, 1991

—— (1994), 'Proust: A Search for Our Time' in Guberman (1996)

—— (1998), *Contre la Dépression nationale: Entretien avec Philippe Petit*, Paris: Editions Textuel

Kuhn, Annette (1982), *Women's Pictures: Feminism and Cinema*, London: Routledge & Kegan Paul

Kuhn, T. S. (1957), *The Copernican Revolution: Planetary Astronomy in the Development of Western Thought*, Cambridge, MA: Harvard University Press

—— (1962), *The Structure of Scientific Revolutions*, Chicago: University of Chicago Press

Lacan, Jacques (1932), *De la Psychose paranoïaque dans ses rapports avec la personnalité*, Paris: Seuil, 1975

—— (1936), 'Au-delà du principe de réalité' in Lacan (1966)

—— (1938), *Les Complexes familiaux dans la formation de l'individu. Essai d'analyse d'une fonction en psychologie*, Paris: Navarin, 1984

—— (1946), 'Propos sur la causalité psychique' in Lacan (1966)

—— (1948), 'Aggressivity in Psychoanalysis' in Lacan (1977)

—— (1949), 'The Mirror-Stage as Formative of the I as Revealed in Psychoanalytic Experience' in Lacan (1977)

—— (1951a), 'Intervention on Transference' in Lacan (1982)

—— (1951b), 'Some Reflections on the Ego', *International Journal of Psychoanalysis* 34

—— (1953), 'The Function and Field of Speech and Language in Psychoanalysis' in Lacan (1977)

—— (1955a), 'The Freudian Thing, or the Meaning of the Return to Freud in Psychoanalysis' in Lacan (1977)

—— (1955b), 'The Seminar on "The Purloined Letter"', tr. Jeffrey Mehlman, *Yale French Studies* 48, 1973

—— (1955c), 'Variants de la cure-type' in Lacan (1966)

—— (1957), 'The Agency of the Letter in the Unconscious, or Reason Since Freud' in Lacan (1977)

——(1957–8), 'On a Question Preliminary to Any Possible Treatment of Psychosis' in Lacan (1977)

—— (1958a), 'The Significance of the Phallus' in Lacan (1977)

—— (1958b), 'The Direction of the Treatment and the Principle of its Power' in Lacan (1977)

—— (1958–9), 'Desire and the Interpretation of Desire in *Hamlet*', tr. James Hulbert, *Yale French Studies* 55–6, 1977

—— (1960), 'The Subversion of the Subject and the Dialectic of Desire in the Freudian Unconscious' in Lacan (1977)

—— (1965), 'Hommage fait à Marguerite Duras, du *Ravissement de Lol V. Stein*', *Cahiers-Renaud-Barrault* 53

—— (1966), *Écrits*, Paris: Seuil

—— (1973), *The Four Fundamental Concepts of Psychoanalysis*, tr. Alan Sheridan, with a new introduction by David Macey, Harmondsworth: Penguin, 1994

—— (1975a), *The Seminar. Book I. Freud's Papers on Technique 1953–54*, tr. with notes by John Forrester, Cambridge: Cambridge University Press, 1987

—— (1975b), *Le Séminaire: Livre XX. Encore 1972–1973*, Paris: Seuil

—— (1977), *Écrits: A Selection*, tr. Alan Sheridan, London: Tavistock

—— (1978), *The Seminar. Book II. The Ego in Freud's Theory and in the Technique of Psychoanalysis 1954–55*, tr. Sylvana Tomaseli with notes by John Forrester, Cambridge: Cambridge University Press, 1988

—— (1981), *The Seminar. Book III. The Psychoses. 1955–56*, tr. Russell Grigg, London: Routledge

—— (1991), *Le Séminaire. Livre XVII. L'Envers de la psychanalyse. 1969–70*, Paris: Seuil

Lacapra, Dominique (1989), 'Two Trials' in Hollier (1989)

Laing, R. D. (1960), *The Divided Self: An Existential Study in Sanity and Madness*, Harmondsworth: Penguin, 1965

—— (1967), *The Politics of Experience and The Bird of Paradise*, Harmondsworth: Penguin

—— and David Cooper (1964), *Reason and Violence*, London: Tavistock

—— and A. Esterton (1964), *Sanity, Madness and the Family*, London: Tavistock

Landry, Donna and MacLean, Gerald, eds (1996), *The Spivak Reader*, London: Routledge

Laplanche, Jean (1987), *New Foundations for Psychoanalysis*, tr. David Macey, Oxford: Blackwell, 1989

—— and Pontalis, J.-B. (1967), *The Language of Psychoanalysis*, tr. Donald Nicholson-Smith, London: Hogarth Press and the Institute of Psychoanalysis, 1977

Lasch, Christopher (1979), *The Culture of Narcissism*, New York and London: Norton

—— (1995), *The Revolt of the Elites and the Betrayal of Democracy*, New York and London: Norton

Lavers, Annette (1982), *Roland Barthes: Structuralism and After*, London: Methuen

Leach, Edmund (1970), *Lévi-Strauss*, London: Fontana

Leavis, F. R. (1932), *New Bearings in English Poetry*, London: Chatto & Windus

—— (1936), *Revaluation: Tradition and Development in English Poetry*, London: Chatto & Windus

—— (1937), 'Literary Criticism and Philosophy', *Scrutiny* vol. 6 no. 1

—— (1948), *The Great Tradition*, London: Chatto & Windus

—— (1952), *The Common Pursuit*, London: Chatto & Windus

—— (1955), *D. H. Lawrence: Novelist*, London: Chatto & Windus

—— (1963), '*Scrutiny*: A Retrospect', *Scrutiny* 20

——, ed. (1968), *A Selection from 'Scrutiny'*, Cambridge: Cambridge University Press, 2 vols

—— (1975), *The Living Principle: English as a Discipline of Thought*, London: Chatto & Windus

—— and Leavis, Q. D. (1970), *Dickens the Novelist*, London: Chatto & Windus

—— and Thompson, Denys (1942), *Culture and Environment: The Training of Critical Awareness*, London: Chatto & Windus

Leavis, Q. D. (1932), *Fiction and the Reading Public*, London: Chatto & Windus

Lecourt, Dominique (1972), *Marxism and Epistemology: Bachelard, Canguilhem and Foucault*, tr. Ben Brewster, London: New Left Books, 1975

Lee, Brian (1970), 'The New Criticism and the Language of Poetry' in Fowler (1970)

Lees, Sue (1993), *Sugar and Spice: Sexuality and Adolescent Girls*, Harmondsworth: Penguin

Lefkowitz, Mary R. and Rogers, Guy MacLean, eds (1996), *Black Athena Revisited*, Chapel Hill and London: University of North Carolina Press

Leith, William (1998), ' "I'm not a real photographer" ', *Observer Life*, 15 February

Lemon, L. T. and Reis, M. J., eds (1965), *Russian Formalist Criticism*, Lincoln: University of Nebraska Press

Lenin, V. I. (1902), *What Is To Be Done?* in Lenin (1963)

—— (1908), 'Marxism and Revisionism' in Lenin (1963)

—— (1918), 'The Proletarian Revolution and the Renegade Kautsky' in Lenin (1964)

—— (1929), 'Conspectus of Hegel's Book, *The Science of Logic*' in *Collected Works* XXXVIII, London: Lawrence & Wishart, 1961

—— (1963), *Selected Works in Three Volumes* I, Moscow: Progress Publishers

—— (1964), *Selected Works in Three Volumes* III, Moscow: Progress Publishers

Lennon, Kathleen and Whitford, Margaret (1994), *Knowing the Difference: Feminist Perspectives in Epistemology*, London and New York: Routledge

Lentricchia, Frank (1980), *After the New Criticism*, London: Athlone Press

Le Roy Ladurie, Emmanuel (1967), *Times of Feast, Times of Famine*, tr. Barbara Bray, London: Allen & Unwin, 1972

—— (1978), *Montaillou: Cathars and Catholics in a French Village 1294–1324*, tr. Barbara Bray, Harmondsworth: Penguin, 1980

—— (1979), *Carnival in Romans: A People's Uprising at Romans, 1579–1580*, tr. Mary Feeney, Harmondsworth: Penguin, 1981

Leslie, Esther (1999), 'Introduction to the Adorno-Marcuse Correspondence', *New Left Review* 233

Levenson, Michael, ed. (1999), *The Cambridge Companion to Modernism*, Cambridge: Cambridge University Press

Lévi-Strauss, Claude (1948), *La Vie familiale et sociale des Indiens Nambikwara*, Paris: Société des Américanistes

—— (1949), *The Elementary Structures of Kinship*, tr. James Harle Bell, John Richard von Sterner and Rodney Needham, London: Eyre & Spottiswoode, 1969

—— (1950), *Introduction to the Work of Marcel Mauss*, tr. Felicity Baker, London: Routledge, 1992

—— (1955a), *Tristes Tropiques*, tr. John and Dorothy Weightman, London: Jonathan Cape, 1973

—— (1955b), 'The Structural Study of Myth', *Journal of American Folklore* vol. 68 no. 270

—— (1956), 'The Family', rev. edn in Lévi-Strauss (1983)

—— (1958), *Structural Anthropology*, tr. Claire Jacobson and Brooker Grundfast Schoepf, New York: Basic Books, 1963

—— (1960), 'Reflections on a Work by Vladimir Propp' in Lévi-Strauss (1973)

—— (1962a), 'Jean-Jacques Rousseau, Founder of the Sciences of Man' in Lévi-Strauss (1963)

—— (1962b), *Totemism*, tr. Rodney Needham, Harmondsworth: Penguin, 1969

—— (1962c) *The Savage Mind*, London: Weidenfeld & Nicolson, 1962

—— (1964), *The Raw and the Cooked*, tr. John and Dorothy Weightman, London: Jonathan Cape, 1970

—— (1965), 'Structuralism and Literary Criticism' in Lévi-Strauss (1973)

—— (1967), *From Honey to Ashes*, tr. John and Dorothy Weightman, London: Jonathan Cape, 1973

—— (1968), *The Origins of Table Manners*, tr. John and Dorothy Weightman, Chicago: University of Chicago Press, 1990

—— (1971), *The Naked Man*, tr. John and Dorothy Weightman, Chicago: University of Chicago Press, 1981

—— (1973), *Structural Anthropology* II, tr. Monique Layton, London: Allen Lane, 1976

—— (1975), *Way of the Masks*, tr. Sylvia Modelski, Seattle: University of Washington Press, 1988

—— (1983), *The View from Afar*, tr. Joachim Neugroschel and Phoebe Hess, Harmondsworth: Penguin, 1987

—— (1993), *Regarder, écouter, lire*, Paris: Plon

Levin, Thomas Y. (1989), *Siegfried Kracauer: Eine Bibliographie seiner Schriften*, Marbach-am-Necker: Deutsche Schillergesellschaft

Levinas, Emmanuel (1930), *Théorie de l'intuition dans la phénoménologie de Husserl*, Paris: Alcan

—— (1961), *Totality and Infinity*, tr. Alphonso Lingis, Pittsburg, KS: Duquesne University Press, 1969

—— (1968), *Quatre Lectures talmudiques*, Paris: Minuit

—— (1972), *Humanisme de l'autre homme*, Montpellier: Fata Morgana

—— (1974), *Autrement qu'être ou au delà de l'essence*, The Hague: Martinus Nijhoff

—— (1983), *Difficult Freedom: Essays on Judaism*, tr. Sean Hand, London: Athlone Press, 1990

—— (1995), *Nouvelles lectures talmudiques*, Paris: Minuit

Levy, Bernard-Henri (1977), *Barbarism with a Human Face*, tr. George Holoch, New York: Harper & Row

Leyda, Jay (1960), *Kino: A History of the Russian and Soviet Film*, London: George Allen & Unwin

Liddington, Jill and Norris, Jill (1978), *One Hand Tied Behind Us: The Rise of the Women's Suffrage Movement*, London: Virago

Lin Chun (1993), *The British New Left*, Edinburgh: Edinburgh University Press

Lipietz, Alain (1987), *Mirages and Miracles: The Crises of Global Fordism*, tr. David Macey, London: Verso, 1987

Lippard, Lucy (1966), *Pop Art*, London: Thames & Hudson

—— (1976), *From the Center: Feminist Essays on Women's Art*, New York: Dutton

Lipstadt, Deborah (1993), *Denying the Holocaust: The Growing Assault on Truth and Memory*, New York: Free Press

Locke, John (1690a), *Two Treatises of Government*, ed. Peter Laslett, Cambridge: Cambridge University Press, 1988

—— (1690b), *Essay Concerning Human Understanding*, London: Everyman, 1993

Loomba, Ania (1998), *Colonialism/Postcolonialism*, London: Routledge

Lovibond, Sabina (1990), 'Feminism and Postmodernism' in Boyne and Rattansi (1990)

Lucretius, *The Nature of the Universe*, tr. R. E. Latham, Harmondsworth: Penguin, 1951

Lukács, Georg (1920), *The Theory of the Novel: A Historic-Philosophical Essay on the Forms of Great Epic Literature*, tr. Anya Bostock, London: Merlin Press, 1971

—— (1923), *History and Class-Consciousness*, tr. Rodney Livingstone, London: Merlin Press, 1971

—— (1937), *The Historical Novel*, tr. Hannah and Stanley Mitchell, London: Merlin Press, 1962

—— (1938), 'Realism in the Balance', tr. Rodney Livingstone, in Bloch et al. (1977)

—— (1950), *Studies in European Realism: A Sociological Survey of the Writings of Balzac, Stendhal, Zola, Tolstoy, Gorki and Others*, London: Merlin Press

—— (1970), *Writer and Critic and Other Essays*, tr. Arthur Kahn, London: Merlin Press

Lukes, Steven (1973), *Emile Durkheim. His Life and Work: A Historical and Critical Study*, Harmondsworth: Penguin, 1992

Lyons, John (1968), *Introduction to Theoretical Linguistics*, Cambridge: Cambridge University Press

—— (1970), *Chomsky*, London: Fontana

Lyotard, Jean-François (1954), *La Phénoménologie*, Paris: PUF

—— (1971), *Discours, figure*, Paris: Klincksieck

—— (1973a), *Dérive à partir de Marx et Freud*, Paris: Union Générale des Editions

—— (1973b), 'Newman: The Instant', tr. David Macey in Benjamin (1989)

—— (1973c), *Les Dispositifs pulsionnels*, Paris: Christian Bourgois

—— (1974), *Libidinal Economy*, tr. J. H. Grant, London: Athlone Press, 1993

—— (1977a), *Rudiments païens: genre discursif*, Paris: UGE

—— (1977b), 'Lessons in Paganism', tr. David Macey in Benjamin (1989)

—— (1979a), *The Postmodern Condition: A Report on Knowledge*, tr. Geoffrey Bennington and Brian Massumi, Manchester: Manchester University Press, 1984

—— (1979b), *Just Gaming*, tr. Wlad Godzich, Manchester: Manchester University Press, 1985

—— (1980), 'Discussions, or Phrasing after Auschwitz', tr. Georges van den Abbeele in Benjamin (1989)

—— (1983), *The Differend: Phrases in Dispute*, tr. George van der Abbeele, Minneapolis: Minnesota University Press, 1988

—— (1984a), 'The Sublime and the Avant-Garde', tr. Geoffrey Bennington and Marian Hobson in Benjamin (1989)

—— (1984b), 'Philosophy and Painting in the Age of their Experimentation: Contribution to an Idea of Postmodernity', tr. Mária Minich Breuer and Daniel Breuer in Benjamin (1989)

—— (1985), 'Anamnesis of the Visible, or Candour', tr. David Macey in Benjamin (1989)

—— (1988), *Le Post-moderne expliqué aux enfants*, Paris: Galilée

—— (1992), *Peregrinations: Law, Form, Event*, New York: Columbia University Press

—— (1993), *Political Writings*, tr. Bill Readings and Kevin Paul Geiman, Minneapolis: University of Minnesota Press

Macey, David (1988), *Lacan in Contexts*, London: Verso, 1988

—— (1993), *The Lives of Michel Foucault*, London: Hutchinson

—— (1994), 'Thinking with Borrowed Concepts: Althusser and Lacan' in Elliott (1994)

—— (1998), '*Insoumis*: Nizan, Sartre, Fanon' in Dolamore (1998)

—— (2000), *Frantz Fanon: A Life*, London: Granta Books

Macherey, Pierre (1966), *A Theory of Literary Production*, tr. Geoffrey Wall, London: Routledge & Kegan Paul, 1978

—— (1990), *The Object of Literature*, tr. David Macey, Cambridge: Cambridge University Press, 1995

Mackay, Hugh (1997), *Consumption and Everyday Life*, London: Sage

MacKenzie, Iain (1997), 'Creativity as Criticism: The Philosophical Constructivism of Deleuze and Guattari', *Radical Philosophy* 86

MacKillop, Ian (1995), *F. R. Leavis: A Life in Criticism*, London: Allen Lane

MacKinnon, Catherine A. (1994), *Only Words*, London: HarperCollins

Macksey, Richard and Donato, Eugenio (1972), *The Structuralist Controversy: The Languages of Criticism and the Sciences of Man*, Baltimore and London: Johns Hopkins University Press

Macleod, Glenn (1999), 'The Visual Arts' in Levenson (1999)

Magarshack, David (1961), 'Stanislavski' in Bentley (1968)

Magee, Bryan (1973), *Popper*, London: Fontana

Magnus, Bernd and Higgins, Kathleen M., eds (1996), *The Cambridge Companion to Nietzsche*, Cambridge: Cambridge University Press

MAHRO (1983), *Visions of History*, Manchester: Manchester University Press

Malcolm, Janet (1984), *In the Freud Archives*, London: Jonathan Cape

Mâle, Louis (1902), *The Gothic Image: Religious Art in France of the Thirteenth Century*, tr. Dorn Nussey, New York: Harper Torchbooks, 1958

Malinowski, Bronislaw Kasper (1923), 'The Problem of Meaning in Primitive Languages' in Ogden and Richards (1923)

Mandel, Ernest (1972), *Late Capitalism*, tr. Joris De Bres, London: New Left Books, 1975

Mann, Michael (1995), 'As the Twentieth Century Progresses', *New Left Review* 214

Mannheim, Karl (1929), *Ideology and Utopia*, tr. Louis Wirth and Edward Shills, London: Routledge & Kegan Paul, 1936

Marcus, Steven (1966), *The Other Victorians: A Study of Sexuality and Pornography in Mid-Nineteenth Century England*, London: Weidenfeld & Nicolson

Marcuse, Herbert (1937), 'The Affirmative Character of Culture' in Marcuse (1965)

—— (1941), *Reason and Revolution: Hegel and the Rise of Social Theory*, London: Oxford University Press

—— (1955), *Eros and Civilization*, London: Sphere, 1955

—— (1964), *One-Dimensional Man*, London: Routledge & Kegan Paul

—— (1965a), *Negations: Essays in Critical Theory*, tr. Jeremy J. Shapiro, Harmondsworth: Penguin, 1972

—— (1965b), 'Repressive Tolerance' in Wolff, Moore and Marcuse (1965)

—— (1969), *An Essay on Liberation*, London: Allen Lane

—— (1977), *The Aesthetic Dimension: Towards a Critique of Marxist Aesthetics*, Boston: Beacon Press

Marinetti, F. T. (1971), *Let's Murder the Moonshine: F. T. Marinetti, Selected Writings*, ed. R. W. Flint, Los Angeles: Sun and Moon

Markov, Vladimir (1969), *Russian Futurism: A History*, London: MacGibbon & Kee

Marks, Elaine and de Courtivron, Isabelle (1979), *New French Feminisms*, Brighton: Harvester

Martinet, André (1960), *Elements of General Linguistics*, tr. Elisabeth Palmer, London: Faber & Faber, 1964

Marx, Karl (1843a), 'Critique of Hegel's Doctrine of the State' in Marx (1975)

—— (1843b), 'On the Jewish Question' in Marx (1975)

—— (1843–4), 'A Contribution to the Critique of Hegel's Philosophy of Right' in Marx (1975)

—— (1844), 'Economic and Philosophical Manuscripts' in Marx (1975)

—— (1845), 'Theses on Feuerbach' in Marx (1975)

—— (1847), *The Poverty of Philosophy*, New York: International Publishers, 1963

—— (1853), 'The Future Results of the British Rule in India' in Marx (1973b)

—— (1859), *A Contribution to the Critique of Political Economy*, Moscow: Progress Publishers, 1970

—— (1865), 'Wages, Price and Profit' in Marx and Engels (1969)

—— (1867), *Capital* I, tr. Ben Fowkes, introduction by Ernest Mandel, Harmondsworth: Penguin, 1976

—— (1973a), *The Revolutions of 1848: Political Writings I*, ed. David Fernbach, Harmondsworth: Penguin

—— (1973b), *Surveys from Exile: Political Writings II*, ed. David Fernbach, Harmondsworth: Penguin

—— (1975), *Early Writings*, tr. Rodney Livingstone and Gregor Benton, Harmondsworth: Penguin

—— and Frederick Engels (1845–6), *The German Ideology: Critique of Modern German Philosophy According to its Representatives Feuerbach, B. Bauer and Stirner, and of German Socialism According to its Various Prophets* in Marx and Engels (1976)

—— (1847–8), 'The Communist Manifesto' in Marx (1973a)

—— (1965), *Selected Correspondence*, Moscow: Progress Publishers

—— (1969), *Selected Works in One Volume*, New York: International Publishers

—— (1973), *On Literature and Art*, ed. L. Baxandal and S. Morawski, St Louis: Telos Press

—— (1976), *Collected Works V: Marx and Engels 1845–47*, London: Lawrence & Wishart

Marxist Feminist Literature Collective (1978), 'Women's Writing: Jane Eyre, Shirley, Villette, Aurora Leigh' in Barker et al. (1978)

Masereel, Frans (1925), *The City ('Die Stadt'): 100 Woodcuts*, New York: Dover, 1972

Massey, Anne (1995), *The Independent Group: Modernism and Mass Culture in Britain, 1945–1959*, Manchester: Manchester University Press

Masson, Jeffrey Moussaieff (1984), *The Assault on Truth: Freud's Suppression of the Seduction Theory*, New York: Farrar, Straus & Giroux

Masters of Seventeenth-Century Dutch Genre Painting, Philadelphia: Philadelphia Museum of Art, 1984

Matejka, Ladislav and Pomorska, Krystyna, eds (1971), *Readings in Russian Poetics: Formalist and Structuralist Views*, Cambridge, MA: MIT Press

Mathews, Harry and Bratchie, Alastair (1998), *OULIPO Compendium*, London: Atlas Press

Matthews, J. H. (1973), *The Imagery of Surrealism*, New York: Syracuse University Press

Mauss, Marcel (1923), *The Gift: The Form and Reason for Exchange in Ancient Societies*, tr. W. D. Halls, London: Routledge, 1990

Mayakovsky: Twenty Years of Work, Oxford and Moscow: Museum of Modern Art and State Museum of Literature, 1982

McCarney, Joseph (1993), 'Shaping Ends: Reflections on Fukuyama', *New Left Review* 202

McCarthy, Thomas (1984), *The Critical Theory of Jürgen Habermas*, Cambridge: Polity Press

—— (1993), 'The Idea of a Critical Theory and its Relation to Philosophy' in Benhabib, Bonns and McCole (1993)

MacInnes, Colin (1957), *City of Spades*, London: MacGibbon & Kee

—— (1959), *Absolute Beginners*, London: MacGibbon & Kee

McLuhan, Marshall (1962), *The Gutenberg Galaxy: The Making of Typographic Man*, Toronto: University of Toronto Press

—— (1964), *Understanding Media: The Extensions of Man*, London: Routledge & Kegan Paul

—— (1967), *The Medium is the Massage*, San Francisco: Hardwired, 1996

—— (1968), *War and Peace in the Global Village*, San Francisco: Hardwired, 1997

McRobbie, Angela (1991), *Feminism and Youth Culture: From 'Jackie' to 'Just Seventeen'*, London: Macmillan

—— and Garber, Jenny (1975), 'Girls and Subcultures: An Exploration' in *Working Papers in Cultural Studies* (1975)

Meinenke, Friedrich (1936), *Historicism: The Rise of a New Historical Outlook*, tr. J. E. Anderson, London: Routledge & Kegan Paul, 1972

Merleau-Ponty, Maurice (1942), *The Structure of Behaviour*, tr. Alden L. Fisher, London: Methuen, 1965

—— (1945), *Phenomenology of Perception*, tr. Colin Smith, London: Routledge & Kegan Paul, 1982

—— (1947), *Humanism and Terror*, tr. John O'Neil, Boston: Beacon Press, 1969

—— (1948), *Sense and Non-Sense*, tr. Hubert Dreyfus and Patricia Allen Dreyfus, Evanston, IL: Northwestern University Press, 1973

—— (1955), *Adventures of the Dialectic*, tr. Joseph Bie, Evanston, IL: Northwestern University Press

—— (1960), *Signes*, Paris: Gallimard

—— (1964a), *L'Oeil et l'esprit*, Paris: Gallimard

—— (1964b), *The Visible and the Invisible*, tr. Alphonso Lingis, Evanston, IL: Northwestern University Press, 1968

—— (1969), *The Prose of the World*, tr. John O'Neil, Evanston, IL: Northwestern University Press, 1973

—— (1995), *La Nature*, Paris: Seuil

—— (1997), *Parcours 1935–1951*, Paris: Verdier

Merquior, J. G. (1986), *From Prague to Paris: A Critique of Structuralist and Post-Structuralist Thought*, London: Verso

Meszaros, Istvan (1971), *Marx's Theory of Alienation*, London: Merlin Press

Metz, Christian (1966), 'La Grande Syntagmatique du film narratif', *Communications* 8

—— (1968), *Film Language: A Semiotics of the Cinema*, tr. M. Taylor, New York: Oxford University Press, 1974

—— (1971), *Language and Cinema*, tr. D. J. Umiker-Seboek, The Hague: Mouton, 1974

—— (1977), *Psychoanalysis and Cinema: The Imaginary Signifier*, tr. C. Britton, A. Williams, B. Brewster and A. Guzzetti, London: Macmillan, 1982

Mill, John Stuart (1843), *A System of Logic Ratiocinative and Inductive: Being a Connected View of the Principles and Methods of Scientific Investigation*, London: Longman, 1970

Miller, Alice (1988), *Banished Knowledge: Facing Childhood Injuries*, tr. Leila Vennewitz, London: Virago, 1991

Millett, Kate (1969), *Sexual Politics*, London: Abacus, 1972

—— (1971), *The Prostitution Papers: A Candid Dialogue*, New York: Basic Books

—— (1974), *Flying*, New York: Alfred A. Knopf

—— (1977), *Sita*, New York: Farrar, Straus & Giroux

—— (1990), *The Loony Bin Trip*, New York: Simon & Schuster

—— (1998), 'The Feminist Time Forgot', *The Guardian*, 23 June

Mirza, Heidi Safia, ed. (1997), *Black British Feminism: A Reader*, London and New York: Routledge

Mishra, Vijay and Hodge, Bob (1991), 'What is (Post-)Colonialism?', *Textual Practice* vol. 5 no. 3

Mitchell, Juliet (1966), 'Women: The Longest Revolution', *New Left Review* 40

—— (1971), *Women's Estate*, Harmondsworth: Penguin

—— (1974), *Psychoanalysis and Feminism*, London: Allen Lane

—— (1984), *Women: The Longest Revolution: Essays in Feminism, Literature and Psychoanalysis*, London: Virago

—— and Rose, Jacqueline, eds (1982), *Jacques Lacan and the École freudienne: Feminine Sexuality*, tr. Jacqueline Rose, London: Macmillan

Moers, Ellen (1976), *Literary Women: The Great Writers*, Garden City, NY: Anchor Press/Doubleday

Moi, Toril (1985), *Sexual/Textual Politics: Feminist Literary Theory*, London: Methuen

——, ed. (1986), *The Kristeva Reader*, Oxford: Blackwell

——, ed. (1987), *French Feminist Thought: A Reader*, Oxford: Blackwell

—— (1994), *Simone de Beauvoir: The Making of an Intellectual Woman*, Oxford: Blackwell

Mongin, Olivier (1998), *Paul Ricoeur*, Paris: Seuil

Monk, Ray (1990), *Wittgenstein: The Duty of Genius*, London: Jonathan Cape

Montrose, Louis A. (1986), 'Renaissance Literary Studies and the Subject of History', *English Literary Renaissance* 16

—— (1989), 'Professing the Renaissance: The Poetics and Politics of Culture' in Veeser (1989)

Moore, G. E. (1903), *Principia Ethica*, Cambridge: Cambridge University Press

Moore-Gilbert, Bart (1997), *Post-Colonial Theory: Contexts, Practices, Politics*, London: Verso

Moreno, J. L. (1946), *Psychodrama*, New York: Beacon House

Morgan, Robin, ed. (1970), *Sisterhood is Powerful: An Anthology of Writings from the Women's Liberation Movement*, New York: Vintage Books

Morley, David and Kuan-Hsing, Chen, eds (1996), *Stuart Hall: Critical Dialogues in Cultural Studies*, London: Routledge

Morrison, Blake (1980), *The Movement: English Poetry and Fiction of the 1950s*, Oxford: Oxford University Press

Morrison, Toni (1992), *Playing in the Dark: Whiteness and the Literary Imagination*, Cambridge, MA: Harvard University Press

Moszynska, Anna (1990), *Abstract Art*, London: Thames & Hudson

Motion, Andrew (1993), *Philip Larkin: A Writer's Life*, London: Faber & Faber

Mudimbe, V. Y., ed. (1992), *The Surreptitious Speech: 'Présence africaine' and the Politics of Otherness, 1947–1987*, Chicago: University of Chicago Press

Mukarovsky, Jan (1932), 'Standard Language and Poetic Language' in Garvin (1964)

—— (1941), 'Structuralism in Esthetics and in Literary Studies', tr. Olga Hasty in Steiner (1982)

Mulhern, Francis (1979), *The Moment of 'Scrutiny'*, London: New Left Books

—— (1990), 'English Reading' in Bhabha (1990)

—— (1996), 'A Welfare Culture? Hoggart and Williams in the Fifties', *Radical Philosophy* 77

Mulvey, Laura (1975), 'Visual Pleasure and Narrative Cinema', *Screen* vol. 16 no. 3

Murdoch, Iris (1958), 'A House of Theory' in Murdoch (1997)

—— (1997), *Existentialists and Mystics: Writings on Philosophy and Literature*, ed. Peter Conradi, London: Chatto & Windus

Musser, Charles (1996), 'Cinéma-vérité and the New Documentary' in Nowell-Smith (1996)

Muthesios, Angelica (1992), *Jeff Koons*, Cologne: Benedikt Taschen

Nairn, Tom (1964), 'The British Political Elite', *New Left Review* 24

—— (1995), 'Breakwaters of 2000: From Ethnic to Civic Nationalism', *New Left Review* 214

Naremore, James (1998), *More than Night: Film Noir in its Contexts*, Berkeley: University of California Press

Nayar, Radhakrishnan (1998), 'Vernacular Spectacular', *Times Higher Education Supplement*, 6 February

Neue Sachlichkeit and German Realism of the Twenties, London: Arts Council of Great Britain, 1979

Neumann, Franz L. (1944), *Behemoth: The Structure and Practice of National Socialism*, New York: Oxford University Press

Neurath, O., Carnap, R. and Morris, C., eds (1938), *International Encyclopedia of Unified Science*, Chicago: University of Chicago Press

Neville, Richard (1970), *Playpower*, London: Paladin

New Formations 26: 'Special Issue on Psychoanalysis and Culture', 1995

New Fowler's English Usage, 3rd edn, ed. R. W. Burchfield, Oxford: Clarendon Press, 1996

New German Critique 17: *Special Walter Benjamin Issue*, 1979

—— 34: *Second Walter Benjamin Issue*, 1986

—— 54: *Special Issue on Siegfried Kracauer*, 1991

Ngugi wa Thiong'o (1968), 'On the Abolition of the English Department' in Ngugi wa Thiong'o (1972)

—— (1972), *Homecoming: Essays*, London: Heinemann

—— (1977), *Petals of Blood*, London: Heinemann

—— (1981), *Detained: A Writer's Prison Diary*, London: Heinemann

—— (1984a), 'The Language of African Fiction' in Ngugi Wa Thiong'o (1986)

—— (1984b), 'The Language of African Theatre' in Ngugi Wa Thiong'o (1986)

—— (1986), *Decolonising the Mind: The Politics of Language in African Literature*, Oxford: James Currey; Nairobi: EAEP; Portsmouth, NH: Heinemann

—— (1997), *Writers in Politics: A Re-Engagement with Issues of Literature and Society*, Oxford: James Currey; Nairobi: EAEP; Portsmouth, NH: Heinemann

Nietzsche, Friedrich (1872), *The Birth of Tragedy*, tr. Shaun Whiteside, Harmondsworth: Penguin, 1993

—— (1874), 'On the Uses and Disadvantages of History for Life' in *Untimely Meditations*, tr. R. J. Hollingdale, Cambridge: Cambridge University Press, 1983

—— (1878), *Human, All Too Human*, tr. Marion Faber and Stephen Lehmann, introduction and notes by Marion Faber, Harmondsworth: Penguin, 1994

—— (1886), *Beyond Good and Evil*, tr. R. J. Hollingdale, Harmondsworth: Penguin, 1990

—— (1887), *On The Genealogy of Morals and Other Writings*, tr. K. A. Pearson and C. Dicthe, Cambridge: Cambridge University Press, 1994

—— (1892), *Thus Spoke Zarathustra*, tr. R. J. Hollingdale, Harmondsworth: Penguin, 1961

—— (1901), *The Will to Power*, tr. Walter Kaufmann and R. J. Hollingdale, New York: Vintage Books, 1968

Nochlin, Linda (1968), 'The Invention of the Avant-Garde: France, 1830–1880' in Nochlin (1991)

—— (1971a), *Realism*, Harmondsworth: Penguin

—— (1971b), 'Why Have There Been No Great Woman Artists?' in Nochlin (1989)

—— (1989), *Women, Art and Power and Other Essays*, London: Thames & Hudson

—— (1991), *The Politics of Vision: Essays on Nineteenth-Century Art and Society*, London: Thames & Hudson

—— and Harris, Ann Sutherland (1976), *Women Artists 1550–1950*, Los Angeles: Los Angeles County Museum of Art

Nolte, Ernst (1985), 'Between Myth and Revisionism? The Third Reich in the Perspectives of the 1980s' in Koch (1985)

Norris, Christopher (1978), *William Empson and the Philosophy of Literary Criticism*, London: Athlone Press

—— (1982), *Deconstruction: Theory and Practice*, London: Methuen

Nowell-Smith, Geoffrey, ed. (1996), *The Oxford History of World Cinema*, Oxford: Oxford University Press

Oakley, Ann (1972), *Sex, Gender and Society*, London: Temple Smith

—— (1974), *Housewife*, London: Allen Lane

—— (1996), 'A Brief History of Gender' in Oakley and Mitchell (1997)

—— and Mitchell, Juliet (1997), *Who's Afraid of Feminism? Seeing through the Backlash*, London: Hamish Hamilton

O'Connor, Garry (1975), *French Theatre Today*, London: Pitman

Ogden, C. K. and Richards, I. A. (1923), *The Meaning of Meaning: A Study of the Influence of Language on Thought, with Supplementary Essays by B. Malinowski and F. C. Crookshank*, London: Kegan Paul, Trench & Trübner

Oliver, Kelly, ed. (1997), *The Portable Kristeva*, New York: Columbia University Press

Oliver, Paul (1960), *Blues Fell This Morning*, New York: Horizon Press

Onis, Frederico de (1934), *Antología de la poesía española e hispanoamericana (1882–1932)*, New York: Las Americas Press, 1961

Orwell, George (1937), *The Road to Wigan Pier*, Harmondsworth: Penguin, 1962

—— (1938), *Homage to Catalonia*, Harmondsworth: Penguin, 1962

—— (1939), 'Boy's Weeklies' in Orwell (1968, I)

—— (1941), 'The Lion and the Unicorn' in Orwell (1968, II)

—— (1942), 'The Art of Donald McGill' in Orwell (1968, II)

—— (1945), *Animal Farm*, Harmondsworth: Penguin, 1951

—— (1949), *Nineteen Eighty-Four*, London: Secker & Warburg

—— (1968), *The Collected Essays, Journalism and Letters of George Orwell*, London: Secker & Warburg, 4 vols

Ott, Hugo (1988), *Martin Heidegger: A Political Life*, tr. Allan Blunden, London: Harper-Collins, 1993

OULIPO (1973), *La Littérature potentielle*, Paris: Gallimard

—— (1981), *Atlas de littérature potentielle*, Paris: Gallimard

Owen, Ursula (1998), 'The Speech that Kills', *Index on Censorship* 1

Oxford Literary Review vol. 8: *Sexual Difference*, 1986

Packard, Vance (1957), *The Hidden Persuaders*, London: Longman Green

Paddison, Max (1993), *Adorno's Aesthetics of Music*, Cambridge: Cambridge University Press

Paglia, Camille (1990), *Sexual Personae: Art and Decadence from Nefertiti to Emily Dickinson*, New Haven: Yale University Press

—— (1992), *Sex, Art and American Culture*, New York: Vintage

—— (1994), *Vamps and Tramps*, New York: Random House

Panofsky, Erwin (1939), *Studies in Iconology: Humanistic Themes in the Art of the Renaissance*, New York: Oxford University Press

—— (1943), *The Life and Art of Albrecht Dürer*, Princeton: Princeton University Press, 1971, 4th edn

—— (1953), *Early Netherlandish Painting*, New York: Harper & Row, 1971, 2 vols

—— (1955), *Meaning in the Visual Arts: Papers in and on Art History*, New York: Doubleday

—— (1957), *Gothic Architecture and Scholasticism*, New York: Meridian, 1973

—— (1965), *Renaissance and Renascences in Western Art*, London: Paladin, 1970

Parallax 4. Kojève's Paris/Bataille Now, 1997

Paris Post War: Art and Existentialism 1945–55, London: Tate Gallery, 1993

Parker, Rozsika and Pollock, Griselda (1981), *Old Mistresses: Women, Art and Ideology*, London: Routledge

—— (1987), *Framing Feminism: Art and the Women's Movement 1970–1985*, London: Pandora Books

Parsons, Talcott (1937), *The Structure of Social Action*, New York: McGraw Hill

—— (1951), *The Social System*, London: Routledge & Kegan Paul

—— (1971), *The System of Modern Societies*, Englewood Cliffs, NJ: Prentice-Hall

Pascal, Blaise (1669), *Pensées*, tr. A. J. Krailsheimer, Harmondsworth: Penguin, 1966

Patton, Paul, ed. (1996), *Deleuze: A Critical Reader*, Oxford: Blackwell

Pavel, Thomas (1989), *The Feud of Language: A History of Structuralist Thought*, English version by Linda Jordan and Thomas Pavel, Oxford: Blackwell, 1992

Pears, David (1971), *Wittgenstein*, London: Fontana

Pêcheux, Michel (1975), *Language, Semantics and Ideology*, tr. Harbans Nagpal, London and Basingstoke: Macmillan, 1982

—— et al. (1995), *Automatic Discourse Analysis*, ed. Tony Hak and Niels Helsloot, tr. David Macey, Amsterdam and Atlanta, GA: Rodopi

Peirce, C. S. (1932), *Collected Papers* II, Cambridge, MA: Harvard University Press

—— (1934), *Collected Papers* IV, Cambridge, MA: Harvard University Press

—— (1955), *Philosophical Writings of Peirce*, ed. Justus Buchler, New York: Dover

Perec, Georges (1965), *Things: A Story of the Sixties*, tr. David Bellos and Andrew Leak, London: Harvill Press, 1990

—— (1969), *A Void*, tr. Gilbert Adair, London: HarperCollins, 1994

—— (1973), 'Histoire du lipogramme' in OULIPO (1973)

—— (1978), *Life: A User's Manual*, tr. David Bellos, London: Collins Harvill, 1987

Peristiany, J. G., ed. (1965), *Honour and Shame: The Values of Mediterranean Society*, London: Weidenfeld & Nicolson

Phelan, Shane, ed. (1997), *Playing with Fire: Queer Politics, Queer Theory*, New York and London: Routledge

Phillips, Angela (1998), 'At War with the Sisters', *Guardian Saturday Review*, 19 September

Picard, Raymond (1965), *Nouvelle Critique ou nouvelle imposture?*, Paris: Pauvert

Pierre, José (1990), *Investigating Sex: Surrealist Research 1928–32*, tr. Malcolm Imrie, London: Verso, 1982

Piscator, Erwin (1925), *The Political Theatre*, tr. H. Robinson, London: Eyre Methuen, 1980

Pivcevic, Edo (1970), *Husserl and Phenomenology*, London: Hutchinson

Plant, Sadie (1992), *The Most Radical Gesture: The Situationist International in a Postmodern Age*, London: Routledge

Pleynet, Marcelin (1977), *Painting and System*, tr. Sime N. Godfrey, Chicago: University of Chicago Press, 1984

Plato, *Cratylus*, tr. H. C. J. Fowler in *Plato in Twelve Volumes*, Cambridge, MA: Harvard University Press, 1926, IV

—— *The Symposium*, tr. W. Hamilton, Harmondsworth: Penguin, 1951

—— *Protagoras* in *Protagoras and Meno*, tr. W. K. C. Guthrie, Harmondsworth: Penguin, 1956

—— *Timaeus*, tr. H. D. P. Lee, Harmondsworth: Penguin, 1965

—— *Phaedrus and Letters VII and VIII*, tr. Walter Hamilton, Harmondsworth: Penguin, 1973

—— *Philebus*, tr. Robin A. H. Waterfield, Harmondsworth: Penguin, 1982

—— *The Republic*, tr. A. D. Lindsay, London: Everyman, 1992

Poirié, François (1987), *Emmanuel Levinas: Essai et entretiens*, Lyon: La Manufacture

Pollock, Griselda (1995), *Vision and Difference: Femininity, Feminism and the Histories of Art*, London: Routledge

——, ed. (1996), *Generations and Geographies in the Visual Arts: Feminist Readings*, London and New York: Routledge

—— (1998), *Mary Cassatt: Painter of Modern Women*, London: Thames & Hudson

Pomorska, Krystyna (1968), *Russian Formalist Theory and the Poetic Ambiance*, The Hague: Mouton

Ponge, Francis (1998), *Selected Poems*, ed. Margaret Gution, tr. John Montague and C. K. Williams, London: Faber & Faber

Pope, Alexander (1704), 'Pastorals, with a Discourse on Pastoral' in *The Poems of Alexander Pope*, ed. John Butt, London: Methuen, 1963

Popper, Karl R. (1934), *The Logic of Scientific Discovery*, London, Hutchinson, 1959

—— (1945), *The Open Society and its Enemies*, London: Routledge & Kegan Paul

—— (1957), *The Poverty of Historicism*, London: Routledge & Kegan Paul

—— (1963), *Conjectures and Refutations: The Growth of Scientific Knowledge*, London: Routledge & Kegan Paul

—— (1976), *Unended Quest: An Intellectual Autobiography*, London: Fontana

Porter, Roy (1987), *Mind-Forg'd Manacles: A History of Madness in England from the Restoration to the Regency*, Harmondsworth: Penguin, 1990

Portoghesi, Paolo (1983), *Postmodern: The Architecture of the Post-Industrial Society*, New York: Rizzoli

Prendergast, Christopher (1986), *The Order of Mimesis: Balzac, Stendhal, Nerval, Flaubert*, Cambridge: Cambridge University Press

Press, John, ed. (1965), *Commonwealth Literature: Unity and Diversity in a Common Culture*, London: Heinemann

Prince, Gerald (1973a), *A Grammar of Stories*, The Hague: Mouton

—— (1973b), 'Introduction à l'étude du narrataire', *Poétique* 14

Propp, Vladimir (1928), *Morphology of the Folktale*, tr. Lawrence Scott, Bloomington: Indiana University Press, 1958

Putman, H. (1988), *Representation and Reality*, Cambridge, MA: Harvard University Press

Queneau, Raymond (1937), *Odile*, tr. Carol Sanders, Elmwood Park, IL: Dalkey Archive Press, 1988

Quine, W. V. O. (1953), *From a Logical Point of View*, Cambridge, MA: Harvard University Press

Racine, Daniel (1983), *Léon-Gontran Damas: L'Homme et l'oeuvre*, Paris and Dakar: Présence africaine

Radicalesbians (1972), 'The Woman-Identified Woman' in Schneier (1995)

Radway, Janice A. (1984), *Reading the Romance: Women, Patriarchy and Popular Literature*, Chapel Hill, NC and London: University of North Carolina Press

Ransom, John Crowe (1941), *The New Criticism*, Norfolk, CT: New Directions

—— (1955), *Poems and Essays*, New York: Vintage

Raspaud, Jean-Jacques and Voyer, Jean-Pierre (1972), *L'Internationale situationiste: Protagonistes/chronologie/bibliographie (avec un index des norms insultés)*, Paris: Éditions Champ Libre

Rattansi, Ali (1997), 'Postcolonialism and its Discontents', *Economy and Society* vol. 26 no. 4

Rawls, John (1972), *A Theory of Justice*, New York: Oxford University Press

Rawson, Judy (1976), 'Italian Futurism' in Bradbury and McFarlane (1976)

Rayner, Eric (1991), *The Independent Mind in British Psychoanalysis*, London: Free Association Books

Re, Lucia (1990), *Calvino and the Age of Neorealism: Fables of Estrangement*, Stanford: Stanford University Press

Read, Alan, ed. (1996), *The Fact of Blackness: Frantz Fanon and Visual Representation*, London and Seattle: ICA/Institute of International Visual Arts, Bay Press

Readings, Bill (1991), *Introducing Lyotard: Art and Politics*, London: Routledge

Recherches (1973), *Grande Encyclopédie des homosexualités: Trois milliards de pervers*

Reich, Wilhelm (1933), *Character Analysis*, New York: Farrar, Straus & Giroux, 1972

—— (1935), *The Sexual Revolution*, tr. Theodore P. Wolfe; London: Vision Press, 1972

—— (1942), *The Function of the Orgasm: Sex-Economic Problems of Biological Energy*, tr. Theodore P. Wolfe, London: Panther, 1968

Renan, Ernest (1882), 'What Is a Nation?', tr. Martin Thom in Bhabha (1990)

Resistance through Rituals (1975), *Working Papers in Cultural Studies* 7/8

Revel, Jean-Jacques (1960), *Sur Proust*, Paris: Julliard

Richard, Jean-Pierre (1954), *Littérature et sensation*, Paris: Seuil

—— (1955), *Poésie et profondeur*, Paris: Seuil

—— (1961), *L'Univers imaginaire de Mallarmé*, Paris: Seuil

—— (1974), *Proust et le monde sensible*, Paris: Seuil

Richards, I. A. (1924), *Principles of Literary Criticism*, London: Routledge & Kegan Paul

—— (1925), *Science and Poetry*, London: Routledge & Kegan Paul

—— (1929), *Practical Criticism: A Study of Literary Judgement*, London: Routledge & Kegan Paul

Richardson, Michael (1994), *Georges Bataille*, London: Routledge

——, ed. (1996), *Refusal of the Shadow: Surrealism and the Caribbean*, tr. Michael Richardson and Krzysztof Fijalkowski, London: Verso

Richter, Hans (1964), *Dada: Art and the Anti-Art*, tr. David Britt, London: Thames & Hudson, 1965

Ricoeur, Paul (1947), *Karl Jaspers et la philosophie de l'existence*, Paris: Seuil

—— (1948), *Gabriel Marcel et Karl Jaspers: Philosophie du système et philosophie du paradoxe*, Paris: Seuil

—— (1963), 'Structure and Hermeneutics' in Ricoeur (1969)

—— (1965), *Freud and Philosophy: An Essay on Interpretation*, tr. Denis Savage, New Haven: Yale University Press, 1970

—— (1969), *The Conflict of Interpretations: Essays in Hermeneutics*, ed. Don Ihde, Evanston: Northwestern University Press

—— (1975), *The Rule of Metaphor: Multi-Disciplinary Studies in the Creation of Meaning*, tr. Robert Czerny with Kathleen McLaughlin and John Costella, London: Routledge, 1978

—— (1983–5),*Time and Narrative*, tr. Kathleen McLaughlin and David Pellauer, Chicago: University of Chicago Press, 1984–6, 3 vols

—— (1986), 'Ce qui me préoccupe depuis trente ans', *Esprit*, August–September

—— (1990), *Oneself as an Other*, Chicago: University of Chicago Press, 1992

Riesman, David with Galzer, A. and Densey, R. (1950), *The Lonely Crowd: A Study of the Changing American Character*, New Haven: Yale University Press

Rimbaud, Arthur (1873), 'Une Saison en enfer', in *Oeuvres complètes*, Paris: Bibliothèque de la pléïade, 1951

Rimmon-Kenan, Shlomith (1983), *Narrative Fiction: Contemporary Poetics*, London: Methuen

Rivière, Joan (1929), 'Womanliness as Masquerade', *International Journal of Psychoanalysis* 10

Robbe-Grillet, Alain (1953), *The Erasers*, London: Calder & Boyars, 1966

—— (1963), *Snapshots and Towards a New Novel*, tr. A. M. Sheridan-Smith, London: John Calder, 1965

Robbins, Bruce (1991), 'Tenured Radicals, the New McCarthyism and PC', *New Left Review* 188

Robbins, Derek (1991), *The Work of Pierre Bourdieu: Recognizing Society*, Milton Keynes: Open University Press

Robert, Marthe (1972), *Origins of the Novel*, tr. Sacha Rabinovitch, Brighton: Harvester 1980

Robinson, Cedric J. (1998), 'Blaxploitation and the Misrepresentation of Liberation', *Race and Class* vol. 4 no. 1

Robinson, Paul A. (1972), *The Sexual Radicals*, London: Paladin

Robinson, Victoria and Richardson, Diane, eds (1997), *Introducing Women's Studies*, London: Macmillan, 2nd edn

Rockmore, Tom (1989), *Habermas on Historical Materialism*, Bloomington and Indianapolis: Indiana University Press

—— (1995), *Heidegger and French Philosophy: Humanism, Antihumanism and Being*, London and New York: Routledge

—— and Margolis, Joseph, ed. (1992), *The Heidegger Case: Philosophy and Politics*, Philadelphia: Temple University Press

Rodney, Walter (1972), *How Europe Underdeveloped Africa*, London: Bogle L'Ouverture

Rorty, Richard, ed. (1967), *The Linguistic Turn: Recent Essays in Philosophical Method*, Chicago: University of Chicago Press

—— (1980), *Philosophy and the Mirror of Nature*, Oxford: Basil Blackwell

—— (1991a), *Objectivity, Relativism and Truth: Philosophical Papers* I, Cambridge: Cambridge University Press

—— (1991b), *Essays on Heidegger and Others: Philosophical Papers* II, Cambridge: Cambridge University Press

Rose, Jacqueline (1986), *Sexuality in the Field of Vision*, London: Verso

Rothgeb, C. L., ed. (1991), *Abstracts of the Collected Works of C. G. Jung*, London: Karnac Books

Rouch, Jean and Morin, Edgar (1962), 'Chronique d'un été', *Domaine cinéma* 1

Roudinesco, Elisabeth (1982), *La Bataille de cent ans: Histoire de la psychanalyse en France 1885–1939*, Paris: Ramsay

—— (1986), *Jacques Lacan & Co.: A History of Psychoanalysis in France 1925–1985*, tr. with a foreword by Jeffrey Mehlman, London: Free Association Books, 1990

—— (1993), *Jacques Lacan*, tr. Barbara Bray, Cambridge: Polity Press

Rowbotham, Sheila (1972), *Women: Resistance and Revolution*, Harmondsworth: Penguin

—— (1973a), *Hidden from History: 300 Years of Women's Oppression and the Fight Against It*, London: Pluto Press

—— (1973b), *Women's Consciousness, Man's World*, Harmondsworth: Penguin

—— (1974), 'Search and Subject, Threading Circumstance' in Rowbotham (1983)

—— (1983), *Dreams and Nightmares: Collected Writings*, London: Virago

—— (1997), *A Century of Women: The History of Women in Britain and the United States*, London: Viking

——, Segal, Lynne and Wainwright, Hilary (1979), *Beyond the Fragments: Feminism and the Making of Socialism*, London: Merlin Press

Rousseau, Jean-Jacques, *A Discourse on the Origin of Inequality* in Rousseau (1973)

—— (1973), *The Social Contract and Discourses*, tr. G. D. H. Cole, London: Everyman

Rudy, Stephen (1984), *A Complete Bibliography of Roman Jakobson's Writings 1912–1982*, The Hague: Mouton

Russell, B. A. W. (1918), *Philosophy of Logical Atomism* in Russell (1986)

—— (1986), *The Collected Papers of Bertrand Russell* VIII: *The Philosophy of Logical Atomism and Other Essays 1914–1918*, ed. John G. Slater, London: George Allen & Unwin

—— and Whitehead, A. N. (1910), *Principia Mathematica*, Cambridge: Cambridge University Press

Rustin, Michael (1994), 'Incomplete Modernity: Ulrich Beck's *Risk Society*', *Radical Philosophy* 67

Rycroft, Charles (1971), *Reich*, London: Fontana

Ryle, Gilbert (1949), *The Concept of Mind*, London: Hutchinson

—— (1966–7), 'Thinking and Reflecting' in Ryle (1971)

—— (1968), 'The Thinking of Thoughts: What is *Le Penseur* Doing?' in Ryle (1971)

—— (1971), *Collected Papers* II: *Collected Essays 1929–1968*, London: Hutchinson

Sadler, Simon (1998), *The Situationist City*, Cambridge, MA and London: MIT Press

Said, Edward W. (1966), *Joseph Conrad and the Fiction of Autobiography*, New Haven: Harvard University Press

—— (1975), *Beginnings: Intentions and Method*, London: Granta Books, 1997

—— (1978), *Orientalism*, London: Routledge & Kegan Paul

—— (1981), *Covering Islam*, New York: Pantheon

—— (1983), *The World, the Text and the Critic*, New Haven: Harvard University Press

—— (1993), *Culture and Imperialism*, London: Chatto & Windus

—— (1994a), *Representations of the Intellectual: The 1993 Reith Lectures*, London: Vintage

—— (1994b), *The Politics of Dispossession*, London: Vintage

Samuel, Raphaël (1980), 'British Marxist Historians 1880–1980', *New Left Review* 120

——, ed. (1981a), *East End Underworld: South-West Bethnal Green*, London: Routledge & Kegan Paul

——, ed. (1981b), *East End Underworld: Chapters in the Life of Arthur Harding*, London: Routledge & Kegan Paul

—— (1985–7), 'The Lost World of British Communism', *New Left Review* 154, 155, 156, 165

——, ed. (1992), *History Workshop: A Collectanea 1967–1991*, Oxford: Ruskin College

—— (1994), *Theatres of Memory* I: *Past and Present in Contemporary Culture*, London: Verso

—— (1998), *Island Stories: Unravelling Britain*, London: Verso

Samuels, A., Shorter, B. and Plaut, F. (1986), *A Critical Dictionary of Jungian Analysis*, London: Routledge & Kegan Paul

Santoni, Ronald E. (1995), *Bad Faith, Good Faith and Authenticity in Sartre's Early Philosophy*, Philadelphia: Temple University Press

Sapir, Edward (1921), *Language: An Introduction to the Study of Speech*, New York: Harcourt Brace

Sarraute, Nathalie (1939), *The Age of Suspicion* in *Tropisms and The Age of Suspicion*, London: John Calder, 1963

Sarris, Andrew (1968), *The American Cinema: Directors and Direction, 1929–1968*, New York: Dalton

Sartre, Jean-Paul (1936), *The Transcendence of the Ego: An Existentialist Theory of Consciousness*, tr. Forrest Williams and Robert Kirkpatrick, New York: Noonday Press, 1962

—— (1938), *Nausea*, tr. R. Baldwick, Harmondsworth: Penguin, 1965

—— (1939), 'Une Idée fondamentale de la phénoménologie de Husserl: L'Intentionalité' in Sartre (1947d)

—— (1940), *The Psychology of the Imagination*, tr. Bernard Frechtman, New York: Philosophical Library, 1948

—— (1943a), *Being and Nothingness*, tr. Hazel Barnes, London: Methuen, 1957

—— (1943b), 'Explication de *l'etranger*' in Sartre (1947d)

—— (1944a), 'Paris sous l'occupation' in Sartre (1949b)

—— (1944b), *Huis-clos*, tr. Stuart Gilbert, London: Hutchinson, 1990

—— (1945a), *The Age of Reason*, tr. Eric Sutton, Harmondsworth: Penguin, 1990

—— (1945b), *The Reprieve*, tr. Eric Sutton, Harmondsworth: Penguin, 1990

—— (1945c), 'Presentation' in Sartre (1948b)

—— (1946), *Anti-Semite and Jew*, tr. G. Becker, New York: Schocken, 1965

—— (1947a), *Baudelaire*, tr. Martin Turnell, London: Hamish Hamilton, 1964

—— (1947b), *Existentialism and Humanism*, tr. Philip Maiet, London: Methuen, 1957

—— (1947c), *What Is Literature?*, tr. Bernard Frechtman, London: Routledge, 1993

—— (1947d), *Situations* I: *Essais critiques*, Paris: Gallimard

—— (1948a), 'Orphée noir' in Senghor (1948)

—— (1948b), *Situations* II, Paris: Gallimard

—— (1949a), *Iron in the Soul*, tr. Gerard Hopkins, Harmondsworth: Penguin, 1990

—— (1949b), *Situations* III, Paris: Gallimard

—— (1952), *Saint Genet, Actor and Martyr*, tr. Bernard Frechtman, New York: Braziller, 1963

—— (1960), *Critique of Dialectical Reason*, tr. Alan Sheridan Smith: London: Verso, 1982

—— (1964), *Words*, tr. I. Clephand, Harmondsworth: Penguin, 1991

—— (1966), 'Jean-Paul Sartre répond', *L'Arc* 30

—— (1971–2), *The Idiot of the Family*, tr. Carol Cormann, Chicago: University of Chicago Press, 1981–9, 3 vols

—— (1973), *Pour un théâtre de situations*, Paris: Gallimard

—— (1983a), *Notebooks for an Ethics*, tr. David Pellauer, Chicago and London: University of Chicago Press, 1992

—— (1983b), *The War Diaries of Jean-Paul Sartre*, tr. Quintin Hoare, London: Verso, 1985

—— (1985), *Critique of Dialectical Reason* II, tr. Quintin Hoare, London: Verso, 1990

Saussure, Ferdinand de (1916), *Course in General Linguistics*, tr. Wade Baskin, introduction by Jonathan Culler, London: Fontana Collins, 1974

Savage, Jon (1991), *England's Dreaming: Sex Pistols and Punk Rock*, London: Faber & Faber

Sayers, Janet (1982), *Biological Politics: Feminist and Anti-Feminist Perspectives*, London: Tavistock

—— (1991), *Mothering Psychoanalysis: Helene Deutsch, Karen Horney, Anna Freud, Melanie Klein*, London: Hamish Hamilton

Sayers, Sean (1997), 'Is the Truth out There?', *Times Higher Education Supplement*, 6 June

Sayres, Sohnya (1990), *Susan Sontag: The Elegiac Modernist*, New York and London: Routledge

Schacht, Richard (1983), *Nietzsche*, London: Routledge

Schleifer, Ronald (1987), *A. J. Greimas: Linguistics, Semiotics and Discourse Theory*, London: Croom Helm

Schleiermacher, Friedrich (1808), *Hermeneutics and Criticism and Other Writings*, ed. Andrew Bowie, Cambridge: Cambridge University Press

Schmidt, James (1985), *Maurice Merleau-Ponty: Between Phenomenology and Structuralism*, Basingstoke: Macmillan

Schneir, Miriam (1995), *The Vintage Book of Feminism*, London: Vintage

—— (1996), *The Vintage Book of Historical Feminism*, London: Vintage

Schopenhauer, Arthur (1818), *The World as Will and Idea*, tr. R. B. Haldane and K. Kemp, London: Kegan Paul, Trench & Trübner, 1891

Schrift, Alan D. (1995), *Nietzsche's French Legacy: A Genealogy of Poststructuralism*, New York and London: Routledge

Schur, Max (1972), *Freud: Living and Dying*, New York: International Universities Press

Schutte, Anne Jacobson (1976), 'Carlo Ginzburg', *Journal of Modern History* 48

Schutz, Alfred (1953), 'Concept and Theory Formation in the Social Sciences' in Schutz (1967)

—— (1967), *Collected Papers* I: *The Problem of Social Reality*, The Hague, Martinus Nijhoff

Scott, Andrew Murray (1991), *Alexander Trocchi: The Making of the Monster*, Edinburgh: Polygon

Scott, Bonnie Kime (1990), *The Gender of Modernism: A Critical Anthology*, Bloomington and Indianapolis: Indiana University Press

Scott, David (1992), *Paul Delvaux: Surrealizing the Nude*, London: Reaktion Books

Screech, M. A. (1958), *The Rabelaisian Marriage: Aspects of Rabelais's Religion, Ethics and Comic Philosophy*, London: Edward Arnold

Screen (1973), *Special Double Issue: Cinema Semiotics and the Work of Christian Metz* vol. 14 nos 1/2

—— (1974), *Special Number: Brecht and a Revolutionary Cinema* vol. 15 no. 2

—— (1975–6), *Brecht and the Cinema* vol. 16 no. 4

Scrutiny (1963), Cambridge: Cambridge University Press, 20 vols

Searle, John R. (1969), *Speech Acts: An Essay in the Philosophy of Language*, Cambridge: Cambridge University Press

—— (1977), 'Reiterating the Differences: A Reply to Derrida', *Glyph* 1

—— (1979), *Expression and Meaning: Essays in the Theory of Speech Acts*, Cambridge: Cambridge University Press

—— (1983), *Intentionality: An Essay in the Philosophy of Mind*, Cambridge: Cambridge University Press

—— (1995), *The Construction of Social Reality*, New York: Free Press

—— (1999), *Mind, Language and Society: Philosophy in the Real World*, London: Weidenfeld & Nicolson

Sebeok, Thomas (1994), *An Introduction to Semiotics*, London: Pinter

Sedgwick, Eve Kosofsky (1985), *Between Men: English Literature and Male Homosexual Desire*, New York: Columbia University Press

—— (1990), *Epistemology of the Closet*, Harmondsworth: Penguin, 1994

Segal, Hanna (1979), *Klein*, London: Fontana

Segal, Lynne (1987), *Is the Future Female? Troubled Thoughts on Contemporary Feminism*, London: Virago

Segal, Ronald (1995), *The Black Diaspora*, London: Faber & Faber

Seidman, Steven, ed. (1996), *Queer Theory/Sociology*, Oxford: Blackwell

Seitz, William C. (1985), *Abstract Expressionist Painting in America*, New Haven: Harvard University Press

Sellers, Susan, ed. (1988), *Writing Differences: Readings from the Seminar of Hélène Cixous*, Milton Keynes: Open University Press

——, ed. (1994), *The Hélène Cixous Reader*, London: Routledge

—— (1996), *Hélène Cixous: Authorship, Autobiography and Love*, Cambridge: Polity Press

Selz, Peter (1957), *German Expressionist Painting*, Berkeley, CA: University of California Press

Senghor, Léopold Sédar, ed. (1948), *Anthologie de la nouvelle poésie nègre et malgache de langue française*, Paris: PUF

—— (1964a), *Liberté* I: *Negritude et humanisme*, Paris: Seuil

—— (1964b), *The Collected Poetry*, tr. with an introduction by Melvin Dixon, Charlottesville, VA: University of Virginia Press, 1991

Sharpe, Sue (1976), *'Just like a Girl': How Girls Learn to be Women*, Harmondsworth: Penguin

Shattuck, Roger (1969), *The Banquet Years: The Origins of the Avant-Garde in France 1885 to World War One*, London: Jonathan Cape, rev. edn

Sheridan, Alan (1980), *Michel Foucault: The Will to Truth*, London: Tavistock

Sherwood, Richard (1973), 'Victor Shklovsky and the Development of Early Formalist Theory on Prose Literature' in Bann and Bowlt (1973)

Shiach, Morag (1991), *Hélène Cixous: A Politics of Writing*, London: Routledge

Shipley, Joseph T., ed. (1942), *Dictionary of World Literature: Criticism, Forms, Techniques*, New York: Philosophical Library

Shirikov, M. (1937), *A Textbook of Marxist Philosophy*, London: Gollancz

Shklovsky, Viktor (1914), 'The Resurrection of the Word', tr. Richard Sherwood in Bann and Bowlt (1973)

—— (1917), 'Art as Technique' in Lemon and Reis (1965)

—— (1923a), *Sentimental Journey*, tr. Richard Sheldon, Ithaca: Cornell University Press, 1969

—— (1923b), *Zoo, Letters Not About Love, or the Third Eloise*, tr. Richard Sheldon, Ithaca: Cornell University Press

—— (1925), *Theory of Prose*, tr. Benjamin Sher, Elmwood Park, IL: Dalkey Archive Press

—— (1940), *Mayakovsky and his Circle*, tr. Lily Feiler, London: Pluto Press, 1974

Showalter, Elaine (1977), *A Literature of their Own: British Women Novelists from Brontë to Lessing*, Princeton: Princeton University Press

—— (1979), 'Towards a Feminist Poetics' in Jacobus (1979)

—— (1981), 'Feminist Criticism in the Wilderness' in Showalter (1985b)

—— (1985a), *The Female Malady: Women, Madness and English Culture 1830–1980*, London: Virago, 1987

—— (1985b), *The New Feminist Criticism: Essays on Women, Literature and Theory*, New York: Pantheon

—— (1991), *Sexual Anarchy: Gender and Culture at the Fin de Siècle*, London: Bloomsbury

—— (1997), *Hystories: Hysterical Epidemics and Modern Culture*, London: Picador

Simon, Claude (1957), *The Wind*, New York: Braziller, 1960

Sinclair, Iain (1997), *Lights out for the Territory*, London: Granta Books

Sinfield, Alan (1994), *Cultural Politics – Queer Reading*, London: Routledge

Singer, Peter (1976), *Animal Liberation*, London: Jonathan Cape

Skinner, B. F. (1957), *Verbal Behaviour*, London: Methuen

Smith, J. H. and Kerrigan, W. (1983), *Interpreting Lacan*, New Haven: Harvard University Press

Smith, Roger (1997), *The Fontana History of the Human Sciences*, London: Fontana

Socialist Realism in Literature and Art: A Collection of Articles, Moscow: Progress Publishers, 1971

Sokal, Alan (1996), 'Transgressing the Boundaries: Towards a Transformative Hermeneutics of Quantum Gravity', *Social Text* 46–7

—— and Bricmont, Jean (1997), *Impostures intellectuelles*, Paris: Éditions Odile Jacob

—— (1998), *Intellectual Impostures*, London: Profile Books

Solanas, Valerie (1967), *SCUM Manifesto*, Edinburgh and San Francisco: AK Press, 1996

Sollers, Philippe (1958), *A Curious Solitude*, tr. Richard Howard, London: Eyre & Spottiswoode, 1961

—— (1973), *H*, Paris: Seuil

—— (1983), *Women*, tr. Barbara Bray, London: Quartet, 1991

—— (1994), *Portrait du joueur*, Paris: Gallimard

—— (1996), *La Guerre du goût*, Paris: Gallimard

Sommerfield, John (1936), *May Day*, London: Lawrence & Wishart, 1984

Sontag, Susan (1966), *Against Interpretation*, London: Vintage, 1994

—— (1967), *Death Kit*, London: Vintage, 1994

—— (1969), *Styles of Radical Will*, London: Vintage, 1994

—— (1977), *On Photography*, Harmondsworth: Penguin, 1979

—— (1978a), *I, Etcetera*, London: Vintage, 1996

—— (1978b), *Illness as Metaphor*, Harmondsworth: Penguin, 1983

—— (1978c), 'Under the Sign of Saturn' in Sontag (1980)

—— (1980), *Under the Sign of Saturn*, London: Vintage, 1996

—— (1989), *AIDS and its Metaphors*, Harmondsworth: Penguin, 1990

Soper, Kate (1986), *Humanism and Anti-Humanism*, London: Hutchinson

Soviet Socialist Realist Painting 1930–1960, Oxford: Museum of Modern Art, 1992

Soyinka, Wole (1976), _Myth, Literature and the African World_, Cambridge: Cambridge University Press

Spender, Dale (1980), _Man-Made Language_, London: Routledge

Spinoza (1677), _The Ethics and De Intellectus Emendatione_, tr. George Santayana, London: Everyman, 1910

Spitzer, Leo (1948a), _Linguistics and Literary History_, Princeton: Princeton University Press

—— (1948b), _Essays in Historical Semantics_, Princeton: Princeton University Press

Spivak, Gayatri Chakravorty (1985a), 'Can the Subaltern Speak?' in Barker (1985)

—— (1985b), 'Subaltern Studies: Deconstructing Historiography' in Spivak (1987)

—— (1985c), 'Three Women's Texts and a Critique of Imperialism', _Critical Inquiry_ 12

—— (1986), 'Strategy, Identity, Writing' in Spivak (1990)

—— (1987), _In Other Worlds: Essays in Cultural Politics_, New York and London: Methuen

—— (1990), _The Post-Colonial Critic: Interviews, Strategies, Dialogues_, ed. Sarah Harasym, New York and London: Routledge

—— (1993), _Outside in the Teaching Machine_, New York and London: Routledge

Stalin, J. V. (1938), 'Dialectical and Historical Materialism' in Stalin (1958)

—— (1958), _Problems of Leninism_, Moscow: Foreign Languages Publishing House

Stanislavski, Constantin (1926), _An Actor Prepares_, tr. Elizabeth Reynolds Hapgood, Harmondsworth: Penguin, 1967

Starobinski, Jean (1971), _Words upon Words: The Anagrams of Ferdinand de Saussure_, New Haven: Yale University Press, 1979

Steiner, George (1960), _Tolstoy or Dostoyevsky_, London: Faber & Faber

—— (1961), _The Death of Tragedy_, London: Faber & Faber

—— (1962), 'F. R. Leavis' in Steiner (1967)

—— (1963), 'Humane Literacy' in Steiner (1967)

—— (1965), 'A Kind of Survivor' in Steiner (1967)

—— (1967), _Language and Silence_, London: Faber & Faber, 1984, 2nd edn

—— (1971), _In Bluebeard's Castle_, London: Faber & Faber

—— (1989), _Real Presences_, London: Faber & Faber

—— (1992), _After Babel: Aspects of Language and Translation_, Oxford: Oxford University Press, rev. edn

——, ed. (1996), _Homer in English_, Harmondsworth: Penguin

—— (1997), _Errata: An Examined Life_, London: Faber & Faber

Steiner, Peter, ed. (1982), _The Prague School: Selected Writings, 1929–1946_, Austin: University of Texas Press

Stevens, Antony (1990), _On Jung_, London: Routledge

Stevens, Mary Anne, ed. (1984), _The Orientalists, Delacroix to Matisse: European Painters in North Africa and the Middle East_, London: Royal Academy of Arts

Stirk, Peter M. R. (1992), _Max Horkheimer: A New Perspective_, Hemel Hempstead: Harvester Wheatsheaf

Stoekl, Allan (1989), 'The Avant-Garde Embraces Science' in Hollier (1989)

Stoller, Robert J. (1968), *Sex and Gender*, New York: Science House

Stone, Lawrence (1982), 'Madness', *New York Times Review of Books*, 16 December

Strossen, Nadia (1995), *Defending Pornography: Free Speech, Sex and the Fight for Women's Rights*, New York: Simon & Schuster

Subaltern Studies (1982–   ), ed. Ranajit Guha, Delhi: Oxford University Press

Sullivan, Robert R. (1989), *Political Hermeneutics: The Early Thinking of Hans Georg Gadamer*, University Park: Pennsylvania State University Press

Sulloway, Frank L. (1979), *Freud, Biologist of the Mind: Beyond the Psychoanalytic Legend*, New York: Basic Books

Surrealism and Dada Reviewed, London: Arts Council of Great Britain, 1978

Surrealism in Britain in the Thirties, Leeds: Leeds City Art Galleries, 1986

Sussex, Elizabeth (1969), *Lindsay Anderson*, London: Studio Vista

Sutton, Nina (1995), *Bruno Bettelheim: The Other Side of Madness*, tr. David Sharp, London: Duckworth, 1995

Sylvester, David (1954), 'The Kitchen Sink', *Encounter*, December

Szasz, Tomas A. (1961), *The Myth of Mental Illness: Foundations of a Theory of Personal Conflict*, New York: Harper & Row

Tate, Allen (1958), *Collected Essays*, Denver: Swallow

Taylor, Barbara (1983), *Eve and the New Jerusalem: Socialism and Feminism in the Nineteenth Century*, London: Virago

Taylor, Brandon and van der Wil, Wilfried, eds (1990), *The Nazification of Art: Art, Design, Music, Architecture and Film in the Third Reich*, Winchester: The Winchester Press

Taylor, Charles (1989), *Sources of the Self: The Making of the Modern Identity*, Cambridge: Cambridge University Press

Taylor, Frederick W. (1914), *The Principles of Scientific Management*, New York: Harper

Taylor, John Russell (1963), *Anger and After: A Guide to the New British Drama*, Harmondsworth: Penguin, rev. edn

Temps modernes: Témoins de Sartre 531–3, October–December 1990, 2 vols

Tennenhouse, Leonard (1986), *Power on Display: The Politics of Shakespeare's Genres*, New York and London: Methuen

Teresa de Avila, *The Life of Saint Teresa, By Herself*, tr. J. M. Cohen, Harmondsworth: Penguin, 1957

Theory, Culture and Society vol. 5 nos 2–3: 'Special Issue on Post-Modernism', 1988

Therborn, Gören (1970), 'A Critique of the Frankfurt School', *New Left Review* 63

—— (1995), 'The Autobiography of the Twentieth Century', *New Left Review* 214

Thompson, E. P. (1955), *William Morris: Romantic to Revolutionary*, London: Lawrence & Wishart

—— (1963), *The Making of the English Working Class*, Harmondsworth: Penguin, 1968

—— (1965), 'The Peculiarities of the English' in Thompson (1978)

—— (1975), *Whigs and Hunters: The Origins of the Black Act*, Harmondsworth: Penguin, 1977

—— (1978), *The Poverty of Theory and Other Essays*, London: Merlin Press

—— (1980a), *Writing by Candlelight*, London: Merlin Press

—— (1980b), 'Notes on Exterminism, the Last Stage of Civilization', *New Left Review* 121

—— (1983), *Persons and Polemics*, London: Merlin Press

—— and Dan Smith, eds (1986), *Protest and Survive*, Harmondsworth: Penguin

Thompson, Kenneth, ed. (1997), *Media and Cultural Regulation*, London: Sage

Thomson, Peter and Sacks, Glenys, eds (1994), *The Cambridge Companion to Brecht*, Cambridge: Cambridge University Press

Thönnessen, Werner (1969), *The Emancipation of Women: The Rise and Decline of the Women's Movement in German Social Democracy 1863–1933*, tr. Joris de Bres, London: Pluto Press, 1973

Tiles, Mary (1984), *Bachelard: Science and Objectivity*, Cambridge: Cambridge University Press

Tilman, Rick (1992), *Thorstein Veblen and his Critics, 1891–1963: Conservative, Liberal and Radical Perspectives*, Princeton: Princeton University Press

Tocqueville, Alexis de (1835–40), *Democracy in America*, London: Everyman's Library, 1994

Todorov, Tzvetan (1965), *Théorie de la littérature: Textes des formalistes russes, réunis, présentés et traduits par Tzvetan Todorov*, Paris: Seuil

—— (1968), 'Poétique' in Ducrot (1968)

—— (1969), *Grammaire du Décaméron*, The Hague: Mouton

—— (1970), *The Fantastic: A Structural Approach to a Literary Genre*, tr. Richard Howard: Cleveland, OH: Case Western Reserve University Press, 1982

—— (1971a), *Poétique de la prose*, Paris: Seuil

—— (1971b), 'Some Approaches to Russian Formalism' in Bann and Bowlt (1973)

—— (1972), *Théorie du symbole*, Paris: Seuil

—— (1981), *Mikhail Bakhtin: The Dialogical Principle*, tr. Wlad Godzich, Minneapolis: Minnesota University Press, 1984

—— (1982), *The Conquest of America: The Question of the Other*, tr. Richard Howard, New York: Harper & Row

—— (1989), *On Human Diversity: Nationalism, Racism and Exoticism in French Thought*, tr. Catherine Porter, Cambridge, MA: Harvard University Press

—— (1991), *Facing the Extreme: Moral Life in the Concentration Camps*, tr. Arthur Denner and Abigail Pollack, London: Weidenfeld & Nicolson, 1999

—— (1993), *Éloge du quotidien: Essai sur la peinture hollondaise du XVIIe siècle*, Paris: Société Nouvelle Adam Biro

Tomalin, Clair (1974), *The Life and Death of Mary Wollstonecraft*, New York and London: Harcourt, Brace Jovanovich

Tomashevsky, Boris (1925), 'Thematics' in Lemon and Reis (1965)

Tompkins, Jane P., ed. (1980), *Reader-Response Theory: From Formalism to Post-Structuralism*, Baltimore and London: Johns Hopkins University Press

Tönnies, Ferdinand (1887), *Community and Society*, tr. C. P. Loomis, New York: Harper Torchbooks, 1963

Toolis, Kevin (1995), 'A Queer Verdict', *Guardian Weekend*, 25 November

Toumson, Roger and Henry-Valmore, Simone (1993), *Aimé Césaire, le nègre inconsolé*, Paris and Fort-de-France: Syros and Vent des Îles

Touraine, Alain (1969), *The Post-Industrial Society: Tomorrow's Social History. Class, Conflict and Culture in the Programmed Society*, tr. Leonard Fox Mayhew, New York: Random House, 1971

Traub, Valery (1992), *Desire and Anxiety: Circulations of Sexuality in Shakespearean Drama*, London: Routledge

Trevelyan, G. M. (1949–52), *Illustrated English Social History*, Harmondsworth: Penguin, 1964, 4 vols

Trier, J. (1931), *Der deutsche Wortschatz Sinnbezirk des Verstandes*, Heidelberg: Carl Vintner Verlag

Trubetzkoy, Nikolai (1939), *Principles of Phonology*, tr. C. Baltaxe, Berkeley: University of California Press, 1969

Truffaut, François (1954), 'A Certain Tendency in French Cinema' in Caughie (1981)

Tufts, Eleanor (1974), *Our Hidden Heritage: Five Centuries of Women Artists*, New York and London: Paddington Press

Turgenev, Ivan (1861), *Fathers and Sons*, tr. Rosemary Edmonds, Harmondsworth: Penguin, 1965

Turkle, Sherry (1978), *Psychoanalytic Politics: Jacques Lacan and Freud's French Revolution*, New York: Basic Books

Tynjanov, Jurij and Jakobson, Roman (1928), 'Problems in the Study of Language and Literature', tr. Herbert Eagle in Matejka and Pomorska (1971)

Tzara, Tristan (1924), *Seven Dada Manifestoes*, tr. Barbara Wright, London: John Calder, 1981

Vachek, Josef, ed. (1964), *A Prague School Reader in Linguistics*, Bloomington: Indiana University Press

Vaillant, Janet G. (1990), *Black, French and African: A Life of Léopold Sédar Senghor*, Cambridge, MA: Harvard University Press

Vallières, Pierre (1968), *Nègres blancs d'Amérique*, Montréal: Parti-pris

Vaneigem, Raoul (1967), *The Revolution of Everyday Life*, tr. John Fullerton and Paul Sieveking, London: Rising Free, 1979

—— (1995), *Avertissement aux écoliers et lycéens*, Paris: Mille et une nuits

Vattimo, Gianni (1981), *Al de là del soggetto: Nietzsche, Heidegger e l'ermeneutica*, Rome: Laterza

—— (1985), *Introduzione a Nietzsche*, Rome: Laterza

—— (1985), *The End of Modernity: Nihilism and Hermeneutics in Postmodern Culture*, tr. Jon R. Snyder, Baltimore: Johns Hopkins University Press

—— (1987), 'Hermeneutics as *Koine*', tr. Peter Caravetta, *Theory, Culture and Society* vol. 5 nos 2–3, 1988

—— (1994), *Beyond Interpretation: The Meaning of Hermeneutics for Philosophy*, tr. David Webb, Cambridge: Polity Press, 1997

—— and Rovatti, Pier Aldo, eds (1983), *Il Pensiero debole*, Milan: Feltrinelli

Veblen, Thorstein (1899), *The Theory of the Leisure Class*, London: Unwin Books, 1970

—— (1904), *Theory of Business Enterprise*, New York: New American Library

Veeser, H. Aram, ed. (1989), *The New Historicism*, London and New York: Routledge

Veith, Ilza (1965), *Hysteria: The History of a Disease*, Chicago: University of Chicago Press

Venturi, Robert (1966), *Complexity and Contradiction in Architecture*, London: The Architectural Press

——, Scott, Denise and Izenour, Steven (1972), *Learning from Las Vegas: The Forgotten Symbolism of Architectural Form*, Cambridge, MA: MIT Press

Verdi, Richard (1992), *Cézanne*, London: Thames & Hudson

Vergès, Françoise (1996), 'To Cure and To Free: The Fanonian Project of Decolonized Psychiatry' in Gordon et al. (1996)

Vian, Boris (1947), *Froth on the Daydream*, tr. S. Chapman, London: Quartet, 1988

Vickers, Brian (1988), *In Defence of Rhetoric*, Oxford: Clarendon Press

Vidal-Naquet, Pierre (1985), 'Thèses sur le révisionisme' in Vidal-Naquet (1987)

—— (1987), *Les Assassins de la mémoire. 'Un Eichmann de papier' et autres essais sur le révisionisme*, Paris: La Découverte

Vintges, Karen (1992), *Philosophy as Passion: The Thinking of Simone de Beauvoir*, tr. Anne Lavelle, Bloomington and Indianapolis: Indiana University Press, 1996

Vorticism and its Allies, London: Arts Council of Great Britain, 1974

Vovelle, Michel (1978), 'The *Longue Durée*' in Vovelle (1990)

—— (1990), *Ideologies and Mentalities*, tr. Eamon O'Flaherty, Cambridge: Polity Press

Waismann, Frederick (1965), *The Principles of Linguistic Philosophy*, London: Macmillan

Walcott, Derek (1974), 'The Muse of History' in Walcott (1998)

—— (1982), 'The Antilles: Fragments of Epic Memory' in Walcott (1998)

—— (1990), *Omeros*, London: Faber & Faber

—— (1992), *Collected Poems 1948–1984*, London: Faber & Faber

—— (1997), 'A Letter to Chamoiseau' in Walcott (1998)

—— (1998), *What the Twilight Says: Essays*, London: Faber & Faber

Walker, Alice (1983), *In Search of our Mothers' Gardens: Womanist Prose*, New York: Harcourt Brace Jovanovich

Wallon, Henri (1947), *Les Origines du caractère chez l'enfant*, Paris: PUF

Walter, Natasha (1998), *The New Feminism*, London: Little, Brown

Walters, Margaret (1978), *The Nude Male: A New Perspective*, London: Paddington Press

Wandor, Micheline, ed. (1972), *The Body Politic: Women's Liberation in Britain 1969–1972*, London: Stage 1

—— (1990), *Once a Feminist: Stories of a Generation. Interviews with Micheline Wandor*, London: Virago

Ware, Vron (1992), *Beyond the Pale: White Women, Racism and History*, London: Verso

Warhol, Rubya and Herndl, Diana Price, eds (1992), *Feminisms: An Anthology of Literary Theory and Criticism*, Basingstoke: Macmillan, 1977, rev. edn

Warner, Marina (1976), *Alone of all her Sex: The Myth and Cult of the Virgin Mary*, London: Weidenfeld & Nicolson

—— (1981), *Joan of Arc: The Image of Female Heroism*, London: Weidenfeld & Nicolson

—— (1985), *Monuments and Maidens: The Allegory of the Female Form*, London: Weidenfeld & Nicolson

—— (1994a), *From the Beast to the Blonde: On Fairy Tales and their Tellers*, London: Chatto & Windus

—— (1994b), *Managing Monsters: Six Myths of our Time. The Reith Lectures 1994*, London: Vintage

Washton Long, Rose Carol, ed. (1993), *German Expressionism: Documents from the End of the Wilhelmine Empire to the Rise of National Socialism*, Berkeley: University of California Press

Watney, Simon (1980), 'The Ideology of GLF' in Gay Left Collective (1980)

—— (1986), 'The Banality of Gender' in *Oxford Literary Review* (1986)

—— (1987), *Policing Desire: Pornography, Aids and the Media*, London: Comedia

Watson, Sean (1998), 'The New Bergsonism: Discipline, Subjectivity and Freedom', *Radical Philosophy* 92

Watt, Ian (1957), *The Rise of the Novel: Studies in Defoe, Richardson and Fielding*, Harmondsworth: Penguin, 1976

Weber, Max (1904–05), *The Protestant Ethic and the Spirit of Protestantism*, tr. Talcott Parsons, London: Routledge, 1992

Weber, Samuel (1990), *Return to Freud: Jacques Lacan's Dislocation of Psychoanalysis*, tr. Michael Levine, Cambridge: Cambridge University Press, 1991

Weeks, Jeffrey (1977), *Coming Out: Homosexual Politics in Britain from the Nineteenth Century to the Present*, London: Quartet

Weinsheimer, J. C. (1985), *Gadamer's Hermeneutics*, Cambridge, MA: MIT Press

Wellek, René (1955–91), *A History of Modern Criticism*, New Haven: Yale University Press, 7 vols

—— (1963), *Concepts of Criticism*, New Haven: Yale University Press

—— (1986), 'The New Criticism' in Wellek (1955–91), VI (1986)

—— and Warren, Austin (1949), *Theory of Literature*, Harmondsworth: Penguin, 1966, rev. edn

White, Hayden (1973), *Metahistory: The Historical Imagination in Nineteenth-Century Europe*, Baltimore: Johns Hopkins University Press

—— (1978), *Tropics of Discourse: Essays in Cultural Criticism*, Baltimore: Johns Hopkins University Press

Whitford, Margaret (1991a), *The Irigaray Reader*, Oxford: Blackwell

—— (1991b), *Luce Irigaray: Philosophy in the Feminine*, London: Routledge

Whorf, Benjamin Lee (1956), *Language, Thought and Reality*, ed. J. B. Carrol, Cambridge, MA: MIT Press

Widdowson, Peter, ed. (1982), *Rereading English*, London: Methuen

Wilcox, Helen, McWatters, Keith, Thompson, Ann and Williams, Linda R. (1990), *The Body and the Text: Hélène Cixous, Reading and Teaching*, London: Harvester Wheatsheaf

Wildenstein, Daniel (1996), *Monet*, Cologne: Taschen and the Wildenstein Institute, 4 vols

Willett, John (1977), *The Theatre of Bertolt Brecht: A Study from Eight Aspects*, London: Methuen, rev. edn

—— (1978), *The Theatre of Erwin Piscator*, London: Methuen

Williams, Bernard and Montefiore, Alan, eds (1966), *British Analytic Philosophy*, London: Routledge & Kegan Paul

Williams, P. and Chrisman, L., eds (1994), *Colonial Discourse and Post-Colonial Theory: A Reader*, New York: Columbia University Press

Williams, Raymond (1954), *Drama in Performance*, London: C. A. Watts

—— (1958), *Culture and Society 1780–1950*, London: Chatto & Windus

—— (1960), *Border Country*, London: Chatto & Windus

—— (1961), *The Long Revolution*, London: Chatto & Windus

—— (1966), *Modern Tragedy*, London: Chatto & Windus

—— (1968), *Drama from Ibsen to Brecht*, London: Chatto & Windus

—— (1970), *The English Novel: From Dickens to Lawrence*, London: Chatto & Windus

—— (1971), *George Orwell*, London: Fontana

—— (1972), 'Ideas of Nature' in Williams (1980)

—— (1973a), *The Country and the City*, London: Chatto & Windus

—— (1973b), 'Base and Superstructure in Marxist Cultural Theory' in Williams (1980)

—— (1974), *Television: Technology and Cultural Form*, London: Fontana

—— (1976), *Keywords: A Vocabulary of Culture and Society*, London: Fontana, expanded edn, 1983

—— (1977), *Marxism and Literature*, Oxford: Oxford University Press

—— (1979), *Politics and Letters: Interviews with New Left Review*, London: New Left Books

—— (1980), *Problems in Materialism and Culture: Selected Essays*, London: Verso

—— (1989), *What I Came to Say*, ed. Neil Belton, Francis Mulhern and Jenny Taylor, London: Hutchinson Century

—— and Orram, Michael (1954), *Preface to Film*, London: Film Drama

Willis, Paul (1972), 'The Motorbike within a Subcultural Group', *Working Papers on Cultural Studies* 2

—— (1979), *Learning to Labour*, London: Saxon House

Wilson, Edmund (1931), *Axel's Castle: A Study in the Imaginative Literature of 1870–1930*, London: Fontana, 1961

Wilson, Elizabeth (1992), 'The Invisible Flâneur', *New Left Review* 191

Wimsatt, W. K. (1954), *The Verbal Icon: Studies in the Meaning of Poetry, with Two Preliminary Essays Written in Collaboration with Monroe C. Beardsley*, London: Methuen, 1970

—— and Beardsley, Monroe C. (1942), 'Intention' in Shipley (1942)

—— (1954a), 'The Intentional Fallacy' in Wimsatt (1954)

—— (1954b), 'The Affective Fallacy' in Wimsatt (1954)

Winnicott, D. W. (1958), *Collected Papers: Through Paediatrics to Psycho-Analysis*, London: Tavistock

—— (1971), *Playing and Reality*, Harmondsworth: Penguin, 1980

Wiseman, Mary Bittner (1989), *The Ecstasies of Roland Barthes*, London and New York: Routledge

Wittfogel, Karl August (1955), *Oriental Despotism: A Comparative Study of Total Power*, New Haven: Yale University Press

Wittgenstein, Ludwig (1921), *Tractatus Logico-Philosophicus*, tr. D. F. Pears and B. F. McGuiness, London: Routledge & Kegan Paul, 1961

—— (1929), 'Some Remarks on Logical Form', *Proceedings of the Aristotelean Society*, supplementary vol. IX

—— (1953), *Philosophical Investigations*, Oxford: Basil Blackwell

—— (1958), *The Blue and Brown Books: Preliminary Studies for the 'Philosophical Investigations'*, Oxford: Basil Blackwell

—— (1974), *Philosophical Grammar*, Oxford: Blackwell

Wittig, Monique (1969), *The Guerillieres*, tr. D. Le Vay, London: Peter Owen, 1971

—— (1973), *The Lesbian Body*, tr. David Le Vay, Boston: Beacon Press, 1986

—— (1981), 'One is Not Born a Woman . . .', *Feminist Issues* vol. 1 no. 1

—— (1996), *The Straight Mind and Other Essays*, foreword by Louis Turcotte, Hemel Hempstead: Harvester Wheatsheaf

—— and Zeig, Sande (1980), *Lesbian Peoples: Materials for a Dictionary*, London: Virago

Wolf, Naomi (1990), *The Beauty Myth*, London: Chatto & Windus

—— (1993), *Fire with Fire: The New Female Power and How it Will Change the 21st Century*, London: Chatto & Windus

Wolff, Janet (1985), 'The Invisible Flâneuse; Women and the Literature of Modernity', *Theory, Culture and Society* vol. 2 no. 3

Wolff, Robert Paul, Moore, Barrington Jr and Marcuse, Herbert (1965), *A Critique of Pure Tolerance*, London: Jonathan Cape, 1969

Wölfflin, Heinrich (1898), *Renaissance and Baroque*, tr. Kathrin Simon, Ithaca: Cornell University Press, 1968

—— (1899), *Classic Art: An Introduction to the Italian Renaissance*, tr. Peter and Linda Murray, London: Phaidon Press, 1953

—— (1915), *Principles of Art History: The Problem of the Development of Style in Art*, tr. M. D. Huttinger, New York: Dover, 1950

Wolin, Richard (1982), *Walter Benjamin: An Aesthetic of Redemption*, New York: Columbia University Press

——, ed. (1993), *The Heidegger Controversy*, Cambridge, MA: MIT Press

Wollen, Peter (1989), 'The Situationist International', *New Left Review* 174

Wollstonecraft, Mary (1792), *A Vindication of the Rights of Woman*, Harmondsworth: Penguin

—— (1797), *Maria; or the Wrongs of Women*, London: Oxford University Press, 1980

Women's Images of Men, London: Institute of Contemporary Arts, 1980

Woods, David, *Derrida: A Critical Reader*, Oxford: Blackwell

Woodwood, Kathryn, ed. (1997), *Identity and Difference*, London: Sage

Woolf, Virginia (1919), 'The Tunnel' in Woolf (1979)

—— (1923), 'Romance and the Heart' in Woolf (1979)

—— (1924), 'Mr Bennet and Mrs Brown' in *Collected Essays* III

—— (1929), *A Room of One's Own* in Woolf (1992)

—— (1931), 'Professions for Women' in Woolf (1979)

—— (1938), *Three Guineas* in Woolf (1992)

—— (1979), *Women and Writing*, introduction by Michèle Barrett, London: The Women's Press

—— (1986–94), *Collected Essays*, ed. Andrew McNeillie, London: The Hogarth Press, 4 vols

—— (1992), *A Room of One's Own and Three Guineas*, Oxford: World's Classics

Working Papers in Cultural Studies (1975): *Resistance through Rituals*

Working Papers in Cultural Studies (1977): *On Ideology*

Worringer, Wilhelm (1908), *Abstraction and Empathy: A Contribution to the Psychology of Style*, tr. Michael Bullock, London: Routledge & Kegan Paul, 1963

Worton, Michael and Still, Judith, eds (1990), *Intertextuality: Theories and Practices*, Manchester: Manchester University Press

Wright, Elizabeth (1984), *Psychoanalytic Criticism: Theory in Practice*, London: Methuen

——, ed. (1992), *Feminism and Psychoanalysis: A Critical Dictionary*, Oxford: Blackwell

Wright, Patrick (1985), *On Living in an Old Country: The National Past in Contemporary Britain*, London: Verso

—— (1991), *A Journey through Ruins: The Last Days of London*, London: Random Century

—— (1993), 'Beastly Trials of the Last Politburo', *Guardian*, 17 July

Yale French Studies 24 (1959): *Midnight Novelists*

Yale French Studies 36/37 (1966): *Structuralism*

Yale French Studies 55/56 (1977): *Literature and Psychoanalysis: Reading Otherwise*

Yale French Studies 78 (1990): *On Bataille*

Young, Jock (1972), *The Drugtakers: The Social Meaning of Drug Use*, London: Paladin

Young, Julian (1997), *Heidegger, Philosophy, Nazism*, Cambridge: Cambridge University Press

Young, Robert (1990), *White Mythologies: Writing History and the West*, London and New York: Routledge

Young-Bruehl, Elisabeth (1982), *Hannah Arendt: For Love of the World*, New Haven: Yale University Press

—— (1988), *Anna Freud: A Biography*, New York: Summit Books

Zhdanov, Andrey Alexandrovich (1950), *On Literature, Music and Philosophy*, London: Lawrence & Wishart

Zizek, Slavoj (1989), *The Sublime Object of Ideology*, London: Verso